# PUBLIC SPEAKING

### 3rd Edition

## Michael Osborn
Memphis State University

## Suzanne Osborn
Memphis State University

HOUGHTON MIFFLIN COMPANY ■ BOSTON ■ TORONTO

Geneva, Illinois ■ Palo Alto ■ Princeton, New Jersey

**To Roy and Inez Parrish Osborn and Donald and Martha Larson Smith**

Sponsoring Editor: Margaret Seawell
Basic Book Editor: Karla Paschkis
Senior Project Editor: Cathy Labresh Brooks
Production/Design Coordinator: Jill Haber
Marketing Manager: Karen Natale

Cover design by Karen Lehman.
Cover image by Dick Hannus.

Text and photo credits begin after page G8.

As part of Houghton Mifflin's ongoing commitment to the environment, this text has been printed on recycled paper.

Printed in the U.S.A.
Library of Congress Catalogue Number: 93-78696
ISBN: 0-395-67578-2

1 2 3 4 5 6 7 8 9-DC-97  96 95 94 93

# Contents

*Preface xiv*
*List of Speeches xxvi*

## PART ONE    THE FOUNDATIONS OF PUBLIC SPEAKING                                   1

### 1    *Public Speaking as Communication*                                          3

Personal Benefits of Public Speaking    5

Social Benefits of Public Speaking    6

Cultural Benefits of Public Speaking    8

The Communication Process    9

*The Speaker as Source    10*
*Idea    11*
*Message    11*
*Medium    12*
*The Audience as Receiver    13*
*Response    13*
*The Communication Environment    13*

What Makes a Good Public Speech?    14

*Speaker Commitment    14*
*Well-Chosen Topic    15*
*Clear Sense of Purpose    16*
*Audience Involvement    16*
*Substance    17*
*Appropriate Structure    17*
*Skillful Language Use    19*
*Effective Presentation    20*

The Ethics of Public Speaking    21

*Respect for the Audience    21*
*Responsible Knowledge    22*
*Concern for Consequences    23*
*Responsibilities of Listeners    24*

In Summary    24    ■    Terms to Know    25    ■    Discussion    25    ■
Application    26    ■    Notes    27

■ **Speaker's Notes:** How to Create a Good Public Speech  15

How to Avoid Plagiarism  23

## 2 *Your First Speech*  29

Understanding the Impressions You Make  31

*Competence  31*
*Integrity  31*
*Likableness  33*
*Power  34*

Introducing Yourself and Others  35

Developing the Introductory Speech  39

*Designing Your Speech  40*
*Introduction  41*
*Body  42*
*Conclusion  43*

Outlining the Introductory Speech  44

Presenting the Introductory Speech  45

*Spotlight the Ideas  46*
*Sound Natural  46*
*Key-Word Outline  46*
*Practice Your Speech  47*
*Make Nervousness Work for You  48*

In Summary  51  ■  Terms to Know  52  ■  Discussion  52  ■
Application  53  ■  Notes  55

■ **Speaker's Notes:** Self-Awareness Inventory  39

Preparing Your First Speech  43

Ten Ways to Control Communication Apprehension  50

---

**Sample Speech of Self-Introduction:**
Sandra Baltz, *"My Three Cultures"*  56

---

## 3 *Critical and Constructive Listening*  59

Benefits of Critical and Constructive Listening  61

Overcoming Listening Problems  64

*Personal Reactions  64*
*Attitudes  67*
*Bad Habits  69*

Critical Thinking and Listening  72

*The Importance of Critical Thinking to Listening  73*

*Questions for Critical Thinking and Analysis*   73

Developing Constructive Listening Skills   75

*Empathetic Listening*   76
*Synergistic Listening*   77

Evaluating Speeches   79

In Summary   81  ■  Terms to Know   82  ■  Discussion   82  ■
Application   82  ■  Notes   83

■  **Speaker's Notes:**   Guides for Effective Listening   70

               Guidelines for Critical Thinking and Listening   75

               Questions for Evaluating Constructive
Listening Experiences   78

## PART TWO    PREPARATION FOR PUBLIC SPEAKING      85

### 4   *Audience Analysis and Adaptation*      87

Adjusting to the Communication Environment   89

*Time*   89
*Place*   89
*Context*   90
*Nature and Purpose of the Occasion*   92
*Size of Audience*   93

Adjusting to Audience Demographics   94

*Age*   95
*Gender*   95
*Educational Level*   97
*Group Affiliations*   98
*Sociocultural Background*   100

Adapting to Audience Dynamics   101

*Motivation*   101
*Attitudes, Beliefs, and Values*   105

In Summary   108  ■  Terms to Know   109  ■  Discussion   109  ■
Application   110  ■  Notes   111

■  **Speaker's Notes:**   Check List for Analyzing the Speech Setting   94

               Guidelines for Long-Range Audience Analysis   106

### 5   *Selecting and Researching Your Topic*      115

Selecting a Good Topic   117

*Charting Interests*   117
*Analyzing Your Topic*   119

*Selecting Your Topic    121*

Determining Your Purpose    122

*General Purpose    122*
*Specific Purpose    123*
*Thematic Statement    125*

Acquiring Responsible Knowledge    127
*Personal Experience    129*
*Library Research    129*
*Interviewing for Information    135*

Recording Information    139

*Information Cards    140*
*Source Cards    140*
*Testing Information    140*

In Summary    142    ■    Terms to Know    143    ■    Discussion    143    ■
Application    143    ■    Notes    144

■    **Speaker's Notes:**    Check List for Topic Selection    122

Guidelines for Evaluating My Specific Purpose    124

Interviewing for Information    139


6    *Use of Supporting Materials*    147

Facts and Figures    149

*Facts    149*
*Statistics    151*
*Evaluating Facts and Figures    152*
*Using Facts and Figures    154*

Testimony    155

*Expert Testimony    155*
*Prestige Testimony    156*
*Lay Testimony    157*
*Evaluating Testimony    157*
*Using Testimony    158*

Examples    159

*Types of Examples    160*
*Evaluating Examples    162*
*Using Examples    163*

Narratives    163

*Evaluating Narratives    166*
*Using Narratives    167*

In Summary    168    ■    Terms to Know    169    ■    Discussion    169    ■
Application    170    ■    Notes    170

■ **Speaker's Notes:** Evaluating Facts and Figures 154

Evaluating Testimony 158

Evaluating Examples 162

Using Narratives 167

## 7 *Structuring Your Speech* 173

Principles of Good Form 174

*Simplicity 174*
*Symmetry 176*
*Orderliness 177*

Structuring the Body of Your Speech 177

*Determining Your Main Points 178*
*Arranging Your Main Points 178*
*Selecting Your Supporting Materials 182*

Using Transitions 185

Preparing an Effective Introduction 187

*Capturing Attention and Interest 187*
*Establishing Your Credibility as a Speaker 192*
*Previewing Your Message 193*
*Deciding What Introductory Techniques to Use 194*

Developing an Effective Conclusion 195

*Functions of the Conclusion 195*
*Concluding Techniques 196*

In Summary 198 ■ Terms to Know 199 ■ Discussion 199 ■
Application 200 ■ Notes 200

■ **Speaker's Notes:** Determining and Arranging Your Main Points 181

Capturing the Attention of Your Audience 192

## 8 *Outlining Your Speech* 203

Developing a Preparation Outline 205

*Audience-Centered Outlining 210*

Developing a Formal Outline 211

*Title 211*
*Topic, Purposes, and Thematic Statement 215*
*Separation of Speech Parts 215*
*Coordination and Subordination 215*
*Wording Your Main Points 218*
*Supporting Your Main Points 219*
*Reference Citations 223*

Developing a Key-Word Outline 224

In Summary   225   ■   Terms to Know   226   ■   Discussion   226   ■
Application   227   ■   Notes   228

■ **Speaker's Notes:**   Developing a Formal Outline   219

**Sample Formal Outline:**
Dawn Williams, *"Making Sense and Saving Cents When You
Buy a Computer"*   220

## PART THREE   DEVELOPING PRESENTATION SKILLS   229

### 9   *Visual Aids*   231

Uses and Advantages of Visual Aids   232

Kinds of Visual Aids   233

*People*   233
*Objects and Models*   234
*Graphics*   235
*Photographs and Pictures*   241

Ways of Presenting Visual Aids   242

*Chalkboard*   243
*Flip Chart*   245
*Poster Board*   246
*Handouts*   246
*Slides and Transparencies*   247
*Computer-Generated Materials*   248
*Films, Videotapes, Audiotapes, and Laser Disks*   248

Preparing Visual Aids   249

*Principles of Visual Aid Design*   250
*Principles of Color*   251
*Making Visual Aids*   253

Using Visual Aids   254

In Summary   255   ■   Terms to Know   256   ■   Discussion   257   ■
Application   257   ■   Notes   257

■ **Speaker's Notes:**   Planning and Preparing Visual Aids   252

### 10   *The Speaker's Language*   259

The Power of Language   260

*The Power to Make Listeners See*   261
*The Power to Awaken Feelings*   262

*The Power to Bring Listeners Together   265*
*The Power to Encourage Action   266*
*The Power to Help Listeners Remember   267*

The Tools of Language   267

*Tools to Help Listeners See   267*
*Tools to Make Listeners Feel   270*
*Tools to Create Togetherness   273*
*Tools to Make Listeners Act   276*
*Tools to Help Listeners Remember   277*

Using Language Effectively   279

*Clarity   279*
*Color   281*
*Concreteness   282*
*Correctness   282*
*Conciseness   283*
*Cultural Sensitivity   284*

In Summary   285   ■   Terms to Know   287   ■   Discussion   287   ■
Application   288   ■   Notes   288

■   **Speaker's Notes:**   How Language Helps Us See: The Three *R*'s (Relating,
Replacing, Representing)   271

Using Language to Create Togetherness   275

The Six *C*'s of Effective Language Use   280

Avoiding Racist and Sexist Language   285


**11   *Presenting Your Speech***   *293*

What Is Effective Presentation?   294

Methods of Presentation   295

*Impromptu Speaking   295*
*Memorized Text Presentation   297*
*Reading from a Manuscript   298*
*Extemporaneous Speaking   300*

Using Your Voice Effectively   301

*Pitch   302*
*Rate   304*
*Loudness   305*
*Variety   307*
*Patterns of Speaking   307*

Using Your Body Effectively   310

*Facial Expression and Eye Contact   310*
*Movement and Gestures   312*

*Personal Appearance   313*

The Importance of Practice   314

Making Video Presentations   316

*Adapting for Video Presentations   316*
*Practicing for Video Presentations   317*
*Making Your Media Presentation   318*

In Summary   319   ■   Terms to Know   320   ■   Discussion   320   ■
Application   321   ■   Notes   321

■   **Speaker's Notes:**   Suggestions for Using Different Methods
of Presentation   299

Practicing for Presentation   315

## PART FOUR   TYPES OF PUBLIC SPEAKING   323

### 12   *The Nature and Kinds of Informative Speaking*   325

Functions of the Informative Speech   327

*Sharing Information and Ideas   327*
*Shaping Perceptions   328*
*Setting the Agenda   328*
*Clarifying Options   329*

Informative Speaking and the Learning Process   330

*Motivation   330*
*Attention   331*
*Retention   333*

Types of Informative Speeches   334

*Speeches of Description   334*
*Speeches of Demonstration   335*
*Speeches of Explanation   336*

Speech Designs   337

*Spatial Design   337*
*Categorical Design   339*
*Comparison and Contrast Design   340*
*Sequential Design   342*
*Historical Design   343*
*Causation Design   345*
*Combined Speech Designs   346*

In Summary   347   ■   Terms to Know   348   ■   Discussion   348   ■
Application   348   ■   Notes   349

■   **Speaker's Notes:**   Helping Listeners Learn New Information   334

Designing an Informative Speech   346

**Sample Informative Speech with Visual Aids:**
Stephen Huff, *"The New Madrid Earthquake Area"* *350*

## 13  The Nature and Kinds of Persuasive Speaking  *357*

Characteristics of Persuasive Speaking  359

The Process of Persuasion  361

The Challenges of Persuasion  364

    *Enticing a Reluctant Audience to Listen  365*
    *Removing Barriers to Commitment  368*
    *Moving from Attitude to Action  369*

Types of Persuasive Speeches  371

    *Speeches Addressing Attitudes  371*
    *Speeches Urging Action  372*
    *Speeches of Contention  373*

Designs for Persuasive Speaking  374

    *Problem-Solution Design  374*
    *Stock Issues Design  376*
    *Motivated Sequence Design  378*
    *Refutative Design  380*
    *Analogy Design  382*

In Summary  384  ■  Terms to Know  385  ■  Discussion  385  ■
Application  385  ■  Notes  386

■  **Speaker's Notes:**  Applying McGuire's Model of the Persuasive Process
        to Your Speeches  364

        Meeting the Challenge of a Reluctant Audience  367

        Meeting the Challenge of an Uncommitted Audience  368

        Meeting the Challenge of Moving an Audience
        to Action  370

        Designing Your Persuasive Speech  383

**Sample Persuasive Speech:**
Anna Aley, *"We Don't Have to Live in Slums"* *389*

## 14  Evidence, Proof, and Argument  *393*

Using Evidence Effectively  394

    *Facts and Figures  395*
    *Examples  396*

*Narratives* *397*
*Testimony* *397*

Proving Your Points   399

*Logos* *399*
*Pathos* *400*
*Ethos* *401*
*Mythos* *402*
*Using Proofs in Combination* *405*

Forming Arguments   406

*Deductive Argument* *406*
*Inductive Argument* *408*
*Analogical Argument* *410*
*The Importance of Defining Terms* *411*

Avoiding Defective Persuasion   412

*Defective Evidence* *412*
*Defective Proofs* *415*
*Defective Arguments* *416*
*Fallacies Related to Particular Designs* *418*

In Summary   419   ■   Terms to Know   421   ■   Discussion   421   ■
Application   421   ■   Notes   422

■   **Speaker's Notes:**   Guidelines for the Ethical Use of Evidence   398

Developing Powerful Arguments   411


**15   *Ceremonial Speaking*** *425*

Techniques of Ceremonial Speaking   427

*Identification* *427*
*Magnification* *428*

Types of Ceremonial Speeches   429

*The Speech of Tribute* *429*
*The Speech of Acceptance* *432*
*The Speech of Introduction* *434*
*The Speech of Inspiration* *436*
*The After-Dinner Speech* *438*

In Summary   441   ■   Terms to Know   442   ■   Discussion   442   ■
Application   442   ■   Notes   442

■   **Speaker's Notes:**   Making an Acceptance Speech   434

Introducing Main Speakers   436

**Ceremonial Speeches:**
Thomas P. O'Neill, Jr., *"Tribute to Jesse Owens"* 430
Jesse Owens, *"The Meaning of the Olympics"* 437

**Sample After-Dinner Speech:**
Dick Jackman, *"Address at Awards Dinner of the National Football Foundation"* 444

## *Appendix A    Group Communication*                                   *A1*

The Problem-Solving Process    A4

*Step 1: Defining the Problem    A4*
*Step 2: Generating Solution Options    A4*
*Step 3: Evaluating Solution Options    A5*
*Step 4: Planning for Action    A6*
*Step 5: Planning for Evaluation    A6*

Participating in Small Groups    A7

Leadership in Small Groups    A9

*Developing a Meeting Plan    A10*
*Conducting an Effective Meeting    A11*

Guidelines for Formal Meetings    A11

## *Appendix B    Speeches for Analysis*                                   *B1*

*Rodney Nishikawa,* **"Free at Last"** B3
*Scott Champlin,* **"My Twenty-First Birthday Party"** B4
*Cecile Larson,* **"The 'Monument' at Wounded Knee"** B6
*Jane Doe,* **"Rape by Any Other Name"** B8
*Stephen Lee,* **"The Trouble with Numbers"** B11
*Bonnie Marshall,* **"Living Wills: Insuring Your Right to Choose"** B13
*Elizabeth Glaser,* **"AIDS: A Personal Story"** B16
*Mary Fisher,* **"AIDS: A Personal Narrative"** B19
*Bill Clinton,* **"Inaugural Address"** B22
*Elie Wiesel,* **"Nobel Peace Prize Acceptance Speech"** B26
*Bill Cosby,* **"University of South Carolina Commencement Address"** B28
*Ronnie Davis,* **"The Trials of Malcolm X"** B31

**GLOSSARY    G1**

**INDEX    I-1**

# Preface

We are grateful to the many instructors and their thousands of students who have justified this new edition of *Public Speaking*. The opportunity to touch so many lives is exhilarating, but it is also quite sobering. Accordingly, we have approached this revision of our book with both excitement and caution.

Over the past three years we have spoken with many teachers and students and listened to their suggestions and reflections on their classroom experience with the text. This new revision is enriched by what we have learned from them, and records our own growth in the discipline. We especially have gained appreciation for the role of public speaking in a multicultural society. A sentence from the preface to our Second Edition is even more true than we realized then: "An effective public speech is like a bridge that joins people who otherwise would be quite separate." Moreover, we have strengthened our conviction that the ethical importance of speaking must never be absent from the communication enterprise. Finally, our appreciation for the vital, creative role of listening in public communication has intensified.

While this edition reflects this new consciousness, we have not changed the basic orientation that so many users have endorsed. We continue to honor a study that ancient educators thought belonged at the center of liberal education. What other discipline, they argued, requires students to think clearly, to organize their thoughts, to select and combine words judiciously, and to express themselves with power and conviction, all under the direct scrutiny of a live audience? In our own time, the study of public speaking should empower us as speakers and listeners in the many social, economic, and political situations that require open discussion. Not only our personal success but the fate of our communities may depend upon the outcomes of such discussions.

For these reasons we believe that a college or university course in public speaking should offer more than practical advice, as useful as such advice may be. The student must also understand why certain techniques work and don't work in certain situations or under certain conditions. Therefore we continue to emphasize both the *how* and the *why* of public speaking—*how* so that beginners can achieve success as quickly as possible, and *why* so that they may add flexibility, understanding, and a sense of responsibility to their new skill.

The third edition of *Public Speaking* offers both practical instruction and an introduction to the principles underlying effective communication. Many new examples and models of successful speaking help bring the material to life. The Roman educator, Quintilian, held forth the ideal of "the good person speaking well" as the goal of all such instruction. We follow in his path as we stress the value of speech training in the development of the whole person. We also emphasize that successful public speaking is leadership-in-action and that improving one's speaking skills is excellent training for leadership roles. In addition, a solid understanding of the basics of public communication makes students more resistant to unethical speakers and more intelligently critical of daily communication. Our goal is to help students become both better producers and better consumers of public communication.

##  FEATURES OF THE TEXT

In pursuit of these objectives, we have developed a number of special features.

### *Step-by-Step Presentation*

Our presentation of topics helps students build knowledge and skills step-by-step to achieve positive results. It is especially important for beginners to have a successful first speaking experience. For this reason, Chapter 2 offers an elementary overview of required skills so that students can develop good speeches introducing themselves or others. This overview helps students present introductory speeches that build a sense of classroom community and trust. In the chapters that follow, students learn how to listen critically and constructively, to analyze their audiences, to select, refine, and research speech topics, to develop supporting materials, to arrange these materials in appropriate structures, to outline their thinking in disciplined patterns, and to create effective visual aids. They also learn how to manage words and how to present their messages. They then learn about the major forms of public speaking, the nature of information and how to present it, the process of persuasion and how to engage it, and the importance of ceremonial speaking. Appendix A, "Group Communication," offers concise practical advice on how to participate effectively in small groups. Individual instructors may rearrange this pattern to suit different syllabi and course strategies.

### *The How and the Why of Public Speaking*

Consistent with our "how and why" philosophy, we base our practical advice on underlying principles of human communication. The book begins with a concept of public speaking as a dynamic circle that links speakers, listeners, language, the time and place of the speech, and the overall communication environment. As we offer advice on structuring speeches, we show how various structural designs can be explained by simple concepts of Gestalt psychology such as "good form." In Chapter 10, when we tell students how to manage words, we also discuss the basic functions words perform. In Chapters 12 and 13, we ground our advice on informative speaking in learning theory, and our advice on persuasive speaking in a model adapted from social psychology. We show further, in Chapter 14, how evidence, proof, and argument function together as an integrated system that makes persuasion work. As we consider ceremonial speaking in Chapter 15, we show how two basic principles, one derived from classical and the other from contemporary theory, provide essential techniques for successful ceremonial speaking. We draw from the past and present, from the social sciences and the humanities, in our effort to provide the most useful coverage of the elements of public speaking for the beginning speaker.

### Focus on Planning and Structuring Speeches

We give special attention to selecting worthwhile topics and to preparing and structuring speeches. Chapter 5 introduces a systematic method of topic selection that ties together personal and audience interests and the requirements of the assignment. The chapter leads the student step-by-step through the process of analyzing and refining the selected topic. Chapter 6 explains four major forms of supporting material and their strengths and limitations. Chapter 7 shows how to combine these materials into an effective structure by determining, arranging, and developing the main points of a speech. The concept of good form helps us explain why some speeches succeed while others fail. Because outlining is such an important part of planning a speech, Chapter 8 guides students through its processes, including preparation, formal, and key-word outlines.

### Emphasis on Ethics

*Public Speaking* introduces students to the ethics of communication and the responsibilities of the speaker. Chapter 1 discusses the problem of plagiarism and challenges each class to develop a code of ethical conduct to be observed during the term. Chapter 5 introduces the concept of *responsible knowledge* as an ethical requirement for all public speakers. Throughout the text, we warn against abuses of supporting materials, evidence, proofs, arguments, and potent stylistic forms. We encourage students to respect cultural differences both in themselves and others, recognizing our national diversity. In addition, the book encourages thorough deliberation of critical public issues.

### Learning Tools

The book provides models to guide students in their classroom speaking experiences. Sample annotated speeches and outlines illustrate the techniques appropriate to particular assignments; for example, the student speech at the end of Chapter 12 illustrates both informative speaking methods and the use of visual aids. In addition, the book abounds with contemporary examples that help students see the application of communication techniques and principles to the world in which they live. The four-color design and the carefully selected photographs facilitate learning by making the book colorful and appealing.

We have designed each chapter to enhance knowledge. Learning objectives cue students to the content and prepare them for productive reading. The epigram and vignette that open each chapter point up its significance and motivate readers. Speaker's Notes such as "Developing a Formal Outline" and "Evaluating Examples" reinforce learning as the chapters develop. Model speeches throughout the text and additional speeches for analysis in Appendix B represent an interesting variety of speech topics, contexts, and speakers, and illustrate the major forms of self-introductory, informative, persuasive, and ceremonial speeches. Chapter summaries and Terms to Know remind the student of important points, and discussion and application exercises help put the knowledge to work. A glossary at the end of the book defines all the Terms to Know.

## CHANGES IN THE THIRD EDITION

This new edition has given us the chance to refine and reinforce old themes and introduce new ideas.

### *Cultural Diversity*

We believe that the public speaking class provides an ideal laboratory to explore and discover the different cultures that make up America. Students learn to tolerate and respect the many voices that make up what Lincoln once described as "the chorus of the Union." They also learn to accept and even cherish the many voices within themselves, for most of us have been fashioned by many cultures.

The representation of different cultures in most audiences also can present the speaker with a formidable practical problem in speech adaptation. How can we speak in a manner that invites these cultures to share a common understanding? Throughout the book, we return to this question.

For these reasons, the values of cultural diversity, strongly implicit in the first two editions, have become explicit in the Third Edition. We are convinced that respect for diversity and sensitivity to cultural differences are essential for effective, ethical speaking. We discuss these values directly and select our examples and model speeches in light of their importance. Chapter 1 discusses "cultural benefits" along with personal and social benefits. As the book proceeds, topics such as audience analysis in Chapter 4, the speaker's language, and the selection of supporting materials in Chapter 6 offer opportunities to emphasize the speaker's concern for cultural diversity. In particular, we add "cultural sensitivity" to our standards for effective language usage discussed in Chapter 10.

## Balanced Approach to Listening

Recently we worked with the Kettering Foundation on a project to improve public communication. That experience, plus our reading of the recent literature, has led us to develop a more balanced approach to listening. In the past, textbooks including our own have focused on critical listening as a defensive skill for protection from exploitive or defective communication. While understandable, this emphasis neglects the creative, constructive dimension of listening that makes the audience a vital partner in communication. The balanced ideal of critical and constructive listening invites audiences to participate more fully in the co-creation of meaning. As we describe this ideal in Chapter 3, our goal is to offer a more healthy, holistic view of listening that will encourage better listening behavior and a more expansive view of public speaking as an important social force.

## Highlights of Specific Changes

Throughout the Third Edition, the reader will encounter fresh writing, improved examples, and new sample speeches. Chief among these specific changes are the following:

- more attention to the pervasive importance of ethics. For example, Chapter 1 now highlights ethics as the most important criterion of speech evaluation.

- enriched discussion of communication apprehension in Chapter 2 so that the beginning student receives more support on this problem early in the course.

- change from "target audience" to "primary audience" to remove any suggestion that manipulation is an acceptable practice and to match our new emphasis on constructive listening.

- expanded and updated section in Chapter 5 on the use of "Electronic Data Bases" in library research.

- significant use of examples from award-winning student speeches in the 1991 Houghton Mifflin public speaking contest.

- greater emphasis in Chapter 8 on the process nature of outlining and on the role of audience in speech design.

- simplified, more accessible chapters on language and persuasion.

- added section on video presentations in Chapter 11 on "Presenting Your Speech."

- enriched discussion of informative speaking in Chapter 12, including a new chart matching types of speeches with design options, model outlines for each design option, fresh examples, and incorporation of recent research.

# PLAN OF THE BOOK

The plan of the book is both logical and flexible. We have found that the present sequence of topics works well in the classroom, beginning with an overview of the communication process and gradually building toward more complex skills and deeper understanding. Teachers who prefer a different sequence, however, will find the book easy to use because each chapter covers a topic thoroughly and completely.

Part One, "The Foundations of Public Speaking," provides basic information that students need for their first speaking and listening experiences. Chapter 1 highlights the personal, social, and cultural benefits of speaking effectively and explains the ethical responsibilities speakers must always bear in mind. We use a model to emphasize the dynamic interaction of speakers, listeners, ideas, the occasion and situation, and the overall communication environment. The chapter concludes with criteria for evaluating public speaking.

Chapter 2 offers students procedures for planning, outlining, practicing, and presenting their first speeches. The chapter helps them develop credibility for later speeches and cope with communication apprehension. It describes a speech assignment for introducing the self or others that can help break the ice and establish a constructive atmosphere in the class. An annotated student speech of self-introduction completes the chapter. Chapter 3, on critical and constructive listening, redefines the role of the audience in public communication. The chapter identifies common listening problems and explains ways to overcome these problems. The chapter concludes by developing the criteria introduced in Chapter 1 into a useful listener's guide for evaluating speeches.

Part Two, "Preparation for Public Speaking," provides in-depth coverage of the basic skills needed to prepare an effective speech: audience analysis, topic selection, research techniques, the development of supporting materials, and structuring and outlining. Chapter 4 emphasizes the importance of the audience one anticipates when preparing and developing a speech. We explain how to adapt to the speech occasion, to audience characteristics (including demographic information), and to audience dynamics. Chapter 5 provides systematic ways to select and refine topics so that the speech purpose is clearly framed. We also identify the library resources most useful for public speeches and offer suggestions for interviewing. Chapter 6 covers the types of supporting materials speakers must gather as they research their topics. The chapter discusses facts and figures, examples, and testimony. Responding to recent research, it introduces the narrative as another basic form of supporting material.

Chapter 7 shows students how to determine the main points in the body of the speech, how to make transitions from point to point, and how to prepare effective introductions and conclusions. Extended examples guide students through the outlining process in Chapter 8, from developing an initial preparation outline to completing a formal outline and a key-word outline for use during presentation.

Part Three, "Developing Presentation Skills," covers the use of visual aids, language, voice, and body for an effective presentation. Chapter 9 explains the development and appropriate use of visual aids to augment the message of a speech; examples illustrate the strengths and weaknesses of each type of aid. This chapter's discussion of computer graphics and of the role of color in the visual communication of ideas is distinctive. Chapter 10 provides a comprehensive understanding of the powerful role language plays in communication and offers many practical suggestions for using language effectively. Chapter 11 helps students develop presentation skills, offering useful exercises to develop both voice and body language. The aim of this chapter is to help students build an extemporaneous style that is adaptable to most public speaking situations. The chapter concludes with a section devoted to video presentations.

Part Four, "Types of Public Speaking," discusses informative, persuasive, and major ceremonial types of public speaking. Chapter 12 covers the principles and practices of speeches designed to share information and increase understanding. The chapter explains the functions of informative speaking and presents designs suitable for structuring such speeches. We go beyond the mechanics to show how informative speaking serves listeners' basic desire to learn, and conclude the chapter with an annotated student speech.

Chapter 13 describes the principles underlying the persuasive process and the skills needed for persuasion. The chapter focuses on the types and challenges of persuasive speaking, covers designs that are appropriate to persuasive speeches, and offers an annotated student speech for analysis. This chapter demonstrates how persuasion operates in our daily lives. In Chapter 14 we explain the uses of evidence, proof, and argument and how to combine them in effective persuasion. The object is to show students how to form powerful arguments to support their positions on policies or proposals. The chapter concludes by identifying the major forms of fallacy that can discredit persuasion, so that students can avoid such errors in their own speeches and detect them in the messages of others.

Chapter 15 discusses speaking on ceremonial occasions. The chapter shows the relationship of such speaking to cultural values and centers on the important techniques of identification and magnification. We consider many types of ceremonial speeches, such as speeches of introduction, tribute, acceptance, inspiration, eulogy, and celebration, including the after-dinner speech. A special section shows the uses and possible dangers of humor in such speaking. The chapter includes annotated speech excerpts and an annotated after-dinner speech to illustrate the major techniques.

Appendix A, "Group Communication," introduces students to the problem-solving process and the responsibilities of group participants. This appendix also provides guidelines for managing informal and formal meetings, and introduces students to the basic concepts of parliamentary procedure. Appendix B contains sample speeches by professional and student speakers for classroom analysis and discussion.

## SUPPLEMENTARY MATERIALS

The following are available to users of *Public Speaking:*

- The *Instructor's Resource Manual with Test Items* was written by Suzanne Osborn and Randall Parrish Osborn. In Part I, the manual includes sections on the purpose and philosophy of the course, preparing a syllabus, various sample syllabuses, an assortment of speech assignment options, a discussion of evaluating and grading speeches, a troubleshooting guide and teaching strategies for new instructors, and an extensive bibliography of resource readings. Part II of the manual offers a chapter-by-chapter guide to teaching *Public Speaking,* including learning objectives, suggestions for teaching, lecture/discussion outline, guidelines for using end-of-chapter items, additional activities, ancillary materials, transparency masters and handouts, and a bibliography of readings for enrichment. Part III offers test items for all chapters, and Part IV provides annotations for the speeches in Appendix B. The manual is the most comprehensive of its kind available, and can be used as a text for training teaching assistants.

- *Speech Designer,* a computer program designed to accompany the text, has been carefully revised for this edition. It offers students a self-directed, step-by-step electronic tour of outlining their speeches, and includes formats for each major speech design discussed in the text. This unique feature should improve the structure of student speeches, and should also result in better knowledge of speech design options.

- Transparencies may be used to enhance lectures and class discussions on such topics as the Dynamic Circle of Communication and the Step-by-Step Guide to Preparing a Self-Introductory Speech.

- Test-generating software is available.

- Teachers can arrange for an additional chapter, "Classical Origins of Public Speaking," to be included with the books they order. This chapter offers a summary and appreciation of the ideas developed by the early Greek theorists on the nature and importance of public speaking.

- Videotapes, two featuring student speeches, and one showing major public addresses on vital contemporary issues, are available to adopters. The special topic for the third edition's contemporary issues tape is "The Contentious Society." The tape offers controversial speeches by President Bill Clinton at the Vietnam Veterans Memorial, Barbara Bush and Hillary Rodham Clinton on the identity and values of women, Robert Redford on environmental problems, Elizabeth Glaser on the agony of AIDS, and Arthur Ashe and Michael Crichton on the quality and ethics of contemporary mass communication.

  The videotapes are accompanied by a *Guide to the Video Program* prepared by the authors. The *Guide* contains the text of each student speech, an evaluation, suggested discussion questions, and a commentary. In addition, both the videotapes and the *Guide* continue a theme introduced in the supplementary materials for the previous edition, "Prominent Speakers on Contemporary Issues." The *Guide* introduces the background for each prominent speech, provides its text, develops a discussion guide, and offers critical commentary. Users should contact Houghton Mifflin representatives for details.

## ACKNOWLEDGEMENTS

Many people have helped improve *Public Speaking* as it has passed through its revisions. The editors at Houghton Mifflin Company have been richly supportive in both professional and personal ways: Molly Faulkner made the success of the First Edition an obsession, and Ruth Gillies loved the book through several editions as our Basic Book Editor. Greg Tobin was a devoted, innovative counselor for the Second Edition. Jean Woy, Editor in Chief, and Margaret Seawell, Sponsoring Editor, have been immensely supportive of the present edition. Other editors who have left their wise marks upon the book include Beth Frankel, Project Editor for the first edition, Christina Horn, Project Editor for the second edition, and Susie Yanchus, who worked on the Speech Designer software for the second edition. For the present edition, we thank Karla Paschkis, Basic Book Editor, Cathy Brooks, Senior Project Editor, and Michele Casey, Editorial Assitant. Many of the marketing personnel for Houghton Mifflin have also encouraged us and offered advice. Finally, we would like to offer particular thanks to Nader Darehshori, the Chief Executive Officer and Chairman of the Board of Houghton Mifflin Company, who became our number one supporter and cheerleader many years ago. This book is a testament to Nader's faith.

We thank our colleagues listed below, whose thoughtful and helpful critical readings guided our revisions for the Third Edition.

Mike Allen
University of Wisconsin at Milwaukee

Scott Britten
Indiana University—South Bend

Donald R. Browne
University of Minnesota—Twin Cities Campus

Ann L. Darling
The University of Utah

David Evans
Navarro College

William David Fusfield
University of Pittsburgh at Pittsburgh

Susan A. Hellweg
San Diego State University at San Diego

Rachel L. Holloway
Virginia Polytechnic Institute and State University

Michele Horner Jackson
University of Minnesota—Twin Cities Campus

Joyce Jessa
Loyola Marymount University

Delton R. McGuire
Crowleys Ridge College

Stephen F. Nielsen
University of Nevada—Las Vegas

Mabry M. O'Donnell
Marietta College

Kenna J. Reeves
Emporia State University

Sandra Berkowitz Stafford
University of Minnesota—Twin Cities Campus

Ralph B. Thompson
Cornell University

Jay Pence
University of North Carolina at Chapel Hill

Janice Peterson
Santa Barbara City College

Judy Pier
Slippery Rock University

Nancy J. Wendt
Oregon State University

John L. Vohs
University of California—Davis

We again extend our gratitude to the reviewers of the First and Second Editions: Phillip Anderson, Kansas State University; James R. Andrews, Indiana University; John Bee, University of Akron; Cecile S. Blanche, Villanova University; Don M. Boileau, George Mason University; Barry Brummett, University of Wisconsin—Milwaukee; Carl Burgchardt, Colorado State University; Francis E. Cheslik, Seton Hall University; Patrick J. Collins, John Jay College of Criminal Justice; Jo Ellen Cox, Northwest Mississippi Community College; James Darsey, Ohio State University; Jimmy T. Davis, Belmont College; Michael DeSousa, University of California—Davis; L. Patrick Devlin, University of Rhode Island; Robert J. Doolittle, University of Tulsa; Clyde Faries, Western Illinois University; Elizabeth Faries, Western Illinois University; Susan Fiechtner, Texas A & M University; Patricia Friel, University of Cincinnati—Clermont College; Darla Germeroth, University of Scranton; James Gibson, University of Missouri, Columbia; Ethel Glenn, University of North Carolina at Greensboro; Keith Griffin, BelSouth Services Incorporated; Clair O. Haugen, Concordia College; Susan A. Hellweg, San Diego State University; Judith S. Hoeffler, Ohio State University; Richard J. Jensen, University of New Mexico; Madeline M. Keaveney, California State University, Chico; Harold J. Kinzer, Utah State University; Robert S. Littlefield, North Dakota State University; Suzanne McCorkle, Boise State University; Patricia Palm McGillen, Mankato State University; Michael McGuire, University of Nevada—Las Vegas; Andrea Mitnick, Pennsylvania State University, Delaware Campus; Virginia Myers, West Texas State University; Donovan Ochs, University of Iowa; Mary F. O'Sullivan, Western Wisconsin Technical Institute; Charles J. Pecor, Macon Junior College; James W. Pence, Jr., University of North Carolina at Chapel Hill; James Phipps, Cedarville College; Ralph S. Pomeroy, University of California—Davis; Meredith Rouseau, Pennsylvania State University, York Campus; Thomas Seibert, College of Mount Saint Joseph; Aileen Sundstrom, Henry Ford Community College; Charles O. Tucker, Northern Illinois University; Beth M. Waggenspack, Virginia Polytechnic Institute and State University; Donald H. Wulff, University of Washington.

Special appreciation goes to the following: Phillip Anderson at Kansas State University, who brought Anna Aley's speech to our attention; Anna Aley, Bonnie Marshall, and Stephen Lee, who travelled to Memphis so that we could videotape their speeches; Roxanne Gee, Valerie Banes, and Tom Dean, colleagues at Memphis State, who expertly prepared videotapes of student speeches; Robert X. Browning, Director of the Public Affairs Video Archives of C-Span at Purdue University, who helped us select the speeches for "Prominent Speakers on Contemporary Issues"; Pamela Palmer, Memphis State University librarian, who offered invaluable advice concerning resources of the reference room; Marshall Swanson, assistant director of Information Services, University of South Carolina, who helped us contact Bill Cosby; and Hal Phillips, film writer and novelist from Corinth, Mississippi, who went out of his way to help us. Thanks also to Richard Fiordo of Penn State University—Erie and Cynthia Smith of Keene State College. In addition, we want to acknowledge the generous support and advice of colleagues at Memphis State University, especially John Bakke, Keith Kennedy, and Richard Ranta.

M.O.

S.O.

# List of Speeches

**SELF-INTRODUCTORY**     *Sandra Baltz,* **"My Three Cultures"**    **56**

*Rodney Nishikawa,* **"Free at Last"**    **B3**

*Scott Champlin,* **"My Twenty-First Birthday Party"**    **B4**

**INFORMATIVE**    *Stephen Huff,* **"The New Madrid Earthquake Area"**    **350**

*Cecile Larson,* **"The 'Monument' at Wounded Knee"**    **B6**

*Jane Doe,* **"Rape by Any Other Name"**    **B8**

*Stephen Lee,* **"The Trouble with Numbers"**    **B11**

**PERSUASIVE**    *Anna Aley,* **"We Don't Have to Live in Slums"**    **389**

*Bonnie Marshall,* **"Living Wills: Insuring Your Right to Choose"**    **B13**

*Elizabeth Glaser,* **"AIDS: A Personal Story"**    **B16**

*Mary Fisher,* **"AIDS: A Personal Narrative"**    **B19**

**CEREMONIAL**    *Thomas P. O'Neill, Jr.,* **"Tribute to Jesse Owens"**    **430**

*Jesse Owens,* **"The Meaning of the Olympics"**    **437**

*Dick Jackman,* **"Address at Awards Dinner of the National Football Foundation"**    **444**

*Bill Clinton,* **"Inaugural Address"**    **B22**

*Elie Wiesel,* **"Nobel Peace Prize Acceptance Speech"**    **B26**

*Bill Cosby,* **"University of South Carolina Commencement Address"**    **B28**

*Ronnie Davis,* **"The Trials of Malcolm X"**    **B31**

PART ONE

# The Foundations
# of Public Speaking

*Speeches are actions among people, and, indeed, most effective ones.*
    *—Georg Wilhelm Friedrich Hegel*

# Public Speaking as Communication

**This Chapter Will Help You**

- develop a greater appreciation for the personal, social, and cultural benefits of public speaking.
- understand how the communication process works.
- appreciate what makes a public speech effective.
- become aware of the ethical responsibilities of public speaking.

Professor Parrish has just informed your mechanical engineering class that the research project he has assigned must be presented orally as well as submitted in writing. You can expect questions and should be ready to defend your conclusions. The oral presentation will count as 25 percent of the project grade.

You just had a phone call from Ms. Foster, the personnel recruiter who interviewed you last week for a marketing position with Dynamic Products, Inc. You have been invited to Atlanta for an on-site interview. As Ms. Foster closed the conversation, she added, "By the way, we'd like you to make a short presentation to our managers on that marketing project you told me about. Our director of promotions thinks it sounds exciting and wants to hear more about it. Let me know what audiovisual equipment you'll need."

You may find yourself in a position like that of Anna Aley, an undergraduate student at Kansas State University. Anna was living in substandard off-campus housing, and she wondered what she, as an individual student, could do about it. She heard that the Department of Speech was sponsoring a public forum of outstanding student speeches on local problems. Anna hoped that she could win a place on the program and call attention to the issue.

till wonder why you are in this public speaking course? Learning about public speaking can prepare you for some important moments in your life — times when a grade may be decided, when your chance for the job you really want hangs in the balance, or when a public problem that affects you directly needs action. Even speeches given in classes can result in changes that benefit the public good. Anna Aley's speech (the text of which follows Chapter 13), first heard in her public speaking class, was selected by her classmates to be presented in the public forum. Her speech made such an impression that the local newspaper, the *Manhattan Mercury,* reprinted it and began an investigation of the off-campus housing problem. The newspaper then followed up with a strongly worded editorial, and the mayor responded by calling for implementation of a rental inspection program. Of course, most of the speeches we give and hear are not so momentous, but our words create ripples of meaning that can spread far beyond the time and place in which we voice them. We never know how the speeches we give might affect distant lives.

From a practical point of view, the skills you build in this class can help you in whatever career you may undertake. A recent Office of Academic Affairs study in Wisconsin identified oral communication skills as a basic factor considered by employers when they assess job candidates. The study also found that such skills correlate highly with success in employment. Similarly, 250 companies surveyed by the Center for Public Resources rated speaking and listening problems, along with mathematical and science deficiencies, as the most critical areas in need of improvement among high school graduates and dropouts coming into the work force. An American Council on Education report, *Employment Prospects for College Graduates,* advises readers that "good oral and written skills can be your most prized asset" in getting and holding a desirable position.[1]

Finally, the abilities you acquire can help you later in life as well. Picture the following scenarios:

> The local school board has just announced that it will eliminate "frills" in order to balance next year's budget. Art and music classes must go! Your child is talented in drawing and painting, and you want to see her artistic training continue. Moreover, you believe that education in the arts is important for all children. A public hearing on next year's budget has been scheduled for the school board meeting next Thursday evening. Someone must speak out in favor of keeping art and music in the public school curriculum. Because you feel so strongly about the issue and others refuse to step forward, you must be that spokesperson.

> A real estate developer is planning to build a shopping center and office complex on fifteen acres of undeveloped land near your home. You believe that such a development will not only devalue your property but also destroy the beauty and serenity of your neighborhood. The Land Use Control Board has scheduled a public hearing for next Tuesday afternoon. To protect your pocketbook as well as your lifestyle, you need to speak at that hearing.

At such vital moments, family, spiritual, and material values may all depend on your ability to speak effectively in public. As you become more confident and skilled in public speaking, you may notice that you also improve in small-group and private communication situations. As we develop in one dimension of oral communication, we develop in others as well.

## PERSONAL BENEFITS OF PUBLIC SPEAKING

Beyond such practical applications, education in public speaking can help develop your sensitivity and creativity. Public speaking requires you to explore your own interests and positions on issues and to become more sensitive to the needs and interests of others. What issues concern you most? What makes them important to you? How might others react when you speak about these issues? What personal experiences can you draw upon to make these issues engaging to your listeners? What information is available to sharpen your understanding? Preparing an effective speech involves self-discovery and creative self-expression as you combine ideas and information in new ways.

One thing you will learn is the power of speech itself. There is a magic to the art of speaking well that has been acknowledged since civilization began. From the time of Homer, poets have marveled over the mysterious force that can move a speaker to eloquence. The Oglala Sioux, for example, thought that such speaking must have divine origins. They believed that "the ability to make a good speech is a great gift to the people from their Maker, Owner of all things."[2] As you speak before a group, you become aware of people responding to you. A responsive audience can make your thoughts and feelings come to life in a way you have never experienced before.

In addition to sensitizing and broadening you as a person and teaching you the technical arts of preparing and presenting speeches, education in public speaking can help you listen better and critically evaluate what you hear. Becoming a sophisticated consumer of messages is increasingly important in our society. The daily barrage of media messages directed at us makes the ability to sort out honest from dishonest public communication a basic survival skill. People who cannot make such distinctions are open to exploitation. You will also learn how to become a constructive listener. As a listener, you play an essential role in the creation of meaning. Listening constructively draws you closer to speakers and to others whose lives may be affected by their words. As a creative, constructive listener, you will be alert to the positive potentials in messages as well as to their defects. We examine listening in more detail in Chapter 3.

A final bonus of your public speaking class is that you become an active participant in the learning process. *You* put communication to work. The speeches you give illustrate the strategies, the possibilities, and the problems of human communication. As you join in the discussions that follow these speeches, you learn to identify elements that can promote or block communication. Your public speaking class may develop its own vital sense of community. It is no accident that the words *communication* and *community* have a close relationship: they both derive from the Latin word for *common,* meaning "belonging to many" or "shared equally."

## SOCIAL BENEFITS OF PUBLIC SPEAKING

The benefits you derive from studying public speaking go beyond developing your personal skills. Public communication takes place in a social setting. Richard Sennett in *The Fall of Public Man* presents eloquent reasons for ordinary people to develop public speaking skills. He argues that civilization, serving the best interests of the many, cannot survive without the active participation of citizens. Sennett further notes that "the first recorded uses of the word 'public' in English identify the 'public' with the common good in society."[3]

The political system of the United States is built on faith in communication. Without open and responsible communication there can be no freedom of choice, no informed decisions, and no representative lawmaking by elected legislators. Thus, the nation's founders realized the crucial impor-

*The United States Constitution and Bill of Rights protect rights to assemble and speak out on issues without fear of retaliation. Public speaking is vital to the survival of a free society.*

tance of freedom of speech when they wrote the First Amendment to the Constitution:

> Congress shall make no law respecting an establishment of religion, or prohibiting the free exercise thereof; or abridging the freedom of speech, or of the press; or the right of the people peaceably to assemble, and to petition the government for a redress of grievances.

Such freedom is not without its risks, as noted by Supreme Court Justice William Brennan:

> Rulers always have and always will find it dangerous to their security to permit people to think, believe, talk, write, assemble and particularly to criticize the government as they please. But the language of the First Amendment indicates that the founders weighed the risks involved in such freedoms and deliberately chose to stake this Government's security and life upon preserving the liberty to discuss public affairs intact and untouchable by the government.[4]

To be able to speak without fear of retaliation, to have the opportunity to hear all sides of an issue, and to be free to make informed judgments that affect our lives are rights basic to a democracy. Acquiring the presentation and evaluation skills you need to keep this freedom alive is a central value of this course.

## CULTURAL BENEFITS OF PUBLIC SPEAKING

One hears a good deal these days about "multiculturalism" and "cultural diversity." Should we value — and emphasize — the unity and commonality of the American experience, or should we instead appreciate those things that make us different and define us as individuals? Although this controversy seems quite recent, it reaches back into our country's history.

There are at least two fundamentally different ways to talk about American identity. The first, commonly known as the "melting pot" theory, suggests that various ethnic and national groups came to this country, where they were blended and melted down in a vast cultural "pot," emerging as a powerful alloy — the American Character. This "melting pot" metaphor, which was especially popular in the first half of this century, originated in the great steel mills of the industrial East. It held out the promise that all the immigrants who had come to our shores might be absorbed easily into our national life and forged into a powerful new cultural unity.

The "melting pot" metaphor, however, has some fairly obvious problems. For one thing, it expressed a basic cultural arrogance — American was best! For another, its stereotype of the ideal American citizen always had a decidedly white, definitely male face. Oriental, Hispanic, and African American peoples did not mix very readily into a common pot where they might easily lose racial identity. There simply was no such pot. Moreover, often these people, joined by Native Americans and others, *did not wish* to lose their original identities. Within the melting pot image, women simply disappeared. It was hard to champion the economic and political rights of women when the ideal citizen was always depicted as a man.

A much different kind of metaphor for the American cultural experience entered into public dialogue at the conclusion of Abraham Lincoln's first inaugural address, as the president sought to hold the nation together on the eve of the Civil War:

> The mystic chords of memory, stretching from every battlefield, and patriot grave, to every living heart and hearthstone, all over this broad land, will yet swell the chorus of the Union, when again touched, as surely they will be, by the better angels of our nature.[5]

Lost in the immediate crisis of that war, Lincoln's image of America as a harmonious chorus implied themes that are dear to multiculturalism: that the individual voice can survive in society and that this voice has unique values.

However, the metaphor also suggests, in a far less arrogant and more estheti-cally pleasing way, that the individual voices of America, when heard to-gether, can create a music, a chorus, that is somehow more rich and beautiful than the voices when heard alone.

Lincoln's image of a harmonious chorus may seem out of place beside the noisy contemporary American scene, but it holds forth a continuing dream of a society in which individualism and the common good can not only survive, but enhance each other. Within these pages you will hear many voices in the examples and speeches we offer: Native Americans and New Americans, women and men, conservatives and liberals, Americans of all different colors and lifestyles. Sometimes these voices may seem bitter, alienated, dispos-sessed, but all of them are a part of the vital chorus of American life.

The importance of public speaking for multiculturalism is that it allows us to listen to each other directly, to experience and savor that which makes each of us distinct and valuable. The public speaking class provides a setting in which we can experience cultural diversity, and an opportunity for us all to develop tolerance and appreciation for the various ways we may choose to live.

## THE COMMUNICATION PROCESS

Why does a public speaking class offer such important personal, social, and cultural benefits? To answer this question, we must understand the communi-cation process. As an important form of that process, public speaking has a distinct set of characteristics that can be visualized as a *dynamic circle* (see Figure 1.1). To illustrate how these characteristics relate to each other, let's consider the speech by Anna Aley mentioned earlier. As the model shows, communication begins with a source, in this case, Anna herself. The source has an idea that should justify both speaking and listening, in this case, the problem of substandard student housing and the need to do something about it. This idea is formed into a message, a carefully designed structure of thoughts that is presented through the words, voice, and gestures of the speaker. A medium, or channel, usually the air through which the sounds and sights of speaking must travel, carries the message. The medium connects the source with a receiver, an audience that considers the merits of the idea. In the case of Anna Aley's speech, the audience was extended through the pub-lication of the text of her speech in the local newspaper. The message pro-duces a response that can be both immediate and delayed. The immediate audience response provides feedback that can help speakers adapt their mes-sage during presentation. The delayed response is what happens as a result of the speech. The delayed response to Anna Aley's speech was the involve-ment of the mayor and the subsequent change in rental housing policy.

This entire process occurs within a communication environment, which can help or impede a speech's effectiveness. For example, a recent airline disaster might create a favorable environment for a speech on improving our air traffic control system because the audience is acutely aware of the problem. In contrast, a speech scheduled the day before spring break may suffer because the audience is distracted.

Anna Aley gave her speech in a receptive communication environment. Many other students had suffered from the same problem and were ready to listen to her message. Aware of the quality of work demonstrated in previous forums, the local press provided press coverage, thus extending the influence of her thoughts.

### The Speaker as Source

Every message has a **source,** or a point of origin. The source of a speech is the speaker. This is no mere technicality, for as Aristotle pointed out more than two thousand years ago, what we think about speakers affects profoundly how we respond to their messages. We are far more inclined, Aristotle observed, to react favorably to speeches when we think speakers are competent in their subject matter and when we trust them. These ancient qualities of competence and integrity form the basis of the modern term *credibility.* Aristotle also noted that audiences respond more favorably when

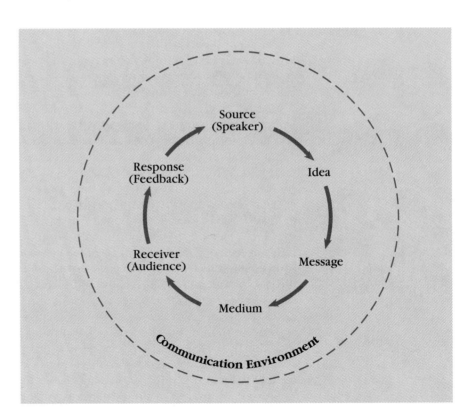

FIGURE 1.1
Communication as a
Dynamic Circle

speakers seem likable — when they seem to be people of good will. Modern researchers have uncovered still another important source characteristic, perceived power.[6] Some speakers strike us as forceful, action-oriented people. They may also occupy positions of power, from which (we perceive) they might reward or punish us in significant ways. These qualities of likableness and power combine to form the basis for another modern term, *charisma*. Taken together, credibility and charisma make up what Aristotle called the **ethos** of the speaker, a force that can determine whether we accept or reject a speech.[7]

Speakers who rate high on the various measures of ethos are likely to emerge as our leaders. Leaders are those who have some special knowledge to offer or advice to give, or who may inspire us by recalling important values and traditions. When we listen closely to speakers, and take their advice seriously, we acknowledge their leadership.

### Idea

For successful communication, you must develop a meaningful **idea** — a fabric of thoughts, feelings, information, and recommendations. What makes an idea meaningful in public speaking?

First, the idea should be important to you. It is something you want to share with others. Substandard housing conditions were important to Anna Aley because she was living in them. Second, listeners must find the idea useful and valuable. Anna's speech was oriented to her student audience. If her speech had impact, it would benefit other students living in substandard off-campus housing. Next, you should be qualified to present the idea through your previous knowledge or experience. And, finally, you must have done research that makes you an informed, authoritative, responsible speaker. Anna enhanced her personal experience with research about her problem.

Generating meaningful ideas for speaking is essential. We deal with this problem in Chapter 2, "Your First Speech," and Chapter 5, "Selecting and Researching Your Topic."

### Message

The **message** is the carefully designed structure of thoughts, presented through the speaker's words, visual aids, vocal patterns, and body language, that conveys the idea of the speech to a specific audience. Shaping a message is basic to the art of speaking. It is also a complex intellectual challenge that involves considering the needs and interests of your listeners, finding and organizing information, selecting supporting materials, and determining which words to use for maximum impact.

The speaker prepares the message by building a structure of thoughts in which each point seems to follow naturally and appropriately the point that precedes it until the idea is completed. We cover the art of speech organization in Chapter 7, "Structuring Your Speech." Within this overall structure, supporting materials — facts, examples, testimony, and narratives — make a message convincing. We address the use of supporting materials in Chapter 6, "The Use of Supporting Materials." To strengthen or clarify a message and add energy and variety to a speech, the speaker may use visual aids, such as maps, models, or charts. We consider visual aids in Chapter 9, "Visual Aids."

The wording of a message is very important. The meanings of words are often tricky — sometimes highly technical, sometimes very confusing. The use of the wrong word before a certain audience can destroy your ethos and the effect of your speech. For instance, a speaker who talked about "fraud" when he meant "Freud" left the audience puzzled over his meaning, caused them to question his competence, and diminished the effectiveness of his message. But the right words can work just as powerfully for you. We discuss the effective use of language in Chapter 10, "The Speaker's Language."

Finally, speakers convey their messages by the way they use their voices, facial expressions, and gestures. We cover these topics in Chapter 11, "Presenting Your Speech." Becoming a master of the message is a complicated process, but it is a goal you can achieve through practice and constructive advice from your teacher and classmates.

### *Medium*

Your message travels to the audience through a **medium.** Because public speaking is typically a direct, face-to-face encounter between a speaker and an audience, the medium is usually the air that surrounds the participants. If a speech is to be presented outside or in a large auditorium, a microphone and amplifiers may be part of the medium. We tend to take the medium for granted — until we discover something wrong with it, like poor acoustics. When such problems arise, the speaker must make immediate adjustments, such as speaking more distinctly and slowly.

Given an opportunity to speak on radio or television or to tape a presentation, speakers quickly learn that the change to an electronic medium can have profound effects on the entire communication process. Radio emphasizes the attractiveness, clarity, and expressiveness of the speaker's voice. Television brings a speaker into a close relationship with unseen viewers, so personality and physical appearance become important determinants of ethos. When speakers hope for coverage on television or radio news, they must be able to compress their ideas into fifteen- or twenty-second segments, or "sound bites," to fit the time constraints of electronic journalism. The language used must be immediately clear and colorful, so that casual listeners will be able to understand and remember the message. For speakers accustomed to audience eye contact, the impersonal microphone and the cold eye of the television camera may be disconcerting. To be effective, speakers must be able to imagine the audience beyond the microphone and the camera, and speak to those listeners.

A change in medium can thus complicate the speaker's job. But effective speakers also know that the electronic media present a rare opportunity to extend their message to mass audiences. We cover media presentations in Chapter 11.

## The Audience as Receiver

The audience is the **receiver** in the process we are describing, but we must not think of listening in mechanical terms. Ideal listening requires creativity as well as critical judgment. Because the fate of a message depends on how listeners respond to it, the audience is never far from the speaker's mind. Indeed, intelligent speech preparation begins by considering listeners. What kinds of subjects might interest them? What special experiences have they had? What biases might warp their reception of certain messages? These questions may be critical to the selection of your topic and to the way you frame your message. For example, it would be a waste of time and energy to inform people about something they already know or to persuade them to accept something they already believe. We consider the audience further in Chapter 4 and discuss critical and constructive listening in Chapter 3.

## Response

The **response** to a speech can be both immediate and delayed. The immediate response, called **feedback,** can take the form of puzzled looks, smiles or frowns, nods of agreement, and looks of intense interest or boredom. Effective speakers are sensitive to feedback from their listeners and adjust their messages accordingly. Does the audience appear "into the speech"? Good, you are getting through to them. Go on confidently to your conclusion. Do listeners seem puzzled? You may need to explain your point more fully or to provide an illustrative example. We discuss using feedback more fully in Chapter 11.

Every speaker hopes for a speech to have a desirable delayed response that has a positive impact on audience behavior. As a result of the speech, the lives of listeners are enriched in some way. The speech and the speaker have made a difference.

## The Communication Environment

Public speaking takes place within a **communication environment** of events and audience moods, attitudes, and expectations that can encourage or discourage speech effectiveness. Recent events can change this environment almost overnight. Your carefully planned presentation attacking "oppressive campus security" could be jeopardized if a major crime occurs on campus shortly before your speech. On the other hand, a campus incident illustrating overreaction by security forces could be a real bonanza. An effective speaker learns to cope with adverse events and to make ethical use of helpful ones.

Audience expectations are another important part of the communication environment. If your listeners are anticipating an interesting self-introductory speech and instead receive a tirade against tax reform, the communication environment may become a bit chilly. In another time, another place, perhaps, your speech might work — but not in that particular circumstance.

Another key aspect of the communication environment is **interference** that can disturb speech effectiveness. Interference can be any physical noise that impedes the hearing of a speech, such as a plane flying over the building. Interference can also be psychological "noise" within listeners that can cause them to be inattentive, such as worries about an upcoming test. We discuss interference further in Chapter 4.

Although the environment of a speech affects how it is processed and received, we must not forget that we are describing a *dynamic* circle. Speaking is shaped by events, but good speaking also shapes events. More than any other creatures, humans control and create their own environment, and they do so largely through words.

## WHAT MAKES A GOOD PUBLIC SPEECH?

What determines if a speech will be dynamic, if it will shape people and events? What standards should we use to judge the quality of a speech? These are important questions for all who are preparing to speak or listen. The following criteria can help us evaluate the quality and effectiveness of a speech: (1) speaker commitment, (2) a well-chosen topic, (3) a clear sense of purpose, (4) audience involvement, (5) substance, (6) appropriate structure, (7) skillful language use, and (8) effective presentation. In addition, a final criterion, ethical consequences, is so important that it deserves special consideration.

### Speaker Commitment

**Commitment** is the dedication that listeners can sense in you and your speech. Commitment is caring; you must let your listeners know that both the subject and their well-being mean a great deal to you. Commitment means allowing enough preparation time. A good speech generally cannot be prepared at ten-thirty the night before you are scheduled to speak. You need time to consider the needs of your audience, select and analyze your topic, do an adequate amount of research, organize your thinking, and practice your presentation.

Anna Aley's speech on off-campus housing problems, mentioned earlier in this chapter, is a good example of commitment. The topic was important to her personally and to the welfare of other students. It took her more than two weeks to research her topic and prepare her speech for classroom presenta-

## How to Create a Good Public Speech

1. Choose a subject that is important to you and vital to your listeners.

2. Select a topic that interests you, that you know something about, and that you can bring to life for your audience.

3. Decide on a clear purpose. What would you like your audience to do as a result of your speech?

4. Involve your listeners by asking for their response and relating your topic directly to them.

5. Use testimony, facts, examples, and stories to add substance to your speech.

6. Organize your ideas into a logical design.

7. Use clear, colorful, concrete language.

8. Practice your speech until you can present it smoothly.

9. Be concerned about ethical consequences of your speech.

tion. Then she revised and polished it some more for the public forum on campus. Her commitment was rewarded when her speech was successful.

Commitment also suggests that you respect your listeners, that you see them as people who can be helped by your speech and who can help the cause it may represent. Such commitment provides the personal motivation that makes a speech effective. Motivated speakers communicate enthusiastically, and enthusiasm is contagious. Commitment is the spark in the speaker that can touch off fire in the audience.

### *Well-Chosen Topic*

A well-chosen topic is one that interests you and should interest your audience once you bring it to life with facts, examples, and stories that show listeners how it affects their lives. Generally you should already know something about the topic you select. This knowledge serves as the foundation for further research that will enable you to speak responsibly and authoritatively.

A well-chosen topic is also one that can be handled within the time limits for your speech. Time passes quickly when you are talking about something that is important to you. You may have to narrow your topic and time your speech as you practice. You won't be able to tell listeners all they need to know about your subject in a short time, but you can acquaint them with an important part of it.

Finally, a well-chosen topic is appropriate to the communication environment and to your assignment. If your community is suffering from a crime wave, a good choice might be "What You Can Do to Prevent Crime." If your assignment is to inform your audience, you might discuss "Five Ways to Keep Your Home Safe"; if you are to persuade, you could advocate tough new laws with a speech titled "Let's Crack Down on Criminals."

### Clear Sense of Purpose

The kind of speech you present will depend on your general purpose. **Informative speeches** aim at extending understanding. **Persuasive speeches** are intended to influence the attitudes or actions of listeners. **Ceremonial speeches** emphasize the importance of common values. Figure 1.2 summarizes the major differences among these types of speeches. We look at informative speeches in Chapter 12, persuasive speeches in Chapter 13, and ceremonial speeches in Chapter 15. Beyond these general purposes, speeches should also have a specific purpose. For example, an informative speech may have the specific purpose of increasing listeners' knowledge of what they should do if an earthquake hits.

A speech that lacks a clear sense of purpose will seem to drift and wander as though it were a boat without a rudder, blown this way and that by whatever thought occurs to the speaker. Developing a clear purpose begins with thinking about your audience. Deciding precisely what you want to accomplish with listeners helps give direction to your preparation.

### Audience Involvement

Effective speakers are listener centered. This means that during preparation you should weigh each possible technique and each potential piece of data or evidence in terms of audience reaction. Will this example interest your listeners? Is this information important for them to know? How can you get them involved? The audience should always be at the center of your thinking as you plan and prepare your presentation.

One way to involve your audience is by asking questions at the beginning of your speech: "Have you ever thought about what it would be like not to have electricity?" Also, using the pronoun *we* throughout a speech seems to draw the audience, speaker, and subject closer together. The close involvement of subject, speaker, and listener is called **identification.** It is vital for effective speaking.

Being listener centered brings another advantage as you present the speech. If you concentrate on sharing your message with your audience, you will be less aware of your own natural nervousness about speaking before a group. Focusing on the audience can help relieve communication apprehension.

| Type | Functions | Examples |
|------|-----------|----------|
| Informative | Share ideas and knowledge, extend understanding, shape perceptions, clarify options | Speeches that describe, explain, or demonstrate |
| Persuasive | Influence attitudes or behavior, urge commitment, encourage change | Speeches that address attitudes, urge action, or contend with others' positions |
| Ceremonial | Celebrate events and occasions, recognize heroes and heroines, renew values, revitalize group commitment | Speeches that offer tribute, accept rewards, introduce other speakers, inspire listeners, or celebrate achievements |

FIGURE 1.2
Types of Public Speeches

## Substance

A good speech has **substance.** This means the speech has an important message, a carefully thought-out plan of development, and enough facts, examples, and testimony to support its claims. Your personal experiences can be a valid source of information and can make your speech seem more meaningful and real. Library research or interviews of other people can provide additional substance. A substantive speech shows that you care about your subject and your listeners, that you have invested your time and energy in an effort to do justice to the one and to reward the other.

*Examples,* which may either be based on actual experiences or developed out of your imagination, can help the audience better understand what you are talking about and can bring problems to life in moving ways. *Facts and figures* add authority to a speech and provide needed backing for conclusions. Skillful speakers often combine statistical data with a comparative example to relate the unfamiliar to the better known. For instance, you can say, "The base of the Great Pyramid at Giza measures 756 feet on each side." This information will be more meaningful for many audiences if you add, "More than eleven football fields could fit in its base."

*Testimony* adds the authority, prestige, and support of others to the substance of your speech. In many cases you will use the authoritative words of experts on your topic or quote the eloquent statements of famous people. At other times you may cite the "voice of the people," using testimony from ordinary people with whom listeners might identify.

## Appropriate Structure

A good speech follows a planned design so that each part seems to belong exactly where it is placed and contributes to the overall effect. Without such structure a speech may seem to consist of random parts that move in no purposeful direction. A well-structured speech will be organized in a manner that is appropriate to the subject, assignment, audience, speaker, and occasion. Consider this introduction to a self-introductory speech:

> I note with some interest and sorrow that our instructor has made me the first speaker of the day. Let me tell you about another time I went first — first down Devil's Canyon in our new campus white-water canoeing club!

This introduction suggests that the speech will be a personal narrative. As most of us enjoy listening to good stories, the design should produce an interesting speech. Moreover, since it pokes fun at the speaker's coming first, it relieves some of the tension speakers and listeners may initially experience.

Every speech needs an *introduction,* which should arouse interest and draw listeners into the topic. A second essential part is the *body* of the speech, which presents your main points and the material needed to develop and support them. The final necessary design element is a *conclusion,* which summarizes the main points of the speech, reflects upon the meaning of the message, and ties the speech into a satisfying whole.

The introduction may begin with an example, a quotation, or a question that draws the audience into the topic, such as "Do you think there's no need to be worried about global warming?" Once you have gained their attention, you will usually prepare listeners for what is to come in the body of your speech by disclosing your purpose. More suggestions for developing introductions can be found in Chapter 7.

The organization of the body of your speech will vary according to your material and purpose. If your speech tells your audience how to do something — for instance, how to mat and frame a picture — your main points should follow the order, or *sequence,* in which it is done. If the subject breaks naturally into parts, such as your three favorite authors, you can use *categories* to discuss them in an order that seems most appropriate and effective. Chapters 12 and 13 discuss these and other designs for speeches.

A variety of concluding techniques can be used to tie the speech up nicely. If you have covered several points in the body, you may want to summarize them into a final statement that will remain with your listeners. Another effective concluding technique is to connect the end of the speech with its beginning. This provides a strong sense of closure for the audience. Note how the following conclusion echoes the introduction:

> So, first down Devil's Canyon, first to speak today. You're not as tough as white water, but I can tell you that both trips were exciting!

Chapter 7 provides additional information on developing conclusions.

Effective speeches also contain *transitions* that link the various parts of the speech. They signal the audience that something different is coming and help the speech flow better. Transitions should be used between the introduction and body of a speech, between the body and conclusion, and between the main points within the body. Transitions can be a single word, such as *next* or *finally,* or they can be whole sentences, such as "Now that you can see the problem clearly, let's turn to how we can solve it." Transitions bridge ideas and aid understanding. You will learn more about them in Chapter 7.

## Skillful Language Use

Communication does not take place unless meaning is shared with listeners through language. In oral communication, listeners don't have an instant-replay button they can push if they don't understand. Your sentence structure should be simple and direct. Avoid long sentences with complex chains of dependent clauses. Compare the following examples:

> Working for a temporary employment service is a good way to put yourself through school because there are always jobs to be found and the places you get to work are interesting—besides, the people you work for treat you well, and you don't have to do the same thing day after day — plus, you can tailor the hours to fit your free time.

> Working for a temporary employment service is a good way to put yourself through school. Jobs are readily available. You can schedule your work to fit in with your classes. You don't stay at any one place long enough to get bored. And you meet a lot of interesting people who are glad to have your services.

Which is easier to follow? The first example is rambling; the information is presented in no particular order, and the speaker pauses only to catch a breath. In the second example, the sentences are short, and the meaning is clear.

Concrete words are generally preferable to abstract ones because they create vivid pictures for your audience and enhance understanding of your meaning. Consider the following levels of abstraction:

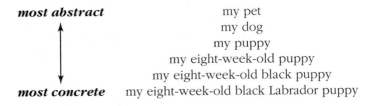

As the language goes from abstract to concrete, the audience is better able to visualize what is being talked about, and there is less chance of misunderstanding. We discuss other language factors that help improve communication in Chapter 10.

*An extemporaneous pre-
sentation sounds sponta-
neous and natural. It
allows the speaker to adapt
to her audience and elaborate on ideas that need further explanation.*

## Effective Presentation

A good speech is one that is presented effectively. Effective presentation
sounds natural and enthusiastic. It draws attention to the speaker's ideas
rather than to the speaker, and avoids distracting mannerisms.

To achieve these qualities, most class assignments call for an **extemporaneous presentation.** In this style of speaking, the speech is carefully prepared and practiced but *not* written out or memorized. You may speak from
an outline. Extemporaneous speaking allows you to be spontaneous and to
adapt to your audience during the presentation of your speech. If listeners
seem confused, you can rephrase what you have said or provide another example. This kind of speaking requires practice, however. Extemporaneous
does *not* mean "off the top of your head." In addition to analyzing your audience, doing research, organizing materials, and outlining what you want to
say, you must practice your presentation.

Practice may not make perfect, but it certainly improves your chances of
doing a good job. Some techniques that may look good on paper may not
sound good at all. It helps if you can tape-record your speech, leave it alone
overnight, then play it back to yourself. Get your roommate or friends to listen to the speech. See if they can identify your purpose and your main
points. Imagine your audience in front of you as you practice. If possible,
find a time when your classroom is not being used so that you can try out
your speech where you will actually be giving it. The more you practice your

presentation under these conditions, the better it should flow when you stand before your audience in class.

When you actually present your speech, speak loudly enough to be heard in the back of the room. It is hard to hold the attention of an audience if you speak too softly. Body language is also an important part of effective presentation. Your posture should be relaxed. Keep your hands out of your pockets; it is difficult to gesture when they are stuck there. Keep your movements natural. Speakers who point to their heads every time they say "think" or who spread their arms out wide every time they say "big" will appear more contrived than natural. Gestures should complement what you have to say, not compete with it for attention. Additional suggestions for effective presentation can be found in Chapter 11.

 ## THE ETHICS OF PUBLIC SPEAKING

The final and most important measure of a speech is its **ethical consequences** — whether it is good or bad for listeners and for the causes and people it discusses. If there is a Golden Rule for speaking, it might be: *Do unto listeners as you would have speakers do unto you.* Above all, an ethical speech is one that listeners are the better for having heard.

Because ethical responsibility is so vital, we should understand what constitutes an ethical speech. *An ethical speech is based on (1) respect for the audience, (2) responsible knowledge of the topic, and (3) concern for the consequences.* In addition, listeners must be willing to assume an important ethical role in the speaking situation.

### Respect for the Audience

Because people have different backgrounds, experiences, and interests, their opinions will often vary widely. Ethical speakers are sensitive to such differences and accept the possibility that bright and well-meaning listeners may disagree with their arguments. Consider two speakers: One comes before an audience with the attitude "I have the truth. Those of you who disagree are either stupid or ignorant." The other approaches listeners with the attitude "You are intelligent people. I have some information and ideas to share with you. I trust your judgment upon them." As we consider the probable results of these two approaches, we see that the more ethical speaker should also be the more effective.

Respect for the audience also means that speakers do not conceal their motives or their reasoning. Ethical speakers acknowledge all viable options, even as they argue for their own position and explain why they prefer it. Such practice is again not only ethical but practical. Research has shown that these multisided presentations usually have a more stable and lasting influence than messages that reveal only the side of the issue the speaker prefers.[8]

## *Responsible Knowledge*

Responsible knowledge of a topic requires that the speaker invest the time and effort necessary to speak with authority. Assertions and conclusions are based on a comprehensive view of all sides of the issue. An ethical speaker avoids absolute claims like "We must not support the government of Iran" and provides instead qualified claims that fit the situation, for example: "*As long as these conditions do not change,* we must not support the government of Iran."

Responsible knowledge also means that a speaker should assess the accuracy and objectivity of sources of information and be aware of the possibility of **bias.** A biased source of information has such strong self-interest in an issue that it cannot be expected to give a report or opinion that is entirely objective. For example, the American Cancer Society might be an excellent source of information on the relationship between cancer and smoking. However, on the question of government funding for medical research, the same organization might be biased because of self-interest.

Not only must speakers examine sources of information for bias, but they must be aware of their own personal prejudices as well. Ethical speakers try to be accurate and objective in the presentation of information, recognizing that there are some subjects on which they simply cannot speak without strong bias. For example, a speaker's opinion that mandatory drug testing for athletes is unfair may be based on a vivid and unforgettable personal incident that makes objectivity impossible. Ethical speakers need not avoid such subjects, but they do have a special obligation to reveal their biases so that these can be taken into consideration by listeners. Rather than making the speech ineffective, candor often creates respect for the speaker's integrity. Examples growing out of personal experience can also help a speech seem compelling and authentic.

The requirement of responsible knowledge also means a speaker must draw careful distinctions among facts, opinions, and inferences and meet the obligations of each kind of statement. It is unethical to present an opinion or assertion as a fact. For instance, the statement that "drug testing of student athletes is widespread" is a fact that can be documented. The contention that "drug testing of student athletes is unfair" is an opinion that requires more extensive support. The assertion that "drug testing is intended to protect the reputations of institutions more than the health of athletes" is an inference that must be supported by a full array of evidence. An ethical speaker will report the sources of factual data, present the qualifications of those who offer opinions, and demonstrate the legitimacy of evidence.

Finally, a speech built on responsible knowledge will represent the original work of the speaker and acknowledge all sources of information. Not doing so — *presenting the ideas and words of others as if they were your own, and without acknowledging their origin—is called* **plagiarism.** Colleges and universities consider plagiarism a major infraction of the student code and impose penalties ranging from grade reduction to suspension. Perhaps

### How to Avoid Plagiarism

1. Never summarize a single article for a speech. You should not simply parrot other people's language and ideas.

2. Get information and ideas from a variety of sources; then combine and interpret these to create an original approach to your topic.

3. Introduce your sources as lead-ins to direct quotations: "Studs Terkel has said that a book about work 'is, by its very nature, about violence — to the spirit as well as the body.'"

4. Indentify your sources of information: "According to *The 1990 Information Please Almanac*, tin cans were first used as a means of preserving food in 1811" or "The latest issue of *Time* notes that. . . . "

5. Credit the originators of ideas that you use: "John Sheets, director of secondary curriculum and instruction at Duke University, suggests that there are three criteria we should apply in evaluating our high school."

the worst result of plagiarism is its damage to your credibility once it is discovered. During the 1988 presidential primaries, Senator Joseph R. Biden, Jr., who was campaigning for the Democratic party nomination, was accused of "lifting the words of others" and using them in speeches as his own. Further investigation revealed that he had been disciplined for plagiarism while in college. The negative publicity surrounding these incidents forced him to withdraw from the campaign.[9]

## Concern for Consequences

Having concern for the consequences of speaking means recognizing that words can influence the reputations and fate of others. During times of war, for example, speakers sometimes give the impression that the enemy is more animal than human. Once we start thinking of people as animals, it becomes easier to destroy them without our usual regard for the taking of human life. We may even feel justified in the "extermination" of large populations. Speakers who use such language must realize how powerful words can be. Whoever started the saying "Sticks and stones can break my bones, but words can never harm me" was surely one of the great fools of all time. Words can really hurt! The greater the possible consequences, the more careful speakers must be to assess the potential effects of their language, to support what they say, and to season their conclusions with due regard for the humanity of others.

## *Responsibilities of Listeners*

Listeners also have ethical responsibilities. Ethical listeners should not prejudge a speech. It is irresponsible to say or think, "My mind is made up on that issue. Don't try to persuade me." John Milton, in his *Areopagitica,* observed that listening to those who disagree with us can be enlightening. We may learn that they know more than we do and thus gain a new and better perspective. Or, as we question and argue with them, we may learn *why* we believe as we do. Like our muscles, our ideas and beliefs become flabby if they are not used; they grow in substance and power when they are exercised. To protect ourselves from hostile ideas is to deprive ourselves of the chance to develop our own convictions.

Just as we should be open to ideas, we should also be receptive to the lifestyles and cultural backgrounds of others. Prejudice can prevent us from realizing that people should be judged as individuals, not as members of races, classes, or cultural groups. Moreover, we may have warped ideas about different races or cultures that block us from appreciating how others really live. While we may hear others, it may be hard for us to *listen* to them. When this happens, we are the poorer, for we are then deprived not only of the chance to encounter other worlds, but also of the opportunity to understand our own more clearly. In comparing and contrasting our lifeways with others, we learn more about ourselves.

An ethical listener is an active listener. Ethical listening means testing what we hear, noting its strengths and weaknesses. An ethical listener seeks to apply ideas in constructive ways, and to consider their possible impact on others. As you respond to other speakers, try to provide helpful reactions to their speeches. All sides benefit when speakers and listeners take their ethical roles seriously.

**IN SUMMARY**    *Personal, Social, and Cultural Benefits of Public Speaking.*   Your study of public speaking should help you develop practical skills and your personal potential. It should also make you a more effective member of society. Self-government cannot work without responsible and effective public communication, and public speaking is the basic form of such communication. The public speaking class can also become a forum for cultural diversity as we hear others express their individual lifestyles, values, and special concerns.

*The Communication Process.*   The communication process may be described as a dynamic circle that begins with the *source,* or speaker. Audience impressions of the speaker's competence, character, personality, and power can affect the fate of the speech. At the heart of every significant speech is an *idea,* a complex of thoughts and feelings concerning a subject. The idea is contained in a *message,* which is projected through words, illustrations, voice, and body language. The message travels through a *medium* that connects the source with the *receiver,* the audience that considers the idea.

This consideration results in an immediate *response* in the form of *feedback*. The communication process occurs within an overall *environment* that can promote or impede the speech.

***What Makes a Good Public Speech?*** The quality of a speech can be measured by the following basic criteria: (1) speaker commitment, (2) a well-chosen topic, (3) clear sense of purpose, (4) audience involvement, (5) substance, (6) appropriate structure, (7) skillful language use, and (8) effective presentation. In addition, ethical consequences deserve special emphasis in the evaluation of speaking.

***The Ethics of Public Speaking.*** Public speaking places special moral demands on both speakers and listeners. Speakers must understand the potential consequences of their messages and be willing to accept responsibility for them. An ethical speaker shows respect for the audience, demonstrates responsible knowledge of the subject, and understands the power of speech to influence the lives of others. Listeners should strive to be both critical and constructive, and should especially offer a fair hearing to speakers and points of view that may at first seem wrong or obnoxious.

**TERMS TO KNOW**

| | |
|---|---|
| source | commitment |
| ethos | informative speeches |
| idea | persuasive speeches |
| message | ceremonial speeches |
| medium | identification |
| receiver | substance |
| response | extemporaneous presentation |
| feedback | ethical consequences |
| communication environment | bias |
| interference | plagiarism |

**DISCUSSION**

1. Discuss how the ethics of communication might be applied to advertising. Bring to class an example of an advertisement that you think is unethical and explain why.

2. During the revolutionary takeover of a country, the means of public communication is usually one of the first things to be controlled by the new government. Why is this so?

3. What personal and social benefits are lost in societies that do not encourage the free and open exchange of ideas?

4. Is it better to think of American culture as a "chorus" rather than as a "melting pot"? Can you think of other desirable metaphors that might express the many-in-oneness of our nation? What might be the result of

emphasizing these metaphors in our public communication about our own identity?

**APPLICATION**   1. The Speech Communication Association has adopted the following code of ethics concerning free expression:

### Credo for Free and Responsible Communication in a Democratic Society

Recognizing the essential place of free and responsible communication in a democratic society, and recognizing the distinction between the freedoms our legal system should respect and the responsibilities our educational system should cultivate, we the members of the Speech Communication Association endorse the following statement of principles:

We believe that freedom of speech and assembly must hold a central position among American constitutional principles, and we express our determined support for the right of peaceful expression by any communicative means available.

We support the proposition that a free society can absorb with equanimity speech which exceeds the boundaries of generally accepted beliefs and mores; that much good and little harm can ensue if we err on the side of freedom, whereas much harm and little good may follow if we err on the side of suppression.

We criticize as misguided those who believe that the justice of their cause confers license to interfere physically and coercively with the speech of others, and we condemn intimidation, whether by powerful majorities or strident minorities, which attempts to restrict free expression.

We accept the responsibility of cultivating by precept and example, in our classrooms and in our communities, enlightened uses of communication; of developing in our students a respect for precision and accuracy in communication, and for reasoning based upon evidence and a judicious discrimination among values.

We encourage our students to accept the role of well-informed and articulate citizens, to defend the communication rights of those with whom they may disagree, and to expose abuses of the communication process.

We dedicate ourselves fully to these principles, confident in the belief that reason will ultimately prevail in a free marketplace of ideas.

Working in small groups, discuss how you would adapt this credo into a code of ethics for use in your public speaking class. Each group should present the code it proposes to the class, and the class should determine a code of ethics to be used during the term.

2. Attend a public speech and analyze it using the communication process model described in this chapter. How did the source rate in terms of

ethos? Were the ideas clear? Was the message well structured? Did the medium pose any problems? How did listeners respond? Did the communication environment have an effect on the speech? Report your analysis to the class.

3. Begin keeping a speech analysis notebook in which you record comments on effective and ineffective speeches you hear both in and out of class. Use the criteria for evaluating speeches discussed in this chapter.

**NOTES**

1. From "Statements Supporting Speech Communication," ed. Kathleen Peterson (Annandale, Va.: Speech Communication Association, 1986).
2. "The Lakota Family," *Bulletin of Oglala Sioux Community College, 1980–81* (Pine Ridge, S.Dak.), 2.
3. Richard Sennett, *The Fall of Public Man* (New York: Knopf, 1977), p. 16.
4. William Brennan, "Commencement Address," Brandeis University, 1986; cited in *Time,* 9 June 1986, p. 63.
5. T. Harry Williams, ed., *Abraham Lincoln: Selected Speeches, Messages, and Letters* (New York: Holt, Rinehart and Winston, 1964), p. 148.
6. Gary Cronkhite and Jo Liska, "A Critique of Factor Analytic Approaches to the Study of Credibility," *Communication Monographs* 43 (1976): 91–107.
7. Book 2.1 of the *Rhetoric,* trans. Lane Cooper (New York: Appleton-Century-Crofts, 1932), p. 92.
8. For a recent summary of research supporting this conclusion, see Mike Allen et al., "Testing a Model of Message Sidedness: Three Replications," *Communication Monographs* 57 (1990): 275–90.
9. Memphis *Commercial Appeal,* 17 Sept. 1987, p. A-1.

*Without speech
there would be no
community. . . .
Language, taken as
a whole, becomes
the gateway to a
new world.*
      *— Ernst Cassirer*

# 2

# Your First Speech

## This Chapter Will Help You

- understand the impressions you make on others as a speaker.
- select the best approach for a speech introducing yourself or someone else.
- develop an effective introduction, body, and conclusion for your first speech.
- compose full and key-word outlines for your first speech.
- build effective presentation skills, keeping the focus on ideas, speaking conversationally, and controlling communication apprehension.

Jimmy Green worried about his introductory speech assignment. How could he give a speech about himself when nothing exciting had ever happened to him? Jimmy opened his speech on his life in Decatur County by referring to a popular song, "A Country Boy Can Survive." Then he captivated his urban audience with delightful descriptions of jug fishing for catfish and night-long barbecues where "more than the pig got sauced." Jimmy was surprised that the class found his speech not only interesting but fascinating.

In the discussion following her introductory speech, Sandra Baltz told her classmates that she was taking the course on a pass-fail option. She had dreaded the class and had put it off as long as possible because she felt she wasn't good at talking to groups and was afraid she would do poorly. Her successful speech of self-introduction appears at the end of this chapter.

Mary Gilbert, an engineering student, was assigned to introduce Spider Lockridge, defensive halfback on the football team. She told the class that although Spider was best known for his fierce tackles in the open field, there was another side to his personality. Spider's hobby was writing poetry. Mary read several of his poems to the class, revealing him as a sensitive and witty person. Later, Mary said she was surprised her audience was not more aware of how nervous she had felt.

Many of us do not appreciate the value of our experiences or realize that others can find us quite interesting. Most of us underestimate our speaking ability. Even though we spend a lot of time talking each day, the idea of "public speaking" seems intimidating. We worry that everyone will know how anxious we are and are amazed when we discover that listeners are so caught up with what we are saying that they don't even notice our anxiety. *All the students just described surprised themselves by giving excellent introductory speeches.*

The initial speeches in a class can help build a communication environment that nurtures both effective speaking and healthy listening. No matter what the exact nature of your assignment, your first challenge is to present yourself as a credible source of ideas. In this chapter we show you how to begin building credibility and charisma as you introduce yourself or others. We discuss how to find the best topic for such speeches and how to develop and present them convincingly.

Before the first speeches, you and your classmates are usually strangers. You may even be a stranger to yourself! Introductory speeches give you a chance to explore your personality. These speeches also serve as an ice-breaker, giving members of the class a chance to know each other better. You will probably find that your classmates are a diverse and interesting group, and you should be able to develop an appreciation for each of them as an individual. What you learn about other class members will help you prepare your later speeches. It will give you insights into the knowledge, interests, attitudes, and motivations of your listeners that you can use to adapt your messages. Because it is easier to communicate effectively with people you know, you should also feel more comfortable about speaking before the class. Most important, your introductory speech can be helpful in establishing your credentials for later messages. As we noted in Chapter 1, people are more likely to respond favorably to those whom they respect and like.

Speeches of self-introduction perform an important preparatory role whenever speakers plan a campaign or a sequence of speeches. In short, speakers must establish favorable ethos *before* they go on to advocate programs of reform and change. Sometimes even professional speakers forget this vital rule. That criticism was made in the early days of Bill Clinton's 1992 campaign for the presidency: "At the campaign's start, he treated personal history as secondary to policy specifics, never properly introducing himself before the rumors about his private life did the job for him."[1] To compensate, Clinton's acceptance speech at the Democratic nominating convention focused on his personal ethos. It was a speech of *self-reintroduction,* preparing for the campaign that would lie ahead.

Gaining skill in introducing yourself also may help you outside the classroom. Making a favorable first impression at a job interview or at a social gathering can be important. You will learn how to present your best self to others. You deserve to make a good impression on others, just as people deserve to have their best cases presented in a court of law. The analogy is good, because others are constantly judging us from such impressions.

## UNDERSTANDING THE IMPRESSIONS YOU MAKE

When you stand before others to offer information, ideas, or guidance, you are enacting a natural leadership role. Indeed, the functions of public speaking and leading are closely connected. You may never have thought of yourself as a leader, but as you develop speaking ability, you will also be growing in leadership potential.

Both leading and communicating begin with listeners forming favorable impressions of speakers based on perceived qualities of competence, integrity, likableness, and power. In this section we explore ways you can convey these desirable qualities of ethos.

### *Competence*

Competent speakers come across as informed, intelligent, and well prepared. You can seem competent only if you know what you are talking about. People listen more respectfully to those who speak from both knowledge and personal experience. You can build this perception of **competence** by selecting topics that you already know something about and by doing research to qualify yourself as a responsible speaker.

You can further enhance your expertise by citing authoritative sources. For example, if you are speaking on the link between nutrition and heart disease, you might quote a prominent medical specialist or a publication of the American Heart Association: "Dr. Milas Peterson heads the Heart Institute at Harvard University. Last week in his visit to our campus, he told me. . . ." Note the factors of effectiveness here. The speaker has introduced the qualifications of the expert and has connected him with a prestigious institution. The quotation is recent, suggesting that the information it conveys is the very latest on the subject. The connection between the expert and the speaker is direct and personal, suggesting a favorable association. When you cite authoritative sources in this way, you are in effect "borrowing" their ethos to enhance your own as you strengthen the points you make in the speech.

Personal experience related as stories or examples can also help a speech seem authentic, bring it to life, and make you seem more competent. "I lived this myself" can be a very dramatic technique. Your competence will be further enhanced if your speech is well organized, if you use language ably and correctly, and if you have practiced your presentation.

### *Integrity*

A speaker who conveys **integrity** appears ethical, honest, and dependable. Listeners are more receptive when speakers are straightforward, responsible, and concerned about the consequences of their words. You can enhance your integrity by presenting all sides of an issue and then explaining why you have chosen your position. It also helps if you can show that you are willing to follow your own advice. In a speech that calls for commitment or action, it should be clear to listeners that you are not asking more of them than you would of yourself. The more you ask of the audience, the more important your integrity becomes.

Let us look at how integrity can be conveyed in a speech:

Mona Goldberg was preparing a speech on welfare reform. The more she learned about the subject, the more convinced she became that budget cuts for welfare programs were unwise. In her speech Mona showed that she took her assignment seriously by citing many authorities and statistics. She reviewed arguments both for and against cutting the budget and then showed her audience why she was against reducing aid to such social programs.

Finally, Mona revealed that her own family had had to live on unemployment benefits at one time. "I know the hurt, the loss of pride, the sense of growing frustration. I didn't have to read about them in the library." Her candor showed that she was willing to trust her listeners to react fairly to this sensitive information. The audience responded in kind by trusting her and what she had to say. She had built an impression of herself as a person of integrity.

This example also shows how competence and integrity are often closely linked in judgments of speaker credibility. Speakers who rank high in one quality often get positive evaluations in the other.

### *Likableness*

Speakers who receive high marks for **likableness** seem to radiate goodness and good will and inspire audience affection in return. Audiences are more willing to accept ideas and suggestions from speakers they like. A smile and direct eye contact can signal listeners that you want to communicate. Likable speakers share their feelings as well as their thoughts. They enjoy laughter at appropriate moments, especially laughter at themselves. Being able to talk openly and engagingly about your mistakes can make you seem more human and appealing.

The more likable speakers seem, the more audiences want to identify with them.[2] *Identification* is the feeling of sharing or closeness that can develop between speakers and listeners despite their often diverse cultural backgrounds. Audiences may identify with speakers who talk or dress the way they do. Audiences also respond well to speakers who use gestures, language, and facial expressions that are natural and unaffected. When talking to an audience, you should speak a little more formally than you do in everyday conversation, but not much more. Similarly, you should dress well for your speech, but not extravagantly, just simply and nicely. Although superficial, these identification factors can be important. You do not want to

*The character and personality of a speaker can influence how well a message is received. Speakers who know what they're talking about and who seem trustworthy, warm, friendly, and self-confident are most likely to be effective.*

create distance between yourself and listeners by language or dress that seems either too formal or too casual.

When there are obvious cultural differences between the audience and the speaker, identification may yet be built on shared experiences, values, or beliefs. In such situations, speakers can invite identification by telling stories or by using examples that help listeners focus on what they share in common. Such stories may also help the audience appreciate their differences. For example, Jimmy Green's tales of his outdoor life helped his audience understand both him and his background. By educating them and engaging their interest, he bridged the gap between his rural background and their urban experiences. Here is how another speaker handled the problem of creating a feeling of closeness with her audience despite a strikingly different cultural background:

> Even though she still had some difficulty with spoken English, Kim Sung enchanted her American audience with fairy tales from her native Korea. "All of us," she said, "dream about a better life, and our dreams are reflected in the tales we tell our children." As she told these stories and interpreted their meaning, Kim Sung both explained her unfamiliar cultural background and revealed basic similarities in feelings and values between herself and listeners. She built identification with her audience.

Speaker likableness is under your control and can be developed in your class presentations.

### *Power*

As a student you may not have much **formal power,** but you can have a great deal of **informal power.** Formal power comes from assigned responsibility, status, or position, such as that enjoyed by the instructor of a class. People, however, earn informal power from their manner of dealing with others. Informal power can arise from the other qualities we have discussed. If you are perceived as likable, trustworthy, and competent, listeners will respect you. You will have the power to influence their attitudes and actions.

Informal power often depends on how you handle the challenge of speaking. Jimmy Green, who gave the speech on the joys of country living described at the beginning of this chapter, later confessed to us that before his speech he lacked confidence, was not sure how his speech would be received, and worried that he might make a mistake. But when Jimmy walked to the front of his class to speak, he appeared confident, decisive, and enthusiastic. Whatever he might have secretly felt, his audience responded only to what they saw and gave him high marks for his sense of command. You also can gain power if you appear confident, decisive, and enthusiastic.

At first you may not feel confident about public speaking, but it is important for you to *appear* so. If you strive to appear self-assured, listeners may respond to you as if you are, and you may find yourself *becoming* what you appear to be. In other words, you can trick yourself into developing a very desirable characteristic! When you appear in control of the situation, you also help put your listeners at ease. This feeling comes back to you as positive feedback and further reinforces your confidence.

To achieve informal power, you must also be decisive. In persuasive speeches, you should consider all the important options available to your audience, but there should be no doubt by the end of the speech where you stand and why. Your commitment to your position must be strong.

Finally, you gain informal power from the enthusiasm you bring to your speech. Your face, voice, and gestures should indicate that you care about your subject and about the audience. Your enthusiasm endorses your message. We discuss more specific ways of developing confidence, decisiveness, and enthusiasm in speech presentations at the end of this chapter and in Chapter 11.

Just as integrity often connects with competence in judgments of speaker credibility, power often associates with likableness in overall impressions of speaker charisma. The work you do to improve any of these qualities of ethos tends to favorably affect the others as well. All of these factors work together to help you present credible, effective speeches.

## INTRODUCING YOURSELF AND OTHERS

A speech of introduction is often the first assignment in a public speaking class because it helps warm the atmosphere and provides an opportunity to develop credibility. Of course there is no way to tell your entire life history or another person's history in a short speech. At best, such an effort relates a few superficial facts, such as where you went to high school or your major. This information reveals very little about a person and is usually not very interesting.

Fortunately, there are better ways to give a speech of introduction. One good approach is to isolate the one thing that best defines and identifies you or your classmate. Answer the question *What is it that describes you or the person you are introducing as a unique person?* Then develop a speech around the answer that builds positive credentials for later speeches. Jimmy Green introduced himself as a person with strong outdoor interests and later gave interesting, effective speeches on environmental problems. Sandra Baltz's "My Three Cultures" prepared her audience for the speeches she would later give about Middle Eastern ideas, customs, and issues. Mary Gilbert not only introduced Spider Lockridge as a multidimensional person but also established herself as an individual who enjoyed both sports and literature.

There are a number of questions you can ask to help you isolate essential traits about yourself or the person you will be introducing. As you ask these questions, you will be conducting a **self-awareness inventory** of yourself or your subject.

1. *Is the most important thing about you the **environment** in which you grew up?* Were you shaped more by your cultural background than by anything else? How so? What stories or examples demonstrate this influence? How do you feel about its effect on your life? Are you pleased by it, or do you feel that it limited you? If the latter, what new horizons would you like to explore?

   As he accepted the Democratic nomination for the presidency in 1992, Bill Clinton sought to "reintroduce" himself to the American people. He had just emerged from a hard-fought primary campaign in which his ethos, especially his integrity, had sustained damage. To restore his character he emphasized the formative influence of his early childhood in Hope, Arkansas, and what he had learned in his grandfather's country store: "There were no food stamps back then, so when his customers — whether white or black — who worked hard and did the best they could came in with no money, he'd give them food anyway. Just made a note of it. So did I. Before I was big enough to see over the counter, I learned from him to look up to people other folks looked down on."[3]

2. *Was there some particular **person** — a friend, relative, or childhood hero — who had a major impact on your life?* Why do you think this person had such influence? Often you will find that some particular person was a great inspiration to you. Here is a chance to share that inspiration and to honor that person. As you honor others, you will be telling much about yourself.

   Renee Myers told how the members of her high school basketball team became "closer than family" when her brother was in a coma after an automobile accident. They brought food to the home, drove her family back and forth to the hospital, and came in and did the laundry and housework — all without being asked. For Renee these people defined the meaning of friendship: "Being a friend means doing something for someone without being asked." Through her speech the audience gained an impression of Renee as a sincere, trustworthy person.

3. *Have you been marked by some unusual **experience?*** Why was it important? How did it affect you? What does this tell us about you as a person? The experiences that shape people's lives are often dramatic. If you have had such an experience, it could provide the theme for a very effective speech.

   George Stacey, a student in an evening class, told of an incident that happened while he was working as a security guard at a bank. A customer had

*As you plan your self-introductory speech, consider your experiences and activities. Personal narratives bring a speech to life and help develop a sense of closeness between the speaker and the audience.*

a heart attack in the bank, and George wasn't trained to handle such a crisis. The customer died before emergency services arrived. "I felt my ignorance had killed him." As a result of that experience, George enrolled in first aid and CPR courses and now works as a volunteer with the county emergency services. He concluded his speech by telling about a person whose life he had saved, using his new skills. "She lived, and I felt redeemed." This speech gave the audience a glimpse of George's humanity and also established his credentials for presenting a later successful informative speech on CPR.

Experiences need not be this dramatic to be meaningful. Rod Nishikawa related how an encounter with prejudice at an early age changed his life and helped him develop personal inner strength. His self-introductory speech is reprinted in Appendix B. Sharing such experiences can help establish an atmosphere of trust in the classroom.

4. *Are you best characterized by an **activity** that brings pleasure and meaning to your life?* Remember, what is important is not the activity itself but *how* and *why* it affects you. The person being introduced must remain the focus of the speech. Talk about the specific elements in the activity

that relate to your personality, needs, or dreams. When you finish, the audience should have an interesting picture of you.

David Smart told his audience how golf had taught him useful lessons: "I don't let the little frustrations bother me and I keep going, no matter what happens. In golf, even though you hit a bad shot, you still have to go and hit the next one. You can't walk off the course just because things aren't going your way. College life is the same way. If you have a bad day or do poorly on a test, you can't just give up and go home. You have to get up the next day and keep trying." David brought his speech to life by telling a story about getting caught in a thunderstorm. "We weren't worried about getting hit by lightning because we all had our one irons over our heads. Even God can't hit a one iron." After the speech, his classmates felt that they knew David well.

5. *Is the* **work** *you do a determining factor in making you who you are?* If you select this approach, focus on how your job has shaped you rather than simply describing what you do. What have you learned from your work that has changed you or made you feel differently about others?

In introducing Mike Peterson, Mary Solomon told how his work as a bartender had influenced him. She explained that his job involved more than just mixing drinks—that it had taught him how to get along with many different, and sometimes difficult, people. "He learned to spot 'land sharks,' men who are trying to pick up any woman in the bar. 'They might as well have a fin sticking out of their backs,' he told me. And he learned how to listen, because everybody's got a story." After her speech the audience saw both Mike and his work in a new light. Mary's introduction helped him earn the respect of listeners.

6. *Are you best characterized by your* **goals** *or* **purpose in life?** A sense of commitment to a purpose will usually fascinate listeners. If you choose to describe some personal goal, again be sure to emphasize *why* you have this goal and *how* it affects you.

Tom McDonald had returned to school after dropping out for eleven years. In his self-introductory speech he described his goal of finishing college. Tom originally started college right after high school but "blew it" because he was interested only in athletics, girls, and partying. Even though he held a responsible job, Tom had always felt bad because he didn't have a degree. His wife's diploma hung on their den wall, but he was represented "only by a stuffed duck." As he spoke, many of the younger students began to identify with Tom; they saw a similarity between what caused him to drop out of school and their own feelings at times. Although he wasn't "preachy," Tom's description of the rigors of working forty hours a week and carrying nine hours a semester in night school carried its own clear message.

**SPEAKER'S NOTES**

## Self-Awareness Inventory

1. Have you been influenced by your *environment?*

2. Did some *person* have an impact on your life?

3. Were you shaped by some unusual *experience?*

4. Is there some *activity* that reflects your personality?

5. Can you be characterized by the *work* that you do?

6. Do you have some special *goal* or *purpose in life?*

7. Does some *value* have great meaning for you?

7. *Are you best described by some **value** that you hold dear?* How did it come to have such meaning for you? Why is it important to you? Often such speeches also describe environmental, cultural, or family factors, because many of our principles grow out of early life experiences. Values are abstract, so you must rely on concrete examples to bring them to life.

As he introduced her, Dan Johnson noted that Velma Black grew up in a large family on a small farm in Missouri. That experience, he said, shaped her values. "When you are one of thirteen, you have to learn to get along with others. You have no choice. You learn to work together without whining and complaining. And you learn to love, not noisy shows of affection, just quiet caring that fills the house with warmth and strength." Through the stories he told of Velma's early life, he was able to reveal her values and why they meant so much to her.

As you explore your own background or that of a classmate, we suggest that you ask *all* these questions. Don't be satisfied with the first idea that comes to you. As you explore your subject thoroughly, you will get to know yourself or a classmate better. The self-awareness inventory may even lead you to a different approach than those we have identified. Beth Riley worked through the questions and came up with a unique idea. She described herself as she talked about certain qualities of her favorite color, red.

## DEVELOPING THE INTRODUCTORY SPEECH

Once you have found the right approach, you can begin to develop your speech. The introductory speech is usually short, so you must keep its design simple. The speech must move quickly to its purpose and develop it concisely. Plan carefully so that every word counts.

## *Designing Your Speech*

The overall design of your speech will be shaped by the topic you select, your purpose, and the main points you wish to make. Different topics or purposes will suggest different selections from the design options we discuss in Chapters 12 and 13. Let us look at how a design might develop in an introductory speech that focuses on your childhood environment.

If you decide that the major factor in your life was the neighborhood in which you grew up, then you might select a *categorical* design. In this design you develop different points that advance your overall purpose. You could begin with the setting, a description of a street scene in which you capture the sights, sounds, and smells of the locale: "I can always tell a Swedish neighborhood by the smell of *lutefisk* on Friday afternoons." Next you might describe the people, focusing on a certain neighbor who influenced you—perhaps the neighborhood grocer, who loved America with a patriotic passion, helped those in need, and always voted stubbornly for the Socialist party. Finally, you might talk about the street games you played as a child and what they taught you about people and yourself. This "setting-people-games" categorical design structures your speech in an orderly manner.

The example also suggests how the introduction, body, and conclusion of your speech should be closely related. Your introduction could be the opening street scene that sets the stage for the rest of your speech. In the body of the speech you could describe the people, using the grocer as an extended example, then go on to describe the childhood games that reinforced the lessons of sharing. Your conclusion should make clear the point of the speech:

> I hope you have enjoyed this "tour" of my neighborhood, this "tour" of my past. If you drove down this street tomorrow, you might think it was just another crowded, gray, urban neighborhood. But to me it is filled with colorful people who care for each other and who dream great dreams of a better tomorrow. That street runs right down the center of my life.

Other topics and purposes might suggest other designs. If you select an experience that influenced you, such as "An Unforgettable Adventure," your speech might follow a *sequential* pattern as you tell the story of what happened. You would talk about events in the actual time sequence in which they occurred. Again, you could use the introduction to set the scene and the conclusion to summarize the effect this experience had on you. Should you decide to tell about a condition that has had a great impact on you, a *cause-effect* design might be most appropriate. Maria One Feather, a Native American student, used such a design in her speech "Growing Up Red — and Feeling Blue — in White America." In this instance she treated the condition as the cause and its impact on her as the effect.

*The stepping stones to success in your first speech are to select your topic, decide on your purpose, focus what you want to say, and determine the design best suited to develop the speech.* The design you choose will suggest how you should proceed to open the speech, develop its body, and bring it to a satisfactory conclusion.

Let us consider some additional examples of how this process of developing the introduction, body, and conclusion may work in introductory speeches. Although we discuss these parts of the speech separately, keep in mind that they are part of a larger organic whole. To be effective, they must fit and work together in the finished product.

## Introduction

The basic purposes of an **introduction** are to arouse the interest of your audience, to prepare them for the rest of the speech, and to build a good relationship between yourself and listeners. Randy Block captured the attention of his audience when he opened his introductory speech with this statement:

> I want to tell you about a love affair of mine that won't upset my wife, even if she finds out about it!

This opening *startled* his audience into listening and aroused curiosity about what would follow. Randy next revealed his main theme: his "love affair" was with a bicycle. This central idea of the speech is called the **thematic statement.** Randy used a categorical design to explain the main reasons he was fond of his bicycle. Fortunately, Randy's speech was colorful and interesting, for any speaker who creates such intense curiosity in an introduction must justify that interest with the substance of the speech. An introduction should never upstage the message of a speech.

Eric Whittington engaged his listeners by reciting a list of place names, pausing after each name:

> Guam . . . Hawaii . . . California . . . Washington . . . Michigan . . .
> Virginia . . . South Carolina . . . Florida . . . Tennessee. I'm twenty years old. I've lived in eight different states and one trust territory. I've moved eighteen times in my life and attended schools in nine different school systems. You might think that moving so much wouldn't be good for a person, but it provided me with the opportunity to get to know and appreciate many different lifestyles. Come with me on this journey through my life that brought me to where I am and made me what I am today.

This introduction prepared the audience for the speech's *spatial* design; Eric showed how three of these areas in particular had enriched his life.

Suzette Carter opened her introductory speech by establishing a personal relationship with her listeners:

> Last Monday Elizabeth told us how she enjoyed being an "obedient wife." I admire her honesty and her courage for saying that. I too was an obedient wife and daughter most of my life. But the result was that it took a long time for me to learn who I was and how I could be independent. I'd like to tell you about my quest for myself, in hopes that it may help some of you who have the same problem.

Suzette's speech followed a sequential design, tracing major relevant events in her life.

### Body

The **body** is the most important part of your speech because it is where you present and develop your main points, the most important ideas in your message. In a short presentation you cannot cover many main points and support them adequately. Limit their number so you can develop them in depth. For a three- to five-minute assignment, you should restrict yourself to two or three main points. (Determining and wording main points is covered in more detail in Chapter 7).

Returning to our student examples, Randy developed two main points explaining why he loved his bike: (1) biking gave him a sense of freedom, and (2) biking provided him with an opportunity for adventure. Eric explained his appreciation for diversity with three main points: (1) living in the relaxed multicultural society of Hawaii, (2) living in an industrial town in Michigan, and (3) living in Charleston, South Carolina — a city steeped in the tradition of the Old South. Eric's use of *examples* to develop these points provided interesting, specific detail that illustrated and enlivened his theme. Had he tried to talk about all the places he mentioned in his opening, he would have gone well over the time limit assigned by his teacher and might have bored his listeners as well. Suzette described three main phases in her quest for self: (1) her life in an overprotective home, (2) her life with a domineering husband, and (3) finally finding herself on her own. Her speech used *narratives* to illustrate the main points.

Every main point in your speech should be bolstered with some form of supporting material — facts and figures, testimony, examples, or narratives. *Supporting materials* provide content and substance to your message, especially in the body of a speech (see Chapter 6 for further information). *Facts and figures* help build the impression that the speaker possesses *responsible knowledge.* For example, Randy might have mentioned the number of bicycles sold in the United States last year to suggest that others shared his passion for biking. These figures would not only have added an interesting bit of information: they would also have enhanced his perceived competency.

*Testimony* involves citing what others, especially experts in the field, have to say about your subject. Had Eric cited child development experts on the connection between exposure to many cultures and the development of desirable qualities in children, he could have provided even more in-depth knowledge about his subject and himself.

Examples and narratives are especially useful in the introductory speech because they help develop a feeling of closeness between the audience and the speaker. They hold the interest of the audience while revealing some important truth about the speaker or the topic. Narratives should be short and to the point, moving in natural sequence from the beginning of the story to the end. The language of narration should be colorful, concrete, and active; the presentation, lively and interesting. Randy used a narrative effectively to show how his bicycle provided him with an opportunity for adventure. He told about the time he traveled 130 miles in fourteen hours of continuous biking, and of what happened when he crawled under a bridge to escape the blazing midafternoon sun. As Randy told the story, his voice and face came alive, and he began to gesture spontaneously.

By concentrating on two or three main points in the body of your speech and developing them with facts and figures, testimony, examples, or narratives, you can provide your audience with useful and appealing listening experiences.

## Conclusion

Finally, these students all concluded by showing how the experiences they related had affected their lives. The **conclusion** often includes a **summary statement,** which restates the main points and the central idea, and

---

**SPEAKER'S NOTES**

### Preparing Your First Speech

1. Select a design appropriate to your topic and purpose.

2. Develop an introduction that arouses attention and interest as it leads into your topic.

3. Limit yourself to two or three main points.

4. Develop each main point with narratives, examples, facts and figures, and/or testimony.

5. Prepare a conclusion that ties your speech together and reflects on your meaning.

**concluding remarks,** which reflect on the meaning of the speech. Randy used these techniques to end his speech:

> Now you know why I have this "love affair" with my bike. I love the sense of freedom and the opportunity for adventure that it gives me. Perhaps you would also enjoy this kind of affair. Give it a fling!

Eric concluded his speech by explaining that moving so much had allowed him to develop an appreciation for different cultures. Suzette explained that although she now considers herself liberated and independent, she does not think of herself as a stereotype. She is not so much a feminist as an individual. "I'm not Gloria Steinem," she said in her conclusion. "*My* name is Suzette Carter."

## OUTLINING THE INTRODUCTORY SPEECH

An outline using complete sentences will help you organize your thoughts. It should display your introduction, thematic statement, main ideas and their supporting materials, and your conclusion so that you can see if all these vital elements work together. You should also prepare a **key-word outline,** a shorthand version of your full outline, which serves to remind you of the order of ideas as you practice and present the speech. As the name suggests, this outline contains only key words that prompt your memory as you speak. Although the full outline may require several pages to complete, the key-word outline often fits on one or two small index cards. We shall say more about outlining in Chapter 8.

In the following full outline for a self-introductory speech, several critical parts of the speech — the introduction, thematic statement, and conclusion — are written out word for word. They anchor the meaning of the speech and determine whether your entrance into and exit from the speech will be smooth and effective. Thus, it is important that they be planned exactly. Note, however, that the entire speech is not written out, leaving room for spontaneity in the actual presentation.

### "FREE AT LAST"

#### *by Rod Nishikawa*

*Introduction*

    I.   *Attention-arousing and orienting material:* Three years ago I presented the valedictory speech at my high school graduation. As I concluded, I borrowed a line from Dr. Martin Luther King's "I Have a Dream" speech: "Free at last, free at last, thank God almighty we're free at last!" The words had a joyful, humorous place in that speech, but for me personally, they were a lie.

II. *Thematic statement:* I was not yet free, and would not be free until I had conquered an ancient enemy, both outside me and within me—that enemy was racial prejudice.

*Body*

I. When I was eight years old I was exposed to anti-Japanese prejudice in a brutal way.

A. I was a "Jap" who didn't belong in America.

B. The bully's words burned into my soul.

1. I was ashamed of my heritage.

2. I hated having to live in this country.

II. My parents helped me put this problem in perspective.

A. They survived terrible prejudice in their youth during World War II.

B. They taught me to accept the reality of prejudice.

C. They taught me the meaning of *gaman:* how to bear the burden within and not show anger.

III. Practicing *gaman* has helped me develop inner strength.

A. I rarely experience fear or anger.

B. I have learned to accept myself.

C. I have learned to be proud of my heritage.

*Conclusion*

I. *Summary Statement:* Practicing *gaman* has helped me conquer prejudice.

II. *Concluding Remarks:* Although my Japanese ancestors might not have spoken as boldly as I have today, I am basically an American, which makes me a little outspoken. Therefore, I can talk to you about racial prejudice and of what it has meant to my life. And because I can talk about it, and share it with you, I am finally, truly, "free at last."

> Rod uses three main points to structure the problem-solution design of his speech. Each main point is supported with facts, examples, or narratives.

 **PRESENTING THE INTRODUCTORY SPEECH**

Once you have analyzed your topic and outlined your ideas for your first speech, you are ready to prepare for presentation. An effective presentation spotlights the ideas, not the speaker, and is delivered as though you were talking with the audience, not reading to them or reciting from memory. Also, it is normal, *even desirable,* to feel nervous before giving a speech. In effective presentations, the speakers use the energy from this natural apprehension to make the speech more exciting and interesting.

### Spotlight the Ideas

The presentation of a speech is the climax of planning and preparation — the speaker's time to stand in the spotlight. Though presentation is important, it should never overshadow the speech. Have you ever had this kind of exchange?

> "She's a wonderful speaker — what a beautiful voice, what eloquent diction, what a smooth delivery!"
>
> "What did she say?"
>
> "I don't remember, but she sure sounded good!"

Sometimes the skills of presentation are used to cover up a lack of substance or may even disguise unethical speaking. When this happens, the audience can lose sight of the basic purpose of public speaking: *the presentation of ideas in messages that have been carefully prepared so that they deserve the attention they receive from an audience.*

As you practice speaking from your outline and when you present your speech, concentrate on the thoughts you have to offer. *You should have a vivid realization of these ideas during the moments of actual presentation.*[4] In other words, the thoughts should come alive as you speak, joining you and your listeners.

### Sound Natural

An effective presentation preserves the best qualities of conversation. It sounds natural and spontaneous, yet has a depth, coherence, and quality that are not normally found in social conversation. The best way to approach this ideal of *improved conversation* is to present your speech extemporaneously. An *extemporaneous presentation* is carefully prepared and practiced but not written out or memorized. If you write out your speech, you will be tempted either to memorize it word for word or to read it to your audience. Reading or memorizing usually results in a stilted presentation. *Do not read your speech!* That defeats the purpose of public communication because it robs the audience of its chance to participate in the creation of ideas. *Audience contact is more important than exact wording.* The only parts of a speech that should be memorized are the introduction, the conclusion, and other critical phrases or sentences, such as the punch lines of humorous stories.

### Key-Word Outline

To sound conversational and spontaneous, use your key-word outline while speaking. *Never make the mistake of using your full outline as you present your speech*. You may lapse into reading it and lose contact with your audience. (The following key-word outline is based on the outline presented earlier.)

## "FREE AT LAST"

*Introduction*

    I.   "Free at last" — high school speech

    II.  Not free — enemy was prejudice

*Body*

    I.   Encounter with bully

        A. "Jap," didn't belong here

        B. Words burned

            l. Ashamed of self

            2. Hated U.S.

    II.  Parents help

        A. Survived much worse

        B. Taught me to accept reality

        C. Taught me *GAMAN*

    III.  *Gaman* — inner strength

        A. No fear or anger

        B. Accepted self

        C. Proud of heritage

*Conclusion*

    I.   *Gaman* conquers prejudice

    II.  Can talk about it: therefore "free at last"

### *Practice Your Speech*

Speech classrooms often have a speaker's lectern mounted on a table at the front of the room. Lecterns often present problems for beginning speakers. Lecterns seem very formal and can create a barrier between a speaker and an audience. If you are presenting a speech designed to build identification and good feelings, standing behind a lectern may be inappropriate. In addition, short people can almost disappear behind a lectern. Because their gestures are hidden from view, their messages lose much of the reinforcing power of body language. For these reasons, it is sometimes good to speak from the side of the lectern or even in front of it.

    If you plan to use the lectern, place your outline high on its surface so that you do not have to noticeably lower your head to look at it. That way, you reduce the loss of direct eye contact with your listeners. Print your key-word outline in large letters that you can read easily with a glance. Use 3 × 5 inch index cards. Don't try to hide the cards or feel embarrassed if you need to refer to them. Most of your listeners probably won't even notice it when you use them. Remember, your audience is far more interested in what you have to say than in any awkwardness you may feel.

As you practice, imagine your audience in front of you. Maintain eye contact with your imaginary listeners, just as you will during the actual presentation. Look around the room so that everyone feels included in your message. Try to be enthusiastic about what you are saying. Let your voice suggest that you are confident. Strive for variety and color in your vocal presentation: avoid speaking in a monotone, which never changes pace or pitch. Pause to let important ideas sink in. Let your face, body, and voice respond to your ideas as you speak them.

### *Make Nervousness Work for You*

As you give your first speech, it is only natural to have some **communication apprehension.** In fact, there would be something wrong with you if you didn't have feelings of anxiety. The absence of any nervousness could suggest that you do not care about the audience or your message. Almost everyone who faces a public audience experiences some kind of concern. We once attended a banquet where an award was presented to the "Communicator of the Year." Before sitting down to eat, the recipient of this award confessed privately to us, "I really dread having to make this acceptance speech!" We were not at all surprised when he made an effective presentation.

There are many reasons why public speaking can be frightening. Speaking before large groups of people, where one is the center of attention, is not an everyday occurrence for most people. We may feel strange and uncomfortable when we confront it. Moreover, the importance of communication in such moments is usually great; much depends on how well we express our ideas. This element of risk, combined with the feeling of strangeness, can explain why many people dread public speaking. The important thing is not to be too anxious about your apprehension. Accept it as natural, and remind yourself that you can convert these feelings into positive energy. *One of the biggest myths about public speaking classes is that they can or should rid you of any natural fears.* Instead, you should learn how to harness the energy generated by apprehension so that your speaking is more dynamic. No anxiety often means a flat, dull presentation. Transformed anxiety can make your speech sparkle.

How can you put this energy to work for you? If you find yourself building to an uncontrollable state of nervousness before a speech, go off by yourself and practice relaxation exercises. While breathing deeply and slowly, concentrate on tensing and then relaxing your muscles, starting with your neck and working down to your feet. These techniques will help you control the physical symptoms of apprehension.[5] While you are relaxed, identify any negative thoughts you may harbor about yourself as a speaker, such as "Everybody will think I'm stupid" or "Nobody wants to listen to me." Replace them with positive messages that focus on your ideas and your audience, such as "These ideas are important and useful" or "Listeners will really enjoy this story." This approach to controlling communication anxiety by deliberately replacing negative thoughts with positive, constructive statements is called **cognitive restructuring.**[6] A final technique to help you control apprehension is **visualization,** in which you systematically picture yourself succeeding as a speaker and practice with that image in mind. Athletes often employ visualization to improve their performances.[7] Using this technique, you picture in your mind a day of success, from the moment you get up to the moment you enjoy the congratulations of classmates and teacher for an excellent speech.[8]

There are other things you can do to control communication apprehension. First, select a topic that interests and excites you, so that you will get so involved with it that there is little room in your mind for worry about yourself. Second, choose a topic that you already know something about so that you will be more confident. Then build on that foundation of knowledge. Visit the library and interview experts. The better prepared you are, the more confident you will be that you have something worthwhile to say. Third, consider whether you might use a visual aid — a chart, graph, or model. Referring to a visual aid encourages gesturing, and gesturing helps release excess energy in constructive ways. (For advice on preparing a visual aid, see Chapter 9.) Fourth, practice, practice, and then practice some more. The more you master your message, the more comfortable you will be. Fifth, develop a positive attitude toward your listeners. Don't think of them as "the enemy." Expect them to be helpful and attentive.

Finally as we stated earlier, *act* confident, even if you don't *feel* that way. Don't discuss your anxiety with classmates before you speak. When it is your turn, walk briskly to the front of the room, look at your audience and establish eye contact. If appropriate to your subject, smile at the audience, then begin your presentation. Whatever happens during your speech, remember that listeners cannot see and hear inside you. They know only what you show them. Show them a controlled speaker communicating well-researched and carefully prepared ideas. *Never place on your listeners the burden of sympathy for you as a speaker* — their job is to listen to what you are saying. Don't say anything like "Gee, am I scared!" Such behavior may make the audience uncomfortable. If you put your listeners at ease by acting confident yourself, they can relax and provide the positive feedback that will make you a more assured and better speaker.

When you reach your conclusion, pause, and then present your summary statement and concluding remarks with special emphasis. Maintain eye contact for a moment before you move confidently back to your seat. This final impression is very important. *You should keep the focus on your message, not on yourself.* Even though you may feel relieved that the speech is over, don't say "Whew!" or "I made it!" and never shake your head to show disappointment in your presentation. Even if you did not live up to your aspirations, you probably did better than you thought.

Do these techniques really work, and is such advice helpful? Research on communication apprehension has established the following conclusions: *(1) such techniques do work,* and *(2) they work best in combination.* If you practice these techniques and follow this advice, you should improve your ability to control communication apprehension and convert it into positive, constructive energy.[9]

Thus far, we have discussed controlling communication apprehension in terms of what the speaker can do, but the audience also can help speakers by creating a positive communication climate. As an audience member, you should listen attentively and look for something in the speech that interests you. Even if you are not excited about the topic, you might pick up some techniques that will be useful when it is your turn to speak. When you discuss or evaluate the speeches of others, be constructive and helpful. Listen to others the way you would have them listen to you.

---

**SPEAKER'S NOTES**

### Ten Ways to Control Communication Apprehension

1. Learn and use speech skills to develop confidence.

2. Practice relaxation exercises to control tension.

3. Replace negative, self-defeating statements with positive statements.

4. Visualize yourself being successful.

5. Select a topic that interests and excites you.

6. Select a topic you know something about and research it thoroughly.

7. Use a visual aid to release energy through movement.

8. Practice, practice, practice!

9. Expect your audience to be helpful and attentive.

10. Act confident, even if you don't quite feel that way.

**IN SUMMARY**     Many of us underrate our potential for public speaking. Starting with your first speech, you can work to build a positive communication environment for yourself and others. You can also develop your ethos as a speaker.

*Understanding the Impressions You Make.*     Listeners acquire positive impressions of you based on your ability to convey *competence, integrity, likableness,* and *power.* You can build your perceived competence by citing examples from your own experience, by quoting authorities, and by organizing and presenting your message effectively. You can earn an image of integrity by being accurate and complete in your presentation of information. You can promote likableness by being a warm and open person with whom your listeners can easily identify. *Informal power* comes as a result of your competence, integrity, and likableness and from listeners' perceptions of you as a confident, enthusiastic, and decisive speaker.

*Introducing Yourself and Others.*     The speech of introduction helps establish you or the person you introduce as a unique person. It may focus on environmental influences, a person who inspired you, an experience that affected you, an activity that reveals your character, the work you do, your purpose in life, or some value you cherish.

*Developing the Introductory Speech.*     In developing your introductory speech, determine the appropriate design to organize your thoughts. Organizational strategies include categorical divisions, sequences of events, cause-effect relationships, and spatial patterns. Your speech should begin with an *introduction* that gains attention as it leads into the body of your message. Your introduction will also include your *thematic statement,* which expresses the central idea of your speech. The design you select determines how the *body* of your speech will be structured and developed. Narratives and examples are especially useful in developing speeches of introduction. Other forms of supporting material useful in developing the body are facts and figures and testimony. Finally, your speech should come to a satisfying *conclusion.* Your conclusion should include a *summary statement* and *concluding remarks* that highlight the meaning.

*Outlining the Introductory Speech.*     You can improve your chances for presenting a well-developed and well-structured speech by building an outline. As you practice and present the speech, use a *key-word outline* to jog your memory.

*Presenting the Introductory Speech.*     When presenting your first speech, keep the spotlight on the message, strive for a conversational presentation, and use your natural anxiety as a source of energy. Never let presentation skills overshadow your ideas. Cope with *communication apprehension* by practicing relaxation exercises and *cognitive restructuring,* which replaces negative messages to yourself with positive ones. Using *visualization,* imagine your audience in positive terms, and picture yourself as being successful. The skills training you receive in class will make you more comfortable and confident. In addition, you should select a topic that interests you and that you already know something about so that you can build on this foundation. Use visual aids to give your nervous energy a constructive outlet through gesture. You should practice until you feel confident. During actual presentation you should act confident and avoid expressions of personal discomfort.

**TERMS TO KNOW**

| | |
|---|---|
| competence | body |
| integrity | conclusion |
| likableness | summary statement |
| formal power | concluding remarks |
| informal power | key-word outline |
| self-awareness inventory | communication apprehension |
| introduction | cognitive restructuring |
| thematic statement | visualization |

**DISCUSSION**

1. Although we have defined *ethos* in terms of public speakers, other communicators also seek to create favorable impressions of competence, integrity, likableness, and power. Advertisers always try to create favorable ethos for their products. Bring to class print advertisements to demonstrate each of the four dimensions of ethos we have discussed. Explain how each ad uses ethos.

2. Select a prominent public speaker and analyze his or her ethos. On which dimensions is this speaker especially strong or weak? How does this affect the person's leadership ability? Present your analysis for class discussion.

3. Political ads often do the work of introducing candidates to the public and disparaging their opponents. Study the television ads in connection with a recent political campaign. Bring to class answers to the following questions:
   a. What kinds of positive and negative identities do the ads establish?
   b. Which of these ads are most and least effective in creating the desired ethos? Why?
   c. Which of the self-inventory questions discussed in this chapter might explain how the candidates are introduced?

4. Identify any negative messages you might send yourself concerning public speaking. How might you change these messages, using the principles of cognitive restructuring? Share the original self-defeating messages and their positive counterparts with your classmates.

**APPLICATION**

1. As the introductory speeches are presented in your class, build a collection of portraits of your classmates as revealed by their speeches. At the end of the assignment, analyze this group of portraits to see what you have learned about the class as a whole. What kind of topics might they prefer? Did you detect any strong political or social attitudes to which you might have to adjust? Submit one copy of your analysis to your instructor, and keep another for your own use in preparing later speeches.

2. At the end of the introductory speeches in your class, use the criteria suggested in Chapter 1 for speech evaluation, and decide which was the best speech presented (excluding your own). Write a brief paper defending your choice.

3. Build full and key-word outlines of your self-introductory speech. On a separate sheet of paper, identify the design you are using and discuss why this design is most appropriate. Turn in a copy of your outlines and your rationale to your instructor.

4. To help visualize yourself succeeding as a speaker, write a script in which you describe specific details of an ideal experience of speaking. Start with getting up in the morning on the day of your speech to the moments of satisfaction after you have concluded. Once you have completed your script, relax, concentrate on it, and bring it to life in your mind. As a model both for your own script and for your mental enactment of it, consider the following script and instructions for an informative speech developed by Professors Joe Ayres and Theodore S. Hopf:

> Close your eyes and allow your body to get comfortable in the chair in which you are sitting. Move around until you feel that you are in a position that will continue to be relaxing for you for the next ten to fifteen minutes. Take a deep, comfortable breath and hold it . . . now slowly release it through your nose (if possible). That is right . . . now take another deep breath and make certain that you are breathing from the diaphragm (from your belly) . . . hold it . . . now slowly release it and note how you feel while doing this . . . feel the relaxation fluidly flow throughout your body. And now, one more REALLY deep breath . . . hold it . . . and now release it slowly . . . and begin your normal breathing pattern. Shift around, if you need to get comfortable again.
>
> Now begin to visualize the beginning of a day in which you are going to give an informative speech. See yourself getting up in the morning, full of energy, full of confidence, looking forward to the day's challenges. You are putting on just the right clothes for the task at hand that day. Dressing well makes you look and feel good about yourself, so you have on JUST what you want to wear, which clearly expresses your sense of inner well-being. As you are driving, riding, or walking to the speech setting, note how clear and confident you feel, and how others around you — as you arrive — comment positively regarding your fine appearance and general

demeanor. You feel thoroughly prepared for the task at hand. Your preparation has been exceptionally thorough, and you have really researched the target issue you will be presenting today. Now you see yourself standing or sitting in the room where you will present your speech, talking very comfortably and confidentially with others in the room. The people to whom you will be presenting your speech appear to be quite friendly, and are very cordial in their greetings and conversations prior to the presentation. You feel ABSOLUTELY sure of your material and of your ability to present the information in a forceful, convincing, positive manner. Now you see yourself approaching the area from which you will present. You are feeling very good about this presentation and see yourself move eagerly forward. All of your audio visual materials are well organized, well planned, and clearly aid your presentation.

Now you see yourself presenting your talk. You are really quite brilliant and have all the finesse of a polished, professional speaker. You are also aware that your audience is giving head nods, smiles, and other positive responses, conveying the message that you are truly "on target." The introduction of the speech goes the way you have planned. In fact, it works better than you had expected. The transition from the introductory material to the body of the speech is extremely smooth. As you approach the body of the speech, you are aware of the first major point. It emerges as you expected. The evidence supporting the point is relevant and evokes an understanding response from the audience. In fact, all the main points flow in this fashion. As you wrap up your main points, your concluding remarks seem to be a natural outgrowth of everything you have done. All concluding remarks are on target. When your final utterance is concluded, you have the feeling that it could not have gone better. The introduction worked, the main points were to the point, your evidence was supportive, and your conclusion formed a fitting capstone. In addition, your vocal variety added interest value. Your pauses punctuated important ideas, and your gestures and body movements were purposeful. You now see yourself fielding audience questions with brilliance, confidence, and energy equal to what you exhibited in the presentation itself. You see yourself receiving the congratulations of your classmates. You see yourself as relaxed, pleased with your talk, and ready for the next task to be accomplished that day. You are filled with energy, purpose, and a sense of general well-being. Congratulate yourself on a job well done!

Now — I want you to begin to return to this time and place in which we are working today. Take a deep breath . . . hold it . . . and let it go. Do this several times and move slowly back into the room. Take as much time as you need to make the transition back.[10]

5. Prepare a full outline of the student speech at the end of this chapter. Do the ideas flow smoothly? Might the structure have been improved? Is supporting material used effectively?

**NOTES**

1. Donald Baer, "Bill Clinton, Political Victim," *U. S. News & World Report,* 15 June 1992, p. 32.
2. Kenneth Burke, *A Rhetoric of Motives* (Berkeley and Los Angeles: University of California Press, 1969), pp. 20–23.
3. Bill Clinton, "Acceptance Address, Democratic National Convention," Presented 16 July 1992, text published in *Vital Speeches of the Day,* 58, No. 21 (15 August 1992), 643.
4. Donald C. Bryant and Karl R. Wallace, *Fundamentals of Public Speaking,* 4th ed. (New York: Appleton-Century-Crofts, 1969), p. 233.
5. Gustav Friedrich and Blaine Goss, "Systematic Desensitization," in John A. Daly and James C. McCroskey, eds., *Avoiding Communication: Shyness, Reticence, and Communication Apprehension* (Beverly Hills, Calif.: Sage, 1984), pp. 173–188.
6. William J. Fremouw and Michael D. Scott, "Cognitive Restructuring: An Alternative Method for the Treatment of Communication Apprehension," *Communication Education* 28 (May 1979): 129–133.
7. Joe Ayres and Theodore S. Hopf, "Visualization: Is It More Than Extra-Attention?" *Communication Education* 38 (January 1989): 1–5.
8. Tim Hopf and Joe Ayres, "Coping with Public Speaking Anxiety: An Examination of Various Combinations of Systematic Desensitization, Skills Training, and Visualization," *Journal of Applied Communication Research* 20 (1992): 183–198.
9. Mike Allen, John E. Hunter, and William A. Donohue, "Meta-Analysis of Self-Report Data on the Effectiveness of Public Speaking Anxiety Treatment Techniques," *Communication Education* 38 (January 1989): 54–76.
10. Ayres and Hopf, pp. 2–3.

## My Three Cultures

### *Sandra Baltz*

Sandra's introduction identifies the three cultures that have influenced her life. Her opening example stirs up interest and curiosity. Her awareness of public affairs and fluency in Spanish suggests that she is a competent, complex, and interesting individual.

This transition into the body of the speech establishes Sandra's integrity while foreshadowing the idea that serious problems may arise from cross-cultural misunderstandings. Sandra's thematic statement helps to overcome negative perceptions of the Arabic influence on her life.

By comparing and contrasting the advantages and disadvantages of growing up bilingual, Sandra continues to build her ethos. We learn that she has traveled widely and is a premed student (competence). We find that she wants to serve people (integrity). As Sandra talks about her dialect problems and family reunions, the light humor increases her attractiveness. Her statement that "there really is no language barrier among family and friends" is the key to the deeper meaning of her speech.

Several years ago I read a newspaper article in the *Commercial Appeal* in which an American journalist described some of his experiences in the Middle East. He was there a couple of months and had been the guest of several different Arab families. He reported having been very well treated and very well received by everyone that he met there. But it was only later, when he returned home, that he became aware of the intense resentment his hosts held for Americans and our unwelcome involvement in their Middle Eastern affairs. The journalist wrote of feeling somewhat bewildered, if not deceived, by the large discrepancy between his treatment while in the Middle East and the hostile attitude that he learned about later. He labeled this behavior hypocritical. When I reached the end of the article, I was reminded of a phrase spoken often by my mother. "Sandra," she says to me, *"respeta tu casa y a todos los que entran en ella, trata a tus enemigos asi como a tus amigos."*

This is an Arabic proverb, spoken in Spanish, and roughly it translates into "Respect your home and all who enter it, treating even an enemy as a friend." This is a philosophy that I have heard often in my home. With this in mind, it seemed to me that the treatment the American journalist received while in the Middle East was not hypocritical behavior on the part of his hosts. Rather, it was an act of respect for their guest, for themselves, and for their home — indeed, a behavior very typical of the Arabic culture.

Since having read that article several years ago I have become much more aware of how my life is different because of having a mother who is of Palestinian origin but was born and raised in the Central American country of El Salvador.

One of the most obvious differences is that I was raised bilingually — speaking both Spanish and English. In fact, my first words were in Spanish. Growing up speaking two languages has been both an advantage and a disadvantage for me. One clear advantage is that I received straight A's in my Spanish class at Immaculate Conception High School. Certainly, traveling has been made much easier. During visits to Spain, Mexico, and some of the Central American countries, it has been my experience that people are much more open and much more receptive if you can speak their language. In addition, the subtleties of a culture are easier to grasp and much easier to appreciate.

I hope that knowing a second language will continue to be an asset for me in the future. I am currently pursuing a career in medicine. Perhaps by knowing Spanish I can broaden the area in which I can work and increase the number of people that I might reach.

Now one of the disadvantages of growing up bilingually is that I picked up my mother's accent as well as her language. I must have been about four years old before I realized that our feathered friends in the trees are called "birds" not "beers" and that, in fact, we had a "birdbath" in our back yard, not a "beerbath."

Family reunions also tend to be confusing around my home. Most of my rela-

tives speak either Spanish, English, or Arabic, but rarely any combination of the three. So, as a result, deep and involved conversations are almost impossible. But with a little nodding and smiling, I have found that there really is no language barrier among family and friends.

In all, I must say that being exposed to three very different cultures — Latin, Arabic, and American — has been rewarding for me and has made a difference even in the music I enjoy and the food I eat. It is not unusual in my house to sit down to a meal made up of stuffed grape leaves and refried beans and all topped off with apple pie for dessert.

I am fortunate in having had the opportunity to view more closely what makes Arabic and Latin cultures unique. By understanding and appreciating them I have been able to better understand and appreciate my own American culture. In closing just let me add some words you often hear spoken in my home — *adios* and *allak konn ma'eck* — goodbye, and may God go with you.

*"When people talk, listen completely. . . . Most people never listen. Nor do they observe."*

— *Ernest Hemingway*

# 3

# Critical and Constructive Listening

## This Chapter Will Help You

- develop an appreciation for critical and constructive listening skills.
- identify and work on overcoming your listening problems.
- build critical thinking skills to analyze what you hear.
- develop a constructive orientation to listening.
- establish criteria for evaluating speeches.

Carrie Bolden, the city's first woman candidate for mayor, was scheduled to speak at the campus political forum. Mary Beth Jackson could hardly wait to hear the candidate in person. Mary Beth just knew that she would agree with everything Ms. Bolden had to say. She relished the opportunity to meet her and planned to volunteer to work in her campaign.

On the other hand, Mark Levinson didn't care much for politics or politicians, and he was especially dubious about a woman running for mayor. He would attend the forum only because he was required to write a report on the speech for his class. Mark also was annoyed because he would miss Monday night football on television.

In contrast, Sarah Thomas had an open mind on the Bolden candidacy. She had read some of Ms. Bolden's statements that interested her but had decided to withhold judgment until she actually heard the candidate. Sarah didn't expect to agree with everything she heard but looked forward to a stimulating message that would help her decide whether to support Ms. Bolden.

Only one of the students described above will be a critical, constructive listener at the political forum. Although Mary Beth will be enthusiastic, it's doubtful she will critically evaluate what she hears. Her initial attitudes will predispose her to agree with almost anything the candidate has to say — she will be a rubber-stamp listener. Mark's listening ability also will be affected by his attitudes. Indifference toward the subject and hostility toward the speaker make for less than effective listening. Only Sarah has a healthy, balanced listening orientation. She will listen carefully to what the speaker says, and her constructive attitude should make the experience meaningful.

Although the first two students represent extremes, it is true that a good listener can be hard to find. And without effective listeners, the dynamic circle of communication is broken. When audiences don't listen well, they can't provide useful feedback for speakers, nor is the meaning process completed in their minds. Without such feedback, speakers can't adapt their messages so that audiences understand them better. Communication is most effective when audiences practice critical and constructive listening.

**Critical listening** involves hearing, paying attention, comprehending and interpreting, analyzing and evaluating, responding, and remembering. First, you must be able to hear a message in order to listen, even though you don't necessarily listen to everything you hear. *Hearing* is an automatic process in which sound waves stimulate nerve impulses to the brain. *Listening* is a voluntary process that goes beyond simply reacting to sounds. You must decide to listen. Second, you must focus on the sounds of the message and block out other noises, distractions, thoughts, or feelings that may compete for your attention. Third, you need to comprehend and interpret what you hear. You must understand both the language and point of view of the speaker. The next step in critical listening is analysis and evaluation, in which you examine the message rather than accept it at face value. As you comprehend and evaluate, you may offer *feedback,* visual cues such as smiles or frowns, puzzled looks, or nods of agreement that let a speaker know how you are responding. Remembering is the final phase, as you mentally store what you have heard for future use. In short, critical listening allows you to extract much of the potential value from messages to which you are exposed.

**Constructive listening** is the other dimension necessary to healthy, balanced listening behavior. It suggests the vital role of the listener in the creation of meaning, which involves (1) discovering the speaker's intention from the words, vocal inflections, and body language we hear and see; (2) tracing out the implications and consequences of the message, perhaps even beyond the speaker's awareness; and (3) applying the message to our lives, figuring how we might make use of it. Obviously, meaning is not confined to the speech and ladled out by the speaker. Rather, speaker and listeners share responsibility for the co-creation of meaning. Constructive listeners are always alert to meaning possibilities within speeches that will enrich their lives as well as improve the lives of others. Their careful, probing questions and comments at the ends of speeches can help a better meaning-product emerge.

In healthy listening, the critical and constructive dimensions work together. Just as constructive listening makes us want to listen, and expands the horizons of our awareness, critical listening allows us to judge more carefully the new subjects and issues that come to our attention. In this chapter we aim for a balance between critical and constructive listening.

Listening is the most pervasive communication activity in our lives. Adults spend approximately half of their communication time listening; the remainder is divided among speaking, reading, and writing.[1] Yet we are seldom taught listening skills. This chapter will consider the benefits of critical and constructive listening, listening problems, and ways to improve listening skills. We shall also relate critical and constructive listening to the evaluation of classroom speeches.

## BENEFITS OF CRITICAL AND CONSTRUCTIVE LISTENING

Listening may be an underappreciated skill in our society because we often associate it more with following than with leading. We frequently emphasize speaking and leading while neglecting the fact that listening is a necessary part of any communication interaction. There can be no meaning without listening. Moreover, through their immediate feedback, good listeners help speakers become more sensitive and responsive to the needs of the audience.

*Effective listening requires advance preparation. Familiarizing yourself with the subject can help make listening easier and more effective.*

Listeners who understand, analyze, and respond critically to messages are less vulnerable to unscrupulous leaders. Such speakers may try to cover up a lack of information or faulty reasoning with a glib, overpowering presentation. The best defense against such charlatans is the ability to listen critically to what they say. The Hitlers of the world are created more by uncritical listening than by proficient speaking. Critical listeners learn not to accept anyone or anything at face value, but to analyze and evaluate messages for themselves.

Critical listening skills also are important because much of the mass communication to which we are exposed is highly sophisticated. Each day we are inundated with a barrage of advertising, much of which may rely on irrelevant or misleading appeals. Such ads make you think that their products will satisfy all your basic needs, even when the products have no relationship to such needs. How many times have you seen attractive, scantily clad women appearing in ads to sell everything from soft drinks to automatic transmission repair services? Similarly, these ads may ask you to buy what "doctors" recommend without telling you anything about the credentials of these "doctors." These are obvious examples, but less transparent abuses may be more difficult to detect. Critical listening skills will make you more aware of such deceptive attempts.

As important as critical listening skills may be, too much emphasis on critical listening may make us suspect that *all* communication is manipulative and unethical. That attitude can reinforce a view of listeners as mere consumers of meaning, mental manual laborers, whose work is simply to unpack the prefabricated meaning within the speaker's words. Not only does this view underestimate the creative role of healthy listening — it also understates the listener's ethical responsibility and misrepresents the basic process of meaning formation.

Constructive listening is an essential component of **participative communication.** In participative communication the speaker and listener share the responsibility for creating meaning. The creation of meaning is a "process of discovery, in which the speaker's words and gestures, interacting with audience knowledge and feeling, stimulate the dynamic construction of social meaning. . . . In participative communication, speaker and listener become collaborators, members of the meaning cooperative, joint builders of the edifice of public knowledge."[2] Although the worlds of the speaker and listener may be similar, they are never identical. As speakers offer messages and listeners respond, these worlds interact to produce meaning.

Constructive listeners look for the useful as well as defective elements in a speaker's message. They balance seeing the positive possibilities in messages with avoiding misconceptions and misinterpretations. Becoming a constructive as well as a critical listener helps you to assume responsibility for your own life as well as to contribute as a citizen.

Critical, constructive listeners enjoy many practical benefits as well. You can enhance your performance as a student by developing your listening skills. College students spend close to 60 percent of their communication time listening.[3] Research indicates that students who listen effectively earn better grades and achieve beyond what their intelligence levels might have predicted.[4] A good listener learns to concentrate on what is being said, to identify the main points and most important information, and to evaluate supporting materials. Responsible listeners read assigned materials before a lecture. The information they gain from reading provides a foundation for understanding what they hear. Critical, constructive listeners also question the ideas that they hear to look for neglected possibilities. Through questioning they gain greater understanding and stimulate their own creative thinking.

At work, improved listening skills may mean the difference between success and failure, both for individuals and companies. A survey of Fortune 500 organizations found that poor listening is "one of the most important problems" and that "ineffective listening leads to ineffective performance. . . ."[5] If you listen effectively on the job, you will make fewer mistakes. You will improve your opportunities for advancement. Companies that encourage the development of balanced listening skills enjoy many dividends. They suffer less from costly misunderstandings. Employees are more innovative when they sense that management is receptive to new ideas. Morale improves, and the work environment becomes more pleasant and productive. As a result, the company becomes more dynamic and creative. The all-important "bottom line" — improved profits — looks a lot better! For these reasons many prominent companies, such as the Sperry Corporation, have invested substantially in listening training for their employees.[6]

**OVERCOMING LISTENING PROBLEMS**

The road to critical, constructive listening starts with acknowledging our listening problems. To become more effective listeners, we first need to become aware of what causes poor listening behavior. Listening problems are often a function of our personal reactions, our attitudes, and bad habits we have acquired. At best, these problems pose a challenge to the careful listener; at worst, they defeat communication. Once we understand what our listening problems are, we can begin to correct them. Figure 3.1 should help you identify some of your listening problems. Read through the list and make a check mark next to the problems you need to work on.

### Personal Reactions

One of the most common listening problems is not paying attention. How many times have you found yourself daydreaming, even when you know you should be listening to what is said? One cause of this problem is that our minds can process information much faster than most people speak. Most people speak at about 125 words per minute in public, but process information at about 500 words per minute.[7] This time gap provides an opportunity for listeners to drift away to more delightful or difficult personal concerns. Too often daydreaming listeners will smile and nod encouragingly even though they haven't heard a thing the speaker has said. Such deceptive feedback is a major cause of failed communication. Both personal reactions to words and distractions can trigger such reactions.

**Reactions to Words.**   As you listen to a message, you react to more than just the **denotative meanings,** or dictionary definitions, of words. You also respond to the **connotative meanings,** the emotional or attitudinal reactions that certain words arouse in you. You may react adversely, for example, to the use of the word *girls* in reference to adult females. The term *girls* acts as a **trigger word** that sets off a strong emotional response. As insensitive as such language may be, you should not let it prevent you from hearing the entire message. Suppose a speaker is describing opportunities for advancement in the Crypton Corporation and makes reference to "one of the girls in the typing pool" who moved up into a personnel management position. His use of *girls* makes you think this is a sexist organization. As you sit there stewing over this semantic blunder, you miss his later statement that over the past three years two-thirds of all promotions into management have gone to women and that an aggressive affirmative action program is in place.

Attention also can be disrupted by chance associations you make with some words. The speaker may mention the word *desk,* which reminds you that you need to fix a better place to study in your room, which reminds you that you have to buy a new lamp, which starts you thinking about where you should shop for the lamp. By the time your attention drifts back to the

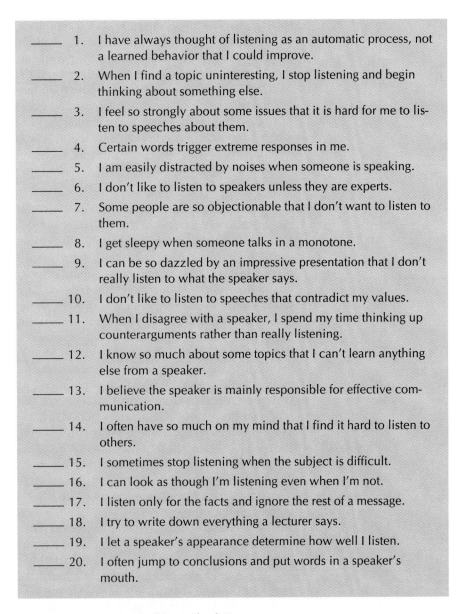

_____ 1. I have always thought of listening as an automatic process, not a learned behavior that I could improve.

_____ 2. When I find a topic uninteresting, I stop listening and begin thinking about something else.

_____ 3. I feel so strongly about some issues that it is hard for me to listen to speeches about them.

_____ 4. Certain words trigger extreme responses in me.

_____ 5. I am easily distracted by noises when someone is speaking.

_____ 6. I don't like to listen to speakers unless they are experts.

_____ 7. Some people are so objectionable that I don't want to listen to them.

_____ 8. I get sleepy when someone talks in a monotone.

_____ 9. I can be so dazzled by an impressive presentation that I don't really listen to what the speaker says.

_____ 10. I don't like to listen to speeches that contradict my values.

_____ 11. When I disagree with a speaker, I spend my time thinking up counterarguments rather than really listening.

_____ 12. I know so much about some topics that I can't learn anything else from a speaker.

_____ 13. I believe the speaker is mainly responsible for effective communication.

_____ 14. I often have so much on my mind that I find it hard to listen to others.

_____ 15. I sometimes stop listening when the subject is difficult.

_____ 16. I can look as though I'm listening even when I'm not.

_____ 17. I listen only for the facts and ignore the rest of a message.

_____ 18. I try to write down everything a lecturer says.

_____ 19. I let a speaker's appearance determine how well I listen.

_____ 20. I often jump to conclusions and put words in a speaker's mouth.

FIGURE 3.1   Listening Problems Check List

speaker, you have lost the gist of what is being said. Feeling hopelessly lost, you may just give up listening altogether.

**_Distractions._**    Both internal and external distractions can disrupt attention. If you are tired, hungry, angry, worried, or pressed for time, you may find it difficult to concentrate. Your personal situation may take precedence over listening to a speaker. Physical noises can divert attention if they drown out the speaker's voice or are unusual or unexpected. A room that is uncomfortably hot or cold may make it hard for people to concentrate. Visual aids left out during a speech can steal attention from the message. Materials distributed before a speech can also compete for attention.

Inconsistencies between the verbal and nonverbal messages of a speech can be even more distracting. Some time ago an IBM executive appeared before a large group of employees to report that the company wished to relax its strict dress code. Only problem was, the speaker himself was dressed in a very formal dark suit. His attire contradicted his words and left his audience very much confused.

***Controlling Reactions and Distractions.***   We all have problems from time to time with attention. To improve your ability to concentrate, you need to become aware of those situations that cause you to "drift away" from a speaker. One way you can do this is to keep a **listening log** in your lecture classes. As you take notes, put a minus mark ($-$) in the margin each time you notice your attention wandering. By each mark, jot down a word or two pinpointing the cause, perhaps a distraction or a trigger word. After class, note the number of times your mind drifted and reconstruct in more detail the causes. Is there a pattern to your behavior? How might you control your daydreaming? This exercise will help you identify the conditions that lead to inattention and will also make you more consciously aware of your tendency to daydream. Once you realize how often and why you are mentally drifting, you can more easily redirect your attention to the message.

If you find yourself reacting emotionally to trigger words, ask yourself: *What is this reaction doing to my listening ability? Is the speaker unaware of the power of these words, or are they being used for a purpose? What effect is the speaker seeking?* By concentrating on such questions, you can defuse much of the power of such words and psychologically distance yourself from your own emotional reactions. Then it will be easier to refocus your attention on the message.

You can also control inattention created by internal distractions. Come to your classes well rested, well fed, and ready to listen. Remind yourself that you can't really do your homework for another class when someone is talking. Leave your troubles at the door even if it means scheduling a time to worry later in the day. Clear your mind and your desk of everything except paper on which to take notes. Sit erect, establish eye contact with the speaker, and start to listen.

Do what you can to control external distractions as well. Try to sit near the front of the room for psychological as well as physical reasons. You will be able to hear better, and you will also be indicating a commitment to listen. Speakers will appreciate this positive signal that you want to help make communication successful. Moreover, you are less likely to daydream if you are sitting front and center. If outside noises distract you, unobtrusively get up and close a door or window. Do not try to read charts or handouts unless and until the speaker refers to them. Constantly remind yourself that you are there to listen.

## *Attitudes*

You may have strong positive or negative attitudes toward the speaker, the topic, or even the act of communication itself that can diminish your listening ability. All of us have biases, or prejudices, of one kind or another. Listening problems arise when our biases prevent us from receiving messages accurately. Some of the ways that bias can distort messages are through filtering, assimilation, and contrast effects.[8]

**Filtering** means that you simply don't process all of the information to which you are exposed. You unconsciously screen the speaker's words so that only some of them reach your brain. In other words, you hear what you want to hear. Listeners who filter will hear only one side of "good news, bad news" speeches — the side that confirms their prejudices. When you engage in **assimilation,** you interpret positions that are similar to your own as being closer to it than they actually are. Assimilation most often occurs when you have a strong positive attitude toward a speaker or topic. For example, if you believe that the president can do no wrong, you may be tempted to assimilate everything he says so that it seems consistent with all your beliefs.

A **contrast effect** occurs when you see positions that differ from yours as being even more distant. For example, if you are a staunch Democrat, you may think anything Republicans say is far removed from what you believe, even if that may not always be the case. Bias can make you put words in a speaker's mouth, or take them away. If you hear something that does not fit your expectations, you may rationalize it away with an excuse.

***Attitudes Toward Speakers.*** If you have had previous contact with speakers or have heard about them from others, you may have developed attitudes toward them that cause listening problems. The more competent, interesting, and attractive you expect speakers to be, the more attentive you will probably be and the more likely you will be to accept what they have to say. If your positive feelings are extremely strong, like those of the first listener in our chapter opening example, you may accept anything you hear without considering its merits. But if you anticipate incompetent, uninteresting, or unattractive speakers, you may be less attentive and less likely to accept their information or advice. You may dislike speakers because of positions they have previously defended or groups with which they are associated. If you are intolerant of other races, genders, or religious or social groups, your attitudes may block your listening ability. You may even develop strong positive or negative feelings about speakers based on such extraneous factors as hair style, dress, delivery, accent, or mannerisms.[9]

***Attitudes Toward the Topic.*** Your attitudes toward certain topics also can affect how well you listen. If you believe that a topic is relevant to your life, you may listen more carefully than if you are indifferent. Speeches about retirement planning usually fall on deaf ears with young audiences. You may listen more attentively, although less critically, to speeches that support positions you already hold. If you feel strongly about a subject and oppose the speaker's position, you may find yourself developing counterarguments instead of listening. For example, if you have strong feelings against gun control, you may find yourself silently reciting the Second Amendment to the U.S. Constitution instead of listening to a speaker's arguments in favor of gun control. When you engage in such behaviors, you may miss much of what the speaker actually has to say and deprive yourself of a learning experience. Finally, you may think that you already know enough about a topic. In such cases, you are not likely to listen effectively and may miss out on new, interesting information.

***Attitudes Toward Communication.***    You also may have attitudes about communication that can affect how well you listen. You may mistakenly equate listening with hearing. Remember that hearing is automatic and involves no effort on the part of the receiver. Listening is voluntary and requires energy and effort for it to be effective. If you confuse hearing and listening, you may become a mere passive recipient of messages.

If you believe that the speaker is solely responsible for the effectiveness of communication, you are likely to neglect your role as a listener and break the dynamic circle of communication. A good listener is an active participant in the communication process. Looking at the speaker and responding hon-

*Effective listeners provide feedback for speakers through body language and facial expressions. Without effective listeners the dynamic circle of communication is broken.*

estly with nods, smiles, or other forms of body language can improve the quality of communication and keep the dynamic circle intact.

***Controlling Your Attitudes.***    Biases are not easy to control. The first step in overcoming their influence is admitting that you may have them. Strive for objectivity by delaying judgments and reactions until you have given a message a full and careful hearing. Being objective does not mean that you must agree with a message. It simply means you recognize that others may hold different positions and that you can learn something from listening to them. Try not to prejudge a speaker, but rather go into communication situations with an open mind. Exposure to opposing points of view may cause you to reevaluate your position, but you may also find yourself strengthening what you already believe. Don't let yourself be distracted by extraneous characteristics, such as the speaker's appearance or mannerisms. Tell yourself it's all right if Kate wears blue nail polish or John has long hair — this doesn't mean they have nothing worthwhile to say.

Motivate yourself to listen. Even if you have little or no interest in a topic, look for something in the speech that will benefit you personally. You may surprise yourself by acquiring new knowledge, developing new interests, or learning things that will prove useful at some later time. Even poor speeches can provide valuable learning experiences through negative examples of what not to do when you are presenting a speech. Remember that good listeners are rewarded in both work and school.

If you are prone to developing counterarguments when you should be paying attention, practice the Golden Rule of listening: *Listen to others as you would have them listen to you.* Keep in mind that listening is an opportunity for learning. Reserve judgment until you have heard all of a message. Always remember that you, as a listener, are an integral part of the communication process. Without your participation there can be no effective communication.

## Bad Habits

Many listening problems stem from bad habits. Since we do so much listening and very few of us have been trained in listening skills, we probably have acquired some bad habits. We may feign attention or avoid listening to difficult materials. Our attention spans may have been shortened from too much television viewing. Unless a message is entertaining, we may try to "change the channel" even when the message is not on television. Our experiences as students may have conditioned us to listen just for facts or to try to write down everything we hear. Such habits can interfere with effective listening.

***Feigning Attention.***    Although sincere, constructive feedback is important to speech effectiveness, we all have learned how to *look* attentive to stay out of trouble. We know how to sit erect, focus our eyes on the speaker, even

## Guides for Effective Listening

1.  *Be conscious of your listening behavior.* Identify your listening problems and work to solve them.

2.  *Motivate yourself to listen.* Be opportunistic. Get all you can out of the messages you hear.

3.  *Prepare yourself to listen.* Put problems and biases aside so that you can be more attentive and open to new learning experiences.

4.  *Control your reactions.* Learn to recognize situations that cause you to daydream and strive to control them. Identify your trigger words so that they become less powerful. Resist distractions. Postpone evaluations and judgments until you have heard all the speaker has to say.

5.  *Work at listening.* Develop a plan to extend your attention span. Seek out new and varied listening experiences that exercise your mind.

6.  *Listen for ideas.* Do not try to write down everything you hear. Focus on identifying the main points the speaker is making.

7.  *Concentrate on the message.* Don't allow extraneous factors to interfere with listening effectiveness.

nod or smile from time to time (although not always at the most appropriate times), and not listen to one word that is being said! You may find that you revert to such behavior when a message is difficult, technical, or abstract. If the speaker asks, "Do you understand?" you may nod brightly, sending false feedback just to be polite or to keep from appearing unintelligent.

***Avoiding Difficult Material.***   It is not uncommon to want to avoid listening to difficult material. This tendency may be related to a fear of failure. Rather than exerting the effort needed to understand such material, we may lapse into inattention. If we are asked questions later, we can always say "I wasn't really listening," instead of, "I didn't understand." Additionally, our desire to have things simplified so that we can understand them without much effort makes us susceptible to "snake oil" pitches, those oversimplified remedies for everything from fallen arches to failing government policies.[10]

***Listening Only for Facts.***   Your experiences as a student may contribute to another bad habit: listening only for facts and trying to write down everything that is said. If you do this, you may miss the forest because you are so busy counting the leaves on the trees. Placing too much emphasis on fact and detail and too little emphasis on understanding ideas can make you a poor consumer of messages. Listening just for facts also keeps you from attending to the nonverbal aspects of a message. Effective listening includes integrating what you hear and what you see. Gestures, facial expressions, and tone of voice communicate nuances that are vital to the meaning of a speech.

***Television-Trained Listener Habits.***   Many of our poor listening habits may stem from heavy television viewing. Ninety-eight percent of American homes have at least one television set, and the average set is on for over seven hours a day.[11] Heavy television viewing may result in a shortened attention span and a strong desire to be entertained by everything we see or hear. Television messages are characterized by fast action and the presentation of short bits of information at a time. Habitual television viewing may lead us to want all messages to follow this format. William F. Buckley has commented that "the television audience . . . is not trained to listen . . . to 15 uninterrupted minutes."[12] Our television-watching experiences may also lead us into "the entertainment syndrome," in which we demand that speakers be lively, interesting, funny, and charismatic to hold our attention.[13] Unfortunately, not all subjects lend themselves to such treatment, and we can miss much if we only listen to those who put on a "dog and pony show."

***Coping with Bad Habits.***   Overcoming bad habits requires effort. When you find yourself feigning attention, ask yourself, "Why am I doing this?" and "What is this doing to my listening ability?" Keep in mind that honest feedback helps speakers, but that inappropriate responding deceives them.

When you know you will be listening to difficult or complicated material, do some advance preparation so that you will be familiar with the ideas and vocabulary you may encounter. Don't try to remember everything or write down all that you hear. Instead, concentrate on absorbing the important information. Listen for the thematic statement and the overall idea of the speech and identify the main points. Use the difference between speaking and mental-processing speeds to paraphrase what you hear so that it makes sense to you. Consider the choice of examples and the way they are related to the main points. Also look for nonverbal cues. Does the speaker's tone of voice change the meaning of the message? Are gestures and facial expressions consistent with words? If not, what does this tell you?

Practice extending your attention span. If your original listening log shows that you drifted away from a lecturer twenty times in one class session, see if you can reduce this to fifteen, then to ten, then to five. To become a more effective listener, you need to keep in mind the differences between good and poor listeners. These differences are summarized in Figure 3.2 on the following page.

| Poor Listeners | Good Listeners |
|---|---|
| 1. allow their minds to wander. | 1. focus attention on the message. |
| 2. respond emotionally to "trigger words." | 2. control reactions to "trigger words." |
| 3. let personal problems keep them from listening effectively. | 3. leave their worries at the door. |
| 4. succumb to distractions. | 4. work to reduce distractions. |
| 5. are unaware that their biases may distort messages. | 5. guard against letting personal biases distort messages. |
| 6. react strongly to a speaker's style or reputation. | 6. don't let the speaker's style or reputation impair listening. |
| 7. "tune out" dry topics. | 7. listen for what they can use. |
| 8. hold the speaker responsible for effective communication. | 8. recognize the important role of the listener in communication. |
| 9. listen passively. | 9. listen actively. |
| 10. mentally rehearse counterarguments during a speech. | 10. reserve judgment until a speaker is finished. |
| 11. feign attention, giving false feedback to the speaker. | 11. provide honest feedback. |
| 12. avoid difficult material. | 12. become familiar with topic ahead of time. |
| 13. listen only for facts. | 13. listen for main ideas. |
| 14. seek out entertaining messages. | 14. exercise their minds by listening to many kinds of communication. |

FIGURE 3.2
Differences Between
Good and Poor Listeners

## CRITICAL THINKING AND LISTENING

You can enhance your ability to listen effectively by developing your critical thinking skills. **Critical thinking** is an integrated process of examining information, ideas, and proposals. It involves

- using your intelligence and knowledge to question, explore, and deal effectively with yourself, others, and life's problems.
- developing your own view of the world by examining ideas and arriving at your own conclusions.
- being receptive to new ideas and willing to analyze issues from different perspectives to develop greater understanding.
- supporting your personal views with reasons and evidence and understanding the reasons and evidence that support alternative viewpoints.
- discussing your ideas with others to test and enrich your thinking.[14]

## *The Importance of Critical Thinking to Listening*

Throughout this course the skills and knowledge you acquire as you learn to prepare speeches will be useful also for analyzing and evaluating messages you receive. You will learn how to use and evaluate supporting materials and different language resources in speeches. As you learn to prepare responsible arguments, you will also be learning how to evaluate the arguments of others. Although these topics will be covered in more depth in later chapters, we will preview some questions that should start you on the path to critical listening skills.

## *Questions for Critical Thinking and Analysis*

*Does the speaker simply make assertions and claims?* Responsible, ethical communicators back up assertions and claims with supporting materials such as facts and figures, examples, testimony, and narratives. Whenever speakers claim, "This statement is beyond dispute!" that might be a very good time to start a dispute. Listen for what is not said, as well as to what is said. No evidence, no proof should be your motto. Don't hesitate to ask such speakers challenging questions.

*Is the supporting material relevant, representative, recent, and reliable?* Supporting materials should relate directly to the issue in question. They should be representative of the situation as it exists rather than exceptions to the rule. The speaker who shouts, "Hollywood is destroying family values!" and then offers statistics that demonstrate a rising divorce rate in the nation, has not supported a causal relationship between the film industry and family values. Similarly, the divorce rate is not necessarily related to such values. Facts and figures also should be timely. This is particularly important when knowledge about a topic is changing rapidly. Supporting materials should come from sources that are trustworthy and competent in the subject area. Controversial material should be verified by more than one source.

*Are credible sources cited?* Responsible, ethical speakers present the credentials of their sources so that listeners can make independent judgments. When credentials are left out or described in vague terms, their testimony may be questionable. We recently found an advertisement for a health food product that contained "statements by doctors." A quick check of the current directory of the American Medical Association revealed that only one of the six "doctors" cited was a member of AMA and that his credentials were misrepresented. Always ask yourself, "Where does this information come from?" and "Are these sources qualified to speak on the topic?"

*Is there a clear distinction among facts, inferences, and opinions?* Facts are verifiable units of information that can be confirmed by independent observations. Inferences make projections based on facts. Opinions add interpretations or judgments to facts: they tell us what someone thinks about a subject. For example, "Mary was late for class today" is a fact. "Mary will probably be late for class again tomorrow" is an inference. "Mary is an irresponsible student" is an opinion. It may sound easy to make these distinctions among facts, inferences, and opinions, but you must be constantly alert as a listener to detect accidental or intentional confusions of them in messages.

*Is the language concrete and understandable or purposely vague?* When speakers have something to hide, they often use vague or incomprehensible language. Introducing people who are not physicians as "doctors" to enhance their testimony on health subjects is just one form of such deception. Another trick is to use pseudoscientific jargon such as "This supplement contains a gonadotropic hormone similar to pituitary extract in terms of its complex B vitamin-methionine ratio." If it sounds impressive but you don't know what it means, be careful.

*Am I being asked to ignore reason?* Although it is not unethical to use emotional appeals in a speech, reason should always support feelings. Examples that stress the emotional aspects of a situation may be used to humanize a topic, but speakers should also include valid information and logic to justify the claims of a message. In speeches, this problem can take many forms. One problem occurs when speakers *think* they are being reasonable but actually are using questionable premises or applying such premises in doubtful ways. One of the most fateful moments in President John F. Kennedy's justly celebrated Inaugural Address came when he made the following bold statement: "We shall pay any price, bear any burden, meet any hardship, support any friend, oppose any foe in order to assure the survival and success of liberty." When government officials later used that statement to justify the United States' involvement in South Vietnam, their thinking may have been driven more by passion than by reason. At the very least, they did not stop to define precisely the meaning of that "liberty" we were sworn to protect. At the time the statement was made, South Vietnam was hardly a model of political freedom or democratic institutions.

*Is the reasoning plausible?* Plausible reasoning looks and sounds sensible. When reasoning is plausible, conclusions appear to follow from the points and supporting materials that precede them. The basic assumptions that support arguments are those on which most rational people agree. Whenever reasoning doesn't seem plausible, ask yourself why, and then question the speaker or consult with independent authorities before you make decisions or commit yourself.

*Is the message believable, or does it promise too much?* If an offer sounds too good to be true, it probably is. The health-food advertisement described previously contained the following claims: "The healing, rejuvenating and disease-fighting effects of this total nutrient are hard to believe, yet are fully documented. Aging, digestive upsets, prostrate [*sic*] diseases, sore throats, acne, fatigue, sexual problems, allergies, and a host of other problems have been successfully treated. . . . [It] is the only super perfect food on this earth. This statement has been proven so many times in the laboratories around the world by a chemical analyst that it is not subject to debate nor challenge." Maybe the product is also useful as a paint remover and gasoline additive.

**SPEAKER'S NOTES**

**Guides for Critical Thinking and Listening**

1. *Require that statements and claims be supported* with facts and figures, testimony, examples, or narratives; insist that these be relevant, representative, recent, and reliable.

2. *Do not accept what anyone says at face value.* Examine the credentials of sources, particularly in terms of their competence and trustworthiness.

3. *Differentiate among facts, inferences, and opinions.*

4. *Be wary of language that seems purposely vague or incomprehensible.*

5. *Be on guard against claims that promise too much.*

6. *Look for plausible reasoning,* especially when messages arouse emotion.

7. *Be receptive to new ideas and new perspectives,* but scrutinize them carefully.

8. *Ask questions.* Responsible advocates welcome serious questions; unethical speakers fear them and usually become defensive.

*How does this message fit in with what I already know or believe?* A good test of any message is whether it fits in with our previous knowledge or beliefs. Of course, we should be open to the possibility of new knowledge and realize that we have been wrong before. But when a message contradicts what we know and believe, we should be ready to apply critical thinking skills. Ask questions of the speaker and use the library to check information in the speech.

These questions together make up the discipline of critical thinking. When we add this discipline to the improved listening skills that result from solving our listening problems, we are on the way to becoming sophisticated listeners. Then when we add the additional ingredient of a constructive listening orientation, we can approach the balanced ideal of becoming critical, constructive listeners.

##  DEVELOPING CONSTRUCTIVE LISTENING SKILLS

The first step in developing constructive listening skills is to realize the absolute necessity of healthy listening to the communication enterprise. We have mentioned, for example, that the feedback offered by listeners to speakers at times can be deceptive. But honest feedback is one of the most important aspects of healthy listening behavior. As mentioned in Chapter 1, *feedback* is the ongoing response behavior of listeners that lets speakers know how their messages are being received. It is vital because of the interactive nature of communication. For example, if the speaker is not clear or is speaking too softly or too loudly, listeners may frown with uncertainty, strain forward to hear, or push backwards to escape the irritating loudness. Adept speakers will recognize these feedback messages and attempt to clarify the point or increase or reduce their volume. Good speakers monitor audience feedback for signs of successful or flawed communication. Good listeners provide honest feedback so that speakers can make their messages more effective.

As important as good feedback can be, it is only the most obvious part of constructive listening. We can better understand the totality of such listening in terms of two other concepts, empathetic listening and synergistic listening.

### Empathetic Listening

**Empathetic listening** involves a feeling of closeness or identity that listeners can develop for speakers or for others whom the speaker's words might affect.[15] Good listeners look beyond the speaker's words for the motives that

*Constructive listeners evaluate ideas, are sensitive to the humanity of others, and respond fully and creatively to ideas that are put forth. President Bill Clinton listens closely in a discussion with adult literacy students.*

prompt them. They seek the humanity in speakers, even when they may disagree with the speaker's position. An empathetic listener tries to communicate the following message: "I understand why you are saying these things, even if I can't accept them. I look forward to the times when I can agree with you." This type of attitude will underlie whatever specific feedback the listener offers.

Empathetic listeners encourage and share in the satisfaction of a successful classroom speech. We once taught a class in which a student — we shall call her Marta — seemed unable to complete her presentations. She was obviously talented and intelligent, yet approximately two-thirds of the way through her presentations, Marta would stop, even though the speech seemed to be going well, and declare that she could not continue. It quickly became an unstated class goal to have Marta complete a speech before the end of the term. We counseled with her repeatedly and offered our encouragement. Finally, there came the day when Marta, in the midst of a fine speech, paused, breathed deeply, and went on to finish her speech on a high note. That class of empathetic listeners broke into loud and sustained applause while Marta beamed. Her victory was their victory. At the end of the class Marta came up to us, her face glowing, to ask if there were other speech classes she might take. Every speech instructor could offer similar stories of small but meaningful personal triumphs in classrooms before empathetic listeners.

True empathy, however, goes beyond identification with the humanity of the speaker. To experience empathetic listening in the fullness of its meaning, we must also consider the impact of the speaker's words on others and feel their involvement as well. It was in such an elevated consciousness that Nelson Mandela described himself as "a particle of a people."[16] Although they are members of a particular audience, empathetic listeners also sense their role as surrogates for humanity. In this role, they place high ethical demands upon speakers. Martin Luther King, Jr., in his final speech in Memphis the night before he was assassinated, captured such an attitude quite well: "The question is not, 'If I stop to help this man in need, what will happen to me?' The question is, 'If I do *not* stop to help the sanitation workers, what will happen to them?' That's the question."[17] This is the kind of question the truly empathetic listener asks.

To summarize, empathetic listening directs our attention both to the humanity of the speaker and to the larger human family, whose fate is always involved when serious words are spoken on public occasions.

### *Synergistic Listening*

One of the ways that we talk about the meaning of words trivializes the communication process. We sometimes treat meaning as something the speaker decides upon, then carefully packs into words. Thus we talk about "the meaning of her words" as though meaning belonged exclusively to the speaker. From such a perspective the duty of the listener is to "unpack" the words and receive the meaning. From this perspective the major responsibility of the listener is to avoid distorting the meaning during the unpacking.

The idea of participative communication provides a different view of meaning. In participative communication, speakers and listeners are not packers and unpackers of a product, but rather creative collaborators who make meaning together. The role of listeners is elevated in this view. If the speaker supplies the meaning potentials, it is the listener who completes and often even improves these potentials. **Synergistic listening** is the process by which listeners respond fully and creatively to the speaker's words in order to find the richest possible meaning within them. Synergistic listening expands our awareness of the world and its problems, and sharpens and deepens the ideas generated by the speech. The speaker's words become an invitation to a dialogue, carried on within the minds of listeners or even in actual questions and answers after a speech. Such dialogues often produce discoveries, better realizations of public values, and better answers to public problems. Synergistic listening, therefore, is that process by which speaker and listener, interacting together, make each other better than either could be alone. Synergistic listening makes it possible for 1 + 1 to equal 3.

The results of synergistic listening are often surprising and unpredictable. Andy Atkinson delivered a passionate appeal in class asking for donations to a relief fund for victims of "a far more sinister Andy — Hurricane Andrew." During the class discussion after the speech, Heather Martin asked if there

**SPEAKER'S
NOTES**

## Questions for Evaluating Constructive Listening Experiences

1. Did the speech draw you closer to the speaker and to other members of the audience?

2. What might be the impact of the speaker's message on others?

3. Did this speech stimulate you to think about its subject?

4. Were you able to relate this speech to your life?

5. Did the speech raise ideas or possibilities in your mind that the speaker had not considered?

6. What will you carry away from your experience of this speech?

could be a campuswide effort. After class Heather, Andy, and several other interested students met and laid plans for a fund-raising effort that raised a significant amount of money for the hurricane victims. Their campaign also brought the university community together, created close personal friendships, and taught these students a valuable lesson about the power of dedicated individuals to bring about change. Andy's strong speech had combined with Heather's synergistic listening to produce a result far more meaningful than either could have predicted.

Synergistic and empathetic attitudes together make up that constructive orientation that can make listening such a satisfying human experience. The ideal of critical, constructive listening can light our way as we seek to improve our listening behavior.

## EVALUATING SPEECHES

You can use your critical and constructive listening skills to evaluate the speeches you hear in your class. During the discussion following a speech, you may ask questions, comment on effective techniques, or offer suggestions for improvement. Your feedback always should be aimed at helping the speaker improve.

There is a difference between criticizing a speaker and giving a **critique,** or evaluation, of a speech. Criticism often suggests an emphasis on what someone did wrong. This approach can create a negative, competitive communication environment. When you give a critique, your manner should be helpful and supportive. Give credit where credit is due. Point out strengths as well as weaknesses. Whenever you point out a weakness or problem, also try to point out remedies or solutions. This type of interaction creates a classroom environment that stresses the willingness of students to help each other.

To participate in the evaluation of speeches, you need a set of criteria or standards to guide you. Your instructor may have a special set of criteria for grading your presentations, and the criteria may be weighted differently from assignment to assignment. For example, your instructor may assess your informative speeches primarily in terms of their structure and the adequacy of information and examples, and may evaluate your persuasive speeches based on your use of evidence and reasoning.

Regardless of what special criteria are involved, there are some general guidelines you can use to evaluate speeches. In Chapter 1 we discussed the factors that make a speech effective. You may wish to review that discussion at this time. These same factors may also be used to assess classroom speeches. Figure 3.3 on the following page presents these standard criteria.

**Commitment**
Did the speaker seem committed to the topic?
Had the speaker done enough research?

**Topic**
Was the topic inherently worthwhile?
Did the topic fit the assignment and the time limit?
Was the topic handled imaginatively?

**Purpose**
Was the purpose of the speech clear?

**Audience involvement**
Was the topic adapted to the audience?
Were you able to identify with the speaker and the topic?
Did the speech stimulate you to make creative applications?

**Substance**
Were the main points supported by evidence?
Were the examples clear and interesting?
Was the reasoning clear and correct?

**Structure**
Did the introduction spark your interest?
Was the speech easy to follow?
Was important information emphasized?
Were transitions used to tie the speech together?
Did the conclusion help you remember the message?

**Language**
Was the language clear, simple, and direct?
Were grammar and pronunciations correct?
Was the language concrete and colorful?

**Presentation**
Was the speaker enthusiastic?
Was the speech presented extemporaneously?
Did gestures and body language complement ideas?
Was the speaker's voice expressive?
Did the speaker maintain good eye contact?
Were notes used unobtrusively?
Were the rate and loudness appropriate to the material?

**Ethics**
Did this speech reveal its actual purpose?
Did the speaker discuss all options?
Would the consequences of this speech be desirable?

FIGURE 3.3
Guidelines for Evaluating
Speeches

**IN SUMMARY**  Listening is as vital to effective communication as speaking. The ideal listener balances the skills of critical and constructive listening. *Critical listening* involves hearing, attending, comprehending, analyzing, responding to, and remembering a message. *Constructive listening* suggests the vital role of the listener in the creation of meaning. To become better listeners, we must first overcome our listening problems. Then we must combine the skills of effective listening and critical thinking with a constructive orientation.

*Benefits of Critical and Constructive Listening.*  Critical listening skills make us less vulnerable to unethical advertising or to dishonest political communication. The critical listener is especially on guard against irrelevant or misleading appeals. Constructive listening skills enable us to play our role in *participative communication,* in which both speaker and listener become co-creators of meaning. The constructive listener looks for positive, useful elements in messages. We should be able to play both critical and constructive roles, because a balance of such skills helps us lead successful, fulfilling lives. Skilled listening especially correlates with success in school and in our careers.

*Overcoming Listening Problems.*  Listening problems may arise from personal reactions, attitudes, or bad listening habits. Personal reactions to *trigger words* that set off strong negative or positive emotions can block effective listening. Both internal and external distractions can also interfere with listening, as can biased attitudes toward the speaker or topic. Bad habits, such as pretending we are listening when we are not or listening only for facts, can also impair our listening behavior.

Effective listening skills can be developed. The first step is to identify your listening problems. Concentrate on the main ideas and the overall pattern of meaning in the speech. Strive for objectivity, withholding value judgments until you are certain you understand the message.

*Critical Thinking and Listening.*  *Critical thinking* skills help you analyze and evaluate messages more effectively. Critical listeners question what they hear, require support for assertions and claims, and evaluate the credentials of sources. Critical listeners differentiate among facts, inferences, and opinions. They become wary when language seems incomprehensible or overly vague, when reason and rationality are absent in a message, or when a message promises too much. When what they hear does not fit with what they know, critical listeners pause, consider the message very carefully, and ask questions.

*Developing Constructive Listening Skills.*  *Constructive listening* includes both empathetic and synergistic elements. *Empathetic listening* is that feeling of closeness or identity listeners may develop both for speakers and for others whom the speaker's words might affect. Empathetic listeners place high ethical demands on speakers because they realize how words can influence the fate of others, absent as well as present. *Synergistic listening* is the process by which listeners respond creatively and fully to the speaker's words in order to find the richest possible meaning within them. Such listening invites dialogue and inquiry, so that the speech becomes an episode in a cooperative quest for meaning.

***Evaluating Speeches.***   Speech evaluation takes the form of a *critique,* a positive and constructive effort to help the speaker improve. Criteria for speech evaluation include speaker commitment, choice of topic, clarity of purpose, audience involvement, substance, structure, language, presentation, and ethics.

**TERMS TO KNOW**

| | |
|---|---|
| critical listening | filtering |
| constructive listening | assimilation |
| participative communication | contrast effect |
| denotative meaning | critical thinking |
| connotative meaning | empathetic listening |
| trigger word | synergistic listening |
| listening log | critique |

**DISCUSSION**

1. Complete the "Listening Problems Check List" on page 00 of this chapter. Working in small groups, discuss your listening problems with the other members of the group. Develop a listening improvement plan for the three most common listening problems in your group. Report this plan to the rest of the class.

2. List three positive and three negative trigger words that provoke a strong emotional reaction when you hear them. Have someone write these words on the chalkboard. Try to group the words into categories, such as sexist or ethnic slurs, political terms, ideals, and so forth. Discuss why these words have such a strong impact on you. Do you feel your reactions to them are justified?

3. Think of a person (public speaker, teacher, and so forth) to whom you like to listen. List all the adjectives you can that describe this person. Think of another person to whom you do not like to listen. List the adjectives that describe this person. Compare the two lists and share your conclusions with the class.

**APPLICATION**

1. Review the notes you have taken in one of your lecture courses. Are you able to identify the main points, or have you been trying to write down everything that was said? Compare your note taking before and after studying listening behavior. Can you see any difference?

2. Read the following paragraph carefully:

Dirty Dick has been killed. The police have rounded up six suspects, all of whom are known criminals. All of them were near the scene of the crime at the approximate time that the murder took place. All had good motives for wanting Dirty Dick killed. However, Larcenous Lenny has been completely cleared of guilt.

Now determine whether each of the following statements is true (T), false (F), or is an inference (?).[18]

T F ?   1. Larcenous Lenny is known to have been near the scene of the killing of Dirty Dick.

T F ?   2. All six of the rounded-up criminals were known to have been near the scene of the murder.

T F ?   3. Only Larcenous Lenny has been cleared of guilt.

T F ?   4. The police do not know who killed Dirty Dick.

T F ?   5. Dirty Dick's murderer did not confess of his own free will.

T F ?   6. It is known that the six suspects were in the vicinity of the cold-blooded assassination.

T F ?   7. Larcenous Lenny did not kill Dirty Dick.

T F ?   8. Dirty Dick is dead.

The answers are found following the Notes at the end of the chapter. Were you able to distinguish between inferences and facts?

3. Prepare a critique of a speech by a prominent political or religious leader. What advice would you offer this person?

4. During the next round of speeches in your class, choose a day in which you determine to be an especially exemplary listener. As you listen to the speeches, try to balance your critical and constructive listening skills. Test the ideas you hear and seek to develop and apply them creatively. Try to identify with the speakers and to imagine the impact of their words on others. Keep notes, and write a full report of your experiences as soon as you can after class while your memory is still fresh. How close were you able to approach the ideal of critical, constructive listening? What problems did you encounter? Submit your report to your instructor.

**NOTES**     1. James J. Floyd, *Listening: A Practical Approach* (Glenview, Ill.: Scott, Foresman, 1985), p. 2.

2. Michael and Suzanne Osborn, *Alliance for a Better Public Voice: The Communication Discipline and the National Issues Forums* (Dayton, Oh.: National Issues Forums Institute, 1991), pp. 14–17.

3. Walter Pauk, *How to Study in College* (Boston: Houghton Mifflin, 1989), pp. 121–133.

4. W. B. Legge, "Listening, Intelligence, and School Achievement," in *Listening: Readings,* ed. S. Duker (Metuchen, N.J.: Scarecrow Press, 1971), pp. 121–133.

5. Gary T. Hunt and Louis P. Cusella, "A Field Study of Listening Needs in Organizations," *Communication Education* 32 (October 1983): 399.

6. Andrew D. Wolvin and Carolyn Gwynn Coakley, *Listening,* 2nd ed. (Dubuque, Iowa: William C. Brown, 1985), p. 22.

7. Ibid., p. 177.

8. J. J. Makay and W. R. Brown, *The Rhetorical Dialogue: Contemporary Concepts and Cases* (Dubuque, Iowa: William C. Brown, 1972), pp. 125–145.

9. Jill Scott, "What Did you Say? I Was Listening to Your Tie," *English Journal* 73 (1984): 88.

10. Waldo Braden, "The Available Means of Persuasion: What Shall We Do About the Demand for Snake Oil?" in *The Rhetoric of Our Times,* ed. J. Jeffry Auer (New York: Appleton-Century-Crofts, 1969), pp. 178–184.

11. Kathleen Hall Jamieson and Karlyn Kohrs Campbell, *The Interplay of Influence: Mass Media and the Public in News, Advertising, Politics,* 2nd ed. (Belmont, Calif.: Wadsworth, 1988), p. 4. Anthony M. Casale and Phillip Lerman, *USA Today: Tracking Tomorrow's Trends* (Kansas City, Kans.: Andrews, McMeel & Parker, 1986), p. 19.

12. William F. Buckley, "Has TV Killed Off Great Oratory?" *TV Guide,* 12 Feb. 1983, p. 38.

13. Floyd, pp. 23–25.

14. John Chaffee, *Thinking Critically,* 2nd ed. (Boston: Houghton Mifflin, 1988), p. 59.

15. See the discussion in *Alliance for a Better Public Voice,* pp. 26–3l. We use this term deliberately to distinguish it from a closely related phenomenon, *empathic listening,* which occurs in interpersonal communication.

16. Nelson Mandela, "Address to the United States Congress," Congressional Record — House, 26 June 1990, pp. 4136–4138.

17. Martin Luther King, Jr., "I've Been to the Mountaintop," *Texts in Context: Critical Dialogues on Significant Episodes in American Political Rhetoric,* ed. Michael C. Leff and Fred J. Kauffeld (Davis, Calif.: Hermagoras Press, 1989), p. 319.

**Answers to Application item #2:** (1) ?, (2) T, (3) ?, (4) ?, (5) ?, (6) ?, (7) ?, (8) T.

# PART TWO

# Preparation for Public Speaking

*Oratory is the art of enchanting the soul, and therefore one who would be an orator has to learn the differences of human souls.*

— *Plato*

# 4

# Audience Analysis and Adaptation

## This Chapter Will Help You

- adapt your speech to environmental factors such as time, place, context, occasion, and audience size.

- adjust your message to audience demographics such as age, gender, education, group affiliations, and sociocultural background.

- plan for audience dynamics such as motivations, beliefs, values, and attitudes that influence the reception of your message.

It's the beginning of the fall term and as president of the newly formed Students for Environmental Action you have a busy day coming up next Tuesday. At eight o'clock in the morning you will introduce your group to the incoming freshmen assembled at the soccer field. Your major goal will be to inform them about SEA's projects for the coming year and to motivate some of them to join the organization. Later that day you face what you fear will be a more daunting task. You just received a letter from the director of the Coahoma County Industrial Development Board. She wants you to attend their luncheon meeting at the Executive Club to let the members know "what you students are up to." You must convince the board that SEA's work will help rather than hurt the business climate in the area.

You will speak on the same general topic, but the different audiences will create different challenges and goals for you. The listeners you anticipate — their needs and interests — must occupy the center of your thinking as you plan and develop your speech. Moreover, the setting for your speech can make a big difference in how you present it: your manner of presentation, as well as the language you choose, may vary from the soccer field to the board room.

In this chapter we consider the audience for your speech and the setting in which you will speak. In particular, you need to develop a special sensitivity to your audience, so that your adaptation is intelligent, effective, and ethical.

A sensitive audience analysis can help you make both *long-range* and *immediate* adjustments to your speech. You make long-range adjustments as you plan and prepare your speech, and immediate adjustments either right before or while you speak. Both are important elements of successful presentations. For example, you may wish to give a speech opposing recreational drug use but fear that your classmates have grown tired of the barrage of emotional antidrug appeals. You start to think, "Maybe I should choose another topic." Then the lights go on in your head. You can focus your speech precisely on the local drug scene and how it affects *your* community. Instead of an emotional approach, you can emphasize facts, policy options, and ways listeners can get personally involved. On the day of your speech, you discover you must make some immediate adjustments. The room is hot and stuffy. The speech before yours was tedious, and the audience is drowsy. You realize you must speak more dramatically than you had planned, awaken listeners with your introduction, and cut any material that is not absolutely necessary.

In this chapter we discuss (1) *external factors* in the communication environment, many of which may require immediate adjustments; (2) *demographic factors,* which are objective, observable traits of audience members; and (3) *audience dynamics,* or internal factors that influence listeners from within. The demographic and dynamics factors typically affect the long-range planning of the speech. We will consider these factors both in relation to your classroom audience and to other types of audiences you may encounter in the world beyond.

## ADJUSTING TO THE COMMUNICATION ENVIRONMENT

The communication environment includes the time of your presentation, place in which you will speak, context of your speech, nature and purpose of the occasion, and anticipated size of your audience. You should take all these factors into account as you design your speech.

### *Time*

The time of day when you present your speech should be considered as you plan for your presentation.[1] If you are speaking early in the morning, like the speaker in our opening example, or right after any meal, many of your listeners may be half asleep, and you will need some lively or startling examples to keep them awake. If your speech is scheduled on a Monday, when people have not readjusted to going back to work or school, you may need a light, bright touch to hold their attention. On a Friday you may need to be more direct and to the point to keep listeners' minds from drifting to the weekend ahead.

Even the time of year can influence audience response. Gloomy winter days or balmy spring weather can put people in different frames of mind. As you plan your speech, think of adjustments you might make to compensate. For example, a bit more humor or a more forceful presentation might enliven an audience on a dreary day.

### *Place*

You should also consider the physical surroundings for your speech. Will you be speaking indoors or outside? If you are outside, you may have to cope with weather problems or other distractions, such as passing traffic or the beauty of the scenery. Your speech needs to be interesting or dramatic to hold your audience's attention in such surroundings.

Even in the classroom, speakers must learn to cope with distractions — construction and traffic noises may filter in from outside or students in the hall may be raucous and loud. How can you handle such distractions? If the noise is temporary or intermittent, such as passing traffic or audience applause, you should pause and wait until it stops, repeat your last words, then go on with your message. With constant noise the obvious solution is to speak louder. However, if the noise is so loud that you must shout, you should pause and ask someone to close the window or door. The important consideration is to take such problems in stride and not let them distract you or your audience from your message.

Will your listeners be seated or standing? If seats are hard or people must stand, your message must be short and lively so that you don't lose your audience. If listeners are wriggling in their seats or beginning to wander away, you will need to make immediate adjustments. A dramatic statement, vigorous gesture, or change in vocal pitch or loudness may help you recapture their attention.

The size of the room can also affect the audience's ability to hear you. Will you have access to a microphone? Is there a lectern and a place to display visual aids? Will electronic equipment be available? Check out where you will be speaking so that you can make adjustments in advance.

### Context

Anything that happens near the time of your presentation becomes part of the context of your speech. Both recent speeches and recent events can influence how the audience responds to you.

***The Context of Recent Speeches.***   The speeches presented before yours create an atmosphere in which you must work. This atmosphere has a **preliminary tuning effect** on listeners, predisposing them to respond in certain ways to you and your message.[2] Outside the classroom, preliminary tuning for speeches is often carefully planned. At political rallies, patriotic music and introductions prepare the audience for the appearance of the featured speaker. The same effect can be seen at evangelical meetings where

*Elie Wiesel, recipient of the 1986 Nobel Peace Prize, had to overcome many distractions when speaking at this Holocaust memorial service. But a compelling message, a sincere commitment, and a forceful presentation can help speakers cope with such problems as traffic noise and inclement weather.*

music and prayer tune the congregation, or at concerts where warm-up groups put listeners in the mood for the star. Such planned preliminary tuning creates a sense of anticipation that favors the featured speaker or entertainer.

In the classroom, preliminary tuning can be more difficult to control. Sometimes instructors encourage an effective speaker to lead off, knowing that a good speech can create a positive atmosphere and stimulate others to do their best. This type of positive momentum also helps listeners become more receptive audiences. However, less successful speeches, especially if they come one after another, can set off a downward spiral that both speakers and listeners must work to reverse.

Sometimes previous speeches affect the mood of an audience. If the speech immediately before yours was on a sensitive topic, it may have aroused strong emotions. In this case you may need to ease the tension before you can expect listeners to turn their minds to your message. One way of handling such a problem is to acknowledge the reactions and use them as a springboard into your own speech:

> Obviously, many of us feel very strongly about abortion. It's a subject that is important to most of us. What I'm going to talk about is also very important — but it is something I think we can all agree on — the challenge of finding a way to stop the AIDS epidemic now spreading through our community.

If your speech is considerably lighter than the one that preceded it, you might decide to begin with a story to involve listeners and refocus their attention. Sometimes humor can help relieve the tension, but humor can also be risky. People who are upset may be in no mood for laughter; but on the other hand, they may welcome your effort to relieve their somber feelings. Your decision on whether to use humor must be based on your reading of each situation: the mood of listeners, the subject under discussion, and your own ability to use the technique constructively and effectively. Humor will certainly *not* be appropriate in many situations. Additionally, some types of humor, such as racial or ethnic jokes or gender jibes, are always out of bounds. If the humorous material you are considering might be offensive to anyone in the audience, avoid it like the plague.

If the speech that preceded yours was light and yours covers a more serious topic, you may also have to modify your introduction to get the audience in the proper frame of mind:

> Well, we've all enjoyed Margaret's descriptions of the horrors of Halloween, but today I'd like to talk with you about a more serious horror — the horror of being hooked on crack cocaine.

In addition to dealing with the mood created by earlier speeches, you may also need to adapt your message to their content. Suppose you have spent the past week preparing to discuss the importance of extending endangered species legislation. You are scheduled to speak third, and the first speaker gives a convincing presentation on the *problems* of extending endangered species legislation. What can you do? Try to use this negative preliminary tuning to your advantage by adjusting your introduction. Point out that the earlier speech has established the importance of the topic but that — as good as that effort was — it did not give the total picture: "Now you will hear the *other* side of the story."

***The Context of Recent Events.*** As listeners enter the room the day of your speech, they bring with them information about recent local, national, and international events. They will use this knowledge to evaluate and react to what you say. If you are not up-to-date on recent events relevant to your topic, your credibility will suffer. A student in one of our classes once presented a very interesting and well-documented speech comparing public housing in Germany with that in the United States. She was able to add a personal touch to her message since she had lived in Germany for several years. Unfortunately, she was unaware of a current scandal with local public housing. For three days before her presentation, the story had made front-page headlines in the local paper and was the lead story in area newscasts. Everyone in the class seemed to know about it but she, and everyone expected her to mention it. Her failure to incorporate this important local material weakened her credibility.

In contrast, Rod Nishikawa used a recent tragedy to lead into his persuasive speech urging greater controls on the sale and ownership of automatic weapons. Shortly before he gave his speech, a gunman using such a weapon had injured and killed a number of children in a school yard in Stockton, California. Rod presented an effective speech urging his classmates at the University of California – Davis to contact their local representatives in support of pending gun-control legislation. Because Stockton is near Davis, his references to the nearby massacre evoked vivid images. The message is clear: as a speaker you should stay abreast of news relevant to your subject.

At times the context of events to which you must adjust your speech may be quite unexpected. Then you must make on-the-spot adjustments so that the situation works in your favor. During the 1985 graduation at Loyola Marymount University, the school's president fell off the platform immediately before the commencement address. The speaker, Peter Ueberroth, organizer of the 1984 Los Angeles summer Olympic Games, recaptured the audience's attention and brought down the house by awarding the president a 4.5 in gymnastics.[3]

## Nature and Purpose of the Occasion

As you plan and prepare your message, you need to take into account *why* people have gathered to listen. If you have a "captive" audience that has been required to attend, as in a mandatory employee meeting or a public speaking class, you may have to work extra hard to arouse interest and maintain attention. Additionally, listeners often have definite ideas about what is and is not appropriate for specific speech occasions. If the speaker does not offer the kind of speech they expect, listeners may be puzzled or even annoyed. For example, if they have been led to expect an informative talk and instead are bombarded by a sales pitch, their expectations will be violated. This could result in irritation rather than persuasion.

## Size of Audience

The larger your audience, the more diverse it is apt to be. Your listeners may differ in many ways: sex, age, education level, interests, attitudes, motivations, and cultural background. The more diverse your audience, the more difficult it will be to reach everyone with your message. Consequently, when faced with a diverse group, you should concentrate on your **primary audience,** *those listeners who are capable of making your words effective.* For example, the entire audience for a speech you are planning against recreational drug use may be made up of users, susceptible nonusers who might be tempted to start, and adamant nonusers. The users and susceptible nonusers would be the primary audience for your message because these are the listeners you hope to influence or change. Your speech may reinforce the beliefs and attitudes of the adamant nonusers, but they are not the primary audience for your persuasive efforts. Determining who constitutes the primary audience for your message allows you to focus your efforts most effectively.

The size of the audience also can call for modifications in your manner of presentation. With small audiences (under twenty people), you get more direct feedback and can interact more effectively because you can make and maintain eye contact with nearly everyone present. Small audiences often call for less formal presentations. You can even ask questions and solicit responses, modifying your presentation on the spot if necessary. Standing behind a lectern and never deviating from a prepared presentation may create barriers to effective communication.You should not be the prisoner of a rigidly planned speech.

On the other hand, the larger your audience, the more formal your presentation should be. With a larger audience, casualness may be seen as lack of preparation or seriousness. You should speak more deliberately and enunciate your words more carefully when addressing a large group. Because you cannot make or sustain eye contact with everyone, choose representative listeners in various sections of the audience and change your visual focus from time to time. Establishing eye contact with listeners in all sections of the room helps more people feel included. With a larger group your gestures must be more emphatic so that everyone can see them, and any visual aids you use must be large enough that those in the back of the audience can understand them without strain.

**SPEAKER'S NOTES**

### Check List for Analyzing the Speech Setting

1. Will the time or timing of my speech pose any problems?

2. Will room arrangements be adequate? Will I have the equipment I need for visual aids?

3. What does the audience expect on this occasion?

4. Is there any late-breaking news on my topic?

5. Will there be other speakers before me that I may have to adjust to?

6. How large and diverse will the audience be?

7. Who is my primary audience?

## ADJUSTING TO AUDIENCE DEMOGRAPHICS

The demographic make-up of your audience includes their age range, gender, education level, group affiliations, and sociocultural background. The more you know about these audience factors, the better you can adapt your speech to the needs and interests of your listeners. If you are familiar with the group you are addressing, you can determine their demographics rather easily. If not, try to get as much information as you can from the person who invited you to speak. You might also talk with group members or contact others who have addressed them.

Gathering such information systematically is called **demographic audience analysis.** During political campaigns, demographic analyses are used to help candidates address specific audience concerns in their speeches. In your speech class, such information can help you estimate audience interest in your topic, how much listeners may already know about it, how they may feel about it, and how you might best motivate them to listen. Your instructor may conduct such an analysis early in the term and distribute the results to the class. If introductory speeches were presented in your class, they should also have provided useful information. This material, combined with timely insights from public opinion and consumer surveys, can help you adjust your message more precisely to your audience.[4] The relevance of specific demographic factors may vary from topic to topic. For example, if you were speaking on "Government Services — Yours for the Taking," age might be an important consideration, but gender or religious preference might be irrelevant.

## Age

Age has been used to predict audience reactions since the time of Aristotle, who suggested that young listeners are pleasure loving, optimistic, impulsive, trusting, idealistic, and easily persuaded. The elderly, he said, are more set in their ways, more skeptical, cynical, and concerned with maintaining a comfortable existence. Those in the prime of life, Aristotle suggested, present a balance between youth and age, being confident yet cautious, judging cases by the facts, and taking all things in moderation.[5]

Contemporary communication research supports the relationship between age and persuasibility that Aristotle described. Maximum susceptibility to persuasion occurs during childhood and declines as people grow older.[6] Research also suggests that younger people are more flexible and open to new ideas, but older people tend to be more conservative and less receptive to change.[7]

What expectations might you have about your classroom audience? To begin with, the average college student is getting older. In 1987, 16 percent of college students were over 35; by 1997 this figure is expected to rise to 22 percent.[8] If your audience contains both younger and older students, you may need to consider your topic selections and speech strategies with this in mind. For example, if your audience consists mainly of eighteen-year-olds, they may be interested in a speech on campus social activities. But if your audience is composed more of older students, this topic could seem trivial or uninteresting.

What else does contemporary research tell us about college students? They define themselves as politically moderate, yet express fairly liberal attitudes about sexual freedom, sexual equality, and racial issues.[9] Traditional values remain important to them: over 80 percent attended church in 1991, two-thirds performed volunteer work, and over three-quarters voted in student elections and planned to vote in the 1992 presidential election (even though they mistrust government!). Such survey information can be helpful as you design a speech, but keep in mind that these impressions are based on national data and may not apply to the students in your public speaking class. For example, in 1991 the American Council on Education Survey contained the questions found in Figure 4.1. Answer these questions for yourself and see how your responses compare with the national results.[10]

## Gender

In our society, notions of gender differences are changing rapidly.[11] The changes are especially marked in the areas of "gender appropriate" roles and interests. During the 1950s, when your authors were in college, *Life* magazine interviewed five (male) psychiatrists, who suggested that women's ambitions were the "root of mental illness in wives, emotional upset in husbands, and homosexuality in boys."[12] As late as 1981, this same publication introduced the first female Supreme Court justice, Sandra Day O'Connor, with the headline, "President Goes A-courtin'."[13] Many people still think of

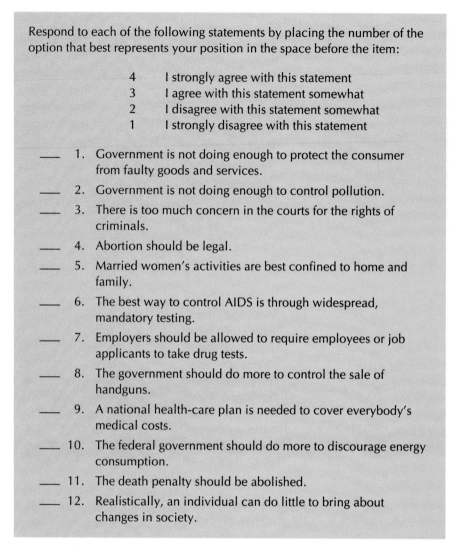

Respond to each of the following statements by placing the number of the option that best represents your position in the space before the item:

4     I strongly agree with this statement
3     I agree with this statement somewhat
2     I disagree with this statement somewhat
1     I strongly disagree with this statement

____ 1. Government is not doing enough to protect the consumer from faulty goods and services.

____ 2. Government is not doing enough to control pollution.

____ 3. There is too much concern in the courts for the rights of criminals.

____ 4. Abortion should be legal.

____ 5. Married women's activities are best confined to home and family.

____ 6. The best way to control AIDS is through widespread, mandatory testing.

____ 7. Employers should be allowed to require employees or job applicants to take drug tests.

____ 8. The government should do more to control the sale of handguns.

____ 9. A national health-care plan is needed to cover everybody's medical costs.

____ 10. The federal government should do more to discourage energy consumption.

____ 11. The death penalty should be abolished.

____ 12. Realistically, an individual can do little to bring about changes in society.

FIGURE 4.1
College Student Attitude
Questionnaire

automobiles as a traditionally "male domain," yet in 1988 women bought 40 percent of all new cars and helped decide on the purchase of another 40 percent.[14] Similarly, 57 percent of all first-time New York Stock Exchange investors are women.[15] Politics have also changed: in the 1992 presidential election, 54 percent of the voters were women, and more females sought and won public office than ever before.[16] Formerly "male" professions are now attracting women at a rapid rate; the number of women working as engineers and computer programmers is increasing dramatically.[17] It also has become more acceptable for men to enter traditionally female occupations, such as nursing and teaching young children.

During the spring of 1992, a national Gallup poll survey tried to project what America would be like if it were run by women.[18] The results suggested that women place *somewhat* higher values on a caring society that offers more government support for families. The results also suggest that women in power would be tougher on gun control and less tolerant of crimes against persons. Women also would insist more forcefully on equal pay for equal work.[19] A survey of college student attitudes confirmed the same value inclinations among the women questioned.[20] But, as the researchers cautioned, "It's not that men don't care about these issues. It's simply that women care more."[21]

Given minimal value differences between the genders and the rapid changes in gender roles, is there any way you can use gender as a reliable factor in audience analysis? Begin by being certain that any assumptions you make are based on the most current data available from reliable sources, because the differences are often a matter of "now you see them, now you don't."[22]

One assumption you can safely make is that many in your audience — men and women — will find gender stereotyping and sexist language highly objectionable. **Gender stereotyping** occurs when broad generalizations are made about men or women based on outmoded assumptions, such as "men don't know how to take care of children" or "women don't understand business." Such stereotyping often implies that whatever differences do exist between men and women justify discrimination. You should be especially careful not to portray gender roles in ways suggesting superiority and inferiority.

**Sexist language** involves making gender references in situations where the gender is unknown or irrelevant. It may involve the generic use of masculine nouns or pronouns, such as referring to "man's advances in science" or using *he* when the intended reference is to both sexes. You can avoid this problem simply by saying "she or he" or by using the plural "they." Sexist language use may also involve **marking,** or adding a gender reference when none is needed. For example, if you referred to "the woman engineer Thompson," you might be trivializing her contribution by drawing attention to gender when it is irrelevant. Some audience members may interpret your remarks as suggesting that "Thompson is a pretty good engineer *for a woman,*" whether you intend that or not. As we noted in Chapter 3, sexist language may also involve using emotional trigger words, such as calling adult females "girls." Prevent unnecessary damage to your cause and credibility by avoiding gender stereotyping and sexist language.

### Educational Level

You can better estimate your listeners' knowledge of and interest in a topic from their educational level than from their age or gender. The more educated your audience, the more you can assume they know about general topics and current affairs. Research also suggests that better-educated audiences are more concerned with social, consumer, political, and environmental issues. Similarly, the higher the educational level of an audience, the broader their range of interests is apt to be. Finally, better-educated audiences tend to be more open minded. They are more accepting of social and technological changes and more supportive of women's rights and alternative lifestyles.[23]

Educational differences can also affect how you plan and prepare for a speech. For example, if there are several positions or options on an issue, you should assume that a better-educated audience will be aware of them. Therefore, you should be especially careful to acknowledge alternatives and explain why you have selected your position.[24] Although you should always speak from responsible knowledge, knowing that your listeners are highly educated places even more pressure on you for careful preparation. A well-educated audience will require that you supply evidence and examples that can stand up under close scrutiny. If you are not well prepared, such listeners will question your credibility.

## Group Affiliations

The groups people belong to often reflect their interests, attitudes, and values. Knowing the occupation, political preference, religious affiliation, and social group memberships of an audience can provide useful information, helping the speaker design a speech that better fits the interests and needs of listeners. Such information can make your message more relevant to a particular audience and can promote identification between listeners and the speaker's cause.

***Occupational Groups.*** Members of occupational groups are united by special career or employment interests. For example, members of the Speech Communication Association share concerns about educational policies and practices, freedom of speech, and communication ethics. In business organizations, union members typically care about seniority, salary, benefits, and working conditions as well as the overall health of the company that provides their livelihood.

The similar interests of occupational groups, however, go beyond job-related concerns. Occupational group members often share leisure activities, civic concerns, and even reading and television-viewing habits.[25] Knowing your listeners' occupational affiliations, or in the case of your classmates their occupational aspirations, can suggest the kinds of examples that should work best in your speeches or the authorities your audience will find most credible. If many of your classmates are business majors, for instance, they may place more credence in information drawn from the *Wall Street Journal* than from *USA Today*.

Occupational group membership can also provide insight into how much your listeners know about a topic and which aspects of it should be more interesting to them. It can even suggest the wording of your speech. For example, speeches on tax-saving techniques given to professional writers and then to certified public accountants should not have the same focus or use the same language. With the writers you might stress record keeping and business deductions and avoid using technical jargon. With the CPAs you might concentrate on factors that invite audits by the IRS, and you would not have to be so concerned about translating technical terms into lay language.

Unless you are attending a highly specialized school, your classroom audience will probably contain students majoring in everything from accounting to zoology. It will be helpful for you to know the occupational aspirations of your classmates and what type of jobs they hold while attending college. Use this information to guide your selection of topics and choice of examples. It will also help you determine what authorities your listeners respect most and may even suggest the kind of language you should use.

***Political Groups.*** Members of organized political groups are generally quite interested in policies and problems of public life. Knowing how interested in politics your listeners are and their political party preferences can be useful in planning and preparing your speech.[26] For example, Democrats often show greater interest in social and domestic programs than do Republicans, who more often emphasize business interests.

People with strong political ties usually make their feelings known. Some of your classmates may be members of the Young Democrats or Young Republicans. Your college may conduct mock elections or take straw votes on issues of political interest, reporting the results in the campus newspaper. Be on the alert for such information.

***Religious Groups.*** Knowing the religious affiliations of listeners can provide useful information because religious training often underlies the social and cultural values that form the foundation of attitudes. Members of fundamentalist religious groups are likely to have conservative social and political as well as religious attitudes. Baptists tend to be more conservative than Episcopalians, who in turn are often more conservative than Unitarians. In addition, a denomination may advocate specific beliefs that most of its members accept as a part of their religious heritage. You might expect audiences that are primarily Roman Catholic to have fairly negative attitudes toward abortion and birth control because these are part of the church's traditional teachings.

Audiences are usually quite sensitive about topics that touch their religious convictions. As a speaker you should be aware of this sensitivity and be attuned to the religious make-up of your anticipated audience. Appealing to "Christian" values before an audience that includes members of other religious groups is one way to insult listeners unnecessarily and diminish the effectiveness of your message. In today's multicultural world, your classroom audience will probably be made up of students from many different religious and cultural backgrounds.

Despite the power of religious affiliation, even in church-sponsored colleges you cannot always rely on uniformity of religious belief or on the influence of religion on social attitudes. A recent *USA Today* survey of college students indicated no differences in alcohol or drug use between students attending religious and those attending nonreligious institutions, although those enrolled in church-affiliated colleges were twice as likely to have a "great deal of faith in organized religion" and only half as likely to have a live-in romantic relationship.[27] However, since religious affiliation may be a strong indicator of values, it is wise not to ignore its potential importance as a demographic factor.

***Social Groups.*** Membership in social groups can be as important to people as any other kind of affiliation. Typically, we are born into a religious group, raised in a certain political environment, and end up in an occupation as much by chance as by design. But we choose our social groups on the basis of our interests. Photographers join the Film Club, business people become involved with the Chamber of Commerce, outdoor enthusiasts may be members of the Sierra Club, feminists may join the National Organization for Women.

Knowing which social groups are represented in your audience and what they stand for is important for effective audience adaptation. A speech favoring pollution control measures might take a different focus depending on whether it is presented to the Chamber of Commerce or to the Audubon Society. With the Chamber of Commerce you might stress the importance of a clean environment in inducing businesses to relocate in your community; with the Audubon Society you might emphasize the effects of pollution on wildlife. People tend to make their important group memberships known to others around them. Be alert to such information from your classmates and consider it in planning and preparing your speeches.

### Sociocultural Background

An audience's sociocultural background may include anything from the section of the country in which the audience lives to its racial composition. People from different sociocultural backgrounds have different experiences, interests, and ways of looking at things. If your audience is composed primarily of urbanites, it may be difficult for you to create much interest in farm support programs. Similarly, a rural audience might find it hard to identify with the problems of rush hour commuting. A basically white, middle-class audience could have difficulty understanding what it means to grow up as a member of a minority. Midwesterners and southerners may have misconceptions about each other.

If your topic involves interests or issues that are unfamiliar to your audience, you will need to bridge the cultural gap by using examples, stories, and testimony that bring the subject closer to home. Stories help create a sense of identification and bring diverse factions together.[28] It will also help if you can demonstrate to listeners that they share a common interest in problems. Those who want to arouse international concern for a famine in Africa must often overcome barriers of race, culture, and physical distance. Examples that highlight the plight of individuals can create more of a sense of closeness.

Since most college classes represent a diversity of backgrounds, you must strive to reach the majority without offending the minority. Remember that two of the major pillars of ethical speaking are respect for your audience and concern over the consequences of your words. With diverse audiences your appeals and examples may have to be more general, calling on those experiences, feelings, and motivations that people hold in common. It also may be helpful to envision smaller audiences within the larger group. You may even want to direct specific remarks to these smaller groups. You might say, for example, "Let me tell you liberal arts majors what computer skills you'll need to survive the '90s," or "Let me warn you business majors that large corporations are looking for people with the breadth of perspective that comes from a liberal arts education." Direct references to specific subgroups within the audience can keep your speech from seeming too general.

If your classmates gave introductory speeches, you should have a good idea of the diversity of their backgrounds and interests. When you accept invitations to speak outside the classroom, ask questions about the demographic make-up of your anticipated audience. The more information you have about listeners, the better you should be able to adapt your message and the better it should be received.

## ADAPTING TO AUDIENCE DYNAMICS

As the preceding discussions show, audience demographics are seldom considered in isolation. Such data are almost always combined with information on **audience dynamics:** the motivations, attitudes, beliefs, and values that influence the behavior of listeners. Survey researchers have developed the area of psychographics, which ties together demographics and dynamics.[29] Although not all of the information from national surveys will be applicable to your specific audience, an understanding of how these dynamics function is critical to successful speech preparation. The better you understand your audience, the better you can adapt your message to fit their needs and values. Such adaptation helps audiences respond synergistically and brings you closer to the ideal of participative communication.

### *Motivation*

Our needs, wants, and wishes make up our **motivation,** the force that impels us to action and directs our behavior toward specific goals. Motivation explains *why* people behave as they do.[30] When we think of applying motivation to public speaking, we may think first of its use in persuasive messages designed to move people to action. Indeed, the word *motive* comes from the Latin word *movēre,* which means "to move." Making people aware of a need, and then showing them a way to satisfy it, is a major persuasive strategy. But motivational appeals are also vital in informative speeches. *People will listen,* *learn, and retain your message only if you can relate it to their needs, wants, or wishes.* You must understand these aspects of human behavior so that you can adapt your speeches to accommodate them.

All people share certain motivations, but these can vary in importance according to particular personal and social situations.[31] People are most motivated by things they don't have, but that they want, need, or value. For example, if you have recently entered a new school or moved to a new town, your desire to make friends may be very important and may lead you to seek out places where you can meet others. At such times you may be unusually susceptible to advertising that links products to friendship. Similarly, if you find yourself living on a minimum-subsistence budget, you may be more receptive to information on how to "make it through the crunch." When your financial status improves, this need will become less important.

The importance of specific motivations also can change with changing social or political conditions in the culture as a whole. For example, one group of psychologists reported that between 1957 and 1976 women developed increasing needs for achievement and autonomy.[32] These changes were consistent with the increasing feminist consciousness in the American culture. The sensitive speaker must be aware of such societal changes.

Motivations can be aroused purposefully or accidentally. Suppose you have just eaten a very satisfying meal. If someone enters the room with a tray of warm, freshly baked cookies, the sight and smell can be enough to make you want some, even though you are not really hungry. Astute speakers use motivational appeals to make their ideas and proposals enticing, even for listeners who might not originally have been interested.

In an extensive classic study of human motivation, Henry A. Murray and his associates at the Harvard Psychological Clinic catalogued more than twenty-five different human motives.[33] Some contemporary psychologists treat these motives as intrinsic elements of the human personality.[34] You can appeal to many of them in your speeches. The motives listed below will help you better understand audience dynamics so that you can adapt your speeches in light of them.

***Comfort.*** The need for comfort involves such things as having enough to eat and drink, keeping warm when it's cold and cool when it's hot, and being free from pain. Most middle-class Americans take "comfort" for granted, so advertisements based on this need must awaken an awareness of potential problems. Storm window manufacturers contrast a warm interior scene with cold, snowy weather outside. Over-the-counter-drug ads stress the way to spell *relief!* If you can show your audience that your topic could increase their comfort, you'll have most of them sitting up and listening. Such speech topics could include "Meals in Your Room: The Alternative to Cafeteria Food" or "No Pain, No Gain? How to Stay Fit Without Hurting."

***Safety.*** All of us need to feel free from threats. Rising crime rates, environmental pollution, natural disasters, and accidents are major sources of concern. Appeals to such needs are based on arousing a sense of fear. Water filtration system ads stress security from contamination. Air bags are proclaimed "the latest and best safety device for cars." In the midst of the Great Depression Franklin Delano Roosevelt advised listeners that "the only thing we have to fear is fear itself."[35]

You should be cautious when using fear appeals because if you arouse too much anxiety in listeners, they may resent you and reject your message. If you use appeals to safety in your speech, be sure to provide clear instructions on how dangers can be averted or overcome. The student speech at the end of Chapter 12 shows how the need for safety can be used effectively in an informative speech. The speaker paints a vivid word picture of the potentially disastrous effects of a large earthquake along the New Madrid fault line, then reassures the audience by providing detailed instructions for earthquake preparedness.

***Friendship.*** People need other people to give and receive affection and companionship. This need explains our desire to join groups and take pride in our affiliations. It also may increase our longing for romantic relationships. The need for friendship is probably the most prevalent appeal in contemporary American advertising.[36] If we don't use the "right" deodorant, serve the "right" soft drink, or drive the "right" car, we'll be left out in the cold — friendless and lonely. Some speech topics based on the need for friendship include "New Interests, New Friends: Finding Your Place on Campus," "Love Makes the World Go 'Round: A Look at Computer Dating Services," and "Overcoming Loneliness: Volunteers Help Themselves While Helping Others."

***Recognition.*** Most people want to be treated as valuable and important; they like others to acknowledge their existence and accomplishments. Advertisements that associate products with visible symbols of success and recognition, such as elegant homes or expensive cars, appeal to this need. Even more directly, we are told that using MasterCard will give us "clout," and our American Express card tells others that we are important people (even if they don't recognize our face). Speakers utilize the need for recognition when they find ways to compliment the audience — an advisable tactic if the speaker is not well known or uncertain of acceptance.

***Variety.*** Too much of anything — even a good thing — can be dull. If you eat steak every night, you might find yourself hungry for hot dogs. The need for variety also can include a longing for adventure, a desire to do something different or exciting, or a yen to travel to exotic places. A recent Roper poll suggested that the most prevalent topic of people's daydreams was traveling abroad.[37] Advertisers recognize our need for variety when they present their products against a background of exotic places. Offering your listeners an opportunity to satisfy this desire can help you attract and hold their attention. Speech topics that appeal to this need include "Break Away over Spring Break: Try Skiing for a Change!" or "Around the World at the Dinner Table!"

***Control.*** We don't like to feel buffeted by forces we can't control. All of us like to feel we have some say over our destiny. Data from a *USA Today* survey suggest that taking control of our lives is one of the major motivations of the 1990s.[38] The need for control also heightens our competitive impulses: part of the appeal of victory is gaining control of situations. Thus razor blade manufacturers promise that their product will give you "that winning edge." Speeches that show listeners how they can gain control typically have strong appeal. Examples of such speech topics are "Five Steps to Leadership" or "Secrets of Time Management Experts: Taking Control of Your Life."

***Independence.*** Although we need other people, we also need to feel that we do not always have to rely on others to help us. The idea that we can improve ourselves is so deeply ingrained in our society that we find it difficult to resist in advertising or speeches. Virginia Slims ads trace women's climb from subservience to independence — and connect that somehow with smoking! Speeches that show the audience how to "do it yourself" often appeal to this need.

***Curiosity.*** We want to understand the world and the people around us, so we look for the causes of events and try to figure out why people act as they do.[39] According to a group of prominent psychologists, we are most likely to try to discover the causes of highly unusual or unpleasant events or anything that creates doubt about the future.[40] We may be drawn to catastrophes, not because we enjoy watching people suffer, but because we are curious about such events and sympathize with the victims (especially if we live in an area subject to storms or earthquakes). Speech topics that are unusual, that explain the causes of events or behaviors, or that discuss fears about the future may satisfy this need.

***Tradition.*** Although we may seek novelty or variety in some areas of our lives, there are certain things we don't want to change. Thanksgiving dinner is supposed to be turkey and dressing, cranberries, and pumpkin pie. Even couples who have lived together for a long period of time may want a traditional wedding ceremony to signal the totality of their commitment. Advertisements often draw on such traditions or call on cultural heroes or myths. Even products as contemporary as cordless phones may be enhanced by such appeals. Showing your audience that you share its traditions, that you value many of the same things it values, can help create identification in speeches.

***Success.*** The need for achievement and accomplishment is one of the most thoroughly studied human motives.[41] Although winning may not be everything, most of us feel that losing doesn't have much to recommend it. Thus, self-improvement books glut the market. We can share the success of our sports heroes if we wear the right shoes or eat the right cereal. Speeches that show your audience how they can improve themselves and enhance their chances in life touch on this important motivator. Some sample topics include "Making It in the '90s: The Jobs for the Future" or "Six Tips for Better Studying: How to Improve Your Grades."

***Nurturance.*** It makes people feel good to be able to care for, protect, and comfort the helpless or the less fortunate. Have you ever noticed how many ads have babies, small children, or animals in them? Speech topics that depend on our desire to nurture might include "Help Yourself and Others by Donating Blood" and "Wanted for Worthy Cause: Student Volunteers!"

***Enjoyment.*** People need to have fun occasionally, especially college students, who often find themselves buried under tests and papers, not to mention full- or part-time work. Advertisers appeal to this need when they associate their products with leisure activities. If you can show listeners how to bring pleasure into their lives, you can be sure of sustaining their attention. Here are some sample topics: "Fifteen-Minute Time-outs: Life's Short Pleasures" and "Weekend Break-aways: The Alternative to Long, Expensive Vacations."

Incorporating any of these motivational appeals into your speeches can help arouse attention, sustain interest in your message, and influence or persuade listeners. These appeals can be enhanced by certain forms of powerful language, which we discuss in Chapter 10. They are also basic to the persuasive speech design known as the *motivated sequence,* which we discuss in detail in Chapter 13, "The Nature and Kinds of Persuasive Speaking."

## Attitudes, Beliefs, and Values

When we use the word *attitude,* we are typically referring to our feelings about something — whether we like or dislike, approve or disapprove of people, places, events, or ideas. Actually, attitudes are more than just feelings. **Attitudes** also include our **beliefs** — what we know or think we know about something — and the way we are predisposed to act toward it.[42]

Our important social attitudes are anchored by our **values,** how we think we should behave or what we regard as an ideal state of being.[43] These ideals guide much of our thinking and behavior. Because they underlie our important beliefs and attitudes, values are frequently invoked in political speeches.[44] In his speech accepting the nomination as Republican presidential candidate in 1992, George Bush emphasized the following family-oriented values: getting back to our roots, families sticking together and fathers sticking around, the worth of individual human lives — both born and unborn, teaching children the difference between right and wrong, respect for work, and love for neighbors and God.[45]

Information about your audience's beliefs and values can be useful in planning your speeches. Knowledge of your audience's beliefs can reveal what new information you need to supply or what misinformation you must correct. References to shared values can increase identification between the

**SPEAKER'S NOTES**

## Guidelines for Long-Range Audience Analysis

- Which audience demographics may be relevant to my topic?

- How important is my topic to this audience? Do listeners already care about it? If they don't, how can I motivate them to care?

- What particular aspects of the topic will be most relevant for them? How can I best gain and hold their interest and attention?

- What do my listeners already know about my topic? What will they want to know? What do they need to know?

- How does my audience feel about the topic? Are they positive, neutral, or negative? How open will they be to new ideas?

- What needs, interests, beliefs, attitudes, or values do I share with my listeners? How can I build on this common ground?

speaker and the audience and can enhance the persuasive impact of a speech.[46] The American Council on Education Survey, mentioned earlier in this chapter, contained a series of items that tapped student values. The most important values for the first-year students included becoming well-off financially, earning professional recognition and becoming an authority in one's field, raising a family, and helping others who are in difficulty.[47]

Understanding your listeners' attitudes toward your topic can be of major importance in preparing persuasive speeches. Such information can suggest strategies to get a fair hearing for your message. For example, suppose you are preparing a speech opposing capital punishment, and you know that most members of your audience strongly favor this practice. Audiences that have negative attitudes toward your position may distort your message, discredit you as a communicator, or even refuse to listen to you. Audience attitudes can affect the way listeners receive informative as well as persuasive messages. Understanding these facts, how can you maintain your position and still reach listeners? One way to deal with a negative audience stresses establishing identification between speaker and audience, avoiding the use of emotion and relying instead on rational appeals, limiting what you hope to accomplish, and acknowledging opposing positions.[48] These and other strategies for handling reluctant audiences are discussed in detail in Chapter 13.

How can you find out about your audience's values, beliefs, and attitudes? In the classroom it is not very difficult because people can hardly open their mouths without revealing this kind of information. Classroom discussions

*An audience that is demographically diverse may share important motivations, beliefs, and values. The need for achievement and accomplishment bridges cultural and social differences.*

following earlier speeches should provide valuable cues. Outside the classroom such information may be harder to obtain. However, as you question the person who invites you to speak concerning audience demographics, insights about audience attitudes should also emerge. You also can ask specific questions about audience values that may be related to your topic.

If knowledge of your particular audience's attitudes is critical to your presentation, you would be well advised to seek information by survey. You will want to find out about listeners' knowledge of the subject, their relevant beliefs and values, and how they might respond to sources of information or opinion that might be used in your speech. Classroom surveys will not be as reliable as those conducted by professional pollsters, but they can yield useful results if you use the following guidelines for preparing your questionnaire:

- Use language that is concrete, simple, and clear.
- Keep your questions short and to the point.
- Don't tip your hand: keep bias out of your questions so you don't skew the results.
- Provide room for comments.
- Keep the questionnaire short.

Ask your instructor's permission to hand out the survey at the beginning of the class period and to take it up at the end. Figure 4.2 on the next page is a sample survey questionnaire on capital punishment.

For each question, please circle the number that most closely represents your position.

1. How interested are you in the topic of capital punishment?

| Very Interested | | | Unconcerned | | | Not Interested |
|---|---|---|---|---|---|---|
| 7 | 6 | 5 | 4 | 3 | 2 | 1 |

2. How important do you think the issue of capital punishment is?

| Very Important | | | No Opinion | | | Very Unimportant |
|---|---|---|---|---|---|---|
| 7 | 6 | 5 | 4 | 3 | 2 | 1 |

3. How much do you know about capital punishment?

| Very Little | | | Average Amount | | | Very Much |
|---|---|---|---|---|---|---|
| 7 | 6 | 5 | 4 | 3 | 2 | 1 |

4. How would you describe your attitude toward capital punishment?

| Total Opposition | | | "On the Fence" | | | Total Support |
|---|---|---|---|---|---|---|
| 7 | 6 | 5 | 4 | 3 | 2 | 1 |

5. Please place a check beside the sources of information on capital punishment that you would find most acceptable.

_____ attorney general's office

_____ FBI

_____ local police department

_____ criminal justice department of the university

_____ American Civil Liberties Union

_____ local religious leaders

_____ Conference of Christians and Jews

_____ NAACP

_____ other (please specify) _____

Comments:

FIGURE 4.2
Sample Survey
Questionnaire

**IN SUMMARY**  Preparing an effective speech begins with an analysis of the audience and of the communication environment. Knowledge and understanding of these factors can help you make long-range, in-depth adjustments to your message. The situation you encounter at the time of your speech may also necessitate immediate, on-the-spot adjustments of the message you present.

*Adjusting to the Communication Environment.* Environmental factors you should consider include the time and place of your speech. Previous speeches and current events form a context that influences the interpretation and reception of your message. Additionally, audiences often have specific expectations about what types of speeches are appropriate for certain occasions. If you violate these expectations, you may have problems. Finally, the size of your audience may affect how you present your speech.

*Adjusting to Audience Demographics.* Your *primary audience* includes those listeners whose responses can make your words effective. As you consider this audience, analyze its interest in, knowledge of, and attitudes toward your topic. Knowing the demographic composition of your audience provides insights into its interests, knowledge, and attitudes. Important factors that you should consider in *demographic audience analysis* include age, gender, educational level, group membership, and sociocultural factors such as race and social class.

*Adapting to Audience Dynamics.* An understanding of human *motivation* can also enhance your ability to adapt your message to your audience. Tying your topic to the needs, wants, and wishes of your listeners can help you gain their attention and maintain their interest, as well as move them toward action. Some motivational appeals you may want to use in speeches are comfort, safety, friendship, recognition, variety, control, independence, curiosity, tradition, success, nurturance, and enjoyment.

Your audience's *attitudes, beliefs,* and *values* can affect the way your message is received and interpreted. If your audience is very negative toward your topic, you may have to adjust your presentation to receive a fair hearing.

**TERMS TO KNOW**

preliminary tuning effect

primary audience

demographic audience analysis

gender stereotyping

sexist language

marking

audience dynamics

motivation

attitudes

beliefs

values

**DISCUSSION**

1. How might the following situations affect a speech you are about to give, and how would you adapt to them?
   a. You are the last speaker during the last class period before the Thanksgiving holiday.
   b. A lost student walks into the class right in the middle of your speech, looks around, says, "Excuse me," and walks out.
   c. The speaker right before you gives an incredibly successful speech, which brings spontaneous applause from the class and high praise from the instructor.
   d. The speaker right before you bombs badly. The speech is poorly prepared, the speaker is very nervous and simply stops in the middle and sits down, visibly upset.
   e. (It rarely happens, but . . . ) The speaker right before you gives a speech on the same topic, taking the same general approach.

2. Bring to class an example of an advertisement that exemplifies gender stereotyping. Discuss why such an approach might be used and who the primary audience might be. Would the ad succeed in selling its product? In your opinion, what is the effect of such practice?

3. Rank the twelve human needs discussed in this chapter in terms of their power as motivators for you. Discuss how the three needs you ranked highest might make you susceptible to certain speech topics and approaches.

4. Construct a hypothetical person who represents the average student at your school in age, gender, educational background, group affiliations, and sociocultural background. What speech topics would this hypothetical person find most interesting? What motives, values, and attitudes might this person bring to these topics?

**APPLICATION**

1. Explain how you would tailor a speech on the general topic of food for an audience of
   a. high school sophomores
   b. senior citizens
   c. student dietitians
   d. football players

2. If you were to speak on the general topic of food, what kinds of examples might you develop to appeal to the following audience needs?
   a. safety
   b. friendship
   c. variety
   d. tradition

3. You have been invited to speak before the Futures Club of your city. Using the following information about your audience, what will be your topic and purpose, and what major strategies will you follow in your speech?
   a. *Speech occasion:* The occasion will be a weekly meeting of the Futures Club, a group of business people interested in forecasting trends and encouraging those that seem most beneficial to the community. The meeting consists of a luncheon, an officer's report, and your speech, in that order. You should plan for a fifteen-minute presentation. There will be a time for questions and discussion following your speech. The luncheon will be held in a large dining room of a downtown hotel. A speaker's lectern will be provided, and distractions should be minimal. There will be fifty to sixty people present. At the meeting before your speech, the Futures Club heard an advocate of "gray rights" urge reforms that will help older Americans. Before that, they heard a state senator present an agenda for major legislation in the next decade. They should be interested in your view as a student of what should be conserved and what should be changed in the future. However, you are free to select your own topic and frame your own purpose.

   b. *Demographics:* The typical Futures Club member is thirty-five years old, a highly successful, rapidly rising executive in a local firm. Membership is 60 percent male, 40 percent female. The typical member is a college graduate. Many graduated with honors, and a few have advanced degrees. The members are "joiners" — many are boating, golf, and tennis enthusiasts and belong to various clubs promoting these interests. Republicans outnumber Democrats two to one. Religious commitments are not particularly intense: if there is any preferred faith, it is Episcopalian. Most of the members come from white, upper-middle-class families that expected them to succeed. A few have rebelled against this background and are tolerated in the club as a kind of maverick element. The club has five or six African American members. Three years ago members realized (with some embarrassment) that there were no Asian or Hispanic members. These ethnic groups are now represented.

   c. *Dynamics:* Economically, the club members are well off, although their marriages are often unstable. They have intense needs for friendship, recognition, and success. The Futures Club itself helps to satisfy these needs. The members do not fear change, and they have powerful impulses toward control and independence. Their attitudes and values are flexible and somewhat pragmatic: they value programs that produce measurable results. They share a desire to see qualitative improvements in the life of the community, and they want to be part of a positive movement toward such change.

**NOTES**

1. James W. Gibson and Michael S. Hanna, *Audience Analysis: A Programmed Approach to Receiver Behavior* (Englewood Cliffs, N.J.: Prentice-Hall, 1976), pp. 25–26.
2. For more about preliminary tuning, see Theodore Clevenger, Jr., *Audience Analysis* (Indianapolis: Bobbs-Merrill, 1966), pp. 11–12.
3. Reported in *Time,* 17 June 1985, p. 68.
4. Such data are readily available in popular periodicals. The *Washington Post National Weekly Edition* devotes one page of each issue to "What Americans Think"; *Harper's* magazine regularly includes "Harper's Index," a compilation of unusual and interesting statistics; *USA Today* provides tidbits of poll results on a daily basis; each January the American Council on Education releases the results of a survey of college freshmen.
5. *The Rhetoric of Aristotle,* trans. George Kennedy (New York: Oxford University Press, 1992), pp. 163–169.
6. William J. McGuire, "Attitudes and Attitude Change," in *The Handbook of Social Psychology, vol. 2, Second Ed.* Gardner Lindzey and Elliot Aronson (New York: Random House, 1985), pp. 287–288.
7. Milton Rokeach, *The Open and Closed Mind* (New York: Basic Books, 1960).
8. Anita Manning, "Adults Are Giving the Old College Try," *USA Today,* 12 Sept. 1989, pp. D1–2.
9. Michele N-K Collison, "More Freshmen Say They Are Choosing Colleges Based on Costs," *Chronicle of Higher Education,* 22 Jan. 1991, pp. 33–37;

Mary Jordan, "More Freshmen Lean to the Left," *Washington Post,* 20–26 Jan. 1992, national weekly edition, p. 37; John Leo, "The Unplugged Generation," *U.S. News & World Report,* 10 July 1992, p. 22; "Student Survey," *Esquire,* Apr. 1992, pp. 112–114. *American Demographics* is also an excellent source of timely survey information.

10. Percentage of first-year students agreeing with the items as reported in the 1992 survey as reported in the *Chronicle of Higher Education* were (1) 69, (2) 86, (3) 65, (4) 63, (5) 26, (6) 66, (7) 81, (8) 78, (9) 76, (10) 79, (11) 21, (12) 31.

11. Carol Tavris, in her recent book, *The Mismeasure of Woman* (New York: Simon & Schuster: 1992), suggests that focusing on differences between the sexes strengthens the myths that perpetuate misunderstandings.

12. Cited in Allison Adato and Melissa G. Stanton, "If Women Ran America," *Life,* June 1992, p. 40.

13. James R. Gaines, "A Note from the Editor," *Life*, June 1992, p. 6.

14. Anthony M. Casale and Philip Lerman, *USA Today: Tracking Tomorrow's Trends* (Kansas City, Mo.: Andrews, McMeel & Parker, 1986), p. 47.

15. Ibid.

16. "Exit Poll Results 1992," *Newsweek: Special Election Issue,* Nov./Dec. 1992, p. 10.

17. Casale and Lerman, p. 56.

18. Adato and Stanton, p. 40.

19. Richard Morin, "The Gender Gap Revisited," *The Washington Post National Weekly Edition,* 25–31 May 1992, p. 37.

20. Collison, p. 35.

21. Adato & Stanton, p. 41.

22. Kay Deaux and Brenda Major, "Putting Gender into Context: An Interactive Model of Gender-related Behavior," *Psychological Review* 94 (1987): 369.

23. James Atlas, "Beyond Demographics," *Atlantic Monthly,* Oct. 1984, pp. 49–58; Arnold Mitchell, *The Nine American Lifestyles: Who We Are and Where We're Going* (New York: Macmillan, 1983); Rokeach, *The Open and Closed Mind;* P. Schonback, *Education and Intergroup Attitudes* (London: Academic Press, 1981).

24. McGuire, pp. 271–272.

25. Vernon G. Zunker, *Career Counseling: Applied Concepts of Life Planning* (Monterey, Calif.: Brooks Cole, 1981), pp. 120–123.

26. For a detailed analysis of this topic, see Donald R. Kinder and David O. Sears, "Public Opinion and Political Action," in *The Handbook of Social Psychology,* vol. 2, pp. 659–741.

27. Casale & Lerman, pp. 172–183.

28. Michael and Suzanne Osborn, *Alliance for a Better Public Voice* (Dayton: National Issues Forum, 1991), pp. 33–35.

29. See, for example, James Atlas, "Beyond Demographics," pp. 49–58; Tom and Nancy Biracree, *Almanac of the American People* (New York: Facts on File, 1988); "Marketers Say Clusters Are Us," *USA Today,* 16 March 1989, pp. B1–2; Arnold Mitchell, *Nine American Lifestyles: Who We Are and Where We're Going* (New York: Macmillan, 1983).

30. Douglas A. Bernstein et al., *Psychology,* 2nd ed. (Boston: Houghton Mifflin, 1991), p. 431.

31. The material in this section is based on the work of Bernstein, *Psychology;* P. Evans, *Motivation and Emotion* (New York: Routledge), 1989; John P. Houston et al., *Invitation to Psychology,* 3rd ed. (San Diego: Harcourt Brace Jovanovich, 1989); Abraham H. Maslow, *Motivation and Personality,* 2nd ed. (New York: Harper & Row, 1970); D. W. Rajecki, *Attitudes: Themes and Advances,* 2nd ed. (Sunderland, Mass.: Senauer Associates), 1990; Janusz Reykowski, "Social Motivation," *Annual Review of Psychology* 33 (1982): pp. 128–130.

32. J. Veroff et al., "Comparison of American Motives: 1957 Versus 1976," *Journal of Personality and Social Psychology* 39 (1980): 1249–1262.

33. Henry A. Murray, *Explorations in Personality* (New York: Oxford University Press, 1938).

34. Motivations form the scales for two personality measures: the *Edwards Personal Preference Schedule Manual* (New York: Psychological Corporation) and the *Personality Research Form* (Goshen, NY: Research Psychologists Press).

35. Franklin Delano Roosevelt, "First Inaugural Address," in *The World's Great Speeches,* 3rd ed., ed. L. Copeland and L. W. Lamm (New York: Dover, 1973), p. 508.

36. Jib Fowles, "Advertising's Fifteen Basic Appeals," *Et Cetera* 39, No. 3 (Fall 1982); reprinted in Robert Atwan, Barry Orton, and William Vesterman, *American Mass Media: Industries and Issues,* 3rd ed. (New York: Random House, 1986), pp. 43–54.

37. Tom Biracree and Nancy Biracree, *Almanac of the American People* (New York: Facts on File, 1988), p. 35.

38. Casale and Lerman, pp. 34–35.

39. B. Weiner, "A Cognitive (Attribution)-Emotion-Action Model of Motivated Behavior," *Journal of Personality and Social Psychology* 39 (1980): 186–200.

40. Houston et al., p. 366.

41. J. W. Atkinson, *Personality, Motivation, and Action* (New York: Praeger, 1983).

42. McGuire, pp. 235–253.

43. Milton Rokeach, *Beliefs, Attitudes and Values: A Theory of Organization and Change* (San Francisco: Jossey-Bass, 1970), pp. 109–32; and *The Nature of Human Values* (New York: Free Press, 1973K), pp. 26–52.

44. See, for example, Henry E. McCuckin, Jr., "A Value Analysis of Richard Nixon's 1952 Campaign Fund Speech," *Southern Speech Communicaton Journal* 33 (1968): 259–269; Wayne N. Thompson, "Barbara Jordan's Keynote Address: The Juxtaposition of Contradictory Values," *Southern Speech Communication Journal* 44, (1979): 223–232.

45. George Bush, "Acceptance Address," *Commercial Appeal,* 21 Aug. 1992, A-11.

46. Henry Z. Scheele, "Ronald Reagan's 1980 Acceptance Address: A Focus on American Values," *Western Speech Communication Journal* 48 (1984): 51–61.

47. Collison, p. 36.

48. Herbert W. Simons, *Persuasion: Understanding, Practice, and Analysis,* 2nd ed. (Reading, Mass.: Addison-Wesley, 1986), pp. 121–139.

*Learn, compare,
collect the facts! . . .
Always have the
courage to say to
yourself — I am
ignorant.*

*— Ivar Petrovich
Pavlov*

# 5

# Selecting and Researching Your Topic

## This Chapter Will Help You

- select a topic that is meaningful and that suits the audience and occasion.
- determine the general purpose, specific purpose, and thematic statement for your speech.
- develop responsible knowledge to add credibility and substance your speech.

"I have to speak for *five whole minutes?* What can I talk about for that long? What do I know enough about to sound reasonably intelligent?" Your instructor has just given you your assignment. You are to prepare an informative speech on a subject of your choice. Your stomach starts to tighten as you worry. "Speech about what? How do I *begin?*"

on't succumb to panic and head for the "drop" office or the High Sierras! There are systematic ways to find a good topic, develop your speech purpose, and expand your knowledge so that you can make an informed and responsible presentation. This chapter will introduce you to these techniques.

In order to find the right approach, you must first understand the nature of a good speech topic. Your topic must be meaningful and substantive — one that is important both in its own right and to you personally. Your topic must also be adapted to your audience. The final test of a good topic is whether you can acquire responsible knowledge and speak credibly about it.

*A good topic is meaningful.* Your speech topic need not concern an earth-shaking issue to be worthwhile, but it should affect your audience or community, or be an issue on which you believe the audience should be informed. Trivial topics, such as "How to Make Popcorn in a Microwave," waste the time of both speakers and listeners. Your topic also should be important to you personally. It takes a lot of time to think through your ideas, research your topic, organize your materials, and practice your presentation. This requires a real commitment on your part. If your topic is not important to you, you will find it hard to invest the time and effort needed to speak responsibly. Personal commitment also helps the presentation of your speech. People who speak on topics to which they are committed are more sincere and enthusiastic. Their enthusiasm is contagious. It carries over to listeners and gets them involved in the message.

*A good speech topic is adapted to its audience.* Analysis of your audience should go hand in hand with topic selection. As you put together your information on audience demographics and dynamics, ask yourself such questions as "What are their interests and concerns? What is happening that they should know about?"

If you combine what you have learned from your audience analysis with information from earlier speeches and class discussions, you should have a good idea of your listeners' interests. Perhaps one of your classmates gave a speech honoring his family doctor's sense of caring. The speech sparked a lively discussion and started you thinking about your own less pleasant experiences with doctors. There could be a potential speech topic lurking in these related ideas. You could develop an informative speech on the relationship between personal physician care and patient recovery or a persuasive speech advocating training in interpersonal skills for physicians. If you have a topic in mind but are not sure your audience will share your enthusiasm, then you must try to generate interest. You may need to show your listeners how this topic affects them personally and what they stand to gain from your message.

A good topic also fits the time, place, and purpose of the speech. It should meet the audience's expectations about what is appropriate for the occasion. A celebration in honor of a friend is *not* the time to deliver a political tirade.

*The final test of a good topic is whether you can acquire enough responsible knowledge to speak credibly about it.* The time you have for the preparation and presentation of your message is limited. Consequently, you should select a topic you already know something about, then focus on developing some *manageable aspect* of it for your presentation. Instead of trying to cover all the problems involved in the disposal of nuclear waste, it would be better to limit yourself to discussing your state's role in nuclear waste disposal. The limited topic would be more manageable, would be adapted more precisely to your audience, and should lend itself to responsible preparation.

## SELECTING A GOOD TOPIC

The goal of a topic search is to identify an idea that justifies your speaking and others' listening. To find the right topic, you may need to work through several stages of discovery, including:

1. charting your own interests and the interests of your listeners
2. analyzing potential topics to refine and focus them
3. selecting one topic on the basis of its meaningfulness, its audience appropriateness, and your ability to acquire responsible knowledge of it

### Charting Interests

The best way to begin your search is to develop lists of your own interests and those of your listeners as revealed in class discussions and earlier speeches. You can employ the same kind of questions you used to generate ideas for introductory speeches:

1. Are you interested in *places?*
2. Are you interested in *people?*
3. What *activities* do you enjoy?
4. What *events* are foremost in your mind?
5. What *work* do you do or hope to do?
6. What are your long- and short-range *goals?*

| Places | People | Activities | Events |
|--------|--------|-----------|--------|
| Great Smokies | Pauline Gore | hiking | Olympic games |
| Yellowstone Park | Jesse Owens | collecting birds | hurricanes |
| Freeport, Maine | Chief Seattle | photography | float trip on Snake |
| Epcot Center | Mother Teresa | camping | River |
| Avenue of the Giants | Charles Kuralt | see the USA | spring break |
| | | | Smoke-Out |

| Work | Goals | Values | Problems |
|------|-------|--------|----------|
| archaeology | finish school | peace in world | air & water pollution |
| public relations | work in NYC | close family ties | TV influences |
| volunteer work | marry, have a family | equality | substance abuse |
| library assistant | visit Mexico | physical fitness | time pressures |
| temporary agency | own a boat | kindness | sexism |

**FIGURE 5.1  Interest Chart**

7. What *values* are important to you?

8. What *problems* concern you most?

A chart of your interests might look like that in Figure 5.1.

***Getting Ideas from the Popular Media.***   Sometimes it is hard to come up with a list of potential topics in the abstract. If your mind seems to have gone blank, you can sometimes spur it by using newspapers, magazines, or television to generate ideas. Go through the Sunday paper, scan *Time* or *Newsweek,* or watch the evening news. Study the headlines, titles, advertisements, and pictures. What catches your attention? What might be adapted to the interests or needs of your audience?

One student developed an idea for a speech after seeing an advertisement for bank services. The ad stirred some unpleasant memories of writing a check that bounced. This experience suggested a speech on keeping better personal records. His problem was getting listeners to see the importance of this topic to their lives. His solution was to develop an introduction that startled the audience into attention.

Last month I committed a crime! I wrote a bad check, and it bounced. The check was for $4.67 to a local grocery store where I bought the ingredients for a spaghetti supper. The bank charged me $15.00 for the overdraft, and the store charged me $10.00 to retrieve my bad check. That was the most expensive spaghetti dinner I've ever eaten!

The headline "Travel Money Tips Offered" might inspire a speech entitled "Champagne Travel on a Beer Budget." The personals section in the classifieds might prompt a speech on the dangers of computer dating services.

You must be careful not to misuse media sources for generating topics. The media can direct you to ideas for speeches, but they do not provide the speeches for you. You can't simply read an interesting article, then summarize it for presentation. Use the article as a starting point. Search out more information. *Your* speech must be *your* message, designed to appeal to *your* specific audience. You should always bring something new to your subject — a fresh insight or an application to the lives of your listeners.

***Matching Your Interests to Your Audience.*** After you have charted your own interests, make a similar chart of apparent audience interests as revealed by class discussion and your demographic analysis. What places, people, events, activities, work, goals, values, and problems concern listeners? Now study the two charts together, looking for possible points of convergence in order to pinpoint your best topic possibilities. To do this systematically, make a three-column *topic inventory chart*. In the first column (personal interests), list those topics from your personal interest list and media search that you find most appealing. In the second column (audience interests), list those topics suggested by demographic analysis and class discussion. In the third column (possible topics), match columns one and two to produce speech possibilities. Figure 5.2 on the next page shows a sample topic inventory chart.

In this example, your interests in travel and outdoor activities are matched with the audience's interest in unusual places and developed into a possible speech topic: "Weekend Adventures Within Two Hours of Campus." Similarly, your concern for physical fitness is paired with the audience's interest in deceptive advertising to generate another possibility: "Exercise Spa Rip-offs." Your interest in water and air pollution could combine with audience interests in leisure to lead to the topic "Are Our State Parks at Risk?" Not all of your interests or those of your audience will result in possible topics. It is the *matching* of these interests that concerns you.

## Analyzing Your Topic

In order to come up with specific topic possibilities, you may need to start with general topic areas and subject them to close analysis. One technique is to ask the questions news reporters use to assure that they investigate a story thoroughly. The writer Rudyard Kipling described the questions in this poem:

> I keep six honest serving-men
>
> (They taught me all I knew);
>
> Their names are What and Why and When
>
> And How and Where and Who.[1]

Not all these questions will apply to every topic area, but by working through the list systematically, you should be able to develop a number of

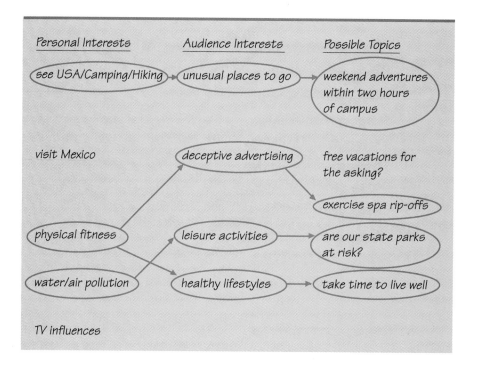

Personal Interests   Audience Interests   Possible Topics

see USA/Camping/Hiking — unusual places to go — weekend adventures within two hours of campus

visit Mexico — deceptive advertising — free vacations for the asking?

exercise spa rip-offs

physical fitness — leisure activities — are our state parks at risk?

water/air pollution — healthy lifestyles — take time to live well

TV influences

**FIGURE 5.2**
**Topic Inventory Chart**

possible topics. Let's take "National Parks" as a topic area and see where these "six honest serving-men" might lead us:

*Who* started the national park system? Who works in national parks? Who uses national parks?

*What* are national parks? Are they mainly for entertainment, public education, or environmental preservation? What are the most popular national parks? What are the least-known national parks? What do people like best in our national parks? What is the difference between a national park and a national forest?

*When* was the first national park established? When was the most recent national park opened? When are the parks most crowded? When are they least crowded?

*Where* is the closest national park? Where are the major attractions in that park? Where can you go to escape the crowds of tourists in the parks? Where can you see the most wildlife in the park?

*Why* were national parks established? Why do people go to national parks? Why are some campgrounds closed to tent campers?

*How* are our national parks financed? How do people train to be a park ranger? How can students get summer work in a park?

As you consider the six prompts, write down as many connections to your topic as you can. As you look over these thoughts, you may notice that certain clusters or themes of ideas emerge: some entries may center on the history of the parks, some on park attractions, others on wildlife and ecological concerns. What would be the best topic for your speech on national parks? That depends a great deal on your audience. If you live near a park and most audience members have already visited there, a speech on the park's major attractions would offer little in terms of new information. Such an audience, however, might be interested in the history of the park or current ecological problems there. On the other hand, if you live far from the nearest park and most audience members have never been there, a speech on major attractions could be interesting. College students might be especially concerned with summer jobs at the park.

Our example describes a search for an informative speech topic. The same types of questions can be used to analyze topics for persuasive speeches. Because persuasion often addresses problems, you can simply change the focus of the questions and add some areas that are specific to persuasive situations:

*Who* is involved in or affected by this problem?

*What* issues are most important?

*Why* did the problem arise?

*Where* is this problem happening?

*When* did the problem begin?

*How* is this problem like or unlike previous problems?

*How* extensive is the problem?

*What* options are available for dealing with the problem?

### Selecting Your Topic

After you have completed your interest charts and analyzed your topic area, two or three specific topics should emerge as important and appealing possibilities. Now you should ask of each:

- Does this topic fit the nature of the assignment or occasion?
- Could I give a speech on this topic in the time available?
- Can I learn enough about this topic to give a responsible speech?
- Why would I want to give a speech on this topic?

As you consider your options in light of these questions, a final choice should become clear. *This* will be your speech topic! The final question on this list is especially important because it tests whether you have a clear idea of your own motives in developing a certain speech and helps you determine your purpose.

**SPEAKER'S NOTES**

## Check List for Topic Selection

1. Does the topic fit the time, place, and occasion of my speech?

2. Have I selected a topic that is meaningful?

3. Have I selected a topic I care about?

4. Have I selected a topic I already know something about?

5. Have I focused my topic so that it matches the concerns and needs of listeners?

6. Have I limited my topic so that I can develop responsible knowledge and make a credible presentation?

## DETERMINING YOUR PURPOSE

*"Why would I want to give a speech on this topic?"* Your answers to this question suggest the **purpose** of your speech. You will be able to develop a successful speech only when your purpose is clear.

To gain a clear understanding of your purpose, you must focus on your topic as though your mind were a microscope. You look through one lens and see the topic and your purpose in a broad, hazy outline. Replace that lens with another, and now you can see this topic-purpose interaction in sharper detail. Replace the second lens with a third, and now you can see to the heart of your message.

### General Purpose

The broad and hazy outline seen through the first lens is the **general purpose** of your speech. The general purpose is often assigned for your classroom speeches. For example, you may be asked to prepare a speech *to inform* or *to persuade*. If you are to inform, your general purpose is to share knowledge with your audience. If you are to persuade, your general purpose is to influence the thinking or behavior of listeners.

The general purpose of a speech is usually stated as an infinitive: *to inform*, *to persuade*. This reflects the nature of public speaking as an activity that has consequences for listeners. It calls attention to the audience because there must be someone *to inform* or *to persuade*. This active way of stating the general purpose symbolizes the importance of the audience as you plan a speech.

When speaking outside the classroom, the general purpose may be left for you to decide. You may be asked to address a group because you are a specialist on a subject, because you are a respected member of the community, or simply because you have a good reputation as a speaker. When this happens, you will have to determine your own general purpose, taking into account the audience and the occasion. For example, if your audience knows very little about your topic, you might decide that your general purpose should be to inform these listeners. If the topic demands a change in public policy, your general purpose could be to persuade them to action. Good sense will usually point you to the right general purpose.

## Specific Purpose

The second lens of your microscope focuses on your **specific purpose.** Your specific purpose indicates what kind of response you want from your audience, what you want to accomplish. It identifies what you want listeners to understand, believe, feel, or do. Having a specific purpose clearly in mind helps direct your research toward relevant information so that you don't waste time searching for materials that will not be useful.

You should be able to state your specific purpose clearly and succinctly as a single idea. Let's look at how a specific purpose statement focuses the topic and general purpose of a speech:

| | |
|---|---|
| *Topic:* | National parks |
| *General purpose:* | To inform |
| *Specific purpose:* | To inform my audience about hiking trails in Shenandoah National Park |
| | |
| *Topic:* | Greenhouse effect |
| *General purpose:* | To persuade |
| *Specific purpose:* | To persuade my audience that the greenhouse effect poses a serious threat to our environment |

How can you tell if you have formed a good specific purpose? Your specific purpose should focus on those aspects of your topic that are most relevant or interesting to your audience. It should also enrich the audience by offering new information and ideas or new advice. You waste time and energy when you try to inform listeners about things they already know or convince them of things they already believe. A good specific purpose also will be ambitious. Audiences appreciate speakers who take risks — who avoid trivial or stale topics. Just as Olympic divers receive higher scores for executing more difficult dives, classroom speeches that take chances usually earn more respect from the audience (and often higher grades!). Finally, your specific purpose should be manageable in the time allotted to you. In a five-minute speech you have only about seven hundred words to get your message across. *If you can't cover the material in the time allowed, then your purpose may not be specific enough*. You will need to narrow your focus to some aspect you can handle.

Let's look at some examples of poor specific-purpose statements and see how they might be improved:

| | |
|---|---|
| *Poor* | To inform my audience about our national parks |
| *Improved* | To inform my audience of the lesser-known attractions in Yellowstone Park |
| *Poor* | To persuade my audience that driving while drinking is dangerous |
| *Improved* | To persuade my audience to accept the idea of *responsible* drinking and driving |

In our first example, the specific purpose to inform the audience about "our national parks" is *poor* because it is too general. It does not narrow the topic sufficiently. Entire books have been written on individual national parks; you could not possibly cover the topic in a short presentation. Moreover, it does not specify what aspect of the national parks you will discuss. With this *nonspecific* purpose you could prepare a speech on the resurgence of grizzly bears in Yellowstone Park, on the differences between national parks and national forests, on the camping areas for backpackers in Smoky Mountain National Park, or on a multitude of other topics. The *improved* specific purpose limits the topic so that it can be handled within the time permitted. This helps you concentrate your research efforts on those materials most useful to your speech.

The second *poor* specific purpose is also too general. Furthermore, it would not enrich the audience. It would be hard to find anyone who would

---

**SPEAKER'S NOTES**

### Guidelines for Evaluating My Specific Purpose

- Does it specify what I want to *accomplish* with my speech?

- Does it identify what I want my listeners to *understand, feel, believe,* or *do*?

- Does it focus on those aspects of my topic that should be most *relevant* and *interesting* to my audience?

- Does it offer fresh, *new* ideas, information, or advice?

- Is it *ambitious*?

- Is it *manageable* in the time available?

argue that driving while drinking is not dangerous. Even more, the subject may be overworked. Unless the speaker can offer a fresh perspective on the subject, there may be problems maintaining attention or motivating the audience. The *improved* specific purpose is more limited in scope and offers something new to the audience: the concept of *responsible* drinking and driving.

### Thematic Statement

The third lens in your mental microscope focuses your **thematic statement.** The thematic statement should bring the heart of your message into sharp detail. *It should specify precisely what you want your audience to learn or accept.* As the name indicates, it identifies the *theme* or central message of your speech. You should be able to condense this statement without strain into a single declarative sentence. The thematic statement frequently is presented at the beginning of the speech so that listeners will understand your intentions. The thematic statement also may preview the body of the speech. The **preview** identifies the main points in the body of the speech and presents an oral agenda for the speech that will follow. In long or complicated speeches, the preview makes it easier for audience members to listen and reduces chances for misunderstanding. When the thematic statement and preview are separate, they usually come sequentially, the thematic statement followed by the preview, as in the following example:

> Date rape — acquaintance rape — social rape — by any other name, it is still rape [*thematic statement*]. Today we will consider the nature of date rape, its causes and effects, and what we can do personally to keep it from happening [*preview*].

At times speakers may leave the thematic statement unstated, to be constructed by listeners from cues within the speech. Note, for example, how Cecile Larson left the thematic statement implicit in her speech, "The 'Monument' at Wounded Knee," which appears in Appendix B. Speakers may leave the thematic statement unstated in order to create a dramatic effect as listeners discover it for themselves. Regardless of how and whether it appears directly in the speech, unless you have a clear thematic statement in mind, your speech is apt to wander and never accomplish its goal.

To construct a clear thematic statement, ask yourself these questions: "If a reporter from the local newspaper were to cover this speech, how would I like the headline to read? What should be the lead sentence into the story?"[2] The following examples show how thematic statements go a step beyond specific purposes in focusing the central ideas of speeches. Note that in these examples the thematic statement functions also as preview.

| | |
|---|---|
| *Specific purpose:* | To inform my audience about the less well-known attractions in Yellowstone Park |
| *Thematic statement:* | Three of the less well-known attractions in Yellowstone are the Fountain Paint Pots, the Grand Canyon of the Yellowstone, and the Firehole River. |
| *Specific purpose:* | To persuade my audience to accept the idea of *responsible* drinking and driving |
| *Thematic statement:* | You should practice responsible drinking and driving by knowing your tolerance for alcohol, having a designated driver, and not letting friends drive while intoxicated. |

Let us now look at the process of moving from general topic area to thematic statement to see how these may evolve in speech preparation:

| | |
|---|---|
| *Topic area:* | Vacations in the United States |
| *Topic:* | Camping in the Rockies |
| *General purpose:* | To inform |
| *Specific purpose:* | To inform my audience that there are beautiful, uncrowded places to camp in the Rockies |
| *Thematic statement:* | Three beautiful, uncrowded camping areas in the Rockies are Bridger-Teton National Forest in Wyoming, St. Charles Canyon in Idaho, and Dinosaur National Monument in Utah. |

With the purposes and major ideas clearly specified, a speech titled "Camping in the Rockies: Getting off the Beaten Path" might take the following form:

| | |
|---|---|
| *Introductory Material* | Page 43 of the tour guide to Grand Teton National Park reveals this idyllic picture of camping [display blow-up of picture]. As you can see, the area is beautiful and uncrowded. With a picture like this in mind, I started my first camping trip to the Rockies two summers ago. Was I ever disappointed! After a long drive I arrived at Jenny Lake campground about two in the afternoon — early enough to set up camp, take a hike, and prepare a leisurely dinner. Not! All of the campsites had been taken since 8:30 that morning. Not only were no sites available, but after driving through the campground, I realized I wouldn't have wanted to camp there anyway. Hundreds of tents were crowded on top of one another. It looked like a refugee relocation center after a disaster. And it wasn't only the crowding that was bad, but the noise! Radios and televisions blasted you with an unholy mixture of music and game shows and soap operas. I might just as well have been back in our freshman dorm. |

| | |
|---|---|
| *Thematic Statement and Preview* | Not every camping area in the Rockies is like this. Let me tell you about some places I found on a camping trip last summer. Three of the most interesting, beautiful, and uncrowded were Bridger-Teton National Forest in Wyoming, St. Charles Canyon in Idaho, and the Dinosaur National Monument in Utah. |
| *Main Points* | 1. Bridger-Teton National Forest at Slide Lake has a magnificent view of the Tetons. |
| | 2. St. Charles Canyon on a white-water stream offers the ultimate in seclusion. |
| | 3. At Dinosaur National Monument you can watch the excavation of gigantic skeletons that are millions of years old. |
| *Transition and Conclusion* | There are interesting, beautiful, and uncrowded places to camp if you know where to look. Try the National Forest Service campgrounds or national monuments rather than the overcrowded national parks. Last summer I enjoyed the peace and serenity of Slide Lake while reveling in its view of the Tetons. I caught and cooked cut-throat trout in secluded St. Charles Canyon, and saw the isolated petroglyphs at Dinosaur National Monument. I can't wait to get back! |

Although the thematic statement appears in the foregoing example, you will note that the speaker *does not* begin with "My thematic statement is. . . ." Rather, it is artfully worked into the introduction, where it indicates the main points the speech will develop. It also suggests that this speech may give us interesting facts, illustrated by vivid examples and perhaps by action stories. Moreover, it tells us what kind of informative speech we will hear (descriptive) and implies the overall design or pattern the speech will follow (categorical).

With a clearly drawn thematic statement in mind, the speaker can focus his or her research to acquire responsible knowledge of the topic. In this case the speaker might use pamphlets, brochures, or books purchased at the sites mentioned; national recreation area attendance figures from almanacs; and materials available in the government documents section of the library.

## ACQUIRING RESPONSIBLE KNOWLEDGE

Although we have discussed selecting a topic and determining your purpose before we have taken up research, your background reading for a speech will often begin before you frame your thematic statement. Indeed, in order to determine your specific purpose and the major points you should address, you will probably have to find out more about your topic. Once you have your specific purpose and thematic statement in mind, you can move on to that concentrated phase of research that will provide you with **responsible knowledge** for your speech. Responsible knowledge of a topic includes information on or about

- its main issues or points of interest
- what the most respected authorities say
- the latest major developments
- local concerns or applications of special interest to *your* audience

Although you cannot become an authority on most topics with ten hours or even ten days of research, you can learn enough to speak responsibly. Your research should result in your knowing more than the rest of the class about your topic. Responsible knowledge allows you to enrich the lives of listeners with good information or advice. It places you in a sound ethical position. The major sources of information available to you are your own

*First-hand experience helps develop responsible knowledge of your topic and adds credibility to your speech. Hillary Rodham Clinton's speeches on educational reform are based on her meetings with students and teachers.*

knowledge and experiences, library resources, and interviews. Each of these sources can supply facts, testimony, examples, or narratives to use as supporting materials in your speech.

### *Personal Experience*

You should begin your research by taking stock of what you already know about your topic. Personal experience adds credibility, authenticity, and freshness to a speech. As valuable as personal knowledge is, however, you should not depend on it as your *sole* source of information because it may be limited or unreliable. Your experiences may not be truly representative, or may be representative only of your cultural background. As you read or hear what others have to say on your topic, you should be willing to expand or correct your previous impressions if they prove to be narrow or distorted.

You can actively seek out personal experience that will add credibility to your speech. Suppose you want to deliver a speech on how television news shows are put together. You could arrange to visit a nearby station that produces a live newscast. Take in the noise, the action, and the excitement that occur before and during a show — this atmosphere can enrich your speech.

You must take the initiative to arrange such experiences. For example, if you want to give a speech on the boredom of assembly line work, you might phone a local union for help in gaining firsthand exposure. To test this recommendation, we phoned the local Labor Council headquarters and talked with a union leader, who said the problem of worker boredom was acute in many local industries. We then asked if his office would help student speakers who wanted to arrange interviews with workers or make visits to plants. He responded enthusiastically, "Just tell the students to give us a call." Such willingness to cooperate is understandable. Any large organization likes favorable publicity. As a speaker, you control part of that publicity. You will never be more aware of the power of public speaking than when someone "rolls out the red carpet" to make the kind of favorable impression they hope will surface in your speech. Just don't be so flattered by the attention you receive that you forget to be on guard against bias on controversial issues.

Although personal experience is often a good starting point for your research, it is rarely enough to support an entire speech. To fill in the gaps and verify your knowledge and information, you should turn next to library resources.

### *Library Research*

Although knowledge obtained from the library may lack the excitement and immediacy that personal experience provides, it has definite advantages. Library research can give you a broad perspective and a sound basis for speaking responsibly. It can extend, correct, and enrich your experience by acquainting you with others' experience and knowledge.

Most college and large municipal libraries have the following major research resources to help you:

1. *Catalog* of books and major publications alphabetized by author, title, and subject, either on cards or on computer terminals

2. *Reference area* containing timely information and bound or computerized indexes to magazines, newspapers, and journals

3. *Government documents area* containing federal, state, and local government publications

4. *Nonprint media archives* of films, videotapes, recordings, and microfilms

5. *Special collections areas* with materials that can help you adapt your topic to local needs and interests

6. *Computerized search services* to provide bibliographic assistance

7. *Holding areas,* or stacks, where books and bound volumes of periodicals are shelved

8. An *interlibrary loan service* that offers access to specific materials that may not be available in your library

With such a multitude of resources available, it can be difficult to know where to begin your research. The most valuable resource in any library is the professional librarian, who can steer you to the most appropriate sources of information in *your* library for *your* topic. The following review of library resources focuses on the special needs of student speakers, who must spend their limited research time to best advantage. Your library may have a printed directory of their resources or may offer guided tours for students. Take advantage of these aids.

**Reference Area.**    The first stop in your quest for responsible knowledge should be the reference area, which has convenient guides to timely and concentrated sources of information. The reference librarian may be able to steer you to the most useful sources of information for your research. Some of the materials you may find useful are described below.

*Encyclopedias.*    Encyclopedias can either be general or about a specific subject area. They are most helpful in providing background information or historical perspectives on your topic. Encyclopedias are less useful on current issues and are not the best sources for testimony or examples. Most contemporary encyclopedias are listed and compared in *Best Encyclopedias: A Guide to General and Specialized Encyclopedias.*[3] Among the more respected general encyclopedias are

> *Encyclopaedia Britannica*
>
> *World Book Encyclopedia*
>
> *Encyclopaedia Americana*

Subject-specific encyclopedias include

> *Encyclopedia of Religion and Ethics*
>
> *International Encyclopedia of the Social Sciences*

*Encyclopedia of World Art*

*Encyclopedia of Education*

***Sources of Current Facts.*** Up-to-date information is important to many topics. If you are not aware of recent events related to your topic, your credibility may be damaged. For the most recent information, start with a newspaper index, such as the *New York Times Index.* The reference librarian can steer you to the best indexing services available in your library. These indexes identify articles published during a given period of time. Who won this year's Nobel Peace Prize? How did Hurricane Andrew indirectly affect the Mexican economy? The index will tell you where articles related to such questions can be found in the newspaper and may also provide a summary of the article. For even more up-to-date information, look through current issues of *Time, Newsweek,* or other relevant weekly or monthly publications. An easy-to-use source of recent information is *Facts on File,* which reports weekly on current events by topical categories.

***Other Indexes and Abstracts.*** Periodical indexes direct you to magazine and journal articles on your topic. These articles may not always be current, but they provide depth of information. They often reduce situations, issues, and arguments to their essentials. In addition, the books and authors mentioned in the articles can lead you to other sources of information. Abstracts provide a summary of the articles that may help you determine their relevance to your purpose.

*Reading the best books on your topic can give you a deeper understanding and make your speech more authoritative. Library research is the key to acquiring responsible knowledge.*

Indexes and abstracts range from the highly specialized to the very general. Your reference librarian can direct you to the source most suitable to your topic. The following indexes and abstracts are frequently used:

*Reader's Guide to Periodical Literature* contains author and subject references to articles in over 175 popular periodicals. This source is especially useful for speakers because the articles are written for a general readership that is probably similar to the type of audience you will have in class. The magazines indexed attract reputable writers and experts and will add credibility to your speech when cited. Where is acid rain a problem, and what is being done about it? How is increased attendance affecting the environment in our national parks? *Reader's Guide* can direct you to articles that might contain the answers to these questions.

*Business Periodicals Index* covers a wide range of business and economic magazines and journals and is helpful for speeches on topics such as career choices, sales techniques, or advertising appeals.

*Public Affairs Information Service (PAIS)* publishes an index that covers periodicals, pamphlets, and other documents reporting on civic and governmental issues that range from land use policy to tax reform.

*Social Sciences Index* covers articles you may find useful on topics involving social problems.

*Index to Journals in Communication Studies* includes references to topics particularly interesting to communication students. What made Abraham Lincoln an effective speaker? What are the major arguments used to promote nuclear disarmament? What can be done about communication apprehension? Articles addressing these and similar questions are indexed here.

***Atlases.*** If your topic calls for geographical information or comparisons among regions and areas, you may wish to consult an atlas like *The National Geographic Atlas of the World*. Such atlases contain more than just maps; they often include information on issues such as religious preference by states, population density of countries, or the agricultural or industrial production of a given area. Such an atlas may also suggest designs for effective visual aids.

***Biographical Information.*** You can find out about noteworthy people by consulting one of the many biographical resources found in most libraries. The *Who's Who* series provides brief information on important living people; the *Dictionary of American Biography* covers famous Americans of the past. *Current Biography* contains longer essays on people who are prominent in the news. *Notable American Women* contains information on women "whose work in some way took them before the public."

***Books of Quotations.*** Quotations are especially useful in speeches. Quotations from famous sources are indexed by topic and author in such books as *Bartlett's Familiar Quotations, The Oxford Dictionary of Quotations,* and *The Quotable Woman.*

***Almanacs, Yearbooks, and Directories.*** Almanacs provide compilations of facts and figures on a wide range of topics. What movies were the biggest hits in the 1940s? What was the strongest earthquake ever to rock the United States? Who is the director of the Boston Pops? You can find this kind of information in an almanac like *The Information Please Almanac, The World Almanac,* or the *Book of Facts.* Yearbooks such as the *Statistical Abstract of the United States* provide data on everything from the annual catch of abalone to the yearly production of zinc. Directories like the *Encyclopedia of Associations* tell you about the members, leaders, and functions of organizations.

***Vertical File.*** Many libraries maintain a clipping and filing service on topics of local interest, usually referred to as the "vertical file." The vertical file might contain pamphlets, newspaper clippings, or magazine stories on prominent people and important happenings in your area. Also check to see if your local or campus newspaper has such a service (often called the "morgue" of the newspaper).

***Government Documents.*** Most government documents are housed in their own section of the library. These documents provide more in-depth information than that found in most almanacs. Such material includes reports on congressional hearings, legislation, and proceedings; the proclamations, orders, and other formal statements of the president; and opinions and decisions of the Supreme Court. Some of the major government publications include

*Congressional Record:* daily account of the proceedings of Congress

*Federal Register:* proclamations and orders of the president and regulations of various departments of government

*United States Reports:* opinions and decisions of the Supreme Court

*Monthly Catalog of United States Government Publications:* the master list of government documents

*Selected Rand Abstracts:* guide to unclassified reports, papers, and books of the Rand Corporation, which conducts government-sponsored studies

*American Statistics Index:* a master guide to government statistical publications

*Undex: (United Nations Document Index):* covers publications issued by the United Nations

***Electronic Data Bases.*** Most libraries now have electronic data bases. In fact, the amount of information that can be accessed through computer terminals has grown at a phenomenal rate. Between 1988 and 1989, over 3.5 *billion* records were added to such databases.[4] Your library may have an on-line card catalog; a computerized newspaper index such as *The National Newspaper Index;* or periodical indexes such as *Infotrac* or *ProQuest,* which can access a variety of data bases. Two of *ProQuest* system's services, the *General Periodicals Ondisc* and the *ABI/Inform Ondisc,* are especially useful for speech preparation. *General Periodicals Ondisc* contains abstracts to articles from over 450 general interest, scientific, and trade or professional periodicals, as well as complete articles from selected journals. *ABI/Inform Ondisc* is a business database containing abstracts and indexing to articles from over 800 business and management journals.

The development of such new technology as the CD-ROM (Compact Disk–Read Only Memory) has made it possible to store enormous amounts of data on disks similar to those used by stereo music systems. For example, a thirteen-volume *Oxford English Dictionary* can be stored on just one CD-ROM disk. Many other data bases, such as the *Art Index, Biography Index, Humanities Index, Social Sciences Index,* and *Periodical Abstracts* are also available on CD-ROM disks.

You do not have to be a computer whiz to use these resources. To conduct a search, you simply type in your subject and push the computer key labeled "Search." The references to articles on your subject then appear on the screen. Some of the references contain abstracts as well as bibliographic information. A printer attached to the computer allows you to print out your references. Many of the articles are available on disks or microcassettes that are part of these programs. The articles are available for immediate viewing and copying. Using such a service, you can find your references, record the bibliographic information, read the article, and make

```
                    General Periodicals Index P

PUBLIC SPEAKING
-technique

Tips on making speeches to international audiences. by Robert T.
Moran  v 44 International Management April '89 p 59 (1)

Speakers who address multicultural audiences need to consider
audiences' native customs and habits. Speakers should be careful
to not alienate audiences by telling jokes, revealing personal
details, or dressing too formally or informally. Japanese speak-
ers always wear proper business suits, begin their speeches with
a sign of respect to their audience, and are careful to speak to
the audience as a whole. French audiences are very skeptical and
they expect opinions to be supported with numbers, while German
audiences focus on technical questions.
```

FIGURE 5.3
Sample *Infotrac* Entry

a copy — all in the same place! Figure 5.3 is an example of an *Infotrac* entry with an abstract.

If your subject is complex, spanning several disciplines and interests, a more detailed computer search conducted through your library's information retrieval service can help you establish a working bibliography. Such a search will generate a list of citations on your topic and may also print out abstracts of the articles listed. For example, suppose you wish to find information on companies involved in medical product development using biotechnology. You instruct the computer to search for articles on biotechnology *and* companies *and* health. The *and* is very important because the computer will cross-check these references against each other and give you a list of articles that link all three topics. On this particular subject, a computer actually identified 93 articles on biotechnology, 31,841 articles on companies, 7,512 articles on health, but only 8 articles on biotechnology *and* companies *and* health.[5] These last eight articles are the ones that should prove most useful. There is typically a charge for this more detailed search service if it must be ordered through the library. Some of the newer electronic data systems such as *Proquest* allow you to conduct such a search yourself.

***Card Catalog.***    Students are often told to start their research with the subject listings in the card catalogue. This advice may not always be best for speakers because on popular subjects you might find fifty or even five hundred books listed, and you have no way to determine which are most relevant or most helpful. However, in the articles you read on your topic, you may encounter references to books that sound particularly interesting. Reading the best books on your topic can give you a deeper understanding that will make your speech more authoritative and impressive.

## Interviewing for Information

Interviewing experts can give you credibility similar to what you acquire through personal experience. If you can say, "The personnel director of Nupak Automotive Parts told me . . . ," listeners will sit up and take notice. Like personal experience, however, interviewing has its limitations. Finding the right person to interview can be a problem. You may have a tendency to accept the word of your expert without further investigation. If you know very little about the subject, it will be difficult for you to evaluate what you hear.

To minimize these problems, check your library's vertical file or the local newspaper morgue to help identify people whose knowledge can enhance your speech. The news clippings and your other research may also help you think of questions to ask during an interview. Prepare for the interview by learning about the topic in advance.

***Establishing Contact.***    If time permits, write the person to request an interview. In your letter state your purpose and demonstrate your seriousness. Follow up with a telephone call to set a time and place for the interview. Figure 5.4 on the following page is a sample interview request letter.

Room 225 Adams Hall
Biltmore College
Detroit, MI 72641
November 7, 19—

Ms. Carol Johnson, Director of Personnel
Nupak Automotive Parts
1427 Beltway Drive
Detroit, MI 72678

Dear Ms. Johnson:

I am a student at Biltmore College enrolled in a public speaking
class. I am preparing an informative speech on company- and
union-sponsored programs aimed at overcoming boredom on the job.
Marcia Thomas, an old family friend, suggested that I could
learn a great deal from the quality circles program you have developed at Nupak. I would appreciate very much the opportunity
to interview you about the program.

I am especially interested in your ideas and opinions on the
following questions:

1. Have the quality circles generated workable programs to counteract boredom?

2. Does job enrichment work in the auto parts industry?

3. Might job restructuring be a possible alternative?

4. Have there been any changes in absenteeism or job turnover
   since starting the program?

I am scheduled to speak at the end of next week, and will call
your office Thursday morning to see if we can arrange an interview. My dormitory phone number is 834-4922. I will be very
grateful for your help and look forward to meeting you.

                              Sincerely,


                              Richard Mardsen

**FIGURE 5.4   Sample Interview Request Letter**

A well-written letter helps establish your credibility. It also establishes an agenda for the interview and gives your expert some idea of what you wish to discuss. It suggests that you are serious enough to have done research on the topic. If you do not have time to establish contact by letter, telephone the expert. Don't be shy. A request for an interview is a compliment.

***Designing the Interview.*** Either in your letter or at the beginning of the interview, establish why you are there and what you hope to learn. Plan questions that invite your expert to discuss the meaning of events. Avoid questions that invite yes or no answers, such as "Do you think quality circles are worthwhile?" Never supply the answer you want in your question, as in "Don't you think that quality circles work because they make employees feel important?" Design your questions in a sequence so that the answers form a coherent line of thought:

"When did you adopt the quality circles idea?"

"Why did you go with the quality circles approach?"

"How did you implement the concept?"

"What have been the results?"

"How would you evaluate the program?"

Allow the person you are interviewing to complete the answer to one question before you ask another. Don't interrupt and don't jump in with another question every time your expert pauses. Your expert may go from one point to another and may even answer a question before you ask it. You should be flexible enough to adapt to a spontaneous flow of information.

Design your questions so that your expert is not made defensive by the way they are worded. Questions such as "When are managers going to stop exploiting workers?" are not only argumentative but ill mannered. Save controversial questions for late in the interview after you have established rapport. Ask such questions honestly but tactfully: "Some union leaders have said that quality circles are just 'the latest ploy to exploit workers.' How do you feel about such criticism?" If asked with sincerity rather than hostility, this kind of question may produce the most interesting part of your interview.

Should you plan to tape-record your interview? A tape recorder can free you from note taking and help you get the exact wording of answers. But setting up and running a tape recorder can be a nuisance that interferes with establishing rapport. Also, many people dislike being tape-recorded. Never attempt to record interviews without obtaining prior consent. A good time to seek such consent is in your follow-up telephone call. If your expert seems reluctant, don't press the point.

***Conducting the Interview.*** Arrive for the interview on time. Dress nicely to show that you take the interview seriously and as a sign of respect for the

*Plan your interview questions to make maximum use of your expert's time. Avoid "yes or no" questions and let the expert do most of the talking.*

person you are interviewing. When you meet your expert, take time to get to know the person on an informal basis before you get into your prepared questions. Try to establish common ground. On one occasion, as we were interviewing the late Supreme Court Justice Hugo Black, the justice discovered during small talk before the interview that our people had come from the hill country of north Georgia. Since these were also his family roots, he felt instant rapport with us. This reduced the tension, and we went on to have a productive interview.

Let the expert do most of the talking while you do the listening. Be alert for opportunities to follow up on responses by using probes, mirror questions, verifiers, or reinforcers.[6] **Probes** are questions that ask the expert to elaborate on a response: "Could you tell me more about how you got the quality circles program started?" **Mirror questions** reflect back part of a response to encourage further discussion. The sequence might go as follows:

> "So I told Melvin, 'If we want to change the workers' attitudes toward us, we're going to have to change our attitudes toward them.'"

> "You said management would have to change first?"

A **verifier** confirms the meaning of something that has just been said, such as "If I understand you correctly, you're saying. . . ." Finally, a **reinforcer** encourages the person to communicate further. A smile, a nod, or a comment such as "I see" are reinforcers that can keep the interview moving.

If you feel the interview beginning to drift off course, you can often steer it back with a transition. As your expert pauses, you can say, "I believe I understand how the quality circles work. Now let me ask you about the results of the program."

Do not overstay your welcome. As the interview draws to a close, summarize the main points you have learned and how you think they may be useful in your speech. A summary allows you to verify what you have heard and reassures the expert that you intend to use the information fairly and accurately. Show your gratitude for the interview as you conclude, then follow up with a telephone call or thank-you letter in which you report the successful results of your speech.

After the interview is concluded, find a quiet place, go over the notes you have taken, and get down the wording of important answers while they are still fresh in your mind. Nothing is more frustrating than to recall that your expert made a striking statement that would be perfect for the conclusion of your speech, but you can't remember what it was.

 ## RECORDING INFORMATION

In the course of your research, you will come across facts and figures, ideas for examples and narratives, or quotations that might be useful in your speech. It is impossible to remember all of these items, or even to remember where you saw them, unless you keep notes. Many researchers use index

---

**SPEAKER'S NOTES**

### Interviewing for Information

1. Select and contact an expert on your topic.

2. Research the topic so that you can develop effective questions.

3. Dress neatly and arrive on time.

4. Let the expert do most of the talking. Do not interrupt.

5. Avoid questions that call for yes or no answers. Do not ask leading questions. Save controversial questions until late in the interview. Use probes, mirror questions, verifiers, and reinforcers to follow up.

6. Summarize what you have heard so your expert can verify it.

7. Go over your notes as soon as possible to assure that you have recorded vital information and quotations correctly.

8. A thank-you note is a valuable professional courtesy.

cards to record the information they discover. These cards are easy to handle and sort by categories. The note cards you prepare during your research should show what the information is and where it was obtained. You will be preparing two major kinds of research note cards: information cards and source cards.

### Information Cards

**Information cards** record ideas and information from an article or book, usually one item to a card. For any single article or book you may have several cards. While you are doing your research, you will not always know whether something will be useful in your speech. When in doubt, write it down. The more information you have to select from, the more responsible your knowledge should be. Avoid getting into situations in which you remember that you read something important but can't remember what it was, and — worse still — you can't remember where you read it.

Each card should contain a *heading* describing the information contained on the card, the *source* where the information was obtained, and the *information* itself, which may be either a direct quotation or a paraphrase of what the author said. Figure 5.5 shows an information card.

### Source Cards

You should also prepare a **source card** for each article or book you use. The source card contains the author, title, place and date of publication, and page references. This information permits you to document precisely your sources of data when you introduce them in your speech. Establishing who said something, where it was reported, and when it was said is important to the credibility of your information.

The source card for a book typically takes the following form: author, title, place of publication, publisher, and date of publication. A source card for an article lists the author, article title, name of the periodical, volume number, date, and pages (see Figure 5.6). The source card may also be used to list important information about the author, book, or periodical that might be helpful. This information can be useful as you introduce sources in support of points you make during your speech. You may also use your source card to write down a *brief* summary of the material, including some comments on its quality and significance.

### Testing Information

Researching a speech is sometimes like mining for gold. First, you have to find what you think might be valuable. Then you must test it to be sure it is authentic. Your research should help you find facts and figures, testimony, examples, and narratives that will add substance to your message. Before you use these materials, you should evaluate them carefully. Detailed

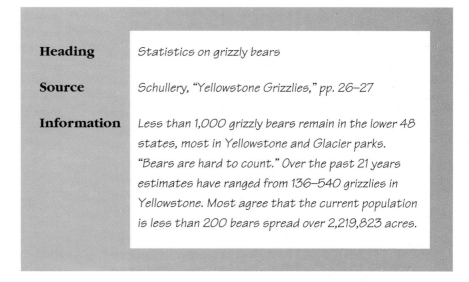

**FIGURE 5.5**
**Information Card**

guidelines for evaluating each kind of supporting material are provided in Chapter 6. Regardless of the type of supporting material your research uncovers, you should check its reliability, thoroughness, recency, and precision.

**Reliability** refers to the trustworthiness of information and is critical to the credibility of a speech. Reliable information comes from sources that are qualified by education or experience and that are free from self-interests that might result in bias. **Thoroughness** of information is also an important consideration. You must try to discover all the important information you need

| **Bibliographic information for an article** | Paul Schullery, "Yellowstone Grizzlies: The New Breed," <u>National Parks</u> (November/December 1989), pp. 25–29. |
|---|---|
| **Summary and comments** | Well-documented information on grizzly population, causes of endangerment, and adaptations the bears had to make when the dumps were closed in 1969 and 1970. Author is a writer with the research division in Yellowstone Park — has written 2 books on the bears. |

**FIGURE 5.6**
**Source Card**

to make a responsible presentation. **Recency** is essential when knowledge is changing rapidly on a subject. **Precision** is important if you are speaking on a topic that varies widely from place to place, such as unemployment rates or the incidence of AIDS. You must be certain that your information applies in the locale where you are speaking. Applying these tests of research to the different types of supporting materials is covered in detail in the next chapter.

**IN SUMMARY**   To give a successful speech, you must find a good topic, determine your general and specific purposes, decide on a thematic statement, and expand your base of knowledge so that you can speak responsibly. A good topic is meaningful to both you and your audience. A good topic will be limited so that you can research it adequately and develop a speech that will fit within the allotted time.

*Selecting a Good Topic.*   One way to discover promising topic areas is to chart your interests. You can also scan television news, magazines, and newspapers for ideas. Next, chart audience interests as disclosed in previous speeches and match them with your interests. To develop topic possibilities, use a topic analysis method based on six key questions: who, what, when, where, why, and how. When applied to a topic area, these questions can guide you to specific topics. As you move toward your selection, consider whether a given topic fits the assignment, whether you can develop a responsible speech on it within the time limit, and what your *purpose* is for speaking upon it.

*Determining Your Purposes.*   Your *general purpose* describes the overall function of the speech. Your *specific purpose* identifies the kind of response you would like to evoke, what you want to accomplish. Your *thematic statement* expresses the central ideas of your speech in a single sentence. It can also *preview* the main points of your speech.

*Acquiring Responsible Knowledge.*   In order to speak responsibly on your topic, you should gather as much relevant information as time allows. You can obtain useful knowledge from personal experience, library resources, and interviews. Personal experience can make your speech seem highly credible and authentic, but you should not rely on it as your only source of information. Library research can add objective, authoritative information to your speech. The aim of such research is to acquire *responsible knowledge,* which means knowing the major features, issues, experts, latest developments, and local applications relevant to your topic. Interviewing puts you in direct contact with experts. The knowledge you obtain through interviewing can add freshness, vitality, and local relevance to your speech.

*Recording Information.*   As you conduct research, record what you learn on index cards so that you can sort your material easily. Use *informa-*

*tion cards,* which separate the ideas and information you find into useful categories, and *source cards* for each article, book, or interview. The source card identifies the author and place of publication fully. It may be used to record background information about the source and an overall summary and evaluation of the material. As you collect research for your speech, you should ask four basic questions: does this material satisfy the tests of *reliability, thoroughness, recency,* and *precision* so that I can use it responsibly in my speech?

**TERMS TO KNOW**

| | |
|---|---|
| purpose | verifier |
| general purpose | reinforcer |
| specific purpose | information card |
| thematic statement | source card |
| preview | reliability |
| responsible knowledge | thoroughness |
| probe | recency |
| mirror question | precision |

**DISCUSSION**

1. Working in small groups, exchange a chart of your interests with your classmates. Discuss the most promising areas for speech topics among your interests. Report these to the class.

2. Using the topic analysis method, analyze the most promising topic areas identified in item 1. As you consider these topic possibilities, discuss what general purposes they might serve.

3. As a follow-up to items 1 and 2, develop specific purposes and thematic statements for the three topics that interest you most. Evaluate them in class, using the criteria for selecting good topics and determining specific purposes described in this chapter.

4. In what ways might personal experience limit and distort your knowledge as well as enrich it? Discuss in class, drawing on examples from your own experience.

**APPLICATION**

1. Working in small groups, scan a variety of resources to generate topic areas for speeches. Each group should be responsible for checking one of the following materials:
   a. the local Sunday newspaper
   b. a television news program over a week's time
   c. a recent issue of a weekly news magazine
   d. a recent issue of a general-interest magazine

In the first part of a class period, meet as groups to generate a list of topic ideas. Each group should select five topic ideas. In the second part of the class period, a representative should present each group's recommendations to the class and explain how and why the topics were chosen. Which kind of media resource produces the best speech topics? What are the strengths and limitations of each?

2. Choose one of the topics you selected from Application 1 and identify the most likely sources of information you could use to develop it.

3. Take a walking tour of your library and locate the various resources described in this chapter. While you are there, try to find the answers for the following questions. Do not ask the librarian for assistance. Record the source of each answer.
   a. What was the population of the city in which you were born in the year of your birth?
   b. What television show had the highest Nielsen ratings when you were six years old?
   c. What contemporary public figure do you admire most? When and where was he or she born? What is he or she most noted for?
   d. Who won the Nobel prize for literature in the year your most admired public figure (MAPF) was born? What was the author's nationality? most noted work(s)?
   e. What actress won the Academy Award for best supporting actress in the year your MAPF was born? What movie was she in?
   f. Who were the U.S. senators of the state in which you were born during the year of your birth?
   g. Who were the Democratic presidential and vice-presidential candidates during the election held nearest the birth year of your MAPF?
   h. What noteworthy event took place during the month and year of your birth? When and where did this happen?
   i. When and where were you born?

4. Discuss the following thematic statements in terms of their effectiveness:
   a. You ought to protect yourself from date rape.
   b. The role of superstitions in our lives.
   c. Young children should not be admitted to horror movies.
   d. Weekend trips are preferable to long vacations.
   e. Nutritious meals you can cook in your dorm room.
   Improve those that do not meet the criteria for effective thematic statements.

**NOTES**  1. Rudyard Kipling, *Just So Stories* (Garden City, N.Y.: Doubleday, 1921), p. 85.
2. Adapted from Brent Filson, *Executive Speeches: 51 CEOs Tell You How to Do Yours* (Williamstown, Mass.: Williamstown Publishing Co., 1991), pp. 47-48.

3. Kenneth F. Kister, *Best Encyclopedias: A Guide to General and Specialized Encyclopedias* (New York: Oryx, 1986).
4. Sherwood Harris, ed., *The New York Public Library Book of How and Where to Look It Up* (New York: Prentice Hall, 1991).
5. From a brochure of Dialog Information Services, Inc.
6. Lois J. Einhorn, Patricia Hayes Bradley, and John E. Baird, Jr., *Effective Employment Interviewing: Unlocking Human Potential* (Glenview, Ill.: Scott, Foresman, 1982), pp. 135–139.

*The universe is made of stories, not of atoms.*
    *—Muriel Rukeyser*

# 6

# The Use of Supporting Materials

## This Chapter Will Help You

- use facts and figures in ethical and effective ways.
- use expert, prestige, and lay forms of testimony when each is most appropriate.
- use examples to enliven your speech and to emphasize important points.
- use narratives to involve your listeners and to illustrate abstract ideas.

Let me tell you about a gentleman who never used the drugs he sold, Darrell Tonnell. He was a very close friend of mine, and he had just been released from active-duty Army. . . . His sister's boyfriend was a dealer and offered him the chance to make some real money. Within a week [tosses what appears to be money to the floor] he had money to buy clothes and food for his mother. Within two weeks [tosses more apparent money to floor] he had a whole new wardrobe, including a beeper to match each outfit [laughter]. Within seven months [tosses a large roll of what seem to be bills to floor] he paid cash for a brand-new BMW.

. . . As the police were getting too close to him, he decided to move to Chicago and to go into business with his cousin Ronnie. . . . I went to visit them in Chicago for a week. . . . The third night of my visit we went out to a club. Here we were approached by a dealer whose profits had been taken by Darrell and Ronnie's business. He told them to give him a commission or else he was going to kill all three of us. . . . So after the threat we had to watch over our backs every minute, and I agreed then to carry a gun wherever I went.

One day we decided to go to Kroger's. We had to do some shopping. We decided that morning would be the least risky time to go, so we went, and we shopped, and after we came out we were walking into the lot, and we looked around cautiously to make sure no one was there. We didn't see anyone, so we proceeded into the lot, and as we did we heard a screech of tires and saw a yellow Cadillac coming around the corner. Out of the window was a man holding an Uzi in his hand pointed right at us. I heard the shots, and I dived behind a concrete pillar, and Darrell and Ronnie decided to fire back. My adrenaline was rushing, I heard my heart pounding, and then I heard silence. I looked up, and Darrell had been shot. He had been hit by five bullets in the chest. I rushed to him screaming for help, but no one came. He died in my arms, never having used any kind of narcotic substance.

People, if the government hopes to win, if we the people of America hope to win, if we the people of this world hope to win this war, then we must confront this problem realistically. . . . As long as children continue to see drug dealers as role models, this cycle will continue to turn.

M atthew Miller, a student at Indiana University South Bend, told this story in a classroom speech that won the Midwest regional competition of Houghton Mifflin's 1991 public speaking contest. Narratives used in speeches are stories with a purpose. Matthew's purpose was to convince his listeners that the national antidrug campaign was inadequate and misdirected. He used a personal narrative to bring both closeness and concreteness to the problem. Matthew's personal involvement made the narrative genuine, credible, and moving. It helped his audience understand and feel the tragic implications for all those whose lives are entangled in the drug trade.

Narratives, facts and figures, testimony, and examples are **supporting materials,** the basic building blocks of speeches. Supporting materials provide the substance, reliability, and appeal a speech must have before listeners will place their faith in it and you. As you research your topic, you should ask yourself: Does an article contain relevant and useful information? Does it cite experts who support your position? Are there any interesting examples that could make your speech more clear and realistic? Can you find stories that might bring your ideas to life? Your quest for responsible knowledge should focus on finding supporting materials that will add substance and interest to your speech.

In general, supporting materials perform four important functions. First, *they demonstrate the meaning of topics.* Second, they *emphasize the importance of ideas.* Third, *they show the relevance of topics to listeners' lives,* often through examples or narratives. And fourth, *they verify controversial statements and claims.* Although this fourth function would seem to relate mainly to persuasive speeches, informative speeches can also make claims that require the support of facts, figures, and expert testimony. If you assert, "American cars are inferior to foreign-made cars," your audience might very well ask, "Says who?" "Says me!" would not be very convincing. You must be able to show where you got your information and demonstrate that your sources are reliable. In persuasive speeches this burden usually is heavier. If you are asking people to change their beliefs or modify their behavior, you must be able to verify your claims with powerful supporting material. A statement without support will not bear the weight of examination that most audiences will place upon it.

As we examine each of the major kinds of supporting materials, we will discuss its nature and significance, how to evaluate it, and how to put it to work for improved speech effectiveness.

 ## FACTS AND FIGURES

When we think of supporting material for speeches, often the first thing that comes to mind is information. Such information takes two basic forms: general facts and statistics.

### Facts

Facts are a powerful form of supporting material. Richard Weaver, a prominent critic of communication, once noted that Americans honor facts as the highest form of knowledge. Facts constitute our *truth.* He further suggested that when facts are confirmed by scientists, they carry even more weight and are less likely to be questioned. The contemporary American audience respects scientific facts and numbers in the way that other societies respect the word of God.[1]

*Facts and figures add substance to a speech. The speaker addressing these Canadian natives in Ottawa may have cited statistics to prove that natives are in the process of recovering their lost lands.*

As a speaker you must master the facts surrounding your topic if you want to be credible. But what exactly are facts? **Facts** are verifiable units of information, which means that independent observers see and report them consistently. The following statements may be considered facts because they can be verified as either true or false:

AIDS is a communicable disease.

Most Metro Tech students work to put themselves through college.

Many students experience communication apprehension when they speak.

Factual statements can stand by themselves, but speakers rarely use facts without interpreting them. Although interpretation aids understanding, it can also be a source of distortion. As soon as you start handling facts so that they serve your purpose in a speech, you create the possibility of distorting them. Biased interpretations can creep into otherwise factual statements with just a few additional words, turning them into opinions:

AIDS is a *shameful* communicable disease.

Most Metro Tech students *have to* work to put themselves through college.

Many students experience *debilitating* communication apprehension when they speak.

Despite their possible misuse, facts serve vital communication functions. Often they are interwoven into a speech as definitions or explanations. Definitions and explanations should help clarify information by translating it into language the audience can easily understand. The following definition of *old growth* could be used effectively in a speech on forest preservation:

> From a traditional forester's view, old growth stands are those where the over-all increase in wood production has reached its peak. . . . Old-growth stands contain significant numbers of large, live, old trees. . . . Generally, old growth is virgin terrain that has never been harvested. The Wilderness Society defines "classic" old growth as "containing at least eight big trees per acre exceeding 300 years in age or measuring more than 40 inches in diameter at breast height."[2]

Because we usually cannot directly verify the accuracy of facts, they are often combined with expert testimony, which we cover in detail later in this chapter. All information comes from somewhere, so you must consider how your audience might react to your sources of information. Periodicals have certain reputations that make them more or less acceptable to different audiences. For instance, William F. Buckley's *National Review* is known as a conservative magazine, and *The Nation* is considered more liberal.[3]

## Statistics

When you use numbers to describe the magnitude of events or to predict future patterns, you are using **statistics.** There are two basic types of statistics: **descriptive statistics,** which explain something in terms of its size or distribution, and **inferential statistics,** which make predictions, show trends, and demonstrate relationships.

Descriptive statistics may describe a topic by its size or average occurrence. The following excerpt shows the use of statistics and contrast to establish the size of a problem:

> Although more than 1,200 of the students on our campus have experimented with cocaine, most of us — nearly 12,000 as reported in a recent University Health Services survey — still get our kicks from that less spectacular drug, alcohol. The average student has not even tried cocaine and has no particular desire to do so. But, that same student has not only tried alcohol — he or she continues to use it each week.

Descriptive statistics also may be used to describe the way something is distributed or spread out:

Most of us work to help pay our way. Information from our Registrar's Office indicates that 18 percent of us don't need to work — we are fully supported by parents or spouses. Twenty-one percent of us work full time — at least forty hours a week — and attend school on a part-time basis. The rest of us — the vast majority, 61 percent of us — work part-time while carrying a full-time course load.

When the numbers you are presenting are large or unfamiliar, it helps if you can tie them to something the audience can relate to more easily. Note how a prominent physician helped his listeners understand the enormity of his statistical information on health care:

> Last year the health-care industry had total expenditures of $384 billion. That is three times the revenue of the American auto industry. Think of it, $1 billion in the last twenty-four hours. When I worked in Washington, I heard Everett McKinley Dirksen, the late Minority Leader of the United States Senate, [say], "A billion here, a billion there, pretty soon it adds up to real money!" One billion per day equals $42 million per hour, and that is real money! Looked at another way, we spent more than $1,600 for every man, woman, and child in the nation last year. For a family of four that's $6,400, the price of a compact automobile. Seldom do we think of the trade-off of a new car each year for health care.[4]

Inferential statistics, which make predictions or claim causal relationships, are based on probability, not on absolute certainty. Therefore, you should be especially cautious as you use and interpret them. Inferential statistics often focus on *correlations,* which show the relationships between two factors, and *trends,* which describe and predict changes over time. John McGervey, a physicist from Case Western Reserve University, has described in detail the probability of common occurrences. For example, in looking at the disasters people commonly worry about, McGervey points out the following correlation: a trip in a commercial jet airplane carries a one-in-a-million risk of death, but 120 miles of driving in a car with a seat belt (or 60 miles unbelted) carries the same level of risk. Therefore, driving 12,000 miles a year is one hundred times riskier than a commercial airline flight.[5] Had McGervey reported significant changes in this correlation over the past decade, he would have been describing a trend.

### Evaluating Facts and Figures

Before you incorporate information into your speech, you should use your critical thinking skills to evaluate it. As you research your speech, you may discover much interesting information about your topic that does not *directly* relate to your specific purpose. No matter how fascinating it may be, if the information does not help develop your thematic statement, don't use it. A speech that is cluttered with interesting digressions is difficult for listeners to follow. You may lose them on one of the side paths!

In evaluating facts and figures, you should consider how current the information is, especially when your topic is one in which information is changing rapidly. Save yourself the embarrassment of a listener's pointing out that your information is out of date. You should also be certain that statistical data apply to your particular situation. If you talk about the "crisis of unemployment" in your area, basing your claim on a national statistical average of 7 percent, you could have a problem if someone points out that the local rate is only 4 percent. Similarly, you might try to take comfort in the national figures, when the local unemployment rate actually might have soared to 10 percent. The lesson is clear: be doubly certain that statistical data fit precisely the time and place and subject you want to talk about.

It is also important to carefully evaluate your sources of information and not rely too much on any single source. Information confirmed by more than one authority is apt to be more reliable. The more controversial your topic, the more critical the reliability of your information and the credibility of your sources. Examine even "factual" material for potential bias, distortions, or omissions. Compare what different expert sources have to say, and look for areas of agreement. Be certain that what you have are facts and not inferences or opinions.

You should also consider whether your information is impressive enough to stand on its own, or whether you must use comparisons, contrasts, or even an example to point out its meaning. A barrage of numbers may impress some listeners, but for statistics to work well as supporting material you should combine them with examples to make them clearer and more memorable. Recent research suggests that good examples may be better than statistics alone at gaining and holding attention and are easier for listeners to comprehend.[6] On the other hand, reliable statistical information provides the firm base of knowledge needed to make the use of examples responsible.

Finally, Stephen Lee, a student at the University of Texas at Austin who won the Southern regional competition of the Houghton Mifflin Company's 1991 public speaking contest, reminds us to ask whether statistical differences truly represent a difference. In his speech Stephen noted:

> Our government is faulted for many problems. Statistical misuse is perhaps one of the greatest. This was clearly demonstrated in March of 1983 when the computation of the unemployment rate was changed to encompass military personnel. Now this had a significant impact, as the number changed from 10.6 to 10.1 percent. Some people said it was a political ploy of President Reagan, trying to make himself look good in the public spectrum, while other people claimed this was a highly justified move, since, after all, military personnel were employed. But I think there's a more important question that needs to be answered. Look at what happened to the number. It changed. Look at what happened to the way the number was computed.

**SPEAKER'S NOTES**

## Evaluating Facts and Figures

1. Are the facts and figures relevant?

2. Is the information recent and does it apply precisely to the locale of the speech?

3. Is the information reliable? Do other authorities confirm it?

4. Are the sources credible? Are they competent, trustworthy, and unbiased?

5. Is the information complete? Has anything important been omitted or withheld?

6. Is this factual information, or is it opinion masquerading as fact?

7. Do statistical differences represent actual differences?

It changed, too. But what happened to the very real problem of civilian unemployment, which we all assumed this number to represent? It had not changed at all. It all goes back to what Lester T. Thurow said in his basic theory of economics: "A difference is only a difference if it truly makes a difference." Many times a difference in a number does not represent a difference in the real world.

### Using Facts and Figures

Once you have found your information and determined that it is sound, you must decide how to use it. You should have an abundance of information pertinent to each main point of your speech, so that you can *select the best* as supporting material for your presentation. Identify your sources of information. Bring statistics to life by using examples or concrete comparisons.

Be sure you use facts ethically in your speeches. Be careful not to distort factual and statistical statements by the way you word them. Be careful not to read into information what you want to find. Don't ignore facts or figures that contradict your ideas by rejecting them as atypical or irrelevant. Do not put blind faith in what *appear* at first glance to be factual statements. In your communication roles as speaker and listener, you should examine all factual statements and statistical data carefully. Chapter 14's discussion of other possible misuses of facts and figures as evidence in persuasive speaking will help you further. Remember that — at best — statistical information is probable, not certain.

# TESTIMONY

**Testimony** involves citing other people, institutions, or publications in your speech, either by quoting them directly or by paraphrasing what they have to say. Three types of testimony are useful as supporting material. **Expert testimony** comes from sources who are authorities on the topic. **Prestige testimony** comes from someone who is highly regarded but not necessarily an expert on the topic. **Lay testimony** involves citing ordinary citizens who may have firsthand experience.

## Expert Testimony

As you research your topic, you will probably run across statements by experts offering important opinions, information, and interesting quotations. Use this type of testimony to establish the validity of your facts and interpretations. When you use expert testimony, you are calling on qualified witnesses to support your case. In a sense, using expert testimony allows you to borrow ethos from those who have earned it through their distinguished and widely recognized work. Expert testimony is especially important when your topic is innovative, unfamiliar, highly technical, or controversial.

When using expert testimony, do not overlook the power of titles such as *scientist* or *doctor* when such terms can be used legitimately to identify a source. Also remember that certain publications and institutions carry more weight than others. Financial information from the *Wall Street Journal* may be better received than the same type of information from your local newspaper. Medical studies conducted at the National Institutes of Health may be more respected than similar studies done in smaller, less prestigious institutions.

Because most beginning speakers are not really authorities on their topics, expert testimony is a very important source of support in student speeches. But even speakers who are highly qualified by education or experience often call on other experts to substantiate their messages. In a speech entitled "Changing Relationships Between Men and Women," Dr. Bernice Cohen Sachs relied on university-conducted surveys and opinions from psychiatrists, sociologists, and other specialists to support her interpretations. Dr. Sachs, herself a noted physician, was always careful to make certain that the audience was aware of the credentials of her sources. She introduced a discussion of the effects of outside employment on women in the following way:

> Mary Howell, M.D., Ph.D., mother of six and coordinator for evaluation and education at the Geriatric Clinical Center at the Bedford, Massachusetts, Veterans' Administration Medical Center, said that employment outside the home. . . .[7]

Be sure to introduce the authorities you quote in the same careful way. You may wish to emphasize their expert background, the nature of their research projects, or where and when they made the statement you are citing, depending on the circumstances of your speech.

### *Prestige Testimony*

Prestige testimony can enhance the general credibility of both you and your speech. When you use prestige testimony, you associate yourself with the source's good name and positive reputation. Often the source of prestige testimony is a respected writer or public figure. Quite frequently, it is the insight provided by the source or the eloquent use of language that makes prestige testimony effective. Geraldine Ferraro used prestige testimony in the introduction to her acceptance speech at the 1984 Democratic National Convention:

> As I stand before the American people and think of the honor this great convention has bestowed upon me, I recall the words of Dr. Martin Luther King, Jr., who made America stronger by making America more free.
>
> He said: "Occasionally in life there are moments which cannot be completely explained by words. Their meaning can only be articulated by the inaudible language of the heart."
>
> Tonight is such a moment for me.
>
> My heart is filled with pride.
>
> My fellow citizens, I proudly accept your nomination for the vice president of the United States.[8]

In her acceptance speech, Ms. Ferraro quoted her source **verbatim;** that is, she used the exact words of the source. Providing a verbatim quotation is preferable to paraphrasing when the citation is short, when the exact wording is important, or when the source has said something with such clarity, grace, and force that you know you cannot improve on it.

If the testimony is taken from a long passage or excerpted from a series of passages, you might find it more advantageous to paraphrase or restate it in your own words, making sure you still cite the source. Consider the following example from a student speech:

> In an article on teen-age pregnancy published in the *Ladies' Home Journal,* Eunice Kennedy Shriver pointed out that over 600,000 teenage girls will become mothers this year and that nearly 40,000 of this number will not have turned fifteen when they become pregnant.

Whether quoted verbatim or paraphrased, prestige testimony does *not* establish the factual validity of a statement. Citing Eunice Kennedy Shriver as a source of information concerning teen-age pregnancy could demonstrate a misuse of prestige testimony. What might the audience know about Eunice Kennedy Shriver? That she is the sister of former president John F. Kennedy or the wife of Sargent Shriver, the first director of the Peace Corps? So how, one might ask, does this qualify her to serve as an expert on teen-age pregnancy? What the speaker failed to do in this example was to present Ms. Shriver's credentials as professional social worker with experience at the House of the Good Shepherd in Chicago and the Federal Penitentiary for Women in West Virginia. Once this background information has been supplied, her testimony carries more authority and is not improperly used. Indeed, her testimony then becomes *both* prestigious and expert, a powerful blend.

### Lay Testimony

Speakers often use lay testimony to add authenticity and humanity to a speech. Lay testimony can be particularly important in speeches presented in the United States, where ordinary people enjoy special status as the source of political power. Therefore, speakers often give high regard to "the voice of the people," so much so, in fact, that *USA Today* features their testimony along with that of experts on its editorial page.[9] If you were preparing a speech on assembly line boredom, you might quote factory workers to add a real-life dimension to your message. Similarly, for a speech on campus security you might find it useful to cite other students and faculty members.

Lay testimony also can be used to increase identification — the sense of close relationship — between your listeners and your speech. If listeners can identify with the sources you use because they are "just like us," then they may be more willing to accept the point you are making. Ronald Reagan made effective use of lay testimony in his first inaugural address as he quoted the diary of Martin Treptow, a young soldier who died on the Western front during World War I:

> On the flyleaf under the heading, "My Pledge," he had written these words: "America must win this war. Therefore I will work, I will save, I will sacrifice, I will endure, I will fight cheerfully and do my utmost, as if the issue of the whole struggle depended on me alone."[10]

Treptow's pledge represented the kind of dedication President Reagan wished to inspire in American citizens.

### Evaluating Testimony

Like facts and figures, testimony must be evaluated in terms of how relevant, how recent, and how accurate it is. You must be particularly careful that a quotation you select reflects the overall meaning and intent of its author. Never twist the meaning of testimony to make it fit your purposes. Such unethical practice is called "quoting out of context." Advertising that accompanies movies or plays is notorious for quoting out of context, especially when citing reviews. A review may slam a play as boring and dull but praise the costuming as the "one brilliant grace in an otherwise disastrous

**Evaluating Testimony**

1. Is the testimony relevant and recent?

2. Is the testimony truly representative of the source's position?

3. Is the source objective, unbiased, and an authority on the topic?

4. Has the proper kind of testimony—expert, prestige, or lay—been used?

production." The advertisement then appears: "'Brilliant,' says the *New York News!*" Be certain you are not guilty of such an ethical misdemeanor in your speeches.

Some sources may also have a vested interest in what they advocate. For example, a doctor who promotes vitamin therapy may be the part-owner of a company that sells vitamins. If you rely on such a source in your speech, it could damage your credibility.

In addition to these basic tests, you must also consider whether the type of testimony is appropriate for your purpose. Lay testimony can be used to humanize a speech and to provide a basis for identification. Prestige testimony can be used to enhance the general credibility of both speech and speaker, but only expert testimony should be used to demonstrate that a statement is factually true. If you are using expert testimony, be sure your source is an authority in the topic area. Expertise is topic-specific. The entire field of medicine is beyond the grasp of any one doctor, and no professor can lay claim to the entire range of human knowledge. Be certain that your source of testimony is qualified to speak on your topic.

## Using Testimony

Testimony can be a powerful form of support, but you should follow certain ethical and practical rules for its use. Be careful to quote or paraphrase your sources accurately. Have direct quotations written out on cards so that you can read them, rather than relying on memory. Use testimony from more than one source, especially when your topic is controversial or there is a possibility of bias. Find the most up-to-date testimony available, and emphasize its recency. As you introduce testimony into your speech, point out the qualifications of your sources so that you establish their credibility. A transition, such as "According to . . ." or "In the latest issue of . . . ," leads gracefully into such material. You can find much useful information about your sources in the biographical resources mentioned in Chapter 5.

## ▶ EXAMPLES

Examples bring a speech to life. Just as pictures serve as graphic illustrations for a printed text, **examples** serve as verbal illustrations for an oral message. In fact, some scholars prefer the term *illustration* to *example.* The word *illustration* derives from the Latin *illustrare,* which means "to shed light" or "to make bright." Good examples illuminate the message of your speech, making it clearer and more vivid for your audience.

In addition to clarifying ideas, examples can also arouse attention and sustain interest. They bring a sense of reality to a speech by the simple concrete applications they provide. In effect, examples demonstrate that what you have said either has happened or could happen. Speakers acknowledge these functions when they say, "Let me give you an example." Similarly, examples may be used to personalize your topic and to humanize both you and your message. Fred Krupp, executive director of the Environmental Defense Fund, used this personal example in a speech presented at an Environmental Marketing Communications Forum:

> Thank you for the kind introduction. I'm a little surprised that you left out my most important qualifying credential. I have three small sons—ages 7, 4, and 14 months. So I do know a great deal about cleaning up after environmental disasters.[11]

Examples about people give the audience someone with whom they can identify, thus involving them in the speech. Personalized examples help the audience to experience the meaning of your ideas, not simply to understand them. Examples that point out common experiences, beliefs, or values also help to bridge gaps in cultural understanding.

Examples may also be used for emphasis. When you make a statement and follow it with an example, you are pointing out that what you have just said is IMPORTANT. Examples amplify your ideas. They say to the audience, "This bears repeating." Examples are especially helpful when you introduce new, complex, or abstract material. Not only can they make such information clearer, they also allow time for the audience to digest and understand what you have said before you move on to your next point.

Examples are especially useful in speech introductions and conclusions. In introductions, examples help the speaker gain attention. In conclusions, they can help give the speech lasting effectiveness because they are easily remembered. Dianne Feinstein, former mayor of San Francisco, opened a speech with the following example to illustrate an outdated perspective of the role of women in politics:

> About thirty years ago, Senator Margaret Chase Smith was asked by
> *Time* magazine what she would do if one day she woke up in the White

House. She replied that she would apologize to Bess Truman and leave immediately.[12]

By using this example Mayor Feinstein did more than just arouse interest. She also lightened the mood of the audience and suggested that for women things had indeed changed for the better. Examples often carry more meaning than their simplicity would suggest. They are equally as effective as support for the main points in your speech. Use them to emphasize a point or to increase understanding.

### Types of Examples

Examples take different forms, and these forms have different functions. An example may be brief or extended and may be based either on an actual event or on something that might have happened.

*Brief Examples.*  A **brief example** mentions a specific instance to demonstrate a more general statement. Brief examples are concise and to the point. Often a speaker will use several of them together. They may be juxtaposed to demonstrate comparison and contrast, as in the following example on teen-age pregnancy:

> Teen-age pregnancy occurs among the rich and the poor. Take Mary Thompson. Mary's father was one of the town's leading doctors, and she lived in a five-bedroom home in Steir Park. She had a child at fifteen. In another case, Janet Reese delivered when she was sixteen. Her father was a sanitation worker, and she grew up in a two-room shack next to the stockyards. Youthful pregnancy does not respect status. There is no group in our society that is not cursed by it. Indeed, we can safely say that teen-age pregnancy is an equal-opportunity disaster.

Brief examples provide support by extending the meaning of an idea. As a rule they refer to something that is more concrete and familiar to the audience than the statement they demonstrate.

*Extended Examples.*  An **extended example** contains more detail and allows you to dwell more fully on a single instance. Our student speaker could have described a teen-age mother with an extended example like the one that follows:

> Alicia Thomas is fifteen years and ten months old. She lives with her mother, father, and younger brother in suburban Bellaire. Alicia is a sophomore at Clearwater Preparatory School. Like many other fifteen-year-old girls, Alicia wears braces. Like many other fifteen-year-old girls, Alicia loves rock music and MTV. Like many other fifteen-year-old girls, Alicia spends a lot of time on the phone. But while most girls her age are looking forward to getting their driver's licenses, Alicia is looking forward

to something else. You see, Alicia is six months pregnant. She is looking forward to being out of school for a year and to the heartbreak of giving her baby up for adoption.

This extended example gives us enough detail that we feel we know Alicia. It allows the speaker to make two indirect points: first, teen-age pregnancies are not confined to the poor, uneducated segments of our society; and second, teen-age pregnancies are deeply disruptive to the lives of young girls. Also, the extended example permits the speaker to convey feeling about a topic that might be lost if the speech relied solely on brief examples.

*Factual Examples.* As the name implies, a **factual example** is based on a real event or person. In the preceding extended example, Alicia could be the cousin of the speaker, a friend or neighbor, or even someone the speaker read about in a newspaper or magazine article. The important consideration is that Alicia is an actual person (whose name may have been changed to protect her identity). Factual examples provide strong support for any assertion because they ground the point you are making in reality. If the speaker's association with topics is direct — when you actually know the persons involved as opposed simply to having read about them — the factual examples are even stronger.

Mark Thompson used a factual example in a classroom speech to define the meaning of generosity:

> Generosity? I'll tell you what it means. Last week, tennis champion Arthur Ashe died — one more innocent victim of AIDS. Yesterday, a retired secretary and grandmother who is dying of lung cancer in Brooklyn gave $400,000 to St. Jude Children's Research Hospital to help create the Arthur Ashe Chair for Pediatric AIDS Research. She wanted his name remembered, not hers. We know only that she is a person "of very modest means" who received the money in a malpractice suit when doctors failed to recognize her symptoms of cancer. She wanted to reach out to children who, like her, are fighting terminal illness.
>
> While she remains anonymous, this obscure woman is a champion too — a champion of the human spirit. She has given us a gift far more precious than her money.

*Hypothetical Examples.* Examples need not be real to be effective. The **hypothetical example** is a composite of actual people, situations, or events. Although invented by the speaker, it represents reality. It is a fiction that may open the door to truth even better than a factual example. Velva White used such a hypothetical example to illustrate the concept of poverty:

> Let me tell you about Mary Jones. Mary lives in a shack that backs up to what the newspaper calls "Sugar Ditch." But that's not what the residents call it. Because none of the houses in the area have inside plumbing, raw

sewage is often dumped into the ditch. That's where it gets the name residents use. Mary, her sister Jasmine, Mary's four children, and Jasmine's two children all live in this three-room shack. The outside walls are covered with tarpaper. Inside, wadded-up newspapers are jammed into cracks to keep out the cold winter winds. An old pot-bellied stove provides heat and a way for Mary to cook. Does Mary Jones exist? Yes and no. There is not *a* Mary Jones, but there are *many* Mary Joneses in Pottsville and in other towns and cities in our nation. We all pay the price for the way they must live.

Hypothetical examples must be true to the reality they represent. To satisfy ethical standards, their hypothetical nature must be acknowledged in the speech ("There is not *a* Mary Jones but there are *many* Mary Joneses. . . ."). They work best and are most ethical when they accompany and bring to life facts and figures and testimony that demonstrate that the situation they illustrate does indeed exist.

### Evaluating Examples

Just as information and testimony must be relevant and representative, so must examples. You should not have to strain to make them fit. If you feel you have to explain their relevance, then the examples are probably not very useful. Examples must also be representative. They should reflect what is typical, or they will not seem plausible to your audience. The more incredible your examples, the more you must buttress them with factual information or expert testimony.

You should also consider whether examples will be interesting and memorable. They should meet acceptable standards of tact and taste and fit the mood and spirit of the occasion. You should risk offending listeners only when you have no other choice — only when listeners must be shocked before they can be informed or persuaded.

### Using Examples

Examples often make a difference between a speech that is humdrum and one that is quite successful. Use examples in your speeches to clarify the meaning of technical or abstract ideas. Bring your examples to life by being as specific as possible. Use contrasting examples, following an *it is this, not this* (or *it is not this, but this*) pattern, to dramatize the meaning of a point. Highlight the authenticity of your examples by providing the names of people, places, and institutions. It is much easier for a listener to relate to Matt Dunn of the local General Motors plant than to some anonymous worker in an unnamed company. Use transitions to move smoothly from statement to example and example to statement. Phrases such as "For instance . . ." or "As you can see . . ." work very nicely. Finally, use examples selectively to emphasize and clarify statements of major importance.

## NARRATIVES

The **narrative** goes beyond the example by *telling a story* within the speech — narratives have plot lines. Because people love stories and get caught up in the action, narratives — perhaps more than any other technique — can capture and hold attention and demonstrate the meaning of what the speaker is trying to communicate. A narrative may be remembered long after the rest of the speech is forgotten.

Narration has a considerable history in public discourse. Aesop's fables have long warned children of the dangers of pride and deception. Jesus used parables to illustrate moral lessons: the parable of the Good Samaritan exemplifies compassion. Narratives usually invite audiences to discover the "truth" for themselves. With narratives the audience becomes involved in the creation of the message — it becomes *their* discovery, *their* truth. Such involvement enhances the impact of the message. Personal narratives are especially powerful because they increase identification between speaker and audience.[13] After the story told in the opening of this chapter, of how Matthew Miller's "dealin'" friend died in his arms, the bond of sympathetic identification between Matthew and his listeners was strong indeed.

A well-told story creates anticipation and suspense and brings a sense of concreteness to abstract concepts or principles. Narratives function like a speech within a speech, beginning with an attention-arousing introduction, continuing with a body in which the story develops, and ending with a conclusion that reinforces the point in question.

Narratives are frequently used as the introduction to a longer speech because they actively involve the audience with the topic. Bonnie Marshall, a student at Heidelberg College and a finalist in the 1991 Houghton Mifflin public speaking contest, began her speech with the following story:

*Narratives help capture and hold the attention of an audience, adding the force of drama to speeches and inviting audience involvement. Mario Cuomo, Governor of the state of New York, is known for his effective use of narratives in speeches.*

Harry Smith was a cranky, obstinate old farmer. He loved bowling, Glenn Miller music, and "Monday Night Football." He was also dying of cancer of the esophagus, which had metastasized to his lungs. Harry didn't like doctors, and he liked hospitals and modern medicine even less. He used to say that he could remember when three square meals, Mom's mustard plaster, and an occasional house call from Doc Jones were all anyone ever needed to stay healthy. Harry didn't want to live in pain, and he hated being dependent on anyone else. Yet like so many others, he never expressed his wishes to his family.

When Harry's illness became so debilitating that he could no longer speak for himself, his family stepped in to make decisions regarding his medical care. His children, out of a sense of guilt over the things they had done and the love they hadn't expressed, refused to let Harry die. He was subjected to ventilators, artificial feedings, and all the wizardry modern medicine can offer. Harry did die eventually, but only after months of agony with no hope of recovery.

Harry's doctor, my husband, agonized too over the decisions regarding Harry's medical care. He knew the children were acting out of a sense of guilt rather than for Harry's benefit, yet because Harry had never documented his wishes, his doctor had no choice but to subject him to the senseless torture he didn't want.

This narrative created the emotional climate in which Bonnie's speech, "Ensuring Your Right to Die," could appropriately develop.

Narratives within the body of the speech are helpful in illustrating abstract concepts that are difficult to define in any other way. They are especially useful in ceremonial speeches, where they also help keep alive the memories and meanings of significant events. President Reagan illustrated these uses of narration in a speech delivered at Pointe du Hoc, Normandy, as a D-Day memorial to the Allied forces who fought there during World War II:

> At dawn, on the morning of the 6th of June, 1944, 225 Rangers jumped off the British landing craft and ran to the bottom of these cliffs. Their mission was one of the most difficult and daring of the invasion: to climb these sheer and desolate cliffs and take out the enemy guns. The Allies had been told that some of the mightiest of these guns were here and they would be trained on the beaches to stop the Allied advance.
>
> The Rangers looked up and saw the enemy soldiers [at] the edge of the cliffs shooting down at them with machine guns and throwing grenades. And the American Rangers began to climb. They shot rope ladders over the face of these cliffs and began to pull themselves up. When one Ranger fell, another would take his place. When one rope was cut, a Ranger would grab another and begin his climb again. They climbed, shot back, and held their footing. Soon, one by one, the Rangers pulled themselves over the top, and in seizing the firm land at the top of these cliffs, they began to seize back the continent of Europe.
>
> Two hundred and twenty-five came here. After two days of fighting, only 90 could still bear arms.[14]

Concluding narratives leave the audience with something to remember and extend the impact of a message. They can establish a mood that will last long after the last words have been spoken. In a speech to the Rotarians of Murray, Utah, David Archambault, Lakota Sioux and president of the American Indian College Fund, used the following narrative as part of his conclusion:

> More than 100 years ago, our great chief Sitting Bull was murdered. His people — frightened that they too would be killed — set out on foot across South Dakota along with Chief Big Foot. Carrying their children, they fled across the frozen prairie through the bitter subzero cold 200 miles to seek refuge on the Pine Ridge reservation in southwestern South Dakota.
>
> On December 29, 1890, near a creek now known to all the world as Wounded Knee, Chief Big Foot and his followers were massacred. No one knows who fired first, but when the shooting was over, nearly 300 Indians — men, women, and children — lay dead and dying across the valley. Their bodies were dumped into a mass grave. The survivors were unable to hold a burial ceremony, a ceremony we call the wiping away of tears. It meant the living could never be free.

On the 100th anniversary of the massacre at Wounded Knee, several hundred of us on horseback retraced the journey of Big Foot and his band during those final days. We arrived at dawn at the site of the mass grave at Wounded Knee and completed the wiping of tears ceremony. The Si Tanka Wokiksuye, the Chief Big Foot Memorial Ride, was a mourning ritual that released the spirits of our ancestors and closed a tragic chapter in our history.

We have the opportunity now to help rebuild our nation. And I do not mean just the Indian nations. On this 500th anniversary of Columbus's voyages, we together can build a better America, a nation enriched by the diversity of its people and strengthened by the values that bring us together as a community.[15]

Some narratives directly involve the audience in the story by making them part of the action. Speakers can create this kind of effect by beginning with "Picture yourself in the following situation . . ." or "Imagine that you are. . . ." The direct assignment of a role within a narrative tends to increase audience involvement with the topic.

In a narrative, **dialogue** is almost always preferable to **paraphrase.** When speakers use dialogue, they reproduce conversation directly. When they paraphrase, they summarize what was said. Paraphrasing can save time, but it can also rob a narrative of power and authenticity. Let people speak for themselves in your narratives. The late Senator Sam Ervin of North Carolina was a master storyteller. Note how he used dialogue in the following narrative, which opened a speech on the Constitution and our judicial system:

Jim's administrator was suing the railroad for his wrongful death. The first witness he called to the stand testified as follows: "I saw Jim walking up the track. A fast train passed, going up the track. After it passed, I didn't see Jim. I walked up the track a little way and discovered Jim's severed head lying on one side of the track, and the rest of his body on the other." The witness was asked how he reacted to his gruesome discovery. He responded: "I said to myself, 'Something serious must have happened to Jim.'"

Something serious has been happening to constitutional government in America. I want to talk to you about it.[16]

Had "Mr. Sam" paraphrased this story as "The witness reported that he knew instantly that the victim had had a serious accident," he would have destroyed its effect. Dialogue makes a narrative come alive by bringing listeners close to the action. Paraphrase distances the audience.

### Evaluating Narratives

You evaluate narratives in much the same way that you test examples. First, you should question whether the narrative is relevant to your purpose.

Speakers sometimes "borrow" a narrative from anthologies of stories or jokes and then have to strain to establish a connection between it and the topic. Narratives should never be used simply for the sake of telling a story or amusing your audience. An irrelevant narrative distracts your audience and may even overpower your actual message.

You should also consider whether the narrative fairly represents the point you wish to make. Is the story typical, or have you selected one that is an exception to the rule? Ethical considerations require that your narratives be representative. In addition, they must seem plausible to the audience. The characters should be believable and the dialogue realistic.

You must also be concerned about whether the narrative will seem appropriate. It should establish a mood consistent with the topic and meet acceptable standards of taste. Stay away from narratives that foster negative stereotypes or contain language your audience would find offensive. Finally, ask yourself whether the narrative will be interesting. If the audience has heard your story before, it may be hard to hold their attention. When in doubt, throw it out!

### Using Narratives

There is an art to telling a story well. Narratives are usually set off from the rest of a speech by oral or physical punctuation marks. For example, you might pause before beginning a narrative or even move physically closer to the audience. Voice and dialect changes may signal listeners that a "character" is speaking, not the actual speaker. Gestures and a change of pace may help convey the action and excitement of the story. Strive for an intimate style of presentation that creates a sense of closeness and good will between you and the audience. Good storytellers seem to be sharing a secret

**SPEAKER'S NOTES**

**Using Narratives**

1. Set the narrative off from the rest of your speech with oral or physical punctuation marks.

2. Strive for an intimate style of presentation.

3. Use colorful, concrete, active language and emphasize dialogue.

4. Avoid digressions, and be economical.

5. Save narratives for special moments. Don't let your speech become a string of loosely connected stories.

or an inside joke with listeners. This impression helps build ethos and establish identification.

The language you use should be colorful, concrete, and vivid. Some verbs convey a sense of action and character better than others. There is a considerable difference, for instance, between someone who "struts" down a street and one who simply "walks." Use active verbs. When the late baseball player and sports announcer Dizzy Dean said, "Bartkowski stole home!" he was using an active verb. Had he said, "Home was stolen by Bartkowski," the passive form would have robbed the sentence of its punch. Remember that in most cases using dialogue is better than paraphrasing.

Finally, be economical. Include only those details necessary to convey the proper mood and get your point across. Develop a linear, progressive form of storytelling. Begin with an introduction that excites curiosity; then develop the narrative in an orderly manner. Avoid digressions such as, "That reminds me . . ." or "Speaking of. . . ." Deliver your punch line with a punch! Don't let your conclusion simply dwindle away.

A well-told narrative can add much to a speech, but its use should be reserved for special occasions. Too many narratives can turn a speech into a rambling string of stories without focus. Use narratives to arouse or sustain attention, to convey a special mood for your message, or to demonstrate some important but abstract truth.

**IN SUMMARY**   Facts and figures, testimony, examples, and narratives are the supporting materials of successful speeches. They demonstrate the meaning and relevance of topics and help verify controversial statements and claims.

*Facts and Figures.*   Information in the form of facts and figures is a powerful type of support, particularly in American society. *Facts* are verifiable units of information, but they can be distorted when speakers interpret them. It is always important to consider the source of your information in terms of its competence, trustworthiness, and acceptability to listeners. *Statistics* are numerical facts. *Descriptive statistics* may be used to describe the size and distribution of an object or occurrence. *Inferential statistics* are used for demonstrating relationships and predicting trends. They are based on probability estimates.

Evaluate information in terms of its relevance, recency, precision, reliability, and completeness. Ask yourself whether the facts and figures can stand alone, or whether you must supplement them with other supporting materials, such as testimony and example, to make them more effective. Have more facts and figures than you need so that you can be selective, and remember that facts and figures put probability — not certainty — on your side.

*Testimony.*   When you use *testimony,* you cite the ideas or words of others in support of your points. Testimony may employ either *verbatim* quotations or a *paraphrase* of what has been said. You can use *expert testimony* from recognized authorities to support the validity of ideas. *Prestige testimony* from well-known public figures can enhance the overall credibility of your speech. *Lay testimony* from peers can help humanize a topic and enhance identification.

Be sure that the sources you cite are objective and unbiased and that the type of testimony you use is appropriate to your purpose. Check to be certain that the experts you cite are speaking within the area of their competence. Be sure to state the qualifications of your sources, especially if these are not well known to listeners.

*Examples.* *Examples* serve as verbal illustrations for an oral message. They may be used to create and sustain interest, to clarify ideas, to aid in the retention of information, to personalize a topic, to provide emphasis, and to demonstrate the truth of your message. *Brief examples* extend the meaning of an idea by identifying specific instances in support of a statement. *Extended examples* contain more detail about a single instance and give the speaker more room to build impressions. *Factual examples* are based on something that actually happened or that really exists. *Hypothetical examples* are a synthesis of what might have happened, of probable persons and events. Use specific names to personalize examples and transitions to integrate examples into the orderly flow of ideas.

*Narratives.* *Narratives* are stories that illustrate some important truth about the topic and are an effective technique for involving the audience. Like good speeches, good narratives have a clear-cut beginning, body, and conclusion. They help establish a mood for a speech. Narratives should be told in language that is colorful and concrete. Active sentence structure and *dialogue* help a narrative come to life. A lively and informal style of presentation can enhance narration.

**TERMS TO KNOW**

| | |
|---|---|
| supporting materials | verbatim |
| facts | example |
| statistics | brief example |
| descriptive statistics | extended example |
| inferential statistics | factual example |
| testimony | hypothetical example |
| expert testimony | narrative |
| prestige testimony | dialogue |
| lay testimony | paraphrase |

**DISCUSSION**

1. Evaluate the use of testimony in two of the student speeches in Appendix B. Is there sufficient use of testimony? What types are used? Are they appropriate to the purpose? Do the speakers introduce source qualifications?

2. President Reagan was known as a speaker who used narrative very effectively. Find examples of his speeches in the *Weekly Compilation of Presidential Documents,* and study his use of narrative as supporting material. What vital functions did narrative perform for him? Did he rely too heavily on it? If so, how did this over-reliance weaken his speeches?

3. Select a speech from a recent issue of *Vital Speeches of the Day* that uses statistical information for support. What kind of statistics are used? Are they used effectively? Did the speaker supplement the statistical information with examples? Share your analysis with your classmates.

4. Look in newspapers or magazines for recent statements by public officials that purport to be factual but that may actually contain distortion. What tips you off to the distortion? Would most people be likely to detect this bias?

**APPLICATION**   1. Develop a hypothetical example or narrative to illustrate one of the following abstract concepts:

love

compassion

charity

welfare

justice

2. Note how television advertisements often give facts and figures, testimony, examples, or narratives in combination with visual aids. Using the criteria provided in this chapter and in Chapter 9, analyze and evaluate a current TV ad with respect to these techniques.

3. Determine which types of testimony might best support the following statements:
   a. Native Americans don't get a square deal in the United States.
   b. Campus security measures are inadequate.
   c. Teen-age pregnancy is a national disaster.
   d. We should open our ports and our hearts to the "boat people" of Haiti.
   e. The proper diet can help prevent cancer.
   f. Asian immigrant children are outperforming their American-born counterparts in public schools.
   g. Religious training is an important part of a child's development.
   h. The "greenhouse effect" poses a real danger to our future.

   Defend your choices in class.

**NOTES**   1. Richard Weaver, "Ultimate Terms in Contemporary Rhetoric," in *The Ethics of Rhetoric* (Chicago: Henry Regnery, 1953), pp. 211–232.

2. Adapted from *The 1992 Information Please Environmental Almanac* (Boston: Houghton Mifflin, 1992), p. 144.

3. For similar commentary on other periodicals, see Howard Kahane, *Logic and Contemporary Rhetoric: The Use of Reason in Everyday Life* (Belmont, Calif.: Wadsworth, 1984), pp. 337–338.

4. William L. Kissick, "Health Care in the '80s: Changes, Consequences and Choices," presented to the Greater Philadelphia Committee for Medical Pharmaceutical Sciences of the Philadelphia College of Physicians, Philadelphia, 26 Sept. 1985, in *Vital Speeches of the Day* 52 (15 Jan. 1986): 213.

5. Reported in Al Sicherman, "Playing the Odds: McGervey Estimates the Risks," *Memphis Commercial Appeal,* 30 Oct. 1989, p. C-1.

6. S. E. Taylor and S. C. Thompson, "Stalking the Elusive 'Vividness' Effect," *Psychological Review* 89 (1982): 155–181.

7. Bernice Cohen Sachs, M.D., "Changing Relationships Between Men and Women," presented to Medical Women's International Congress, Vancouver, B.C., 29 July–4 Aug. 1984, in *Vital Speeches of the Day* 50 (1 Oct. 1984): 757–762.

8. Geraldine Ferraro, "Acceptance Speech," presented at the Democratic National Convention, San Francisco, 19 July 1984, in *Vital Speeches of the Day* 50 (15 Aug. 1984): 644.

9. The power of lay testimony is one possible implication of Michael Calvin McGee's "In Search of the People: A Rhetorical Alternative," *Quarterly Journal of Speech* 61 (1975): 235–249.

10. Ronald Reagan, "Inaugural Address: Putting America Back to Work," presented in Washington, D.C., 20 Jan. 1981, in *Vital Speeches of the Day* 47 (15 Feb. 1981): 258–260.

11. Fred Krupp, "Business and the Third Wave: Saving the Environment," presented to the Environmental Marketing Communications Forum, New York, 12 Mar. 1992, in *Vital Speeches of the Day* 58 (15 Aug. 1992): 656.

12. Dianne Feinstein, "Women in Politics: Time for a Change," presented at Impact '84: A Leadership Conference for Democratic Women, Washington, D.C., 28 Sept. 1983.

13. For a detailed discussion of personal narratives, see Robert Coles, *The Call of Stories* (Boston: Houghton Mifflin, 1989); Kristin M. Langellier, "Personal Narratives: Perspectives on Theory and Research," *Text and Performance Quarterly* 9 (1989): 243–276.

14. Ronald Reagan, "Remarks to Veterans at Pointe du Hoc," Normandy, France, 6 June 1984, in *Weekly Compilation of Presidential Documents* 4 (11 June 1984): 841.

15. David Archambault, "Columbus Plus 500 Years: Whither the American Indian," *Vital Speeches of the Day* 58 (1 June 1992): 493.

16. Sam J. Ervin, Jr., "Judicial Verbicide: An Affront to the Constitution," presented at Herbert Law Center, Louisiana State University, Baton Rouge, 22 Oct. 1980, in *Representative American Speeches 1980–1981,* ed. Owen Peterson (New York: H. W. Wilson, 1981), p. 62.

*Every discourse ought to be a living creature; having a body of its own and head and feet; there should be a middle, beginning, and end, adapted to one another and to the whole.*

*—Plato*

# 7

# Structuring Your Speech

**This Chapter Will Help You**

- appreciate the importance of simplicity, symmetry, and orderliness in speech designs.

- determine your main points and arrange them effectively.

- use transitions to make your speech flow smoothly.

- develop introductions that capture attention, establish credibility, and preview your topic.

- prepare conclusions that summarize your speech, provide a sense of closure, and make a lasting impression on the audience.

*HISTORY 111*

THORNTON, PATRICIA    Professor Thornton's lectures are easy to understand and follow. She covers the most important material point by point, supplementing what is in the text with interesting examples. You don't have to re-organize your lecture notes to make sense of them. She helps you prepare for the departmental examinations.

KRAMER, ROBERT    Professor Kramer has a marvelous repertoire of funny stories. Unfortunately, these don't seem to tie in well with topics covered in the course. When test time comes, you're on your own. Don't rely on his lectures to help you understand the book or pass the exams. When he does cover the material, it's hard to follow him. He is so disorganized that you have problems figuring out where he's coming from and where he's going.

 ou plan to take History 111 this term. At registration, members of Students for Better Education distributed the above evaluations, which demonstrate how important structure is in public communication. When ideas are being explored, most of us will choose the speaker who is well organized and easy to follow over the entertainer. Communication research has confirmed that not only are disorganized messages more difficult to understand, they also negatively affect the way we perceive the speaker.[1] A well-structured message helps convey the message of the speech *and* build the speaker's ethos.

In this chapter we look at the principles that explain why people prefer well-organized messages. We then use these principles to examine the structure of the body of the speech. Next, we consider how to use transitions to connect the different parts of a speech into a cohesive, smoothly flowing finished product. Finally, we discuss how to prepare effective introductions and conclusions.

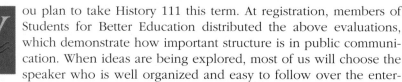 **PRINCIPLES OF GOOD FORM**

The structure of a speech should follow the way people naturally see and arrange things in their minds. According to the Gestalt psychologists, we organize experience according to certain basic perceptual principles.[2] The primary principle of structure is the idea of **good form,** which is based on simplicity, symmetry, and orderliness. You can build good form into your speeches by presenting your material as clearly and simply as possible, developing a well-balanced presentation, and arranging your main points so that they seem to lead naturally from one to another.

### *Simplicity*

*Simple designs are preferable to elaborate designs in public speaking.* Public speaking is based on the sharing of ideas, information, or advice. The more complex your message, the greater the burden of understanding you place upon listeners. You can achieve structural **simplicity** by limiting the number of main points in your speech and by keeping each point short and direct.

***The Number of Main Points.*** In general, the fewer main points you have, the better. Keep in mind that each main point of your message must be bolstered by supporting materials. Information, examples, narratives, and testimony take up time during presentation. Short classroom speeches (under ten minutes) usually should not have more than three main points. Even longer speeches outside the classroom, those that may last up to an hour, should not normally attempt more than five main points. Consider what happens when a speech becomes overburdened with main points:

*Thematic statement:* Government welfare programs aren't working.
*Main points:*
- I. There are too many programs.
- II. The programs often duplicate coverage.
- III. Some people who really need help are left out.
- IV. They are underfunded.
- V. They waste money.
- VI. Recipients have no input into what is really needed.
- VII. The programs create dependence and stifle initiative.
- VIII. They rob the poor of self-respect.

Each of these points may be important, but presented in this way, they could be overwhelming. The audience would have problems remembering them because there are too many ideas and they are not organized into a meaningful pattern. Let's see how these ideas can be clustered into a simpler structural pattern:

*Thematic statement:* Our approach to welfare in America is inadequate, inefficient, and insensitive.
*Main point:*  I. Our approach is inadequate.
*Subpoints:*
    A. We don't fund it sufficiently.
    B. Some people who need help get left out.
*Main point:*  II. Our approach is inefficient.
*Subpoints:*
    A. There are too many programs and too much duplication.
    B. Money is wasted.
*Main point:*  III. Our approach is insensitive.
*Subpoints:*
    A. It creates dependence and stifles initiative.
    B. It robs people of self-respect.

This simpler structure will make the speech easier to follow. The ideas have been arranged so that the general main points follow each other in a logical pattern of development. The main points break down into more specific subpoints that extend and explain their meaning. Overlapping points have been combined and unnecessary ideas omitted. The audience will more likely remember the thrust of the message.[3]

***The Phrasing of Main Points.***    You also should word your main points as simply as possible. In the preceding example not only has the number of main points been reduced, but the wording of these points has been made clear and direct. Parallel phrasing has been used for emphasis. This strategic repetition helps listeners remember the message. It also allows the speaker to refer to the "Three *I*s" (Inadequate, Inefficient, and Insensitive) of welfare in the introduction and conclusion, which should help the audience remember the message.

To achieve structural simplicity, be sure your specific purpose, thematic statement, and main points are very clear to you so that you can express them succinctly. Keep in mind that some of the world's most magnificent structures are simple in design. Greek temples, which have been admired for thousands of years, are models of simplicity that impress observers with their strength, grandeur, and beauty. Think of simplicity as a major goal when building your speech.

### Symmetry

**Symmetry** means proper balance. In a well-balanced speech all the major parts — the introduction, body, and conclusion — receive the right amount of emphasis and fit together smoothly. Proper emphasis depends upon the *timing* of the various parts of your speech. The sense of proper fit, or *coherence,* involves the logical relationship between parts.

***Timing the Speech.***    Instructors frequently time speeches that are presented in class, so you must plan your message with those time limitations in mind. It can be very disconcerting to find yourself finishing the first main point of your speech with only one minute left and two more main points to go. Outside the classroom, working within time limits is equally important. If you are asked to present a fifteen-minute report on a work project and instead take thirty minutes, you risk a poor reception. Time yourself as you practice, cutting and adding material to maintain the proper balance.

There is no clear rule of thumb that establishes time limits for the major parts of speeches. However, the following suggestions may be helpful:

1. *The body should be the longest part.* The body contains the essence of your message — the major ideas you want to communicate. If you spend three minutes on your introduction, a minute and a half on the body, and thirty seconds on the conclusion, your speech will seem badly out of balance.

2. *Your main points should be balanced with respect to time.* You might follow a principle of *equality,* in which each main point receives the same amount of attention. Or you could follow a principle of *progression,* in

which successive main points receive increasing attention proportionate to their importance to your specific purpose. For example, to show that they build in importance, the first main point might receive one minute; the second, one and a half minutes; and the third, two minutes.

3. *The introduction and conclusion should be approximately equal in length.* Neither should seem abrupt, nor should either seem overly prolonged. The total amount of time spent on the introduction and conclusion should be less than that spent on the body of your speech.

***Making the Speech Coherent.*** The coherence of a speech depends on how well the individual parts relate to each other. You should structure the body of your speech first so that you can be certain that your introduction and conclusion fit what you have to say. Your speech is also more coherent when you can tie together the introduction and conclusion. If the introduction asked a question, the conclusion could repeat the question and then supply an answer based on ideas from the speech. Or, if you began with a story of defeat, your conclusion might offer a related story of victory. As you move from introduction to body, from point to point within the body, and from the body to the conclusion, transitions help listeners see the overall logical pattern of the speech.

### *Orderliness*

**Orderliness** calls for a methodical or consistent pattern of development in your speech. For example, if you want to propose a solution to a problem, you would first present the problem and then the solution. Why would you organize this way? Simply because this is how our minds typically work. We usually don't think first of solutions, then go in search of problems to fit them. This type of natural processing also explains the order of a question followed by an answer. We don't usually come up with answers, and then look for their questions. Several other principles are also helpful in ordering the main points in the body of your speech. We discuss them in the next section.

## STRUCTURING THE BODY OF YOUR SPEECH

The body of your speech contains the *substance* of what you have to say. It is where you pursue your purposes and develop your thematic statement. Because the body does the important work of your speech, you should organize it first, and then prepare the introduction and conclusion so that they reinforce it. In developing the body, you have three major tasks to accomplish:

1. You must determine what main points you will make.

2. You must arrange these points in the most effective order.

3. You must decide how to use supporting material to substantiate these points.

## Determining Your Main Points

Preparing a speech is like building a bridge over a canyon so that communication can cross between speaker and listener. Each main point should be a pillar that supports the bridge. As you do your research, you will find that certain ideas are stressed and repeated in the material you read or in the interviews you conduct. These ideas represent the most vital concerns and issues connected with your topic. By reflecting on them and how they affect your listeners, you can decide on the specific purpose and thematic statement of your speech. Shaped by your purpose, these featured ideas may well become the main points of your speech.

Let's look at how you might determine the main points for a speech on selecting a personal computer. To get the best overall picture, prepare a **research overview** that lists the main sources of information and the major ideas from each source identified on your information and source cards, as discussed in Chapter 5. Figure 7.1 presents an overview based on personal experience, an article in *Consumer Reports,* a buyer's guide to personal computers, and an interview with the director of the computer lab on campus.

To find your main points, you would look for repeated ideas or themes across the sources or any information which might be especially relevant for your audience. You might come up with the following themes (the initials refer to column headings in Figure 7.1):

1. Match the computer to your needs [PE 5; CR 1, 2, 5, and 6; BG all; I 1, 2, and 3].
2. Check compatibility with campus equipment and services [I 3].
3. Investigate dependability and service [CR 3 and 4; I 4, 5, and 6].

Constructing main points out of these themes now becomes relatively easy:

I. Determine your needs and which computers might best serve them.
II. Check for compatibility with campus services.
III. Consider the dependability of the computer and the availability of service.

## Arranging Your Main Points

Once you have determined your main points, you must decide how to arrange them in your speech. You need to come up with a way of ordering them that makes sense to your audience, is easy to follow, fits your material, and helps you realize your purpose. As you consider the order of your main points, remember the principles of good form: simplicity, symmetry, and orderliness. Additional Gestalt principles that will help you structure the body of your speech include proximity, similarity, and closure. In this section we discuss basic speech designs as they relate to the way people process information. More detailed examples of speech designs may be found in the chapters on informative and persuasive speaking.

| *Personal Experience* | *Consumer Reports* | *Buyer's Guide* | *Interview* |
|---|---|---|---|
| 1. Early wrong ideas I had. | 1. Determine how you will use the computer. | 1. Compare costs versus features. | 1. Your major will affect your uses and needs. |
| 2. How I started shopping. | 2. Buy what you will need for your uses. | 2. Decide what features you need/want. | 2. Can you upgrade or expand system? |
| 3. How I got on the right track. | 3. Check for local dealer service and assistance. | 3. Check software costs. | 3. What services does your campus offer? Will your computer be compatible? |
| 4. Talks with friends about problems and servicing. | 4. Check dependability/repair record. | | 4. Try to talk with other campus users re: programs and service. |
| 5. How the computer has helped me. | 5. Determine if you can upgrade equipment. | | 5. Check for training/trouble-shooting help. |
| | 6. Find out what peripherals are available. | | 6. Check out company, time in business, service if you move. |

FIGURE 7.1    Sample Research Overview

***Principle of Proximity.***    The **principle of proximity** suggests that things occurring close together in time or space should be presented in the order in which they normally occur. If you are describing a process that involves three steps, you need to present these steps using a *sequential design* that follows a chronological pattern. If you want to discuss events that led to a present-day problem, you might use a historical design. Your research may show that the major incidents occurred in 1945, 1962, and 1975. If you follow this natural pattern, your speech will be easy to understand. But if you start talking about 1975, then jump back to 1945, then leap ahead to the present before doubling back to 1962, you will probably lose most of your listeners on one of these abrupt turns. You will have violated the principle of proximity.

If you are preparing a speech describing the scenic wonders of Yellowstone Park, your speech might best follow a *spatial design*. Such a design is based on physical relationships, such as east-west, up-down, or points around a circle. You might begin with your audience at the south visitor's center, take them up the west side to Old Faithful, continue north to Mammoth Hot Springs, then down the east side through the Grand Canyon of the Yellowstone. This way your audience gets a verbal map to follow as well as a picture of the major attractions in the park.

***Principle of Similarity.*** The **principle of similarity** implies that people group together things that seem alike. This natural tendency underlies the *categorical design* for organizing speeches. Speakers use categorical designs when they discuss "three ways to stop smoking" or "the four characteristics of a good stereo system." Categories can be used to group *similar terms, concepts, or notions,* such as types of diets, or they can be used to represent *major divisions that exist in topics themselves,* such as the symptoms of a disease. Socrates may have been thinking of categories when he advised speakers to divide subjects "according to the natural formation, where the joint is, not breaking any part as a bad carver might."[4]

You also can use a categorical design to talk about a person. For example, you might believe that the public image of Gloria Steinem has been distorted by poor press coverage; therefore, you decide to present a speech that will help the audience understand her feminism. You decide on a categorical design so that you can emphasize the factors leading to her activism. In such a design you might consider (a) personal and family events, (b) professional events, and (c) political events. These categories generate the main points of your speech:

| | |
|---|---|
| *Specific purpose:* | To inform my audience of critical events that contributed to Gloria Steinem's feminism. |
| *Thematic statement:* | To understand why Gloria Steinem is a feminist, one must examine the personal, professional, and political events that shaped her life. |
| *Main points:* | I. Ms. Steinem's personal life laid the basis for her feminism. |
| | II. Ms. Steinem's professional activities exposed her to sexual harassment. |
| | III. Ms. Steinem's political experiences subjected her to discrimination.[5] |

***Principle of Closure.*** We like to have processes and patterns completed so that we know the "whole story." This tendency explains the **principle of closure.** Have you ever gotten engrossed in a magazine article in a waiting room only to find that someone had torn out the last page of the story? Can you remember the annoyance you felt? Your need for closure had been frustrated.

The principle of closure suggests that we like to have patterns in speeches completed. If you omit an important category when developing your topic, listeners may notice its omission. If you leave out an important step in a sequence, audiences often sense the flaw. Although all speeches should satisfy this need, there are two speech designs for which closure is essential. These are *cause-effect* and *problem-solution* speeches. Because we need the world to seem purposeful, coherent, and controllable, we prefer that all events have clear causes and all problems have solutions.

A cause-effect speech can go in two directions: it can begin by focusing on a present situation and then seek its causes, or it can look at the present as a potential cause of future effects. Sometimes these variations can be combined. You might take a current situation such as the budget deficit and develop a speech tracing its origins. If you had enough time, you might continue by predicting the future effects of the deficit. Understanding the causes could help your listeners see what needs to be done to reduce the deficit. Predicting future effects might make them *want* to reduce it. No matter which variation you use, the principle of closure suggests that you should include *both* the causes and effects in your speech.

The problem-solution design is closely related to the cause-effect design, and the two are often used in combination. The problem-solution design focuses the audience's attention on a problem and then provides a solution to it. Such speeches often use motivational appeals to bring the problem home to listeners. Once you have aroused strong feelings, your solutions must promise to satisfy them, or the audience will feel frustrated and resentful. Returning to our previous example, the budget deficit could be presented as a problem, a threat to national security and the well-being of future generations. The speaker then would look to the causes of the problem to find a solution. *Both* problem and solution must be discussed to satisfy listeners' need for closure.

---

**SPEAKER'S NOTES**

### Determining and Arranging Your Main Points

1. Review your research notes to identify repeated ideas for possible main points.

2. Select as main points those ideas most relevant to your specific purpose and most appropriate for your audience.

3. Limit the number of main points to three for a short speech and five for a longer effort.

4. Use the principle of proximity to arrange main points as they naturally occur in sequential or spatial patterns.

5. Apply the principle of similarity to arrange main points in a categorical design.

6. Use the principle of closure to assure completeness in cause-effect and problem-solution designs.

## Selecting Your Supporting Materials

Once you have determined and arranged your main points, you must decide how to develop and support them. As you develop your main points, you must consider whether you need to break them down into subpoints. The subpoints must be established for listeners to understand and accept the main point. For example, if you want to develop the main point "My plan for dealing with hazardous waste materials is both workable and cost-efficient," you would need to establish your subpoints on workability and cost to get listeners to agree with your main point. To support your main points, you must strengthen them or their subpoints with supporting materials. In the example just mentioned, you could support your subpoint on workability by using examples of neighboring communities that successfully used a similar plan. You might even develop a before-and-after narrative to tell the story of how one nearby community improved its handling of such materials. To convince listeners on the cost subpoint, you could use striking facts and expert testimony. At the end of this process of development and support, the main point should stand as a reasonable conclusion.

Viewed in terms of speech structure, supporting materials provide answers to the practical questions, such as

1. Why do you say that? On what basis can you make that statement? (*facts and figures*)
2. How do you know for sure? Who else says so? (*testimony*)
3. I don't quite understand. How does it work? Where is it true? (*example*)
4. Why should I be interested? (*narrative*)

Main points that are grounded securely in supporting materials make the bridge of communication possible: they can carry a message across the canyons of misunderstanding or suspicion that may separate speakers and audiences. On the other hand, an undeveloped main point will not carry much weight.

There is no easy answer to the question of how much or what kind of supporting material effectively establishes a main point. The following guidelines, however, may help:

1. *The more controversial the point you wish to make, the more you should use "hard" supporting material, such as statistical evidence and expert testimony.* When experts disagree on a subject or when expert opinion contradicts the ideas held by your audience, you must have more supporting material. "Dr. Jensen claims that the Japanese have developed a superior standard of living, but three other experts disagree. Let us consider their arguments. . . ." Verifiable facts and figures add objectivity and authority to a controversy. Yukio Matsuyama, former chief writer and member of the editorial board of the *Asahi Shimbun* (newspaper), chose

several "hard" facts to make his point about comparative living standards in Japan and the United States: "Did you know that you have to pay nearly 150 dollars — not yen — for a taxi from the center of Tokyo to Narita Airport, and once there, a government toll of 15 dollars for using the airport facilities? If such a thing were to happen in Boston, it might cause another Boston Tea Party!"[6]

2. *The more complex or abstract a point, the more you should use examples as supporting materials.* Bare statistics are especially difficult to understand when presented in speeches, so you should supplement such information with examples that make the meaning clear. To heighten understanding, examples often use comparison and contrast to relate the abstract to the concrete and the unknown to the known. Calling an earthquake a "burp of the earth" — as was heard during media discussions of the 1989 California quake that rocked San Francisco — illustrates this principle in miniature. Visual aids may also help clarify complex points.

3. *The more you ask from your listeners, the more you must reassure them with supporting material.* You should introduce expert testimony the audience will find impressive and credible, and cite prestige authorities the audience already knows, trusts, and respects. Lay testimony may also reassure listeners because it comes from people like them. Note the combination of these forms of testimony in the following student speech:

> Yes, paying more at the gas pump will be painful, but Dr. Morton Friedman, head of environmental sciences at our university, told me in an interview Monday that the president's new program to clean up and cool off the environment will work, if we can just afford it. In your responses to my questionnaire last week, most of you indicated you were willing to pay more in gas taxes, *if* the money were invested in a program of sound environmental management. We have plans for such a program, and the time to enact it is long past due. Thirty years ago, John F. Kennedy warned us: "The nation's battle to preserve the common estate is far from won." What would Kennedy say if he were here today? I think he would say, "Let's get the lead out of the struggle for a better environment."

4. *The less expertise you bring to an issue, the more you need abundant supporting material.* Although your classmates may like you, your personal opinion on such matters as environmental policy may not carry much weight with them. To speak credibly on complex topics, your ideas should be buttressed with the best and most recent information and with powerful combinations of testimony, such as we saw in the previous example.

5. *The further a subject is from the lives of your listeners, the more you must use examples and narratives that build identification and human interest.*

The impact of drought on human life in Africa cannot be conveyed by numbers alone. Only vivid images created by using examples or by telling the stories of people involved will bring the issues closer to home.

Although the situation varies from topic to topic, speaker to speaker, and audience to audience, it is possible to set up an *ideal model* for the support of each main point. That model includes the main point plus the following supporting materials (not necessarily in this order):

- the most important relevant facts and figures
- the most authoritative judgments about a situation, made by sources the audience will respect
- at least one interesting story or example that helps humanize and clarify the situation

Figure 7.2 provides a model outline format for supporting a main point. Let us look at how this model actually could work in a speech. Assume that you want to demonstrate that suntans are not a sign of good health. Here is one way you could use supporting materials to develop this point:

| | |
|---|---|
| *Statement:* | Suntans are not as "good" *for* you as they look *on* you. |
| *Transition:* | Let's examine some of the evidence. |
| *Facts/statistics:* | According to a 1989 report of the American Cancer Society, prolonged exposure without protection is responsible for about 90 percent of all skin cancers. |

Statement:_____

   Transition into facts or statistics:_____

     1. Factual information or statistics to support statement:_____

     _____

     _____

   Transition into testimony: _____

     2. Expert, prestige, or lay testimony to support statement: _____

     _____

     _____

   Transition into example or narrative: _____

     3. Example or narrative to support statement:_____

     _____

     _____

   Transition into restatement: _____

   Restatement of original assertion: _____

_____

**FIGURE 7.2
Outline Format for
Supporting a Point**

| | |
|---|---|
| *Transition:* | Moreover, radiation also accelerates the aging process. |
| *Expert testimony:* | According to Dr. John M. Knox, head of dermatology at the Baylor University College of Medicine, "If you do biopsies on the buttocks of people ages seventy-five and thirty-five, you won't see any differences under the microscope . . . protected skin stays youthful much longer." |
| *Transition:* | Let's look at one person who suffered the effects of overexposure. |
| *Narrative:* | Jane was a fair-skinned blond-haired girl who loved the sun as a child and teen-ager. She would sunburn often but didn't think there would be any effects other than the short-term pain. Lying in the sun seemed so healthy and appealing, she didn't dream it could harm her. Now at forty-five, she knows better. She couldn't believe her ears when her doctor said she had skin cancer. She felt that she took good care of herself. Now she cannot go out into the sun, even for a few minutes, without using a sunscreen and wearing a hat, a long-sleeved shirt, and long pants. |
| *Transition:* | What does all this mean? |
| *Restatement:* | A suntan may make you look healthy, but it is not healthy. Overexposure to the sun causes cancer and premature aging. Are you willing to take that risk just to look good for a brief time? |

In this example three forms of supporting material — statistical information, expert testimony, and narrative — work together to establish the main point. Each contributes its special strength. If each of your main points is buttressed by supporting materials that work together, your bridge of meaning should carry its message effectively to your listeners.

## ▶ USING TRANSITIONS

The preceding example also illustrates the vital work of transitions. **Transitions** tie your speech together by showing how your points relate to each other. Transitions help your listeners focus on the meaning of ideas already discussed and prepare your audience for new material you will introduce. Transitions serve as signposts that help listeners see the overall logic and cohesion of your message as it develops. Transitions also point up the structure of the message by reminding listeners of the main points and how they are related and by connecting the body of a speech with its introduction and conclusion.

Some transitions are simple, short phrases such as "There is another important point that must be made. . . ." More often, however, transitions are worded as phrases that link ideas, such as "Having looked at why people don't pay compliments more often, let's consider. . . ." This type of transition sums up what you have just said while directing your audience to your next point.

Certain stock words or phrases can be used to signal changes in a speech. For example, transitional words and phrases like *until now, twenty years ago, in the future,* and *only last week* can be used to point out time changes. Transitions can also be used to show that you are expanding on something you have already said. Transitions that signal addition include *furthermore, moreover,* and *in addition.* The use of the word *similarly* indicates that a comparison will follow. Phrases and words such as *on the other hand, unfortunately,* and *however* suggest that a contrast is imminent. Cause-and-effect relationships can be suggested with words like *as a result* and *consequently.* Introductory phrases like *as we step inside* or *as we move west* indicate spatial relationships.

One special type of transition is the **internal summary.** An internal summary reminds listeners of the points you have already covered before you move on to the next part of your message. Internal summaries are especially useful in cause-effect and problem-solution speeches. An internal summary signals your listeners that you have concluded your discussion of the causes or problem and are ready to move on to the effects or solution. In addition, an internal summary condenses and repeats your ideas, which can help your listeners remember your message. If listeners have somehow missed the point, the transition helps put them back on track. They need not be lost for the remainder of the speech. Consider the following example:

> So now we see what the problem is. We know the cost in human suffering. We know the terrible political consequences and the enormous economic burden. The question is, what are we going to do about it? Let me tell you about a solution that many experts agree may turn things around.

The speaker condensed the three main points about the human, political, and economic aspects of a problem into an internal summary that prepared the audience for the next major phase of the speech. Internal summaries should be brief and to the point so that they highlight the major features of your message.

The lack of planned transitions is often apparent when beginning speakers overuse the words *well, you know,* or *okay* to replace transitions. Plan a variety of effective transitions that help your speech flow smoothly and clearly. If you find that you are unable to develop effective transitions, your message may well lack clarity and logical flow. Outline your thoughts to be sure that they move in a clear direction in orderly sequence.

Once you have identified your main points and planned how to develop, support, and connect them with effective transitions, you can prepare an appropriate introduction and conclusion that will assure a symmetrical speech that begins and ends effectively.

## PREPARING AN EFFECTIVE INTRODUCTION

As you stand before your audience, you must quickly cope with two critical questions in your listeners' minds: *Why should I listen to this speech?* and *Why should I listen to this speaker?* The answers to these questions indicate two of the basic functions of speech introductions: to arouse the interest of your listeners and to establish your credibility. The third major function of an introduction is to preview your message.

### *Capturing Attention and Interest*

The speech that opens with "Good evening. Tonight I'm going to talk to you about organ transplants" has already created a problem for itself. It does not make listeners *want* to listen. There are several good ways to attract, build, and hold the interest of your audience. These include (1) asking rhetorical questions, (2) beginning with a quotation, (3) telling a story, (4) involving the audience, (5) developing suspense, (6) relating your subject to personal experience, and (7) shocking or startling the audience. Though these techniques may be especially helpful in the introduction, you can also use them throughout the speech.

***Asking Rhetorical Questions.*** The usual function of a question is to seek information from others. However, the **rhetorical question** is different. Rather than seeking information, the rhetorical question touches audience motivations by arousing curiosity and focusing attention on the speaker's subject. Annette Berrington opened her classroom speech on safety belts by asking the audience:

> How would you like to have your name in the paper? I can tell you a good way to get it there. Don't wear your seat belt while you're riding in a car. Yesterday I called Nashville and talked to Linda Butler in the planning and research department of the state highway patrol. Ms. Butler revealed some startling facts. Of the 899 people killed in automobile accidents in our state last year, 777 were *not* using their seat belts at the time of the crash. How do you like those odds? You have a much greater chance of being killed if you don't wear your safety belt!

These rhetorical questions provided a provocative opening. The listeners' first reaction was to think that they *would* like to have their names in the paper—we all enjoy recognition. However, their positive response quickly changed as listeners realized the circumstances under which their names would appear. Needless to say, Annette had captured her audience's attention.

***Beginning with a Quotation.***   Starting your speech with a striking quotation or paraphrase from a well-known person or respected authority on your topic both arouses interest and gives you some borrowed ethos.

The most effective opening quotations are short and to the point. One student paraphrased a famous author to open his speech comparing and contrasting whole-grain and white breads.

> Henry Miller once said that you can travel 50,000 miles in America without tasting a good piece of bread.

If a quotation contains vital information or if the language is especially eloquent, you will want to cite the exact words. Susie Smith used the following quotation, attributed to the novelist William Faulkner, to introduce her classroom speech on job satisfaction:

> You can't eat for eight hours a day, nor drink for eight hours a day, nor make love for eight hours a day—all you can do for eight hours is work. Which is the reason why man makes himself and everybody else so miserable and unhappy.

Most books of quotations (see Chapter 5) are indexed by key words and subjects as well as by authors. They are an excellent source of striking statements you might use to introduce your topic.

***Telling a Story.***   Long ago around countless campfires, we humans began our love affair with stories. Through stories we remember the past and pass on our heritage to future generations, thus honoring tradition. Stories also entertain and educate us. In introductions, stories help capture audience attention and depict abstract problems in vivid terms. Sandra Baltz, a premed major, introduced the issue of deciding who shall live and who must die with the following story:

> On a cold and stormy night in 1841 the ship *William Brown* struck an iceberg in the North Atlantic. Passengers and crew members frantically scrambled into the lifeboats. To make a bad disaster even worse, one of the lifeboats began to sink because it was overcrowded. Fourteen men were thrown overboard that horrible night. After the survivors were rescued, a crew member was tried for the murders of those thrown overboard.

Fortunately, situations like this have been few in history, but today we face a similar problem in the medical establishment: deciding who will live as we allocate scarce medical resources for transplants. Someday, your fate — or the fate of someone you love — could depend on how we resolve this dilemma.

Humorous anecdotes are also often used in introductions. A touch of humor can put an audience in a receptive mood for your message. Humor is appropriate when your subject is light or the occasion is festive. But humor may also be the most frequently misused technique of introducing speeches. Thinking that being funny will assure success, novice speakers often search through joke books to find something to make people laugh. Unless carefully adapted, such material often sounds canned, inappropriate, or only remotely relevant to the topic or occasion. If you wish to use humor in your introduction, be certain the material is fresh and relevant to your topic.

***Involving the Audience.***    One of the most frequently used involvement techniques is complimenting the audience. People like to hear good things about themselves and their community. In 1962 John F. Kennedy delivered

*The introduction of your speech must engage the attention of your audience and involve them with your topic. If you don't get the audience's attention within the first minute of speaking, they may be lost to your forever.*

an address at a White House dinner honoring Nobel Prize winners. His opening remarks included this statement:

> I think this is the most extraordinary collection of talent, of human knowledge, that has ever been gathered together at the White House, with the possible exception of when Thomas Jefferson dined alone.[7]

With this elegant tribute Kennedy was able to pay homage to his guests without embarrassing them or going overboard with praise. His witty reference to the genius of Thomas Jefferson honored the past as well as the present and helped establish the nature of the dinner as a national celebration.

You can also involve listeners by relating your topic directly to their lives. This is especially important when your topic seems remote from the audience's immediate concerns or experiences. Beth Duncan wanted to speak to her college student audience on Alzheimer's disease, a topic that might have seemed distant to many of them. Beth helped listeners relate to her speech with the following introduction:

> I'd like to share with you a letter my roommate got from her grandmother, an educated and cultured woman. I watched her weep as she read it, and after she showed it to me, I understood why.
>
> > "Dear Sally," she read. "I am finally around to answer your last. You have to look over me. ha. I am so sorry to when you called Sunday why didn't you remind me. Steph had us all so upset leaving and not telling no she was going back but we have a good snow ha and Kathy can't drive on ice so I never get a pretty card but they have a thing to see through an envelope. I haven't got any in the bank until I get my homestead check so I'm just sending this. ha. When you was talking on the phone Cathy had Ben and got my groceries and I had to unlock the door. I forgot to say hold and I don't have Claudette's number so forgive me for being so silly. ha. Nara said to tell you she isn't doing no good well one is doing pretty good and my eyes. Love, Nanny."
>
> Sally's grandmother has Alzheimer's disease. Over 2.5 million older people in the United States are afflicted with it. It could strike someone in our families — a grandparent, an aunt or uncle, or even our mother or father.

When Beth finished this introduction, her classmates were deeply involved with her topic, moved by feelings of sympathy for her roommate and the grandmother. Moreover, realizing that this disease of older people could affect their own families made them want to listen to Beth's speech. You too can involve your listeners by relating your topic to their motivations or attitudes and by using inclusive words such as *we* and *our*.

***Developing Suspense.***   You can attract and hold your listeners' attention by arousing their curiosity, then making them wait before you satisfy it. The following introduction creates curiosity and anticipation:

> Getting knocked down is no disgrace. Champions are made by getting up just one more time than the opponent! The results are a matter of record about a man who suffered many defeats: Lost his job in 1832, defeated for legislature in 1832, failed in business in 1833, defeated for legislature in 1834, sweetheart died in 1835, had nervous breakdown in 1836, defeated for nomination for Congress in 1843, elected to Congress in 1846, lost renomination in 1848, rejected for land officer in 1849, defeated for Senate in 1854, defeated for nomination for Vice-President in 1856, defeated for Senate in 1858. In 1860 Abraham Lincoln was elected president of the United States. Lincoln proved that a big shot is just a little shot who keeps shooting. The greatest failures in the world are those who fail by not doing anything.[8]

***Relating the Subject to Personal Experience.***   An old adage suggests that people are interested first in themselves, next in other people, then in things, and finally in ideas. This may explain why relating a topic to personal experience heightens audience interest. When speakers have been personally involved with a topic, they also gain credibility. We are more willing to listen to others and take their advice if we know they have traveled the road themselves. They bring personal testimony to bear, inviting empathetic listening by their audiences. Self-help groups such as Alcoholics Anonymous and Weight Watchers acknowledge this truth by restricting their leadership to members who have been through their programs.

Viola Brown effectively related her topic to personal experience. She began a speech urging her classmates to contribute to the United Cerebral Palsy Foundation by holding up a ten-dollar bill.

> This money means a lot to me, as I'm sure it would to most of you. College students who are working their way through school don't have money to burn. But I'm going to give this ten dollars away. It's my monthly contribution to the United Cerebral Palsy Foundation. This organization is very important to me because I have a cousin who has cerebral palsy. Today I want to tell you what it is like to have someone with this illness in your family. And I want you to know what the United Cerebral Palsy Foundation can do with this money.

***Shocking or Startling the Audience.***   Anything truly unusual draws attention to itself and arouses curiosity. Consider the headlines from the sensationalist tabloids: "TALKING BEAR SCARES COUPLE!" "FIVE SENATORS ARE ALIENS!" "WHY I WENT FROM HERO TO HEROINE: EX-GI TELLS ALL!"

Evita Moreno used the **shock-and-startle technique** effectively in the opening of her informative speech by combining it with audience involvement:

**SPEAKER'S NOTES**

## Capturing the Attention of Your Audience

- Ask rhetorical questions.
- Use a quotation from a well-known person.
- Tell a story that is related to your topic.
- Show your listeners how your topic applies to them.
- Create suspense and anticipation.
- Call on your personal experience with the topic.
- Startle the audience with something unusual.

If the statistics hold true, more than half of us in this room have risked our lives in the past year. Indeed, millions upon millions of college students have willing exposed themselves to a life-threatening disease in the past year. That disease is cancer. Do you think these numbers are overblown? Do you believe you're not at risk? Let's see.

How many of you smoke or use some form of tobacco? Raise your hands. [*Pauses for a show of hands.*] Okay, that's six. Now, how many of you eat a lot of fatty fast foods — hamburgers, french fries, pizza. Come on, raise your hands. [*Pauses for a show of hands.*] Well, that's fourteen. Now, in the past year, how many of you took a sunbath — or went to a tanning parlor — or worked outside without using a sunscreen oil or lotion? [*Pauses for a show of hands.*] That's seventeen! I guess my numbers were a little bit off, but I actually understated the probability. Today I want to tell you how you can lower your risk and avoid becoming a statistic in someone else's speech.

The shock-and-startle technique must always be used with care. You don't want to arouse more interest in your introduction than the body of your speech could ever possibly satisfy. If your opening is too sensational, you simply will overshadow the rest of your speech.

### Establishing Your Credibility as a Speaker

The second major function of an effective introduction is to establish the credibility of the speaker. We tend to judge others early in our interactions with them. These initial impressions color our later perceptions, both of speakers and of their messages.[9] Therefore, it is important to establish early that you are qualified to speak on your subject. Establishing credibility is often difficult for novice speakers. There is a delicate balance between seeming competent and seeming conceited. If you keep your focus on your commitment to your topic and on sharing a message with your audience, and offer yourself as a messenger, you should be able to create the proper balance.

Your credibility may come from personal experience. As she talked about the problems of a family member who suffered from cerebral palsy, Viola Brown relied on personal knowledge to establish her credibility. You do not have to have such personal experience, however, to be qualified to speak on a topic. In your introduction you can refer to your research to demonstrate your credibility:

> I was amazed to learn in psychology class that research does not support a strong link between exposure to persuasive communications and behavior. This discovery led me to do more reading on the relationship between advertising and consumer activity. What I found was even more surprising, especially when you consider that, according to *Parade* magazine, companies were willing to pay $850,000 for a thirty-second spot commercial during Super Bowl XXVI.

Such an approach creates more credibility (and is much more interesting) than had you said:

> The information for my speech came from my psychology class, two articles in the *Journal of Applied Psychology,* and a feature story in *Parade* magazine.

When you establish favorable ethos, you also create the grounds for one of the most powerful effects of communication: *identification* between you and your listeners. Identification occurs when people break through the personal and cultural walls that separate them as individuals and share thoughts and feelings as though they were one. When you seem likable, sincere, competent, and dynamic, your listeners *want* to identify with you, and your effectiveness as a communicator is magnified. An effective introduction should put you on good terms with your listeners. You can establish identification among yourself, the audience, and your topic by relating personal experiences that put your listeners in a receptive mood for your message.

### Previewing Your Message

The final function of an introduction is to preview what is to follow in the body of the speech. The **preview** foreshadows the main points you will cover and offers your audience an overview of your speech. As we noted in Chapter 5, the preview may immediately follow the presentation of your thematic statement, or that statement itself may also function as a preview. Either way, the preview usually comes near the end of the introduction and may serve also as a transition into the body of your speech. Because it helps the audience focus on your main points, a good preview aids critical listening.

Martha Radner used the following preview for a speech on campus security problems. Note how her preview follows her thematic statement:

> We could be a lot safer on this campus if we adopted a bold new plan to assure campus security [*thematic statement*]. First, I want to show you how dangerous our situation has become. Second, I'll explore the reasons why current security measures on our campus are ineffective. And third, I'll present my plan for a safer campus [*preview*].

By informing her listeners of her intentions as well as her speech design, Martha helped her audience listen more intelligently.

### *Deciding What Introductory Techniques to Use*

There are no hard and fast rules for determining exactly how you should open a speech. As you conduct the research for your speech, look for material that would make an effective introduction. The following guidelines may help you make a wise selection among the available resources and techniques:

1. *Always consider your audience in relation to your topic.* If you are not certain listeners are already motivated to listen to your message, you must provide motivation by giving them a reason to listen to you. Use your introduction to tie *your* topic into *their* needs, interests, or well-being. Show them how they will benefit or what they stand to gain.

2. *Consider the mood you want to establish.* Some topics require more serious consideration than others, so humor may be inappropriate. Certain occasions, such as after-dinner speeches, will mandate a light touch. Other occasions, such as memorials or awards, may call for more solemnity.

3. *Keep time constraints in mind.* Remember the principle of symmetry requires that your speech should be balanced. If you are to speak for seven minutes, you can't get bogged down in a five-minute introduction.

4. *Do what you do best.* Some people are effective storytellers, and others are better using striking statistics and eloquent quotations. Go with your strength! Your introduction must fit you as well as your topic and your audience.

Whatever attention-arousing technique you use in your introduction, be sure that it is relevant to your topic. One student began his speech with the following opener:

> Have you ever thought about what it might be like to die? Have you ever dreamed about death? Have you ever talked with someone who came close to death, yet survived?

These rhetorical questions gained the attention of the audience and prepared listeners for a speech on near-death experiences. Unfortunately, what followed was a speech on taxes. The student tried to tie his introduction to the topic by saying:

> Nothing is certain except death and taxes. This afternoon I want to tell you how you can save money on your income tax.

His speech was carefully prepared and effectively presented, yet the audience felt cheated. The introduction had prepared the audience for something the speech did not deliver. Be sure your attention-getting material is appropriate for your topic.

## DEVELOPING AN EFFECTIVE CONCLUSION

Many beginning speakers seem awkward when they come to the end of their speeches. "That's all, folks!" may be an effective ending for a cartoon, but in a speech such conclusions violate the principles of good form and closure. Saying "That's it, I guess" or "Well, I'm done," accompanied by a sigh of relief, suggests that you have not planned your speech very carefully. You should spend at least as much time developing an effective ending for your speech as you spend on the introduction.

### Functions of the Conclusion

Your conclusion is the final span in your bridge of meaning. Your concluding words should stay with listeners, remind them of your message, and, if appropriate, move them to action. Therefore, your conclusion should (1) summarize the meaning and purpose of your speech, (2) provide a sense of closure, and (3) in some persuasive speeches, motivate listeners to act.

The first task of an effective conclusion is to summarize the meaning of major ideas. This summary often functions as a transition between the body and the final remarks, as in this conclusion to a speech on choosing a personal computer:

> Now you should feel more comfortable about moving into the world of personal computers. Remember, begin by analyzing your needs. Second, be sure the computer you buy will allow you to access campus services. Finally, consider dependability and availability of repairs in making your decision. Whatever you do, don't be taken in by the ads that promise something for nothing. Do some research so that you spend your money wisely.

Such a summary can itself offer listeners a sense of closure. To seal that effect, you can use any one of a number of techniques.

*An effective conclusion summarizes your message and leaves the audience with something to remember. The honorable Patty Murray, United States Senator from Washington, acknowledges her audience's applause at the end of a speech.*

## Concluding Techniques

Many of the techniques that create effective introductions are also useful for developing memorable conclusions. Using the same technique to close a speech as you used to open it can make your speech seem balanced and elegant. This practice also increases the symmetry of form that we discussed earlier in this chapter.

***Asking Questions.*** When used in your introduction, questions help gain attention and excite curiosity. When used in conclusions, questions give your audience something to think about after you have finished. In persuasive speeches they can challenge listeners to action.

Annette Berrington opened her speech on the use of seat belts with a rhetorical question: "How would you like to have your name in the paper?" Her final words were "Are you really sure you'd like to have your name in the paper?" This final question echoed the beginning and served as a haunting reminder to buckle up when you get in the car. Had Annette ended with "Remember, buckled seat belts save lives!" the effect would not have been as dramatic.

When used as a persuasive appeal, concluding questions may be more than rhetorical. They may actually call for a response from the audience. During his 1988 presidential campaign, the Reverend Jesse Jackson often used this technique to register voters. He would end a speech by asking:

> How many of you are not registered to vote? Raise your hands. No, stand up so we can see you! Is that all of you who aren't registered? Stand up! Let me see you!

Such questioning and cajoling would be followed by on-site voter registration. Evangelists who issue an invitation to personal salvation at the end of their sermons often use concluding questions in a similar way. To be effective, this technique must be the climax of a speech that has prepared its audience for action.

***Closing with a Quotation.*** Brief quotations that capture the essence of your message or purpose can make effective conclusions. If one literary quotation is used to open a speech, another on the same theme can provide balance in the conclusion. Susie Smith opened her speech on job satisfaction with a quotation from William Faulkner that linked work and unhappiness. She closed the speech with a more positive quotation from Joseph Conrad that summed up the meaning of satisfying work:

> I like what is in work — the chance to find yourself. Your own reality — for yourself, not for others — what no other . . . can ever know.

***Telling a Story.*** Ending a speech with an anecdote that summarizes your message or purpose is also an effective concluding technique because the story tends to stick in listeners' memories. To conclude his student speech on converting waste materials into usable energy, Dan Martini told this story:

> Last week I was riding with a friend out Walnut Grove Road, and we could see the landfill. The wind was stirring up paper and debris. It was really depressing! My friend shook his head and said, "You know, some archaeologist in the future may rediscover our civilization, buried under a pile of garbage."
>
> What I said to him is what I've said to you today: "Have more faith in our creative imagination. The same technology that makes waste can also show us how to use it productively. Like modern alchemy, our technology can transform garbage into gold — or at least into energy!"

***Ending with a Metaphor.*** A striking metaphor can end your speech effectively.[10] As we will discuss at greater length in Chapter 10, metaphors combine things that are apparently unlike so that we see unexpected relationships. An effective metaphor reveals a hidden truth about the speaker's subject in a memorable way. As a conclusion to a speech, such a metaphor may provide lasting illumination. A good metaphor also allows you to say many things at the same time. Melodie Lancaster, president of Lancaster Resources, used such a metaphor, combined with a narrative, as she concluded a speech of inspiration to the Houston Council, American Business Womens' Association:

> We recall the story of the three stonemasons who were asked what they were doing. The first said, "I am laying brick." The second replied, "I am making a foundation." And the third said: "I am building a cathedral." Let's you and I set our sights that high. Let's build cathedrals of success to-day, tomorrow and the day after tomorrow. [11]

Consider the many possible meanings this metaphor might stimulate in the minds of imaginative listeners. First, the speaker suggests listeners must work hard, as hard as stonemasons. Second, she suggests they must work with a vision of their goals in mind, like the third stonemason. Third, the connection with a religious institution, a cathedral, suggests they must work with the kind of zeal and dedication one connects with religious commit-ment. All these meanings are packed in the same metaphor, making it mem-orable for her audience.

Whatever concluding technique you select should satisfy your audience that what was promised in the opening has now been delivered. The conclu-sion should help listeners remember the meaning of your speech and should encourage them to take its message to heart.

**IN SUMMARY**    A speech that is carefully structured helps the audience understand the mes-sage and enhances the ethos of the speaker.

***Principles of Good Form.***    A well-structured speech has *good form:* it is simple, symmetrical, and orderly. *Simplicity* can be achieved by limiting the number of main points and using clear, direct language. A speech has *sym-metry* when the major parts receive proper emphasis and when they work together effectively. *Orderliness* means that a speech follows a consistent pattern of development.

***Structuring the Body of Your Speech.***    You should structure the body first, so that you can build an introduction and conclusion that fit well with the principal part of your speech. To develop the body, decide on your main points, determine how best to arrange them, and select effective supporting materials. To discover your main points, prepare a *research overview* of the information you have collected. This summary can help you spot major themes that can develop into main points.

You should arrange main points so that they follow natural perceptual patterns based on the principles of proximity, similarity, and closure. *Prox-imity* suggests that things should be discussed as they happen together in space or time. If they occur in a time sequence, use a sequential design for your speech. If they occur in physical relationship to each other, a spatial de-sign might be appropriate. The *similarity* of objects or events may suggest a categorical design for structuring main points. The structure of the body satisfies the principle of *closure* when it completes the design it begins. Cause-effect and problem-solution designs require closure in order to be effective.

Supporting materials fill out the structure of the speech and strengthen main points either directly or indirectly. The kind and type of supporting material you need depends on how controversial your point may be, its complexity, the risk it entails for listeners, your credibility, and its closeness to the actual experiences of listeners. In an ideal arrangement, you should support each main point with information, testimony, and an example or story that emphasizes its human aspects.

*Using Transitions.* Effective *transitions* point up the relationships among ideas in your speech and tie the speech together. *Internal summaries* remind listeners of the points you have made in one part of your speech before moving on to another.

*Preparing an Effective Introduction.* The introduction to a speech should arouse your listeners' interest, establish your credibility, and orient the audience to your message. Some useful ways to introduce a speech include asking rhetorical questions, beginning with a quotation, telling a story, involving the audience with the subject, creating suspense, relating the topic to personal experience, and startling the audience. As you build credibility, you also make possible identification between you and the audience. Your introduction is also the place to preview your topic.

*Developing an Effective Conclusion.* An effective conclusion should summarize the meaning and purpose of your speech, provide a sense of closure, and, if appropriate, motivate listeners to act. Techniques useful for conclusions include asking questions, closing with a quotation, telling a story, and ending with a metaphor. Your speech will seem more symmetrical and satisfying to listeners if your conclusion ties into your introduction.

**TERMS TO KNOW**

| | |
|---|---|
| good form | principle of closure |
| simplicity | transitions |
| symmetry | internal summary |
| orderliness | rhetorical question |
| research overview | shock-and-startle technique |
| principle of proximity | preview |
| principle of similarity | |

**DISCUSSION**

1. Working in small groups, share your research overviews for your next speeches. What main points are suggested by each overview? What can you learn about the selection of main points from these discussions?

2. Share the organizational plan of your next speech with a classmate so that you become consultants for each other. Help each other come up with alternative patterns for the main points, introductions, and conclusions. After the speeches are presented, each consulting team should explain the options it considered and why it chose the particular structures used for each speech.

**APPLICATION**
1. Select a speech from Appendix B and study its symmetry. Are its major parts—introduction, main points, and conclusions—coherent and properly balanced? If not, what would you suggest to improve it?

2. Analyze the structure of your favorite television advertisement. How does it gain attention and establish credibility? What design does it follow? Does the conclusion tie into the introduction? Present your analysis in class.

3. What kind of introductory technique would be most useful for each of the following specific purpose statements?
   a. To inform my audience of the role of student volunteers
   b. To persuade my audience that it is better to marry than to live together
   c. To inform my audience that fluorocarbons are destroying our atmosphere
   d. To persuade my audience that famines in Africa are more often the result of power politics than natural forces

4. Develop a narrative you might use as an introduction for one of the topics in the preceding application. In small groups discuss how these stories might advance the purpose of the speech. Each group should select its best story and present it to the class as a whole.

5. Suggest an appropriate structural design for each of the following specific purposes:
   a. To inform listeners where they might see a grizzly bear in the wild
   b. To inform my audience about sexist advertising practices
   c. To inform listeners about the ideal way to prepare for an examination
   d. To persuade my audiences to vote in the next election
   e. To persuade listeners to vote Democratic (or Republican) in the next election

**NOTES**
1. J. C. McCroskey and R. S. Mehrley, "The Effects of Disorganization and Nonfluency on Attitude Change and Source Credibility," *Communication Monographs* 36 (1969): 13–21.
2. Morton Deutsch and Robert M. Krauss, *Theories in Social Psychology* (New York: Basic Books, 1965), pp. 14–36.
3. Douglas A. Bernstein, Edward J. Roy, Thomas K. Srull, and Christopher D. Wickens, *Psychology,* 2nd ed. (Boston: Houghton Mifflin, 1991), p. 308.

4. Plato, "The Phaedrus," in *The Works of Plato,* ed. Irwin Edman (New York: The Modern Library, 1927), pp. 311–312.

5. Gloria Steinem, *Outrageous Acts and Everyday Rebellions* (New York: Holt, Rinehart & Winston, 1983).

6. Yukio Matsuyama, "Japan's Role in the New World Order," *Vital Speeches of the Day* 58 (15 May 1992): 463.

7. Cited in Arthur M. Schlesinger, Jr., *A Thousand Days: John F. Kennedy in the White House* (Boston: Houghton Mifflin, 1965), p. 733.

8. Bob Lannom, "Patience, Persistence, and Perspiration," *News Leader* (Parsons, Tenn.), 20 Sept. 1989, p. 9.

9. N. H. Anderson and A. A. Barrios, "Primacy Effects in Personality Impression Formation," *Journal of Abnormal and Social Psychology* 63 (1961): 346–350.

10. John Waite Bowers and Michael Osborn, "Attitudinal Effects of Selected Types of Concluding Metaphors in Persuasive Speeches," *Speech Monographs* 33 (1966): 148–155.

11. Melodie Lancaster, "The Future We Predict Isn't Inevitable: Reframing Our Success in the Modern World," *Vital Speeches of the Day* 58 (1 Aug. 1992): 638.

*Our plans miscarry because they have no aim. When a man does not know what harbor he is making for, no wind is the right wind.*

— *Seneca*

# 8

# Outlining Your Speech

**This Chapter Will Help You**

- appreciate the importance of outlining your speeches.
- understand the process involved in developing an effective outline.
- develop preparation outlines to help structure your speech.
- prepare a formal outline following the conventions of coordination and subordination.
- condense your formal outline into a key-word outline to use as you present your speech.

For several years our residential neighborhood was caught up in zoning disputes. We lived on a cove surrounded by woods and undeveloped fields that developers wanted to rezone for commercial use. Once when we were at a zoning board meeting to protest a proposed automobile dealership, we learned that a plan to operate a helicopter port in the neighborhood was on the agenda that same afternoon.

With only minutes to prepare, we organized our arguments against the heliport. Our specific purpose was clear: we wanted to defeat this proposal. Our thematic statement was "A heliport in this neighborhood is both undesirable and illegal." We hastily outlined our main arguments on the back of a civil defense bulletin:

I.   A heliport would be an undesirable intrusion into our neighborhood.

    A.  It would disturb the peace and quiet of the residents.

    B.  It would bother the patients in a nearby nursing home.

II.  The applicants had shown disrespect for the law.

    A.  They had not applied for a license before operating.

    B.  They had violated FAA operating regulations.

Armed with this simple outline, which helped us focus and structure our speaking, we defeated *both* the heliport and the car dealership in the same afternoon!

As this example shows, outlining is not just an academic exercise that instructors like to inflict on students. In the classroom as in real life, outlining is an essential phase of speech preparation. The outline is the logical plan of your speech. Just as there are patterns for suits and dresses and blueprints for bridges, there are outlines for speeches. If we had spoken before the zoning board without first organizing and outlining our thoughts, we could not have presented effective speeches.

Outlining goes hand in hand with structuring, discussed in the previous chapter. As you make decisions on the main points in the body of your speech, it helps if you outline them so that you can see more clearly how they fit together. You can also check to see whether the main points cover everything you have proposed in your thematic statement. As you develop your main points, outlining can help you determine if you have enough supporting material and if it is sufficiently varied. Moreover, the outline can help you see where you need transitions and if the introduction and conclusion tie together effectively.

In short, outlining helps to *discipline* the process of structuring and can point you in new creative directions. A good outline helps you control your material, organize and clarify your thinking, and streamline your speech structure. The discipline of outlining can also reveal if you have not thought through your topic sufficiently, if your ideas don't fit together cohesively, and if you lack sufficient knowledge to develop and support your main points.

In Chapter 2, we suggested that you develop complete sentence outlines to help you prepare for your speech introducing yourself or others. As you plan longer and more complex speeches, think of outlining as a process that evolves from initial preparation outlines to a final formal outline. The formal outline is the most technically complete form of the sentence outline discussed in Chapter 2. As you prepare your informative, persuasive, and ceremonial speeches, you may develop several preparation outlines, a formal outline, and a key-word outline.

## DEVELOPING A PREPARATION OUTLINE

A **preparation outline** is a *tentative* plan of the speech you will eventually give. It can show you how your ideas are evolving and whether they fit together. It can also suggest what more you may need to learn in order to speak responsibly. You may make and discard several preparation outlines as you develop your speech.

Why would you want to make a preparation outline? Assume that you plan to present an informative speech on "selecting a personal computer." You have done some reading and thinking on the topic but are just not sure how your speech will develop. A preparation outline should help reduce your uncertainty.

The first thing you must do is be sure that you have your topic, general and specific purposes, and thematic statement clearly in mind. These constitute the foundation for the speech you will build. Write them out to assure your mastery of them:

| | |
|---|---|
| *Topic:* | Selecting a personal computer |
| *General purpose:* | To inform |
| *Specific purpose:* | To inform my audience of steps to take in selecting a personal computer |
| *Thematic statement:* | Choose a personal computer that meets your needs and offers dependable service |

Keeping in mind that this is a tentative plan for your speech, you will next outline the body of your speech. First identify your main points from your research overview. Next, ask yourself: *Are these the two or three major ideas I must develop in order to satisfy my thematic statement?* In this case you might emerge with something like the following:

I. Determine how you will use your computer.

II. Select a computer that meets your needs.

III. Investigate dependability and service.

Just as your thematic statement is developed by main points, your main points depend on more specific, concrete statements and/or supporting materials to make them meaningful and credible. These more concrete statements and materials show up at the **subpoint** level of your speech outline. To identify subpoints ask yourself: *How does this main point break down? What must I establish before listeners will accept my main points? How should I support each main point?* For example, as you work through your initial preparation outline, you might list the following preliminary subpoints for your first main point ("Determine how you will use your computer"). You may also note on your preparation outline questions about supporting materials.

I.  Determine how you will use your computer.

    A.  Learn what a personal computer can do.

    B.  Learn the language of "computerese."

    C.  Talk with other computer users in your major department [*conduct interviews with faculty members?*].

    D.  Talk with campus computer lab personnel.

    E.  Purchase a good guide to PCs [*recommend and introduce the Bass book?*].

Eventually, as you develop more refined preparation outlines for longer speeches, you may develop the **sub-subpoint** and **sub-sub-subpoint** levels of speech structure, which represent even more detailed and specific breakdowns of the topic under discussion. Theoretically, these breakdowns could go on indefinitely, but in the practice the process usually stops at the sub-sub-subpoint level. To determine how much elaboration you will need, ask yourself:

1.  How much time do I have to develop my ideas?

2.  What is required to give my listeners a responsible picture of the subject?

3.  Must I elaborate to overcome audience doubts on any of my points?

4.  At what point might listeners become bored or confused by too much elaboration?

To complete your first preparation outline, rough in an introduction that fits your main points. Your introduction should include attention-getting material, help establish your credibility, and preview your message. Finally, plan a conclusion that includes a summary and concluding remarks. Figure 8.1 is a sample early preparation outline that shows how these parts relate to one another.

Let us assume that several days go by. You have done more reading and thinking about your topic and are ready to refine your initial preparation outline. You may first notice that your thematic statement refers to only two main points, but you have plotted three main points in the outline. At this point you should revise the thematic statement to correct this problem:

*Thematic statement:* Determine how you will use your computer, and then select one that will meet your needs and offer dependable service.

Next you should return to your main points to consider how the subpoints relate to them and to each other. You are now also ready to extend your thinking to the sub-subpoint level, should this be necessary. Consider the original version of the first main point:

**Main point I:** Determine how you will use your computer.

*Subpoints:* A. Learn what a personal computer can do.
B. Learn the language of "computerese."
C. Talk with other computer users in your major department.
D. Talk with campus computer lab personnel.
E. Purchase a good guide to PC's.

It is clear now that the above subpoints fall into two basic categories: (1) the general uses of personal computers, and (2) how the personal computer might work for you in particular. You can now revise the preparation outline to reflect these categories. Note also that your comments to yourself about how to use supporting materials have changed from questions to qualified conclusions.

**Main point I:** Determine how you will use your computer.

*Subpoint A:* Know the general uses of personal computers [*use quotation from Bass here*].

*Sub-subpoints:* 1. Purchase a good guide to PCs.
2. Learn what a personal computer can do.
3. Learn the language of "computerese" [*provide brief examples*].

*Subpoint B:* Decide how the computer can work for you.

*Sub-subpoints:* 1. Talk with computer users in your major department [*interview Prof. Walker*].
2. Talk with campus computer lab personnel.

You examine the second main point in the same way:

**Main point II:** Select a computer that meets your needs.

*Subpoints:* A. Discuss needs with dealer.
B. Check on available peripherals.
C. Check for training/troubleshooting help.
D. Check guide to identify computers that offer what you need.
E. Check to see which of these are compatible with campus network.

As you consider this cluster of ideas in conjunction with your further research, two dominant subpoints emerge: (1) deciding what kind of equipment you need, and (2) determining the best source for buying a computer.

**PREPARATION OUTLINE**

**Topic:** Selecting a Personal Computer

**General purpose:** To inform

**Specific purpose:** To inform my audience of steps to take in selecting a personal computer

**Thematic statement:** Choose a personal computer that meets your needs and offers dependable service.

**INTRODUCTION**

**Attention-getting material:** *Times Leader* ad: "Buy a Titan PC for $325!" Bargain or not? *Consumer Reports* quote: "A computer that is not compatible with others is little more than an expensive doorstop."

**Establish credibility:** Experience in purchasing my own PC. Spent a lot of time learning how to get the most for my money.

**Thematic statement/preview:** How can you choose a personal computer that will meet your needs and provide dependable service?

**BODY**

**Main point I:** Determine how you will use your computer.
    Subpoints:  A. Learn what a personal computer can do.
                  B. Learn the language of "computerese."
                  C. Talk with other computer users in your major department [*seek interviews with faculty members?*].
                  D. Talk with campus computer lab personnel.
                  E. Purchase a good guide to PCs [*recommend and introduce the Bass book?*].

**Main point II:** Select a computer that meets your needs.
    Subpoints:  A. Discuss needs with dealer.
                  B. Check on available peripherals.
                  C. Check for training/troubleshooting help.
                  D. Check guide to identify computers that offer what you need.
                  E. Check to see which of these are compatible with campus network [*use narrative from Raskin essay?*].

**Main point III:** Investigate dependability and service.
    Subpoints:  A. Talk with other computer users about their experiences.
                  B. Check out dealer, length of time in business, and service availability should you relocate [*summarize advice from Smith book?*].

FIGURE 8.1
Sample Early Preparation Outline

**CONCLUSION**

**Summary:** When you invest in a PC, be sure it meets your needs, that it is dependable, and that service will be available.

**Concluding remarks:** Is that computer advertised for $325 a bargain? Quote from Thomas Jefferson: "Never buy what you do not want because it is cheap; it will be dear to you."

Once more you can revise the preparation outline to reveal a more precise pattern of relationships:

| | |
|---|---|
| ***Main point II:*** | Select a computer that meets your needs [*use facts and figures*]. |
| *Subpoint A:* | Decide what kind of equipment to purchase. |
| *Sub-subpoints:* | 1. Establish minimum acceptable standards. |
| | 2. Determine compatibility with campus and department equipment. |
| | 3. Investigate what peripherals are available. |
| | 4. Decide what software you need. |
| *Subpoint B:* | Determine the best source for buying a computer. |
| *Sub-subpoints:* | 1. Talk with students and faculty about their experiences. |
| | 2. Consider your need for training and trouble-shooting help. |
| | 3. Check prices through mail order, campus bookstore, local dealers, discount outlets, and used computer dealers. |

Next you look at the third main point in the same careful way:

| | |
|---|---|
| ***Main point III:*** | Investigate dependability and service. |
| *Subpoints:* | A. Talk with other computer users about their experiences. |
| | B. Check out dealer, length of time in business, and service availability should you move. |

Here your further reading has again enriched and refined your thinking. You adjust the preparation outline to reflect these changes:

| | |
|---|---|
| ***Main point III:*** | Investigate dependability and service [*Smith guidelines*]. |
| *Subpoint A:* | Check warranty. |
| *Subpoint B:* | Check dependability ratings in *Consumer Reports*. |

*Subpoint C:* Talk with other computer users about their satisfaction with equipment, dealers, and service.

*Subpoint D:* Check availability of service should you relocate.

Now you can put your revised points back together and look at the body of the speech as a whole. As you do so, some doubts begin to rise in your mind. Can you cover this in the allotted time? Do you really need to explain the basic uses of computers to your listeners? Will most of them need lessons in "computerese?" Will they be interested in what you say?

### *Audience-Centered Outlining*

These kinds of questions occurred to Dawn Williams as she prepared her speech "Making Sense and Saving Cents When You Buy a Computer." These questions brought the audience to the center of her thinking. Like Dawn, you should always consider your listeners when you are planning, researching, and outlining a speech. As you develop your outline point by point, you should ask yourself such questions as

- Will this information be clear and convincing for my audience?
- Will that example strike listeners as authentic, and will they be moved by it?
- Does this testimony come from a source the audience respects?
- Will my listeners be able to identify with the people in this story?

As you begin to work on your speech, the audience can easily slip into the background. You may have to work up a complete preparation outline before you can see the limitations of an approach for your particular group of listeners. At that point you may need to revise your outline. This means that speech preparation often proceeds in fits and starts, periods of frustration followed by moments of inspiration and revision.

As you consider your audience, remember the advice given to beginning journalists: *Never overestimate your audience's information, and never underestimate its intelligence!* For example, Dawn knew the audience for her speech on computer selection included twenty-two students — sixteen freshmen and six sophomores. She also knew that most of the high schools in the state and region require a course in computer literacy for graduation. From this information she could safely assume that most of her audience members were already familiar with the general uses of personal computers and with basic computer terminology.

Taking these considerations into account, Dawn concluded that the structure of the speech sketched above was off the mark. She decided to narrow and sharpen her focus so that the speech would better serve her immediate audience as well as meet the time limits of the assignment. She would emphasize the more precise problems of matching personal computers to personal needs in a university setting, and of seeking the best value with limited resources. As she thought about this revised focus, a new preparation outline began to emerge (Figure 8.2, pages 212-213). Note that with the overall logical plan of her speech now firmly in mind, Dawn has plotted in the major transitions of her speech.

By now Dawn was on the right track. Her outlining work was not yet completed, but she was confident with the overall pattern of her speech. If she had not prepared a series of preparation outlines, she might have presented a flawed and poorly adapted speech. It is not unusual for a speech to evolve through several such outlines before you find the right approach for your particular topic and audience.

## DEVELOPING A FORMAL OUTLINE

A **formal outline** is the final outline in a process leading from your first rough ideas for a speech to the finished product. It is the most polished and most complete outline form, and it includes the major forms of supporting materials you will use. The formal outline follows the established conventions of outlining. A basic model of the formal outline, illustrating many of these conventions, is shown in Figure 8.3 on pages 214-215.

The conventions of formal outlining include

1. an optional title, depending on the circumstances of the speech
2. identification of speech topic, general and specific purposes, and thematic statement
3. separation of speech parts: introduction, body, and conclusion
4. adherence to the rules of coordination and subordination
5. proper wording of main points and subpoints
6. indication of major supporting material
7. a bibliography of major references

### Title

The need for a title for your speech varies with the circumstances. Classroom speeches may not require titles. When speaking outside the classroom, titles are often useful for advertising speeches and attracting audiences. Therefore, it may be a good idea to experiment with titles for classroom speeches.

When properly chosen, titles prepare the audience for the speech. They can arouse curiosity, making people want to come and listen. A title can be stated early in the introduction, then repeated throughout the speech as a reminder of the central message. Titles should not promise too much or deceive the audience. Titles that promise everything from the end of war to the end of obesity are too often followed by speeches that disappoint or frustrate listeners. Such titles often damage the speaker's ethos.

**PREPARATION OUTLINE**

**Topic:** Selecting a Personal Computer

**General purpose:** To inform

**Specific purpose:** To inform my audience of steps to take in selecting a personal computer

**Thematic statment:** Choose a personal computer that meets your needs and seek the best value for your money.

**INTRODUCTION**

**Attention-getting material:** *Times Leader* ad: "Buy a Titan PC for $325!" Bargain or not? *Consumers Digest* quote: "A computer that is not compatible with others is little more than an expensive doorstop."

**Establish credibility:** Experience in purchasing my own PC. You can benefit from what I learned.

**Thematic statement/preview:** Today I want to tell you how to match a computer to your needs and get the most for your money when you buy a PC.

[**Transition** from introduction to body: "First let's consider how to . . ."]

**BODY**

**Main point I:** Select a computer that meets your needs.

Subpoint A: Take your major into consideration to determine your needs.

Sub-subpoints:
1. Liberal arts majors may need only basic word processing.
2. Science majors may need the capacity to run statistical programs and graphics.
3. Business majors may need spreadsheets for accounting [*develop brief examples*].

Subpoint B: Know what minimum standards you should look for in equipment [*use facts and figures from Millar interview*].

Sub-subpoints:
1. Check for hardware specifics.
2. Check on availability of peripherals.
3. Check on availability of software.
4. Check on capacity to upgrade.

Subpoint C: Check for compatibility with campus network.

Sub-subpoints:
1. You can save time and money if your system is compatible.

FIGURE 8.2
Sample Revised
Preparation Outline

2. Basic word processors will probably not be compatible.
3. A build-in modem is a definite advantage.

[**Transition** between main points: "Now that we've looked at your needs, let's consider the old bottom line—how to . . ."]

**Main point II:** Select a source that offers the most value for your money [*cite Smith guidelines*].

Subpoint A: Determine how much support and assistance you may need.

Sub-subpoints: 1. The more computer literate you are, the less you need to rely on dealer assistance.
2. Campus computer lab personnel may be able to help you with problems.

Subpoint B: Check out warranty and service contracts.
Sub-subpoints: 1. Check length of warranty.
2. Check how warranty is honored.

Subpoint C: Compare prices across sources.
Sub-subpoints: 1. A computer dealer may be the most expensive source.
2. Look for good deals from mail order companies, discount stores, and the campus bookstore.
3. Secondhand computers may look like the "best deal," but be careful.

[**Transition** from body to conclusion: "So what have we learned today? When you make the big step into computer ownership, . . ."]

## CONCLUSION

**Summary statement:** Be sure you buy a personal computer that meets your needs, and shop around for a source that gives you the most value for your money.

**Concluding remarks:** That word processing computer for $325 may be a bargain only if you will use it to write term papers and only if you don't want to hook up to campus services. Remember, nothing is a bargain if it doesn't meet your needs. Heed the words of Thomas Jefferson, who said, "Never buy what you do not want [and I add 'what you don't need'] because it is cheap; it will be dear to you."

**TITLE** *(optional)*

**Speech topic:** _____

**General purpose:** _____

**Specific purpose:** _____

**Thematic statement:** _____


**INTRODUCTION**

  **I. Attention-getting material** _____

    _____

 **II. Establish credibility** _____

    _____

**III. Thematic statement/Preview** _____

    _____

*[Transition into body of speech]*

**BODY**

  **I. Main point #1:** _____
    **A.** Subpoint or supporting material _____
    **B.** Subpoint or supporting material_____
      **1.** Sub-subpoint or supporting material _____
      **2.** Sub-subpoint or supporting material _____

*[Transition into point A2]*

 **II. Main point #2:** _____
    **A.** Subpoint or supporting material _____
      **1.** Sub-subpoint or supporting material _____
      **2.** Sub-subpoint or supporting material _____
    **B.** Subpoint or supporting material _____

*[Transition into point A3]*

**III. Main point #3:** _____
    **A.** Subpoint or supporting material _____
    **B.** Subpoint or supporting material _____
      **1.** Sub-subpoint or supporting material _____
      **2.** Sub-subpoint or supporting material _____
        **a.** Sub-sub-subpoint or supporting material _____
        **b.** Sub-sub-subpoint or supporting material _____

*[Transition into conclusion]*

FIGURE 8.3
Format for the Formal
Outline

CONCLUSION

  I. Summary: _____

     _____

 II. Concluding remarks: _____

     _____

**Bibliography**

**Books:**
**Articles:**
**Miscellaneous references:**

## Topic, Purposes, and Thematic Statement

Although you won't necessarily state your topic, purposes, or thematic statement directly as you present your speech, the discipline of writing them out in a formal outline helps assure that you know what you want to accomplish with your audience. A clear realization of these elements can help you develop a cohesively structured message that moves with purpose from the opening to the closing words.

As noted earlier, this identification of speech topic, general and specific purposes, and thematic statement in preparation and formal outlines is very much like the foundation of a building: we may never actually see it *in* the speech itself, yet we know it must be present before speakers can build an effective structure of ideas.

## Separation of Speech Parts

Separation of the major parts of the speech in the formal outline helps assure that you give each the full and careful attention it requires. Only when introduction, body, and conclusion are fully developed, and joined by the major transitions of your speech, can they work together to achieve your specific purpose and fulfill the promise of the thematic statement.

## Coordination and Subordination

Figure 8.3 illustrates the principles of coordination and subordination on which formal outlining is based. It demonstrates how you should use letters, numbers, and indentation to set up an outline. The actual number of main points and levels of subpoints you develop in your outline depends on your purpose and your analysis of audience interests, needs, and knowledge of your topic. The less listeners know at the outset about your topic, the simpler your speech structure must be.

**Coordination** requires that statements that are approximately equal in importance (subpoints, sub-subpoints, and so forth) should be placed on the same level in the outline. For example, your *I*'s and *II*'s, your *A*'s and *B*'s, your *1*'s and *2*'s, and your *a*'s and *b*'s should seem about equally significant. In Figure 8.4 on pages 220–223 the main points (I, II) identify major considerations for selecting a personal computer. They are approximately equal in importance. Think how strange it would be if the third main point in this outline was "Consider what games you can play in your spare time." That function would not be equal to selecting a computer that meets your needs or selecting a source that offers the most value for your money. Nor would it be relevant to your specific purpose or thematic statement. The subpoints for each main point also should be of about the same importance.

Coordination also requires that statements at the same level in an outline should receive approximately the same degree of support. If you back up one main point with strong testimony, then other main points should also be supported with important facts, testimony, examples, or narratives. Keep in mind that if you don't support statements equally, they will not seem equal in importance to your audience.

**Subordination** requires that related material descend in importance from the more general, abstract main points to the increasingly concrete and specific subpoints, sub-subpoints, and sub-sub-subpoints. This arrangement follows a standard set of symbols: Roman numerals, capital letters, and Arabic numbers.

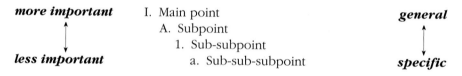

The more important a statement is, the farther to the left it is positioned. If you turn an outline over so that it rests on its right margin, the "peaks" will represent the main points, the highest points of priority in the speech, with all other subpoints arranged under them according to significance.

Each level in your outline must be logically related to the level above it. To check your outline for proper subordination, ask yourself the following question: "Does each subordinate idea make the point above it understandable, believable, compelling, or enjoyable?"[1] One other way to test for coordination and subordination is to ask whether the transitions that tie together the different levels of the speech seem to flow naturally and easily. If you find you have to force them, that can be a clear sign that your system of coordination and subordination is flawed. To find the problem, consider again the overall structure of your speech.

The easiest way to demonstrate the importance of coordination and subordination is to look at a sample outline that violates these principles:

I.   Computers can help you develop writing skills.

    A. PCs can improve your schoolwork.

    B. PCs can be useful for organizing class notes.

*Outlining brings discipline to the process of organizing and structuring a speech. An outline allows you to verify that your main points are adequately supported and that your speech flows smoothly from beginning to end.*

II. Computers can help you keep better financial records.

   A. They can help you plan personal time more effectively.

   B. They can be useful in your personal life.

   C. They can help organize your research notes for class projects.

This collection of thoughts is an outline in name only. It violates the principles of both coordination and subordination in that the levels are not equal in importance, nor are they logically related to each other in descending order. To straighten out this problem, let's look first at the main points. In this outline, they are not the most general, most important statements. The main points are actually I-A and II-B: the ideas that PCs can improve your schoolwork and be useful in your personal life. Putting these points where they belong allows us to correct the outline:

I. Computers can improve your schoolwork.

   A. PCs can help you develop writing skills.

   B. PCs can be useful for organizing class notes.

   C. PCs can help organize your research notes for class projects.

II. Computers can be useful in your personal life.

   A. PCs can help you keep better financial records.

   B. PCs can help you plan personal time more effectively.

### *Wording Your Main Points*

The main points in your outline should be worded as simple, independent sentences. A main-point sentence that starts sprouting clauses should be broken down into subpoints. For example, the following does not make a good main-point sentence because it is too long and complex:

> Bad eating habits endanger health and lower feelings of self-worth, causing us to lose years off our lives and to suffer personal anguish.

It works better if changed and expanded into:

I. Bad eating habits are a threat to our well-being.
   A. Such habits endanger health.
      1. They can result in increased heart disease.
      2. They can shorten the life span.
   B. Such habits can damage self-image.
      1. Obese people sometimes dislike themselves.
      2. They can feel that they have nothing to offer others.

Breaking the complex sentence in the first example down into outline form helps you to focus what you are going to say. It simplifies both the structure and logic of your speech.

Look for opportunities to use **parallel construction** when wording the main points of your speech. If you were developing a speech on the need for reforms in election financing, you might word your main points as follows:

I. We need reform at the national level.
II. We need reform at the state level.
III. We need reform at the local level.
IV. But first we need to reform ourselves.

Parallel construction has many advantages. Each statement leads into a major area for development, and each statement helps build to the dramatic conclusion. Because each sentence has the same basic structure, the variations in each stand out sharply. The preceding example highlights the words *national, state, local, But first,* and *ourselves* because they are the only words that differ in important ways in otherwise similar sentences. The parallel structure emphasizes the way the speech narrows its focus like a zoom lens as it moves from a national to an individual perspective.

Parallel construction also helps to distinguish the main points from the subpoints. It makes possible a series of effective internal summaries as the speech moves toward its conclusion. Since it involves repetition, such structure is easy to remember and may prolong the effect of the speech. It satisfies the principles of good form and closure discussed in Chapter 7. Consider using parallel construction whenever this technique seems appropriate to the subject and to your purpose.

**SPEAKER'S
NOTES**

## Developing a Formal Outline

1. Write out your topic, general purpose, specific purpose, and thematic statement.

2. Outline your main points as complete sentences using parallel wording if possible.

3. Add appropriate subpoints under each main point. Be certain these are clearly related to the main points above them.

4. Include supporting material (at subpoint level or lower) for each main point.

5. Place transitions between introduction and body, main points, and body and conclusion.

6. Check the outline for proper coordination and subordination.

7. Outline your introduction, making sure that it contains attention-getting material, establishes your credibility, and previews your speech.

8. Outline your conclusion, being sure that it contains a summary and concluding remarks to help your audience remember your message.

9. Prepare a bibliography, citing the articles, interviews, or books you used in the preparation of your speech.

## *Supporting Your Main Points*

Your supporting material should be shown in the formal outline. As noted in Chapter 6, supporting materials add credence to the main points or subpoints above them. For example, a subpoint that states "Computer on-line services can save you time preparing for class" might rely on a factual example to demonstrate that claim in dramatic form: "This chart shows how much speech preparation time I saved using my computer to access the library's data base."

As you prepare your formal outline, be sure that each main point receives the type and amount of supporting material it needs to be effective for your audience. If you cannot find or devise any effective supporting materials—any factual information, testimony, examples, or narratives—the claim probably does not deserve to be a main point in your speech.

Figure 8.4 on the next page shows the formal outline for Dawn Williams' ten-minute informative speech. Note that this outline includes her final selections of supporting materials.

### MAKING SENSE AND SAVING CENTS
### WHEN YOU BUY A COMPUTER

Dawn Williams

**Topic:** Selecting a Personal Computer
**General purpose:** To inform
**Specific purpose:** To inform my audience of steps to take in selecting a
personal computer
**Thematic statement:** Choose a computer that meets your needs and buy
from a source that offers the best value for your
money.

## INTRODUCTION

In her introduction Dawn creates interest by using conflicting quotations and a rhetorical question. She also establishes her personal credibility and incorporates her thematic statement into the preview.

**I.** *Times Leader* ad: "Buy a Titan PC for $325!" Bargain or not? *Consumer Reports* quote: "A computer that is not compatible with others is little more than an expensive doorstop."
**II.** I had to learn from experience when I bought my own PC. What I learned might help you avoid some costly mistakes!
**III.** Today I want to help you match yourself with a computer—and get the most for your money!

**Transition** from introduction to body: "So let's turn to your first challenge as a computer buyer."

## BODY

Dawn ties her first main point to her listeners' needs by dividing the audience into three groups based on their majors. To strengthen her first subpoint she uses brief examples, a computer-generated visual aid, and a narrative.

**I.** The first step in buying a PC is finding one that will meet your needs.
  **A.** You should consider your major in deciding how you will use a personal computer.
    **1.** Liberal arts majors will probably use a computer mainly for writing term papers.
      **a.** You could get by with a "less expensive" word processor, but be careful.
      **b.** You may want a computer that can access library materials and other campus services.
      **c.** Present brief examples saving time and money through expanded services.
    **2.** Science majors may need a more powerful computer.
      **a.** You may need to be able to run statistical analyses.
      **b.** You may need graphics software for producing charts and diagrams.

FIGURE 8.4    Sample Formal Outline

       c. Show example of computer-generated chart prepared for lab report.
    3. Business majors may need computers with special business software.
       a. You will probably need an accounting program.
       b. You may need a computer that can handle management simulations.
       c. You may need a modem to hook up with others for group assignments.
       d. Use narrative of business majors from different universities interacting via computer.

B. You should look for certain minimum standards in a computer that you buy.

To support her second subpoint, Dawn uses material from a personal interview. The variety of supporting material is impressive, demonstrating that Dawn has responsible knowledge of her topic.

    1. According to Lee Millar, computer systems specialist on campus, your basic hardware should meet the following specifications:
       a. It should have at least 2 megabytes of RAM.
       b. It should have an 80-megabyte hard-disk drive.
       c. It should have at least one floppy drive to back up your input.
       d. It should have a clock speed range of 20 to 25 megahertz.
    2. Peripherals should fit the kind of work you will do.
       a. You will need a printer to work with your computer.
       b. You may need a modem to access the campus services.
       c. You may not need a color monitor.
    3. Software packages should be available for the functions you will use.
       a. Built-in word processing and graphic programs are available.
       b. Additional software should be available at reasonable prices.
    4. Your computer should have the capacity for upgrading.
       a. You should buy a computer that is slightly stronger than you think you need.
       b. You should be aware of "planned obsolescence."
       c. System updates should be available to you.

C. Your computer should be compatible with campus services.
    1. You can save time and money if your computer is compatible.
       a. You can access information from the library.
       b. You can use the laser printers in the computer lab.
    2. Some basic word processors may not be compatible with campus services.

[**Transition** (internal summary) between main points: "What have we learned so far? First, you ought to consider your major as you assess your computer needs. And second, the computer you buy should meet important minimum standards. Now, let's look at how to shop for a computer."]

Dawn supports her second main point with information from a book. This demonstrates the range of her preparation. This section would have been more lively had she made better use of examples or narratives. But this posed a problem: had Dawn used this more "interesting" supporting material, her speech would have been too long. She either had to restrict the coverage of ideas in her speech or limit her use of stories and examples. Gambling that she could develop intense interest in the first part of her speech, she chose the latter option.

II. Donald W. Smith in *A Buyer's Guide to Personal Computers* suggests that you should select a source that offers the most value for your money.
   A. You should consider how much support and assistance you will need.
      1. If you are computer literate, dealer assistance may not be important.
      2. If you are a computer novice, you can get help from the campus computer lab.
   B. You should check the computer's warranty and service contracts.
      1. Look for a year's warranty and a thirty-day money-back guarantee.
      2. Try to get a guarantee of local repairs.
      3. Require that the dealer offer toll-free telephone calls for troubleshooting.
   C. You should compare the prices of computers from a variety of sources.
      1. Check for "good deals" on secondhand computers.
         a. Be wary of planned obsolescence.
         b. Check the Yellow Pages for dealers that offer refurbished models.
         c. Check the want ads in the campus and local papers for deals from individuals.
      2. Check out mail order sources.
         a. Look for advertisements in computer magazines.
         b. Be aware that service and assistance may be hard to come by.
      3. Check out discount store prices.
         a. Look at "warehouse" stores like Sam's.
         b. Visit specialized discount stores like Circuit City.
         c. Be prepared for meager service and assistance support.
      4. Check the campus bookstore for student discounts.
         a. The brands and models may be limited.
         b. It can take a long time to get delivery.
         c. The money you save may make the wait worthwhile.
         d. Provide an example of possible savings.
      5. Computer dealers may be the most expensive source.
         a. You may be able to bargain for a discount.
         b. They may offer the best service and assistance.
         c. Provide an example of helpful local dealer.

[**Transition** from body to conclusion: "Today's lesson in computer purchasing has taught us an important lesson."]

FIGURE 8.4   Continued

**CONCLUSION**

Dawn concludes with a summary statement and final remarks that tie her speech back to her opening quotations. Her citation from Jefferson makes use of prestige testimony.

I. In choosing a personal computer, keep in mind your needs — not those of the store owner — and search for the best value.
II. That word processing computer for $325 may be a bargain, but it's just as likely, as Lee Millar says, "to be a total waste of money." Remember, nothing is a bargain if it doesn't meet your requirements. Heed the words of Thomas Jefferson, who said, "Never buy what you do not want (and I add, 'what you don't need') because it is cheap; it will be dear to you."

**Bibliography**

**Books:**
Smith, Donald W. *A Buyer's Guide to Personal Computers*. Chicago: Technology Press, 1991.

**Articles:**
Bass, Stephen. "The Practical Guide to Home/Office Computing." *PC World*, Dec. 1991, 332.
"Comparing Computers." *Consumers Digest*, June 1992, 248–262.
Raskin, Robin. "Back to School Again—with a PC." *PC Computing*, Sept. 1989, 128–135.

**Miscellaneous References:**
Millar, Lee. Computer systems specialist, Memphis State University. Telephone interview, Oct. 15, 1992.

## Reference Citations

A bibliography of works you consulted in the preparation of your speech should appear at the end of a formal outline. If you conducted an interview, you should cite that information as well. The following guidelines will help you prepare your bibliography:[2]

***Books.*** All references to books should be arranged alphabetically by the last name of the author(s). List the author's name, last name first, followed by the title and publication information (city of publication: publisher, date). For example:

Conley, Thomas M. *Rhetoric in the European Tradition*. New York: Longman, 1990.

Littlejohn, Stephen W. *Theories of Human Communication.* 3rd ed. Belmont, Calif.: Wadsworth, 1989.

***Articles.*** All references to articles should be arranged alphabetically by the last name of the author, or by title if the author is not specified. List the author's name, last name first, followed by the title of the article, name of periodical, volume number, date of publication, and page numbers. For example:

Rushing, Janice Hocker. "The Rhetoric of the American Western Myth." *Communication Monographs* 50 (1983) 14–32.

"The Starry Sky." *Odyssey,* Jan. 1984, 26–27.

***Miscellaneous References.*** In this category you include interviews, telephone calls, or other sources of information used in your speech. The formats are as follows:

Beifuss, Joan. Interview. *All Things Considered.* National Public Radio. WNYC, New York. 4 Apr. 1986.

Frentz, C. R. Assistant to the President, Happy Valley College. Personal interview. 25 July 1991.

## DEVELOPING A KEY-WORD OUTLINE

You should not use your formal outline as you present your speech. If you try to speak from a formal outline, you will be tempted to read it rather than speak extemporaneously. Instead, use an abbreviated **key-word outline,** which reduces the longer outline to a few words that trace the sequence of your major points. This brief outline can be used to jog your memory.

Even though you may never have to refer to the outline, it is nice to know that it is there if you need it. As a general rule, your key-word outline should fit on a single piece of paper or on two or three index cards. The outline should be written with large letters that can be read easily. Because it will be used strictly as a memory jogger, you may decide not to include the introduction, body, and conclusion headings from the formal outline. You want to keep it as simple as possible. The key-word outline for the speech on personal computers is shown in Figure 8.5.

When you practice your speech, work first from your formal outline. Go through the speech two or three times, referring to this outline until you feel comfortable with what you are going to say and how you are going to say it. Then practice from your key-word outline until your speech flows smoothly. Put your outlines aside for a while, then come back and try giving the speech again, using only the key-word outline. If the key words still work as reminders, your preparation has been effective.

I. INTRODUCTION
   A. AD AND QUOTE
   B. MY EXPERIENCES
   C. MATCH TO NEEDS
II. NEEDS
   A. CONSIDER MAJOR
   B. MINIMUM STANDARDS
      1. 2 MB RAM, 80 MB HARD DRIVE, FLOPPY DRIVE, 20–25 MH SPEED
      2. PRINTER & MODEM
      3. SOFTWARE
      4. UPGRADE CAPACITY
   C. COMPATIBLE WITH CAMPUS SERVICES
III. SELECT FOR VALUE
   A. SUPPORT AND ASSISTANCE?
   B. WARRANTY AND SERVICE?
   C. COMPARE PRICES
      1. SECONDHAND SOURCES
      2. MAIL ORDER
      3. DISCOUNT STORES
      4. CAMPUS BOOKSTORE
      5. COMPUTER DEALERS
IV. CONCLUSION
   A. MEET YOUR NEEDS AND FIND BEST SOURCE
   B. BEWARE OF "BARGAINS"
   C. JEFFERSON QUOTE

**FIGURE 8.5**
Sample Key-Word Outline

During the actual presentation of your speech you may want to have some material written out on separate cards. This is important for quotations or statistics that must be cited exactly. Some speakers find it best to have their introduction on one card, the key-word outline of the body of their speech on a second card, and their conclusion on a third.

You should not try to hide the key-word outline during your actual speech, nor should you feel self-conscious about using it. Hold your outline in your hand or place it on a lectern so that you minimize the loss of eye contact with listeners when you refer to it. We shall have more to say about how to use the key-word outline in Chapter 11, "Presenting Your Speech."

**IN SUMMARY**     An outline gives you an overview of your speech and helps you organize your thoughts for maximum effectiveness.

***Developing a Preparation Outline.*** A *preparation outline* is a tentative plan of the speech you will finally present. It brings together the major parts of your message into a pattern that shows the relative importance of points and how they fit together. A preparation outline arranges main points, sub-points, sub-subpoints, and sub-sub-subpoints in relation to each other. The degree of elaboration depends on your assessment of audience needs, time constraints, and the ethical demands of your topic. As preparation outlines evolve for a particular speech, they indicate how you will use supporting materials. They also point up the role of transitions in the speech. By developing preparation outlines you can judge the effectiveness of your initial research and determine where you may need more work or additional material.

***Developing a Formal Outline.*** The *formal outline* is the final product of the research and planning phase of your speech. It is the most polished and complete outline form. As such, it follows a number of conventions, including coordination and subordination. *Coordination* requires that statements that are approximately equal in importance be placed on the same level in the outline and receive equal support. *Subordination* requires that statements descend in importance and that each level logically include the level below it. As you descend through the various levels, points become more specific and concrete. The numbering, lettering, and indentation system should be consistent throughout the outline.

The main points in a formal outline should be worded as independent sentences. *Parallel construction* highlights the main points and helps the audience remember your message. A formal outline usually requires a bibliography.

***Developing a Key-Word Outline.*** A *key-word outline* can aid in the presentation of a speech. Such an outline reduces the formal outline to a few essential words that remind you of the content and design as you present the speech.

| | |
|---|---|
| **TERMS TO KNOW** preparation outline | coordination |
| subpoints | subordination |
| sub-subpoints | parallel construction |
| sub-sub-subpoints | key-word outline |
| formal outline | |

**DISCUSSION**
1. Working in small groups, share a preparation outline for the next speech you will give in class. Explain the strategy of your structure and show how your outline satisfies the principles of coordination and subordination. Demonstrate that your supporting materials would be adequate. Revise as appropriate in light of the group discussion that follows.

2. Select one of the speeches from Appendix B and prepare a formal outline of it. Does this outline make clear the structure of the speech? Does

it reveal any structural flaws? Can you see any different ways the speaker might have developed the speech? Present your thoughts on these questions in class discussion.

3. If a successful speech is a bridge of meaning that joins speaker and listeners, as we discussed in Chapter 7, how would you describe the importance of an outline for the speech?

**APPLICATION**  1. Assume that the speeches you give in class this semester will be advertised in the campus newspaper. Develop titles that might be useful in attracting an audience to these speeches.

2. See if you can "unjumble" the following outline of the body of a speech using coordination and subordination appropriately. What title would you suggest for this speech?

*Thematic statement:* Deer hunting with a camera can be an exciting sport.

   I.   There is a profound quiet, a sense of mystery.

     A.  The woods in late fall are enchanting.

        1.  The "film-hunter" becomes part of a beautiful scene.

        2.  Dawn is especially lovely.

     B.  Example of big doe walking under my tree stand.

        1.  When they appear, deer always surprise you.

        2.  Example of big buck after long stalk.

  II.   Hunting from a stand can be a good way to capture a deer on film.

     A.  The stalk method on the ground is another way to hunt with a camera.

        1.  Learn to recognize deer tracks and droppings.

           a.  Learn to recognize deer signs.

           b.  Learn to recognize rubs on trees and scrapes on the ground.

        2.  Hunt into the wind and move slowly.

     B.  There are two main ways to hunt with a camera.

        1.  Stands offer elevation above the line of sight and line of scent.

        2.  Portable stands are also available.

        3.  Locating and building your permanent stand.

 III.   The right camera can be no more expensive than a rifle.

     A.  Selecting the right camera for film-hunting is essential.

     B.  Certain features — like a zoom lens — are necessary.

IV.   Display slide of doe.

   A.  You can collect "trophies" you can enjoy forever.

   B.  Display slide of buck.

   C.  Not all hunters are killers: the film-hunter celebrates life, not death.

**NOTES**   1.  Robert T. Oliver, Harold P. Zelko, and Paul D. Holtzman, *Communicative Speaking and Listening* (New York: Holt, 1968), p. 125.

   2.  You can get more extensive directions on bibliography form by consulting Joseph Gilbaldi and Walter S. Achtert, *MLA Handbook for Writers of Research Papers,* 3rd ed. (New York: The Modern Language Association of America, 1988) or the *Publication Manual of the American Psychological Association,* 3rd ed. (Washington D.C.: American Psychological Association, 1983). Your instructor may ask that you follow one of these or another guide.

PART THREE

Developing
Presentation Skills

*Seeing . . . , most of all the senses, makes us know and brings to light many differences between things.*

*—Aristotle*

# 9

# Visual Aids

## This Chapter Will Help You

- appreciate the advantages of using visual aids.
- understand what types of visual aids work best in different situations.
- learn how to present visual aids.
- plan, design, and prepare visual aids.
- use visual aids for greater effectiveness.

If you are like most students, the first "public speeches" you gave involved the use of a visual aid. In kindergarten or first grade, you probably participated in "Show and Tell." You may have brought an object that you were going to talk about — a new toy, something you made, the family pet — or you may have brought something to school that represented the object, such as a picture or a drawing. The visual aid helped you explain or describe your subject. Visual aids in later speech situations may go beyond "Show and Tell" in sophistication but still serve much the same purpose.

## USES AND ADVANTAGES OF VISUAL AIDS

**isual aids** give your audience direct sensory contact with your speech. Usually this contact is visual — hence the term *visual aids*. However, other senses, such as taste and hearing, can also provide such contact. In this chapter the term *visual aids* includes any and all supplemental materials you might use to increase the clarity and effectiveness of your speeches.

Why are such aids so useful? The answer lies in a weakness of words as instruments of communication. As powerful as words can be, they are essentially abstract. They represent objects and ideas, but they are not the objects and ideas they represent. Thus, words can create a barrier of abstraction between listeners and reality. To understand words, listeners must translate them into mental images, a process that can be difficult and confusing. Imagine how hard it would be to describe through words alone the carburetor system of a car. Even with effective graphics — models and charts — it would still be difficult for many of us to comprehend. It can require words *and* visual aids, blended skillfully, to explain some topics to some audiences. Visual aids can help speeches in the following ways:

1. *Visual aids enhance understanding.* Sometimes visual aids work better than words to convey meaning. It is easier to give directions if you can trace the route on a map. Similarly, when you are describing the auditory qualities of stereo-speaker systems, it can be more effective to let audiences actually *hear* the differences.

2. *Visual aids add authenticity.* When you show listeners the points you are making, you do more than just clarify your message. You authenticate or prove it. This type of proof is useful in both informative and persuasive speeches. Research confirms that "visual aids designed to supplement and clarify a persuasive message can affect attitude change and speaker credibility."[1] If audiences can actually hear the difference in stereo systems you have been describing, they are more likely to be convinced that one is better than the other. When you show them the problem you are talking about, they should more readily accept your solution.

3. *Visual aids add variety.* Too much of a good thing, even a well-designed fabric of words, can get tiresome. The use of visual aids at critical points in a speech provides variety. This helps sustain audience interest and attention.

4. *Visual aids may improve presentational skills.* If you have a problem with communication apprehension, try using visual aids during your next presentation. As you identify the parts of a model or point to a graph, you may forget to be nervous. The physical movements needed to interpret a visual aid can release your energy in a constructive way.

5. *Visual aids help your speech have lasting impact.* Visual aids are easier to remember than words because they are more concrete. A photograph of a hungry child may stick in our mind, increasing the influence of a speech urging charitable contributions. Or we may remember the bright red markings on a map that mark dangerous places.

6. *Visual aids can help build your ethos as a speaker.* A neat, attractively designed visual aid reflects your commitment to communicate. It tells the audience that you took extra time to prepare your speech. In some organizational settings, such as training and development workshops, audiences actually expect visual aids to be used. If you don't have them, the audience will be disappointed, and your credibility may suffer.

The skillful use of visual aids takes considerable creativity, planning, preparation, and rehearsal. In this chapter we describe the kinds of visual aids most frequently used in speeches, identify the ways in which they can be presented, offer suggestions for preparing them, and present guidelines for their use.

## KINDS OF VISUAL AIDS

The number and kinds of visual aids are limited only by the speaker's imagination. We shall examine some of the more frequently used visual aids and the speech situations in which they are most helpful.

### People

People can function as visual aids. As the speaker, you cannot avoid being a visual aid for your own speech. Your body, grooming, actions, gestures, voice, facial expressions, and demeanor always provide an added dimension to your speech. Use these factors to help convey your message. Even your clothes can function as a visual aid. If you will be talking about camping and wilderness adventures, blue jeans, a flannel shirt, and hiking boots might be appropriate attire for your speech. What you wear, however, should not be more interesting than what you say. Here as in all other cases, visual aids should accentuate, not overshadow, the verbal message.

You can also use other people as visual aids. Neomal Abyskera used two of his classmates to illustrate the line-up positions in the game of rugger, a game similar to rugby played in his native Sri Lanka. At an appropriate moment in his speech, Neomal said, "Peter and Jeffrey will show you how the opposing team members line up." While his classmates demonstrated the arm-locked shoulder grip position, Neomal briefly explained when and why the position was assumed. This visual demonstration was more interesting and effective than if he had tried to describe the position verbally or drawn it on posterboard with stick figures.

If you plan to use classmates for such a demonstration, be sure that they are willing to help you and will not distract from your speech. Develop good transitions both for the beginning and end of the demonstration, and rehearse with classmates until they fit smoothly into the presentation. On the day of the speech they should sit in the front row so that they can come forward and then sit down again as quickly as possible.

## Objects and Models

Nothing can illustrate something more effectively than the subject itself. But some objects — especially those that are very large or very small — are simply not practical for use in a speech. In such cases, reduced or enlarged scale models may be your only option.

**Objects.**  If you are speaking about something that can be carried easily to class and is large enough that listeners in the back of the room can see it without strain, you may decide to use it as a visual aid. Ideally, it should also be small enough to be kept out of sight until you are ready to use it. If you display the object before you plan to use it, you risk being upstaged by your visual aid. If it is unusual, listeners may get involved in trying to figure out what it is and forget to listen to you. One of our students brought six different objects to class to illustrate an informative speech on the Montessori method of preschool education. When it was her turn to speak, she lined up these objects across the desk in front of the lectern. They were such a distraction that during her speech, a listener in the front row actually scooted his chair closer to the desk and picked up one of the objects to examine it. The speaker had to stop and ask him to put it back. She could have handled this situation more effectively by concealing the objects and bringing them out one at a time as they were being discussed.

Inanimate objects make better visual aids than living things, which you cannot always control. We once had a student present a speech on caring for puppies. She brought a six-week-old puppy to class as her visual aid. At the beginning of her speech, she removed the lectern from the speaker's table, spread some newspapers on it, placed the puppy on the table, and tried to give her speech. We are sure you have already guessed what happened. The first thing the puppy did was wet on the papers (including her note cards, which she had put down on the table while trying to control the puppy). The first thing the audience did was giggle. From there it was all downhill. The puppy squirmed and wiggled happily, tried to jump on the speaker, and alternately whined and yipped throughout the speech. The speaker was totally upstaged by her visual aid. When this fiasco was over, we asked the student why she had brought the puppy to class — what point she had wanted to make with its presence. She said she thought that because she was talking about puppies, it would be "nice to bring one along." Another student brought a realistic looking plastic model of a semiautomatic weapon, which he pulled from beneath the lectern during the introduction of his speech urging gun control. The effect was both dramatic and frightening. Several audience members became quite upset and found it hard to concentrate on his message. Never create these kinds of problems for yourself with a visual aid! If you have any concerns about the appropriateness of an object as a visual aid, check with your instructor in advance of using it.

Objects are frequently used to illustrate speeches that demonstrate how to do something. Indeed, such speeches often cannot succeed without a visual aid. An engaging example of this type of use occurred near Halloween as part of a student speech on jack-o'-lanterns: both how to make them and the folklore behind them. The speaker demonstrated how to draw the face you want on a pumpkin with a magic marker and how to make a beveled cut around the stem so that the top won't fall in. As she was showing how to do these things, she was also telling stories of the ancient myths surrounding jack-o'-lanterns. Her visual aid and her words helped each other: the demonstration enlivened her speech, and the stories gave the demonstration depth and meaning. As she came to her closing remarks, she reached inside the lectern and produced a finished jack-o'-lantern, complete with lighted candle. The effect was memorable.

***Models.***   Sometimes your object may be too large to carry, too small for the audience to see easily, too rare, expensive, or fragile to risk bringing to class, or simply unavailable. In such cases a model of the subject can serve as a visual aid. An additional advantage of a model is that you can also provide a cross section or cutaway example of the object to show the interior of the object.

George Stacey borrowed a slightly smaller than life-size model of a person from the Red Cross to demonstrate how to conduct cardiopulmonary resuscitation. The model folded neatly into a suitcase, so that it could be kept out of sight when not in use. When using a model as a visual aid, be sure that it is truly representative. It should be constructed to scale, maintaining the proper proportions between parts. The model should also be large enough for all listeners to see from their seats. Any visual aid that the audience must strain to see will be more of a distraction than a help.

## Graphics

Graphics are representational visual aids that you prepare for use in a speech. They may include sketches, maps, graphs, charts, or textual graphics.

***Sketches.*** Sketches or diagrams can offer simplified representations of what you are describing. They should be used to stress essential aspects of your message.

Mark Peterson prepared a sketch to illustrate his speech on factors to consider when buying a bicycle. Mark placed the poster board containing his sketch of a bicycle on the ledge of the chalkboard (blank side to the audience) before he began his speech. When he reached the point at which he wanted to talk about making bar-to-pedal and seat-to-handlebar measurements, he said, "Let me show you how to take some basic measurements," as he turned the poster around. When he finished his demonstration, Mark turned the poster board around again to its blank side so that it would not be a distraction during the rest of his speech.

***Maps.*** Commercially prepared maps contain too much detail to serve as visual aids for speeches. Much of this detail is irrelevant, and the map will be difficult, if not impossible, for most listeners to read from their seats. The best maps are those that you make specifically for your speech so that they are large, simple, and relevant to your purpose. Maps are particularly useful in speeches based on spatial design. The map in Figure 9.1 was used to indicate the distance and routes between major attractions at Yellowstone National Park. Having such a map helps the audience put locations and spatial relationships into perspective and makes them easier to understand and remember. Stephen Huff used a map to help his listeners see precisely where a series of devastating earthquakes had occurred along the New Madrid Fault and to understand how a recurrence of such earthquakes might endanger them (see his speech and visual aids at the end of Chapter 12).

Whether a map works as a visual aid depends on the speaker's ability to integrate it into the verbal presentation. Elizabeth Walling used a map of the wilderness canoe area in northern Minnesota to familiarize her Memphis audience with that area. She made a double-sided poster that she was able to keep hidden behind the speaker's table until she was ready for it. On one side she highlighted the wilderness canoe area on an outline map of northern Minnesota, pointing out various places of interest to canoers. To illustrate how large the area is, Elizabeth said, "Let me put this in a familiar context for you." She then turned the poster over, revealing an outline map of western Tennessee on which she had superimposed the wilderness area. At a glance we could see that this area would extend from Memphis to past Jackson, some eighty miles away. By using maps this way, she created a striking visual comparison.

***Graphs.*** Mrs. Robert A. Taft once commented, "I always find that statistics are hard to swallow and impossible to digest. The only one I can ever remember is that if all the people who go to sleep in church were laid end to end, they would be a lot more comfortable."[2] Many people may share Mrs. Taft's feelings about statistics. Masses of numbers recited in a speech may be

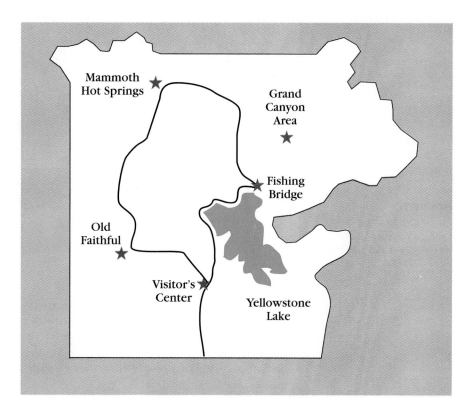

FIGURE 9.1
Map: Yellowstone Park

confusing or even overwhelming. A well-designed graph can help make statistical information easier for listeners to comprehend.

A **pie graph** or circle graph shows the size of a subject's parts in relation to each other and to the whole. The circle, or "pie," represents the whole, and the segments, or "slices," represent the parts. The two pie graphs in Figure 9.2 on page 238 show the dramatic increase in the number of women earning undergraduate college degrees, using the years 1950 and 1989 as bases of comparison.[3] The most effective pie graphs have five or fewer categories. Too many divisions of the pie make the graph cluttered and difficult to read.

A **bar graph** shows comparisons and contrasts between two or more items or groups. Bar graphs are easy to understand because each item can be readily compared with every other item on the graph. Bar graphs also have a dramatic visual impact. Figure 9.3 is a bar graph illustrating units of blood donated by undergraduates by class on a certain campus during a recent year.

A **line graph** demonstrates changes across time and is especially useful for indicating trends of growth or decline. Because you can plot more than one item on a line graph, you can use it for complex and detailed represen-

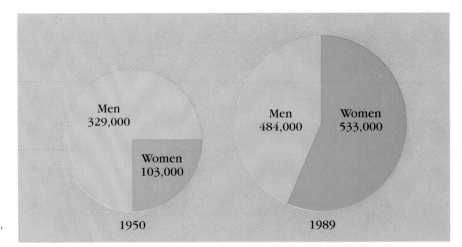

FIGURE 9.2
Pie Graph: Undergraduate
College Degrees Conferred,
by Gender, 1950 and 1989

tations. Consider, for example, how we might represent the information shown in Figure 9.2 in a line graph. Instead of showing undergraduate college degrees earned by men and women for only two years, the line graph (Figure 9.4) allows us to show the intervening years as well and to offer more precise explanations of how these trends develop. The upward-sloping lines confirm the dramatic rise in the number of women earning degrees.

Whenever you plot more than one line on a graph, you must be certain that listeners can distinguish the lines. Use different colors or patterns, such as solid lines, dashes, and dots, to designate specific items. Different colors or patterns are preferable to labeling the lines because they keep the graph from becoming cluttered. Never try to plot more than three lines on a graph.

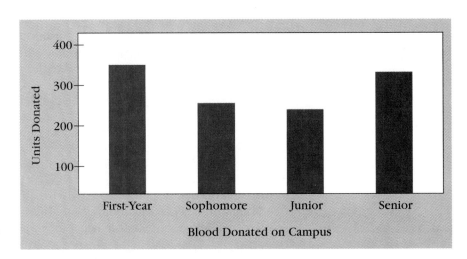

FIGURE 9.3
Bar Graph: Blood Donated
by Undergraduate Classes

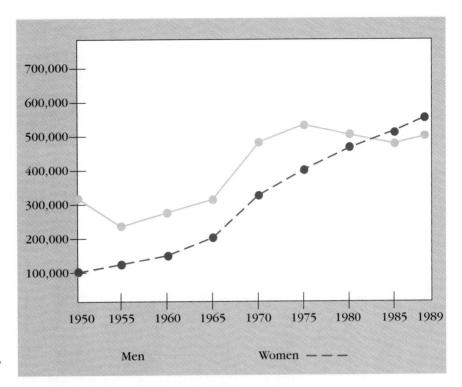

FIGURE 9.4
Line Graph: Undergraduate
College Degrees Conferred,
by Gender, 1950–1989

***Charts.*** Charts provide convenient visual summaries of processes and relationships that are not in themselves visible. However, they are difficult to use as visual aids in speeches because they must often be oversimplified to keep them from being cluttered and distracting. Among the more frequently used types of charts are flow charts, tree charts, and stream charts.

**Flow charts** can show power and responsibility relationships, such as who reports to whom in an organization. Organizational flow charts usually place the most powerful office or person at the top of the chart, the next most powerful offices or people directly underneath, down through the least powerful offices or people. Flow charts can also be used to detail the steps in a process. Using lines and arrows, such a chart indicates what steps occur simultaneously and what steps occur sequentially. Figure 9.5 on page 240 is a flow chart that traces the major steps in the preparation of a speech.

**Tree charts** show processes of development across time, such as how complex family systems may develop across generations from original ancestors, or how one discovery may lead to many spin-off inventions. The emphasis is on diffusion, on how the few can blossom into the many.

**Stream charts** also show development over time, but their purpose is the opposite of a tree chart. Rather than indicating how the few become many, a stream chart shows how the many come together to produce the few, just as many streams make up a river. Stream charts may be used to establish how

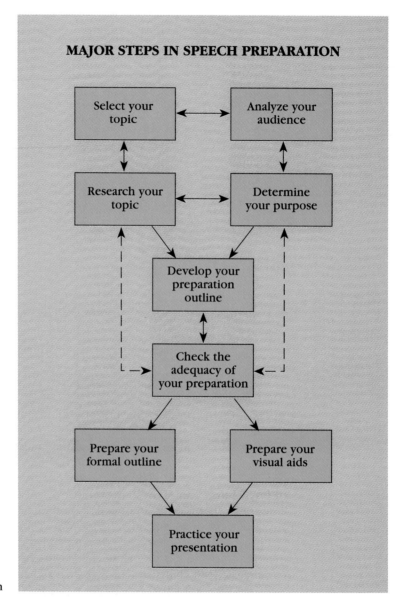

**MAJOR STEPS IN SPEECH PREPARATION**

FIGURE 9.5
Flow Chart: Major Steps in
the Preparation of a Speech

forces converge to make up a person, product, or decision. The stream chart
can offer a sophisticated visual projection of the cause-effect relationship.

   The problem with most charts is that they are usually too complex and detailed for use in speeches, especially if your time is limited. Sequence charts,
however, can be quite helpful, even in a brief speech. **Sequence charts,**
which are presented in a series, show different stages of a process. You can
create suspense by using sequence charts, as the audience anticipates what

the next chart will reveal. For example, you could choose to present material on the awarding of college degrees, divided by gender, in a series of charts. On these charts you might want to use **pictographs,** symbolic representations of information or abstract concepts. In the first chart, representing 1950, you could show the figure of a man three times larger than the accompanying figure of a woman, indicating the 3:1 ratio in earned degrees. Intermediate charts prepared for decade years could show changes in the relative sizes of these figures, until the final chart would indicate the emergence of women into majority status. Figure 9.6 indicates how the first and last charts in the sequence might look.

***Textual Graphics.*** **Textual graphics** are lists of words designed for visual impact. Presenting key words visually as you speak can help an audience track the message of a complicated speech. For example, as you describe a process, you might write on the chalkboard the number "1" and by it a key word or phrase, then "2" and "3" as your speech proceeds. That way you would guide your audience to the main points of your speech. Unfamiliar material becomes more clear and memorable when listeners can both hear and see the message. You can also present textual graphics using poster board, flip charts, transparencies, slides, or handouts.

## *Photographs and Pictures*

The old Chinese proverb that a picture is worth a thousand words is not always true in public speaking. The use of pictures or photographs has both advantages and disadvantages. On the plus side, a good photograph can demonstrate or authenticate a point in a speech in a way that words alone cannot. It can make a situation seem more vivid and realistic. For instance, if

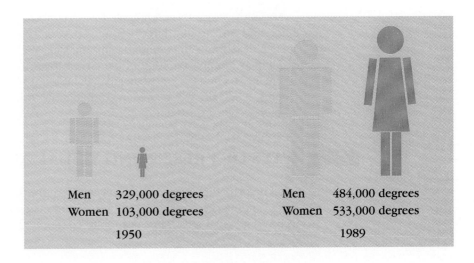

FIGURE 9.6
Sequence Chart:
Undergraduate College
Degrees Conferred, by
Gender, 1950 and 1989

Men     329,000 degrees
Women  103,000 degrees

1950

Men     484,000 degrees
Women  533,000 degrees

1989

you were trying to describe the devastation caused by a flood, tornado, or hurricane, photographs could be quite useful.

On the negative side, photographs and pictures frequently include distracting details that are not relevant to your message. Their vividness can also be a disadvantage, especially when speakers rely on them too heavily to make a point, forgetting that language is the primary medium of communication in a speech. Such aids should reinforce, not replace, the speaker's words.

The major problem with using pictures as visual aids is their size. Unless a picture is large enough for everyone in the room to see easily, it contributes nothing. We once had a student who tried to illustrate his speech on baseball by showing the audience pictures from a book. He used paper clips to mark the pages on which there were pictures he wanted to show the class. Unfortunately, the sequence of pictures in the book did not match the sequence of ideas in his speech, so he kept opening the book to the wrong pages. Additionally, the pictures in the book were too small to be seen except from the front row. This visual aid created considerable problems for the student, both diminishing the effectiveness of his presentation and damaging his ethos. Finally, it is hard to resist the temptation to circulate photographs among the audience as you give your speech. The pictures then compete with you for the attention of listeners.

Despite such limitations, photographs or pictures can work well if they are carefully selected, controlled, and enlarged. They should be selected for their relevance to your speech. They should be controlled just as you control charts, graphs, and maps — revealed only when they serve the point you are making and then put away. Color copiers can now make inexpensive eleven-by-seventeen-inch enlargements from snapshots. These are probably the minimally acceptable size for most classroom speeches. Because they are reproduced on copier paper, you should mount them on poster board for ease of presentation.

Museum prints and commercial posters are made to be seen from a distance and are usually large enough to overcome the size problem. In his speech describing an extended camping trip, Michael McDonald used a print of Thomas Moran's painting of the Green River in the American West to represent his feelings about that area. Paintings can often convey a mood or feeling, especially when used in combination with eloquent words. They can help speeches arouse emotion.

## WAYS OF PRESENTING VISUAL AIDS

Chalkboards, flip charts, poster board, handouts, projections, films, videotapes, audiotapes, and computer-generated materials are often used as ways to present visual aids. Most corporate conference rooms, school classrooms, and public meeting places are equipped with chalkboards or flip charts. They are probably the most frequently used ways to present visual aids.

## Chalkboard

The chalkboard works well when a speaker wants to offer a step-by-step demonstration. Building a visual aid on the board one unit at a time creates suspense and holds the attention of listeners. The spontaneous construction of a visual aid implies that you are in command of a concept — and you prove it by creating the visual aid right before your audience's eyes. You can also use the chalkboard to emphasize certain words and ideas. Writing these terms or names on the board calls the audience's attention to their importance and helps your listeners remember them. This is especially important if the word or name is spelled differently from the way it is pronounced. For example, if you mentioned the leader of the undergound Christianity movement in China, Lin Xiangao, it would be advisable to write the name on the chalkboard. As you turn to the board, you might say, "Let me write this name for you." Write quickly, but legibly, then immediately regain eye contact with your audience.

A chalkboard also can be a good audience-adaptation tool. Despite your best preparation, there may be moments when you look at your listeners

*In his televised "infomercials" during the 1992 presidential campaign, Ross Perot used line graphs to illustrate economic issues. Line graphs show changes across time and are especially useful for indicating trends of growth or decline.*

and realize that some of them have not understood what you have just said. You can respond to this feedback by writing a few words on the board or drawing a simple diagram to help dispel their confusion.

A final advantage of using a chalkboard is that it keeps you from hiding behind the lectern while you are speaking. Once you have moved from the lectern to the chalkboard, you will feel freer to walk about, perhaps presenting your next point from the side of the speaking table or even moving in front of the table to reduce distance between yourself and listeners.

For all these strong advantages, chalkboards can hinder communication more than they help unless you use them carefully. If you are not artistically talented, your visual aids may look sloppy, and your audience may not be able to decipher what you have just put on the board. If you are not able to practice your speech in the actual classroom setting, you may create too small a visual aid on the chalkboard. It frustrates listeners on the back rows when they are not able to see without straining. They may feel alienated from the speech, and simply give up their roles as critical and constructive listeners. You can remedy these problems by practicing in the room when it is not in use. As you practice, look at the visual aid from the back row to be sure it is legible and effective. Preserve the appearance of spontaneity by lightly roughing out your designs in advance. These should not be visible to listeners before your speech. Just be sure to warn earlier speakers not to erase your preparations!

Another possible disadvantage is that chalkboards can become cluttered with writing, which distracts from your speech. Be sure to erase any previous drawings on the board before you begin. As a courtesy to later speakers, erase your own visual aids when you have concluded.

A final problem with chalkboards is that speakers tend to overuse them and to use them poorly. Despite the most careful preparation, including lightly roughing out visual aids in advance, chalkboard visual aids are not as neat and polished as those constructed in advance on flip charts, poster boards, transparencies, slides, or handouts. Additionally, you should not use the chalkboard for any visual aid that will take more than a few seconds to write or draw. If you spend much time with your back to the audience, you will lose contact with them. We have all witnessed speakers who end up talking more to the chalkboard than to the audience. Never use the chalkboard simply because you do not want to take the time to prepare a polished visual aid.

For these reasons chalkboard illustrations should be used sparingly in classroom speeches. Keep the designs or writing simple and to the point. As you practice, try not to turn your back on your imagined audience. Stand to the side of your drawing or writing and maintain eye contact with these imaginary listeners. If the visual aid is too complex to permit you to maintain such contact, this is a clear sign that you should prepare a different type of visual aid. Discover this *before* you make your formal presentation.

## *Flip Chart*

A flip chart is a large, unlined tablet. Most flip charts are newsprint pads that measure about two feet wide by three feet high. They are placed on an easel so that pages can be flipped over the top once you are finished with a page. You use broad-tipped felt markers to draw or write on a flip chart.

Flip charts offer many of the same advantages as chalkboard and minimize many of the disadvantages. They are convenient, inexpensive, and adaptable to most speech settings. With a flip chart you can produce a striking visual aid because felt markers are available in many vivid colors. And because flip-chart pads are portable, you can prepare your materials before your speech. This allows you to draw neater, more complex visual aids and to maintain audience contact throughout your speech. Like the chalkboard, the flip chart can also be used spontaneously should the need arise. Just be certain that you have blank pages left in the pad for this purpose and that you bring felt markers.

When preparing visual aid materials on a flip chart, try to keep each page as simple as possible. Write on every other page because the felt-marker ink may bleed through the paper. Back each page of prepared material with a blank page marked at the bottom with small paper clips. Leave the first page of the flip chart blank so that your written materials are hidden from audience view until you are ready to flip over the blank page and reveal your message or drawing.

Susan Larson used a flip chart effectively to illustrate a speech on nautical navigation. Figure 9.7 shows her first page of flip-chart material. The acronym POSH was her device for remembering how to navigate in relation to river

FIGURE 9.7
Flip Chart: Explanation of
an Acronym

markers. Susan kept her writing to a minimum so that the material stood out clearly and emphatically. Had she tried to write out the message "Keep the marker buoys to your left (port) as you leave the marina and to your right (starboard) coming home," the flip-chart page would have looked cluttered.

Susan's second and third flip-chart sheets contained color drawings of Coast Guard navigation markers found in the inland waterways. Her fourth sheet was a simplified drawing of a navigational chart, showing the placement of buoys marking a river channel. As she talked, Susan drew the path a boat would have to navigate between the buoys, adding the element of spontaneity. The flip-chart technique was less cumbersome than trying to handle four separate posters.

### Poster Board

Poster board has many uses in the construction of visual aids. When you wish to make just one or two highly polished or complex visual aids or when flip charts are not available, poster board can be invaluable. You may be able to tack your poster to the cork border at the top of many chalkboards so that it can be seen easily.

Even if you are not artistic, you can prepare an effective drawing on poster board. Most college bookstores or any office supply store can provide all the materials you need to turn out a professional-looking product: the poster board, a straightedge or ruler, a compass, felt markers, and stick-on letters in a variety of colors and sizes. This basic equipment will enable you to prepare sketches, simplified maps, and charts or graphs.

On the day of your speech, be sure to conceal your visual aid until you need it. Only a moment is required to place the poster board on an easel, on the ledge in front of a chalkboard, or in front of the speaker's lectern. To be certain that things go smoothly, try to practice in your actual classroom. Develop effective transitions that introduce the visual aid (Let's see how a visual model of these relationships might look") and conclude it ("Now that we've seen a representation of these relationships, let's consider their consequences"). As you practice, remember to stand to one side of the poster, facing the imaginery audience as much as possible while referring to your aid. Point to each feature as you speak about it. If you cannot get into the classroom for practice, come early on the day of your speech to be sure you can position the poster board as you want it. Bring masking tape and thumbtacks in case you should need them.

### Handouts

Handouts that you distribute to the audience before your speech are a high-risk way to present a visual aid. The handout can compete with you for attention, and the audience may decide to read instead of listen. Handouts do, however, have many advantages. They are especially useful when speech subjects are complex or or your message contains a lot of statistical information. Handouts are also helpful in speeches that introduce a new vocabulary. When the speech is concluded, the handout remains to remind listeners of your message. Do not distribute handouts during your speech — do it either before or after your presentation, depending on whether the audience needs to refer to the material as you speak.

Dwight Davidson distributed a handout at the beginning of his speech entitled "Job Trends for the Nineties." Dwight's audience was able to follow him as he introduced and explained the statistical tables in the handout. Without such a visual supplement his listeners might have been lost. Stephen Huff distributed the handout called "Earthquake Preparedness Suggestions" *after* he had concluded the speech [both the speech and handout are reprinted at the end of Chapter 12]. Thus he avoided a potential distraction during his speech and also helped his audience remember the important advice he had given. Your decision whether to distribute a handout before or after your speech must be based on case-by-case consideration of the nature of the subject, how confident you are of your ability to control attention, and how you want your handout to function.

## Slides and Transparencies

Slides and transparency projections allow the audience to see graphics or photographs more easily or to look at an outline of your main points while you are making them. This technique helps listeners remain on track during long or complicated presentations. Slides and transparencies are frequently used in organizational presentations.

Slides are difficult to handle in public speeches. Often the room must be darkened while they are being shown, and the illuminated screen — not you — becomes the center of attention. Unless you have remote-controlled equipment, you may have to stand behind or in the middle of the audience to run the projector. The result is that you will always be talking to someone's back. If you do not have remote-controlled equipment, your best solution may be to have a classmate change the slides on cue. You will need to practice coordinating your presentation with the showing of the slides. You will also need specialized equipment to prepare your slides. Check to see if your campus has an audiovisual media center that can help you.

Transparency projections have many advantages over slide presentations. A transparency projector enlarges and transmits an image from a clear acetate original. Transparencies can be made on many copying machines and are quite inexpensive. You can draw, print, or type your original material on plain paper and have it converted to a transparency. Transparencies are also one of the best ways to use computer-generated graphics. You can buy acetate sheets that can be run through a laser printer. Once the transparency has been made, you can highlight various parts with colored markers. The room need not be as dark for projections as for slides. You can also add material to a transparency as it is being shown. A pencil makes a convenient pointer to direct the audience's attention to features you want to emphasize. The major disadvantage of such projections is that you must speak from where your equipment is located. Again, you may find yourself addressing the backs of some listeners.

If you decide to use slides or transparencies as visual aids in a speech, be sure that you check the equipment ahead of time and familiarize yourself with its operation. Practice delivering your speech using the equipment. In some machines, slides or transparencies must be inserted upside down. Be certain you have them in correctly before you make your presentation. Also be sure you have a spare light bulb taped inside the machine. Many a presentation has been ruined by an upside-down slide or a burned-out light bulb. You may need a long extension cord to position your equipment where you want it. Check the location of electrical outlets in advance, and be sure the cord fits. Finally, do not use too many slides or transparencies in a short speech. Any visual aid should do just that — *aid* your speech, not compete with it or replace it.

### Computer-Generated Materials

Many graphics programs are now available for use with personal computers. Using such programs, you can produce professional-looking visual aids. The graphs produced by a computer are much neater and more accurate than most of those drawn freehand. Computer programs can produce textual graphics that are clear, readable, and eye-catching. Some of the more sophisticated programs will even generate colored transparencies or slide masters when a color printer is available. Figure 9.8 shows an excellent computer-generated textual graphic for use as a transparency.

Computers can help you make handouts and slides as well as transparencies. Unless you have access to a blueprint-size enlarger/copier, computer-generated graphics are less appropriate for posters.

### Films, Videotapes, Audiotapes, and Laser Discs

Films, videotapes, audiotapes, and laser discs can help authenticate a speech and add variety to a presentation. One major problem is that they are difficult to incorporate into a speech when time is limited. They also share many of the disadvantages of slide presentations, such as the need for a darkened room, special equipment, and operating skills. Additionally, they may need to be edited for use in presentations, which takes special training and equipment. If not properly cued, they can ruin a presentation and damage your ethos. It is all too easy for a film or tape to dominate the speech and consume so much of your time that you are overwhelmed by your visual aid. When in doubt about the wisdom or practicality of using such aids, consult your instructor.

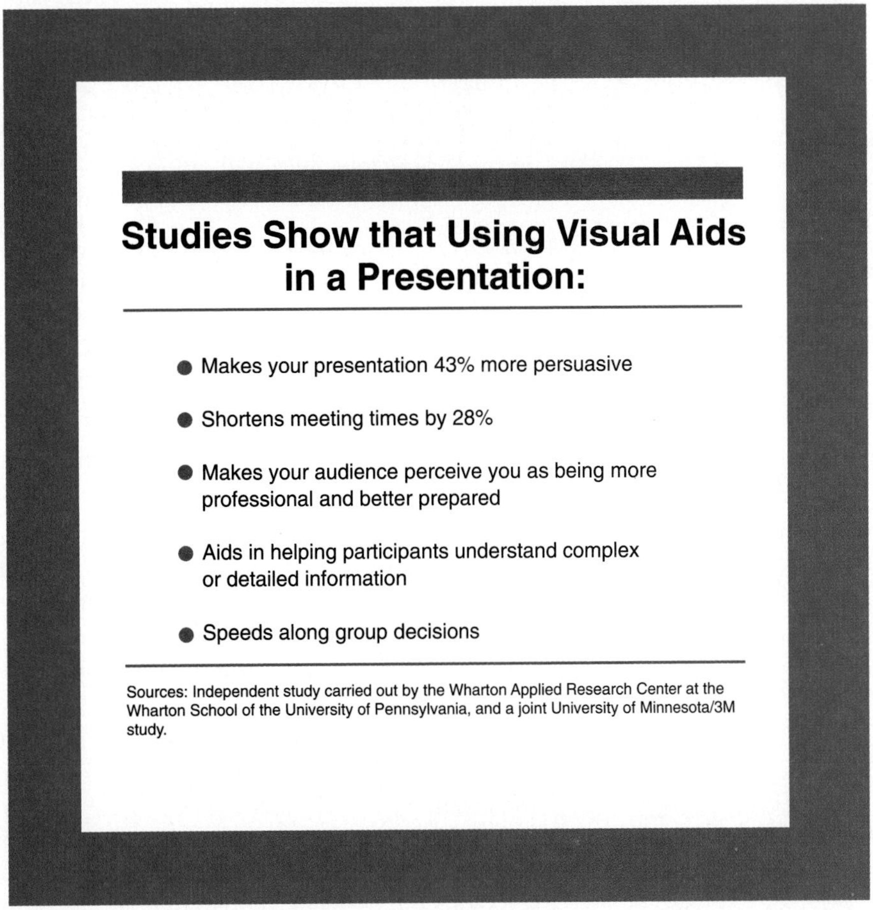

**Studies Show that Using Visual Aids in a Presentation:**

- Makes your presentation 43% more persuasive

- Shortens meeting times by 28%

- Makes your audience perceive you as being more professional and better prepared

- Aids in helping participants understand complex or detailed information

- Speeds along group decisions

Sources: Independent study carried out by the Wharton Applied Research Center at the Wharton School of the University of Pennsylvania, and a joint University of Minnesota/3M study.

**FIGURE 9.8**
Computer-Generated
Transparency

Audiotapes may be more useful than films or videotapes and are not as difficult to handle and integrate into the speech. If you wanted to describe the alarm cries of various animals, for instance, an audiotape could be essential. Consult your instructor about the availability of equipment and materials if your speech would benefit from such a tape.

## PREPARING VISUAL AIDS

Any visual aid worth using requires that you invest adequate time in planning, designing, preparing, and practicing its use. As the planning for your speech evolves through the first and later preparation outlines, you should also be developing and refining the design for your visual aid. As you develop an aid, you should follow basic principles of design and color.

## *Principles of Visual Aid Design*

The basic principles of visual aid design, including visibility, emphasis, and balance, are based on how a visual aid functions before an audience.

***Visibility.***   As we have already noted, your visual aid must be easy for the audience to see. Test your aid to be certain it can be seen from the back of the room. If not, the aid will become a distraction rather than an asset. When preparing a poster or flip-chart visual aid, you should use the following size printed letters for presentations in standard classrooms:

| | |
|---|---|
| Titles: | 3 inches high |
| Subtitles: | 2 inches high |
| Other text: | 1 1/2 inches high |

If you use a computer to generate slides or transparencies, be certain that it can print large letters. Computer print is typically sized in terms of points (pt). Figure 9.9 shows the standard computer print sizes appropriate for preparing transparencies, slides, or handouts.

Such visual aids should use the following sizes of letters:

| | Transparencies | Slides | Handouts |
|---|---|---|---|
| Title | 36 pt | 24 pt | 18 pt |
| Subtitles | 24 pt | 18 pt | 14 pt |
| Other text | 18 pt | 14 pt | 12 pt |

Use boldface type when preparing computer-generated materials.

***Emphasis.***   Your visual aid should emphasize what the speech emphasizes. This means that you should keep visual aids relevant and simple. Your listeners' eyes should be drawn immediately to what you want to illustrate. The map of Yellowstone Park (Figure 9.1) eliminates all information except what the speaker wishes to stress. Had the speaker added pictures of bears to indicate grizzly habitats or drawings of fish to show trout streams, the visual aid would have been more distracting than helpful. Graphics prepared for handouts may be more detailed than those used for posters, slides, or transparencies, but they should not contain extraneous material.

***Balance.***   Your visual aid should seem balanced and pleasing to the eye. The focal point of the aid can be the actual center of the chart or poster, or it can be deliberately placed off-center for the sake of variety. The POSH example shown earlier (Figure 9.7) has a high focal point. You should have a margin of at least two inches at the top of poster boards or standard flip

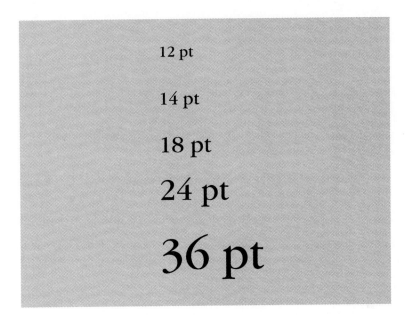

**FIGURE 9.9**
**Standard Computer**
**Print Sizes**

charts. The margin at the bottom of such aids should be at least two and a half inches. On computer-generated graphics you should leave at least an inch and a half of blank space at both the top and bottom. You should also have equal side margins. For poster boards and flip charts, these margins should be about one and a half inches wide. On computer-generated graphics they should be at least an inch wide.

### *Principles of Color*

Color adds impact to visual aids. A colored visual aid attracts and holds attention better than a black and white one. Color also is a subtle way to convey or enhance meaning. For example, a speech detailing crop damage from a drought might use an enlarged outline map showing the least affected areas in green, the moderately damaged areas in orange, and severely affected areas in brown. The natural colors would reinforce the message.

Color can also be used to create moods and impressions. For example, the color blue suggests power and authority (blue chip, blue ribbon, royal blue). Using blue in your graphics can invest them with these qualities. Red is a highly emotional color and may be used to indicate vital life forces or the presence of crisis (in the red, red ink). Line graphs tracing the rise in cases of AIDS or the drop in sales for some company in financial trouble could be portrayed in red to convey a sense of urgency. On his map of the New Madrid Fault area, Stephen Huff showed the earthquake epicenters in red, emphasizing their danger.

**SPEAKER'S NOTES**

## Planning and Preparing Visual Aids

1. Be certain your visual aid enhances the meaning or impact of your speech.

2. Limit the number of aids you will use. Keep the focus on your message.

3. Make a rough draft of your visual aid to check how well it works.

4. Be sure your aid is simple, balanced in design, and easy to see from the back of the room.

5. Use color in your visual aid to increase its effectiveness.

6. Prepare a neat visual aid. A sloppy one can damage your credibility and reduce the effectiveness of your speech.

The manner in which colors are combined can be used to convey subtle nuances of meaning. A **monochromatic color** scheme uses variations of one color to suggest changes in a subject. For example, using deeper shades of blue as you draw the figures representing increases in the number of women receiving college degrees could suggest growth in power.

An **analogous color** scheme uses colors that are adjacent on the color wheel, such as green, blue-green, and blue. Although this type of color scheme shows the differences among the components represented, it also suggests their connection and compatibility. For example, a pie graph could represent the students, faculty, and administration of a university, using analogous colors. The different colors suggest that these parts are indeed separate, but the analogous color scheme and the inclusion of these parts within a circle imply that they belong together. In this subtle way, the visual aid itself makes the statement that the components of a university ought to work together.

A **complementary color** scheme uses colors that are opposites on the color wheel, such as red and green. Complementary color schemes suggest tension and opposition among elements in a speech. Because they heighten the sense of drama, they may enliven informative speaking and encourage change in persuasive speaking. For example, one suggestion for developing the map accompanying the speech at the end of Chapter 12 would be to outline and color the New Madrid Fault area dark red and the surrounding area green, further dramatizing the danger of earthquake.

The colors you use for your graphics should always stand out from the background of the poster. It is best to use white poster board and strong, primary colors such as red, blue, and green, for contrast. Colors like pink, light blue, and pale yellow are not strong enough for good graphic emphasis.

## *Making Visual Aids*

For charts, graphs, or other poster and flip-chart aids, you should begin with a rough draft that allows you to see how your aid will look when it is finished. If you will be using poster board, prepare your draft on cheaper paper of the same size.

Don't try to crowd too much information into a single visual aid. With a light pencil mark off the margins to frame your aid. Divide your planning sheet into four equal sections to help you balance the placement of material. Use a wide-tipped dark felt marker to sketch in your design and words. Now step back to view your visual aid from about the same distance as the back row of your audience. Will your most distant listeners be able to read words without straining? Is everything spelled correctly? Is your eye immediately drawn to the most important elements in the poster? Have you positioned your material so that it will be most effective? Is the poster balanced, or does it look lopsided? Is there anything you can eliminate? If the poster looks cluttered, consider making a series of visual aids instead of just one.

Once you have decided that your rough draft is what you want your finished product to look like, practice presenting your speech using the aid.

*When using visual aids, be sure to maintain eye contact with the audience. Stand to the side of the aid and point to specific elements as you talk about them.*

Does it enhance what you have to say? Is it easy for you to use? When you have decided on a layout and design, take time to prepare a polished final product. If an art room with equipment is available on campus, see if you can get permission to prepare your final product there.

With computer-generated graphics for use as slides, transparencies, or handouts, you might experiment with several different designs, printing yourself copies so that you can see the entire page at one time. Don't get so caught up with what the program can do that you try to incorporate everything into a visual aid. If you do, you will wind up with something that is so "busy" it will detract from your message, rather than supplement it. The computer-generated graphic in Figure 9.10 is too cluttered to be effective for use in a speech. Too much information is crammed into it, and the multiple colors are distracting. The visual aid would have been much more effective had the information been separated into three different graphs.

## USING VISUAL AIDS

As we discussed each of the specific kinds of visual aids, we offered suggestions on how to use them in presentations. Here we review these suggestions and extract some basic guidelines.

- Practice your presentation using your visual aid. Be sure to integrate it smoothly into your speech with transitions.

- Go to the room where you will be speaking to decide where you will place your aid both before and during your speech. Determine what you will need to display it (thumbtacks, masking tape, etc.).

- Check out any electronic equipment you will use (slide projector, overhead projector, VCR, etc.) in advance of your presentation. Be certain that you can operate it and that it is working properly.

- Do not display your visual aid until you are ready to use it. When you have finished with it, cover or remove the aid so that it does not distract your audience.

- Don't stand directly in front of your visual aid. Stand to the side of it and face the audience as much as possible. Maintain eye contact with listeners. You want them to see both you and your visual aid.

- When you refer to something on the visual aid, point to what you are talking about. Don't leave your audience searching for what you are describing.

- Do not distribute materials during your speech. If you have prepared handouts, distribute them before or after you speak.

- Do not use too many visual aids in one speech. Remember, they should help your verbal message, not replace it.

**IN SUMMARY**   *Visual aids* are tools to enhance the effectiveness of speeches. They can increase comprehension, authenticate a point, add variety, and help a speech have lasting impact.

*Kinds of Visual Aids.*   Every speech has at least one visual aid: the speaker. Your appearance, clothing, and body language must all be in concert with your message. Other people may also be used in demonstrations. Another form of visual aid is the actual object. Unless that object is large enough to be seen, small enough to be portable, and strictly under your control, you may have to use a model or a sketch instead.

Maps are useful in speeches based on spatial designs. Draw them specifically for your speech so that they contain only the material you wish to emphasize. Graphs can help make complex data more understandable to an audience. *Pie graphs* illustrate the relationships between parts and a whole. *Bar graphs* highlight comparisons and contrasts. *Line graphs* show changes over time. Charts give form to abstract relationships. Among the most fre-

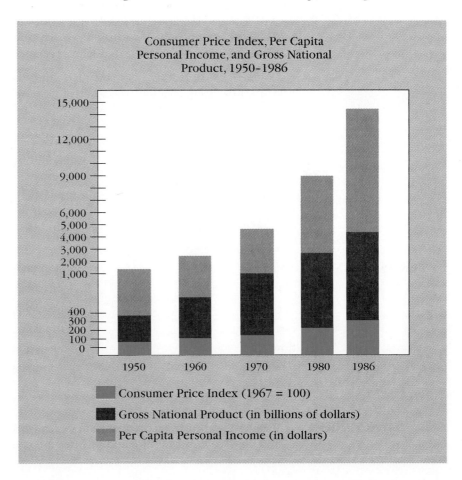

FIGURE 9.10
Ineffective Computer-
Generated Graphic

quently used are *flow charts, tree charts,* and *stream charts. Sequence charts* can be especially effective in speeches to emphasize and illustrate various stages in a process.

Photographs and pictures can add authenticity to a speech if handled correctly. Photographs provide slice-of-life realism but can also include irrelevant detail. Any photograph used in a speech should be enlarged so that everyone in the audience can see it.

*Ways of Presenting Visual Aids.*   Chalkboards and flip charts are popular ways of presenting visual aids. Chalkboards permit step-by-step demonstrations that can build suspense and hold attention. Unless carefully designed and roughed in ahead of time, such spontaneous visual aids may confuse listeners. A better option may be to use flip charts or poster board.

Handouts are effective in explaining complex or unfamiliar material; these should be distributed either before or after a speech. Slides and transparency projections can help the audience stay on track, but they also can be awkward to handle and may compete with you for attention. Though they add variety, films, videotapes, and laser discs can be difficult to integrate into a brief classroom speech. You may find that audiotapes are easier to use. Many visual aids can be generated with special computer software.

*Preparing Visual Aids.*   As you plan your visual aid, be aware of basic principles of design. The visual aid must be easy for the audience to see. It should emphasize what the speech emphasizes, excluding all extraneous material. It should seem balanced and pleasing to the eye. Plan your layout as you develop the speech itself through the preparation outlines. Carefully proofread your visual aid. Consider using strong colors to add interest and impact.

*Using Visual Aids.*   Practice using the visual aid until it seems a natural part of your presentation. Always talk to your audience and not to your visual aid and keep the aid out of sight when not in use.

**TERMS TO KNOW**

| | |
|---|---|
| visual aids | sequence chart |
| pie graph | pictograph |
| bar graph | textual graphics |
| line graph | monochromatic color |
| flow chart | analogous color |
| tree chart | complementary color |
| stream chart | |

**DISCUSSION**   1. Watch news programs on television or read *USA Today* for several days and observe how graphics and pictures are combined with words to convey meaning. What techniques are most and least useful? Be prepared to discuss examples of effective and ineffective usage in class.

2. Recall classes in which your instructors used visual aids. Did these aids serve one or more of the four functions of visual aids (aid understanding, authenticate a point, add variety, or give greater impact to the message)? Why or why not?

3. Describe situations in which speakers either would or would not be effective visual aids for their own speeches. Have you ever seen examples outside your classroom in which the appearance of speakers worked against their message?

4. Look through a recent popular magazine and analyze the advertisements according to the principles of design discussed here. Do the visual aspects of the ads work in concert with the words to emphasize the message? Which of the ads seem most balanced and pleasing to the eye? Do any of the ads violate the rules of simplicity and ease of comprehension? Which of the ads use color most and least effectively? Bring the most interesting ads to class and discuss your findings.

**APPLICATION**

1. Select a speech in Appendix B and prepare the rough draft of a visual aid that might have been used with it. Would the aid have helped the speech? What other options did you consider?

2. What kinds of visual aids might be most useful for the following speech topics?
   a. Nuclear-waste disposal sites in the United States
   b. What to do in case of snake bite
   c. History of the stock market over the last decade
   d. How the federal budget is divided into major categories
   e. Administering your university: who has the power to do what to whom?
   f. How we got the modern telephone: the growth of an invention
   g. Hunger in Africa: the human story
   h. The sounds of navigation and what they mean

**NOTES**

1. William J. Seiler, "The Effects of Visual Materials on Attitudes, Credibility, and Retention," *Speech Monographs* 38 (1971): 334; Douglas R. Vogel, Gary W. Dickson, and John A. Lehman, "Persuasion and the Role of Visual Presentation Support: The UM/3M Study," 3M Corporation (1986), pp. 1–20.
2. Cited in Laurence J. Peter, *Peter's Quotations: Ideas for Our Time* (New York: Bantam, 1979), p. 478.
3. Based on information in *The 1992 Information Please Almanac,* 45th ed. (Boston: Houghton Mifflin Company, 1992).

*Colors fade, temples
crumble, empires
fall, but wise words
endure.*

*—Edward
Thorndike*

# 10

# The Speaker's Language

## This Chapter Will Help You

- understand the power of words.
- express ideas clearly, simply, and correctly.
- dramatize events through powerful images.
- use language to bring listeners together.
- choose words that move people to action.

A legislator was asked how he felt about whiskey. He replied, "If, when you say whiskey, you mean the Devil's brew, the poison scourge, the bloody monster that defiles innocence, dethrones reason, creates misery and poverty—yes, literally takes the bread from the mouths of little children; if you mean the drink that topples Christian man and woman from the pinnacle of righteous, gracious living into the bottomless pit of degradation, despair, shame and helplessness, then certainly I am against it with all my power.

"But if, when you say whiskey, you mean the oil of conversation, the philosophic wine, the ale that is consumed when good fellows get together, that puts a song in their hearts and the warm glow of contentment in their eyes; if you mean Christmas cheer; if you mean the stimulating drink that puts the spring in an old gentleman's step on a frosty morning; if you mean that drink, the sale of which pours into our treasury untold millions of dollars which are used to provide tender care for our crippled children, our blind, our deaf, our dumb, pitiful, aged and infirm, to build highways, hospitals, and schools, then certainly I am in favor of it.

"That is my stand, and I will not compromise."[1]

learly, language can be both deceptive and richly expressive—often at the same time. The very wording of a speech can evade a tough question even while seeming to answer it! Yet words are the basic material of communication, and how well you use language often determines your success as a speaker. This chapter describes the power of language in speeches, identifies certain tools of language that can be especially helpful, and proposes standards for the effective use of spoken language.

## THE POWER OF LANGUAGE

Words can shape attitudes. Whether we believe that a certain action was *murder, justifiable homicide,* or *self-defense* may depend on the words used to describe it. The act does not change, but the words used to refer to it influence how we see it and what it means to us. This power has been discussed since ancient times and across cultures. Confucius noted that "all wisdom is rooted in learning to call things by their right names." Kenneth Burke, a contemporary American rhetorical critic, has suggested that persuasion begins with the names we give things.[2]

Oral language differs from written language.[3] Oral language is more spontaneous and less formal. Sentence fragments and slang expressions that might be inappropriate in written communication are acceptable in speech.

Oral language is more interactive, depending on audience involvement for its effectiveness. Consider the following segment from a speech:

> You want to know what we're going to do? I'll tell you what we're *not* going to do. We're not going to play along. This is a rule that deserves to be broken. Yes, broken! And we're going to do the breaking.

This example illustrates the spontaneous, informal, fragmentary, and interactive qualities of oral language. Moreover, in oral communication, pauses, vocal emphasis, and vocal variations act as punctuation marks to clarify and underscore meaning. Such resources are missing in written communication. Because listeners cannot reread a spoken statement, oral language must strive for simplicity and make greater use of repetition. Examples and illustrations are especially important in oral communication.

When skillfully used in public communication, the spoken word often reaches others in ways that writing cannot. We present five ways that effective oral language can influence the lives of listeners by making them see, feel, come together, act, and remember.[4] These powers of language can be used by ethical listeners to attain positive goals, but they can also be misused either inadvertently or purposely. An understanding of their uses and abuses is important both for effective speaking and critical listening.

### The Power to Make Listeners See

By their skillful use of words, speakers help us see the world as they see it. Their words become windows that can reveal subjects with startling clarity. This power is especially important when a subject is unfamiliar or unusual. For people to comprehend and react to a subject they must have mental images that are retained for later retrieval and use. As listeners we must keep in mind, however, the cautions of Francis Bacon, who warned that the glass in such windows may be "enchanted." The perspective may be shaded or distorted by the speaker's interests, values, and preoccupations. Thus, as critical listeners, we must guard against accepting any speaker's view as THE TRUTH of the matter. Words can color and alter their subjects.

For example, in the ongoing controversy over abortion rights, certain legal and moral issues are evoked by the way a speaker *depicts* the subject, by what the speaker's language allows us to see. Many of these basic questions surround the identity of the fetus. One side depicts the fetus as "an unborn child," calling abortion "legalized murder."[5] The other side suggests that the early fetus is a mass of cells, not a human being, and that our deeper concern should be for "real over potential life." Neither side describes itself as "antichoice" or "antilife." Thus, much of the heat in the abortion controversy centers on attempts to control names and perceptions. This power of words to shape our perceptions is fundamental to persuasion because on the basis of such perceptions we form attitudes, apply values, and decide to take certain actions.

Each power of language has its negative side. If words reveal a subject, they can also hide it. Either by design or lack of skill, speakers can disguise or obscure reality. The English writer George Orwell once complained:

> . . . Political language has to consist largely of euphemism, question-begging and sheer cloudy vagueness. Defenceless villages are bombarded from the air . . . this is called *pacification.* People are imprisoned for years without trial or shot in the back of the neck . . . this is called *elimination of unrealiable elements.* Such phraseology is needed if one wants to name things without calling up mental pictures of them. . . . A mass of Latin words falls upon the facts like soft snow, blurring the outlines and covering up all the details.[6]

Orwell would insist that the power to make us see is also a power that can blind.

### The Power to Awaken Feelings

Language can also arouse intense feelings. It can touch us, move us to action, or convert us to new ways of thinking. Like the power to make people see, the power to make us feel can be used ethically or abused. It is most ethical when it supplements sound reasoning and credible evidence. It is abused when speakers substitute appeals to feelings for evidence or reasoning. To arouse feelings language must overcome the barriers of time, distance, and apathy.

***Overcoming Time.*** Listeners tend to be oriented toward the present. Therefore, it can be difficult to awaken feeling about events that lie in the remote past or distant future. Fortunately, the language of feeling has a time-machine quality. It can bring past and future events into the present and make them seem real.

Let's look at how large corporations can use narratives to evoke the past in the service of present problems. In many organizations, problems arise because employees and customers lack a sense of identification with the company. They may feel that the atmosphere is impersonal and that no one is concerned about them or their problems. Narratives that recapture feelings from the past are often told at company meetings or used in advertisements. Such narratives help establish a sense of corporate heritage and culture. It is more pleasant to do business with a company that seems to have human qualities. Look how the words in the following story awaken feelings. Reconstructed from oft-told legend, these words capture the legend of Federal Express, a pioneer in overnight delivery:

You know, we take a lot for granted. It's hard to remember that Federal Express was once just a fly-by-night dream, a crazy idea in which a few people had invested — not just their time and their money, but their futures and their lives. I can remember one time early on — when things weren't going very well. We were really up against it. Couldn't even make the payroll that week. It looked like we were going to crash. Fred [Smith, founder of the company] was in in a deep funk. Never saw him quite like that before or since. "What the hell," he said, and flew off to Las Vegas. The next day he flew back and his face was shining. "We're going to make it," he said. He had won $27,000 at the blackjack table! And we made it. We met the payroll. Shortly after that things turned around, and Federal Express began to grow into the giant it is today. [7]

Language can also make a bridge to the future. In his inaugural address, Bill Clinton addressed the transition to America's future in these terms:

Our democracy must be not only the envy of the world but the engine of our own renewal. There is nothing wrong with America that cannot be cured by what is right with America. And so today we pledge an end to the era of deadlock and drift, and a new season of American renewal has begun. [8]

Such language can make the future seem close at hand. Because language can cross the barrier of time, we are able to have both a sense of tradition and a vision of tomorrow to guide us through the present.

***Overcoming Distance.*** The closer subjects seem to our lives, the easier it is to develop feelings about them. But what if speakers must discuss events that initially seem far away from listeners' interests? Again, language can telescope such subjects so that they seem close and affecting. Consider how one student reduced the psychological distance between her urban audience and her rural subject by introducing an interesting character and describing his meaning to her life. Her excellent use of graphic language allows her audience to share her feelings and experiences:

James Johnson knows the loveliest, most sparkling springs in Fentres County. He has lived all eighty-four years of his life there, and he taught me the most important things I know: why the mist rises on a lake at night, how to make the best blackberry jam you've ever tasted, and how to take care of baby wild rabbits that are abandoned. Today, I want to tell you more about James — and about myself through him.

By focusing on details that helped the audience envision the place she was describing, the speaker conquered distance and aroused feelings about a subject that otherwise seemed remote.

***Overcoming Apathy.***   We live in an age of communication overkill. Modern audiences have become jaded by an endless barrage of mass-mediated information, persuasion, and entertainment. The personal contact of public speaking, even when mediated, allows speakers to reach out to listeners and touch them with language. Jesse Jackson stirred the audience of the 1988 Democratic National Convention with the following message:

> America's not a blanket woven from one thread, one color, one cloth. When I was a child growing up in Greenville, South Carolina, and grandmother could not afford a blanket, she didn't complain and we did not freeze. Instead, she took pieces of old cloth — patches, wool, silk, gabardine, crockersack on the patches — barely good enough to wipe off your shoes with.
>
> But they didn't stay that way very long. With sturdy hands and a strong cord, she sewed them together into a quilt, a thing of beauty and power and culture.
>
> Now, Democrats, we must build such a quilt. Farmers, you seek fair prices and you are right, but you cannot stand alone. Your patch is not big enough. Workers, you fight for fair wages. You are right. But your patch, labor, is not big enough. Women, you seek comparable worth and pay equity. You are right. But your patch is not big enough. Women, mothers, who seek Head Start and day care and pre-natal care on the front side of life, rather than jail care and welfare on the back side of life, you're right, but your patch is not big enough.
>
> Students, you seek scholarships. You are right. But your patch is not big enough. Blacks and Hispanics, when we fight for civil rights, we are right, but our patch is not big enough. Gays and lesbians, when you fight against discrimination and [for] a cure for AIDS, you are right, but your patch is not big enough. Conservatives and progressives, when you fight for what you believe, right-wing, left-wing, hawk, dove — you are right, from your point of view, but your point of view is not enough.
>
> But don't despair. Be as wise as my grandmama. Pool the patches and the pieces together, bound by a common thread. When we form a great quilt of unity and common ground we'll have the power to bring about health care and housing and jobs and education and hope to our nation.[9]

Jackson's references to poverty and his grandmother's loving care aroused sympathetic feelings from many viewers. The image of a quilt — suggesting the warmth of home and the ability to create things of lasting value and beauty from humble materials — gave the audience a vision of unity to strive for and sparked thunderous applause.

Clearly, at its best, language can overcome the barriers of apathy, time, and distance to make us really care about a subject we should be addressing. At its worst, language can deaden our feelings or distract us from the issues.

*The power of language to bring people together is especially important on ceremonial occasions. Maya Angelou's poetic presentation at the 1993 Clinton inaugural also helped set a mood of reverence and respect befitting the occasion.*

## The Power to Bring Listeners Together

On many issues, individual action is not enough. Only people, acting together, can bring about necessary change. Therefore, speakers must often help listeners discover a group identity for themselves with respect to the problem at hand. For example, in the 1992 presidential campaign, Ross Perot urged his listeners to "band together to save the American dream" of a better economic world for their children. He invited his audience to assume an identity as crusaders for a cause.

Images of heroes and villains are often important to group closeness. Heroes offer leadership. They can be pictured performing unusual deeds or enduring sacrifices for the sake of the group. Adversaries can help establish what the group is *not*. For example, assume that you will speak at a campus rally opposing a rise in tuition. As organizer and main speaker at the event, you may find yourself treated by some as a hero. What you say and do becomes especially important for them. This heroic image places unusually high ethical demands upon you. You must make doubly sure that your arguments are defensible. Can you justify where you stand in light of the

strongest arguments on the other side? You must not lead susceptible follow-
ers down a false path.

You must be just as certain not to picture opponents as enemies or even
villains. If you must speak ill of others, do so only with full knowledge of
their intentions and actions. Take special pains, as the Native American saying gently reminds us, to "walk a mile in their moccasins." Resist the tendency to stereotype people either as heroes or villains. The language of
group identity can work powerfully to assist good causes, but you must be
careful not to abuse it.

### *The Power to Encourage Action*

Audience members may share an identity and yet not be ready to act. In
such cases, speakers must use the power of language to make listeners *want*
to take action. One way to do this is to depict real-life dramas that reveal
what is at stake and challenge listeners to enact certain roles.[10] Such scenarios draw clear lines between right and wrong. In the words of an early union
organizing song, the audience may be asked, "Which side are you on?"[11] If
you script such a drama, be careful to respect the humanity of all involved in
a conflict. Try to avoid melodramas that picture unblemished virtue in conflict with pure evil. The unreality of such representations will make critical
listeners suspicious. In your speech on tuition costs, you may decide after
careful research that you can ethically depict certain legislators as unrespon-
sive to student needs:

> Who wants tuition raised? The same legislators who have continually ig-
> nored our pleas for better teaching. Until we organize and speak with a
> louder, more unified voice, these powerful persons will continue to ne-
> glect us. They must hear us say: "Give us what we pay for! Give us good
> teaching! And don't keep raising the price on us!"

If you want your words to lead to action, you should also offer a positive vision of change:

> Our college can be a great center for learning, but only if the faculty *and*
> the students *and* state government want it to be. Learning happens when
> good, highly motivated teachers and students can interact in a stimulating
> environment. It can happen here. But only if we care enough to make it
> happen.

Whether words move us to action often depends on our trust in speakers,
and on our acceptance of them as leaders. This fact underscores again the
importance of ethos properly earned through careful preparation.

### *The Power to Help Listeners Remember*

Words that invoke the past help us celebrate who we are and can challenge us to be worthy of our best cultural traditions. The presidential inaugural address is a classic example of such ceremonial rhetoric. In his second inaugural, President Reagan called up memories of American heroes and patriotic myths to help listeners recall their heritage:

> . . . hear again the echoes of our past.
>
> A general falls to his knees in the harsh snow of Valley Forge; a lonely President paces the darkened halls and ponders his struggle to preserve the Union; the men of the Alamo call out encouragement to each other; a settler pushes West and sings a song, and the song echoes out forever and fills the unknowing air.
>
> It is the American Sound. It is hopeful, big-hearted, idealistic — daring, decent and fair. That's our heritage. That's our song.[12]

You too can use the power of words to evoke the past. The right words and phrases, used in the right places, can create a lasting picture:

> Twenty-five years ago, one professor — one person alone — faced a cold legislative committee one frigid December day to plead for a new level of support for our university. With his words, Dr. John Frazier painted the better future that would become our present. We now follow in his steps as we seek to lift our university again for the sake of our children. May we be worthy of his tradition.

The power of language is great, ranging from shaping perceptions to revitalizing group culture. How can speakers harness this power in ways that are both ethical and elevating? We turn now to the special techniques you can use to engage these powers.

## ▰ THE TOOLS OF LANGUAGE

Certain language tools can help your listeners see your subject vividly, feel appropriate emotions, identify with one another, act in desirable ways, and remember cultural traditions.

### *Tools to Help Listeners See*

Speakers who want listeners to *see* subjects in certain ways often have problems when subjects are abstract, complex, or vast, or when listeners hold opposing views. To overcome these problems, speakers must use techniques that encourage shared perceptions.

***Abstract Subjects.*** Abstract words refer to ideas, intangible qualities, beliefs, or values. Abstract words like *justice* pose special problems for communication. Because such words are not anchored in concrete reality, people may react to them in different ways. *Honor* may mean one thing to one person, something entirely different to another. When people see things differently, their attempts to understand each other may miss the mark.

One way to handle this problem is to show a *relationship* between the abstract subject and some concrete object of comparison. For example, you might say, "His courage turned on and off like a faucet — first cold, then hot"; here the abstract subject *courage* is related to the concrete object *faucet*. When words such as *like* or *as* are used to connect the abstract and concrete, the comparison is called a **simile.** Similes work when they help listeners understand abstractions more clearly. For example, Russian leader Mikhail Gorbachev once suggested that initial agreements with the United States might "cause *a kind of* peaceful 'chain reaction' in the field of strategic offensive arms" reduction.[13]

When using similes, remember that what you select for comparison can either enhance or diminish a subject. Aristotle noted that if you want to praise a subject, you should relate it to something better. For example, you might say, "She writes like Flannery O'Connor." On the other hand, if you want to diminish a subject, you should select something inferior for comparison, such as "This novel reads like a soap opera." To use similes ethically, you should be able to back up your comparisons with supporting material.

Another tool for overcoming abstraction, **metaphor,** involves the *replacement* of expected words with unexpected words. When using metaphors, we substitute concrete words for abstractions. This helps bring a subject into focus, often in startling and insightful ways. During the Senate hearings on the Watergate burglary committed during President Nixon's 1972 reelection campaign, L. Patrick Gray, who had been director of the FBI, was questioned relentlessly. What did it mean to have one's reputation destroyed in such a prolonged, public way? John Ehrlichman, who was a member of the White House team surrounding the president, used a metaphor to describe that experience. He said that Gray had been left to "twist slowly, slowly in the wind" — a graphic description of the kind of death Gray's reputation had suffered.

You should select metaphors carefully and use them with restraint. If you call a flu epidemic a tornado that devastated the campus, then talk about the need for storm warnings from health services and disaster relief from teachers, you risk carrying the metaphor too far. You may seem more infatuated with your ingenuity than concerned with your subject and audience. That kind of vanity can damage your ethos. Keep your metaphors brief and don't extend them too far.

You should also be careful about mixing metaphors. The speaker who intoned, "Let us march forward into the seas of prosperity," got a laugh he didn't want and hadn't intended. Finally, avoid trite similes and metaphors, such as "dead as a doornail" or "lion-hearted." Overuse has dimmed these comparisons until people are no longer affected by them. They may also damage your ethos because clichés suggest a dull, stale mind.

***Complex Subjects.*** Many subjects are so complex that it is difficult to describe them completely. Descriptions that are too complicated or too detailed may confuse listeners. With such subjects we must use language to *select* and *simplify,* spotlighting relevant features.

One technique of language that helps us deal with complex subjects is **synecdoche.** This tool of communication focuses upon a part of the subject to represent the whole. Such *representation* directs our attention to some strategic aspect of a subject to help us make a point about it. For example, in an antihunting television documentary the camera zoomed in on a hunter's bloody hands to symbolize guilt. Similarly, the word *movement* is an important synecdoche of our time when used to characterize reform campaigns such as the civil rights movement or the women's movement. This term focuses on the marching and demonstrating aspects of such campaigns to point up their activity and strength. A synecdoche can also present the *whole* of which the subject is part. In this secondary use, synecdoche stresses the significance of the subject, such as referring to police officers as "the law."

**Metonymy** is a related language tool that represents a subject by focusing on something closely associated with it. In the antihunting documentary, the close-up featured not just the hunter's bloody hands, but also the knife he was holding. This combined synecdoche and metonymy associated hunting with both guilt and brutality. Traditional metonymies in American rhetoric include the frontier, the cowboy, and the pioneer woman, used to symbolize national character.[14]

In addition to using these techniques, speakers sometimes simplify complex issues by forcing them into verbal molds that offer sharp moral contrasts, such as *good-evil, war-peace,* or *right-wrong.* Such contrasts add drama to communication and help move listeners to action. Be careful when using such language, however, because the price of this simplification is often distortion. Similarly, be wary when speakers try to move you by painting the world in black and white.

***Vast Subjects.*** Because of their monumental size, some subjects defy description. For example, journalists often find it difficult to describe the effects of war and starvation on masses of people. How can one convey the true magnitude of tens of thousands of people fleeing to refugee camps? Merely stating numbers cannot describe the subject adequately. In such situations, examples often give the audience a better picture of the subject. In Chapter 6 we noted that examples may arouse and sustain attention and interest, clarify major ideas, and emphasize specific points. Examples also help to make vast subjects easier to comprehend by supplying vivid images. For instance, if you were describing how war affects civilians, you could talk about an old man and his granddaughter, the only survivors of their family, and describe them trudging wearily down a dusty road to nowhere.

The word *trudge* in the above example demonstrates **onomatopoeia,** the tendency of certain words, like *buzz* or *hiss,* to imitate through sounds the object or action they signify. It suggests the weary, discouraged walk of the survivors and makes the imagery more dramatic.

***Opposing Views.*** Occasionally you may speak to an audience that holds contrary views. In such instances you may wish to use the technique of **perspective by incongruity.**[15] This technique acts as a verbal "shock treatment" to make people see a subject in a radically new way. Roger Tory Peterson, the well-known author of bird identification books, used perspective by incongruity to emphasize the importance of environmental awareness:

> Many people go through life as though they are wearing blinders or are sleep-walking. Their eyes are open, yet they may see nothing of their wild associates on this planet. Their ears, attuned to motor cars and traffic, seldom catch the music of nature — the singing of birds, frogs, or crickets — or the wind. These people are *biologically illiterate — environmentally illiterate —* and yet they may fancy themselves well informed, perhaps sophisticated.[16]

Perspective by incongruity often relies on metaphor for its impact. One student speaker described incidents of gender discrimination on campus and concluded: "This campus is a stinking pigpen of male chauvinism!" Many in the audience were shocked, and a few protested, but the image lingered and challenged more than one listener to rethink the situation. The verbal techniques of relationship, replacement, and representation can help us climb the walls that separate us so that we can share perceptions of our world.

### Tools to Make Listeners Feel

As we noted in Chapter 3, there are two major types of meaning. The *denotative meaning* of a word is its dictionary definition or generally agreed-upon objective usage. For example, the denotative definition of *alcohol* is "a colorless, volatile, flammable liquid, obtained by the fermentation of sugars or starches, which is widely used as a solvent, drug base, explosive, or intoxicating beverage."[17] How different this is from the two connotative definitions of alcohol in the opening example of this chapter! *Connotative meaning* invests a subject with emotional associations. Thus, *alcohol* in the form of whiskey is no longer just a chemical substance but either "the poison

**SPEAKER'S
NOTES**

## How Language Helps Us See: The Three *R*'s (Relating, Replacing, Representing)

1. *Relating* abstract subjects with concrete objects of comparison ("Her heart was as big as a Montana sky" — *simile*).

2. *Replacing* expected, abstract words with unexpected, concrete words ("Fear was the rope that choked him" — *metaphor*).

3. *Representing* complex subjects by focusing on selected features or associations ("There's blood on her hands" — *synecdoche.* "The number-crunchers are taking over the field" — *metonymy*).

4. *Representing* vast subjects by selected examples that imitate mass actions ("Among the countless refugees was an old man, who *trudged* down the dusty road to nowhere" — *onomatopoeia*).

5. *Replacing* a conventional view with a radically different perspective ("You may think you're bright, but your bulb has burned out" — *perspective by incongruity*).

scourge" or "the oil of conversation." Connotative language intensifies feelings, whereas denotative language encourages audience detachment.

Many of the techniques of language that help listeners see things can also help listeners feel things. Simile and metaphor may kindle feelings by the objects they select for relationship or replacement. If they are dramatic, as in the "pigpen" example, such feelings also can affect the speaker's ethos. Synecdoche and metonymy can arouse us by the speaker's choice of focus. For example, during the Vietnam War, demonstrators often chanted: "Hey, hey, LBJ, how many kids did you kill today?" The effect of this metonymy was to concentrate emotional attention on one outcome of American involvement in Southeast Asia.

Finally, well-chosen examples can make us feel as well as see. It is easier to identify emotionally with a frail grandfather and a hungry child than with great masses of people. As John Steinbeck observed: "It means very little to know that a million Chinese are starving unless you know one Chinese who is starving."[18] This is why Save the Children ads present the story of a single child who needs your help rather than overwhelming you with the numbers of starving children in Third World nations. With a problem so vast, the little we can do seems hardly worth the effort. But tell us about little Maria, who lives in a barrio outside Managua and for whom twenty dollars a month will provide food, shelter, clothing, and an opportunity to attend school. We can relate to this desperate child. We can help *her*. The example acts as a lens to bring the subject into clear and compelling focus.

The use of examples to arouse emotions has its origins in classical rhetoric. Some two thousand years ago the Roman rhetorician Longinus called the **image** the natural language of the passions. According to Longinus, an image can intensify feelings when "you think you see what you describe, and you place it before the eyes of your hearers."[19] During the grim days of World War II, when London was bombed every night, the British people needed reassurance of their ability to prevail. Sir Winston Churchill advanced an image of defiance and hope for Britans in his frequent radio speeches. Note how he built this image on a metaphor of fire:

> What he [Hitler] has done is to kindle a fire in British hearts . . . which will glow long after all traces of the conflagration he has caused in London have been removed. He has lighted a fire which will burn with a steady and consuming flame until the last vestiges of Nazi tyranny have been burnt out of Europe.[20]

**Hyperbole,** or purposeful exaggeration, can also be used to arouse feelings. Speakers may use this technique to encourage action or force listeners to confront problems. Note the use of hyperbole in Martin Luther King's speech the night before he was killed:

> Men for years now have been talking about war and peace, but now no longer can they just talk about it. It is no longer the choice between violence and nonviolence in this world, it's nonviolence or nonexistence. . . . And in the human rights revolution, if something isn't done and done in a hurry to bring the colored peoples of the world out of their long years of poverty, their long years of hurt and neglect, the whole world is doomed.[21]

Are the choices really that simple, the consequences really that inescapable? Perhaps not, but King wanted his listeners to understand in their minds *and* hearts what would happen if they neglected their moral responsibility. His use of hyperbole was meant to make his audience think and feel simultaneously. As a speaker you should be careful when using hyperbole. The line between exaggerating and lying is all too easy to cross. Save hyperbole for those moments when it is vital for listeners to get your message.

A final technique that helps to awaken feelings, especially when the subject is abstract, is **personification.** Personification involves treating inanimate subjects, such as ideas or institutions, as though they had human form or feeling. In the late spring of 1989, Chinese students demonstrating for freedom marched in Tiananmen Square carrying a statue they called the "Goddess of Liberty." They were borrowing a personification that has been used in the Western world for about four hundred years: the representation of liberty as a woman.[22] Here is how a student used personification effectively in a classroom speech:

> This university must be more caring. It must see that its investments reflect its morality. When it supports companies that invest in South Africa, it endorses apartheid. It becomes a partner in global inhumanity. It lashes the backs of black people one more time.

This speaker emphasized the moral responsibility of the university by treating it as human. Personification makes it easier to arouse feelings about values and policies that might otherwise seem far removed from the lives of listeners.

Both speakers and listeners should be careful in using and responding to the language of feeling. Words can arouse us, but they can also make us numb. When injected into discussion, some language can deaden our feelings or distract us from their subjects. Our ethical goal should be language that seeks a balance between denotation and connotation, so that we see subjects both clearly and richly.

## Tools to Create Togetherness

Speakers can create feelings of togetherness by using inclusive pronouns, telling stories about shared experiences, calling on a vocabulary of special words, or evoking universal images.

*Inclusive Pronouns.*    Speakers rarely refer to *my* feelings, *my* plans, or *my* cause, but rather *our* feelings, *our* plans, *our* cause. Similarly, they do not say that *I* will do something or *you* will do something, but that *we* will do it together. These inclusive pronouns help unite speakers and listeners. Their importance can be shown by a negative example. When Ross Perot addressed an NAACP convention during the 1992 presidential campaign, he repeatedly referred to his African-American audience as "you people." These words furthered separation, not identification, and alienated many listeners. The incident reinforced an impression that he was inexperienced in political leadership.

*Shared Stories.*    Groups pass on their history to new members through stories.[23] One traditional American narrative portrays our country as a melting pot for immigrants. Another, the Horatio Alger myth, was named for the author of a series of popular nineteenth-century books. This myth suggests that the humblest person can succeed in America by being ambitious, energetic, and thrifty. In an effective student speech, Martha Porter praised one of her friends for overcoming cultural barriers and poverty to graduate with high honors. Her speech drew much of its power from its implicit connections to such stories:

> When Ang Sok came to this country, she owned only the clothes she was wearing — and they were pretty ragged. She could not speak English. All she wanted was a chance to learn, to work, and to succeed — the opportunity to become an American. Our country gave it to her. In three weeks she will graduate magna cum laude. Isn't it ironic that she should have to come all the way from Cambodia to show us what it means to be an American?

***Special Words.*** In addition to narratives, groups also develop a special vocabulary that can be used to sustain their identity. **Culturetypes** are words that are specific to a group's identity — words that express its values and goals, or refer to its heroes and enemies.[24] One contemporary rhetorical critic, Richard Weaver, called these words "god and devil terms."[25] He suggested that *progress* was the primary "god term" of American culture in the 1950s. When used in speeches, *progress* became a rallying cry. People were willing to do almost anything to achieve the benefits the word suggested. Other related god terms of the 1950s, according to Weaver, included *science, modern,* and *efficient.* Such expressions, he suggested, had unusual power because they were rooted in American values. On the other hand, words like *Communist* and *un-American* were "devil terms." Devil terms denigrate a subject and strengthen group ties by pointing out what we are not. Culturetypes can change over time. By the mid-1970s words like *natural, peace,* and *communication* had become god terms; *nuclear* and *pollution* were new devil terms.

Michael Calvin McGee, a scholar of rhetoric at the University of Iowa, has written about **ideographs,** those special culturetypes that express a country's basic political beliefs.[26] He suggests that words such as *freedom, liberty,* or *democracy* are especially potent because they are tied to America's political identity. Expressions like "*freedom* fighters" or "*democracy* in action" have unusual power because they use ideographs.

In addition to national culturetypes, you should also consider whether there may be special culturetypes that express group identity at your school and that might be effective with your classroom audience. In what does your school take pride? Who are its rivals and adversaries? The answers to these questions could alert you to special language that may help advance your purpose. One student at Indiana University strengthened her speech for blood donations by arguing: "Purdue has done it — why can't we?" Presumably, students at Purdue could use Indiana in the same culturetypal way.

**SPEAKER'S NOTES**

### Using Language to Create Togetherness

1. Emphasize inclusive words such as *we* and *our*.

2. Present group narratives and legends.

3. Use culturetypes that express group values and increase identification.

4. Use archetypal metaphors to intensify the meaning of common experiences and create identification.

Culturetypes add strength to a speech when used ethically. They remind us of our heritage, make us proud of who we are, and suggest that we must be true to that identity. However, because they are so potent, culturetypes lend themselves to abuse. To avoid problems, demonstrate how culturetypes apply to your topic and defend their relevance to your position. Respect those who may reject the invitation culturetypes offer into group identity. After all, another principle close to the American heart is that individual rights, especially the right to reject conventional values and lifestyles, must be preserved.

***Universal Symbols.***    Some symbols draw on experiences that persist across time and space and that cross most cultural boundaries. These words express many of the motives discussed in Chapter 4. Such words may be the most potent language tools, especially when we wish to appeal to diverse groups. The universal symbol most frequently used in speeches is the **archetypal metaphor.** An archetypal metaphor connects its abstract subject with a widely experienced source, such as light and darkness, storms, the sea, disease and cure, war and peace, structures, the family, and space. A brief look at three of these metaphors demonstrates their potential power in communication.[27]

*Light and darkness.* From the beginnings of time, people have made negative associations with darkness. The dark is cold, unfriendly, and dangerous. On the other hand, light brings warmth and safety. It restores one's sense of control. When speakers use the light-darkness archetype, they usually equate problems or bad times with darkness and solutions or recovery with light.

President Bush used the words "a thousand points of light" to dramatize an appeal for volunteer service in our communities. Wuer Kaixi, a leader of the Chinese freedom movement, expressed his horror over the Tiananmen Square massacre of 1989 by referring to a "black sun that rose on the day in June that should have belonged to a season of fresh flowers."[28] Because light and darkness is so often used metaphorically, it may be difficult to avoid triteness. However, if you can find a creative way to frame your topic in terms of this metaphor, your audience may listen with special feeling and appreciation.

*Storms and the sea.* The storm metaphor is often used when describing catastrophes. Quite often the storm occurs at sea — a dangerous place under the best of conditions. The student speaker who argued that "our society is cut adrift — it has lost its moorings, and we don't see the dark nuclear cloud on our horizon" was using archetypes to give dramatic expression to his fears of the future.

*Disease and cure.* This archetypal metaphor reflects our fears of illness and our ongoing search for cures. The plague was the great symbolic disease of the past; more recently, cancer is the metaphoric illness that dominates discourse. The speaker using such a metaphor usually offers a cure. If the disease has progressed too far, radical surgery may be the answer. Speaking in Memphis on the night before he was assassinated, Dr. Martin Luther King, Jr., warned that "the nation is sick, trouble is in the land, confusion all around." Only the commitment of his listeners to political, economic, and spiritual reform, he suggested, might cure that illness.

Similarly, metaphors of *war and peace* reflect our fascination with war and our yearning for peace.[29] *Structural* images emphasize the human urge to create better conditions by constructing better policies and institutions. *Family* metaphors often express the dream of a loving relationship among people through such images as "the family of humanity."[30] And *spatial* metaphors reflect striving upward and forward toward goals and the wish to avoid falling or retreating into failure.

Culturetypes and archetypal metaphors can help you develop a speech that appeals to our need for togetherness and that sets the stage for group action. *Be careful not to overdo such language.* If you strain to use these metaphors, they will seem artificial. But if such language fits naturally, it can make your speech both unifying and dynamic.

### Tools to Make Listeners Act

Action requires time and trouble and often involves cost and risk. These barriers may make listeners cautious and unwilling to act, even when the need is urgent. Fortunately, there are language resources that can help overcome such audience inertia.

Many of the tools that awaken feelings can also be used to incite action. Hyperbole, imagery, and personification can picture the possible consequences of not acting. Synecdoche and metonymy show how we should focus our energy. For example, "We will win with our minds, not with our might" could be used to promote education over armaments. Similarly, certain archetypal metaphors, most notably disease or war, can encourage aggressive behavior. Other language techniques that can spur an audience to action include alliteration, anaphora, inversion, and antithesis.

***Alliteration.*** **Alliteration** is the repetition of initial consonant sounds in closely connected words: "Rather than *m*ilitary *m*adness, we need to offer the world *p*eace and *p*rosperity." The repetition attracts attention and reinforces the ideas contained in the words. Alliteration can be very effective in the introductions and conclusions of action-oriented speeches. But, be careful not to overdo alliteration—it can sound artificial and forced if it is too obvious.

***Anaphora.*** **Anaphora** is the repetition of the same initial words in a sequence of phrases or sentences. It is especially useful for formal conclusions in which it seems to seal the thoughts developed in the speech. The speaker who ended with the words "Freedom yesterday, freedom today, freedom tomorrow" was using anaphora.

***Inversion.*** In **inversion** the speaker changes the expected word order to make statements more memorable and emphatic. One student speaker concluded his message with a paraphrase of John Donne, "Ask not for whom the bell tolls. It tolls for thee." The "ask not" was inversion.

***Antithesis.*** **Antithesis** combines opposing ideas in the same sentence or adjoining sentences so that listeners can see their choices clearly. Antithesis suggests that the speaker has a clear grasp of options. One student used antithesis well as she summarized her speech on educational reform:

> The lack of funding does not cheat us as much as the lack of leadership.
> The root of our problem is small people, not small budgets. Shakespeare
> put it well: "The fault is not in our stars but in ourselves."

The following quotation from President Kennedy's inaugural address is a famous example combining antithesis, inversion, and anaphora.

> And so, my fellow Americans: Ask not what your country can do for you—
> ask what you can do for your country.
>
> My fellow citizens of the world: Ask not what America will do for you, but
> what together we can do for the freedom of man.[31]

### Tools to Help Listeners Remember

Some language is particularly appropriate for those special occasions when groups celebrate past events, recognize outstanding achievements, remember

*Patriotic culturetypes were prominent in the speeches of President Reagan. The use of words like* freedom *and* liberty *help people remember their heritage as they celebrate common values.*

their values, and revive their sense of identity. Skillful speakers can make the past come alive by recalling specific achievements. Reference to the midnight ride of Paul Revere may evoke memories of the bold spirit of early Americans. Great research accomplishments or dedication to teaching can represent the essence of a university.

Ceremonial speeches can help revitalize culturetypes. Words like *freedom, liberty,* and *progress* can be renewed by other language tools. The following example illustrates this process:

> What is freedom in our time? I'll tell you how I see it. Freedom is our right to take risks on our own, our right to climb the mountain, and if necessary, our right to fall. Freedom is our right to pick up and go, to decide our own destiny. Freedom is our right to open our mouths and make fools of ourselves without going to jail for it. Freedom is our right to laugh if we want to or pray if we want to. Freedom means a nation that aims at those elusive targets of respect and fairness and tolerance for all. It doesn't mean that we always hit those targets — what nation has? The most important thing is that in our wonderful and naive way, we keep trying.

This excerpt from a ceremonial speech uses metaphor, synecdoche, anaphora, image, and personification to revitalize the culturetype *freedom.* Can you find them?

Because groups value their identity, language that evokes one's heritage can be very effective. Archetypal metaphors can help us appreciate who we are and what we represent in the great scheme of things. "We survived the storm of war" or "we came out of the darkness of depression" or "we watched the sun rise on a new day" are the kinds of phrases that can help us recall, understand, and celebrate the meaning of group experiences.

These tools of language can help you use the power of words to further good causes and demonstrate effective leadership. Keep in mind, however, that these tools can be misused. Learning to recognize them and to understand how they work can alert you to moments when they may obscure issues or divide listeners, when they may serve the forces of darkness.

## USING LANGUAGE EFFECTIVELY

No one can tell you exactly how you should use language. Your style is an expression of your individuality. **Rhetorical style** is the unique way you choose and arrange words in a speech. Your rhetorical style may vary according to the topic, audience, and situation. Formal situations call for more formal language. Words and expressions appropriate to a celebrity roast would be out of place at a memorial service. Your language for a speech on the dangers of nuclear power should be different from that for a speech warning about what one student called "power shopping." Your style for an audience of accountants may vary from that for an audience of artists.

Nevertheless, there are certain standards for language usage you should strive to achieve whenever you communicate. We refer to these standards as the six *C*'s of effective language usage: clarity, color, concreteness, correctness, conciseness, and cultural sensitivity.

### *Clarity*

Clarity comes first in our list for good reason: unless you are clear, your speech will be defeated from the outset. Your language should be as simple and familiar as the topic, audience, and occasion will permit. Although this advice may seem obvious, it is often ignored. Some speakers forget that listeners may not share their technical vocabularies, so they don't translate unusual terms into lay language. Vice President Albert Gore, Jr., has been sensitive to this problem in his many speeches on environmental problems. To show that a gradual deterioration of the environment could prove worse than a sudden catastrophe, the then Senator Gore once used a simple narrative. *U.S. News and World Report* summarized it as follows:

> If dropped into a pot of boiling water, a frog will quickly jump out. But if the same frog is put into a pot and the water is slowly heated, the frog will

**SPEAKER'S NOTES**

## The Six *C*'s of Effective Language Use

1. *Strive for clarity* by using familiar words in a simple, direct way.

2. Use *colorful,* vivid language to make your message memorable.

3. Develop *concrete* images so the audience can picture what you're talking about.

4. Check the *correctness* of the words you use.

5. Be *concise.*

6. Be *culturally sensitive:* avoid stereotyping and racist or sexist language.

stay put until boiled alive. Just so with pollution, the senator told the National Academy of Sciences last week: if we do not wake up to the slow heating of our environment, we may jump too late.[32]

Like Vice President Gore, tell people what they need to know in language they can understand.

One major enemy of clarity is jargon. All of us have been exposed to language that seems purposefully befuddling. Public television commentator Bill Moyers warned his audience at the University of Texas against the dangers of jargon:

If you would . . . serve democracy well, you must first save the language. Save it from the jargon of insiders who talk of the current budget debate in Washington as "megapolicy choices between freeze-feasible base lines." (Sounds more like a baseball game played in the Arctic Circle.) Save it from the smokescreen artists, who speak of "revenue enhancement" and "tax-base erosion control" when they really mean a tax increase. . . . Save it from . . . the official revisionists of reality, who say that the United States did not withdraw our troops from Lebanon, we merely "backloaded our augmentation personnel."[33]

Speakers may use jargon because they actually don't want to communicate the reality of situations. Fearing what may happen if audiences actually understand their meaning, they may hide reality behind clouds of language. In contrast, ethical speaking is clear and direct.

One way to achieve clarity is through **amplification,** the art of strategic repetition in speeches. Amplification allows you to dwell on a central or difficult point. You amplify when you rephrase ideas rather than simply repeating them verbatim. Providing important bits of information or brief examples that compare and contrast the subject are other ways to amplify an idea. In effect, you tell listeners something, then you expand and repeat what you are saying. Observe the techniques of amplification at work in the following speech sample, in which each sentence expands and repeats the meaning of the sentence that precedes it:

> The roadrunner is not just a cartoon character that makes a fool of Wile E. Coyote. It is a member of the cuckoo family and state bird of New Mexico. Still, the cartoon roadrunner and the real roadrunner have much in common. Both are incredibly fast, real roadrunners having been tracked at ground speeds over 15 miles per hour. Neither takes to the air to chase prey or escape a predator. Both look rather awkward as they run, with strides up to 20 inches long—a real feat for a bird that is only 24 inches long with over half its length in its tail.

## Color

Color refers to the emotional intensity or vividness of language. Colorful language is memorable because it stands out in our minds. Malcolm X, the well-known human rights activist of the 1960s, used colorful speech especially well. Consider the following passage transcribed from a tape of one of his best-known speeches:

> What can the white man use now to fool us? After he put down that march on Washington, and you see all through that now. He tricked you. Had you marchin' down to Washington. Yeah! Had you marchin' back and forth between the feet of a dead man named Lincoln and another dead man named George Washington singin' "We Shall Overcome." He made a chump out of you! He made a fool out of you! He made you think you were goin' somewhere and you ended up goin' nowhere but between Lincoln and Washington.[34]

What makes this statement colorful? First, it conveys the speaker's excitement and indignation. It uses the fragments and rhythms of everyday street talk, including such interjections as *"Yeah!"* as Malcolm interacts with listeners. Simple, graphic words like *fool, trick,* and *chump* hit with special force. Although deceptively simple, the passage is quite artful. It uses the contrast between the living, active, singing marchers and the statues of the "dead men," Lincoln and Washington. It also uses a striking antithesis: "He made you think you were goin' somewhere and you ended up goin' nowhere. . . ."

Colorful language can create sensory images. We saw this technique at work in our earlier excerpt from a speech about James Johnson: "[He] knows the loveliest, most sparkling springs. . . . He taught me . . . why the mist rises on a lake at night, how to make the best blackberry jam you ever tasted, and how to take care of baby wild rabbits. . . ." This speaker selected her images deliberately to awaken several of her listeners' senses — to make them "see" the mist, "taste" the jam, "feel" the rabbits' fur. She used adjectives sparingly but with striking pictorial result ("sparkling springs" — notice how the alliteration contributes to the pleasing effect). Adjectives should not be strewn about a speech extravagantly but saved so that they really count when you use them.

Color also can be achieved through synecdoche and metonymy, which direct our attention to exciting aspects of subjects. Color also can be created by personification, hyperbole, and archetypal metaphors. When speakers use colorful language well, we are drawn to them. Therefore, color is an important standard for effective language usage.

### Concreteness

It is virtually impossible to discuss anything of significance without using some abstract words. However, if the language in your speech is overly abstract, listeners may lose interest. Moreover, because abstract language is more ambiguous than concrete language, a speech full of abstractions invites misunderstanding.

Concrete language connects us to subjects through our senses. The more concrete a word is, the more specific information it conveys. For example, consider this continuum of terms describing a cat.

Mehitabel is a/an

creature   animal   mammal   cat   Persian cat   gray Persian cat
*abstract* ─────────────────────────────────────────────→ *concrete*

A similar continuum can be applied to active verbs. If we wanted to describe how a person moves, we could use any of the following terms:

Jennifer

moves                                walks                        strides
*abstract* ─────────────────────────────────────────────→ *concrete*

Again, we see that the more concrete our language, the more pictorial and precise the information we can convey. Concrete words are also easier for listeners to remember. Therefore, your language should be as concrete as the subject permits.

## Correctness

Nothing can sink your ship more quickly than a glaring misuse of language. Mistakes in grammar or word selection can be disastrous to your ethos because most audiences connect such errors with incompetence. They are likely to reason that anyone who misuses language can hardly offer good advice. When you select your words, be careful that they say exactly what you mean to say.

Occasionally beginning speakers, wishing to impress people with the size of their vocabularies, get caught up in the "thesaurus syndrome." They will look up a simple word to find a synonym that sounds more impressive or sophisticated. What they may not realize is that the words shown as synonyms often have slightly different meanings. For example, the words *disorganize* and *derange* are sometimes listed as synonymous, yet their meanings are different enough that to use them interchangeably could cause serious problems. Just try referring to a disorganized person as deranged, and you will see what we mean. Use your dictionary when you have any doubts about word choice.

People often err when using words that sound similar. Such confusions are called **malapropisms,** after Mrs. Malaprop, a character in a play by Richard Sheridan. William J. Crocker of Armidale College in New South Wales, Australia, collected the following malapropisms from student speeches in his classes:

> A speaker can add interest to his talk with an *antidote.*
>
> The disagreements can arise from an unintended *conception.*
>
> The speaker hopes to arouse *apathy* in his audience.
>
> Good language can be reinforced by good *gestation.*
>
> The speaker can use either an inductive or a *seductive* approach.[35]

Students are not the only ones who make such blunders. Elected officials are not above an occasional malapropism. One former United States senator declared that he would oppose to his last ounce of energy any effort to build a "nuclear waste *suppository*" in his state.[36] And a former mayor of Chicago once introduced Carl Sandburg as "the poet *lariat* of the United States."[37] The lesson is clear. To avoid being unintentionally humorous, use a current dictionary to check the meaning and pronunciation of any word you feel uncertain about.

## Conciseness

In discussing clarity we talked about the importance of repetition in speeches. Although it may seem contradictory, you must also be concise, even while you are amplifying your ideas. You must make your points quickly and efficiently. Follow the advice given by Franklin Delano Roosevelt to his son James: "Be sincere . . . be brief . . . be seated!"

Even if you have unlimited time for speaking, conciseness is a virtue. It helps listeners to see more clearly and to feel more powerfully. Long, drawn-out speeches lose audience interest. They can kill the impulse toward action that persuasive speaking must cultivate.

To achieve conciseness, strive for simple, direct expression. Thomas Jefferson once said, "The most valuable of all talents is that of never using two words when one will do." Use the active voice rather than the passive in your verbs: "We demand action" is more concise — and more direct, colorful, and clear — than "Action is demanded by us."

You can also be succinct by using comparisons that reduce complex issues to the essentials. Sojourner Truth, a nineteenth-century human rights activist, once had to counter the argument that society should not educate blacks and women because of their "inferiority." She destroyed that then-powerful position with a simple parable: "If my cup won't hold but a pint, and yours holds a quart, wouldn't you be mean not to let me have a little half-measure full?"[38]

The goal of conciseness encourages the use of **maxims,** those wise but compact sayings that summarize the beliefs of a people. During the Chinese freedom demonstrations of 1989, a sign carried by students in Tiananmen Square adapted the maxim of Patrick Henry, "Give Me Democracy or Give Me Death." Similarly, demonstrators at a nuclear plant in Colorado carried a sign reading "Hell No, We Won't Glow!" a variation on a chant often heard in anti-Vietnam war rallies of the 1960s, "Hell no, we won't go!" As these examples suggest, maxims can have special power in attracting mass-media attention. When printed on posters, they can be easily filmed to satisfy the hunger of the press for visual messages. Their brevity makes them ideally suited to the rigid time constraints of television news. One problem with maxims is that one could be tempted to substitute them for careful, well-supported arguments. Even political sound bites should have strong arguments backing them up. Once you have developed a responsible and substantive speech, consider how you might use maxims to reinforce your message.

### Cultural Sensitivity

In Chapter 1 we suggested that an ethical speech was based on respect for the audience, responsible knowledge of the topic, and concern for the consequences. Two of these ethical imperatives, respect for audience and concern for consequences, are often reflected in the language you choose for your speech.

There is a very high probability that your classroom audience will represent different cultures. Data from the 1990 census shows that nearly 25 percent of Americans are of African, Asian, Hispanic, or Native American an-

**SPEAKER'S NOTES**

## Avoiding Racist and Sexist Language

1.  Do not use slang terms to refer to racial, ethnic, religious, or gender groups.

2.  Avoid using the generic *he* and gender-specific titles such as repair*man*.

3.  Avoid "markers" that introduce irrelevant allusions to race, gender, or ethnicity — e.g., the *black* doctor, the *female* professor.

4.  Do not identify people in terms of their partner's accomplishments or status, e.g., "Mary Thompson, wife of the famous author, Jim Thompson. . . ."

5.  Avoid stereotypical roles that imply inferiority or superiority — i.e., try not to identify all of your authority figures as white males.

6.  Do not use sexist, racist, ethnic, religious humor.

cestry.[39] If you live in New Mexico, California, Hawaii, New York, or the District of Columbia, there is a greater than 50 percent chance that any two randomly selected individuals you encounter will differ ethnically or racially.[40] In addition to ethnic and racial differences, your classmates may represent a diversity of religious affiliations, lifestyles, socioeconomic levels, and geographic identifications as well as gender differences. As listeners, they may be very sensitive to any negative allusions they might take personally. For example, during the 1992 presidential campaign, many southerners were offended by references to Clinton and Gore as "the 'Bubba' ticket."

A lack of cultural sensitivity almost always has negative consequences. At best, audience members may be mildly offended; at worst, they will be irate enough to reject both you and your message. Cultural sensitivity begins with being attuned to the diversity of your audience, appreciative of the differences between cultural groups, and careful about the words you choose when referring to those who may be different from you. Although you must make some generalizations about your audience, avoid getting caught up in stereotypes that suggest that one group is inferior in any way to another. Stay away from racial, ethnic, religious, or gender-based humor. Be especially careful not to use racist or sexist language.

**IN SUMMARY**     ***The Power of Language.***     Language is a powerful instrument of communication. Words help us share our perceptions and feelings with others and develop values and goals together. Words can promote togetherness and help launch programs of action to accomplish worthy goals. Words may also preserve memories of our heritage and help stabilize our culture.

The power to affect perceptions with words carries a great ethical obligation: we must be able to justify the names we give to things. If we want to share feelings with listeners, we must overcome barriers of time, distance, and apathy. Language that builds a sense of group belonging for the sake of action often relies on images of heroes and enemies. Language can also trigger action by showing the consequences of acting and not acting. Finally, language helps us remember our heritage by preserving heroes and patriotic stories.

The power of language requires us to be careful speakers and listeners. When used in abusive ways, words can distract us, defeat rational deliberation, threaten individualism, incite ill-considered action, and falsify the past.

***The Tools of Language.***   Speakers utilize special tools to activate the power of language. To help us see and feel, speakers use techniques based on the three *R*'s: relationship, replacement, and representation. *Simile* helps clarify abstract subjects by relating them to things that are concrete and familiar. *Metaphor* offers new perspectives by replacing anticipated words with surprising, unexpected language. *Synecdoche* and *metonymy* help simplify complex subjects by focusing on certain representative features or associations. Well-chosen examples can reduce vast subjects to representative instances. Such examples add authenticity through the use of *onomatopoeia,* words that sound like their subjects. *Perspective by incongruity* can sometimes shock listeners into new ways of understanding.

To promote the sharing of feelings, effective speakers use words that stimulate connotative meaning. The *image* is the natural language of the emotions. *Hyperbole* can help overcome audience lethargy and kindle powerful feelings. *Personification* helps us relate emotionally to abstractions or impersonal institutions.

To develop group identity, speakers should use inclusive pronouns such as *our* and *we.* A speaker can also promote identity by telling stories that illustrate cultural values and goals. In addition, speakers may use the special vocabulary of symbols — *culturetypes* and universal symbols — to bring people together. Culturetypes express group values in a compact way, and *archetypal metaphors* remind us of our common humanity. Speakers, however, should respect the differences among people even as they attempt to unify them. When properly used, such techniques as *alliteration, anaphora, inversion,* and *antithesis* can enhance appeals for action. Ceremonial language helps us remember our heritage.

***Using Language Effectively.***   *Rhetorical style* is the unique way you choose and arrange words while speaking. Although style varies with the user and with different topics, audiences, and situations, you should strive to satisfy the six major standards of *clarity, color, concreteness, correctness, conciseness,* and *cultural sensitivity.* Clear language is simple and direct and draws its comparisons from everyday life. *Amplification* promotes clarity by dwelling on important, difficult points. Color refers to the emotional intensity and vividness of our language and is especially vital to the sharing of feeling.

The more concrete the word, the more specific the information it conveys. Your language should be as concrete as the subject permits. Correctness is vital to ethos because grammatical errors and improper word choices can lower perceptions of your competence. *Malapropisms,* confusions among words based on similarities of sound, can be very damaging. Concise speakers strive for brevity, often using comparisons that reduce complex issues to the essentials. *Maxims* are the ultimate in conciseness. Cultural sensitivity demands that a speaker be aware of the diversity within an audience and respectful and appreciative of cultural differences.

**TERMS TO KNOW**

| | |
|---|---|
| simile | ideograph |
| metaphor | archetypal metaphor |
| synecdoche | alliteration |
| metonymy | anaphora |
| onomatopoeia | inversion |
| perspective by incongruity | antithesis |
| image | rhetorical style |
| hyperbole | amplification |
| personification | malapropism |
| culturetype | maxim |

**DISCUSSION**

1. The example that opens this chapter presents arguments for and against whiskey, using connotative language. Rephrase these arguments, using denotative language. How does this change affect the power of the arguments? Which speech situations call for more denotative language? How can connotative language be misused? Under what circumstances is it most appropriate?

2. In the 1950s, Richard Weaver suggested that *progress* was the primary culturetype of American society. What words do you nominate as culturetypes in contemporary society? Why? How are they used now in public communication? Find and share examples from speeches, essays, editorials, cartoons, or advertisements.

3. How can specific language techniques be abused in public communication? Bring examples to class.

4. Analyze how you used the power of language in your last speech. What, if any, barriers to perception or feeling did you have to overcome, and what techniques did you use? Could you have improved the effectiveness of your language? How?

**APPLICATION**   1. Use archetypal metaphors to describe the following abstract concepts:

> friendship
>
> freedom
>
> justice
>
> brotherhood
>
> democracy
>
> poverty

Present your descriptions in class. Which work most effectively and why?

2. Study the language customs and strategies in a speech from a political campaign. How is the power of language exercised? What special tools are used? Evaluate the effectiveness of this usage according to the standards discussed here.

3. Using published pamphlets and speeches determine the heroes and villains of the environmental, peace, antiapartheid, gay rights, or women's liberation movements.

4. To explore and help develop stylistic techniques, your instructor will assign different language tools to members of the class and then present a subject. Your task will be to make a statement about this subject using the technique you have been assigned. Share these statements in class. Try this exercise several times, using different subjects and different tools of language. Evaluate in class what this exercise reveals about the power, techniques, and standards of language.

5. Identify and discuss the language techniques used by Elie Wiesel in his Nobel Prize acceptance speech in Appendix B. Specifically discuss what techniques were used to reawaken group memory and identity, and whether and why they were effective for you as an audience.

**NOTES**   1. William Raspberry, "Any Candidate Will Drink to That," *Austin American Statesman* 11 (May 1984): A-10. The "Whiskey Speech," a legend in Southern politics, was originally presented by N. S. Sweat, Jr., during a heated campaign for liquor-by-the-drink in Mississippi. Because about half of his constituents favored the question and the other half were vehemently opposed, Representative Sweat decided to defuse the issue with humor.

2. Kenneth Burke, *Language as Symbolic Action: Essays on Life, Literature, and Method* (Berkeley and Los Angeles: University of California Press, 1966), pp. 44–80.

3. John F. Wilson and Carroll C. Arnold, *Public Speaking as a Liberal Art,* 3rd ed. (Boston: Allyn and Bacon, 1974), pp. 225–228.

4. These five powers of language were first explored in Michael Osborn, *Orientations to Rhetorical Style* (Chicago: Science Research Associates, Inc., 1976), and are developed further in Michael Osborn, "Rhetorical Depiction," in *Form, Genre, and the Study of Political Discourse,* ed. Herbert W. Simons and Aram A. Aghazarian (Columbia: University of South Carolina Press, 1986), pp. 79–107.

5. *The Silent Scream,* documentary film produced by American Portrait Films, 1984. For a detailed analysis of this conflict, see Celeste Michelle Condit, *Decoding Abortion Rhetoric: Communicating Social Change* (Urbana: University of Illinois Press, 1990).

6. George Orwell, "Politics and the English Language," in *Shooting an Elephant and Other Essays* (London: Secker and Warburg, 1950), pp. 96–97.

7. Based on the account in Claire Perkins, "The Many Symbolic Faces of Fred Smith: Charismatic Leadership in the Bureaucracy," *The Journal of the Tennessee Speech Communication Association* 11 (1985): 22.

8. Bill Clinton, "American Renewal: We Must Care for One Another," speech delivered at Inauguration, Washington, D.C., 20 Jan. 1993; text from *Vital Speeches of the Day,* 15 Feb. 1993, p. 259.

9. Jesse Jackson, "Common Ground and Common Sense," *Vital Speeches of the Day* 54 (15 Aug. 1988): 649–653.

10. Listeners whose lives seem dull and unrewarding are especially susceptible to such dramas. See the discussion in Eric Hoffer, *The True Believer: Thoughts on the Nature of Mass Movements* (New York: Harper, 1951).

11. Union organizing song written in 1932 by Florence Reece, wife of a leader of the National Miners Union in Harlan County, Kentucky.

12. Ronald Reagan, "Second Inauguration Address," *Vital Speeches of the Day* 51 (1 Feb. 1985): 226–228.

13. Mikhail Gorbachev, "USSR Foreign Relations," *Vital Speeches of the Day* 54 (15 Dec. 1987): 130–133.

14. For example, see Ronald H. Carpenter, "Frederick Jackson Turner and the Rhetorical Impact of the Frontier Thesis," *Quarterly Journal of Speech,* Apr. 1977, pp. 117–129, and Janice Hocker Rushing, "The Rhetoric of the American Western Myth," *Communication Monographs,* Mar. 1983, pp. 14–32.

15. Kenneth Burke, *Permanence and Change: An Anatomy of Purpose* (New York: New Republic, 1935), pp. 118–164.

16. Roger Tory Peterson, "Commencement Address," presented at Bloomsburg University, Bloomsburg, Pa. Cited in *Time,* 17 June 1985, p. 69.

17. Adapted from *The American Heritage Dictionary,* 2nd ed. (Boston: Houghton Mifflin, 1985), p. 92.

18. John Steinbeck, preface to *The Forgotten Village,* as cited in Peter Lisca, "*The Grapes of Wrath* as Fiction," in *The Grapes of Wrath: Text and Criticism* (New York: Viking, 1977), p. 736.

19. Longinus, "On the Sublime," in *The Great Critics: An Anthology of Literary Criticism,* trans. W. Rhys Roberts and ed. James Harry Smith and Edd Winfield Parks (New York: Norton, 1951), p. 82.

20. Winston Churchill, *Blood, Sweat, and Tears* (New York: Putnam, 1941), pp. 367–369.

21. Martin Luther King, Jr., from a transcription of "I've Been to the Mountaintop," delivered in Memphis, Tenn., 4 Apr. 1968. For complete text, see *Texts in Context: Critical Dialogues on Significant Episodes in American Political Rhetoric,* ed. Michael C. Leff and Fred J. Kauffeld (Davis, Calif.: Hermagoras Press, 1989), pp. 311–321.

22. Michael Calvin McGee, "The Origins of Liberty: A Feminization of Power," *Communication Monographs* 47 (1980): 27–45.

23. Ernest G. Bormann, "Fantasy and Rhetorical Vision: The Rhetorical Criticism of Social Reality," *Quarterly Journal of Speech* 58 (1972): 396–407.

24. Osborn, *Orientations to Rhetorical Style,* p. 16.

25. Richard Weaver, "Ultimate Terms in Contemporary Rhetoric," in *The Ethics of Rhetoric* (Chicago: Henry Regnery, 1953), pp. 211–232.

26. Michael Calvin McGee, "The Ideograph: A Link Between Rhetoric and Ideology," *Quarterly Journal of Speech* 66 (1980): 1–16.

27. For further insights into the function of archetypal metaphors, see Michael Osborn, "Archetypal Metaphor in Rhetoric: The Light-Dark Family," *Quarterly Journal of Speech* 53 (1967): 115–126, and "The Evolution of the Archetypal Sea in Rhetoric and Poetic," *Quarterly Journal of Speech* 63 (1977): 347–363.

28. *Time,* 10 July 1989, p. 32.

29. See Robert Ivie, "Images of Savagery in American Justifications for War," *Communication Monographs* 47 (1980): 279–294.

30. See another side of this image in J. Vernon Jensen, "British Voices on the Eve of the American Revolution: Trapped by the Family Metaphor," *Quarterly Journal of Speech* 63 (1977): 43–50.

31. Kennedy, "Inaugural Address," p. 11.

32. As reported by David R. Gergen, "The Boiling Pot," *U.S. News & World Report,* 15 May 1989, p. 76.

33. Bill Moyers, "Commencement Address," presented at the Lyndon B. Johnson School of Public Affairs, University of Texas, Austin. Cited in *Time,* 19 June 1985, p. 68.

34. Malcolm X, from a transcription of "The Ballot or the Bullet," delivered in Cleveland, Ohio, 3 Apr. 1964.

35. "Malapropisms Live!" *Spectra,* May 1986, p. 6.

36. Richard Lacayo, "Picking Lemons for the Plums?" *Time,* 31 July 1989, p. 17.

37. *New York Times,* 30 Jan. 1960. Cited in James B. Simpson, *Simpson's Contemporary Quotations* (Boston: Houghton Mifflin, 1988), p. 208.

38. Sojourner Truth, "Ain't I a Woman?" in *Feminism: The Essential Historical Writings,* ed. Miriam Schneir (New York: Random House, 1972), p. 95.
39. Felicity Barringer, "Census Shows Profound Change in Racial Makeup of the Nation,"*New York Times,* 11 Mar. 1991, p. A1.
40. "Measuring Diversity: How Does Your State Rate?" *National Education Association Today,* Sept. 1992, p. 8.

*Whosoever hath a good presence and a good fashion carries continual letters of recommendation.*
—*Francis Bacon*

# 11

# Presenting Your Speech

**This Chapter Will Help You**

- understand what makes an effective presentation.
- learn four major methods of presentation.
- develop a more effective speaking voice.
- improve your use of body language.
- learn how to practice presenting your speech.
- prepare for video presentations.

Jeff was deeply concerned about the environment. For his persuasive speech, he wanted to talk on the importance of saving threatened and endangered species. He went to the library to expand his knowledge beyond what he already knew. Jeff also analyzed his audience, narrowed his topic, decided on his strategy, and outlined his speech. He practiced his presentation at least an hour a day for several days, trying to make his voice more emphatic and expressive and to develop forceful gestures to reinforce his ideas. Finally, he felt comfortable presenting his speech.

On the day of his presentation, Jeff walked to the front of the room with an air of confidence he did not totally feel. As he began his presentation, he got caught up with his ideas. All he could think about was sharing his information and suggestions with his audience. Jeff's nervousness was changed into constructive energy that made him more expressive and convincing. Even though they were impressed by his presentation, all the audience could think about was Jeff's sincerity and how much sense he made. When he finished, there was a moment of silence, then a burst of applause. Jeff and his listeners had shared a moment of real communication.

his vignette reminds us that successful speaking involves both *what* you say and *how* you say it. In this chapter we turn our attention to "how you say it," or **presentation.** We consider what makes a presentation effective, the different methods of presentation, the development of an effective speaking voice, using the body to communicate, the importance of practice, and planning for video presentations.

The presentation skills you learn in this class should help you in other communication settings. They will be useful in job interviews, meetings, and even social occasions. Once you gain a sense of poise, it tends to stay with you over the years. It allows you to carry what Francis Bacon called "continual letters of recommendation."

##  WHAT IS EFFECTIVE PRESENTATION?

A speech is not a speech until it has been presented by a speaker and interpreted by an audience. The essence of communication is sharing. As we noted earlier, the word *communicate* derives from the Latin word meaning *common*. Effective presentation makes it possible for the speaker and audience to hold ideas and feelings in common, even if listeners come from different cultural backgrounds. An ineffective presentation can widen the gap between speaker and listeners.

Your attitude is the starting point for effective presentation. You must want to share with the audience. We have purposely used the term *presenting* the speech, rather than *delivering* it, to help you keep this in mind. The speech you prepare is your gift to the audience. You have invested a great deal of yourself in its preparation, so the way you give it is important.

If you have selected a topic that is important to you — one that excites you and that you want to share with others — then you have taken the first step to an effective presentation. Your enthusiasm should color your presentation with energy and forcefulness. It should tell your audience that you really care about your topic and about them.

A skillful presentation does not call attention to itself or distract from your message. A formal, "oratorical" style with its dramatic gestures and eloquent vocal patterns may leave your audience wondering more about where you got your acting training than about what you have to say. Mumbling is equally distracting. Your speech should be readily intelligible and loud enough to be heard in all parts of the room.

An effective presentation sounds natural and conversational, as though you are talking *with* people, not *at* them. When you speak before a group, you should be just a bit more formal and deliberate than when you talk with friends in casual settings. Your manner should indicate that you value this moment of communication and that you have something important to say. A good presentation sounds spontaneous, as though the words and ideas are coming together for the first time. Your tone, loudness, and rate of speaking should be appropriate to your message and the size of your audience.

## METHODS OF PRESENTATION

There are four major methods of speech presentation: impromptu speaking, memorized text presentation, reading from a manuscript, and extemporaneous speaking. Extemporaneous speaking combines careful planning with a conversational and spontaneous style. It is the preferred method for most speaking situations and is emphasized in this chapter. The other modes of presentation may be useful in specific situations as noted in the following discussions.

### Impromptu Speaking

**Impromptu speaking** is also called speaking "off the cuff," a phrase that suggests you could put all the notes for your speech on the cuff of your shirt or blouse. Impromptu speaking is necessary when you have little or no time for preparation or practice. The incident we described at the beginning of Chapter 8, in which we learned during a zoning hearing that developers were proposing a helicopter port in our neighborhood, called for an

*Impromptu speaking skills can be very important in work settings and civic activities such as this school board meeting. You will increase your effectiveness if you can organize, support, and present your ideas on a moment's notice.*

impromptu speech. At work you might find yourself being asked to make a presentation "in fifteen minutes." In meetings you may want to "say a few words" about something. You can also use impromptu speaking skills in some classes — to answer a question or comment on a point your professor has made. Whatever the situation, effective impromptu speaking is grounded in previous knowledge and experience.

When you have just a few minutes to prepare, focus first on your purpose. What contribution can you make? What effect would you like to have? How can you use your time to best advantage? In light of your purpose, determine your main points. If you have access to any type of writing material — a note pad, a scrap of paper, even the cuff of your shirt! — jot down a memory-jogging word for each of these main ideas, either in the order of their importance or as they seem to follow in natural order. This skeletal outline will keep you from rambling or forgetting something that is important. Stick to the main points, enumerating them as you go: "My first point is. . . . Second, it is important to observe. . . . Finally, it is clear that. . . ." Illustrate each point with some type of supporting material: information, stories, or examples. Keep your presentation short and to the point. End with a summary of your remarks.

An impromptu speech often occurs as one in a series of such speeches as people give voice to their ideas and suggestions in meetings. Earlier speeches create a setting for your presentation. Take your cues from other speakers and from the demands of the situation. If others stood at the front of the room to speak and this seems to satisfy audience expectations, you should do so as well. If earlier speakers remained seated, you may wish to follow suit and adjust the tone of your message to this more relaxed setting. Much depends on whether preceding speakers have been successful. If these speakers offended listeners while making standing presentations, you may wish to remain seated to differentiate yourself from them. If seated speakers have made trivial presentations, you may wish to stand to signal that what you are going to say is important.

Standing to speak is a form of emphasis. It affects the formality of your manner. If you remain seated, the audience may expect less from your message and anticipate an informal manner of presentation. If you think that you may be making several impromptu statements during the course of a discussion, you may wish to reserve the more formal standing mode of presentation for your most important statement.

Fortunately, most impromptu speaking situations are relatively casual. No one expects a polished speech on a moment's notice, but the ability to gather your ideas quickly, organize them effectively, and present them confidently puts you at a great advantage. The principles of organizing, developing, and supporting ideas that you learn in this course can help you become a more effective impromptu speaker.

## Memorized Text Presentation

Because the introduction, conclusion, and vital transitions of a speech are important in gaining audience attention, binding a speech together, and leaving a lasting impression, their wording should be carefully planned. Therefore you may want to memorize these parts of an extemporaneous speech. You also should memorize the outline of main points for an extemporaneous presentation. You might memorize short congratulatory remarks, a toast, or a brief award acceptance speech. In general, however, you should avoid trying to memorize entire speeches because this method of presentation poses many problems.

**Memorized text presentations** require considerable skill. Often, novices who try to memorize speeches get so caught up with "remembering" that they forget to communicate with their audience. The memorized presentation then becomes more of a soliloquy than a public speech and can sound either stilted or "singsongy." Even when offered by professionals, memorized presentations can make a speaker sound "programmed." That charge was made during the 1992 presidential debates against both Bush and Clinton. The audience thought they sometimes sounded over-rehearsed — as though they had memorized answers to questions. Speaking from memory also binds a speaker to a prepared text and inhibits adjusting to audience feedback. It can keep speakers from amplifying points that need clarification or from following up on ideas that have been especially effective. This kind of presentation can end up with speakers staring up at the ceiling, at the wall or out the window, as they strain to remember the exact words. Needless to say, such behaviors reduce audience contact.

Another problem with memorized speeches is that they must be written out in advance. Most people do not write in an effective oral style. The major differences between oral and written language, covered in Chapter 10, bear repeating. Good oral style uses short, direct, conversational patterns. Even sentence fragments can be acceptable. Repetition, rephrasing, and amplification are more necessary in speaking than in writing. Imagery can be especially useful to help the audience visualize the point you are making.

If you feel you must memorize a speech, be sure that you compose the speech using good oral style. Then commit the speech so thoroughly to memory that you can communicate confidently with the audience. Should you experience a "mental block" during a memorized presentation, remember that the audience will not know about your difficulty unless you show signs of distress. *Keep talking*. Talk your way through your block. Restate your last point. Since repetition is natural in oral presentation, your audience should not notice your problem. Most of the time, rephrasing a previous point will put your mind back on track. If it doesn't, you may find yourself *forced* to adopt the preferred extemporaneous style and find, to your surprise, that you express your points better when freed from the constraints of exact wording.

### Reading from a Manuscript

**Manuscript presentation** shares many of the same problems of memorized presentation and creates some of its own. Most people do not read aloud well. Their presentations lack vocal variety and they tend to rush through their manuscript, ignoring feedback from the audience. Additionally, when speakers plan to read a speech, they often do not spend enough time practicing. If the speech is written out in front of them, practice may not seem as necessary. But unless speakers are comfortable with the material, they find themselves glued to their manuscripts rather than communicating with listeners. They first lose eye contact and then mental contact with their audiences.

Reading from a prepared manuscript may be necessary when accurate wording is imperative or when time constraints are severe. Official proclamations, legal announcements, professional papers, or mass media presentations that must be timed within seconds usually call for manuscript presentation. Additionally, extemporaneous presentations may include quotations or statistical data that should be read to ensure accuracy. Finally, reading a vital piece of evidence or an eloquent quotation directly from the book in which it was published can add authority and credibility to your speech. You can use such "props" to increase the impressiveness of your speech.

To make an effective manuscript presentation, write your speech in oral style. Use a large-print typewriter or word processor to prepare the final draft of your manuscript so that you can see it clearly without straining. Double or triple space the print. Mark pauses in the manuscript with slashes. Underline or highlight material you want to emphasize. Practice presenting your speech from the manuscript so that you become familiar with it and can maintain frequent eye contact with your audience.

Record yourself as you practice, using videotape if possible, then review these tapes to evaluate your presentation. Do you sound as though you are talking with someone or reading? Did you maintain frequent eye contact with the imaginary audience? If you were stumbling over phrasing or mispronouncing certain words, revise your manuscript and practice until the material flows smoothly. Strive for a conversational style of presentation.

This exercise may help you read better. Practice reading any written prose, increasing your vocal force at the end of each sentence. This imitates the way people normally talk. It helps you avoid the end-of-the-sentence "blahs" that often plague oral reading. The force you generate at the end of

---

**SPEAKER'S NOTES**

## Suggestions for Using Different Methods of Presentation

1. When making an *impromptu speech,* enumerate your main points, support each point with information, an example, or a story, then conclude with a summary. Keep to the point and avoid rambling.

2. Memorize only brief formal remarks like toasts or acceptance speeches, the vital parts of longer speeches, and the order of ideas. If you experience a "mental block" during a *memorized presentation,* go back over your last point.

3. Read material only when accurate wording is important, time constraints are severe, or when a direct citation from a source of information will be impressive. Practice a *manuscript presentation* until you are thoroughly familiar with your material.

4. Use an *extemporaneous presentation* to create more direct, spontaneous contact with your audience. Plan, prepare, and practice extemporaneous presentations.

sentences will impel you into your next sentence, moving your presentation forward.[1]

### Extemporaneous Speaking

**Extemporaneous speaking** *is prepared and practiced but not written out or memorized.* When you speak extemporaneously, you may use a key-word outline to jog your memory. Each time you practice, your wording will differ. Your speech sounds spontaneous and natural because it is not written out word for word. An extemporaneous presentation lets you adjust to your audience as you observe their responses. Do listeners look as though they understand you? Do you need to define a word you have just used? Should you add an example to make an idea clearer? Are you holding their interest? When speaking extemporaneously, you can monitor such feedback from the audience and make changes on the spot. You can develop better contact with your listeners. Moreover, because successful extemporaneous speaking requires mastery of the subject and the confidence to speak directly with listeners, extemporaneous speakers can earn higher marks for ethos.

These advantages of extemporaneous speaking over manuscript speaking were seen clearly in President Clinton's 1993 State of the Union message. Although he spoke from a prepared manuscript, as is customary on such formal occasions, Clinton's presentation had extemporaneous qualities that many listeners admired. The *New Yorker* commented:

> . . . a President delivering a speech of this sort normally seems in some subtle way cut off from his surroundings, as if encased behind the panes of the teleprompter from which he reads his text. This speech was different. The words scrolled up the teleprompter screens, but Mr. Clinton didn't read them: according to the Washington *Post,* he spoke only four consecutive words of his prepared text. . . . Mr. Clinton's address, in other words, was not an exercise in reading aloud. He argued, cajoled, taught, explained—often off the cuff—and was alert in equal measure to the audience in the Capitol and to the one beyond, watching on television. . . . As a performance the speech was masterly. [2]

Because extemporaneous speaking involves preparation and practice, it is more polished than impromptu speaking. You reveal this preparation and practice by the more careful organization of your material, the more complete support you are able to bring to your points, and the greater ease with which you present your speech. Because extemporaneous presentation combines the best characteristics of the forms we have discussed, many instructors prefer that you use it for most of your classroom speeches. We offer much of our advice in this chapter and elsewhere with this style in mind.

## USING YOUR VOICE EFFECTIVELY

If you doubt that your voice can play an important role in the meaning listeners attach to your words, consider the following simple sentences:

I don't believe it.

You did that.

Give me a break.

How many different meanings can you create, just by varying the pace, emphasis, and rising and falling inflections of your voice?

How your message comes across to your audience depends a great deal on the adequacy of your voice. *A good speaking voice conveys your message clearly and enhances your ethos.* This means that you do not cultivate a good speaking voice for its own sake. The age of the golden-voiced orator, in which speakers took more pride in how they sounded than in what they said, has happily passed into oblivion. Some of the more famous speakers of our time have had less than perfect voices and articulation. Franklin Delano Roosevelt had a rather raspy, strident voice, yet his "fireside chats" on the radio comforted many during the Depression and the early days of World War II. Nevertheless, you should be concerned with your voice

*President Kennedy's presentation skills included effective use of emphasis and timing to highlight his ideas. He was the first political leader to master the use of televised presentation.*

because it affects how listeners perceive you and how they receive your message.

Your voice is very personal. It even may represent your personality to many people. Someone who talks in a soft, breathy voice may be labeled "sexy;" another, who speaks in a resonant and forceful voice, may be considered "authoritative." It follows that minor improvements in the way you speak can bring about positive changes in how others may respond to you. No one can give you a new voice, but you may be able to utilize more fully what nature has provided.

Many of us picked up bad vocal habits when we were young. As adolescents we may have discovered that expressing ourselves freely left us open to ridicule from other teen-agers. Consequently, we may have developed flat, inexpressive voices for protection. The stresses and pressures of modern life may show up even now in strained or strident voices. When we are tossed into a public speaking class, such stress is magnified. The result? Voices that do not communicate freely and naturally. In such situations the standard advice to "Just be natural" or "Just be yourself" may not be very useful.

To speak more expressively, your voice needs careful attention. As one voice specialist put it, "Though speech is a human endowment, how well we speak is an individual achievement."[3] We emphasize, however, that unsupervised vocal exercises are not the answer for serious speech impairments. If you have such a problem, contact the speech pathology clinic on your campus or in your community for professional help.

The first step in learning to use your voice more effectively is to evaluate how you usually talk. Tape-record yourself both speaking spontaneously and reading. When you hear yourself, you may say, "Is that really me?" Ask yourself the following questions:

1. Does my voice convey the meaning I intend?

2. Would I want to listen to this voice if I were in the audience?

3. Does this voice present me at my best?

If your honest answers to any of these questions are negative, you may need to work on pitch, rate, loudness, variety, articulation, enunciation, pronunciation, or dialect. Save your original tape so that you can hear yourself improve as you practice.

### *Pitch*

**Pitch** suggests how listeners might place your voice on the musical scale. We know from our own auditory experience that vocal pitch can range from low, deep to high, squeaky levels. For effective speaking, you need to find a pitch level that is comfortable to you and others and that allows maximum flexibility and variety. Each of us has a **habitual pitch,** or level at which we speak most frequently. Additionally, we all have an **optimum pitch,** or a level at which we can produce our strongest voice with minimal effort and that allows variation up and down the scale.

You can use this exercise to help determine your optimum pitch:

> Sing the sound *la* down to the lowest pitch you can produce without feeling strain or having your voice break or become rough. Now count each note as you sing up the scale to the highest tone you can comfortably produce. Most people have a range of approximately sixteen notes. Your optimum pitch will be about one-fourth of the way up your range. For example, if your range extends twelve notes, your optimum pitch would be at the third note up the scale. Again, sing down to your lowest comfortable pitch, and then sing up to your optimum pitch level.

Tape-record this exercise, and compare your optimum pitch to the habitual pitch revealed during your first recording. If your optimum pitch is within one or two notes of your habitual pitch, then you should not experience vocal problems related to pitch level. If your habitual pitch is much higher or lower than your optimum pitch, you may not have sufficient flexibility to raise or lower the pitch of your voice for changes in meaning and emphasis. You can change your habitual pitch by practicing speaking and reading at your optimum pitch.

Once you have determined your optimum pitch, use it as a base or point of departure in your practice. Read the following paragraphs from John F. Kennedy's inaugural address at your optimum pitch level, using pitch changes to provide meaning and feeling. To make the most of your practice, tape-record yourself so you can observe both problems and progress.

> Let the word go forth from this time and place, to friend and foe alike, that the torch has been passed to a new generation of Americans—born in this century, tempered by war, disciplined by a hard and bitter peace, proud of our ancient heritage—and unwilling to witness or permit the slow undoing of those human rights to which this nation has always been committed, and to which we are committed today at home and around the world.
>
> Let every nation know, whether it wishes us well or ill, that we shall pay any price, bear any burden, meet any hardship, support any friend, oppose any foe to assure the survival and the success of liberty.[4]

The purpose of this exercise is to explore the full range of variation around your optimum pitch and to make you more conscious of the relationship between pitch and effective communication. Therefore, you should exaggerate the variation during practice. If you have a problem with a constricted pitch range, you may discover as you listen to your recorded voice that the exaggeration actually makes you more effective!

When you speak before a group, don't be surprised if your pitch seems higher than usual. Your voice is sensitive to emotions and generally goes up in pitch when you are under pressure. If there is a large gap between your habitual and optimum pitch, hum the latter to yourself as you start rehearsing your speech.

## *Rate*

Your **rate** or speed at which you speak should vary with the type of material you are presenting. Rate contributes to the mood of your speech. Serious, complex topics call for a slower, more deliberate rate; lighter topics can be handled best by a faster pace. Variety of rate includes the relative duration of syllables in words and the use of pauses, as well as the overall speed of presentation.

Beginning speakers may encounter problems with rate because they feel intimidated. Typically they will speed up and run their words together as though they are one jump ahead of the sheriff and the sheriff is gaining with every jump. The main idea this communicates is their desire to get done as quickly as possible and sit down! Other speakers may become so slow or deliberate that they sound as though they are drugged. They plod through their speeches. Neither extreme lends itself to effective communication.

As we noted in Chapter 3, the typical rate for extemporaneous speaking is about 125 words per minute. You can check your speed by timing your reading of the excerpt from the Kennedy inaugural. If you were reading at the average rate, you would have taken about forty-five seconds to complete that material. If you allowed time for pauses between phrases, appropriate for such formal material, your reading may have run slightly longer. If you took less than forty seconds, you were probably going too fast or not using pauses effectively. Your tape recording should reveal this problem.

Pauses are an important element in the presentation of speeches and effective speakers use them to emphasize meaning. A pause before or after a word or phrase can highlight its importance. Pausing also gives your listeners time to contemplate what you have said. Moreover, pauses can clarify the relationships among ideas, phrases, and sentences. They are oral punctuation marks, taking the place of the commas and periods, underlinings and exclamation marks, that occur in written communication. Read the following passage aloud again, using pauses where indicated by the slash marks. This exercise will give you an idea of how President Kennedy used pauses to emphasize and clarify the flow of his ideas:

> Let the word go forth from this time and place, / to friend and foe alike, /
> that the torch has been passed to a new generation of Americans — / born
> in this century, / tempered by war, / disciplined by a hard and bitter
> peace, / proud of our ancient heritage — / and unwilling to witness or per-

mit the slow undoing of those human rights / to which this nation has always been committed, / and to which we are committed today / at home and around the world. /

Let every nation know, / whether it wishes us well or ill, / that we shall pay any price, / bear any burden, / meet any hardship, / support any friend, / oppose any foe / to assure the survival and the success of liberty.

When practicing your next speech, be sure to use pauses to emphasize and clarify ideas.

If your natural tendency is to speak too slowly, you can work to develop a faster rate in practice sessions by reading light material aloud. The following selection by Mark Twain calls for a lively pace. Reading at between 160 and 175 words per minute, you should take about 70 seconds to complete this selection. In the story, the narrator knows absolutely nothing about farming but must write a story to meet a deadline for an agricultural newspaper. In his desperation he fabricates an advice column that causes a farmer to burst into his office.

> "There, you wrote that. Read it to me—quick! Relieve me. I suffer." I read as follows:
>
> > "Turnips should never be pulled, it injures them. It is much better to send a boy up and let him shake the tree.
> >
> > "Concerning the pumpkin, the custom of planting it in the front yard with the shrubbery is fast going out of vogue, for it is now generally conceded that the pumpkin as a shade tree is a failure.
> >
> > "Now, as the warm weather approaches, and the ganders begin to spawn. . . ."
>
> The excited listener sprang toward me and said: "There, that will do. I know I am all right now, because you read it just as I did, word for word. But stranger, when I first read it I said to myself, now I believe I *am* crazy: and with that I fetched a howl that you might have heard for two miles, and started out to kill somebody, because I knew it would come to that sooner or later, and so I might as well begin. I burned my house, crippled several people, and have one fellow up a tree where I can get him if I want him. Then I thought I should stop in here to check with you. I tell you, it is lucky for that chap up in the tree that I did. Good-bye, Sir. *Good*-bye."[5]

### Loudness

No presentation is effective if the audience can't hear you. Similarly, your presentation will not be successful if you overwhelm listeners with a voice that is too loud. When you speak before a group, you usually need to speak louder than you do in general conversation. The size of the room, presence or absence of a microphone, and background noise also may call for adjustments. Take your cues from audience feedback. If you are not loud enough, you may see listeners leaning forward, straining to hear. If you are speaking too loudly, they may unconsciously lean back, pulling away from the noise.

To speak at a proper loudness, you must have good breath control. If you are breathing improperly, you will not have enough force to project your voice so that you can be heard in the back of a room. Breathing improperly can also cause you to run out of breath before you finish a phrase or come to an appropriate pause. To check whether you are breathing properly for speaking, do the following exercise:

> Stand with your feet approximately eight inches apart. Place your hands on your lower rib cage, thumbs to the front, fingers to the back. Take a deep breath — in through your nose and out through slightly parted lips. If you are breathing correctly, you should feel your ribs moving *up and out* as you inhale.

Improper breathing affects more than just the loudness of your speech. If you breathe by raising your shoulders, the muscles in your neck and throat will become tense. This can result in a harsh, strained vocal quality. Moreover, you probably will not take in enough air to sustain your phrasing, and it will become difficult to control the release of air. The air and sound then all come out with a rush when you drop your shoulders, leading to unfortunate oral punctuation marks when you neither want nor need them.

To see if you have a problem, try this exercise:

> Take a normal breath and see how long you can count while exhaling. If you cannot reach fifteen without losing volume or feeling the need to breathe, you need to work on extending your breath control. Begin by counting in one breath to a number comfortable for you, then gradually increase the count over successive tries. Do not try to compensate by breathing too deeply. Deep breathing takes too much time and attracts too much attention while you are speaking. Use the longer pauses in your speech to breathe, and practice the rhythm of your breathing during rehearsal.

You should seek to vary the loudness of your speech, just as you strive for variety in pitch and rate. Changes in loudness are often used to express emotion. The more excited or angry we are about something, the louder we tend to become. But don't let yourself get caught in the trap of having only two options: loud and louder. Decreasing your volume, slowing your rate, pausing, or dropping your pitch can also express emotion quite effectively.

To acquire more variety in loudness, practice the following exercise recommended by Hillman and Jewell: "First, count to five holding on to your optimum pitch but at a very soft volume, as if you were speaking to one person. Then holding the same pitch, count to five at medium volume, as if to ten or fifteen people. Finally, holding the same pitch, count to five, as if to thirty or sixty people."[6] If you tape-record your practice, you should be able to hear the clear progression in loudness.

## *Variety*

The importance of vocal variety is most evident in speeches that lack it. Speakers who drone on and on in a monotone, never varying their pitch, rate, or loudness, send a clear message. Rightly or wrongly, they tell us that their topic has little meaning for them and that they have no interest in communicating with listeners. Add variety and see how their speeches come to life! Vocal variety adds color and interest to a speech. It can promote identification between speaker and audience. One of the best ways to develop variety is to read aloud materials that demand variety to express meaning and feeling. As you read the following selection from *the lives and times of archy and mehitabel,* strive for maximum variation of pitch, rate, and loudness. Incidentally, archy is a cockroach who aspires to be a writer. He leaves typewritten messages for his newspaper-editor mentor but, because he is a cockroach, he can't type capital letters and never uses punctuation marks. His friend mehitabel, whom he quotes in this message, is an alley cat with grandiose dreams and a dubious reputation. Have fun!

> archy what in hell have i done
> to deserve all these kittens
> life seems to be just one damn litter after another
> after all archy i am an artist
> this constant parade of kittens
> interferes with my career
> its not that i am shy on mother love archy
> why my heart would bleed if anything happened to them
> and i found it out
> a tender heart is the cross i bear
> but archy the eternal struggle between life and art
> is simply wearing me out[7]

Tape-record yourself while reading this and other favorite poems or dramatic scenes aloud. Compare these practice tapes with your initial self-evaluation tape.

## *Patterns of Speaking*

People often make judgments about others based on their speech patterns. If you slur words together, mispronounce familiar words, or have an unfamiliar dialect, you may be labeled an "outsider" or even considered uneducated or socially undesirable. If you sound "odd" to your listeners, their attention will be distracted from what you are saying to the way you are saying it.

In this section we cover articulation, enunciation, pronunciation, and dialect as they contribute to or detract from speaking effectiveness.

*Articulation.* Your **articulation** refers to the way you produce individual speech sounds. Some people have trouble making certain sounds. For example, they may substitute a *d* for a *th* saying "dem" instead of "them." Other sounds that are often misarticulated include *s, l,* and *r.* Severe articulation problems can interfere with effective communication, especially if the audience cannot understand the speaker or the variations are perceived as signs of low social or educational status. Such problems are best treated by a speech pathologist, who retrains the individual to produce the sound in a more acceptable manner. Minor articulation problems may not disrupt communication and even can be part of a person's oral signature. Barbara Walters's speech is immediately recognizable by her "weak" *r* and *l* sounds, yet these have not hindered her success in television.

*Enunciation.* **Enunciation** refers to the way you articulate and pronounce words in context. In casual conversation it is not unusual for people to slur their words—for example, saying "gimme" for "give me." But careless enunciation can cause credibility problems for the public speaker. Are you guilty of saying "Swatuh thought" for "That's what I thought"; "Harya?" for "How are you?"; or "Howjado?" for "How did you do?" Such lazy enunciation patterns are not acceptable in public communication settings. On the tape-recordings you make of vocal exercises to develop more effective pitch, rate, and vocal variety, check your enunciation patterns as well. If you have developed bad articulation habits, concentrate on careful enunciation as you practice. However, be careful to avoid another problem at the opposite extreme. Equally unacceptable are inflated, pompous, and pretentious articulation patterns in which speakers meticulously enunciate each and every syllable, affecting a language pattern they think is stylish or sophisticated. Very few speakers can make this work without sounding phony. You should strive to be neither sloppy nor overly precise.

*Pronunciation.* Your **pronunciation** refers to whether you say words correctly. Pronunciation includes both the use of correct sounds and the proper stress or accent on syllables. Because written English does not always indicate the correct pronunciation of spoken English, we may not be sure how to pronounce words that we first encounter in print. For instance, does the word *chiropodist* begin with an *sh*, a *ch,* or a *k* sound?

If you are not certain how to pronounce a word, consult a dictionary. An especially useful reference is the *NBC Handbook of Pronunciation,* 4th ed. (New York: Harper, 1991), which contains 21,000 words and proper names that sometimes cause problems. When international stories and new foreign leaders first appear in the news, newspapers frequently indicate the correct pronunciation of their names. Check front-page stories in the *New York Times* for such guidance.

In addition to problems pronouncing unfamiliar words, you may find that there are certain words you habitually mispronounce. For example, how do you pronounce the following words?

|            |           |
|------------|-----------|
| government | library   |
| February   | picture   |
| ask        | secretary |
| nuclear    | just      |
| athlete    | get       |

Unless you are careful, you may find yourself slipping into these common mispronunciations:

|           |           |
|-----------|-----------|
| goverment | liberry   |
| Febuary   | pitchur   |
| aks       | sekaterry |
| nuculer   | jist      |
| athalete  | git       |

Mispronunciation of such common words can damage your ethos. Most of us know what words we chronically mispronounce and are able to pronounce them correctly when we think about it. The time to think about it is when you are practicing your speech.

***Dialect.*** A **dialect** is a speech pattern typical of a geographic region or ethnic group. Your dialect usually reflects where you were raised or lived for any length of time. In the United States there are three commonly recognized dialects: eastern, southern, and midwestern. Additionally, there are local variations within the broader dialects: Tidewater Virginians speak differently from Arkansans, Vermonters differently from New Yorkers. And then there's *"Bab-stabn"* where you buy *"lodge budded pup con"* at the movies!

There is no such thing as right or wrong, superior or inferior dialect. However, there can be occasions when a distinct dialect is a definite disadvantage or advantage. Listeners have esthetic preferences for speech patterns based on their familiarity to the ear. Audiences may also have stereotyped preconceptions about people who speak with certain dialect patterns. For example, those raised in the South often associate a northeastern dialect with brusqueness and abrasiveness, and midwesterners may associate a southern dialect with slowness of action and mind. You may have to work to overcome these prejudices against your dialect.

If your dialect blocks communication between you and your audience, you can plan your speech to overcome this difficulty. Sometimes the best way to tackle such a problem is to acknowledge it. Get it out in the open early in the speech, then move on in a spirit of good will. This kind of direct, disarming approach may not remove the problem, but should reduce its importance:

> We sound different. I know that. I just didn't have the good fortune to be born in Chicago. But we laugh the same way. We care the same way about our families. And when crime comes to our communities, we often cry the same way.

You should be deeply concerned about your dialect only if it creates barriers to understanding and identification between you and your audience. Then you may want to work toward softening your dialect so that you lower these barriers for the sake of your message. If others share your dialect problem, you may be able to form a self-help group in which you assist each other in identifying specific problems and work together to correct them. If you can combine these sessions with actual practice for the speeches you will give in class, so much the better.

## USING YOUR BODY EFFECTIVELY

Communication with your audience begins before you ever open your mouth. Your facial expression, personal appearance, and air of confidence all convey a message. How do you walk to the front of the room to give your speech? Do you move with confidence and purpose, or do you stumble and shuffle? As you begin your speech, do you look listeners directly in the eye, or do you stare at the ceiling as though asking for divine intervention? Are you enthusiastic? Do you move and gesture freely and naturally? All of these visible behaviors form your **body language,** the nonverbal message that accompanies your speech. For public speaking to be effective, your body language must reinforce your verbal language. If your face is expressionless as you urge your listeners to action, you are sending inconsistent messages. Be sure that your body and words both "say" the same thing.

### *Facial Expression and Eye Contact*

> I knew she was lying the minute she said it. There was guilt written all over her face!

> He sure is shifty! Did you see how his eyes darted back and forth? He never did look us straight in the eye!

*During the 1992 presidential campaign debate at the University of Richmond, Bill Clinton frequently left his seat and approached the audience to answer questions. Reducing the physical distance between a speaker and an audience can help increase identification.*

Most of us believe we can judge character, determine people's true feelings, and tell whether they are honest from their facial expressions. If there is a conflict between what we see and what we hear, we will usually believe our eyes rather than our ears.

The eyes are the most important feature of facial expressiveness. In our culture, frequent and sustained eye contact suggests honesty, openness, and respect. We may think of a person's eyes as a window into the self. If you avoid looking at your audience while you are talking, you are drawing the shades on these windows of communication. A lack of eye contact suggests that you do not care about listeners, that you are putting something over on them, or that you are afraid of them.

When you reach the place where you are going to speak, turn, pause, and look at your audience. This signals that you want to communicate and prepares people to listen. During your speech, try to make eye contact with all sectors of your audience. Don't just stare at one or two people. You will make them uncomfortable, and other members of the audience will feel left out. First look at people at the front of the room, then shift your focus to the middle, finally look at those in the rear. You may find that those sitting in the rear of the room are the most difficult to reach. They may have taken a back seat because they don't *want* to listen or be involved. You may have to work harder to gain and hold their attention. Eye contact is one way you can reach them.

Start your speech with a smile unless this is inappropriate to your message. Your face should reflect and reinforce the meanings of your words. An expressionless face in public speaking suggests that the speaker is afraid or indifferent. The frozen face may be a mask behind which the speaker hides. The solution lies in selecting a topic that excites you, concentrating on sharing your message, and having the confidence that comes from being well prepared.

You can also try the following exercise:

Utter these statements, using a dull monotone and keeping your face as expressionless as possible:

I am absolutely delighted by your gift.

I don't know when I've ever been this excited.

We don't need to beg for change—we need to demand change.

All this puts me in a very bad mood.

Now repeat them with *exaggerated* vocal variety and facial expression. You may find that your hands and body also want to get involved. Encourage such impulses so that you develop an integrated system of body language.

### Movement and Gestures

Most actors learn—often the hard way—that if you want to steal a scene from someone, all you have to do is move around, develop a twitch, or swing a leg. Before long, all eyes will be focused on you. This nasty little trick shows that physical movement sometimes can attract more attention than words. All the more reason that your words and gestures should work in harmony and not at cross-purposes! This also means you should avoid random movements, such as pacing back and forth or hair or mustache curling. Once you are aware of such mannerisms, it is easy to control them.

Your gestures and movement should always appear natural and spontaneous, prompted by ideas and feelings. They should never look contrived and artificial. For example, you should avoid making a gesture fit each word or sequence of words you utter. Perhaps every speech instructor has encountered speakers like the one who stood with arms circled above him as he said, "We need to get *around* this problem." That's taking body language too far!

Effective gestures involve three phases: *readiness, execution,* and *return.* In the readiness phase you must be prepared for movement. Your hands and body should be in a position that does not inhibit free action. For example, you cannot gesture if your hands are locked behind your back or jammed into your pockets, or if you grasp the lectern as though it were a life preserver. Instead, let your hands rest in a relaxed position either at your sides, on the lectern, or in front of you, where they can obey easily the impulse to gesture in support of a point you are making. As you execute a gesture, let yourself move naturally and fully. Don't raise your hand halfway, then stop with your arm frozen awkwardly in the air. When you have completed a gesture, let your hands return to the relaxed readiness position, where they will be free to move again when the next impulse to gesture arises.

From **proxemics,** the study of how humans use space during communication, we can derive two additional principles that help explain the effective use of movement during speeches. The first of these principles suggests that *the physical distance between you as speaker and your listeners will have an impact on identification, the feeling of closeness that does or does not develop in a speaking situation.* President Clinton made effective use of this principle during the second of the televised debates of the 1992 campaign. In the town meeting setting of that debate, Clinton actually rose from his seat after one question, and approached the audience as he answered it. His movement towards his listeners suggested that he felt a special closeness for that problem and for them. Clinton's body language broke the barrier that separated candidates and listeners, and enhanced his identification with the live audience and with the larger viewing audience they represented.

It follows also that the greater the physical distance between speaker and audience, the harder it is to achieve identification. This problem gets worse when a lectern acts as a physical barrier. Short speakers may almost disappear behind it! If this is a problem, try speaking from either beside or in front of a lectern so that your body language can work for you. A different problem arises if you move so close to listeners that you make them feel uncomfortable. If they strain back involuntarily in their chairs, you know you have violated their sense of personal space. You should seek the ideal physical distance between yourself and listeners to increase effectiveness.

The second principle of proxemics suggests that *elevation will also affect identification.* When you speak, you often stand above your seated listeners in a "power position." Because we tend to associate *above* us with power *over* us, speakers may find this arrangement at odds with their purpose of achieving identification. Often they will sit on the edge of the desk in front of the lectern in a more relaxed and less elevated position. If your message is informal and requires close identification, you might want to give this a try.

### *Personal Appearance*

Your clothing and grooming affect how you are perceived. These factors also affect how you see yourself and how you behave. A police officer out of uniform may not act as authoritatively as when dressed in blue. A doctor without a white jacket may behave like just another person. You may have a certain type of clothing that makes you feel comfortable and relaxed. You may even have a special "good luck" outfit that raises your confidence.

When you are scheduled to speak, you should dress in a way that puts you at ease and makes you feel good about yourself. Of course, your speech is a special occasion, and you should treat it as such. By dressing a little more formally than you usually do, you emphasize both to yourself and the audience that your speech is important. As we noted in Chapter 9, your appearance can serve as a visual aid that complements your message. Like any other visual aid, it should never compete with your words for attention or be distracting. Outside the classroom it is best to follow audience custom concerning grooming and dress. Always dress in good taste for the situation you anticipate.

## THE IMPORTANCE OF PRACTICE

It takes a lot of practice to sound natural. Although this statement may seem contradictory, it should not be surprising. Speaking before a group is not your typical way of communicating. Even though most people seem spontaneous and relaxed when talking with a small group of friends, something happens when they walk to the front of a room and face a larger audience of less familiar faces. They may sense an icy wall between themselves and listeners and become stilted, awkward, and unnatural. The flow of communication is blocked, and the frustration both speaker and listeners feel increases the strain.

The key to melting this ice is effective rehearsal until you can respond fully to your own ideas as you present them. Your voice, face, and body should all express your feelings as well as your thoughts. On the day of your speech, you then become a model for your listeners, showing them how they should respond in turn. As the audience responds, the wall of separation will disappear.

To develop an effective extemporaneous style, practice presenting your speech until you feel the speech is part of you. During practice you can actually hear what you have been preparing and can try out the words and techniques you have been considering. What looked like a good idea on paper may not seem to work as well when it comes to life in spoken words. It is better to discover this fact in rehearsal than before an actual audience.

You will probably want privacy the first two or three times you practice. Even then you should try to simulate the conditions under which the speech will be given. Stand up while you practice. Imagine your listeners in front of you. Picture them responding positively to what you have to say. Address your ideas to them, and think of those ideas as having impact.

If possible, go to your classroom to practice. If this is not possible, find another empty room where the speaking arrangements are similar. Such on-the-site rehearsal helps you get a better feel for the situation you will face, reducing its strangeness when you make your actual presentation. Begin practicing from your formal outline. Once you feel comfortable, switch to your key-word outline and practice until the outline transfers from the paper to your head.

Keep material to be read to a minimum. Type or print quotations in large letters so you can see them easily. Put each quotation on a single index card or sheet of paper. If using a lectern, position this material so that you can maintain frequent eye contact while reading. If you will speak beside or in front of the lectern, hold your cards in your hand and raise them when it is time to read. Practice reading your quotation until you can present it naturally while only glancing at your notes. If your speech includes visual aids, practice handling them until they are smoothly integrated into your presentation. They should seem a natural extension of your verbal message.

During practice you can serve as your own audience by recording your speech and playing it back. If videotaping equipment is available, arrange to record your speech so that you can see as well as hear yourself. It is sometimes better to review your taped speech at a later time so that you can be more objective in judging it. If you try to evaluate yourself immediately after you make your practice presentation, you may be hearing what you think you said rather than what you actually said. Always try to be the toughest critic you will ever have, but also be a constructive critic. Never put yourself down or give up on yourself. Work on specific points of improvement.

In addition to evaluating yourself, it sometimes is helpful to ask a friend or friends to listen to your presentation. This outside opinion should be more

**SPEAKER'S NOTES**

### Practicing for Presentation

1. Practice your speech using your formal outline.

2. Continue practicing, using the outline less and increasing eye contact with your imagined audience.

3. Practice from your key-word outline, reading only direct quotations.

4. Work on integrating body language and visual aids into your verbal message.

5. Check the timing of your speech.

6. Practice before friends, listen to their advice, and make changes if necessary.

7. Practice some more until you feel comfortable and confident.

objective than your self-evaluation, and you will get a feel for speaking to real people rather than to an imagined audience. Seek constructive feedback from your friends by asking them specific questions. Was it easy for them to follow you? Do you have any mannerisms (such as hair twisting or saying "you know" after every other sentence) that distracted them? Were you speaking loudly and slowly enough? Were your ideas clear and soundly supported?

On the day that you are assigned to speak, get to class early enough to look over your outline one last time so that it is fresh in your mind. If you have devoted sufficient time and energy to your preparation and practice, you should feel confident about communicating with your audience.

## MAKING VIDEO PRESENTATIONS

In a world of advanced communication technology, it is very likely that at some time you will be making a video presentation. You may be speaking live on closed-circuit television, videotaping instructions or training materials, using community access cable channels to promote a cause, or even appearing on commercial television. With some minor adaptations, the training you receive in this class should serve you well in such situations.

### Adapting for Video Presentation

Television brings a speaker close to viewers. It magnifies every visual aspect of you and your message. Dress conservatively. Avoid wearing shiny fabrics, glittery jewelry, prints that might "swim" on the screen, or dangling earrings that might distract viewers. Don't wear white or very light pastels because they may cause glare. Media consultant Dorothy Sarnoff recommends red or royal blue for women.[8] Ask in advance about the color of the studio backdrop. If you have light hair or if the backdrop will be light, wear dark clothing for contrast. If you are African American, request a light or neutral background and consider wearing light-colored clothes. Special studio lighting may be required to make your facial expressions intelligible and effective.

Both men and women will need make-up to achieve a natural look on television. Not using make-up may make you look unnatural. Have powder available to reduce skin shine or hide a five-o'clock shadow. Women should wear thinly applied eyeliner, a nonglossy neutral eye shadow, and medium-colored lipstick. Dark red lipstick may look black; pale pink will make your lips disappear. Avoid glasses with tinted lenses: they will appear even darker on the screen and may make you look like you are hiding something. If you can see well enough to read the monitor without your glasses, leave them off.

Television is an intimate medium that requires a conversational, casual-seeming mode of presentation. Imagine that you are talking to another person in an informal setting. To be effective, you must make that other person comfortable with you. The most important quality to communicate is sincerity.

While intimate, television is also remote. Since you have no immediate feedback, your meaning must be instantly clear and you must react as though you had a responsive listener. Vocal variety and facial expression will become your most important forms of body language. Just remember that television will magnify all your movements and vocal changes — slight head movements and underplayed facial expressions should be enough to reinforce your ideas. Avoid abrupt changes in loudness as a means of vocal emphasis. Rely instead on subtle changes in rate, pitch, and inflection, and on brief pauses to drive your points home. Avoid long pauses that come across as "dead air."

Use language that is colorful and concrete so that your audience can remember your message. Keep in mind the PRER formula: state a **p**oint, give a **r**eason or **e**xample, then **r**estate the point. Use previews and internal summaries to keep viewers on track. You may use visual aids to aid comprehension, but be sure to confer in advance with the studio director to be sure your materials will work in that setting.

Timing is crucial. Five minutes of air time means five minutes, not five minutes and ten seconds. If you run overtime, you will be cut off in midsentence. For this reason, television favors manuscript presentations using a teleprompter. The teleprompter helps to control timing, but also preserves the illusion of direct eye contact between speaker and listeners. Ask studio production personnel how you can make use of the teleprompter equipment they have available.

## *Practicing for Video Presentations*

If at all possible, arrange to practice your presentation in the studio with the help of production personnel. Make it a point to create a positive relationship with studio workers. Your success depends on how well they do their job. Provide them with a script of your speech marked to show when you will move around or use a visual aid. Practice speaking from the teleprompter, striving to make your reading of the script seem spontaneous and direct. Learn to use the microphone correctly — don't tap it or blow into it to see if it's working! Remember that it will pick up *all* sounds, including shuffling papers or tapping on a lectern. If you use a boom microphone, production personnel will control it. If you use a desk or stand microphone, position it about thirty degrees below your mouth and about ten inches away. The closer your mouth is to the microphone, the more it will pick up extraneous noises like whistled *"s"* sounds or tongue clicks. If you use a lavaliere microphone, production personnel will arrange it around your neck or clip it to your clothing (necktie, scarf, or lapel). Don't fiddle with the mike while you are presenting your speech. Keep in mind that microphones with cords will restrict movement. Know where the cord is so you don't trip over it if you plan to move about during your speech.

Don't be put off by distractions in the studio as you practice and later present your talk. Studio personnel may have to confer with each other while you are speaking. Remember, this is a necessary part of their business — they are not being rude. Besides, they are not your audience. Keep your mind on your ideas and your eye on the camera. The camera may at first seem strange and remote, but think of it as a friendly and receptive face waiting to hear what you have to say. Your eye contact with the camera becomes your eye contact with your audience.

## Making Your Media Presentation

Production personnel may need to fit you with a microphone and arrange how you sit or stand for maximum televisual impact. If you are taping your speech, be prepared for several lighting and voice checks before the actual taping begins. Take advantage of these preparations to run through your opening one more time, being sure to set the right conversational tone. As you approach your speech and after your speech, *you should always assume that any microphone near you is "live."*

Relax! If you are standing, stand at ease. If you are seated, sit up straight and lean slightly forward as you might if you were talking to someone in the chair next to you. The floor director will give you a countdown before the camera starts to roll. Clear your throat and be ready to start on cue. Begin with a smile, if appropriate, as you make eye contact with the camera. If several cameras are trained on you, a red light on top will tell you which camera is on.

During your presentation, studio personnel may communicate with you using special sign language. For example, two fingers held up by the side of the camera may indicate that you have two minutes more to speak. A circular movement of the hand tells you to "wind up," and a rapid circular movement means "wrap it up in a hurry." A stretching movement between the camera operator's hands signals you to talk some more to fill up air time. A sharp, horizontal movement across the throat means "stop."

When using a teleprompter, the script will appear directly below or on the lens of the camera. Even though you may be using a teleprompter, practice your speech until you almost have it memorized. This familiarity will allow you to look at the printed script as a whole. If you rely too much on reading, your eyes will be continually shifting, or you will have what producers call a "dead stare." Concentrate on creating a spontaneous lively "conversation" with your unseen viewer. If you make a mistake, keep going. Do not stop your presentation unless the director tells you to. If appropriate, smile when you finish and continue to look at the camera to allow time for a fade-out closing. Don't assume you are off camera until the director says, "Cut."

**IN SUMMARY**

*What Is Effective Presentation?*   An effective *presentation* integrates the nonverbal aspects of voice and body language with the words of your speech. It is characterized by enthusiasm and naturalness. Your voice and bearing should project your sincere commitment but should not call attention to themselves. You should sound and look spontaneous, not contrived or artificial.

*Methods of Presentation.*   The four major methods of speech presentation are impromptu speaking, memorized presentation, reading from a manuscript, and extemporaneous speaking. In *impromptu speaking* you talk with minimal or no preparation and practice. Both *memorized* and *manuscript presentations* require that your speech be written out word for word. An *extemporaneous speech* requires a carefully planned sequence of ideas, but the wording is not predetermined. Instructors usually require that you present speeches extemporaneously.

*Using Your Voice Effectively.*   A good speaking voice conveys your meaning fully and clearly while enhancing your ethos. Vocal expressiveness depends on your ability to control pitch, rate, loudness, and variety. Your *habitual pitch* is the level at which you usually speak. Your *optimum pitch* is the level at which you can produce a clear, strong voice with minimal effort. Speaking at your optimum pitch gives your voice flexibility. The rate at which you speak can affect the impression you make on listeners. You can control rate to your advantage by using pauses and by changing your pace to match the moods of your material. To speak loudly enough, you need proper breath control. Vary loudness for the sake of emphasis. Vocal variety adds color and interest to a speech, makes a speaker more likable, and encourages identification between speaker and audience.

Articulation, enunciation, pronunciation, and dialect refer to the unique way you give voice to words. *Articulation* concerns the manner in which you produce individual sounds. *Enunciation* refers to the way you utter words in context. Proper *pronunciation* means that you say words correctly. Your *dialect* may identify the area of the country in which you learned language and your cultural or ethnic background. Occasionally, dialect can create identification and comprehension problems between a speaker and audience.

*Using Your Body Effectively.*   You communicate with *body language* as well as with your voice. Eye contact signals listeners that you want to communicate. Your facial expressions should project the meanings of your words. Movement attracts attention; therefore, your movements and gestures must complement your speech, not compete with it. *Proxemics* is the study of how humans use space during communication. Two proxemic principles, distance and elevation, can affect your identification with an audience as you speak. Be sure your grooming and dress are appropriate to the speech occasion and do not detract from your ability to communicate.

*The Importance of Practice.*   You should practice your speech until you have the sequence of main points and supporting materials well established in your mind. It is best to practice your presentation under conditions similar to those in which you will give your speech. Keep citations or other materials that you must read to a minimum. Tape-recording or videotaping can be useful for self-evaluation during rehearsal.

*Making Video Presentations.*   When you prepare a video presentation, pay special attention to the visual aspects of your message. Be sure your language is clear and colorful, and remember that timing is crucial. Get comfortable with the setting. Practice using a teleprompter and microphone. Imagine a listener you can see through the eye of the camera. Present your message as though you were speaking to that person in a relaxed setting.

**TERMS TO KNOW**

| | |
|---|---|
| presentation | rate |
| impromptu speaking | articulation |
| memorized text presentation | enunciation |
| manuscript presentation | pronunciation |
| extemporaneous speaking | dialect |
| pitch | body language |
| habitual pitch | proxemics |
| optimum pitch | |

**DISCUSSION**

1. Attend a public speaking event in your community, such as a lecture at your college, a political speech, or a church service. Did the speaker read from a manuscript, make a memorized presentation, or speak extemporaneously? Was the speaker's voice effective or ineffective? Why? How would you evaluate the speaker's use of body language? Discuss your observations with your classmates.

2. Observe nonverbal communication among small groups at a social gathering. Look at people's facial expressions, their gestures, their movements in communication. How are these similar or dissimilar to what you have observed during speeches in class? Record your observations and exchange them with others in class.

3. Comedians often capture the personalities of public figures by accentuating their verbal and gestural characteristics in comic impersonations. Be alert for such impersonations on late-night television. Which identifying characteristics do the comedians exaggerate? What might this indicate about the "real" speaker's style and ethos? Contribute your observations to a class discussion.

4. Assume you have been invited to present your most recent classroom speech on local public television. How would you adapt your message to that medium? Report your ideas in class. What general conclusions can you draw about the impact of video presentations on public communication?

**APPLICATION**

1. Exchange your self-evaluation tape with a classmate and write a critique of the other speaker's voice and articulation. Emphasize the positive, but make specific recommendations for improvement. Work on your classmate's recommendations to you, and then make a second tape to share with your partner. Do you hear signs of improvement in each other's performance?

2. Make a list of words you often mispronounce. Practice saying these words correctly each day for a week. See if you carry over these changes into social conversation.

3. Experiment with reading the same material aloud at different rates of speed and with varying loudness. Do these differences seem to affect the meaning of the material?

4. As you practice your next speech, deliberately try to speak in as dull a voice as possible. Stifle all impulses to gesture. Then practice speaking with as colorful a voice as possible, giving full freedom to movement and gesture. Notice how a colorful and expressive presentation makes your ideas seem more lively and vivid as you speak.

5. Form small groups and conduct an impromptu speaking contest. Each participant should supply two topics for impromptu speeches, and participants should then draw two topics (not their own). Participants have five minutes to prepare a three-minute speech on one of these topics. Each student then presents the speech to the group, which selects a winner.

**NOTES**

1. This exercise was suggested by Professor Jo Lenhart, Memphis State University, who uses it to teach voice and articulation to theater students.
2. *The New Yorker*, 1 Mar. 1993, pp. 4, 6.
3. Jon Eisenson, *Voice and Diction: A Program for Improvement* (New York: Macmillan, 1974), p. vii.
4. John F. Kennedy, "Inaugural Address," in *Presidential Rhetoric: 1961–1980,* ed. Theodore Windt (Dubuque, Iowa: Kendall Hunt, 1980), p. 9.
5. Mark Twain, adapted from "How I Edited an Agricultural Paper," in *Sketches: Old and New* (Hartford, Conn.: American, 1901), pp. 307–315.
6. Ralph Hillman and Delorah Lee Jewell, *Work for Your Voice* (Murfreesboro, Tenn.: Copymatte, 1986), p. 63.
7. Don Marquis, adapted from "mehitabel and her kittens," in *the lives and times of archy and mehitabel* (Garden City, N.Y.: Doubleday, 1950), pp. 76–80.
8. Dorothy Sarnoff with Gaylen Moore, *Never Be Nervous Again* (New York: Ballantine, 1989), pp. 119–120.

# PART FOUR

# Types of
# Public Speaking

*The improvement of
understanding is
for two ends: first,
our own increase
of knowledge;
secondly, to enable
us to deliver that
knowledge to others.
— John Locke*

# 12

# The Nature and Kinds of Informative Speaking

**This Chapter Will Help You**

- understand the basic functions of informative speaking.

- learn how to motivate listeners, hold their attention, and help them remember your message.

- distinguish among speeches of description, demonstration, and explanation and learn the major designs appropriate to each.

- prepare and present effective informative speeches.

Ancient legend tells us of Prometheus, who was punished by the gods for showing humans how to make fire. After people learned to build fires, they could warm themselves, cook their meals, extend the light, feel safer, and share knowledge as they huddled together around the campfires of antiquity. Thus people gradually built civilizations and grew in stature until they challenged those very gods through the power of learning. Prometheus may have given the first significant speech of demonstration.

ithout the sharing of information there would be no civilization as we know it today. Because we cannot personally experience everything that may be important or interesting to us, we must rely on the knowledge of others to expand our understanding and competence. *Sharing knowledge is the essence of informative speaking*.

Shared information can be important to survival. Early detection and warning systems alert us to impending thunderstorms, hurricanes, and tornadoes. News of medical breakthroughs and information on nutrition and hygiene practices that can increase our life span must be communicated so that we can take advantage of them.

Beyond simply enabling us to live, information helps us to live better. Having friends in for dinner this weekend? How did you learn to prepare the special dessert? Starting a new job? How will you find out what you are supposed to do at work? How many of your classes rely primarily on lectures? How many learning experiences have you had in which the sharing of information was not vital?

As those mythical gods who punished Prometheus realized, information is power. Information is a valuable commodity because it can help us operate machines, control the environment, and even manage people. Companies pirate other companies for employees with know-how and creativity. Graduate schools look for students who have the background of knowledge necessary for success. Countries engage in espionage activities to learn what their friends and enemies are doing. An incompetent manager who fears the loss of power may even try to withhold information in an effort to maintain control (a strategy that usually fails).

Throughout our lives we constantly exchange information. In this chapter we look at the functions of informative communication, the relationship between informative communication and learning, and three basic types of informative speeches (speeches of description, speeches of demonstration, and speeches of explanation). We also discuss six speech designs appropriate to these types — spatial, categorical, comparison and contrast, sequential, historical, and causation — and how more than one design can be combined in a speech. Our objective is to help you bring fire to your listeners.

# FUNCTIONS OF THE INFORMATIVE SPEECH

We refer in this section to "the informative speech" as though it were a distinct and separate type of speaking, but speeches rarely break down into such neat categories. In the same speech, you might introduce yourself, provide information, urge action, and celebrate values. However, any speech can be characterized by its major purpose. *If the main purpose of the speech is to share knowledge, then we call the speech informative.*

The informative speech performs four basic functions. First, informative speaking empowers listeners by sharing information and ideas. Second, informative speaking shapes listener perceptions. Third, informative speaking helps set the agenda of public concerns. Finally, informative speaking clarifies options for action.

## Sharing Information and Ideas

An informative speech *gives* to listeners rather than asks of them. The demands on the audience are relatively low. Informative speakers want enthusiastic attention from listeners. They want them to understand and use what they learn, but they do not ask them to change their beliefs or behaviors. For example, one student speaker gave an informative speech in which she revealed the dangers of prolonged exposure to the sun, but she did not go on to urge her audience to boycott tanning salons. Although informative speaking makes modest demands on the listener, the demands on the speaker are high. The speaker must have a thorough understanding of the subject. It is one thing to know something well enough to satisfy yourself. It is quite another to satisfy the demands of responsible knowledge that the public speaker must meet.

By sharing information, an informative speech reduces ignorance. An informative speech does not simply repeat material the audience already knows. Rather, *the informative value of a speech is measured by how much new and important information or understanding it provides the audience.* You begin building the informative value of a speech with your audience analysis and topic selection. Can you add to listeners' knowledge or give them a fresh perspective? Have you selected an important, novel, and interesting topic, avoiding those that have been overworked? Unless you can answer yes to these questions, you should rethink your topic selection.

In informative speaking, the speaker functions basically as a teacher. To teach people effectively, you must arouse and maintain attention by adapting your message to their interests and needs. You must make listeners aware of how important the new information is. When you have finished, they should feel enriched by the communication transaction.

### Shaping Perceptions

It would be wrong to assume that because informative speaking does not attempt to persuade listeners, it has no influence over them. What speakers share with audiences is not just raw information, but *interpretations* of information. They share points of view. Because no subject of any significance can be covered completely in a short presentation, speakers must be selective. They must highlight ideas and material they feel best represent their subject. If the subject is new to the audience, the initial presentation can influence how listeners receive and respond to the topic in the future. Thus, informative speeches shape how listeners *see* subjects (a function also discussed in Chapter 10). This is a "prepersuasive" function of informative speaking because how we see subjects may also determine how we *feel* and eventually *act* concerning them.

Let us suppose that you know very little about political campaigns or the role that student volunteers might play in them. Further suppose that you hear *one* of the following speeches on political campaigning:

> A speech by an enthusiastic, politically active student who describes volunteer campaign activities in an exciting way;
>
> or
>
> A speech by a disgruntled student reporting how college volunteers are given menial and meaningless jobs in political campaigns.

Neither speaker suggests that you should or should not volunteer to work in the upcoming election. Both provide what they believe is an accurate picture of the role of student volunteers. But each speech leaves you with a different predisposition for future behavior. If you were exposed only to the first speaker, you might be more inclined to respond later to a persuasive appeal for volunteers than if you heard only the second speaker.

As you prepare an informative speech, keep in mind that you are shaping perceptions. Be careful not to let your strong feelings about a subject cause you to present a distorted perspective. If listeners feel you are deliberately manipulating their perceptions, or if they conclude that your biases prevent you from making a responsible informative presentation, they may dismiss your message and lower their estimation of your ethos.

### Setting the Agenda

People are becoming more aware of the role that information plays in our lives. One major function of mass media is **setting the agenda** of public concerns.[1] As they present the "news," the media also tell us what we *should* be thinking about and the relative importance of these topics. Informative speaking also performs an agenda-setting role. As it directs our attention to certain subjects and shapes our perceptions about these subjects, informative speaking influences what we regard as important. The act of selecting one topic, and not selecting others, creates a hierarchy of importance among subjects.

Cecile Larson's speech, "The 'Monument' at Wounded Knee," which appears in Appendix B, illustrates both the perception-shaping and agenda-setting functions of informative speeches. Cecile's description of the monument etches a graphic picture in our minds: she both *shapes* and *intensifies* our perceptions so that they are hard to forget. These perceptions can set the stage for future action. After hearing her speech, we may want to know more about our policies toward Native Americans, past and present. And we may be predisposed to favor better treatment for these "first" Americans. Thus, as it sets our mental agenda, informative speaking can prepare us for persuasion.

## *Clarifying Options*

An informative speech can reveal and clarify options for action. Information expands our awareness, opens new horizons, and suggests fresh possibilities. Information can also help us discard irrelevant or unworkable options. The better we understand a subject, the more intelligent choices we can make on issues that surround it.

For example, what should we know about obesity? Informative speeches may tell us about the consequences of doing something or nothing to correct this problem. They may teach us about the medical soundness of different diets. They may also inform us about the roles of exercise and counseling in weight control. Such information would expand our options for dealing with this problem.

A responsible informative speech covers a topic so that all major positions are fairly represented. Speakers may see the same subject in different ways, but it is unethical to deliberately omit or distort information that is vital to audience understanding. Similarly, speakers who are unaware of options because they have not done the research that will *make* them aware are irresponsible. Try to find material from sources that represent different perspectives. A responsible, ethical, informative speaker carefully seeks out and presents all relevant material that may be important for an audience to know.

The two speeches on student political activity mentioned earlier demonstrate possible abuses of the option-clarifying function of informative speaking. If the speeches are presented as *representative* of student political activities, then both speakers are guilty of overgeneralization from limited personal experience. A more responsible approach would include searching out articles on college-student volunteers in political campaigns, interviewing students who have been active in politics, and talking with local political leaders to determine how student volunteers might assist in upcoming elections.

# INFORMATIVE SPEAKING AND THE LEARNING PROCESS

Because sharing information is the essence of informative speaking, its success depends on this critical test: *does the listener learn from the speech?* Indeed, if the informative speaker is a teacher, then the listener must be a learner. An effective informative speaker must know how to facilitate learning. To do this, the speaker must have a good grasp of three basic principles: motivation, attention, and retention.

## *Motivation*

In Chapter 4 we introduced the concept of motivation as an element of audience analysis. Now we show how motivation applies to learning in informative speaking.

Learning requires some work from listeners. If you want them to remember and use the information you provide, then you must give them a reason to learn. Will this information make them more secure, happier, healthier, or more successful? Will it make them feel better about themselves? Can you show them how your topic relates to their needs?

You can relate your subject to the satisfaction of audience needs and interests either by direct statement or indirectly by the use of examples. In a speech on how to interview for a job you might decide to use a direct ap-

*We are constantly presenting or receiving messages that share information and ideas. The instructor in this physics lab must motivate his students to learn and must explain complex principles so that his listeners understand him.*

proach. In your introduction you could talk about the problems of finding a job in today's economy and how a good interview can make a difference in who gets hired. For supporting materials you might use information from magazine articles on interviewing and a quotation from the personnel manager of a well-known local company. As you preview the body of your speech, you might say, "Today, I'm going to describe four factors that can determine whether you get the job of your dreams. First...." In this case you have given your audience a reason for wanting to listen to the remainder of your speech. In short, you have begun the learning process by motivating your listeners.

## *Attention*

In Chapter 7 we discussed the importance of engaging audience attention with your introduction. For a speech to be successful, you also must sustain this attention throughout your presentation. In this section we examine six basic factors that affect attention: intensity, repetition, novelty, activity, contrast, and relevance. We also explain how to use these factors to sustain interest and promote learning.

*Intensity.*  Our eyes are drawn automatically to bright lights, and we turn to investigate loud noises. In public communication, intense language and vivid images can be used to attract and hold attention. You can emphasize a point by supplying examples that magnify its importance. You can also achieve intensity through the use of visual aids and vocal variety. In a televised speech describing his national drug policy, President Bush gained attention through the intensity of his first sentence: "This is the first time since taking the oath of office that I felt an issue was so important, so threatening, that it warranted talking directly with you, the American people."

*Repetition.*  Sounds, words, or phrases that are repeated attract our attention and embed themselves in our consciousness. Skillful speakers frequently repeat key words or phrases to stress the importance of points, to help listeners focus on the sequence of ideas, to unify the message, and to help people remember what they have heard.

Repetition is the strategy that underlies the language tools of alliteration and anaphora. As we saw in Chapter 10, alliteration can lend vividness to the main ideas of informative speeches: "Today, I will discuss the **m**eanderings of the **M**ississippi River, from **M**innesota to the sea." The repetition of the **m** sound catches our attention and emphasizes the statement. In a like manner, anaphora can establish a pattern that sticks in memory. Used in the form of a repeated rhetorical question, such as, "What is our goal? It is to . . . ," anaphora sustains attention. Strategic repetition also may involve parallel construction or a similar pattern of wording. President Bush's drug speech provides another example:

> Who's responsible? Let me tell you straight out. Everyone who uses drugs. Everyone who sells drugs. And everyone who looks the other way.

***Novelty.*** We are attracted to anything new or unusual. A novel phrase can have such a striking impact that it becomes part of our cultural history. In the recent past "the New Frontier," "the Great Society," and "Star Wars" (Strategic Defense Initiative) have gained such status. Metaphors can provide different perspectives. To speak of your college experience as a "war against ignorance" is totally different from referring to it as a "journey out of darkness." However, both archetypal metaphors could be used to spark and sustain the attention of an audience.

***Activity.*** Our eyes are attracted to moving objects. This attraction can be used to gain attention in speeches. Gestures, physical movement, and visual aids can all add the element of activity to your speech. You can also increase a sense of activity in your speeches by using concrete action words, vocal variety, and a narrative structure that moves your speech along. Note the sense of action and urgency, as well as the invitation to act, in the conclusion of this student's speech:

> I don't know what you're going to do, but I know what I'm going to do. I'm going to march right down tomorrow and register to vote. There's too much at stake not to. Want to join me?

A lively example or an exciting story can also bring a speech to life and engage your listeners.

***Contrast.*** Opposites attract attention. If you work in a noisy environment and it suddenly becomes quiet, the stillness can seem deafening. Similarly, abrupt changes in vocal pitch or rate of speaking will draw attention. Presenting the pros and cons of a situation creates a similar effect. You can also highlight contrasts by speaking of opposites, such as life and death, light and dark, or the highs and lows of a situation.

In a speech dramatizing the need to learn more about AIDS, a speaker introduced two or three specific examples with the statement "Let me introduce you to *Death*." Then, as the speech moved to the promise of medical research, she said, "Now let me introduce you to *Life*." This usage combined repetition and contrast to create a dramatic effect.

Surprise is necessary for contrast to be effective. Once people become accustomed to an established pattern, they no longer think about it. They notice any abrupt, dramatic change from the pattern.

***Relevance.*** Things that are personally related to our needs or interests attract our attention. Research has indicated that sleepers respond with changes in brain-wave patterns when their names are mentioned. Parents have been known to sleep through severe thunderstorms, yet be wakened by the faint sounds of their infant crying. Relevance is essential to public speaking as well.

Darren Wirthwein made a speech on selecting running shoes relevant for his Indiana University audience by stressing the distance between places on campus. Darren pointed out that his early morning speech class was held in a campus building over a mile from the freshman dormitory—that without his running shoes he might have missed his speech! Because his listeners shared his situation, they chuckled, then listened attentively. Follow Darren's lead and increase relevance by using examples close to the lives of audience members.

## *Retention*

Information is useless unless your listeners remember and use it. Repetition aids retention as well as attention. The more frequently we hear or see anything, the more likely we are to retain it. Advertisers bombard us with slogans to keep their product names in our consciousness. These slogans may be repeated in all of their advertisements, regardless of the visuals or narratives of the individual messages. We can even remember slogans from our childhood years: "Ivory soap is ninety-nine and forty-four one-hundredths percent pure!" The repetition of key words or phrases within a speech helps the audience remember the message. In his famous civil rights speech in Washington, D.C., Martin Luther King's repetition of the phrase "I have a dream . . ." became the hallmark of the speech and is now used as its title.

Relevance is also important to retention. According to the Dutch scholar Erasmus, efficient minds are like fishing nets, able to keep all the big fish while letting the little ones slip through. Our minds filter new information as we receive it, associating it with things we already know and unconsciously evaluating it for its potential usefulness or importance. The advice that follows seems simple but is profoundly important. *If you want listeners to remember your message, tell them why and how your message relates to their lives.*

Structural factors also affect how readily a message can be understood and retained. Suppose you were given the following list of words to memorize:

north, man, hat, daffodil, green, tulip, coat, boy, south, red, east, shoes, gardenia, woman, purple, marigold, gloves, girl, yellow, west

It looks rather difficult, but see what happens when we rearrange the words:

north, south, east, west
man, boy, woman, girl
daffodil, tulip, gardenia, marigold
green, red, purple, yellow
hat, coat, shoes, gloves

In the first example you have what looks like a random list of words. In the second the words have been organized by categories: now you have five groups of four related words to remember. Material that is presented in a consistent and orderly fashion is much easier for your audience to understand and retain.

The way you organize the information in your informative speeches depends on your purpose and material. In the remainder of this chapter we

**SPEAKER'S NOTES**

### Helping Listeners Learn New Information

1. Approach your topic in a way that is fresh and interesting.

2. Show listeners how they can benefit from your information.

3. Attract and sustain attention by using vivid examples, novel images, exciting stories, and contrasts.

4. Help listeners remember your message by using strategic repetition and clear organization.

look at three functional types of informative speeches and six designs that are frequently used to structure them.

## TYPES OF INFORMATIVE SPEECHES

As we noted earlier, the major purpose of an informative speech is to share knowledge in order to expand our understanding or competence. To accomplish this purpose, an informative speech will typically describe, demonstrate, or explain its subject.

### Speeches of Description

Often the specific purpose of a speech is to describe a particular activity, object, person, or place. A **speech of description** should give the audience a clear picture of your subject, such as the one Stephen Huff painted of the New Madrid earthquakes of 1811 (see the text of his speech at the end of this chapter). This lingering image is more than just a reflection of the subject; it also conveys its meaning. Before television was widely available, the ability to use language to help the audience "see" what was happening was important for radio broadcasting. One of the most successful radio reporters was Edward R. Murrow. The following excerpt from one of his programs describes the nightly bombing of London in the fall of 1940:

> This is London at 3:30 in the morning. This has been what might be called a "routine night" — air-raid alarm at about nine o'clock and intermittent bombing ever since. I had the impression that more high explosives and few incendiaries have been used tonight. Only two small fires can be seen on the horizon. Again the Germans have been sending their bombers in singly or in pairs. The anti-aircraft barrage has been fierce but sometimes

> there have been periods of twenty minutes when London has been silent. . . . That silence is almost hard to bear. One becomes accustomed to rattling windows and the distant sound of bombs, and then there comes a silence that can be felt. You know the sound will return. You wait, and then it starts again. That waiting is bad. It gives you a chance to imagine things.[2]

This excerpt from the Murrow broadcast is rich in detail—it is not just early morning, but "3:30 in the morning." The language is concrete; the sentences are short, clear, and stark. The descriptions of the actual events are colored with the reporter's personal reactions to them. We are aware that we are seeing through his eyes, and we share his uneasiness. This makes the description especially vivid.

Another example of the speech of description is Cecile Larson's "The 'Monument' at Wounded Knee," printed in Appendix B. Other possible topics for such speeches might be "Trout Streams of Montana," "Native American Rug Patterns," or "Tomorrow's Car Is Speeding Toward Us."

The subject of your descriptive speech should suggest the appropriate pattern for its arrangement. The Murrow example above follows a sequential design in which events are reported in the order of their occurrence. Descriptive speeches also may take spatial designs, categorical designs, or comparison and contrast designs, which are discussed later in this chapter.

### Speeches of Demonstration

The **speech of demonstration** shows the audience how to do something or how something works. Dance instructors tell us how to waltz or do the Texas two-step. Others show us how to use computers for word processing or how to study for the Law School Admission Test. The usual tip-off to the speech of demonstration is the phrase *how to*. What these examples have in common is that they demonstrate a process.

Speeches of demonstration aim either at *understanding* or *application,* showing listeners how something is done, or instructing them so that they can perform the process themselves. If your goal is understanding rather than application, you can usually demonstrate more complex processes. For example, you might be able to prepare a seven-minute speech on how grades are collected, recorded, averaged, and distributed at your university, but you certainly would not expect your audience to be able to set up a grade-processing system after your presentation. On the other hand, in the short time allotted for a classroom speech, you might be able to teach your classmates how to read a textbook more efficiently. This is a skill they can *apply* to their lives. Stephen Huff's speech demonstrated to his classmates how to protect themselves in case of a major earthquake. Regardless of whether your specific purpose is to foster understanding or to teach application, most speeches of demonstration follow a sequential design, discussed in the section on speech designs.

Speeches of demonstration are almost always helped by the use of visual aids, especially when your purpose is to teach listeners how to perform the process themselves. For instance, if you were demonstrating how to mat pictures, you might bring some of the knives used, a piece of matting material, and a sample of the finished product. Stephen Huff distributed a handout that listed the steps to follow in case of an earthquake (he circulated this *after* his speech so that it would not compete for his listeners' attention). When demonstrating a process, "show and tell" is usually much more effective than just telling.

## Speeches of Explanation

The **speech of explanation** informs the audience about subjects that are more abstract than those dealt with through description or demonstration. Since abstract subjects, such as ideas or policies, often are difficult to understand, speeches of explanation are challenging to speakers. To meet this challenge, Katherine Rowan, a communication scholar at Purdue University, suggests that speakers should offer "(a) a definition that lists the concept's critical features, (b) a set of examples and nonexamples (i.e., instances one might think are examples but are not), and (c) opportunities to practice distinguishing the examples from the nonexamples."[3] For example, one student speaker defined date rape to include rape by friends or even intimates. She also showed how to separate examples from nonexamples: "It comes down to whether a person respects the idea that 'no' means 'stop.'" She helped her audience apply this principle with other examples. Finally, she explained the causes of "date rape," its devastating effects, and the ways it can be avoided.

Beyond the problems of abstraction, speeches of explanation face a different challenge when the information they offer runs counter to common sense or generally accepted beliefs. For example, at one time it was difficult for the Western world to accept that the earth was not the center of the universe. That idea ran counter to religious doctrine and got many scientists in serious trouble. Less than four hundred years ago, Galileo was persecuted and imprisoned by the Inquisition for advancing such a view. Rowan describes a more contemporary case:

> Perhaps there is no better example of the problems created by lay theories than in research on seat belt safety campaigns. . . . A particularly resilient obstacle to belt use is the erroneous but prevalent belief that hitting one's head on a windshield while traveling at 30 miles per hour is an experience much like doing so when a car is stationary. . . . If people understood that the experience would be much more similar to falling from a three-story building and hitting the pavement face first, one obstacle to the wearing of seat belts would be easier to overcome.[4]

As her example indicates, dramatic analogies — such as comparing an auto accident at thirty miles per hour to falling out of a building — can help break through our resistance to new ideas that defy folk wisdom. Rowan also recommends that speakers (a) state the prevalent view, (b) acknowledge its apparent legitimacy, (c) demonstrate its inadequacy, and (d) show the greater adequacy of the more expert view. Such a strategy of comparisons and contrasts can help listeners accept the new information and use it in their lives.

Speeches of explanation can present quite a challenge to both speaker and listener. But by translating the abstract into the concrete, and by making an audience receptive to new ideas, the speech of explanation can help lift and enrich the lives of listeners. To accomplish this work, speeches of explanation may use any of the designs described in the following section.

## SPEECH DESIGNS

In this section we focus on six designs often used in informative speeches: spatial, categorical, comparison and contrast, sequential, historical, and causation designs. These designs may also be used in persuasive and ceremonial speeches.

### Spatial Design

A **spatial design** is appropriate for speeches that describe places or that locate subjects within a physical arrangement. Most people are familiar with maps and can readily visualize directions. Once you have determined a starting point and direction of movement, you simply take your audience on an *orderly* imaginary journey to some destination. Cecile Larson used a spatial design for much of her speech describing the monument at Wounded Knee. After giving the audience a brief account of what happened there, she located this historic site geographically, then took her audience with her through the Sioux Indian reservation in search of the monument. Cecile concluded by describing the monument and its setting.

In using a spatial design, you should decide on a starting point — from the top or bottom, right or left, north or south, etc. — so that you build interest as you go along. Cecile's speech progressed so that she and her listeners *arrived* at Wounded Knee; she did not start there. Once you begin a pattern of movement for a spatial design, you should stay with it to the end of the speech. If you change directions in the middle, the audience may get lost on your turn. Be sure to complete the pattern you are describing so that you satisfy listeners' desire for closure.

A speech framed within a spatial design might look as follows:

*Thematic statement:* When you visit Yellowstone, stop first at the South Entrance Visitor's Center, then drive northwest to Old Faithful, north to Mammoth Hot Springs, and southeast to the Grand Canyon of the Yellowstone.

I. Your first stop should be at the South Entrance Visitor's Center.

A. Talk with a ranger-naturalist to help plan your trip.

| Type | Major Design Options | Summary of Procedures |
| --- | --- | --- |
| Description | Sequential | Describes an event as it occurs in time by focusing on its major phases. |
| | Spatial | Describes places or subjects as they are experienced in a spatial pattern (circular, north-south, down-up, etc.). |
| | Categorical | Describes a subject by customary topics (as a person by hair color, eyes, height, weight, age, etc.). |
| | Comparison-contrast | Describes what something is by what it is like or what it is not. |
| Demonstration | Sequential | Teaches a pattern of behaviors that produces some product or result. |
| | Comparison-contrast | Shows how to do something by showing how *not* to do it. |
| Explanation | Categorical | Explains a subject by divisions found within it or by common topics (liberal-moderate-conservative, cost-use-efficiency, etc.). |
| | Historical | Traces a concept, movement, or organization across time. |
| | Causation | Accounts for some subject by what caused it or traces its possible effects. |
| | Comparison-contrast | Explains a subject by its similarities to or differences from another well known subject. |

FIGURE 12.1
Types of Informative
Speeches and Major
Options for Designing
Them

   B. Attend a lecture or film to orient yourself to the park.

   C. Pick up materials and maps to make your tour more meaningful.

II.   Drive northwest through the Geyser Valley to Old Faithful.

   A. Hike the boardwalks in the Upper-Geyser Basin.

   B. Join the crowds waiting for Old Faithful to erupt on schedule.

   C. Have lunch at Old Faithful Inn.

III.   Continue north to Mammoth Hot Springs.

   A. Plan to spend the night at the lodge or in one of the cabins.

        B. Attend the evening lectures or films on the history of the park.

  IV.   Drive southeast to the Grand Canyon of the Yellowstone.

        A. Take in the view from Inspiration Point.

        B. Hike down the trail for a better view of the waterfalls.

## *Categorical Design*

Some subjects have natural or customary divisions that suggest **categorical designs.** For example, taxes may be classified as federal, state, county, and city — or as income, property, sales, and excise. Such divisions can provide the main points for speeches. The categories may represent actual divisions of your subject. More often, however, categories represent customary ways of thinking. Thus, we have the conscious and the unconscious minds, primary and secondary factors, reason and emotion. Categories are the mind's way of ordering our world. They help us to reduce and classify information so that it is meaningful and does not overwhelm us.

Louisa DeCarlo used a categorical design for an informative speech explaining nutrition. She discussed four types of food that are essential to health. Four or five are probably the maximum number of categories that can be handled effectively in a short presentation. Any subject that breaks down into more categories will be too complex for most classroom speeches. Unless you can condense these categories into a manageable number, you should probably consider another way to approach the speech or else narrow its focus.

Louisa's speech illustrated another important point: a categorical design should begin and end with the most important categories in the design. She started her speech by discussing the importance of eating a substantial amount of complex carbohydrates and ended with the importance of limiting fats in a diet. The strategy behind such order is clear: the important first category gains attention, the important final category gives the speech a sense of climax.

A categorical speech on the elements of a healthy diet might take the following format:

    *Thematic statement:*  A healthy diet is high in complex carbohydrates, fruits, and vegetables, and low in dairy products, meats and eggs, and fats.

    I.   You should eat from 6 to 11 servings of whole grain breads, cereals, rice, or pasta a day.

        A. They are the major source of dietary fiber necessary for good digestion.

        B. They provide the complex carbohydrates needed for energy.

        C. They help keep you from feeling hungry.

    II.  You should eat from 5 to 9 helpings of vegetables and fruits each day.

        A. They help fill you up without filling you out.

      B.  They may help prevent diseases.

      C.  They are a major source of vitamins and minerals necessary for good health.

III.   Limit dairy products, meats, and eggs to from 4 to 6 servings a day.

      A.  Americans eat too many of these types of foods.

      B.  They are high in cholesterol, which is related to heart disease.

      C.  Choose healthy selections, such as low-fat milks and cheeses, chicken and fish.

      D.  Limit consumption of eggs to 3 or 4 a week.

IV.   Restrict your intake of fats to less than 30 percent of your daily calories.

      A.  Avoid saturated fats found in butter, cheese, and red meats.

      B.  Use low-fat or no-fat salad dressings, or olive or canola oil and vinegar.

      C.  Cut back on "fast foods" and "junk foods" because they are high in fat and limited in nutritional value.

### *Comparison and Contrast Design*

A **comparison and contrast design** can be very effective when your topic is new to your audience, when you want to describe dramatic changes in a subject, or when you wish to describe the right and wrong ways to perform some action. Such design often creates understanding by relating an unfamiliar subject to something the audience already knows and understands. A Sri Lankan student in one of our classes described the game of rugger as played in his homeland by comparing and contrasting it with American football.

In such speeches, comparison and contrast designs make use of **analogy,** drawing relationships between different objects for the sake of clarification. Analogy comes in two forms: literal and figurative. In a **literal analogy,** we relate objects from the same field of experience: rugger and football, for example, are two forms of contact sport, so the comparison between them is literal. In a **figurative analogy,** the speaker draws together different fields of experience: for example, a speaker might relate the body's constant struggle against infection to a military campaign, identifying the nature of the armies, how they fight, and the consequences of victory or defeat. The basis for a figurative analogy is metaphor, which we discussed in Chapter 10. Because comparison and contrast require imagination on the part of the speaker, audiences admire such designs when they are successful. But an analogy can harm the speaker's ethos and the speech if the comparison seems too far-fetched. The advice we gave for metaphor also holds for design by figurative analogy: avoid stretching the comparison too far, or the design will seem strained.

*Success on the job may depend upon your ability to explain your work to others. When your topic is new to your audience, a comparison and contrast design may be most effective.*

Comparison and contrast designs can also reveal dramatic changes in a subject. A speech discussing how women have been portrayed in advertisements developed the following comparison and contrast design:

*Thematic statement:*  Over two decades — from the late 1960s to the late 1980s — the women we saw in advertisements began to change.

I.  Women began to advertise different products.

 A.  In the 1970s, 75 percent of females shown were in ads for domestic products used in the kitchen or bath.

 B.  In 1988, only 45 percent of females shown were in ads for domestic products.

 C.  By 1988, females were appearing in many ads for automobiles, alcohol, phone services, and business equipment.

II.  Women began to appear in different roles.

 A.  In the 1970s, the women we saw were defined in terms of men (as wives or girlfriends) or in domestic roles about two-thirds of the time; in 1988 this was down to 49 percent.

 B.  In the 1970s, only 9 percent of the females in ads had an identifiable occupation; in 1988 this was up to 18 percent.

1. Women in ads in the 1970s were depicted mainly in low-pay-ing, traditionally female occupations.

2. In 1988, the majority of the women shown in occupational roles were in nontraditional jobs.

III. There have been other important qualitative changes.

A. In the 1970s, 77 percent of the women appeared to be under thirty years of age; in 1988, this was down to 52 percent.

B. In the 1970s, most women were portrayed in demeaning ways — as dumb and dependent sex objects; they were less likely to be so portrayed in 1988.

These examples reveal that comparison and contrast design is especially useful in speeches of description, because they make subjects stand out more clearly in audience understanding. Speeches of demonstration make use of this design when they compare and contrast the right and wrong ways to perform some action.

## Sequential Design

A **sequential design** presents the steps in a process. The first task in developing a sequential design is to determine what steps are essential. For example, in a speech on matting a picture you might come up with the following steps:

1. Decide what color mat to use.

2. Get the right equipment.

3. Determine the size of your mat.

4. Cut the mat.

5. Mat the picture.

6. Decide between a straight and bevel cut.

7. Draw the lines before you cut.

8. Back the picture.

Looking over this list, you discover that you have identified eight steps — at least three too many for a short presentation. At this point you should arrange these steps in the order in which they occur to see if any of them can be compressed into more general steps. Your revised order of steps might take this form:

*Thematic statement:*   The four steps in matting and framing a picture are planning the project, obtaining equipment, cutting the mat, and actually matting and framing the picture.

I.   Begin by planning your project.

A. Decide on color you should use.

      B. Determine size for your mat.

  II.  Obtain the proper equipment.

      A. Buy or borrow a drawing pencil and straight edge.

      B. Buy a cutting knife and matting material at an art supply store.

  III.  Cut the mat to the proper size.

      A. Draw lines for cutting on the back of the matting material.

      B. Make an initial straight cut 1/2 inch in from the size you want the mat to be.

      C. Practice making clean cuts on the material you cut out of the middle.

      D. Make your final cut on the lines drawn.

  IV.  Mat the picture and put it in the frame.

      A. Be sure the picture is properly centered.

      B. Clean the glass with alcohol and water.

      C. Place the picture and the mat in the frame.

      D. Back the picture with cardboard cut to size.

Presenting the steps in this orderly manner helps you "walk and talk" the members of your audience through the process. They now understand how to begin and what to do in the proper order.

## *Historical Design*

**Historical designs** place a subject in a time perspective and, like sequential designs, follow an orderly progression. However, the sequential design is best suited to speeches of demonstration or description, whereas the historical design is most appropriate for speeches of explanation. When using historical designs, you may start with the beginning of an idea or issue and trace it up to the present, or you may start with the present and trace the concept back to its origins. For example, if you wanted to present a historical perspective on Unitarianism, you would probably begin by talking about the beliefs of Emerson and the early transcendentalists. Similarly, a speech on contemporary feminism might trace its beginnings to the suffrage movement of the nineteenth and early twentieth centuries.

Because of time limitations, you must be careful to narrow your topic to manageable proportions. Then you must scan the past and select those events that are most relevant to your point. In this way you telescope time into sequences of vital moments that have contributed to the present state of affairs. Although any rhetorical account of the past will always be selective, be certain that the examples you choose are representative of the situation. In your research, consider different points of view so that you avoid biased or one-sided explanations.

A speech on the evolution of the T-shirt might be designed as follows:

*Thematic statement:*   The T-shirt began its life as an undergarment, developed into a bearer of messages, and has emerged as high-fashion apparel.

I.   The T-shirt originated as an undergarment at the beginning of the twentieth century.

  A.  The first undershirts with sleeves were designed for sailors so sensitive people were spared the sight of hairy underarms.

  B.  Sleeved undershirts were first sold commercially by Sears and Hanes in the late 1930s.

  C.  During WW II, T-shirts were standard military issue and were used as outerwear in the tropics.

II.  After World War II, civilians began using T-shirts as outerwear.

  A.  Veterans liked them because they were comfortable and absorbent.

  B.  They were popularized in movies like *A Streetcar Named Desire* and *Rebel Without a Cause.*

  C.  Parents liked them for children because T-shirts were easy to care for.

III. T-shirts soon became embellished with pictures and messages.

  A.  Children's T-shirts had pictures of cartoon characters like Mickey Mouse.

  B.  Adult T-shirt designs were usually related to sports team logos.

  C.  T-shirts soon became used for "political" statements.

    1.  The first "political" T-shirt was made in 1948 and read "Dew-It with Dewey."

    2.  Peace symbols were popular during the 1960s.

    3.  Ideological slogans such as "A Woman's Place Is in the House (and in the Senate)" appeared during the 1970s.

  D.  During the 1980s, T-shirts became walking billboards, especially for sports equipment.

IV.  Today you have a choice of unique designs for T-shirts.

  A.  T-shirt print shops will customize a message for you.

  B.  Craft fairs often offer air-brushed T-shirts.

  C.  Your local copy shop will put your picture on a T-shirt.

  D.  You can buy dressy T-shirts with rhinestone and pearl decorations.

  E.  You can even spend over $800 for a Gianni Versace abstract print of mercerized cotton that feels like silk.

## Causation Design

Speeches of explanation often focus on causes and effects to try to make the world understandable. A speech that attempts to show how some things bring about others follows a **causation design.** Such a speech may begin with a description of an existing condition, then probe for its causes. Or the speech may begin with the present state of affairs and try to predict effects in the future. Causation designs are frequently used to inform people about economic issues. For example, you might prepare a speech on the effects of the late spring freeze on the quality, availability, and price of peaches, or the potential impact on college students of proposed changes in federal aid to education. Causation designs may also be used to explain why hurricanes occur, why wars have been fought, or why exercise makes a person healthier.

Speeches of causation are subject to one very serious limitation — the tendency to oversimplify. Any complex condition will generally have many underlying causes. Be wary of overly simple explanations.

A speech of causation explaining the greenhouse effect might have the following basic structure of main ideas:

*Thematic statement:* The three major causes of the greenhouse effect are loss of forestlands, population growth, and increasing energy consumption.

I. The greenhouse effect is a gradual warming of the earth due to human activity.

   A. It is characterized by a high concentration of carbon dioxide.

   B. Carbon pollutants are producing a hole in the ozone layer.

II. One cause of the greenhouse effect is the loss of forestlands.

   A. Forestlands convert carbon dioxide into oxygen.

   B. One football field–sized area of forest is lost every second from cutting or burning.

III. Population growth also is contributing to the greenhouse effect.

   A. People use oxygen and emit carbon dioxide.

   B. The more people there are, the more energy is consumed.

IV. Increased energy consumption is the single largest cause of the greenhouse effect.

   A. Fossil fuels account for 90 percent of America's energy consumption.

   B. Transportation-related energy consumption accounts for approximately half of our air pollution.

      1. In 1950 there were 40 million cars in the United States.

      2. Today there are more than 140 million cars in use in America.

   C. Industrial emissions contribute to more than 20 percent of our air pollution.

### Combined Speech Designs

Although we have presented these designs as simple patterns for speeches, effective speeches sometimes combine two or more of them. If you believe that a combined design will work best for your material, be certain to plan it carefully so that you do not seem to ramble or jump helter-skelter from one design type to another.

Alan Dunnette presented an informative classroom speech, "The Moscow Summer Games," that combined historical and categorical designs. He opened his speech by providing a historical view of how these "games" originated as a joking response by the citizens of Moscow, Tennessee (population 583), to the American boycott of the 1980 Summer Olympic Games, scheduled for the *other* Moscow. After presenting this historical background, Alan went on to describe the different types of events that make up the games: the serious events, such as the ten-kilometer run and the canoe and kayak races, and the fun events, such as the Great High Noon Tobacco Spitting Showdown, the Women's Skillet Throw, and the Invitational Cow Milking Contest ("invitational because Moscow cows are particular about who grabs them and where"). Alan was able to make this combined pattern work effectively because he planned it carefully. He also used a transition to cue the audience to the shift in design by saying, "So that's how the Moscow games got started. Now what kinds of events take place there?"

---

**SPEAKER'S NOTES**

## Designing an Informative Speech

1.  In a spatial design, move in a consistent direction.

2.  In a categorical design, limit the number of categories to five or fewer.

3.  In comparison and contrast designs, relate unfamiliar subjects to something well known, describe dramatic changes in a subject, or establish right and wrong procedures.

4.  In a sequential design, present the steps in the order in which they normally occur.

5.  In a historical design, focus on relevant events and present them from past to present or present to past.

6.  In a causation design, do not oversimplify cause and effect.

7.  When combining designs, provide clear transitions.

**IN SUMMARY**  Informative speaking shares knowledge to create understanding. Sharing information is important to survival and to effective living. In short, information is power.

*Functions of the Informative Speech.* Four functions characterize the informative speech. First, informative speaking reduces ignorance by providing insight or understanding. Second, informative speaking shapes perceptions that affect later responses. Third, informative speaking *sets the agenda* of what we consider to be important. Finally, informative speaking clarifies options for decision making. In short, informative speaking teaches people something about a subject they need to know better.

*Informative Speaking and the Learning Process.* From the audience's perspective, an informative speech is a learning experience. You can motivate listeners to learn by showing them how your subject relates to their needs or interests. You must also sustain their attention throughout your speech. Six factors that contribute to attention are intensity, repetition, novelty, activity, contrast, and relevance. You also want your audience to remember your message. Repetition, relevance, and structural organization are important factors in retention.

*Types of Informative Speeches.* Informative speeches may be classified as speeches of description, demonstration, and explanation. *Speeches of description* create word pictures that help the audience visualize a subject. *Speeches of demonstration* show the audience how something is done. They may give listeners an understanding of a process or teach them how to perform it. Speeches of demonstration are often more effective when visual aids are used. *Speeches of explanation* inform the audience about abstract and complex subjects, such as concepts or programs. Such speeches normally pose a more difficult challenge, especially when their information contradicts folk knowledge or cherished beliefs.

*Speech Designs.* The patterns most frequently employed in informative speeches are spatial, categorical, comparison and contrast, sequential, historical, and causation designs. A *spatial design* orders the main points as they occur in physical space. Spatial designs are especially appropriate for describing objects or places. *Categorical designs* may represent actual divisions of your subject or traditional ways of thinking. In a short speech you should limit your number of categories to no more than five. *Comparison and contrast designs* are especially effective when your topic is new to the audience, when it has undergone dramatic changes, or when you wish to establish right and wrong procedures. These designs are often based on *literal* or *figurative analogies,* depending on whether the compared subjects are drawn from the same or different fields. Most speeches of demonstration use a *sequential design,* which presents the steps in a process in their proper order. A *historical design* always develops your subject chronologically by following the order of events. Because such history is selective, you must be careful not to present a distorted perspective. A *causation design* explains how one condition generates or is generated by another.

Sometimes you may decide to incorporate two or more designs into a speech. In that case be certain to provide transitions so that listeners are not confused by the changing patterns.

**TERMS TO KNOW**

| | |
|---|---|
| setting the agenda | analogy |
| speech of description | literal analogy |
| speech of demonstration | figurative analogy |
| speech of explanation | sequential design |
| spatial design | historical design |
| categorical design | causation design |
| comparison and contrast design | |

**DISCUSSION**

1. Analyze the speech by Stephen Lee in Appendix B in terms of its functions, type, and design. Discuss how it gains and holds attention and motivates learning. Can you think of different designs for the speech? Would they be more or less effective?

2. Select your nominations for the "best" and "worst" lecturers you have as instructors this semester, excluding your speech instructor. Without naming these individuals, discuss how they design their presentations and encourage or discourage learning in their classes.

3. Discuss the relationship between information and power. Find specific examples of the use and misuse of such power.

4. Watch a television program that purports to be informative. Which informative functions does it fulfill? Does it seem to have a persuasive purpose as well? Is it ethical in the way it proceeds?

**APPLICATION**

1. Select an informative topic, determine a specific purpose, and develop two different outlines for the speech you might give, each illustrating a choice among the six design options (spatial, categorical, comparison and contrast, sequential, historical, and causation). In each design explain how you would motivate listeners to learn.

2. Plan the informative speech you prepare for class to be sure you use at least three of the six factors of attention (intensity, repetition, novelty, activity, contrast, and relevance). Turn in a short statement specifying the techniques you will use and why you believe they will be effective.

3. Find an informative speech in a recent issue of *Vital Speeches of the Day* and identify the function it fulfills and the design it utilizes. Also discuss the major stylistic techniques used in the speech and how they contribute to its effectiveness.

**NOTES**   1. Shearon A. Lowery and Melvin L. De Fleur, *Milestones in Mass Communication Research,* 2nd ed. (New York: Longman 1988), pp. 327–352.
2. *In Search of Light: The Broadcasts of Edward R. Murrow 1938–1961,* ed. Edward Bliss, Jr. (New York: Alfred A. Knopf, 1967), p. 35.
3. Katherine E. Rowan, "Goals, Obstacles, and Strategies in Risk Communication: A Problem-solving Approach to Improving Communication About Risks," *Journal of Applied Communication Research* 19 (1991): 314.
4. *Ibid.,* p. 316.

## The New Madrid Earthquake Area

### *Stephen Huff*

Stephen's introduction sets the scene in graphic detail. He opens with a rhetorical question and involves his audience by repeating, "If you're like me." He motivates listeners by tying the San Francisco quake to the New Madrid Fault area where they live. His admission of ignorance allows his audience to identify with him as an attractive and modest person, and also suggests his substantial preparation for the speech — both important benefits for his ethos. His thematic statement also provides a skillful preview that promises a categorical design that will combine descriptive, explanatory, and demonstrative functions.

Stephen's first main point concerns earthquakes in general and the New Madrid area in particular. The magnitude chart puts the intensity of earthquakes into perspective. His comparisons and contrasts with the atomic bomb and the recent San Francisco quake help make the numbers meaningful, as do his descriptions of the great New Madrid quakes. He uses facts and statistics as primary supporting material, enlivened by vivid examples and stories.

How many of you can remember what you were doing around seven o'clock on the evening of October 17th? If you're a sports fan like me, you had probably set out the munchies, popped a cold one, and settled back to watch San Francisco and Oakland battle it out in the World Series. Since the show came on at seven o'clock here in Memphis for its pregame hype, you may not have been paying close attention to the TV — until — until — until both the sound and picture went out because of the Bay Area earthquake.

If you're like me, you probably sat glued to the TV set for the rest of the evening watching the live coverage of that catastrophe. If you're like me, you probably started thinking that Memphis, Tennessee, is in the middle of the New Madrid earthquake area and wondering how likely it would be for a large earthquake to hit here. And if you're like me, you probably asked yourself, "What would I do if a major earthquake hit Memphis?"

As I asked myself these questions, I was surprised to admit that I didn't know very much about the New Madrid earthquake area or the probability of a major quake in Memphis. And I was really upset to discover that I didn't have the foggiest idea of what to do if a quake did hit. So I visited the Center for Earthquake Research and Information here on campus; talked with Dr. Arch Johnston, the director; and read the materials he helped me find. Today, I'd like to share with you what I learned about the New Madrid earthquake area, how likely it is that Memphis may be hit by a major quake in the near future, what the effects of such a quake might be, and — most important — what you can do to be prepared.

Let's start with a little history about the New Madrid earthquake area. During the winter of 1811 to 1812, three of the largest earthquakes ever to hit the continental United States occurred in this area. Their estimated magnitudes were 8.6, 8.4, and 8.8 on the Richter scale. [He reveals magnitude chart.] I have drawn this chart to give you some idea of how much energy this involves. To simplify things, I have shown the New Madrid quakes as 8.5. Since a one-point increase in the Richter scale equals a thirtyfold increase in energy release, the energy level of these quakes was over nine hundred times more powerful than the Hiroshima atomic bomb and more than thirty times more powerful than the 7.0 quake that hit San Francisco last October. [He conceals magnitude chart.]

Most of the reports of these early earthquakes come from journals or Indian legends. The Indians tell of the night that lasted for a week and the way the "Father of Waters" — the Mississippi River — ran backwards. Waterfalls were formed on the river. Islands disappeared. Land that was once in Arkansas — on the west bank of the river — ended up in Tennessee — on the east bank of the river. Church bells chimed as far away as New Orleans and Boston. Cracks up to ten feet wide opened and closed in the earth. Geysers squirted sand fifteen

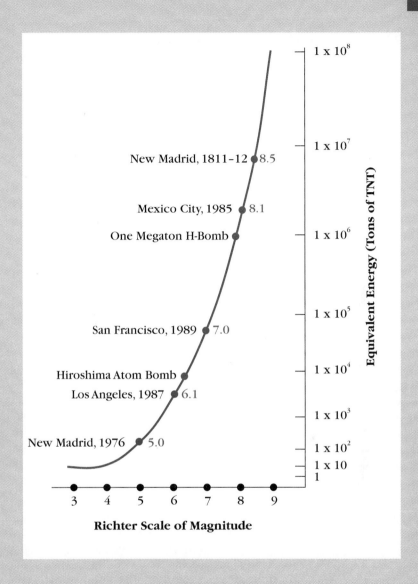

feet into the air. Whole forests sank into the earth as the land turned to quick-sand. Lakes disappeared and new lakes were formed. Reelfoot Lake — over ten miles long — was formed when the Mississippi River changed its course. No one is certain how many people died from the quakes because the area was sparsely settled with trappers and Indian villages. Memphis was just an outpost village with a few hundred settlers.

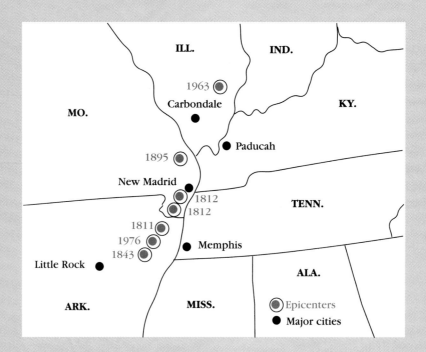

Stephen's simplified map of the New Madrid Fault area helps his audience see the epicenters of earthquake activity in relation to Memphis. He uses contrast between the San Francisco and New Madrid earthquakes to maintain attention and motivate listeners. He continues to document his supporting material carefully.

[He shows map of epicenters.] As you can see on this map, Memphis itself is not directly on the New Madrid Fault line. The fault extends from around Marked Tree, Arkansas, northeast to near Cairo, Illinois. This continues to be a volatile area of earthquake activity. According to Robert L. Ketter, director of the National Center for Earthquake Engineering Research, between 1974 and 1983 over two thousand quakes were recorded in the area. About 150 earthquakes per year occur in the area, but only about eight of them are large enough for people to notice. The others are picked up on the seismographs at tracking stations. The strongest quake in recent years occurred here in 1976. [He points to location on map.] This measured 5.0 on the Richter scale.

The New Madrid earthquake area is much different from the San Andreas Fault in California. Because of the way the land is formed, the alluvial soil transmits energy more efficiently here than in California. Although the quakes were about the same size, the New Madrid earthquakes affected an area fifteen times larger than the "great quake" that destroyed San Francisco in 1906.

Although scientists cannot predict exactly when another major quake may hit the area, they do know that the *repeat time* for a magnitude-6 New Madrid earthquake is seventy years, plus or minus fifteen years. The last earthquake of this size to hit the area occurred in 1895 north of New Madrid, Missouri. [He points to epicenter on map.] According to Johnston and Nava of the Memphis Earthquake Center, the probability that one with a magnitude of 6.3 will occur somewhere in the fault area by the year 2000 is 40 to 63 percent. By the year 2035 this probability increases to 86 to 97 percent. The probabilities for larger quakes are lower. They estimate the probability of a 7.6 quake within the next fifty years to be from 19 to 29 percent. [He conceals map of epicenters.]

What would happen if an earthquake of 7.6 hit Memphis? Allan and Hoshall, a prominent local engineering firm, prepared a study on this for the Federal Emergency Management Agency. The expected death toll would top 2,400. There would be at least 10,000 casualties. Two hundred thousand residents would be homeless. The city would be without electricity, gas, water or sewer treatment facilities for weeks. Gas lines would rupture, and fires would sweep through the city. Transportation would be almost impossible, bridges and roads would be destroyed, and emergency supplies would have to be brought in by helicopter. The river bluff, mid-town, and land along the Wolfe River would turn to quicksand because of liquification. Buildings there would sink like they did in the Marina area during this past year's San Francisco quake. If the quake hit during daytime hours, at least 600 children would be killed and another 2,400 injured as schools collapsed on them. None of our schools have been built to seismic code specifications.

In fact, very few buildings in Memphis have been built to be earthquake resistant, so it would be difficult to find places to shelter and care for the homeless. The major exceptions are the new hospitals in the suburbs, the Omni Hotel east of the expressway, the Holiday Inn Convention Center, and two or three new office complexes. The only municipal structure built to code is the Criminal Justice Center. The new Memphis Pyramid, being built by the city and county, which will seat over twenty thousand people for Memphis State basketball games, is not being built to code. I'd hate to be in it if a major quake hit. The prospects are not pretty.

What can we do to prepare ourselves for this possible catastrophe? We can start out by learning what to do if a quake does hit. When I asked myself what I would do, my first reaction was to "get outside." I've since learned that this is not right. The "Earthquake Safety Checklist" published by the Federal Emergency Management Agency and the Red Cross makes a number of suggestions. I've written them out and will distribute them after my speech.

First, when an earthquake hits, if you are inside, stay there. Get in a safe spot: stand in a doorway, stand next to an inside wall, or get under a large piece of furniture. Stay away from windows, hanging objects, fireplaces, and tall unsecured furniture until the shaking stops. Do not try to use elevators. If you are outside, get away from buildings, trees, walls, or power lines. If you are in a car, stay in it; pull over and park. Stay away from overpasses and power lines. Do not drive over bridges or overpasses until they have been inspected. If you are in a crowded public place, do not rush for the exit. You may be crushed in the stampede of people.

When the shaking stops, check for gas, water, or electrical damage. Turn off the electricity, gas, and water to your home. Do not use electrical switches — unseen sparks could set off a gas fire. Do not use the telephone unless you must report a severe injury. Check to see that the sewer works before using the toilet. Plug drains to prevent a sewer backup.

There are also some things you can do in advance to be prepared. Accumulate emergency supplies: at home you should have a flashlight, a transistor radio

Stephen holds his audience's attention with a frightening scenario, using action and contrast in his descriptions but letting the facts speak largely for themselves. We also see the beginnings of a more critical attitude: although his task is primarily informative, he suggests that city officials are to blame for not preparing Memphis adequately for a major earthquake.

After the grim picture of probable consequences, the next main point, what to do if an earthquake hits, is more reassuring. It suggests ways of surviving. Stephen might have rearranged his subpoints so that the demonstration of what to do in advance preceded rather than followed his subpoints on during and after a quake. In this way the sequence of points — before, during, and after — might have seemed more natural and cohesive. He concludes this section with an appeal that suggests a secondary persuasive focus of the speech.

## Earthquake Preparedness Suggestions

1. If you are inside, stay there. Get in a safe spot: stand in a doorway, stand next to an inside wall, or get under a large piece of furniture. Stay away from windows, hanging objects, fireplaces, and tall unsecured furniture until the shaking stops. Do not try to use elevators.

2. If you are outside, get away from buildings, trees, walls, or power lines. If you are in a car, stay in it; pull over and park. Stay away from overpasses and power lines. Do not drive over bridges or overpasses until they have been inspected.

3. If you are in a crowded public place, do not rush for the exit. You may be crushed in the stampede of people.

4. When the shaking stops, check for gas, water, or electrical damage. Turn off the electricity, gas, and water to your home. Do not use electrical switches — unseen sparks could set off a gas fire. Do not use the telephone unless you must report a severe injury. Check to see that the sewer works before using the toilet. Plug drains to prevent sewer backup.

**There are also some things you can do in advance to be prepared:**

1. Accumulate emergency supplies: at home you should have a flashlight, a transistor radio with fresh batteries, a first-aid kit, fire extinguishers, and enough canned or dried food and beverages to last for 72 hours.

2. Identify hazards and safe spots in your home — secure tall heavy furniture; don't hang heavy pictures over your bed; keep flammable liquids in a garage or outside storage area — look around each room and plan where you would go if an earthquake hit; conduct earthquake drills with your family.

with fresh batteries, a first-aid kit, fire extinguishers, and enough canned or dried food and beverages to last your family for 72 hours. Identify hazards and safe spots in your home — secure tall heavy furniture; don't hang heavy pictures over your bed; keep flammable liquids in a garage or outside storage area — look around each room and plan where you would go if an earthquake hit. Conduct earthquake drills with your family.

There's one more suggestion that I would like to add. One that is specific to Memphis. Let our local officials know that you are concerned about the lack of preparedness. Urge them to support a building code — at least for public structures — that meets seismic resistance standards.

Stephen's conclusion is rather brief. Although his final story is amusing, he might have summarized his major points to make the ending more effective.

In preparing this speech, I learned a lot about the potential for earthquakes in Memphis. I hope you have learned something too. I now feel like I know what I should do if an earthquake hits. But I'm not really sure how I would react. Even the experts don't always react "appropriately." In 1971 an earthquake hit the Los Angeles area at about six o'clock in the morning. Charles Richter, the seismologist who developed the Richter scale to measure earthquakes, was in bed at the time. According to his wife, "He jumped up screaming and scared the cat."

*Because there has been implanted in us the power to persuade each other . . . , not only have we escaped the life of the wild beasts but we have come together and founded cities and made laws and invented arts. . . .*
—Isocrates

# 13

# The Nature and Kinds of Persuasive Speaking

**This Chapter Will Help You**

- appreciate the importance of persuasion in our society.
- understand the characteristics of persuasive speaking.
- recognize the steps in the persuasive process.
- meet the challenges of persuasive speaking.
- understand the different types of persuasive speeches and the designs best suited to each.
- begin preparing effective persuasive speeches.

You awaken daily to a world of persuasion. On your clock radio you hear a disc jockey selling tickets to a rock concert. The weather forecaster urges you to carry an umbrella. Other students ask you to join their organizations. Stores beg for your business. Politicians plead for your vote. Billboards along highways tout everything from bourbon to church attendance. The novels, movies, music, and television shows you encounter may promote social or political causes.

You are constantly persuading as well as being persuaded. You may want your roommate to go out for pizza with you rather than complete an accounting assignment. You think some questions on your last botany test were unfair and would like your instructor to change your grade. You've just met a good-looking guy that you want to date. All of your friends are going to Florida over spring vacation and you have to convince your parents that you need a break. The history department scholarship you are vying for requires a written essay plus an interview. When you go job hunting, you must convince a prospective employer of your abilities. If you want to advance at work, you must be able to promote your ideas.

Whatever path your life takes, you can't avoid persuading and being persuaded.

B eyond its personal importance, persuasion is essential to our society. The right to persuade and be persuaded is the bedrock of our political system, guaranteed by the First Amendment to the Constitution. According to the late Supreme Court Justice Louis D. Brandeis, "Those who won our independence believed that the final end of the State was to make men free to develop their faculties; and that in its government the deliberative forces should prevail over the arbitrary."[1] Free, open discussion and persuasion are required for these "deliberative forces" to operate.

**Deliberation** occurs when groups encourage all sides of an issue to have their say before coming to a thoughtful decision. The contending factions agree to accept the majority decision, unless constitutional principles may be involved. By contrast, when decisions are arbitrarily imposed, they may require force to back them up. Our political system is based on the belief that persuasion is usually more ethical and more practical than force. We should make commitments because we are persuaded, not because we are coerced.

On certain issues you may object to the expression of opposing views, but the freedom to express unpopular views is what liberty is all about. The English philosopher John Stuart Mill put the matter eloquently:

> If all mankind, minus one, were of the one opinion, and only one person were of the contrary opinion, mankind would be no more justified in silencing that one person, than he, if he had the power, would be justified in silencing mankind.

> . . . We can never be sure that the opinion we are endeavoring to stifle is a false opinion; and if we were sure, stifling it would be an evil still.[2]

Other reasons for tolerating minority opinions are more practical in nature. Research suggests that exposure to different viewpoints can stimulate listeners and produce better, more original decisions.[3] For example, even though I may never agree with your view that we should abolish labor unions, your arguments may cause me to reexamine my position, to understand my own convictions better, or perhaps even modify my views.

Although contributing to the dialogue on public issues is an important citizen responsibility, many people shy away from persuasion. They may think: "What difference can one person make? I'm not very important, and my words won't carry much weight." Perhaps not, but words do make ripples, and ripples can come together to make waves. Just ask Anna Aley, whom we first introduced in Chapter 1. Anna was a student at Kansas State University when she gave the persuasive speech on substandard student housing that is reprinted at the end of this chapter. Her speech began as a class assignment and was presented later in a public forum on campus problems. She made such an impression that a text of her speech was reprinted in the local newspaper, the *Manhattan Mercury,* which followed it up with a series of investigative reports and a sympathetic editorial. Brought to the attention of the mayor and city commission, Anna's speech helped promote substantial reforms in the city's rental housing policies. Her words are still reverberating in Manhattan, Kansas.

Perhaps your persuasive speech will not have such dramatic impact, but be assured that the words we utter constantly affect and even create the conditions of our lives. All the more reason to understand how persuasion works. In this chapter we consider the characteristics of persuasive speaking, the process of persuasion, some of the challenges facing persuasive speakers, types of persuasive speeches, and designs appropriate for them.

## CHARACTERISTICS OF PERSUASIVE SPEAKING

The characteristics of persuasive speaking are most clear when viewed in contrast with informative speaking:

*Persuasive speaking urges us to choose from among options: informative speaking reveals and clarifies options.* One of the basic strategies of persuasive speaking is to eliminate alternatives until only one choice remains. The informative speaker might say, "Here are different ways to deal with Eastern Europe"; the persuasive speaker would urge, "We should pursue *this* course of action in dealing with Eastern Europe."

*Persuasive speaking asks the audience for more commitment than does informative speaking.* Although there is some risk in exposure to new information and ideas, there is more at stake when listening to a persuasive speaker.

You risk little as you listen to the informative speaker describe off-campus living conditions. But the persuasive speaker asks you *to do something* about these conditions. What if the speaker isn't honest? What if the actions you take turn out wrong? *Doing* always involves a greater risk than simply *knowing*. The world of persuasion is filled with uncertainty, and your commitment could cost you. Because of the risks involved, audiences for persuasive speeches must practice critical listening skills.

*The ethical obligation for persuasive speakers is even greater than for informative speakers.* When you influence others or ask them to take risks, you assume a large responsibility. Will your plan for improving off-campus housing result in increased safety, or would it merely raise rents? As a persuasive speaker, you carry a special ethical obligation to see that any reforms you urge are sound and well considered. The importance of responsible knowledge looms even larger for you. You should build persuasion on a foundation of facts, figures, and expert testimony. Enliven your ideas and involve the audience with lay and prestige testimony, examples, and narratives.

*The persuasive speaker is a leader: the informative speaker is a teacher.* Informative speakers describe, demonstrate, or explain. Persuasive speakers influence, convince, or inspire listeners to adopt certain attitudes or courses of action. Because of the greater risk, audiences will evaluate persuasive speakers more carefully. Are the speakers competent and sincere? Do they have listeners' interests at heart? As you rally others against the slumlords of student housing, your character and ability will be on public display. Ethos is especially crucial in persuasive situations.

*Persuasive speaking more often depends on exciting emotion than does informative speaking.* You may need to arouse feelings to overcome an audience's reluctance to make a commitment or take action.[4] This is why Bonnie Marshall framed such a strong emotional opening for her speech favoring living wills (see Appendix B). The statement "Studies show that a 10 percent rise in tuition costs will reduce the student population by about 5 percent next fall" may be useful in an informative speech but would not be sufficient in a persuasive speech. Look at another way of putting the matter:

> The people who want tuition increases have a lot of money, so they don't think a few hundred dollars more each term will have much effect on us students. They feel most of us can handle a 10 percent rise in tuition costs. They say that the one in twenty who won't be back will just reduce the surplus enrollment!
>
> Well, let me tell you about a friend of mine — let's call her Tricia. Both of Tricia's parents lost their jobs last year. Tricia is on the Dean's List, and can look forward to a successful career as a chemist when she graduates. But if this rise in tuition goes through, Tricia won't be back next fall. Her dreams deferred — her dreams denied! What do the legislators care about that? What do they care about Tricia's dreams?

> Perhaps you are like Tricia. But even if you are not, she is one of us, and she needs our help *now*.

Emotional language is often needed to help us see human problems and move us to action.

*Persuasive speakers often appeal to groups: informative speakers usually address listeners as individuals.* Persuasion frequently requires group action for its success. If you want your audience to protest a proposed increase in tuition, you must address them as members of a group — in this case, as student-victims. As we noted in Chapter 10, language can be used to create group identity. Persuasive communication can encourage individuals to act together for change.

## THE PROCESS OF PERSUASION

To understand how Anna Aley stirred her audiences to protest poor housing conditions or how Bonnie Marshall hoped to convince people of the value of living wills, we must look at how persuasion works. This understanding can help us both become better persuaders and be less vulnerable to persuasive attempts of others. William J. McGuire, professor of psychology at Yale University, suggests that effective persuasion is a complicated process

*Persuasive speeches can help raise support and funds for worthy causes. Marian Wright-Edelman kicks off the "Leave No Child Behind" campaign with a persuasive message.*

involving up to twelve phases.[5] For our purposes, these phases may be grouped into four stages: awareness, comprehension, acceptance, and integration. Familiarity with these stages helps us recognize that persuasion is not an all-or-nothing proposition — that a persuasive message may be considered successful if it simply moves people along through the process.

*The first stage in the persuasive process is awareness of an issue.* Awareness suggests that we know about a problem, that we pay attention to it, and that we understand how it relates to our lives. Thus, as we noted in the last chapter, informative speaking that builds such awareness can prepare us for persuasion. This stage is especially important when people must be convinced that there actually is a problem. Early feminist speakers, such as Germaine Greer, had to make audiences aware that discrimination against women was a problem. Similarly, Anna Aley had to draw people's attention to substandard student housing, and Bonnie Marshall had to start people thinking about who might be making life-and-death decisions for them if they did not prepare living wills.

Beyond simply acquainting listeners with a problem, persuasion geared to this stage must convince us of the problem's importance and show how it affects us directly. Persuasive speakers must raise audience consciousness before moving on to the next stage in the persuasive process.

*The comprehension stage of persuasion concerns whether listeners understand an argument, are stimulated by its ideas, and know how to carry out its proposals.* Comprehension is crucial in situations where listeners admit there is a problem but lack the understanding needed to do something about it. Persuasion that is both ethical and effective makes listeners more competent. Sound persuasion expands our knowledge of the arguments that bear upon a proposal for action. It demonstrates how some arguments are stronger or weaker than others. Such persuasion presents the proofs and evidence that either support or refute such arguments.[6] In Chapter 14 we discuss how supporting materials become the evidence for proofs and arguments. Anna Aley used all the available forms of supporting materials to build her case for housing reforms.

Effective persuasive messages strike sparks in the minds of listeners. An example may remind them of a similar situation they have encountered. An argument may generate other supporting thoughts or counterarguments. This interplay of ideas engages the audience in synergistic listening (described in Chapter 3), which can deepen the understanding of an issue. Finally, the audience must understand *how* to put the speaker's proposals into effect. For example, Bonnie Marshall clearly spells out the steps she wants her listeners to take, enumerating these as she presents them.

*The third stage in the persuasive process is acceptance of the message.* It concerns whether listeners agree with your recommendations and remember the reasons for their acceptance. Agreement can range from small concessions to total commitment. Lesser degrees of agreement could mean success, especially when listeners have to change their attitudes or risk a great deal by accepting your ideas. You can help listeners remember their commitment by providing vivid images and interesting stories. Narratives and images will stay with your audience long after abstract reasons or arguments are forgotten. A striking conclusion that uses language skillfully can be especially helpful. The story of her neighbor's accident that ended Anna Aley's speech helped embed her message in the minds of her audience.

If you can get listeners to sign a petition, raise their hands, or even voice agreement, you can further strengthen their resolve. The student speaker who mobilized his audience against a proposed tuition increase (a) brought a petition to be signed, (b) encouraged contact with local legislators by providing their addresses and telephone numbers on a handout sheet, and (c) urged listeners to write letters to campus and local newspapers.

*The final stage in the persuasive process is the integration of new attitudes and commitments into the behavior of listeners.* For persuasive speeches to have lasting value, listeners sometimes must modify other attitudes or values to be consistent with the new beliefs. All of us seek consistency among our various values and behaviors. For example, it would be inconsistent for us to march against substandard housing on Monday and contribute to a landlord's defense fund on Tuesday. This is why people sometimes seem to agree with a persuasive message, then change their minds. It dawns on them that this new commitment means they must rearrange the psychological furniture of other behaviors. They may have to give up some valued beliefs and attitudes. They may even lose friends or social status connected with their previous beliefs.

For persuasion to bring about lasting changes in people, it sometimes must evoke emotional reactions and connect these feelings with powerful reasons. There must be compelling reasons to undergo the pain of change. To provide such reasons, speakers must first point out how the new position is consistent with older values. "Our love of liberty is a good reason to adopt a new Marshall Plan for Eastern Europe." Another technique involves reinforcing the acceptance with an immediate action that produces benefits: "If we start the Plan now, these countries will be our trading partners next year!" Finally, knowing the struggle some listeners will experience, plan a response to their objections: "Helping Eastern Europe is certainly hard when there is so much to do at home — when education and health care and our own homeless people need attention. But keep this in mind — investment in Eastern Euope is an investment in world order. It is a gift we give ourselves." There may even be some issues that will require no less than a biblical conversion: listeners must be "born again." To rearrange one's belief system to accommodate some persuasive messages is indeed to be become a new person. Ultimately, those you are persuading may themselves become active advocates for the cause. Obviously, this degree of integration is rarely achieved through a single message. Such dramatic changes may require a campaign of persuasion in which any single speech plays its small but vital role.

## Applying McGuire's Model of the Persuasive Process to Your Speeches

1. Arouse attention with an effective introduction.

2. Involve listeners by relating your message to their interests and needs.

3. Ensure understanding by defining complex terms, using concrete examples, and organizing your material clearly.

4. Build your persuasive efforts on a base of solid information.

5. Be sure listeners know how to carry out your proposal.

6. Help the audience remember your message by using vivid word pictures and a striking conclusion.

7. Ask for a public commitment from your listeners. Give them something to do that starts them on the path to change.

8. Ensure enduring change by stirring deep feelings and connecting them with powerful reasons.

To conclude: persuasion is a complicated process. Any single persuasive effort must focus on where it can make its most effective contribution: to raise awareness, build understanding, seek commitment, or promote the process of integration. To determine where to focus our persuasive efforts, we must carefully analyze our audience, and adapt our messages to the specific challenges of the persuasive situation we anticipate.

## THE CHALLENGES OF PERSUASION

The challenges that confront persuasive speakers range from enticing a reluctant audience to listen to moving a sympathetic audience to action. As you plan a persuasive speech, you need to consider the audience's position on the topic, how listeners might react to you as an advocate, and the situation in which the speech will be presented.

Begin preparing your persuasive speech by determining where your listeners stand on the issue. Do they hold varying attitudes about the topic, or are they united? If listeners are divided, you might hope to unify them around your position. If listeners are already united — but in opposition — you might try to divide them and attract some toward your position. Also consider how your listeners might regard you as a speaker on the subject. If you do not have their respect, trust, and good will, use testimony from highly regarded sources to enhance your ethos and improve your chances for success.

Evaluating the relationships among the audience, the topic, and you as speaker will help you determine how far you can go in a particular speech. These relationships also may suggest what strategies you should use and the kind of supporting materials you will need.

### Enticing a Reluctant Audience to Listen

When attitudes and beliefs are important to your listeners, they are especially hard to change. If you face an audience that opposes your position, success may be measured in small achievements, such as getting thoughtful attention. One way to handle a reluctant audience is to adopt a **co-active approach.**[7] The major steps in this approach include:

1. Establish identification and good will early in the speech.
2. Start with areas of agreement before you tackle areas of disagreement.
3. Work toward the acceptance of underlying values before you propose specific changes.
4. Cite experts the audience will respect and accept.
5. Set modest goals for change.
6. Offer a multisided presentation in which you compare your position with other positions.

Let's look at how you might apply these steps in a speech against capital punishment. You could *build identification* by pointing out the common beliefs, attitudes, and values you share with the audience, such as "We all respect human life. We all believe in fairness." At the same time you would be *starting with areas of agreement* and *working toward the acceptance of common values*. It might also help to take an indirect approach in which you present your evidence and reasoning before you announce your purpose.

> What if I were to tell you that we are condoning unfairness, that we are condemning people to death simply because they are poor and cannot afford a good lawyer? What if I were to show you that we are sanctioning a model of violent behavior in our society that invites more violence and more victims?

As you present evidence, cite authorities that *your audience will respect and accept*. "FBI statistics tell us that if you are poor and black, you are three times more likely to be executed for the crime of murder." *Keep your goals modest*. Only ask for a fair hearing of your position. Your goal might be to give the audience information that could *eventually* change their minds.

> I know that many of you may not like to hear what I'm saying, but think about it. If capital punishment does not deter violent crimes, if indeed it may encourage *more* violent crimes, isn't it time we put capital punishment itself on trial?

Finally, *make a **multisided presentation.*** Acknowledge the arguments in favor of capital punishment, showing that you respect and understand that position, even though you do not accept it.

> I know that the desire for revenge can be strong. If someone I love had been murdered, I would want the killer's life in return. I wouldn't care if capital punishment wasn't fair. I wouldn't care that it condones brutality. I would just want an eye for an eye. But that doesn't mean you should give it to me. It doesn't mean that society should base its policy on my anger and hatred.

A multisided approach is effective when an audience opposes your position. It also helps make those you have persuaded resistant to later counterattacks, because you have shown them how to evaluate and resist such arguments.[8] When you acknowledge and then refute arguments, you help your credibility in two ways. First, you enhance your *trustworthiness* by showing respect for your opposition. You suggest that their position merits consideration, even though you have a better option. Second, you enhance your *competence* by showing your knowledge of the opposing position and of the reasons why people accept it.

After your speech, you should continue to show respect for the audience. Even if some listeners want to argue or heckle, keep your composure. Others may be impressed by your self-control and may be encouraged to rethink their positions in light of your example.

There may be times when you and your audience are so far apart that you decide simply to acknowledge your disagreement. You might say that even though you do not agree with your listeners, you respect their right to their position and hope they will respect yours. Such openness may help establish the beginnings of trust. Even if audience members do not see you as a friend, they may at least start to see you as an honest, committed opponent and may give you a hearing. If you emphasize that you will *not* be asking them to change their minds, but simply to hear you out and to listen to the reasons why you believe as you do, you may be able to have your day in court.

We once heard a student speak against abortion to a class that was sharply divided on that issue. She began with a personal narrative, the story of how her mother had been given thalidomide (a drug that was found to induce birth defects) and was faced with a decision on terminating the pregnancy. The student concluded by saying that if her mother had chosen the abortion route, she would not be there speaking to them that day. She paused, smiled, and said, "Although I know some of you may disagree with my views on abortion, I must say I am glad that you are here to listen and that I am here to speak. Think about it." If your reasons are compelling and your evidence is strong, you may soften the opposition and move "waverers" toward your position.

Another helpful technique for handling opposition involves modifying your specific purpose. Do not try to accomplish too much in a single speech. If too much change is proposed, you may create a **boomerang effect,** in which the audience reacts by opposing your position even more strongly.[9] To hope for a major change on the basis of any single persuasive effort is what McGuire calls the **great expectation fallacy.**[10] Be patient. Try to move your audience a step at a time in the direction you would like them to go.

Do not worry if the change you want does not show up immediately. There often is a delayed reaction to persuasion, a **sleeper effect,** in which change shows up only after listeners have had time to integrate the message into their belief systems.[11] Even if no change is apparent, your message may serve a **consciousness-raising function,** sensitizing your listeners to the issue and making them more receptive to future persuasion.[12] It may require a series of messages to move people through all the steps in the persuasive process.

Facing a reluctant audience is never easy. But you can't predict what new thoughts your speech might stimulate among listeners or what delayed positive reactions to it there might be. Even if it only keeps alive the American tradition of dissent, it will have served a valuable function. Just as Olympic divers often earn higher scores for attempting difficult dives, persuasive speakers can win added credit by confronting reluctant audiences intelligently, courageously, and constructively.

---

**SPEAKER'S NOTES**

## Meeting the Challenge of a Reluctant Audience

1. Establish good will and build arguments based on shared values.

2. Present evidence from sources the audience will accept.

3. Set modest goals. Do not strive for too much change at one time.

4. Use a multisided approach to show respect for the opposition while demonstrating that your position is better.

### *Removing Barriers to Commitment*

Speaking to listeners who have not yet committed to a position also presents a challenge. Listeners may hesitate because they lack important information, or they may not see the connection between their own values and interests and your proposal, or they may not feel certain they can trust what you say. To deal with these challenges you should provide needed information, show listeners how your proposal relates to their values or interests, or strengthen your credibility so that you gain increased trust.

***Provide Needed Information.*** Often a single missing fact or unanswered question can stand in the way of commitment. "I know that many of you agree with me but are asking, 'How much will this cost?'" Anticipating audience reservations and supplying such necessary information can help move listeners toward your position.

***Affirm and Apply Values.*** Persuasive speeches that threaten audience values are not likely to be effective. You must establish that what you urge agrees with what listeners already believe or with their vital interests. For example, if your listeners resist a proposed educational program for the disadvantaged because they think people ought to take care of themselves, you may have to show them that your program represents "a *hand up,* not a *handout.*" Show the audience how people will be able to take care of themselves once the program goes into effect. It is also helpful if you can demonstrate that your proposal will lead to other favorable consequences, such as reductions in public assistance, unemployment compensation, and criminal activities.

As we noted in Chapter 4, values are often resistant to change. If you can reason from the perspective of your listeners' values, using them as the basis for your arguments, you will create identification and remove a barrier to commitment.

***Strengthen Your Credibility.***  When audiences hesitate because they question your credibility, you can "borrow ethos" by citing expert testimony. Call on sources your listeners trust and respect. Uncommitted audiences will scrutinize both you and your arguments carefully. Reason with such listeners, leading them to the conclusion you would like them to form. Provide supporting material each step of the way. Adopt a multisided approach, in which you consider all options fairly, to confirm your ethos as a trustworthy and competent speaker.

When addressing uncommitted listeners, don't overstate your case. Let your personal commitment be evident through your sincerity and conviction, but be careful using appeals to guilt or fear. These might backfire, causing listeners to reject both you and your message[13] It is also important not to push uncommitted listeners too hard. Help them move in the desired direction, but let them take the final step themselves.

## *Moving from Attitude to Action*

When listeners share your position and accept your leadership, they *may* be ready for a speech proposing action. However, it is one thing to agree with a speaker and quite another to accept all the inconvenience, cost, and risk that a commitment to action may require. Just as opponents may be reluctant to listen, sympathetic audiences may be reluctant to act. They may believe that the problem does not affect them personally, they may not know specifically what it is they should do, or they may feel that the situation is hopeless.[14] To move people to action, you must present powerful reasons to act. At the least, you may have to remind listeners of their beliefs, demonstrate the need for their involvement, present a clear plan for them to follow, and make it easy for them to comply.

***Revitalize Shared Beliefs.***  When speakers and audiences celebrate shared beliefs, the result often is renewed commitment. Such occasions may involve retelling traditional stories and resurrecting heroes, giving them new life and meaning. At political conventions Jefferson, Lincoln, Roosevelt, and Kennedy are often remembered in speeches. Such stories and examples invoke a common heritage and relate it to the present.[15] They can be used to bridge diversity in an audience, bringing differing factions together to pursue the same goal.

***Demonstrate the Need for Involvement.***  Present vivid images of the *need* for action. Show your listeners how the quality of *their* lives — how even their survival — depends on prompt action. Demonstrate how the results will be satisfying. It often helps if you can associate the change with a vision of the future. In his final speech, Martin Luther King, Jr., said, "I may not get there with you, but I can see the Promised Land." King's vision of the Promised Land helped justify the sacrifice called for in his plan of action.

Unless people believe that the problem will affect them directly, they may be reluctant to act. Use examples and narratives to bring the issue home to them. During the 1992 presidential nominating conventions, both parties featured well-educated, poised, and eloquent women who spoke in support of aggressive action against AIDS. (See the texts of these speeches in Appendix B.) One speaker had contracted the disease from a contaminated blood transfusion, the other from an infected spouse. The message? By their personal witness, they illustrated that AIDS was not confined to the homosexual population or to the drug-addicted. Rather, it was rapidly becoming an equal-opportunity disease. It could even happen to listeners themselves.

***Present a Clear Plan of Action.*** Listeners may resist action by exaggerating the difficulty of a proposal or insisting that it is impossible. To overcome such resistance, show them how others have been successful. Use examples or narratives that picture the audience undertaking the action successfully. Stress that "we *can* do it, and this is *how* we will do it."

To get people to act, you must give them a clear plan. A speaker hoping to persuade classmates to work to defeat a proposed tuition raise said:

> How many of you are willing to help defeat this plan to raise our tuition? Good! I see your heads nodding. Now, if you are willing to sign this petition to protest this injustice, hold up your hands. Hold them higher so I can see you! O.K.! Good! I'm going to circulate this petition, and I want each of you to sign it. If we act together, we can make a difference.

The plan you present must show listeners what has to be done, who must do it, and how to proceed. Try to anticipate and refute excuses listeners might offer to avoid responsibility. Strong feelings aroused through vivid images

---

**SPEAKER'S NOTES**

### Meeting the Challenge of Moving an Audience to Action

1. Remind listeners of the values and beliefs that are at stake.

2. Stress the need for personal involvement by showing listeners they could be affected by the problem.

3. Present a step-by-step plan of action.

4. Make it easy for listeners to comply with your suggestions.

are often necessary to move people to action. If you can get one person in the audience to make a commitment, others will often follow. Once people have openly voiced their commitment, they are more likely to follow through on it.[16]

Be specific in your instructions. As she urged her audience to support the campaign to defeat a proposed tuition increase, one student speaker said, "Now we're going to march on Monday. We're going to line up at noon outside Student Union, and we're going to march to the steps of the Administration Building." She did *not* say, "Let's all do something to defeat this proposal."

***Make It Easy for Your Audience to Comply.*** Instead of merely urging listeners to write their congressional representatives, provide them with legislators' addresses and telephone numbers, a petition to sign, or preprinted addressed postcards to return. During the 1980s, students at the University of North Alabama lobbied the state legislature for additional funding for the school. Volunteers set up tables at the entries of all classroom buildings and the student center. The students had preprinted postcards for others to sign and a list of legislators broken out into the counties they represented. Over three-fourths of the students at the university signed the cards, which were hand delivered to the state capitol. Result? The school got more money.

 ## TYPES OF PERSUASIVE SPEECHES

In this section we discuss three major types of persuasive speeches: those that address attitudes, those that urge action, and those that contend with opposition. Although a speech may perform all these functions, most of the time one will dominate.

### Speeches Addressing Attitudes

The basic goal of **speeches addressing attitudes** is to form, reform, or reinforce audience attitudes. Sometimes a speaker may simply wish to raise discontent by addressing a topic such as "Have We Played Fair with Haiti?" Later speeches can then build on this discontent and urge specific programs of reform. Thus, speeches addressing attitudes often pave the way for speeches urging action.

When they are most ambitious, speeches addressing attitudes aim for a total change of conviction. A speech on the topic "Beyond the United Nations" might attempt such far-reaching influence. Such speeches can be appropriate when the problems they address require more than surface remedies.

Obviously, the greater the change of attitude you aim for, the more difficult it will be to achieve your goal. As we noted in Chapter 4, beliefs, attitudes, and values are an integral part of our personality. Deep changes in any of these can have a revolutionary impact on lives, so audiences are usually highly resistant to proposals calling for such reform. There is always the possibility that such persuasive efforts will cause audiences to reject the speaker and cling more stubbornly to their previous beliefs.

To be effective, speeches addressing attitudes must begin on common ground. Betty Nichols's classroom speech on responsible drinking and driving began by assuming that she and her listeners shared the belief that drunk driving is a serious problem. She reinforced that shared belief and then proposed a change in attitude as part of a solution for the problem. To encourage such change, offer audience members good reasons for modifying their convictions.[17]

### Speeches Urging Action

**Speeches urging action** go beyond attitude change and encourage listeners to take action either as individuals or as members of a group. Bonnie Marshall asked audience members to take individual action to assure their right to die with dignity: to write their state representatives, draw up a living will, assign durable power of attorney to a trusted friend or family member, and let their personal physicians know their wishes. When a persuasive speech urges individual commitment, audience members must see the value or necessity of action in personal terms.

*When your goal is to move people to action, you must remind listeners of the values and beliefs that are at stake.*

In contrast, when a speech advocates group action, the audience must see itself as having common identity and purpose. As we noted in Chapter 10, the speaker can reinforce group identity by using inclusive pronouns (*we, our, us*), telling stories that emphasize group achievements, and referring to common heroes, opponents, or martyrs. Anna Aley used an effective appeal to group identity as she proposed specific actions:

> What can one student do to change the practices of numerous Manhattan landlords? Nothing, if that student is alone. But just think what we could accomplish if we got all 13,600 off-campus students involved in this issue! Think what we could accomplish if we got even a fraction of those students involved!

Speeches advocating action usually involve some risk. Therefore, the speaker must present compelling reasons to overcome the listener's natural caution. The consequences of acting and not acting must be clearly spelled out. The plan presented must seem practical and reasonable, and listeners should be able to see themselves enacting it successfully.

### Speeches of Contention

In **speeches of contention** you directly refute opposing arguments to clear the way for attitudes and actions you are proposing. "There are those who say that we cannot afford to land explorers on Mars in the next decade," said Marvin Andrews to his public speaking class. "I say we can't afford not to." Marvin then went on to describe the costs of a space journey to Mars and the benefits we might expect from such exploration. "But we really can have no idea of all the benefits, any more than Queen Isabella could have foreseen all the results of the voyage of Columbus. Fortunately, she did not listen to advisers who said his trip would cost too much," Marvin concluded.

On highly controversial topics such as abortion or the legalization of drugs, you often can't avoid a speech of contention. If some audience members hold opposing views, a speech of contention may offend them, place them on the defensive, and make them even more difficult to persuade. Why, then, would you give such a speech? In situations when danger threatens and immediate action is needed, milder argumentative techniques such as the co-active approach may simply take too long to be effective. To secure immediate action, you may have to address opposing beliefs directly and discredit the arguments that support them with indisputable facts and figures or expert testimony.

Speeches of contention also may be the best strategy when your audience is split in terms of their attitudes toward the topic. In such cases your primary audience will be uncommitted listeners and reasonable opponents. By presenting tactful, carefully documented counterarguments, you may reach some of them. A refutational approach may also help strengthen the resolve of supporters who need assurance that an opposing position can be effectively countered.

Finally, in some situations that are extremely important to you personally, such as support for gun control legislation, you may want to make a speech of contention as a last-ditch tactic. You may feel that listeners are so strongly entrenched in their opposition that your only hope is to shock them with a direct, frontal attack that shows them why they are wrong. You hope for a positive delayed effect after their first negative reaction. Or you may even decide that your chances for persuasion are small but that your position deserves to be heard with all the power, reason, and conviction you can muster. You can have your say and feel better for it.

## DESIGNS FOR PERSUASIVE SPEAKING

As you consider the type of persuasive speech you will develop, you must decide how to structure your speech. Many of the designs used for informative speeches are also appropriate for persuasive speeches. The categorical design can provide reasons for accepting changes in attitude, taking action, or rejecting the arguments of others. The sequential design may be used to specify the steps in a plan of action. Similarly, the comparison and contrast design works well for speeches of contention in which you contrast the weaknesses of an opposing argument with the strengths of your own. In the remainder of this chapter, we look at designs especially suited to persuasive speeches. Figure 13.1 explains the relationship between types of persuasive speeches and their major design options.

### Problem-Solution Design

The **problem-solution design** first convinces listeners that they face a problem, then shows them how to deal with it. The solution can involve changing an attitude or taking an action and is particularly appropriate for those types of persuasive speeches. Although this approach sounds simple, it is sometimes difficult to convince listeners that a problem exists. People often ignore problems until they reach a critical stage. You can counteract this tendency by depicting the crisis that surely will emerge unless your audience makes the changes you suggest.

When you prepare a problem-solution speech, do not overwhelm your listeners with details. Cover the most important features of the problem, then show the audience how your solution will work. A problem-solution speech opposing a proposed tuition increase might use the following design:

| Type | Major Design Options | Summary of Procedures |
|------|---------------------|----------------------|
| Form, reform, or reinforce attitudes | Categorical | Justifies attitudes or change in attitudes by presenting categories or reasons. |
| | Problem-solution | Reveals an attitude as central to a problem and a change in attitude as the key to its solution. |
| | Analogy | Creates favorable or unfavorable attitude shifts by associating a topic with an object of comparison. |
| Urge action | Sequential | Shows how a proposed plan will work as a systematic sequence of actions. |
| | Problem-solution | Promotes the need for action to solve some serious social or personal problem. |
| | Stock issues | Addresses questions reasonable listeners want answered before they will take action. |
| | Motivated sequence | Calls directly for action as the final phase of a process that involves arousing attention, demonstrating need, satisfying need, and visualizing results. |
| Contend with opposing views | Comparison-contrast | Attacks an opposing position by comparing and contrasting its weaknesses with the advantages of one's own proposal. |
| | Refutative | Follows a systematic five-step method of attacking an opposing position. |
| | Analogy | Justifies rejection of an opposing approach by connecting it with some disliked similar proposal or situation. |

FIGURE 13.1  Types of Persuasive Speeches and Major Options for Designing Them

*Thematic statement:*  We need to defeat the proposal to raise tuition next fall.

I.  Problem: The proposal to raise tuition is a disaster!

　　A. The plan will create serious hardships for many students.

　　　　1. Many current students may have to drop out.

　　　　2. New students will be discouraged from enrolling.

　　B. The proposed increase will cause additional problems for the university and the community.

　　　　1. Decreased attendance will mean decreased revenue.

    2. Decreased revenue will reduce the university's service to the community.

    3. Reduced service will mean reduced support from the contributors.

II.  Solution: Defeat the proposal to raise tuition!

    A.  Get signatures on a petition against the tuition increase.

        1.  Send copies to state legislators.

        2.  Deliver to the president of the university (alert TV stations).

    B.  Start a letters-to-the-editor campaign.

    C.  Organize a rally on campus.

When the problem can be identified clearly and the solution is concrete and simple, the problem-solution design works well in persuasive speeches.

### Stock Issues Design

The **stock issues design** is a variation on the problem-solution design. Derived from debate theory, the stock issues design attempts to answer the major general questions a reasonable person would ask before agreeing to a change in policies or procedures.[18] General questions related to the problem and its solution form the framework for the stock issues design:

I.  Is there a need for change because of some significant problem?

    A.  How did the problem originate?

    B.  What caused the problem?

    C.  How widespread is the problem?

    D.  How long has the problem persisted?

    E.  What harms are associated with the problem?

    F.  Are these harms inherent to the problem?

    G.  Will these harms continue and grow unless there is change?

II.  What is the solution to this problem?

    A.  Will the solution actually solve the problem?

    B.  Is the solution practical?

    C.  Would the cost of the solution be reasonable?

    D.  Might there be additional desirable or undesirable consequences?

III.  Who will put the solution into effect?

    A.  Are these people responsible and competent?

    B.  What role might listeners play?[19]

These general questions help the speaker identify specific issues relevant to the problem in question. A stock issues speech advocating responsible drinking and driving might use the following design:

*Thematic statement:* We need to replace the old notion of "If you drink, don't drive" with the idea of responsible drinking and driving.

I. The traditional approach — "If you drink, don't drive"—does not work with the college-age population. [*failure of earlier solution identified*]

    A. The "Don't drive if you've been drinking" campaign in Stillwater County, has been a failure.

        1. A campus survey shows that 65 percent of our students admit to driving after drinking during the past six months. [*extent of problem*]

        2. Alcohol-related accidents involving drivers under twenty-five years of age in Stillwater County have risen steadily over the past five years. [*persistence/growth of problem*]

    B. It ignores the real problem — ignorance about the risks involved in drinking and driving. [*origin and cause of problem*]

        1. A campus survey showed that only 24 percent of our students understood how drinking affects reaction time and judgment.

        2. The same survey showed that only 17 percent of our students were aware of the legal consequences of drinking and driving.

    C. The problem will not clear up by itself. [*inherency and harms*]

        1. Without a change in behavior, over half of us in this room will be involved in an alcohol-related accident.

        2. At least one of us will be killed or crippled for life.

        3. That's too high a price to pay for an evening on the town.

II. A campaign for "responsible drinking and driving" is the answer to this problem. [*introduces solution*]

    A. "Responsible drinking and driving" is an educational campaign. [*ties solution to origin and cause of problem*]

        1. It will teach people how alcohol affects them.

        2. It will make people aware of the legal consequences of driving under the influence.

        3. It will teach people to "plan in advance" to manage their drinking behavior.

            a. It advocates a "designated driver" system.

            b. It stresses not letting a friend drive under the influence.

B. A similar campaign was tried in Marlin County. [*demonstrates workability*]

1. The year after it was tried, alcohol-related accidents decreased by 8 percent in the county.

2. A survey of students at Marlin County Community College showed that over 75 percent understood the basics of alcohol impairment.

3. The same survey showed that over 80 percent of those students also knew the legal consequences of drinking and driving.

C. The "Responsible Drinking and Driving" campaign has special advantages. [*identifies other favorable consequences*]

1. It treats young people as responsible adults.

2. Young people respond well to it because it doesn't moralize.

3. It provides them with a workable plan that still allows them to party.

III. The Office of Student Affairs could manage this campaign very well. [*answers who can put plan into effect*]

A. We need to apply some pressure to get them involved. [*spells out role of audience*]

1. Write or call the Dean of Student Affairs and the university president.

2. Ask instructors to request department chairs to make some contacts for us.

3. Sign this petition for presentation to the Office of Student Affairs.

B. I have here some fact sheets on the campaign as it worked in Marlin County. [*facilitates audience involvement*]

1. Use them in your contacts.

2. Distribute them to your friends.

### Motivated Sequence Design

The **motivated sequence design,** introduced by Alan Monroe, also is a variation on the problem-solution design.[20] This design has five steps, beginning with arousing attention and ending with a call for action. Therefore, it is especially suited for speeches that have action as their goal. The design also emphasizes the role of skillful language in stimulating audience perceptions and feelings. The steps in the motivated sequence are as follows:

1. *Arouse attention.* As in any speech, you begin by stimulating interest in your subject. In Chapter 12 we discussed six factors related to attention:

intensity, repetition, novelty, activity, contrast, and relevance. These same techniques may be used in persuasive speeches.

2. *Demonstrate a need.* Show your listeners what they might win or lose if they accept or reject your proposal. Tie your demonstration to the basic needs discussed in Chapter 4.

3. *Satisfy the need.* Present a way to satisfy the need you have demonstrated. Set forth a plan of action and explain how it would work. Offer examples showing how it has worked in other places.

4. *Visualize the results.* You can visualize results with either positive or negative images. You could show your listeners how their lives will be changed for the better when your plan is enacted. A positive image of the future can help overcome resistance to action. You could also paint a dire picture of what life will be like if they do not go along with your plan. You might even put these positive and negative verbal pictures side by side to strengthen their impact through contrast.

5. *Call for action.* Your call for action may be a challenge, an appeal, or a statement of personal commitment. The call for action should be short and to the point. Give your listeners something specific that they can do right away to start the process of change. If you can get them to take the first step in the proposal, the next will come more easily.

Let's look at how this model might work in a persuasive speech that appeals to audience motivations for recognition, friendship, and nurturance, using language that activates feelings of sympathy and identification:

|  |  |
|---|---|
| Arouse attention | Have you ever dreamed about being a hero or heroine? Have you ever wished you could do something great, something that would really make a difference in our world? Well, I'm here to tell you you can if you're willing to give just three hours a week. |
| Demonstrate need | Our community needs volunteers to help children who are lonely and neglected. Big Sisters and Big Brothers of Omaha have a program for these children, but only people can make the program work. Last year they had forty-eight student volunteers. This year only thirty have signed up to help. They need at least thirty more. They need you. |
| Satisfy need | Volunteering to be a big brother or a big sister will help this program of after-school activities keep going. It will also make you a hero or heroine in the eyes of a child. |
| Visualize results | Maybe you can have an experience that will be as rewarding as mine has been. Last year I worked with ten-year-old Kevin two afternoons a week. He needed a lot of help with his homework because his grades were just borderline passing. I tutored him in math and science. But more than that help, he just needed someone to be his friend, someone to talk with, |

someone who cared about him. The first six weeks his grades went from D–'s to C–'s, and I took him to a basketball game one weekend. The next six weeks his grades went up to C's and C+'s and I took him to a movie. This year Kevin is doing well in school. He's making C's and B's in all his courses, but we still work together and I still have the satisfaction of knowing I'm doing something worthwhile. I'm making a contribution to our community, and I'm a hero in the eyes of an eleven-year-old boy.

Call for action

Won't you join me and become one of the unsung heroines or heroes of our town? If you can give just one or two afternoons a week, you can make a difference in the life of a child and in the future of our community. I've got the applications with me and will be waiting for you to sign up after class.

If you plan to use the motivated sequence, first determine where your listeners stand on the issue, then focus on the steps that will carry persuasion forward. For example, if you were speaking to an audience that was already convinced of the need for a change but lacked a plan to make it work, you could focus on step 3, "satisfy the need." However, if you faced an audience that contested the need, your emphasis should be on step 2, "demonstrate the need." In the latter situation, you might simply mention that ways to satisfy the need are available and stop short of a call for action. These final steps could be addressed in later speeches.

The major problem with the motivated sequence design is that it may tempt a speaker into trying too much in a single speech. If you expect to move from introducing a problem, to showing how it can be solved, to energizing listeners to solve it—all in one short speech—you may be committing the great expectation fallacy we mentioned earlier. This is especially true if the problem is complex and involves risk. Also, when beginning speakers use such a rigid model to structure their speeches, they may be tempted to follow the formula as though they were baking a cake using a generic mix. Just as the best cooks turn out culinary masterpieces by modifying recipes, the best speakers adapt designs to fit their subjects, audiences, purposes, and their own personalities.

### Refutative Design

In the **refutative design,** used in speeches of contention, the speaker tries to raise doubt about an opposing position by revealing its inconsistencies and deficiencies. To bring off an effective refutation, you must understand the opposition's motivations, arguments, and evidence. It is often wise to take on the opposition's weakest point first. Your refutation then raises doubt about other opposing arguments. The point of attack may be illogical reasoning, flimsy or insufficient evidence, or even the self-interest of an opposing speaker. However, to keep the dispute as constructive as possible, avoid personal attacks unless credibility issues are inescapable.

There are five steps in developing an effective refutation. These five steps should be followed in sequence for each point you plan to refute.

1. State the point you are going to refute and explain why it is important.
2. Tell the audience how you are going to refute this point.
3. Present your evidence using facts and figures, examples, and testimony. Cite sources and authorities the audience will accept as competent and credible.
4. Spell out the conclusion for the audience. Do not rely on listeners to figure out what the evidence means. Tell them directly.
5. Explain the significance of your refutation — show how it discredits or damages the position of the opposition.

For example, you might refute an argument against sex education in public high schools in the following manner:

| | |
|---|---|
| State the point you will refute and explain its importance | Our well-intentioned friends would have you believe, and this is their biggest concern, that birth-control information increases teen-age sexual activity. |
| Tell how you will support this point | I want to share with you some statistical evidence that contradicts this contention — a contention that is simply not supported by the facts. |
| Present your evidence using credible sources | The latest study on this issue, conducted in 1992 by the National Department of Human Services, compared sexual activity rates in sixty high schools across the United States — thirty with sex education programs and thirty without. Their findings show that there are no significant differences in sexual activity rates between these two groups of schools. |
| State your conclusion | Therefore, the argument that access to birth-control information through sex education programs increases sexual activity simply does not hold water. |
| Explain the significance of your demonstration | That's typical of the attack on sex education in the schools — a lot of sound and fury, signifying nothing. |

You can strengthen this design if you follow your refutation by proving a similar point of your own, thus balancing the negative refutation with a positive demonstration. The result supplies the audience with an alternative belief to substitute for the one you have refuted. Use the same five-step sequence to support your position. For example, you might follow the preceding refutation with the following demonstration:

| | |
|---|---|
| State the point you will support and explain its importance | I'm not going to try to tell you that birth-control information support reduces sexual activity. But I want to tell you what it does reduce. It reduces teen-age pregnancy. |
| Tell how you will support this point | There is reliable evidence that fewer girls become pregnant in high schools with sex education programs. |

| | |
|---|---|
| Present your evidence using credible sources | The same study conducted by the National Department of Human Services demonstrated that in high schools with sex education programs the pregnancy rate dropped from one out of every sixty female students to one out of ninety within two years of the program's going into effect. |
| State your conclusion | Therefore, sex education is a good program. It attacks a devastating social problem — teen-age pregnancy. |
| Explain the significance of your refutation | Any program that reduces unwanted teen-age pregnancy is valuable — valuable to the young women involved, valuable to society. We all pay in so many ways for this personal and social tragedy — we should all support a program that works to reduce it. And we should reject the irrational voices that reject the program. |

## Analogy Design

In a persuasive speech using an **analogy design,** the body of the speech consists of an extended comparison supporting the speaker's proposal. We have already seen how analogies can serve informative speeches by relating the unknown to the known to increase understanding. In a persuasive speech, analogies go beyond this function to affect attitudes as well. Therefore, analogy design is well suited for persuasive speeches urging changes of attitude. Because this design can cast an opposing position in an unfavorable light, it can also serve persuasive speeches that contend with other views.

For analogy to work as a persuasive design, the audience must have an attitude toward the object of comparison that will serve your purpose. For example, if your audience has a positive attitude toward the efficiency of Japanese industry, then drawing an analogy between Japanese management techniques and an open management style for American industry might be an effective technique. Of course, if your audience has negative feelings about Japan, the analogy could backfire. On the other hand, if you wish to discredit an opposing position, you can connect it to something that your listeners are likely to reject. When you compare a proposed plan to "taxation without representation," you are using a negative analogy to the conditions that inspired the American Revolution. Because you can develop both positive and negative analogies, this can be a very useful design for persuasive speeches.

As we observed in the previous chapter, analogies may be either literal or figurative, depending on whether you are comparing things of the same or different kinds. A speech based on an extended analogy between American and Japanese business cultures would follow a literal analogy design. Such a speech would emphasize a rational pattern of persuasion, based on precise points of similarity and difference. On the other hand, speeches based on figurative analogy design are often quite emotional, based on the transfer of attitudes and feelings. Let us see how a speech against a proposed tuition increase might be structured using a figurative analogy. Arguing that "the pro-

**SPEAKER'S NOTES**

## Designing Your Persuasive Speech

1. Use a categorical design to provide reasons for changing attitudes or actions.

2. Use a sequential design to specify the steps in a plan of action.

3. Use a comparison and contrast design to contrast the weaknesses of an opposing position with the strengths of your own.

4. When using a problem-solution design, focus on the main features of a problem, and then present a simple, clear solution.

5. In a stock issues design, develop your speech in response to a set of questions that are basic to persuasive deliberation.

6. In a motivated sequence design, emphasize the most relevant points in a five-step process from "arousing attention" to "calling for action."

7. In a refutative design, attack the weakest points of the opposition first, concentrating on defects in evidence, proof, and argument. Avoid personal attacks unless credibility issues are inescapable.

8. In an analogy design, compare your proposal with something listeners favor to encourage acceptance. Attack an opposing position by comparing it to something listeners dislike.

posal to raise tuition treats students more like slaves than like members of a free society," you might follow this plan:

I. A slave state does not consult slaves: who consulted you?

    A. How the proposal originated.

    B. When it was planned.

    C. Who planned it.

II. A slave state does not care about the welfare of slaves: who cares about your welfare?

    A. How students in general will be affected.

    B. Specific cases of hardship in our class.

III. A slave state does not see the consequences of its acts: who has measured the impact on our university?

    A. Prospect of diminished revenue.

B. Loss of outstanding faculty and programs.

C. Decreased support from state.

In this example the speaker aims for a transfer of emotion — from the behavior of a "slave state" to the unjust conduct of the university. If the analogy works, it is likely to have a profound impact on listener attitudes. When using the figurative analogy design, the speaker must still be able to demonstrate that the analogy fits the situation, or it will seem far-fetched and inappropriate.

**IN SUMMARY**   Persuasive communication is inescapable. Persuasion is also vital to our political system, which is based on the principle of rule by *deliberation* and choice rather than by force. The right to express opinions — no matter how unpopular — also serves practical goals. Groups that have been exposed to different positions usually make better decisions because they are stimulated to examine a situation and to think about their options.

*Characteristics of Persuasive Speaking.* In contrast to informative speaking, persuasive speaking urges a choice among options and asks for a commitment. The persuasive speaker acts as a leader and often emphasizes group over individual action. Persuasive speeches rely more on emotional involvement than informative speeches do, and they carry a heavier ethical burden.

*The Process of Persuasion.*   When persuasion is successful, people listen, learn, agree, and change as a result of what they hear. These behaviors parallel McGuire's categories of awareness, comprehension, acceptance, and integration of persuasive material. Awareness suggests that we know of a problem, that it commands our attention, and that we understand its connection with our lives. Comprehension concerns whether we understand an argument, are stimulated by its ideas, and know how to carry out its proposals. Acceptance includes our agreeing with and retaining a message and recalling the reasons for the agreement. Integration involves consolidating the new attitudes and commitments into our overall behavior system.

*The Challenges of Persuasion.* Persuading others poses many challenges.  You must assess the situation to determine the nature of your challenge. You may have to entice a reluctant audience to listen, remove barriers that block commitment, or move listeners from agreement to action.

*Types of Persuasive Speeches.*  The three major types of persuasive speeches address attitudes, urge action, and contend with opposition. *Speeches addressing attitudes* may aim for small changes or radical conversion. The latter change is difficult, and runs the risk of a *boomerang effect.*

*Speeches urging action* call upon listeners to become change agents. Such speeches may strive for group action and emphasize identification, or for individual action and emphasize self-interest. *Speeches of contention* confront the opposition by systematically refuting its claims. Such speeches usually do not seek to convert opponents but rather to win over the uncommitted and to influence opinion leaders.

*Designs for Persuasive Speaking.*   Problem-solution, stock issues, motivated sequence, refutation, and analogy designs are particularly suited for persuasive speeches. In a *problem-solution design,* you must first convince the audience that a problem exists, and then advance a solution that corrects it. In a *stock issues design,* you anticipate and answer the general questions a reasonable person would want to ask before agreeing to a change. The *motivated sequence design* has five steps: arousing attention, demonstrating need, satisfying need, visualizing results, and calling for action. To use the *refutative design,* state the point you intend to refute, tell how you will refute it, present your evidence, draw a conclusion, and explain the significance of the refutation. Refutation is often followed by demonstration, in which you prove a point to replace the one you have disproved. In an *analogy design,* construct an extended comparison that will transfer attitudes favoring your position.

**TERMS TO KNOW**

deliberation

co-active approach

multisided presentation

boomerang effect

great expectation fallacy

sleeper effect

consciousness-raising function

speech addressing attitudes

speech urging action

speech of contention

problem-solution design

stock issues design

motivated sequence design

refutative design

analogy design

**DISCUSSION**

1. Examine magazine ads and newspaper articles for "infomercials" — persuasive messages cloaked as information. What alerts you to the persuasive intent? In what respects does such pseudo-information possess the characteristics of persuasion discussed in this chapter? In what respects does it possess the characteristics of informative discourse discussed in Chapter 12?

2. The letters-to-the-editor section of the Sunday newspaper is often a rich (and raw!) source for the study of persuasive material. Using a recent Sunday paper, analyze the persuasion attempted in these letters. Which do you think are most and least effective and why?

3. The speech on slum housing that appears at the end of this chapter was prepared for a student audience at Kansas State University. What changes might you suggest in this speech if it were to be presented to a luncheon meeting of realtors in Manhattan, Kansas? Why?

4. When should a speaker give up trying to persuade a hostile audience and simply confront listeners directly with the position they oppose? Why would a speaker bother to do this? Is it possible that both speaker and audience might gain something from such a confrontation? Find an example of such a speech. Do you agree with the strategy used in it? Discuss in class.

**APPLICATION**   1. Keep a diary of your day, identifying all the moments in which you confront and practice persuasion. Evaluate your adventure in persuasion. When were you most and least persuaded and most and least persuasive? Why? Did you encounter (or commit!) any ethical abuses?

2. Read one of the persuasive speeches in Appendix B and identify the following:
   a. the challenge the speaker confronted
   b. the type of persuasive speech
   c. the design of the speech

Suggest an alternative design for the speech and discuss why you think that approach would work as well or better.

3. Select a controversial subject and outline the persuasive speeches you would present on the subject to
   a. an uncommitted audience
   b. an audience in agreement
   c. an audience in opposition

Discuss the differences among your approaches.

**NOTES**   1. *Whitney* v. *California,* 274 U.S. 357, 375 (1927).
2. *On Liberty* (Chicago: Henry Regnery, 1955 [originally published 1859]), p. 24.
3. Charlan Jeanne Nemeth, "Differential Contributions of Majority and Minority Influence," *Psychological Review* 93 (1986): 23–32.
4. Mark A. Hamilton and John E. Hunter, "The Effect of Language Intensity on Receiver Attitudes Toward Message, Source, and Topic," in *Persuasion: Advances Through Meta-Analysis,* ed. M. Allen and R. W. Preiss (Beverley Hills, Calif.: Sage [in press]).
5. William J. McGuire, "Attitudes and Attitude Change," in *The Handbook of Social Psychology,* ed. Gardner Lindzey and Elliot Aronson, vol. 1 (New York: Random House, 1985), I, 258–261.

6. John C. Reinard, "The Persuasive Effects of Testimonial Assertion Evidence," in *Persuasion: Advances Through Meta-Analysis* (in press). See also J. C. Reinard, "The Empirical Study of the Persuasive Effects of Evidence: The Status After Fifty Years of Research," *Human Communication Research* 15 (1988): 3–59.

7. Herbert W. Simons, *Persuasion: Understanding, Practice, and Analysis* (New York: Random House, 1986), p. 153.

8. Mike Allen, "Meta-Analysis Comparing the Persuasiveness of One-sided and Two-sided Messages," *Western Journal of Speech Communication* 55 (1991): 390–404; M. Allen et al., "Testing a Model of Message Sidedness: Three Replications," *Communication Monographs* 56 (1990): 275–291; Jerold L. Hale, Paul A. Mongeau, and Randi M. Thomas, "Cognitive Processing of One- and Two-sided Persuasive Messages," *Western Journal of Speech Communication* 55 (1991): 380–389; Carl I. Hovland, Arthur A. Lumsdaine, and Fred D. Sheffield, "The Effects of Presenting 'One Side' versus 'Both Sides' in Changing Opinions on a Controversial Subject," in *Experiments on Mass Communication* (Princeton, N.J.: Princeton University Press, 1949), pp. 201–227; William J. McGuire, "Inducing Resistance to Persuasion," in *Advances in Experimental Social Psychology,* ed. L. Berkowitz (New York: Academic Press, 1964), pp. 191–229.

9. N. H. Anderson, "Integration Theory and Attitude Change," *Psychological Review* 78 (1971): 171–206.

10. McGuire, p. 260.

11. Mike Allen and James B. Stiff, "Testing Three Models for the Sleeper Effect," *Western Journal of Speech Communication* 53 (1989): 411–426; T. D. Cook et al., "History of the Sleeper Effect: Some Logical Pitfalls in Accepting the Null Hypothesis," *Psychological Bulletin* 86 (1979): 662–679.

12. M. E. McCombs, "The Agenda-setting Approach," in *Handbook of Political Communication,* ed. D. D. Nimmo and K. R. Sanders (Beverly Hills, Calif.: Sage, 1981), pp. 121–140.

13. Franklin J. Boster and Paul Mongeau, "Fear-arousing Persuasive Messages," in *Communication Yearbook 8,* ed. R. Bostrom (Beverly Hills, Calif.: Sage, 1984), 330–377; T. W. Milburn and K. H. Watman, *On the Nature of Threat: A Social Psychological Analysis* (New York: Praeger, 1981).

14. Katherine E. Rowan, "Goals, Obstacles, and Strategies in Risk Communication: A Problem-solving Approach to Improving Communication About Risks," *Journal of Applied Communication Research* 19 (1991): 322.

15. Michael Osborn, "Rhetorical Depiction," in *Form, Genre, and the Study of Political Discourse,* ed. Herbert W. Simons and Aram A. Aghazarian (Columbia: University of South Carolina Press, 1986), pp. 79–107.

16. R. A. Wicklund and J. W. Brehm, *Perspectives on Cognitive Dissonance* (Hillsdale, N.J.: Erlbaum, 1976).

17. See Walter R. Fisher, "Toward a Logic of Good Reasons," *Quarterly Journal of Speech* 64 (1978): 376–384; Karl R. Wallace, "The Substance of Rhetoric: Good Reasons," *Quarterly Journal of Speech* 49 (1963): 239–249.

18. J. W. Patterson and David Zarefsky, *Contemporary Debate* (Boston: Houghton Mifflin, 1983), p. 23.

19. The structure of the stock issues design has been adapted from Charles U. Larson, *Persuasion: Reception and Responsibility,* 6th ed. (Belmont, Calif.: Wadsworth, 1992), pp. 202–203, and Charles S. Mudd and Malcolm O. Sillars, *Public Speaking: Content and Communication* (Prospect Heights, Ill.: Waveland, 1991), pp. 100–102.

20. This design was introduced in Alan Monroe's *Principles and Types of Speech* (New York: Scott, Foresman, 1935) and has been refined in later editions.

## We Don't Have to Live in Slums

*Anna Aley*

Anna's speech uses a problem-solution design to urge action. She gains attention and involves her listeners by asserting that slum conditions exist and that they pose a threat. Anna supports these assertions by describing her personal experience through a superb selection of concrete examples.

Anna shows that hers was not an isolated experience but rather a larger problem requiring reform. She orients her audience by presenting facts on the extent of the problem. Then she appeals to her listeners' own observations. Anna also describes students as a likely group of victims, whom slumlords will take advantage of because of their vulnerability. She cites the number of renters' complaints to reinforce this conclusion.

Slumlords — you'd expect them in New York or Chicago, but in Manhattan, Kansas? You'd better believe there are slumlords in Manhattan, and they pose a direct threat to you if you ever plan to rent an off-campus apartment.

I know about slumlords; I rented a basement apartment from one last semester. I guess I first suspected something was wrong when I discovered dead roaches in the refrigerator. I definitely knew something was wrong when I discovered the leaks: the one in the bathroom that kept the bathroom carpet constantly soggy and molding and the one in the kitchen that allowed water from the upstairs neighbor's bathroom to seep into the kitchen cabinets and collect in my dishes.

Then there were the serious problems. The hot water heater and furnace were connected improperly and posed a fire hazard. They were situated next to the only exit. There was no smoke detector or fire extinguisher and no emergency way out — the windows were too small for escape. I was living in an accident waiting to happen — and paying for it.

The worst thing about my ordeal was that I was not an isolated instance; many Kansas State students are living in unsafe housing and paying for it, not only with their money, but their happiness, their grades, their health, and their safety.

We can't be sure how many students are living in substandard housing, housing that does not meet the code specifications required of rental property. We can be sure, however, that a large number of Kansas State students are at risk of being caught in the same situation I was. According to the registrar, approximately 17,800 students are attending Kansas State this semester. Housing claims that 4,200 live in the dorms. This means that approximately 13,600 students live off-campus. Some live in fraternities or sororities, some live at home, but most live in off-campus apartments, as I do.

Many of these 13,600 students share traits that make them likely to settle for substandard housing. For example, many students want to live close to campus. If you've ever driven through the surrounding neighborhoods, you know that much of the available housing is in older houses, houses that were never meant to be divided into separate rental units. Students are also often limited in the amount they can pay for rent; some landlords, such as mine, will use low rent as an excuse not to fix anything and to let the apartment deteriorate. Most importantly, many students are young and, consequently, naive when it comes to selecting an apartment. They don't know the housing codes; but even if they did, they don't know how to check to make sure the apartment is in compliance. Let's face it — how many of us know how to check a hot water heater to make sure it's connected properly?

Adding to the problem of the number of students willing to settle for substandard housing is the number of landlords willing to supply it. Currently, the Consumer Relations Board here at Kansas State has on file student complaints

against approximately one hundred landlords. There are surely complaints against many more that have never been formally reported.

In this section the problem-solution design emerges clearly. Anna has already established the concrete reality of the problem; now she turns to an analysis of causes, which she must identify before she can advance a solution.

There are two main causes of the substandard student housing problem. The first —and most significant —is the simple fact that it is possible for a landlord to lease an apartment that does not meet housing code requirements. The Manhattan Housing Code Inspector will evaluate an apartment, but only after the tenant has given the landlord a written complaint and the landlord has had fourteen days to remedy the situation. In other words, the way things are now, the only way the Housing Code Inspector can evaluate an apartment to see if it's safe to be lived in is if someone has been living in it for at least two weeks!

A second cause of the problem is the fact that campus services designed to help students avoid substandard housing are not well known. The Consumer Relations Board here at Kansas State can help students inspect apartments for safety before they sign a lease, it can provide students with vital information on their rights as tenants, and it can mediate in landlord-tenant disputes. The problem is, many people don't know these services exist. The Consumer Relations Board is not listed in the university catalogue; it is not mentioned in any of the admissions literature. The only places it is mentioned are in alphabetically organized references such as the phone book, but you have to already know it exists to look it up! The Consumer Relations Board does receive money for advertising from the student senate, but it is only enough to run a little two-by-three-inch ad once every month. That is not large enough or frequent enough to be noticed by many who could use these services.

Anna appeals to the group identity of her listeners and assures them that there is power in numbers. She spells out what they should do. Her petition provides immediate action. She might have strengthened her appeal to "join the Off-Campus Association" if she had membership forms and a roster for her listeners to sign.

It's clear that we have a problem, but what may not seem so clear is what we can do about it. After all, what can one student do to change the practices of numerous Manhattan landlords? Nothing, if that student is alone. But just think of what we could accomplish if we got all 13,600 off-campus students involved in this issue! Think what we could accomplish if we got even a fraction of those students involved! This is what Wade Whitmer, director of the Consumer Relations Board, is attempting to do. He is reorganizing the Off-Campus Association in an effort to pass a city ordinance requiring landlords to have their apartments inspected for safety before those apartments can be rented out. The Manhattan code inspector has already tried to get just such an ordinance passed, but the only people who showed up at the public forums were known slumlords, who obviously weren't in favor of the proposed ordinance. No one showed up to argue in favor of the ordinance, so the city commissioners figured that no one wanted it and voted it down. If we can get the Off-Campus Association organized and involved, however, the commissioners will see that someone does want the ordinance, and they will be more likely to pass it the next time it is proposed. You can do a great service to your fellow students — and to yourself — by joining the Off-Campus Association.

A second thing you can do to help ensure that no more Kansas State students have to go through what I did is sign my petition asking the student senate to increase the Consumer Relations Board's advertising budget. Let's face it — a service cannot do anybody any good if no one knows about it. Consumer Relations Board's services are simply too valuable to let go to waste.

An important thing to remember about substandard housing is that it is not only distasteful, it is dangerous. In the end, I was lucky. I got out of my apart-

Anna concludes her speech with a true-life narrative to help assure that listeners will retain her message and integrate it into their belief systems. Her speech ends with a forceful appeal to action.

ment with little more than bad memories. My upstairs neighbor was not so lucky. The main problem with his apartment was that the electrical wiring was done improperly; there were too many outlets for too few circuits, so the fuses were always blowing. One day last November, Jack was at home when a fuse blew — as usual. And, as usual, he went to the fuse box to flip the switch back on. When he touched the switch, it delivered such a shock that it literally threw this guy the size of a football player backwards and down a flight of stairs. He lay there at the bottom, unable to move, for a full hour before his roommate came home and called an ambulance.

Jack was lucky. His back was not broken. But he did rip many of the muscles in his back. Now he has to go to physical therapy, and he is not expected to fully recover.

Kansas State students have been putting up with substandard living conditions for too long. It's time we finally got together to do something about this problem. Join the Off-Campus Association. Sign my petition. Let's send a message to these slumlords that we're not going to put up with this any more. We don't have to live in slums.

### Bibliography

Kansas State University. *K-State! Campus Living.*

Registrar's Office, Kansas State University. Personal interview. 10 Mar. 1989.

State of Kansas. Residential Landlord and Tenant Act, 1975.

Whitmer, Wade, director, Consumer Relations Board. Personal interview. 10 Mar. 1989.

*Speech is power:*
*Speech is to*
*persuade, to*
*convert, to compel.*
*—Ralph Waldo*
*Emerson*

# 14

# Evidence, Proof, and Argument

## This Chapter Will Help You

- use supporting materials as evidence in persuasive speeches.
- develop powerful proofs based on evidence.
- form arguments by selecting and combining proofs.
- recognize and avoid fallacies of evidence, proof, and argument.
- use evidence, proof, and argument to make persuasion effective.

Every four years we, the people of the United States of America, subject ourselves to a barrage of persuasive messages. From the first primaries in cold, blustery New Hampshire until the final vote is cast in sunny Hawaii, we are inundated by political rhetoric. 1992 may have been a banner year in terms of both the amount and variety of such persuasion. Three major contenders vied for the public's attention, creating intense media interest. While we still heard "sound bites" from traditional campaign speeches on the nightly news and watched the usual spate of spot commercials, new communication strategies and formats were the rule rather than the exception. Candidates appeared on television talk shows. Town meeting debates provided an opportunity for interactive communication. Thirty-minute "infomercials" attracted record audiences.

 hy do we expose ourselves to such a cacophony of persuasion? Why is it that we sometimes listen to speakers with whom we disagree? Why do we absorb facts and testimony that may contradict our previous attitudes? What moves us to integrate new convictions into our belief systems and adopt a change in outlook? In short, what is it that *drives* the process of persuasion discussed in Chapter 13?

To answer these questions, we must introduce three new terms: evidence, proof, and argument. **Evidence** consists of supporting materials as they are used in persuasion. **Proofs** use evidence to produce reasons for accepting a speaker's recommendations. Finally, **arguments** combine evidence and proofs into strategic patterns designed to persuade undecided or reluctant listeners and to reinforce the views of those who already support the speaker's position. Together, these elements form an integrated system—from the simplest piece of evidence to the most complex array of arguments—that drives the persuasive process and explains its power. In this chapter we discuss the nature of evidence, proof, and argument; show how they work together; explain how you can use them ethically and effectively; and demonstrate how to avoid some of the major mistakes that can rob persuasion of its power.

##  USING EVIDENCE EFFECTIVELY

In Chapter 6 we discussed the functions of supporting materials and the ways they could be used in all kinds of speeches. When supporting material is used in persuasive speaking, it becomes evidence to substantiate a claim. In this section we will examine the persuasive functions of evidence to supplement what you learned from Chapter 6.

Evidence is the most simple, most basic component of persuasion, yet it is absolutely vital. Consider a hypothetical situation. A speaker stands and says, "I want us all to sign up as organ donors." A listener responds, "Why?" The speaker replies, "Well, I just think we should. I'm entitled to my opinion." Now consider a different approach. Paul B. Fowler, a student at Alderson-Broaddus College, presented a speech urging his classmates to become organ donors. Instead of just voicing his personal opinion, Paul said:

> According to the *Transplant Organ Procurement Foundation Manual,* more than 25,000 kidney transplants have been performed since 1963. Pittsburgh surgeons alone transplant over 100 kidneys per year. However, only 25 percent of kidney patients can receive a kidney from a living family member. Most must wait for several years for an organ from a donor. In the Pittsburgh area alone, over 120 patients are waiting right now for a phone call telling them a kidney has become available. Nationwide, over 5,000 people are waiting.

The contrast is clear. The person listening to our hypothetical speaker might respond, "You are entitled to your opinion, but I am also entitled to ignore it." Paul Fowler's audience *had* to listen and take his message seriously, even if it did not agree with all his recommendations. The combination of facts and expert testimony lifted his message above personal opinion. His evidence added strength, authority, and objectivity to his speech. *Evidence, therefore, is the most basic ingredient in the persuasiveness of a speech.*

Because you are asking your listeners to take a risk when you present a persuasive speech, audiences will demand support for your assertions. As you do research, look for evidence that is relevant, recent, and derived from sources your audience will respect and accept.

To better understand the force of evidence, let us look briefly at each of the forms of supporting material identified in Chapter 6 and contrast the work they do in informative and persuasive speeches.

## Facts and Figures

In informative speeches, facts and figures illustrate and clarify points. In persuasion, facts and figures also help justify the conclusions and recommendations speakers ask listeners to accept. Facts and figures are especially important during the awareness phase of persuasion, when they prepare listeners for the conclusions that follow. Information is the foundation for the structure of persuasion; without it that structure will be shaky and may tumble when challenged by opposing speakers. Juli Pardell, arguing for more effective safety regulations in air travel, showed how a judicious use of facts and figures, interwoven with testimony and example, can lay the foundation for persuasion:

*Ethical and effective persuasion combines compelling evidence into a variety of proofs to support a position. This speaker has found a dramatic way to present statistical evidence as he encourages recycling at a town meeting.*

In order to fully comprehend the problem of congested skies, we can focus on a specific airport's situation. The Los Angeles airport deserves special attention. The *Christian Science Monitor* of October 29th this year contends that it "exemplifies the growing congestion that decreases safety margins." Thirty other airports lie within a ninety-mile radius of Los Angeles airport, creating a hubbub of planes in the sky. Within a forty-five-mile radius, 197 planes vie for space in the skies at any given moment. Overcongestion only enhances the chance for planes to crash, such as they did last October.

By the time Juli finished presenting these and other carefully documented facts and figures, her audience felt she was justified in recommending reforms in air safety regulation.

## *Examples*

In informative speeches, examples illustrate ideas and create human interest. In persuasive speeches, examples also may move listeners by exciting emotions such as sympathy, fear, or anger. Factual examples are especially useful. When you can say, "This really happened," you strengthen the power of the example. Hypothetical examples are less powerful because they did not actually occur. LaDell Patterson demonstrated the value of factual examples in a speech opposing discrimination against women in news organizations.

In her speech she cited the experiences of Laura Stepp, a reporter for the *Washington Post:*

> Ms. Stepp recalled an incident that happened to her. She said while a *Washington Post* lawyer was reading one of her stories, she commented that she hoped it would land on the front page because of its importance. His reply to her was, "All you have to do is shake your little fanny and they'll put it on the front page." When she objected, he said he had no idea that the remark was offensive.

This example, one of many in LaDell's speech, helped arouse the indignation of her listeners against such behavior and prepared them emotionally for the reforms she recommended.

### Narratives

In informative speeches, narratives illustrate the meaning of major points. In persuasive speeches, narratives help create a sense of reality and build identification between listeners and the speech subject. Narratives may also carry listeners to the scene of a problem and engage listeners in a living drama. Kirsten Lientz illustrated these functions when she opened her persuasive speech with the following narrative:

> It's a cold, icy December afternoon. You hear a distant crash, then screams, and finally the unending moan of a car horn fills the silence. You rush the short distance to the scene of the crash, where you find a Ford Bronco overturned with a young woman and two small boys inside. The woman and one of the boys climb from the wreckage unhurt; the other boy, however, is pinned between the dashboard and the roof of the car, unconscious and not breathing. Would you know what to do? Or would you stand there wishing you did? These events are real. Bob Flath saved this child with the skills he acquired at his company's first aid workshop.

After this dramatic narrative introduction, Kirsten's listeners were prepared to listen to her speech urging them to take the course in first aid offered at her university.

### Testimony

Testimony is even more critical in persuasive than in informative speaking. When you use testimony in a persuasive speech, you are calling upon witnesses to confirm your position. Introduce these witnesses carefully, describing their credentials. To support her call for air safety improvements, Juli Pardell cited eight authoritative sources of information. Paul Fowler in his plea for organ donors cited four reputable books. It was not just Juli and Paul speaking — it was all these sources of testimony together.

If the witnesses you cite testify against their self-interest, evidence is even more powerful. For example, if student reform leaders admit that the latest street demonstrations have gone too far or when government officials confirm that they have made mistakes, their statements provide strong evidence for opposing speakers to use.

In ethical persuasive speaking, you should rely mainly on expert testimony, using prestige and lay testimony as secondary sources of evidence. You can use prestige testimony to stress values you want listeners to embrace. You can use lay testimony to relate your subject to the lives of listeners and increase identification. Remember that when you quote others in your speeches, you are associating yourself with them — for better or for worse. Be careful with whom you associate!

Since all ethical persuasion must be grounded in evidence, select your supporting materials with special care. Do enough research to assure that you have responsible knowledge of your subject. Search out sources of information that represent different perspectives on the problem. Gather more materials than you think you will need so you can select the very best evidence to bolster your presentation. Be sure you have facts, figures, or expert

---

**SPEAKER'S NOTES**

### Guidelines for the Ethical Use of Evidence

1. Does my evidence come from credible sources that are free from bias?

2. Is my evidence relevant to the points I wish to make?

3. Would my evidence be verified by other expert sources?

4. Is my evidence complete? Has anything been purposely withheld?

5. Is my evidence the most recent available?

6. Have I adequately identified the sources of my evidence?

7. Has testimony been used properly — i.e., expert testimony to establish facts, prestige testimony to enhance general credibility, lay testimony to humanize a subject and create identification?

8. Are my "experts" qualified to speak on my subject?

9. Have I quoted or paraphrased testimony accurately?

10. Are my examples and narratives representative of the situation and not exceptions to the rule?

testimony for each of your main points. Use multiple sources and types of evidence to strengthen your case.

## PROVING YOUR POINTS

*Proofs are interpretations of evidence that provide listeners with reasons for accepting a speaker's recommendations.*[1] The work of proofs has been studied since the Golden Age of Greece. In his *Rhetoric* Aristotle suggested that there are three types of proofs: **logos,** which emphasizes rational evidence; **pathos,** which appeals to *personal* motives and emotions; and **ethos,** based on the perceived competence, character, and attractiveness of the speaker. In our time the work of many scholars points to a fourth major form of proof, **mythos.**[2] Appeals to mythos rely on the *social* traditions and values important to an audience and the narratives that have grown up around them.

A persuasive speech rarely relies on a single type of proof. Each kind of proof brings its own special strength to a speech, and the different kinds are often even stronger in combination. Figure 14.1 summarizes the relationships between forms of evidence and types of proof.

### Logos

Logos is very important to persuasion both ethically and practically. The primary work of logos is to prove that a situation is *real,* that it is not some fiction invented by the speaker. Therefore, logos calls upon facts, figures, and expert testimony to ground the problem in the world of reality. The second important task of logos is to show the audience what the facts *mean.* The speaker interprets the facts and reasons from them to a conclusion.

FIGURE 14.1
Basic Relationships
Between Evidence and
Proof

| Form of Evidence | Type of Proof |
| --- | --- |
| Facts and figures ⟷ (justify as well as clarify) | Logos (builds rational appeals) |
| Example ⟷ (moves as well as illustrates) | Pathos (builds emotional appeals) |
| Testimony ⟷ (witnesses as well as confirms) | Ethos (rests on credibility) |
| Narrative ⟷ (creates identification as well as interest) | Mythos (shows connection to culture and tradition) |

How does logos use evidence to develop reasons? To understand this, we must consider how all proofs are structured. As a general rule, proofs follow a simple basic pattern:

1. A *claim* (or assertion) is made that must be proved.
2. *Evidence* is provided to support the claim.
3. A *conclusion* is drawn that ties together the claim and evidence.

In a classroom speech on drinking and driving responsibly, Betty Nichols wanted to demonstrate that the sense of security people may feel in a car can be dangerous. To prove this claim, Betty presented these facts:

Drunk driving causes 24,000 deaths per year and 65,000 serious injuries.

Although this evidence is strong, she recognized that the facts alone might not be compelling enough to fully support the claim. She would have to interpret them for listeners. Therefore, she added a dramatic contrast to make these figures come to life:

Let's compare these numbers with the risk of being a homicide victim. We have a 1 in 150 chance of being murdered, but we have a 1 in 33 chance of being killed or crippled in an alcohol-related accident.

This evidence enabled her to come to this striking conclusion:

Therefore our car — which makes us feel so safe, so secure, so powerful — can become our assassin, our coffin.

Betty's example demonstrates how proof by logos can validate a speech. *The practical result is that the proof gives listeners a vivid sense of the reality behind the message.*

The use of logos demonstrates the speaker's faith in the audience's intelligence. It implies that if people are offered facts and shown how to interpret them, they will come to the proper conclusion.

## *Pathos*

Proof by pathos recognizes that we act on feelings as well as thoughts. People usually respond strongly when they feel angry, afraid, guilty, excited, or compassionate toward others. Ethically used, these proofs can help change attitudes or advance causes. Examples and narratives are the types of evidence most often used to establish proof by pathos.

When speakers tell personal stories, proof by pathos can be especially effective. Personal examples combine the power of pathos with the authenticity of ethos. During a recent congressional debate on hand gun control legislation, James Brady, the presidential press secretary who was shot during the assassination attempt on President Reagan, testified before the U.S. Senate Judiciary Subcommittee. Speaking from his wheelchair he said:

> There was a day when I walked the halls of this Senate and worked closely with many of you and your staffs. There was a wonderful day when I was fortunate enough to serve the President of the United States in a capacity I had dreamed of all my life. And for a time, I felt that people looked up to me. Today, I can tell you how hard it is to have people speaking down to me. But nothing has been harder than losing the independence and control we all so value in life. I need help getting out of bed, help taking a shower, and help getting dressed.
>
> There are some who oppose a simple seven-day waiting period for handgun purchases because it would inconvenience gun buyers. Well, I guess I am paying for their convenience. And I am one of the lucky ones. I survived being shot through the head. Other shooting victims are not as fortunate.[3]

Often, proof by pathos is the only way to convince people of the human dimensions of a problem or of the need for immediate action. Still, as powerful as emotional proofs may seem, they must be used with caution. If the appeal to feeling is too obvious, audiences may resent the speaker's manipulative intent. Appeals to negative emotions such as fear or guilt are especially tricky since they can boomerang, discrediting both the subject and speaker. If you use proof by pathos, be sure you can back up what you say with facts and figures. Bolster pathos with logos as you develop the proofs for your speech. In your presentation, let your voice and body language *understate* rather than overstate the emotional appeal. Don't engage in theatrics!

### *Ethos*

Proof by ethos assumes that listeners are persuaded by the credibility of message sources. As a speaker, you are one such source. The sources you cite are another.

In Chapter 2 we discussed ways to establish your personal ethos. Here we are concerned with the ethos of your sources of evidence. Listeners will also evaluate these sources in terms of their competence, integrity, likableness, and power. If the evaluation of your sources is positive, audiences will be more inclined to accept your arguments.

Appeals based on ethos are popular in advertising. When the credibility of Tylenol suffered after several product-tampering incidents, the company relied heavily on proof by ethos to overcome marketing problems. Its public relations people developed an aggressive advertising campaign that featured lay testimony, showing ordinary people "witnessing" that they trusted Tylenol. The company also introduced prestige and expert testimony stressing the use of Tylenol by doctors and in hospitals. Other advertisers rely on source attractiveness to sell their products.

How might proof by ethos work in your speeches? Let's look at how Heide Nord used such proof to persuade her listeners to change their attitudes about suntanning. To support the claim "We should avoid prolonged exposure to the sun," Heide emphasized expert testimony supplemented with lay testimony:

> The April 24, 1988, *Consumer Report* of the Food and Drug Administration tells us that "Prolonged exposure to sunlight without protection is responsible for about 90 percent of skin cancer." It describes the case of Wendell Scarberry, a skin cancer patient with over a hundred surgeries behind him. Wendell talks about the seriousness of the disease and urges that we be careful about sun exposure. "You can't cure skin cancer," he says, "by just having the doc whack it off." Finally, the American Cancer Society in its pamphlet *Fry Now Pay Later* says that skin cancer most often occurs among people who spend a lot of time in the sun, especially if they have been exposed in their teens or twenties. Well, that's where most of us are right now.

This combination of expert and lay testimony empowered Heide as she urged listeners to protect themselves from prolonged exposure to the sun.

Proofs based on the testimony of reliable, competent, and trustworthy sources are extremely important in persuasive speaking. Identify your sources and point out why they are qualified to speak on the subject. It is also helpful if you can say that their testimony is recent. For maximum effect, quote experts directly rather than paraphrasing them.

### Mythos

Mythos has emerged as an important source of proof in contemporary society. *Mythos* refers to the stories and sayings that illustrate the values, faith, and feelings that make up the social character of a people. Proof by mythos assumes that people value their membership in a society and share its cultural heritage. Martha Solomon, a communication scholar at the University of Maryland, has noted, "Rhetoric which incorporates mythical elements taps into rich cultural reservoirs."[4]

Proof by mythos often calls on patriotism, cultural pride, and heroes or enemies as evidence. In the United States we are raised on political narratives, such as those that stress the hardships of Washington's winter at Valley Forge or the triumphs of the suffragists who won women the right to vote. Such stories impress on us the meaning and value of political freedom. We may think of our country as "a frontier" or "the land of opportunity."[5] Proof by mythos also may be based on economic legends, such as the stories of

*The Western frontier is a major source of proof by mythos in American speeches. The frontier offered pioneers the opportunity to begin a new life and represents such values as freedom, individualism, initiative, and courage.*

success through hard work and thrift made popular by the Horatio Alger books of the late nineteenth century. The continuing power of the Horatio Alger myth was evident during President Clinton's preinaugural economic conference when delegate after delegate proclaimed a rise from humble beginnings. Proof by mythos may also be derived from religious narratives. Religious documents such as the Bible or the Koran provide a rich storehouse of parables, often used as proofs — not just in religious sermons but also in political discourse.[6]

Although the type of evidence most often used in proof by mythos is the narrative, stories need not be retold in their entirety each time they are invoked. Because they are so familiar, allusions to them may be sufficient. The culturetypes discussed in Chapter 10 are often called into service because they compress the myths into a few choice words that are easily recognized throughout the culture. In his speech accepting the Democratic presidential nomination in 1960, John F. Kennedy called on the myth of the American frontier to move Americans to action:

> The New Frontier of which I speak is not a set of promises — it is a set of challenges. It sums up not what I intend to offer the American people, but what I intend to ask of them.[7]

This proof by mythos emerged as a central theme of Kennedy's presidency. He didn't need to refer directly to the legends of Daniel Boone and Davy Crockett or to the tales of wagons pushing west to meet the dangers and challenges that lay ahead — he was able to conjure up those thoughts in listeners with the phrase "the New Frontier." Similarly, President Clinton's use of "the New Covenant" echoes both Kennedy's "New Frontier" and adds biblical connotations as well.

How can you use proof by mythos in a classroom speech? Let us look at how Robert Owens used mythos to urge stronger action against drug traffic in urban slums. In his classroom speech, presented during the spring of 1990, Robert wanted to establish the claim "We must win the battle against drugs on the streets of America." He supported this statement by creating a sense of outrage in listeners over the betrayal of the American dream in urban America:

> Read *Time* magazine of September 11, 1989, and you'll meet an America you never sang about in the songs we learned in school. It's an America in which hope, faith, and dreams are nothing but a bitter memory. They call America a land of hope, but it's hard to hope when your mother is a cocaine addict on Susquehanna Avenue in North Philadelphia. They call America a land of faith, but what faith can you cling to when even God seems to have abandoned the street corners to the junkies and the dealers! They call America a land of dreams, but what kind of dreams can you have when all you hear at night as you lie in bed are the curses and screams of the players in the deadly game.
>
> We might be able to redeem the hope, the faith, and the dream Americans like to talk about. But we're going to have to move in a hurry. President Bush said we've got to declare war on drugs, but we need to do more than declare war. We've got to *go* to war, and we've got to win! If we don't, the crack in the Liberty Bell may soon symbolize—not freedom—but a deadly drug that is destroying the American spirit all over this land.

These appeals to a betrayed mythos justified Robert's concluding plea for a broad-based, aggressive campaign to rid America of its drug culture. Such proof by mythos is powerful when you invoke traditions that are important to listeners and when the action you advocate seems consistent with cultural values. *The unique function of proof by mythos is to help listeners understand how the speaker's recommendations fit into the total belief and behavior patterns of the group.* This gives it a special role in terms of the persuasive process model we discussed in the last chapter. It can help integrate new attitudes and action into the group's culture.

Proof by mythos is similar to proof by pathos in that it is capable of both great good or considerable evil. At its best, mythos heightens our appreciation for our social identity and promotes consistency between community values and public policy. However, when misused, appeals to mythos can make it seem that there is only one *legitimate* culture. It can make us forget that the freedom we honor must encompass cultural pluralism and different lifestyles. The broth of American culture is rich with diverse flavors. The misuse of mythos could also justify action against those who do not conform to dominant group values. Had Robert Owens followed his attack on the drug culture with the conclusion that we ought to muzzle those who wish to see drugs legalized, he would have violated another important social value: freedom of speech. There is a delicate ecology among our social values — they live together in sometimes difficult and fragile harmony. Speakers may do grave damage by their careless use of proof by mythos.

## *Using Proofs in Combination*

Much of the art of persuasion lies in the way speakers combine proofs to make their points convincing. To combine forms of proof artfully, you must (1) determine which forms are most appropriate to your message, and (2) understand how these proofs can work together effectively.

To the extent that audience awareness and comprehension of a problem are uncertain, persuasion must begin with proof by logos. Thereafter, depending on what is crucial, the other forms of proof become important. If a problem calls for human understanding, proof by pathos with moving examples may be needed. If a situation is uncertain or confusing, proof by ethos, based on expert testimony, rises in importance. If traditions and values are relevant to a situation, proof by mythos becomes vital.

You should also consider how combining different forms of proofs can increase the persuasive power of a message. Although logos reassures listeners that they are dealing with a real, factual problem, pathos extends the human meaning of the facts. Ethos makes an audience more confident of a speaker's recommendations, and mythos can bridge the differences between people and even create a group spirit that will be receptive to a message. Using different forms of proofs in combination in a particular speech is usually superior to using one form alone.

**FORMING ARGUMENTS**

Can you imagine a world without argument? It would have to be a world in which everyone always agreed on attitudes, values, or proposed actions. All beliefs would have to be shared in common, and the voice of protest would never be heard. However desirable such a world might be (we happen to think it would be deadly dull!), it is certainly not the world in which we live. Our world is full of disagreement as different sides strive for control. Our world of argument also suggests, however, that listeners have the power to resolve conflict by favoring one side over the other. While it is undeniably noisy, the world of argument is also one in which disagreements can be solved by words rather than by force.

Although the word *argument* has many meanings, we shall define it as an arrangement of evidence and proofs designed to form a compelling case in support of a speaker's position. There are three major forms of argument: deductive, inductive, and analogical.

### Deductive Argument

**Deductive argument** begins with a generally accepted principle or belief ("We all believe in free speech"), then ties a specific issue to that principle to reach a conclusion ("We should allow George to speak"). Because it is based on widely shared principles, deductive argument is especially useful for establishing common ground with reluctant audiences. In such cases, deductive argument can point up inconsistencies between beliefs and behaviors, what we profess and what we practice. Because people like to be consistent and maintain the integrity of their values, deductive argument can be quite powerful in changing specific attitudes and behaviors.

Deductive argument follows a pattern that is either visible or implicit in a speech. This pattern, called a **syllogism,** includes a major premise, a minor premise, and a conclusion. The **major premise** is the generally accepted principle or belief on which the argument rests. Major premises represent the essence of what we have learned from the past. Collectively, they are the faith by which we live. For this reason, they may seem self-evident. For example, in an anti-abortion film, *The Silent Scream,* the narrator, Dr. Bernard Nathanson, says at one point, "Traditional medical ethics and precepts command us that we must not destroy our patients, that we are pledged to preserve their lives." Who would argue with such a seemingly innocent statement? It becomes the major premise of the deductive argument that develops in the film.

The **minor premise** of a syllogism focuses on the specific issue at hand and relates it to the major premise. The connection between major and minor premise is crucial to the success or failure of deductive argument. All the resources of persuasion will be mobilized to defend or destroy it, depending on one's side in a controversy. For example, the minor premise in *The Silent Scream* can be summarized as follows: "The fetus is a patient." The crucial connection rests on what the word *patient* represents. For if the fetus is a patient, then the fetus must also be a human being in the fullest possible sense. The humanness of the fetus was the major contested point in the controversy surrounding *The Silent Scream*. The film defends the human identity of the fetus with proof by pathos. Phrases such as "unborn child" build sympathy for the fetus. In his narration Dr. Nathanson asserts, "Beyond question the unborn child is simply another human being, another member of the human community, indistinguishable in every way from any of us." The film also uses proof by ethos, based on our respect for physicians and how their technical language can sometimes intimidate us. For example, Dr. Nathanson says that the humanity of the fetus is confirmed by "great new technologies, such as ultrasound imaging, electronic fetal heart monitoring, fetology, hysteroscopy, radio immunochemistry, and a host of other dazzling technologies which today constitutes in fact the corpus of the science of fetology."

Planned Parenthood, an organization that supports elective abortion as a last resort in family planning, responded to *The Silent Scream* in a PBS documentary, *The Abortion Battle*. Planned Parenthood presented a number of University of Washington Medical School staff physicians, among them several women. These speakers sought to undermine the credibility of *The Silent Scream* by pointing out alleged flaws and distortions in the proof structure of its arguments. Their strategy was to concentrate on the proofs and evidence that supported the connection between the major and minor premises. In effect, they wanted to show that the twelve-week-old fetus had not yet developed into a human. To do this, they countered proof by pathos with proof by logos, using charts to show the differences in brain development between the early fetus and the fully developed infant. They argued that there are no neural pathways in the fetal brain that can produce either the awareness of danger or the consciousness of pain claimed in *The Silent Scream*. They further argued that the pathos in the film was deceptive, suggesting that phrases like "the unborn child" were verbal tricks that did not *prove* the humanity of the fetus. The group also attacked Dr. Nathanson's ethos, contending that he was an irresponsible and unethical physician who misused semantic and cinematic techniques to support his position. Sophisticated technology, they said, could show us the two-inch fetus in the womb but could not answer the moral question of when human life actually begins.

Once the minor premise is established by evidence and proofs, and its connection to the major premise defended, a deductive argument carries through to its **conclusion.** If we accept the major and minor premises, the argument forces us to accept its conclusion. The conclusion tells us what to believe or do. *The Silent Scream* arrived at this conclusion: "Therefore, doctors should not perform abortions." The Planned Parenthood physicians rejected that conclusion. They charged that in the film's concern for the "second patient," it ignored the medical community's responsibility to its first patient, the woman. The film's effect, they argued, was to divert attention from what they saw as the "real" issue: the fate of living people whose lives are caught up in desperate situations.

***Using Deductive Argument.*** Deductive argument can have great impact on listeners and so offers a large opportunity to speakers. If deductive argument seems appropriate for your persuasive speech, take the following cautions into account:

1. *Be certain your audience will accept your major premise.* If you are not certain that listeners already agree with the value, belief, or principle of your major premise, you will have to use substantial evidence and a variety of proofs to document its validity. Only then can you proceed to build a deductive argument.

2. *Even if you believe the audience will accept your major premise, do not take it for granted.* Remind listeners *why* they believe as they do. Colorful examples, stirring prestige testimony, and exciting narratives may help bring that premise to life for your listeners.

3. *Once your major premise is established, concentrate on demonstrating the relationship between your major and minor premises.* Use evidence and proof to support that connection. Remember, both critical listeners and opponents will inspect this connection very carefully.

4. *Be certain your syllogism is free from logical errors and fallacies.* We discuss such flaws of argument in the final section of this chapter.

5. *Be sure that your conclusion offers a clear direction for your listeners.* Give them a definite action to take immediately in order to reinforce their acceptance and commitment.

## Inductive Argument

As we noted earlier, deductive argument works from general principles to particular issues. In contrast, **inductive argument** works from specific cases to general conclusions about them. Deductive reasoning is anchored in the experience and wisdom of the past as revealed in the major premise. Inductive reasoning keeps our focus on the present, on what is now as opposed to what has been. Inductive thinking begins with careful, responsible observations. For this reason, induction is the principal method of scientific investigation.

Although these two forms of argument may seem like opposites, they actually can work together to complete and correct each other. Inductive argument develops major premises that are verified rather than handed down as items of faith. The syllogisms based on premises drawn from induction may lead us to more reliable conclusions. Therefore, a combined inductive/deductive argument may provide the strongest form of reasoning.

There are two major advantages to inductive arguments. First, *they build a powerful sense of need by accumulating evidence and proofs until any reasonable listener could no longer deny the urgency of the situation.* Second, *because inductive arguments are based on factual observations, their conclusions seem authentic and reliable.*

Inductive argument is especially useful in problem-solution speeches. Paul Fowler emphasized this kind of argument in his student speech proposing a national organ transplant program. Paul first identified and examined three categories of acute need: kidney, heart, and liver transplants. In each category he presented an impressive array of facts and testimony from medical experts to depict the magnitude of the problem. From these particular observations Paul moved to the solution phase of his speech, which included his general conclusions and recommendations.

In inductive arguments, logos and ethos based on expert testimony are the most useful forms of proof. These proofs emphasize the factual aspects of problems. Although proof by pathos may be secondary in inductive arguments, it can add the human dimension to what observations reveal. Paul, for example, concluded his speech on organ donation with a moving story told by a mother whose son's suicide became a "gift of life" to others.

In addition to its usefulness in problem-solution designs, inductive argument also serves refutative and comparison and contrast designs to develop speeches of contention. Refutative speeches closely examine opposing, competing positions and criticize specific weaknesses in their evidence and proofs in order to minimize their appeal. Comparison and contrast persuasive speeches list specific strengths and weaknesses of contending positions before concluding that one is superior to the other. The usefulness of inductive argument is so widespread that it seems the very foundation of reasonableness in public discussions. Perhaps it is grounded in the common sense "show-me" and "seeing-is-believing" attitudes of healthy skepticism that many people carry with them when they listen to debate over public controversies.

Would inductive arguments work in your persuasive speech? That depends first on whether you possess responsible knowledge, whether your observations adequately justify the conclusions you draw from them. Have you read and observed enough? Are your observations recent and reliable? Are you objective enough to see the situation clearly? Are your observations representative of the situation, reflecting the usual rather than the unusual? Do you draw the right conclusions? Do you qualify the strength of your conclusions with words such as *possibly, probably,* or *certainly?* These are the kinds of questions that critical listeners will ask as they evaluate inductive arguments. Ask them first of yourself, and be a tough critic. Your argument should then withstand such scrutiny as it is actually presented.

### *Analogical Argument*

**Analogical argument** creates a special perspective on a subject by relating it to something similar. For example, in a speech urging the values of meditation, you could argue that it "is *like* athletic training — it takes hard work and discipline" or that "to meditate is to take flight, to see things that one could not see before." As these examples indicate, simile and metaphor can be especially useful in analogical thinking.

Analogical argument rises out of the need to focus an unfamiliar, abstract, or difficult subject by relating it to something that is familiar, concrete, and easily understood. But in persuasion, analogical argument emphasizes attitude more than understanding. For example, analogical argument can take the mystery out of threatening situations to encourage audience action ("He may look like a giant but we're going to cut him down to size"). Or analogical argument may associate one subject with another that already has strong positive or negative feelings attached to it, or associate a proposed plan with one that worked or didn't work.

For example, in the ongoing debate over our nation's drug policy, those who favor legalizing "recreational" drugs frequently base their arguments on an analogy to Prohibition.[8] They contend that the Prohibition amendment caused more problems than it solved in that it led to the rise of a criminal empire. They further suggest that our efforts to outlaw recreational drugs have had the same result. In developing their analogical argument, prolegalization forces claim it is impossible to ban a human desire—that to try to do so encourages contempt for the law. Moreover, they assert, legalizing drugs would help put the international drug dealers out of business just as the repeal of Prohibition helped bring about the downfall of the gangsters of the 1930s. Finally, they argue, if drug sales were legal it would be easier to control the quality of drugs, thus reducing the danger to users (parallel to the health problems associated with bootleg whiskey during Prohibition).

As this example shows, analogical argument emphasizes strategic points of comparison between similar situations. People on both sides of an issue will focus on these points, using evidence and proofs to defend or attack them. Opponents to legalizing drugs claim that there are many important differences between drugs and alcohol.[9] They say that alcohol is not as addictive for casual users as heroin or cocaine. They contend that legalization would multiply the drug problem, not reduce it. They further suggest that since many drug abusers are prone to violence, the cost to society would be increased. Moreover, they argue, the campaign against drugs can point to some success, whereas enforcement of the Prohibition laws was a disaster from the beginning. Thus, the public debate rages on, argument clashing with counterargument over these crucial points of comparison.

What makes an analogical argument work? This type of argument is similar to induction in that we seek insight through careful observation. Analogy differs from induction in that *our observations are concentrated on one simi-*

*lar situation* rather than ranging across many. This means that although analogical argument may seem more concrete and interesting than inductive argument, it also may be less reliable. Before you decide to use analogical argument, be certain that the important similarities between the situations outweigh the dissimilarities. To satisfy critical listeners and to disarm opposition, acknowledge major dissimilarities in your speech, but point out how they don't destroy the analogy. If you must strain to make the analogy fit, look for a new one or try a different form of argument.

## *The Importance of Defining Terms*

All the forms of argument we have covered depend on clear definitions of terms. Have you ever had a heated discussion with someone, and then discover you were not even talking about the same thing? Socrates suggested that all persuasive messages should start with definitions of terms, so that speakers and listeners can share understanding from the beginning. Opening definitions clarify what you mean, reveal your intentions, and show the audience how you perceive a subject. When the speaker and audience come from different backgrounds, careful definitions are even more important.

Many problems of definition are based more on fundamental disagreements than on simple misunderstanding. Should alcohol be defined as a

**SPEAKER'S NOTES**

### Developing Powerful Arguments

1. Base deductive arguments on an accepted truth, then lead your audience to the desired conclusion.

2. In deductive arguments, provide adequate proofs and evidence for the minor premise.

3. In inductive arguments, base your conclusions on representative observations.

4. In argument by analogy, create a strategic perspective on a subject by relating it to a similar situation.

5. Remember that argument by analogy may be less reliable than deductive or inductive argument.

6. Be sure to provide adequate definitions of basic terms to achieve clarity and force.

drug? Should the fetus be defined as a human being? Such questions often lead speakers to argue for *ethical* definitions. In the 1968 Memphis sanitation strike that lead to the assassination of Dr. Martin Luther King, Jr., the workers often marched carrying signs that read, "I Am a Man." This simple-looking statement was actually just the tip of an extensive underlying moral argument. The strikers, all of whom were African-American, were claiming that they were not treated like men, both in social and economic terms. As you develop your arguments, keep in mind that definitions can be the *fundamental issues at the heart of controversies.* Define key terms clearly, and support all controversial definitions with evidence and proof.

## AVOIDING DEFECTIVE PERSUASION

It takes hard work to prepare a persuasive speech — analyzing your audience, researching your topic, and planning your strategy. Do *not* ruin the effectiveness of this work or cause listeners to question your credibility by committing the errors in persuasion called **fallacies.** Such mistakes may crop up in the evidence you use, the proofs you develop, or the reasoning of your arguments. There are also fallacies particular to some of the specific designs discussed in the previous chapter. In this section we identify some of these major errors so that you are able to guard against them, as both a producer and consumer of persuasive messages.

### Defective Evidence

Evidence is defective if the speaker misuses facts, statistics, or testimony.

***Misuse of Fact.***   One major misuse of evidence involves the confusion of fact and opinion. A fact is verifiable information. An opinion is a personal interpretation of information: a statement of belief, feeling, attitude, or value. "The university enrolled 15,000 students last year" is a statement of fact. Anyone can look at the records and verify it. "The university is too stringent in its admission policy" is an opinion, a personal interpretation that may or may not be justified. Opinions can be useful in persuasive speeches, but treating an opinion as though it were a fact, or a fact as though it were an opinion, can be the source of many problems. It can make you seem to claim too much or too little and can raise real questions about your competence and ethics.

A second misuse of facts is the **slippery slope fallacy,** which assumes that once something happens it will establish an irreversible trend leading to disaster. During the Vietnam War, government officials who accepted the "domino theory" argued that if Vietnam fell to the Communists, all of Southeast Asia would soon be lost. The slippery slope fallacy often involves oversimplification and outlandish hyperbole. For example, a prominent religious leader recently suggested that feminism was "a socialist, anti-family political movement that encourages women to leave their husbands, kill their children, practice witchcraft, destroy capitalism and become lesbians."[10] In the slippery slope fallacy it is not logic that drives the prediction of events, but rather our darkest fears.

The **red herring** fallacy occurs when irrelevant material is injected into an argument to divert attention from the real issue. Usually the diverting material is sensational or emotional. In 1952 Richard Nixon, then candidate for vice president, spoke on national television to refute charges that he had used $18,000 of campaign contributions for personal expenses. In this speech Nixon diverted attention by talking about his dog Checkers, a gift he said he would not return because his children loved it. Nixon also related his entire financial life history in terms of what he owned and what he owed, matters at best vaguely related to the $18,000. He then launched a counterattack on the Democrats, accusing his opponent of having his wife on the payroll and suggesting that Adlai Stevenson, the Democratic presidential candidate, was "soft on communism." These techniques were red herrings because they diverted attention from what really happened to the $18,000.

***Statistical Fallacies.***　　Audiences are often intimidated by numbers. We've all been taught that "figures don't lie" without being advised that "liars figure." Speakers sometimes exploit our weakness by creating statistical deceptions. For example, consider the **myth of the mean,** or the "illusion of the average." If you've ever vacationed in the mountains, you are well aware that a stream may have an "average depth" of six inches, yet a person could drown in one of its deep pools. The Chamber of Commerce reports that the "average July temperature" in Memphis is eighty-five degrees, but this includes low nighttime as well as high daytime temperatures and omits the humidity factor. A speaker could tell you not to worry about poverty in Plattsville because the average income is well above the poverty level. Yet this average could be obtained because a few families are very wealthy, whereas the majority have incomes below the poverty level. Such "average-income" information creates an illusion of well-being that does not reflect reality. Averages are useful to summarize important statistical information, but be sure they do not hide the reality of a situation.

Another statistical fallacy is the use of **incomparable percentages.** It is misleading to compare percentages *when the bases of comparison are unequal*. We once heard a speaker argue, "The gross national product of the United States is growing at an annual rate of only 6 percent, while that of the Soviet Union is growing at a rate of 14 percent. Therefore, the Soviets are rapidly overtaking us." The speaker had fallen prey to misinterpretation: a 6 percent rise in the American GNP represented more actual economic growth than a 14 percent rise in the Soviet GNP: 6 percent of $500 billion is greater than 14 percent of $200 billion. It was not the Americans who were losing ground! Figure 14.2 illustrates these defective uses of facts and figures.

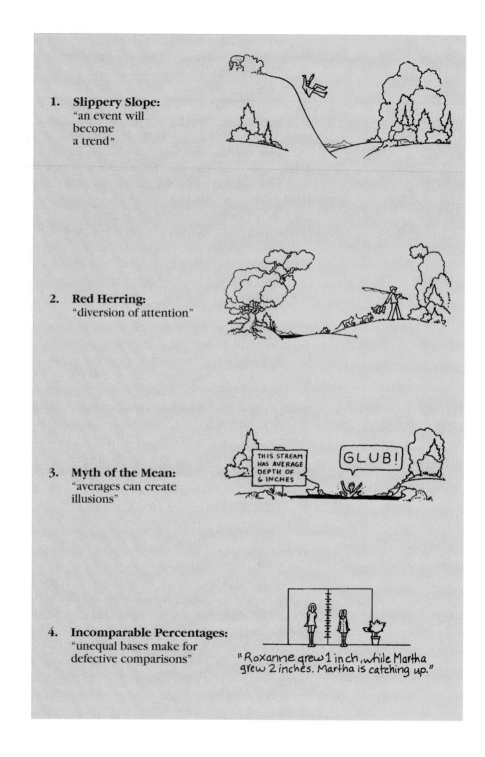

FIGURE 14.2
Examples of Defective
Evidence

***Defective Testimony.*** Testimony can be misused in many different ways. Speakers may omit when a statement was made to hide the fact that testimony is outdated. Speakers may deceive us when they leave out important facts about their experts, intimidating us instead with titles such as *"Dr. Michael Jones reported that smoking does not harm health."* What the speaker *didn't* reveal was that Dr. Jones was a marketing professor who was writing public relations material for the Tobacco Growers Association. Speakers also abuse testimony when they cite words out of context that are not representative of a person's position. As we noted in Chapter 6, prestige and lay testimony can be misused if they replace expert opinion when facts must be established. Finally, the "voice of the people" can be easily misrepresented, depending on *which* people you choose to quote.

***Inappropriate Evidence.*** Other abuses occur when speakers deliberately use one form of evidence when they should be using another. For example, you might use facts and figures when examples would bring us closer to the human truth of a situation. Welfare statistics are sometimes misused in this way. It is as though the speaker preferred to talk about poverty in the abstract, distancing listeners from its concrete reality. On the other hand, speakers may give examples to arouse emotions when what is needed is the dispassionate picture of a situation established by facts and figures. Testimony is abused when it is intended to compensate for weak or inadequate facts. Narratives may also be used inappropriately. Calling someone a "Robin Hood who steals from the rich to give to the poor" has been used to justify more than one crime.

## Defective Proofs

Any form of proof can be defective. We have already pointed out, for example, the danger of overreliance on proof by pathos, when the appeal to feelings overwhelms good judgment and clouds the perception of issues. A related problem comes when speakers get so caught up with the brilliance of their own performance, so intoxicated by their own verbosity, that the focus of the speech shifts to them rather than to serious problems in the world that call for reform. Speakers might also misuse proof by mythos to promote intolerance and work against individualism ("When are Native Americans going to start being good Americans?").

Similarly, speakers misuse proof by ethos when they commit the fallacy of **argument ad hominem** (person-centered rather than issue-centered argument). Such persuaders try to discredit a position by calling the opposition derogatory names. For example, during a recent environmental dispute, one side charged that its opponents were "little old ladies in tennis shoes" and "outside agitators." Not to be outdone, the other side labeled their antagonists as "rapists of public parkland."[11] Proof by ethos also can be abused when speakers overuse it—when they try to intimidate listeners by citing an overwhelming number of authorities while neglecting to present information or good reasons for accepting their claims. Avoid such practices in your own persuasive efforts.

Finally, speakers neglect their responsibility to prove their points when they merely assert what they have not proved, thereby committing the fallacy of **begging the question.** Those who "beg the question" usually rely on colorful language to disguise the inadequacy of their proofs, so that the words themselves *seem* to establish the conclusion. Some antiabortion advocates may be guilty of this practice when they refer to the fetus as the "unborn child" without bothering to address first the difficult moral question of when human life actually begins.

### *Defective Arguments*

Major fallacies may infest all forms of argument. It is unethical to commit them purposely, irresponsible to commit them accidently. In your role as critical listener, you should be on guard against them at all times.

***Errors of Deduction.*** Because deductive reasoning builds on the major premise, an argument can only be as good as the premise is sound. Therefore, you should carefully consider each word in the major premise as you plan an argument. If the major premise of a syllogism suffers from **categorical imprecision,** or vagueness in its key terms, the entire argument could crumble. We once heard a student begin with the premise "college athletes don't really want to learn." She was instantly in trouble. When her speech was over, the class assailed her with questions. How did she define *athletes?* Was she talking about intercollegiate or intramural athletes? How about the tennis team? How did she define learning? Had she taken into account comparative grade-point averages? Was she aware of the negative stereotype at the center of her premise? It's safe to say that the speaker did not persuade too many people that day. To avoid such a fiasco, be sure that you know what you mean by each word in your major premise and that you can defend what each word claims.

The **confusion of probability and certainty** is another error common to deductive argument. Suppose a friend from the Tau Beta fraternity calls you to set up a blind date. If the premise "Tau Betas are handsome" holds about 90 percent of the time and if you are about 90 percent certain that your blind date is a Tau Beta, then your assumption that your date will be attractive must be qualified by two factors of uncertainty. There is a 10 percent chance that your date is not a Tau Beta, and even if he is, there is another 10 percent chance he is not one of the handsome ones. If you assert probabilities as though they were certainties, you are guilty of a reasoning error. It is better to use qualifiers that point out the uncertainty: "There is a *good chance* that my date will be handsome." If you point out the uncertainty in advance, you may not lose the audience's trust if a prediction does not come true.

Another error common in deductive argument is the **post hoc ergo propter hoc fallacy,** or reasoning that if something happens after an event, it was therefore caused by the event. This fallacy confuses association with causation and is the basis of many superstitious beliefs. The same people who wear their lucky boots and shirts to ball games may also argue that we should have a tax cut because the last time we had one we avoided war, increased employment, or reduced crime. A speaker always must demonstrate that events are causally connected, not just make the assumption.

Finally, a **non sequitur fallacy** occurs when the minor premise is not related to the major premise, when the conclusion does not necessarily follow from the relationship between premises, or when the evidence presented is irrelevant. For example, if from the major premise "Tau Betas are handsome" and the minor premise "John is a Tau Beta" one drew the conclusion "Therefore, we should go to a drive-in movie," this would be a non sequitur. The premises would not justify that particular conclusion.

In 1989 Joe Foss, the president of the National Rifle Association, argued against pending gun control legislation to the National Press Club in Washington, D.C. See if you can identify the non sequiturs and other fallacies in this excerpt from the speech:

> You see, back when the country was founded — if you look back that far into history you'll find that they needed guns. And they defeated an outfit that was trying to disarm them. And, as a result of our having guns and being able to use them, we won. That was the start of the United States of America. We won a war. And of course, ever since that time we've been involved, and there've been people that would like to take us over. If you've read Marx and Lenin you know that one of their great ambitions is to disarm a nation. And so here you have a reason to be armed: to see to it that no one is going to disarm us, even in today's world. . . .[12]

***Errors of Induction.*** A common error in inductive reasoning is a **hasty generalization,** which may be based on insufficient or nonrepresentative observations. Suppose you announced: "Eighty percent of our students are in favor of abolishing the foreign language requirement." To determine whether this claim is justified, we would have to consider the supporting evidence: how extensive it is and how it was obtained. If you questioned ten students on the way to class, we might challenge the adequacy of your sample. If you surveyed only freshman business majors (who may not be required to take a foreign language), we would question the representativeness of your sample. Even when and where you collected your supporting data could create a problem. If you surveyed students outside the "drop" office on the last day for dropping and adding classes, your results could well differ from what you might obtain in the language department lounge early in the semester.

Another type of inductive error involves **contamination of the conclusion** by the inclusion of emotionally loaded words. For example, suppose you concluded, "Eighty percent of the *immature* students on campus favor abolishing the foreign language requirement." Do you mean that all students on the campus are immature? Does the claim cover all students or *only* the immature ones? Are you implying that "mature" students have a different opinion? Are you suggesting that being against the foreign language requirement is a sign of immaturity? The intrusion of just one ill-considered word can ruin an entire argument. When such words tap into the mythos of the audience without adequate justification or preparation, the problem can be compounded. A conclusion such as "Be *patriotic!* Support the *American way of life!* Speak out against gun control!" might illustrate such abuse.

*Defective Analogy.* A final type of flaw that can ruin an argument is a **faulty analogy,** which occurs when things are compared that are dissimilar in some important way. When the points of dissimilarity outweigh the similarities, an analogy is in trouble. For example, assume that you have transferred from a college with 1,500 students to a university with 15,000 students. You present a speech proposing new campus security measures, arguing that because they worked well at the college they should also help the university. Would such an analogical argument be valid? That would depend on similarities and dissimilarities between the two schools. Is the size difference important? Are the crime problems similar? Is one located in an urban, the other in a rural, setting? Are the students from the same social and economic backgrounds? Dissimilarity on any of these points could raise doubts about the analogy. You would have to overcome these doubts with evidence for the analogy to be convincing.

### Fallacies Related to Particular Designs

In addition to fallacies of evidence, proof, and argument, there are at least two major fallacies related to particular persuasive designs. **Either-or thinking** may crop up in problem-solution speeches if a speaker tells listeners they have only two options—one desirable, the other not. "Give me liberty, or give me death!" — though a dramatic statement of American mythos — illustrates this kind of fallacy. In either-or thinking, the speaker blinds listeners to other options, such as compromise or creative alternatives not yet considered. Perhaps there *are* only two options for listeners, but as speaker you have a special obligation to investigate a problem thoroughly before you decide this. After all, you assume responsibility for the fate of listeners when you advise them how to behave.

The **straw man fallacy** is most often found in speeches of contention. This fallacy consists of understating or distorting the position of opponents to simplify refutation. Extreme controversies seem to invite this kind of fallacy. In the abortion debate, cries of "women-haters" and "baby-killers" sometimes rise from the contending positions. As a persuasive speaker, you have an obligation to represent an opposing position fairly and fully as you refute it. Only then will your audience respect you and your arguments. The straw man fallacy is an implicit admission of weakness or desperation and can damage what may well be a legitimate case.

Persuasion is constantly threatened by flaws and deception. In a world of competing views, we often see human nature revealed in its petty as well as its finer moments. As you plan and present your arguments or listen to the arguments of others, be on guard against fallacies.

**IN SUMMARY**     Persuasion relies on an integrated system of evidence, proof, and argument for its effectiveness.

*Using Evidence Effectively.*    *Evidence* is supporting material used in persuasion. Facts and figures justify the interpretations a speaker offers of a problem situation. Examples move listeners, creating a favorable emotional atmosphere for the speaker's recommendations. Narratives bring a sense of reality, and help listeners identify with the issue. Testimony calls upon witnesses to support the speaker's position. When you use evidence, strive for recent facts and figures, emphasize factual examples, engage listeners through stories that make your point, and rely primarily on expert testimony.

*Proving Your Points.*    *Proofs* are interpretations of evidence that provide listeners with good reasons for accepting the speaker's recommendations. The forms of proof are logos, pathos, ethos, and mythos. *Logos* emphasizes rational appeals based upon facts and figures. *Pathos* stirs feelings through the use of examples. *Ethos* makes persuasion credible when the speaker cites effective testimony. *Mythos* relates a subject to the culture and tradition of a group through its narratives. Proofs are often stronger when used in combination.

*Forming Arguments.*    An *argument* arranges proofs and evidence into a compelling case in support of the speaker's position. Arguments may be based on deductive, inductive, and analogical patterns of reasoning. *Deductive argument* develops around a *syllogism,* which includes a *major premise, minor premise,* and *conclusion.* The major premise is a generally accepted principle or belief on which the argument rests. The minor premise focuses on the specific issue at hand and connects it with the major premise. The conclusion, drawn from the relationship between major and minor premises, tells us what to believe or do. *Inductive argument* works from specific cases to general conclusions about them, and prizes careful, disciplined observation as the basis of all responsible thinking. *Analogical argument* creates a special perspective on a subject by relating it to something similar. Such argument centers on specific points of comparison. All three forms of argument depend on clear, persuasive definitions for their effectiveness.

*Avoiding Defective Persuasion.*   Fallacies are common in persuasion. Even when unintentional, they can ruin the effectiveness of a speech and damage the credibility of a speaker. If they seem deliberate, they raise doubts about the speaker's ethics. Evidence can be defective when the speaker misuses facts, statistics, and testimony. Common errors include the confusion of fact with opinion; the *slippery slope fallacy,* which assumes that a single instance will establish a trend; and the *red herring,* the use of irrelevant material to divert attention. Statistical fallacies include the *myth of the mean,* in which averages create illusions that hide reality, and *incomparable percentages,* which attempt comparisons when the bases of the comparisons are unequal. Evidence can also be used inappropriately, featuring facts and figures when the situation calls for examples, examples when the audience needs facts and figures, testimony to hide the weakness of information, or narratives to justify unethical behavior.

Among all the problems that can plague proofs, those surrounding proof by ethos seem especially troubling. Proof by ethos is defective when it depends on a negative stereotype to discredit an opposing position. Likewise, *argument ad hominem,* or name calling, can divert attention from the issues to those who present them. In such cases disgusted audiences may decide not to trust *any* persuasive efforts in the situation.

Fallacies are common in all forms of argument. *Categorical imprecision* occurs in deductive reasoning when the wording of the major premise has not been carefully considered. Another error occurs when probability is passed off as certainty. The *post hoc ergo propter hoc fallacy* confuses association with causation. It can lead speakers to assert that one thing causes another when actually it only comes before it in time. A *non sequitur* fallacy occurs when irrelevant conclusions or evidence are introduced into argument. Inductive reasoning can suffer from a *hasty generalization* drawn from insufficient or nonrepresentative observations. *Contamination of the conclusion* occurs when emotional, power-packed words intrude into a claim without adequate preparation or justification. Argument by analogy is defective when important dissimilarities outweigh similarities.

*Either-or thinking* can be a special problem in speeches calling for action. This fallacy reduces audience options to only two, one advocated by the speaker, the other undesirable. When speeches of contention understate, distort, or misrepresent an opposing position for the sake of easy refutation, they commit the *straw man fallacy.*

**TERMS TO KNOW**

evidence

proofs

argument

logos

pathos

ethos

mythos

deductive argument

syllogism

major premise

minor premise

conclusion

inductive argument

analogical argument

fallacy

slippery slope fallacy

red herring

myth of the mean

incomparable percentages

argument ad hominem

begging the question

categorical imprecision

confusion of probability and certainty

post hoc ergo propter hoc fallacy

non sequitur fallacy

hasty generalization

contamination of the conclusion

faulty analogy

either-or thinking

straw man fallacy

**DISCUSSION**

1. Find examples of effective and ineffective uses of testimony in the student speeches in Appendix B. Are the sources carefully documented? Are expert, prestige, and lay forms of testimony used appropriately? How might these have been used more effectively?

2. Bring to class examples of advertisements that demonstrate the four basic types of persuasive proof: logos, pathos, ethos, and mythos. Discuss the ways in which these proofs are used and why you think they are or are not effective.

3. Look for examples of the misuse of evidence, proof, and argument in newspaper and magazine advertising. In your judgment, do these misuses reflect badly on the credibility of the product? Do the ads seem effective nonetheless?

4. Look for examples of defective persuasion in the letters-to-the-editor section of your local newspaper. Bring them to class for discussion.

**APPLICATION**

1. Find a news story that interests you. Taking the information provided, (1) show how you might use this information as evidence in a persuasive speech, (2) structure a proof that would make use of this evidence, and (3) design an argument in which this proof might be functional.

2. In *The Ethics of Rhetoric,* Richard Weaver observed that frequent arguments over the definitions of basic terms in the major premises of

syllogisms are a sign of division within a social group. Look for examples of public argument over the definition of one of the following terms:

    a. community-based schooling
    b. new world order
    c. tax fairness
    d. abortion
    e. gun control
    f. alternative lifestyles
    g. political correctness

Do the arguments reflect the kind of social division Weaver suggested?

3. For your next persuasive speech, consider how you might emphasize deductive argument. Then revise your strategy so that you place the emphasis on inductive argument. Consider finally how you might focus instead on an analogical argument. Which of these approaches seems most promising and why?

**NOTES**

1. Walter R. Fisher, "Toward a Logic of Good Reasons," *Quarterly Journal of Speech* 64 (1978): 376–84; Karl R. Wallace, "The Substance of Rhetoric: Good Reasons," *Quarterly Journal of Speech* 49 (1963): 239–249.

2. Representative of this scholarship is Ernest G. Bormann, "Fantasy and Rhetorical Vision: The Rhetorical Criticism of Social Reality," *Quarterly Journal of Speech* 58 (1972): 396–407; Walter R. Fisher, "Narration as a Human Communication Paradigm: The Case of Public Moral Argument," *Communication Monographs* 59 (1984): 1–22; Michael C. McGee, "In Search of 'The People': A Rhetorical Alternative," *Quarterly Journal of Speech* 61 (1975): 235–249; Michael Osborn, "Rhetorical Depiction," in *Form, Genre, and the Study of Political Discourse,* ed. Herbert W. Simons and Aram A. Aghazarian (Columbia: University of South Carolina Press, 1986), pp. 79–107; Janice Hocker Rushing, "The Rhetoric of the American Western Myth," *Communication Monographs* 50 (1983): 14–32.

3. From a brochure distributed by Handgun Control, Inc., 1225 Eye Street NW, Washington, DC 20005, 1990.

4. Martha Solomon, "The 'Positive Woman's' Journey: A Mythic Analysis of the Rhetoric of STOP ERA," *Quarterly Journal of Speech* 65 (1979): 262–274.

5. Rushing, 14–32.

6. Roderick P. Hart, *The Political Pulpit* (West Lafayette, Ind.: Purdue University Press, 1977).

7. John Fitzgerald Kennedy, "Acceptance Address, 1960," in *The Great Society: A Sourcebook of Speeches,* ed. Glenn R. Capp (Belmont, Calif.: Dickenson Publishing Company, Inc., 1969), p. 14.

8. Lisa M. Ross, "Buckley Says Drug Attack Won't Work," *Commercial Appeal* (Memphis, Tenn.), 14 Sept. 1989, p. B-2.

9. Mortimer B. Zuckerman, "The Enemy Within," *U.S. News & World Report,* 11 Sept. 1989, p. 91.
10. Gilbert Cranberg, "Even Sensible Iowa Bows to the Religious Right," *Los Angeles Times,* 17 Aug. 1992, p. B-5.
11. Michael M. Osborn, "The Abuses of Argument," *Southern Speech Communication Journal* 49 (1983), 1–11.
12. Joe Foss, "The Right to Bear Arms," speech presented to the National Press Club, Washington, D.C., 14 Mar. 1989. (C-Span transcript of the telecast of the speech).

*[People] who celebrate . . . are fused with each other and fused with all things in nature.*

*—Ernst Cassirer*

# 15

# Ceremonial Speaking

## This Chapter Will Help You

- appreciate the importance of ceremonial speaking.
- use the techniques of identification and magnification in ceremonial speeches.
- understand the purposes and procedures for speeches of tribute, acceptance, introduction, and inspiration.
- prepare a toast or an after-dinner speech.

Your college has just reached a great moment in its history. An ambitious fund-raising campaign to create scholarships and attract outstanding teachers, researchers, artists, and lecturers has successfully concluded. As the leader of student volunteers who spent many hours telephoning for contributions, you are invited to be master of ceremonies at a banquet celebrating the campaign. In this capacity you are likely to both give and hear many kinds of speeches: speeches of tribute, speeches accepting awards, speeches of introduction, speeches of inspiration, and after-dinner speeches. During the evening there will be moments both of seriousness and of hilarity. They are all part of what we call ceremonial speaking.

t is easy to underestimate the importance of ceremonial speaking. After all, informative speaking shares knowledge, and persuasive speaking affects our attitudes and actions. In comparison, ceremonial speaking, with its occasional moments of humor or inspiration, may not seem that significant.

Only when we look beneath the surface does the true importance of ceremonial speaking appear. **Ceremonial speaking** stresses the sharing of identities and values that unites people into communities. The philosopher John Dewey observed that people "live in a community in virtue of the things which they have in common; and communication is the way in which they come to possess things in common. What they must have in common . . . are aims, beliefs, aspirations, knowledge—a common understanding. . . ."[1] It is ceremonial speaking that celebrates and reinforces our common aims, beliefs, and aspirations.

Ritual and ceremony are important to all groups because they draw people together.[2] Ceremonial speaking imprints the meaning of a community on its members by providing larger-than-life pictures of their identity and ideals.[3] It answers four basic questions: "Who are we?" "Why are we?" "What have we accomplished?" and "What can we become together?" As it answers these questions, ceremonial speaking provides people with a sense of purpose and helps create an "ordered, meaningful cultural world."[4]

There is also a very practical purpose served by ceremonial speaking. As our opening example indicates, ceremonies put the spotlight on the speaker. As you conduct the college's celebration of its fund-raising campaign as master of ceremonies, others will be looking at you and thinking, "Wouldn't she make a good student body president?" or "Wouldn't he be a fine candidate for city council?" From the time of Aristotle, scholars have recognized that ceremonial speaking puts leadership on display.

Ceremonial speeches also serve to establish standards for action or provide the ethical and moral basis for future arguments.[5] Because such speaking centers on the values and beliefs within the traditions of a community, it contributes to the integration phase of persuasion described in Chapter 13. In this chapter we discuss the techniques and major forms of ceremonial speaking.

# TECHNIQUES OF CEREMONIAL SPEAKING

Many of the techniques of ceremonial speaking are simply variations on those we have already discussed. Two techniques, however, are basic to all forms of ceremonial speaking and deserve special attention: identification and magnification.

## *Identification*

We have already defined **identification** as the creation of close feelings among the members of the audience and between the audience and the speaker. Because the function of ritual and ceremony is to draw people closer together, identification is the heart of ceremonial speaking. Without it, ceremonial speaking cannot achieve its desired effects. Speakers may promote identification through the use of narratives, through the recognition of heroes, or through a renewal of group commitment.

***Use of Narrative.*** Ceremonial speaking is the time for reliving shared golden moments. For example, if you were preparing a speech for the fund-raising celebration, you could recall certain things that happened during those long evenings when student volunteers were making their calls. You might remember moments of discouragement, followed by other moments of triumph, when the contributions were especially large or meaningful. Your story would reflect the meaning of the celebration and would be a tribute both to donors and to the student volunteers who endured frustration and discouragement on their way to success.

***Recognition of Heroes.*** As you speak of the trials and triumphs of fund raising, you may want to single out those who made outstanding contributions, but be careful! If hard work was performed by many, you run the risk of leaving out someone who deserves recognition. This omission could create resentment, a divisive feeling that defeats identification. Therefore, *recognize specific individuals only when they have made truly unusual contributions or when they are representative.* You might say, for instance, "Let me tell you about Mary Tyrer. She is just one of the many who for the last two months have spent night after night on these phones — talking, coaxing, winning friends for our school, and raising thousands of dollars in contributions. Mary, and all the others like you, we salute you!"

***Renewal of Group Commitment.*** Ceremonial speaking is a time both for celebrating accomplishments and for renewing commitment. Share with your listeners a vision of what the future can be like for your college if their commitment continues. Plead with them not to be satisfied with present accomplishments. Renew their identity as an action group moving toward even greater goals. Now is *not* the time to present specific new programs and challenges — after all, there is a time for relaxation and celebration as well as a time for action. But you should at least leave listeners thinking about the brighter future they are shaping.

In his first inaugural address, delivered on the eve of the Civil War, Abraham Lincoln used the technique of identification in an effort to reunite the nation.

> I am loth to close. We are not enemies, but friends. We must not be enemies. Though passion may have strained, it must not break our bonds of affection. The mystic chords of memory, stretching from every battle-field, and patriot grave, to every living heart and hearthstone, all over this broad land, will yet swell the chorus of the Union, when again touched, as surely they will be, by the better angels of our nature.[6]

## Magnification

In the *Rhetoric* Aristotle noted that by selecting certain features of a person or event and dwelling on them, we can magnify them until they fill the minds of listeners and seem to characterize the subject. This technique is called **magnification,** and its effect is to emphasize certain values the selected features represent. For example, imagine that you are preparing a speech honoring Jesse Owens's incredible track and field accomplishments in the 1936 Olympic Games. In your research you come up with a variety of facts, such as:

- He had a headache the day he won the medal in the long jump.
- He had suffered from racism in America.
- He did not like the food served at the Olympic training camp.
- He won his four gold medals in front of Adolf Hitler, who was preaching the racial superiority of Germans.
- Some of his friends did not want him to run for the United States.
- After his victories he returned to further discrimination in America.

If you used all this information, your speech might seem aimless. Which of these items should you magnify, and how should you proceed? To make your selection among the data you have collected, you need to know what themes are best to develop when you are magnifying the actions of a person. These themes include the following:

1. The person must seem to overcome great obstacles.
2. The accomplishment must be unusual.
3. The performance must be superior.
4. The person's motives must be pure, not selfish.
5. The accomplishment must benefit society.

As you consider these themes and your purpose, it becomes clear which of the items concerning Jesse Owens you should magnify and how you should go about it. To begin, you would stress that Owens *had to overcome obstacles* such as racism in America to make the Olympic team. Then you would point out that his *accomplishment was unusual,* that no one else had ever won four gold medals in Olympic track and field competition. Moreover, *the performance was superior,* resulting in world records that lasted many years. Because Owens received no material gain from his victories, *his motives were pure,* his performance driven solely by personal qualities such as courage, competitiveness, and determination. Finally, you would demonstrate that because his victories repudiated Hitler's racist ideology, causing the Nazi leader public humiliation, *Owens's accomplishments benefited our society.* The overall effect would be to magnify the meaning of Jesse Owens's great performances both for himself and for his nation.

In addition to these basic themes, magnification also uses certain tools of language to create dramatic word pictures. *Metaphor* and *simile* can magnify a subject through creative associations, such as, "He was a whirlwind, roaring down the track in search of world records." *Anaphora* can also help magnify a subject by repeating key words in a certain order, until these words become representative of the subject. If you were to say of Mother Teresa, "Whenever there was hurt, she was there. Whenever there was hunger, she was there. Whenever there was human need, she was there," you would be magnifying her dedication and selflessness. This technique should make those qualities seem to resonate in the minds of listeners.

Magnification often favors certain speech designs over others. Comparison and contrast designs promote magnification by making selected features stand out. For example, you might contrast the purity of Owens's motives with those of today's well-paid athletes. Historical designs enhance magnification by dramatizing certain events as stories unfold over time. The causation design serves magnification when the selected features are emphasized as the powerful causes of certain effects: Jesse Owens's victories, a speaker might say, *caused* Nazi propaganda to lose its appeal for many people.

Whatever designs ceremonial speeches use, it is important that *they build in effect until they conclude.* Speakers should save their best stories, their most telling points, until the end of the speech. Ceremonial speeches must never dwindle to a conclusion.

## TYPES OF CEREMONIAL SPEECHES

Ceremonial speeches include the speech of tribute (including the eulogy and the toast), acceptance speeches, the speech of introduction, the speech of inspiration, and the after-dinner speech.

### *The Speech of Tribute*

If you had developed a speech honoring Jesse Owens's Olympic victories, you would have prepared a **speech of tribute.** The speech of tribute, which may center on a person or on events, recognizes and celebrates accomplishments.

For example, you might be called on to honor a former teacher at a retirement ceremony.

Accomplishments and events are usually celebrated for two basic reasons. First, they are important in themselves: the influence of the teacher may have contributed to the success of many of her former students. Second, they are important as symbols. The planting of the American flag at Iwo Jima during some of the most intense fighting of World War II came to symbolize the fortitude of the entire American war effort; it represented commitment and was more important as a symbol than as an actual event. Sometimes the same event may be celebrated for both actual and symbolic reasons. A speech honoring the raising of $60 million for African famine relief would celebrate both aspects. This achievement was important in itself because it helped feed many starving people; it was also a symbol of global generosity. When you plan a speech of tribute, you should consider both the actual and the symbolic values that are represented.

***Developing Speeches of Tribute.*** As you prepare a speech of tribute, there are several guidelines that you should keep in mind. First, do not exaggerate the tribute so that it becomes unbelievable. If you are too lavish with your praise or use too many superlatives, you may embarrass the recipient. Second, focus on the honoree rather than yourself. Even if you know what effort the accomplishment required because you have done something similar, don't mention that at this time. It will just seem as though you are praising yourself when the focus should be on the honoree. Third, create vivid, concrete images of accomplishments. Speeches of tribute are occasions for illustrating what someone has accomplished, the values underlying those accomplishments, and their consequences. Tell stories that make those accomplishments come to life. Finally, be sincere. Speeches of tribute are a time for warmth, pride, and appreciation. Your manner should reflect these qualities as you present the tribute.

***The Eulogy: An Illustration.*** Earlier we asked you to imagine yourself preparing a speech to honor Jesse Owens. Following his death in 1980, many such speeches were actually presented. A speech of tribute presented upon the death of a person is called a **eulogy.** The following comments by Congressman Thomas P. O'Neill, Jr., then Speaker of the House, illustrate how some of the major techniques we have discussed can work in a eulogy:

O'Neill's opening highlights the themes of unusual and superior accomplishment. He begins with the actual value of Owens's victories, and then describes their symbolic value.

. . . I rise on the occasion of his passing to join my colleagues in tribute to the greatest American sports hero of this century, Jesse Owens. . . . His performances at the Berlin Olympics earned Jesse Owens the title of America's first superstar. . . .

No other athlete symbolized the spirit and motto of the Olympics better than Jesse Owens. "Swifter, higher, stronger" was the credo by which Jesse Owens performed as an athlete and lived as an American. Of his performances in Hitler's Berlin in 1936, Jesse said: "I wasn't running against

Hitler, I was running against the world." Owens' view of the Olympics was just that: He was competing against the best athletes in the world without regard to nationality, race, or political view. . . .

Jesse Owens proved by his performances that he was the best among the finest the world had to offer, and in setting the world record in the 100-yard dash, he became the "fastest human" even before that epithet was fashionable. . . .

*These comments magnify the values represented by Owens's life and develop the theme of benefit to the community.*

In life as well as on the athletic field Jesse Owens was first an American, and second, an internationalist. He loved his country; he loved the opportunity his country gave him to reach the pinnacle of athletic prowess. In his own quiet, unassuming, and modest way — by example, by inspiration, and by performance — he helped other young people to aim for the stars, to develop their God-given potential. . . .

*That Owens remained a patriotic American in the face of racism and indifference magnifies his character.*

As the world's first superstar Jesse Owens was not initially overwhelmed by commercial interests and offered the opportunity to become a millionaire overnight. There was no White House reception waiting for him on his return from Berlin, and as Jesse Owens once observed: "I still had to ride in the back of the bus in my hometown in Alabama."

*O'Neill's conclusion emphasizes the symbolic, spiritual values of Owens's life.*

Can one individual make a difference? Clearly in the case of Jesse Owens the answer is a resounding affirmative, for his whole life was dedicated to the elimination of poverty, totalitarianism, and racial bigotry; and he did it in his own special and modest way, a spokesman for freedom, an American ambassador of good will to the athletes of the world, and an inspiration to young Americans. . . . Jesse Owens was a champion all the way in a life of dedication to the principles of the American and Olympic spirit.[7]

When presented at memorial services, eulogies should also express the pain of loss and offer comfort.[8] Rabbi Robert Schreibman, speaking at the funeral of an eight-year-old boy who was killed in Chicago, said: "So deep is our sorrow, so great is our loss, that we know that God is weeping." At the funeral of young Ryan White, a hemophiliac who had contracted AIDS from a blood transfusion, Rev. Raymond Probasco comforted his listeners with this reflection:

> Ryan and his family always believed there would be a miracle. But that didn't happen. I believe God gave us that miracle in Ryan. He healed a wounded spirit in the world and made it whole.

***Making Toasts.*** You may find yourself in situations in which you may be called upon to offer a **toast,** which is a minispeech of tribute. You might be asked to toast a co-worker who has been promoted, a friend who has won an award, or a couple at a wedding reception. The occasion may be formal or informal, but the message should always be eloquent. It won't do simply to mutter, "Here's to Tony, he's a great guy!" Such a feeble toast is "a gratuitous betrayal—of the occasion, its honoree, and the desire [of the audience] to clink glasses and murmur, 'Hear, hear' in appreciation of a compliment well fashioned."[9]

Whenever you think you might be called upon to offer a toast, plan your remarks in advance. Keep your toast brief. Select one characteristic or event that epitomizes your message, illustrate it with a short example, then conclude. You might toast the "coach of the year" in the following way:

> I always knew that Larry was destined for greatness from the time he led our junior high basketball team to the city championship. In one game in that tournament, Larry scored twenty-eight points, scrambled for eight rebounds, and dished off thirteen assists. And he was only five feet two inches tall! Here's to Larry, coach of the year!

Because a toast is a speech of celebration, you should refrain from making negative remarks. For example, it would be inappropriate at a wedding reception to say, "Here's to John and Mary. I hope they don't end up in divorce court in a year as I did!" Although most public speeches are best presented extemporaneously, a toast should be memorized. Practice presenting your toast with glass in hand until it flows easily. If you have difficulty memorizing your toast, it is probably too long. Cut it.

## The Speech of Acceptance

If you are receiving an award or honor, you may be expected to respond with a **speech of acceptance.** A speech of acceptance should express gratitude for the honor and acknowledge those who made the accomplishment possible. In addition, a speech of acceptance should focus on the values the award represents and be presented in language that matches the dignity of the occasion.

Consider a situation in which you are being awarded a scholarship by your hometown historical society. The award is being presented at a banquet, and you must make a public acceptance. You would not go amiss if you began with, "Thank you. I appreciate the honor of this award." Let others praise; you should remain modest. When Elie Wiesel was awarded the 1986 Nobel Peace Prize, he began his acceptance speech with these remarks: "It is with a profound sense of humility that I accept the honor you have chosen to bestow upon me."[10] Follow his lead and accept an award with grace and modesty.

You should also give credit where credit is due. If your hometown historical society is awarding you a scholarship, it would be appropriate for you to mention some teachers who prepared you for this moment. You might say something like, "This award belongs as much to Mr. Del Rio as it does to me. He opened my eyes to the importance and relevance of history in our world today." When Martin Luther King, Jr., accepted his Nobel Peace Prize in 1964, he did so in these words:

*Election night victory cele-
brations give rise to
speeches of acceptance,
which express gratitude
and acknowledge those
who made the accomplish-
ment possible. Diane Feinstein celebrated her
election to the Senate by
thanking her supporters.*

I accept this prize on behalf of all men who love peace and brotherhood. . . . Most of these people will never make the headlines and their
names will not appear in *Who's Who*. Yet when years have rolled past . . .
men and women will know and children will be taught that we have a
finer land, a better people, a more noble civilization—because these humble children of God were willing to suffer for righteousness' sake.[11]

As you accept your award, express your awareness of its deeper meaning.
If you were accepting a history scholarship, you might wish to focus on the
values of a liberal arts education and the contributions of history to our
understanding of present-day problems. In their acceptance speeches, both
Mr. Wiesel and Dr. King stressed the value of freedom and the importance of
involvement — of overcoming hatred with loving concern.

Finally, your language should fit the situation. An acceptance speech is an
occasion for dignity. Your remarks should be carefully planned and styled in
appropriate language. Slang and jokes are usually out of place because they
might suggest that you do not value the award or take the occasion seriously.

The stylistic techniques of magnification are especially useful in speeches
of acceptance. Dr. King relied heavily on an extended movement metaphor
in his acceptance speech. He spoke of the "tortuous road" from Mont-
gomery, Alabama, to Oslo, Norway, a road on which, in his words, "millions

---

### Making an Acceptance Speech

1. Express your appreciation for the honor.

2. Acknowledge those who made your accomplishment possible.

3. Highlight the values the award represents.

4. Be sure your language fits the formality of the occasion.

5. Be modest.

---

of Negroes are traveling to find a new sense of dignity." In a similar manner Mr. Wiesel told the story of a "young Jewish boy discovering the kingdom of night" during the Holocaust. This personal, metaphorical narrative was introduced early in the speech and repeated in the conclusion when Mr. Wiesel remarked, "No one is as capable of gratitude as one who has emerged from the kingdom of night."

Although your rhetorical style may not be as eloquent as these Nobel Prize winners, you should make a presentation that befits the dignity of the occasion.

### *The Speech of Introduction*

One of the more common types of ceremonial speeches is the **speech of introduction,** in which you introduce a featured speaker to the audience. The importance of this speech can vary, depending on how well the speaker and listeners know each other. At times the introduction can be very brief: "We are very pleased and honored today to have as guest speaker the president of our university, Dr. Sally Sorenson." At other times the introduction can be more elaborate as you work to accomplish three goals: first, to make the speaker feel welcome; second, to establish or strengthen the ethos of the speaker; and third, to tune the audience for the speech that will follow.

You make a speaker feel welcome both by what you say and how you say it. Let the speaker know that the audience wants to hear the message and feels honored by his or her presence. For example, you might open with, "We feel very fortunate to have Kelvin Andrews as our guest today. We know how busy he is, so it's a special treat and a real compliment to us that he should be here." When such words are delivered with honest warmth and sincerity, the speaker should feel truly welcome.

Once you have welcomed the speaker, you can begin to establish or strengthen the speaker's ethos. As soon as you know you will be introducing a speaker, find out as much as you can about the person. Often guest speakers will provide a resume listing their experiences and accomplishments. Talk with the speaker beforehand to see what he or she would like you to emphasize. If this is not possible, or if the speaker is noncommittal ("Oh, just say anything you want to"), there are still some good guidelines to follow that will help create respect for the speaker and lay the groundwork for speaker-audience identification:

- Create respect by magnifying the speaker's main accomplishments.

- Don't be too lavish with your praise. An overblown introduction can be embarrassing and make it difficult for speakers to get into their messages. One featured speaker was so overcome by an excessive introduction that he responded, "If you do not go to heaven for charity, you will certainly go somewhere else for exaggeration or downright prevarication."[12]

- Mention achievements that are relevant to either the speaker's message, the occasion on which the speech is being presented, or the audience that has assembled.

- Be selective! If you try to present too many details and accomplishments, you may take up some of the speaker's time and make listeners weary. Introducers who drone on too long can create real problems for the speakers who follow.

You can lay the groundwork for speaker-audience identification by mentioning aspects of the speaker's background that are familiar to the audience. The following introduction welcomes the speaker, establishes her ethos, and humanizes her by talking about her family and her connection to the community where the speech is being presented:

> Not only is tonight's speaker the state's foremost expert on criminal liability. As the mother of two children, Judge Polisky also shares our deep concern for the rights of children. Her grandfather lived in Maryville, and she tells me she still remembers our delicious Maryville strawberries that she enjoyed as a child. Let's welcome back Judge Mary Polisky and share her thoughts on the topic "Law and Disorder."

The final function of an effective introduction is to tune the audience for the speech that will follow. In Chapter 4 we discussed how preliminary tuning can establish a mood predisposing an audience to respond positively or negatively to a speech. You can tune the audience as you introduce a speaker by arousing a sense of anticipation in listeners and making them want to listen. However, this does not mean that you should preview the speech in your introduction. Unless you have special knowledge of what the speaker is going to say, previewing can create problems. You might miss the point completely, in which case the speaker may have to begin with a disclaimer. Even if you have seen the speech ahead of time and are aware of

### Introducing Main Speakers

1. Be sure you know how to pronounce the speaker's name.

2. Ask the speaker what he or she would like you to emphasize.

3. Make the speaker feel welcome. Be warm and gracious.

4. Focus on those parts of the speaker's background that are relevant to the topic, audience, and occasion.

5. Spotlight the title of the speech and tune the audience for it.

6. Be brief!

its content, leave the presentation to the speaker. *Introduce the speaker; don't present the speech.*

### The Speech of Inspiration

The **speech of inspiration** arouses an audience to appreciate, commit to, and pursue a goal, purpose, or set of values or beliefs. Speeches of inspiration help listeners see subjects in a new light. Therefore, these speeches serve the acceptance and integration functions we discussed in Chapter 13 in relation to persuasive speeches. Inspirational speeches may be commercial, political, or social. When a sales manager introduces a new product to marketing representatives, pointing up its competitive advantages and its glowing market potential, the speech is both inspirational and persuasive. The marketing reps should feel inspired to push that product with great zeal and enthusiasm. Speeches at political conventions that praise the principles of the party, such as keynote addresses, are inspirational in tone and intent. As different as these speech occasions may seem, they have important points in common.

First, speeches of inspiration are enthusiastic. Inspirational speakers accomplish their goals through their personal commitment and energy. Both the speaker and the speech must be active and forceful. Speakers must set an example for their audiences through their behavior both on and off the speaking platform. They must practice what they preach. Their ethos must be consistent with their advice.

Second, speeches of inspiration often draw upon past success to encourage future accomplishment. In the later years of his life, when his athletic prowess had faded, Jesse Owens became known as a great inspirational speaker. According to his obituary in the *New York Times,* "The Jesse Owens best remembered by many Americans was a public speaker with the ringing, inspirational delivery of an evangelist.... [His speeches] praised the virtues of patriotism, clean living and fair play."[13]

Third, whatever their specific purpose, speeches of inspiration seek to revitalize appreciation for values or beliefs. In the Owens speech that follows, we shall see the ideals of brotherhood, tolerance, and fair competition set forth in an exciting story. The effect of such revitalized values can be to strengthen our sense of mythos, the distinctive code of values underlying our society. A strengthened mythos in turn creates a resource for persuasive proofs, such as we discussed in Chapter 14. For example, an audience that heard the Owens speech might listen more favorably to a speech extolling the values of competition in everyday life. Thus, speeches of inspiration can contribute to the effectiveness of other speeches that follow.

***Speeches of Inspiration: An Illustration.*** In his inspirational speeches to budding athletes, Jesse Owens frequently talked of his Olympic achievements. The following excerpts, taken from a statement protesting America's withdrawal from the 1980 Summer Olympic Games, illustrate his inspirational style. Jesse Owens was unable to deliver this message orally. It was prepared shortly before his death from cancer.

|  |  |
|---|---|
| Owens's introduction suggests the larger meaning of his victories and sets the stage for identification. | What the Berlin games proved ... was that Hitler's "supermen" could be beaten. Ironically, it was one of his blond, blue-eyed, Aryan athletes who helped do the beating. |
| | I held the world record in the broad jump. Even more than the sprints, it was "my" event. Yet I was one jump from not even making the finals. I fouled on my first try, and playing it safe the second time, I had not jumped far enough. |
| Note the use of graphic detail to recapture the immediacy of the moment. | The broad jump preliminaries came before the finals of my other three events and everything, it seemed then, depended on this jump. Fear swept over me and then panic. I walked off alone, trying to gather myself. I dropped to one knee, closed my eyes, and prayed. I felt a hand on my shoulder. I opened my eyes and there stood my arch enemy, Luz Long, the prize athlete Hitler had kept under wraps while he trained for one purpose only: to beat me. Long had broken the Olympic mark in his very first try in the preliminaries. |
| Owens's use of dialogue helps listeners feel they are sharing the experience. | "I know about you," he said. "You are like me. You must do it all the way, or you cannot do it. The same that has happened to you today happened to me last year in Cologne. I will tell you what I did then." Luz told me to measure my steps, place my towel 6 inches on back of the takeoff board and jump from there. That way I could give it all I had and be certain not to foul. |
| | As soon as I had qualified, Luz, smiling broadly, came to me and said, "Now we can make each other do our best in the finals." |

This narrative leaves open the meaning of Owens's "inside" victory: perhaps it was over self-doubt or his own stereotype of Germans. Perhaps it was *both*.

And that's what we did in the finals. Luz jumped, and broke his Olympic record. Then I jumped just a bit further and broke Luz's new record. We each had three leaps in all. On his final jump, Luz went almost 26 feet, 5 inches, a mark that seemed impossible to beat. I went just a bit over that, and set an Olympic record that was to last for almost a quarter of a century.

I won that day, but I'm being straight when I say that even before I made that last jump, I knew I had won a victory of a far greater kind—over something inside myself, thanks to Luz.

This scene presents an inspirational model of international cooperation.

The instant my record-breaking win was announced, Luz was there, throwing his arms around me and raising my arm to the sky. "Jazze Owenz!" he yelled as loud as he could. More than 100,000 Germans in the stadium joined in. "Jazze Owenz, Jazze Owenz, Jazze Owenz!"

Owens shows how individuals can rise above ideologies, as Long's final message invites identification.

Hitler was there, too, but he was not chanting. He had lost that day. Luz Long was killed in World War II and, although I don't cry often, I wept when I received his last letter—I knew it was his last. In it he asked me to someday find his son, Karl, and to tell him "of how we fought well together, and of the good times, and that any two men can become brothers."

Owens ends with a metaphor of the "road to the Olympics."

That is what the Olympics are all about. The road to the Olympics does not lead to Moscow. It leads to no city, no country. It goes far beyond Lake Placid or Moscow, Ancient Greece or Nazi Germany. The road to the Olympics leads, in the end, to the best within us.[14]

## The After-Dinner Speech

Occasions that celebrate special events, or that mark the beginning or end of a process, often call for an **after-dinner speech.** Political rallies or award banquets, the kickoff for a fund-raising campaign, or the end of the school year may provide the setting for such speaking.

The after-dinner speech is one of the great rituals of American public speaking and public life. In keeping with the nature of the occasion, after-dinner speeches should not be too difficult to digest. Speakers making these presentations usually do not introduce radical ideas that require listeners to rethink their values or that ask for dramatic changes in belief or behavior. Nor are such occasions the time for anger or negativity. They are a time for people to savor who they are, what they have done, or what they wish to do. A good after-dinner speech, however, leaves a message that can act as a vision to guide and inspire future efforts.

**The Role of Humor.** Humor is an essential ingredient in most after-dinner speeches. In the introduction humor can place both the speaker and audience at ease. It can also relieve tension. Enjoying lighter moments can remind us that there is a human element in all situations and that we should not take ourselves too seriously. At least one study has discovered that the use of humorous illustrations helps audiences remember the message of the speech.[15] In addition, humorous stories can create identification by building an "insider's" relationship between speaker and audience that draws them closer together. In sharing humor, the audience becomes a community of listeners.[16]

However, humor cannot be forced on a speech. If you decide to begin with a joke simply because you think one should start that way, the humor may seem contrived and flat. Rather, humor must be functional in a speech, useful to make a point.

Humor may develop out of the immediate situation. Dick Jackman, the director of corporate communications at Sun Company, opened an after-dinner speech at a National Football Foundation awards dinner (the complete text appears at the end of this chapter) with a pointed reference to the seating arrangements, and then warned those in the expensive seats under the big chandelier that it "had been installed by the low bidder some time ago." His speech also contained lighthearted references to well-known members of the audience, including some who were there to receive an award. In her keynote address at the Democratic National Convention in 1988, Texas state treasurer Ann Richards used pointed humor as she took her party to task for not involving women more directly:

> Twelve years ago Barbara Jordan, another Texas woman, . . . made the keynote address to the convention, and two women in 160 years is about par for the course.

*Appropriate humor can relax both speakers and audiences. Speakers who tell amusing stories about themselves help create bonds of identification with an audience.*

But if you give us a chance, we can perform. After all, Ginger Rogers did everything that Fred Astaire did. She just did it backwards and in high heels.[17]

Humor requires thought, planning, and caution to be effective in a speech. If it is not handled well, it can be a disaster. For example, religious humor is usually dangerous, and racist or sexist humor is absolutely forbidden. The first runs the risk of offending some members of the audience and can make the speaker seem intolerant. The second reveals a devastating truth about the speaker's character and can create such negative reactions from the audience that the rest of the speech doesn't stand a chance. In general, avoid any anecdotes that are funny at the expense of others.

Often the best kind of humor centers on speakers themselves. Speakers who tell amusing stories about themselves sometimes rise in the esteem of listeners.[18] When this technique is successful, the stories that seem to put the speakers down are actually building their ethos. A rural politician once told the following story at a dinner on an urban college campus:

> You know, I didn't have good schooling like all of you have. I had to work real hard to educate myself for public office. Along the way I just tried not to embarrass myself like another fellow from around here once did. This man wanted to run for Congress. So he came up here to your college to present himself to all the students and faculty. He worked real hard on a speech to show them all that he was a man of vision and high intellect.
>
> As he came to the end of his speech, he intoned very solemnly, "If you elect me to the United States Congress, I'll be like that great American bird, the eagle. I'll soar high and see far! I won't be like that other bird that buries its head in the sand, the oyster!" There was a wonderful reaction from the audience to that. So he said it again — said he wasn't going to be no oyster.
>
> Well, I've tried hard not to be an oyster as I represent you, even though I know there's some folks who'd say, "Well, you sure ain't no eagle, either!"[19]

This story, which led into a review of the politician's accomplishments, was warmly appreciated for both its humor and its modesty. It suggests that humor takes time to develop and must be rich in graphic detail to set up its punch line. The story would not have been nearly as effective had the speaker begun with, "Did you hear the one about the politician who didn't know an ostrich from an oyster?"

***Developing an After-Dinner Speech.*** After-dinner speeches are more difficult to develop than their lightness and short length might suggest. Like any other speech, they must be carefully planned and practiced. They must have an effective introduction that commands attention right away, especially since some audience members may be more interested in talking to table companions than in listening to the speaker. After-dinner speeches should be more than strings of anecdotes to amuse listeners. The stories told must either establish a mood, convey a message, or carry a theme forward. Such speeches should build to a satisfying conclusion that conveys the essence of the message.

Above all, perhaps, after-dinner speeches should be mercifully brief. Long-winded after-dinner speakers can leave the audience fiddling with coffee cups and drawing pictures on napkins. After being subjected to such a speech, Albert Einstein once commented: "I have just got a new theory of eternity."[20]

**IN SUMMARY**   *Ceremonial speeches* serve important social functions. They reinforce the values that hold people together in a community and give listeners a sense of order and purpose in their lives. They also promote effective leadership.

*Techniques of Ceremonial Speaking.* Two major techniques of ceremonial speaking are identification and *magnification.* The first creates close feeling, and the second selects and emphasizes those features of a subject that will convey the speaker's message. Themes worthy of magnification include overcoming obstacles, achieving unusual goals, performing in a superior manner, having pure motives, and benefiting the community.

*Types of Ceremonial Speeches. Speeches of tribute* may recognize the achievements of individuals or groups or commemorate special events. Speeches of tribute should help us understand and appreciate the values these achievements represent. Accomplishments and events may be significant in themselves or in what they symbolize. *Eulogies* are speeches of tribute presented on the death of a person or persons. *Toasts* are mini-speeches of tribute that may be given on special occasions. *Speeches of acceptance* should begin with an expression of gratitude and an acknowledgment of others who deserve recognition. They should focus on the values that the honor represents. Acceptance speeches often call for more formal language than other speeches and for simple eloquence that suits the occasion.

*Speeches of introduction* should welcome the speaker, establish his or her ethos, and tune the audience for the message to follow. Introductions should focus on information about the speaker that is relevant to the speech topic and the occasion or that has special meaning for the audience. *Speeches of inspiration* help listeners appreciate values and make them want to pursue worthy goals. Such speeches often call on stories of past successes. *After-dinner speeches* should be lighthearted, serving up humor and insight at the same time. Humor should be functional in such speeches, illustrating a point or serving some larger purpose.

**TERMS TO KNOW**

ceremonial speaking

identification

magnification

speech of tribute

eulogy

toast

speech of acceptance

speech of introduction

speech of inspiration

after-dinner speech

**DISCUSSION**

1. The speeches in Appendix B by Bill Cosby and Elie Wiesel are ceremonial addresses. How do they relate to the basic questions of "Who are we?" "Why are we?" "What have we accomplished?" and "What can we become together?" What values do they celebrate? How do they achieve identification and magnification? Which tools of language do they use? Which speech designs do they follow?

2. Is there a speech of inspiration you heard some time ago that you still remember? Why do you feel it made such an impression on you?

3. List five heroes who are often mentioned in ceremonial speeches. Why do speakers refer to them so frequently? What does this tell us about the nature of these heroes, about contemporary audiences, and about the ceremonial speech situation? Be prepared to discuss this in class.

4. When someone has died, eulogies often begin a process of "mythifying" the deceased, speaking in ideal rather than real terms about the person's life. Can this process of idealization be justified? Why or why not?

**APPLICATION**

1. Prepare a speech of introduction that you might give for the next speech of one of your classmates. Which features would you select for magnification? How would you go about promoting speaker-audience identification? How would you tune the audience for the speech?

2. Develop a speech of tribute in honor of a classmate, friend, or family member in which you celebrate the real and/or symbolic importance of some achievement. Remember to consider the five themes of magnification as you plan your tribute.

3. Prepare a toast for a classmate who you feel either (a) has made the most progress as a speaker this semester or (b) has given a speech you will likely remember long after the class is over. Strive for brevity and eloquence in your toast. Be ready to present your toast in class.

**NOTES**

1. John Dewey, *Democracy and Education* (New York: Macmillan, 1916), p. 4.
2. Bronislaw Malinowski, "The Problem of Meaning in Primitive Languages," in C. K. Ogden and I. A. Richards, *The Meaning of Meaning: A Study of the Influence of Language upon Thought and of the Science of Symbolism,* 8th ed. (New York: Harcourt, Brace & World, 1946), p. 315.
3. Michael Osborn, *Orientations to Rhetorical Style* (Chicago: Science Research Associates, 1976), p. 32.

4. James W. Carey, "A Cultural Approach to Communication," *Communication* 2 (1975): 6.
5. Christine Oravec, "Observation in Aristotle's Theory of Epideictic," *Philosophy and Rhetoric* 9 (1976): 162–174.
6. *American Speeches,* ed. Wayland Maxfield Parrish and Marie Hochmuth (New York: Longmans, Green, 1954), p. 43.
7. *Congressional Record,* 1 Apr. 1980, pp. 7459–60.
8. For a more detailed account of the functions of eulogies see Karen A. Foss, "John Lennon and the Advisory Function of Eulogies," *Central States Speech Journal* 34 (1983): 187–194.
9. Owen Edwards, "What Every Man Should Know: How to Make a Toast," *Esquire,* Jan. 1984, p. 37.
10. Elie Wiesel, "Nobel Peace Prize Acceptance Speech," 10 Dec. 1986, reprinted in *New York Times,* 11 Dec. 1986, p. A-8.
11. Martin Luther King, Jr., "Nobel Peace Prize Acceptance Statement," reprinted in *The Cry for Freedom: The Struggle for Equality in America,* ed. Frank W. Hale, Jr. (New York: Barnes, 1969), pp. 374–377.
12. Cited in Morris K. Udall, *Too Funny to Be President* (New York: Holt, 1988), p. 156.
13. *Congressional Record,* 1 Apr. 1980, p. 7249.
14. Ibid., p. 7248.
15. Robert M. Kaplan and Gregory C. Pascoe, "Humorous Lectures and Humorous Examples: Some Effects upon Comprehension and Retention," *Journal of Educational Psychology* 69 (1977): 61–65.
16. For more on the social function of laughter, see Henri Bergson, *Laughter: An Essay on the Meaning of the Comic,* trans. Cloudsley Brereton and Fred Rothwell (London: Macmillan, 1911).
17. Ann Richards, "Keynote Address," delivered at the Democratic National Convention, Atlanta, Ga., 18 July 1988, in *Vital Speeches of the Day* 54 (15 Aug. 1988): 647–649.
18. Some support for these claims comes in Christi McGuffee Smith and Larry Powell, "The Use of Disparaging Humor by Group Leaders," *Southern Speech Communication Journal* 53 (1988): 279–292.
19. Thanks for this story go to Professor Joseph Riggs, Slippery Rock University.
20. *Washington Post,* 12 Dec. 1978.

## Address at Awards Dinner of National Football Foundation

### Dick Jackman

Jackman begins on a light note, using the seating arrangements as a source of humor. The impromptu nature of these remarks builds his ethos as a clever person.

Jackman moves into the major theme of his speech: leadership, teamwork, and optimism make a good football team and a good country. "O.K." is not a transition we normally recommend.

Jackman narrows his theme to optimism and urges listeners to "export" optimism to others.

This humorous narrative illustrates the importance of optimism in daily affairs. Note how the use of dialogue helps the story move along.

Thank you. Sorry I'm so late getting up here. It's about a $2 cab ride from the back row. All of us back there in the cheap seats admire these young athletes, and some of us remarked that we have underwear older than they are.

I'm pleased to be here to share this moment. I look at the logistics here on the dais—Doug Flutie seated alongside Joe Greene. That's like parking a Volkswagen alongside a school bus. And for those of you sitting under the chandelier, you should be aware that it was installed by the low bidder some time ago.

O.K. A football team seems to do best when it produces a combination of leadership and teamwork, and America seems to do best when it produces that same combination. Teamwork being that special quality that helps us look at life not from the standpoint of what's in it for us but from the standpoint of what we can do to help, and leadership being that special quality that helps an awful lot of people in and out of this room stand up on their tiptoes and look over the horizon and lead people there.

You cannot possibly leave this hotel tonight without a great deal of optimism about the future of not only football but America, because there's so much of it in here, and optimism is not meant to be stored. It's meant to be exported. You export it to other people. You make them determined to do that something extra in life that brings a response from others.

Let me mention the finest illustration I've ever heard of doing something extra. We had a teenage neighbor back home, a nice fellow. One day he got home at midnight. His mother said, "Where have you been?" He said, "I was out with my girl." His mother said, "I ought to give you a whipping for staying out so late, but you're being honest with me. I admire your honesty. Have some cookies and go to bed." The next night the kid got home at 1:00 A.M. His mother said, "Where were you tonight?" He said, "Same place. Out with my girl." His mother said, "I ought to give you the whipping of your life, but since you're being honest with me, have some more cookies and go to bed." The next night, he came home at 2:00 A.M. His father was waiting up for him. The kid walked into the house. The father picked up a huge frying pan and turned to face him. The mother leaped to her feet and screamed, "Please don't hit him!" The father said, "Who's going to hit him? I'm going to fry him some eggs. He can't keep this up on cookies." So good people, if you sometimes have difficulty keeping up the pace and the love and the concern for other people on cookies, then let me encourage you to fry some eggs.

Presented at an awards dinner of the National Football Foundation and Hall of Fame held at the Waldorf-Astoria Hotel, New York City, 4 Dec. 1984.

The story of the bumblebee and the other brief examples that follow function as evidence for the claim that people, through optimism, can overcome their limitations.

By this time we've all learned that, aerodynamically, the bumblebee shouldn't be able to fly. The body is too large. The wings are too small. Every time it takes off it should plunge back to the earth. But fortunately, the bumblebee does not understand its engineering limitations. And it's a good thing it doesn't, or we'd be living in a world of plastic flowers and putting mustard on our pancakes. It's a good thing that Scott Hamilton, at 5'3" and 115 pounds, did not realize that he could not possibly become the world's greatest ice skater, and that Mary Lou Retton, at 4'10", and Doug Flutie, who is here with us tonight, about a foot taller than that, did not realize that they could not possibly become the best at what they do, and that Shakespeare, whose mother could not read or write, did not realize that he couldn't possibly become the world's most honored writer.

And perhaps it's a great thing that 208 years ago, Betsy Ross took out her needle and thread. She did not realize that she could not possibly be sewing together an emblem that would one day umbrella the greatest experiment in human opportunity ever tried on this planet.

Let us not look at our limitations tomorrow morning. Let us pursue our possibilities.

Jackman finishes on a note that is both inspirational and humorous. The humor keeps his speech from ending on too serious a note.

On our track team at the University of Iowa we had a cross-eyed javelin thrower. He didn't win any medals, but he certainly kept the crowd alert. Perhaps part of our mission tonight and all the nights and days to follow is to keep the crowd in our homes, in our schools, and in our country alert to their possibilities and not their limitations.

That's far enough. Have an exciting life. Good night.

APPENDIX

A

# Group
# Communication

hen we listen to a speaker present information or make recommendations concerning a problem, what we hear is one person's perception and interpretation of a situation. That point of view may be distorted by bias or self-interest, or it could just be wrong. What can we do to minimize the risk of listening to just one person's opinion on vital issues?

One solution is to empower a group of people working together to investigate, analyze, share information and perspectives, and make recommendations about the problem. Group problem solving reduces the risk inherent in a single point of view and has other advantages as well. When people from different cultural backgrounds share their unique ways of seeing a problem, they enrich the common understanding. We then see the world through the eyes of others, and have the opportunity to learn from them. We may become aware of blind spots in our thinking or of bad habits we have acquired. Hearing different points of view can stimulate more creative thinking about the problems that surround us.

In effective problem-solving groups, people on all sides of an issue have an opportunity to discuss the similarities and differences of their perspectives on that issue. Through discussion, the participants may discover some things they can agree on. These areas of agreement can become the foundation for resolving differences. Additionally, people are often more willing to examine their differences in small group meetings than in larger, more public settings. In small groups they may feel freer to explore compromises or new options. For these reasons, social or business organizations often use a small group approach to problem solving and decision making. In fact, it is estimated that executives normally spend from 500 to 700 hours each year in group meetings.[1]

Although group deliberations have many advantages, there are also some disadvantages inherent in problem-solving groups. First, there is the possibility that one participant may dominate the group through the force of his or her personality. When this happens, the group may simply endorse that individual's suggestions without seriously questioning them or investigating other options. This can result in **groupthink,** the development of a single-focused, uncritical frame of mind that leads to ill-considered decisions.[2] Groupthink is especially dangerous because outsiders are apt to assume that the problem-solving group has deliberated carefully and responsibly.

**Cultural gridlock** is another problem that can impede group deliberations. Along with their different cultural perspectives on a problem, participants also bring different agendas, priorities, and procedures to the table. The potential for disagreement and conflict can cause tension in the group and may even prevent constructive discussions. The possibility of cultural gridlock makes it even more important for us to acquire group communication skills. Also, unless groups are ably led they can be aimless and unproductive. Ineffective leadership may be one reason why executives often complain that their meetings take too long and accomplish too little.[3]

How can you participate effectively in group deliberations? This appendix offers suggestions for group participants and leaders.

##  THE PROBLEM-SOLVING PROCESS

Group deliberations that are orderly, systematic, and thorough help people reach high-quality decisions through consensus.[4] Problem-solving groups can use a variety of methods to achieve their goal.[5] To be effective, groups must decide how they will proceed to assure maximum fairness and efficiency.[6] The approach we suggest modifies the reflective-thinking technique proposed by John Dewey in 1910.[7] This systematic approach to solving problems has five steps. The amount of time devoted to each of these steps depends on the depth and complexity of the problem.

### Step 1: Defining the Problem

Groups often mistakenly assume that the "assigned" problem is the real problem. However, sometimes the assigned problem is only a symptom, or just one aspect of the actual problem. So even if a problem may seem obvious, the group needs to define it carefully before looking for solutions. The following questions may help define the problem:

1. *Precisely* what is the nature of the problem? (*Be as concrete and specific as possible.*)
2. Why has the problem occurred?
3. What is its history?
4. Who is affected by the problem and to what degree?
5. What if the problem is solved? Would things automatically be better? Could they become worse?
6. Does the group have the information it needs to understand the problem completely? If not, how and where can it get this information? (*Do not proceed further until this information is in hand.*)
7. Has the problem been defined and stated so that everyone understands what the group will work on? (*Do not proceed further until you reach consensus on definition.*)

### Step 2: Generating Solution Options

Once a group has determined the nature and extent of the problem, members can begin generating solutions. **Brainstorming,** a group technique that encourages all members to contribute freely to the range of options, can help stimulate ideas. Brainstorming aims at producing a large number of potential solutions. At this stage in the problem-solving process, any attempt to evaluate the options or to settle on the right or best option is premature. The following rules of brainstorming may work as a guide:

1. The leader asks each member in turn to contribute an idea. If members do not have an idea when it is their turn, they pass.

2. A recorder writes down all the ideas members suggest. These should be recorded on flip-chart sheets or a blackboard so that members can see the ideas as they accumulate.

3. Participants offer any ideas that come to mind, no matter how far-fetched they may seem. The objective at this stage is to generate as many ideas as possible. Once expressed, ideas can be elaborated on by others.

4. No criticism of ideas should occur during the brainstorming process. The leader should tactfully discourage any critical comments by calling for other ideas.

5. Brainstorming continues until all members have offered an idea or have passed. The leader should discourage any one person from dominating the discussion.

6. The list of ideas is reviewed for clarification. At this time participants may expand the list of options or combine related ideas into other alternatives.

7. Once the group is satisfied that all options have been exhausted, the final list of alternatives is posted for everyone to see.

### Step 3: Evaluating Solution Options

If at all possible, the group should take a break between generating and evaluating solution options. During the break, the group can develop information about the feasibility of each option and determine whether and how it has been used elsewhere. When the group reconvenes, it should discuss options in the order in which they were proposed. The following questions provide a guide for evaluating options:

1. How costly is the option?

2. How likely is the option to be successful?

3. How difficult will it be to enact the option?

4. When would the option take effect?

5. Would the solution solve the problem completely?

6. What additional benefits might the solution produce?

7. What additional problems might the solution create?

You may wish to use a flip-chart sheet to summarize the answers to these questions for each option. Post these summaries so that participants can refer to them as they compare options. As options are evaluated, some of them will seem weak and be dropped, while others may be strengthened and re-fined. The group also may combine options to generate new alternatives. For example, if the group is caught between Option A, which promises im-proved efficiency, and Option B, which promises lower cost, it may be pos-sible to generate hybrid Option C, which combines the best features of both. After each alternative has been thoroughly considered, participants should rank the solutions in terms of their acceptability. The option receiving the highest overall rank becomes the proposed solution.

During the evaluation step, the group leader should keep the focus of the discussion on ideas and not on participants. It is not unusual for group mem-bers to become personally involved with the solutions they propose. Resist this impulse in yourself and be tactfully aware of it in others. Keep your comments focused on ideas, not on those who propose them. Discussing the strengths of an option before talking about its weaknesses can take some of the heat out of the process. Accept differences of opinion as a natural and necessary part of problem solving.

## Step 4: Planning for Action

Once the group has selected a solution, it must determine the steps needed to implement it. For example, to improve company morale, a group might recommend a three-step plan: (1) better in-house training programs to in-crease upward mobility of employees, (2) a pay structure that rewards suc-cess in the training programs, and (3) increased participation in decision making for the newly trained employees as they move into more responsible positions. As the group develops this plan, it should consider what might help or hinder it, the resources needed to enact it, and a timetable for com-pletion.

If the group cannot develop a sequential action plan for the solution, or if insurmountable obstacles appear, the group should return to Step 3 and re-consider its options.

## Step 5: Planning for Evaluation

Not only must a problem-solving group plan how to implement a solution, it must also determine how to evaluate its results. In essence, the group must answer three questions:

1. *What* constitutes success?
2. *When* can we expect results?
3. What will we do *if* the plan doesn't work as expected?

The first two questions require the group to specify the desired out-comes and indicate how they can be recognized once the solution goes into effect. To monitor the ongoing success of a solution, such as the three-part plan to improve company morale presented in Step 4, the group would have to decide on a reasonable set of expectations for each stage in the process. That way, the company could detect and correct problems as they occur, before they damage the plan as a whole. Having a scheduled sequence of expectations also provides a way to determine results while the plan is being enacted, rather than having to wait for the entire project to be completed. Positive results along the way can encourage group members by showing them they are on the right track. The third question indicates the importance of contingency plans: what to do if things don't go as expected.

## PARTICIPATING IN SMALL GROUPS

In addition to understanding the problem-solving process, you must also understand your responsibilities as a group participant. First, *you should come to meetings prepared.* You should have read background materials and performed the tasks assigned to you by the group leader. If you are not prepared, you will be perceived as less than competent. You may also find yourself vulnerable to the other members of the group. They may be able to dominate the discussion and turn it to their ends.

Second, *you should be open-minded*—willing to listen and learn from others. You should be concerned with contributing to the overall effort rather than with dominating the discussion. Although you may have a well-defined point of view, do not be afraid to concede a point when you are wrong and don't become defensive when challenged. Willingness to change one's views is not a sign of weakness, nor is intractability a strength.

Third, *be a constructive listener.* Speak only when you need information or can add clarification to an issue. Allow others to complete their points without interruption. Don't be afraid to raise an objection if you see consensus forming too quickly around a position. You might save the group from making a bad mistake. In short, each participant should strive to make a positive contribution to group effectiveness.

Analyzing your group communication skills can help you become a more effective group communicator. Use the self-analysis form (Figure A.1) to steer you toward more constructive group communication behaviors.

As you participate in groups, you should also keep in mind the following questions:

1. What is happening now in the group?
2. What should be happening in the group?
3. What can I do to make this come about?[8]

If you notice a difference between what the group is doing and what it should be doing to reach its goals, you have the opportunity to assume group leadership.

|  | Need to DO LESS | Doing FINE | Need to DO MORE |
|---|---|---|---|
| **1.** I make my points concisely. | ___ | ___ | ___ |
| **2.** I am forceful and definite rather than hesitant and apologetic. | ___ | ___ | ___ |
| **3.** I provide specific examples and details. | ___ | ___ | ___ |
| **4.** I synthesize and make explanations. | ___ | ___ | ___ |
| **5.** I let others know when I do not understand what they have said. | ___ | ___ | ___ |
| **6.** I let others know when I agree with them. | ___ | ___ | ___ |
| **7.** I let others know tactfully when I disagree with them. | ___ | ___ | ___ |
| **8.** I express my opinions. | ___ | ___ | ___ |
| **9.** I suggest solutions or courses of action. | ___ | ___ | ___ |
| **10.** I listen to understand rather than to prepare my next remarks. | ___ | ___ | ___ |
| **11.** I check to make sure I understand before agreeing or disagreeing. | ___ | ___ | ___ |
| **12.** I ask questions in ways that get more information than just "yes" or "no." | ___ | ___ | ___ |
| **13.** I ask others for their opinions rather than assuming I know them. | ___ | ___ | ___ |
| **14.** I check for group agreement as discussion proceeds. | ___ | ___ | ___ |
| **15.** I try to reduce tension and hostility. | ___ | ___ | ___ |
| **16.** I accept help from others. | ___ | ___ | ___ |
| **17.** I offer help to others. | ___ | ___ | ___ |
| **18.** I let others have their say. | ___ | ___ | ___ |
| **19.** I stand up for myself. | ___ | ___ | ___ |
| **20.** I urge others to participate. | ___ | ___ | ___ |

FIGURE A.1
Group Communication
Skills Self-Analysis Form

##  LEADERSHIP IN SMALL GROUPS

What does it mean to be a leader? For over thirty-five years, social scientists have been studying leadership by analyzing group communication patterns.[9] Our interest in leadership is very practical: *leaders help others to become effective group members who get the job done.* Accordingly, research suggests that two basic types of leadership behaviors emerge in groups: **task leadership behavior,** which directs the activity of the group toward a specified goal, and **social leadership behavior,** which builds and maintains positive and productive relationships among group members.

Task leaders initiate goal-related communication, including both giving and seeking information, opinions, and suggestions. A task leader might say, "We need more information on just how widespread grade inflation is on this campus. Let me tell you what Dean Johnson told me last Friday. . . ." Or the task leader might say, "I know Gwen has some important information on this point. Tell us about it, Gwen." Social leaders initiate positive social communication behaviors, such as expressing agreement, helping the group release tension, or behaving in a generally friendly and supportive manner toward others. The social leader looks for chances to bestow compliments: "I think Gwen has made a very important point. You have really helped us by finding that out." The supportive effect of sincere compliments helps keep members from becoming defensive and helps maintain a constructive communication atmosphere. In a healthy communication climate the two kinds of leadership behavior support each other and work to keep the group moving toward its goal in a positive way. When one person combines both styles of leadership, that person is likely to be highly effective.

Are just a favored few born for leadership? Can you be a leader? To us, the "favored few" theory is primarily an ego trip for those who think they belong to this elite. Most of us have leadership potential that emerges in certain situations. To understand this potential, consider the major components of **ethos:** at the heart of leadership are competence, trustworthiness, likeableness, and power. In addition, the ideal leader would

- have experience, knowledge, and insight into the problems confronting the group.
- help the group confront and define its problems, set goals, initiate action, and follow its plans to a successful conclusion.
- be considerate of and sensitive to the needs, talents, and limitations of participants.
- mediate and reduce conflicts that can arise during deliberations.
- articulate group consensus as it emerges during discussion.
- be adaptable in the face of unpredictable circumstances.

- represent the group to others and negotiate on its behalf.
- be self-confident and see leadership as an opportunity for self-actualization.

Don't be intimidated by this idealized portrait. Most of us have many of these qualities in varying degrees and can use them as the need for leadership arises. To be an effective leader, remember these simple functional goals: *help others become effective and get the job done.* Cultivate an **open leadership style** that encourages all sides to air their views and resists premature closure. Much of the training you have received in this course will help you become a successful leader. You may even find you enjoy the experience.

## *Developing a Meeting Plan*

Effective leadership techniques include knowing when to call meetings and how to plan and run them. You should call meetings when members need to

- share information and interpret its meaning face-to-face.
- decide on a common course of action.
- lay out a plan of action.
- report on the progress of a plan, evaluate its effectiveness, and revise it if needed.

The following guidelines should help you plan more effective meetings:

1. *Have a specific objective and purpose for holding a meeting.* Unnecessary meetings waste time. If your goal is simply to increase interaction, plan a social event rather than a meeting.

2. *Prepare an agenda for the meeting* and distribute it to participants at least twenty-four hours before the meeting. Having a list of topics to be covered gives members time to prepare and assemble any information or materials they might need. Be sure to solicit agenda items from participants.

3. *Keep meetings short and to the point.* After about an hour groups usually grow weary and tempers get short. Don't try to cover too much ground in any one meeting.

4. *Keep groups small.* You will get more participation and interaction in smaller groups. In larger groups people may be inhibited from asking questions or contributing ideas.

5. *Assemble groups that invite open discussions.* In business settings, the presence of an employee's direct supervisor may inhibit honest interaction. You will get better participation if group members come from the same or near the same working level in the organization.

6. *Plan the site of the meeting.* Try to arrange for privacy and freedom from interruptions. A circular table or seating arrangement contributes to member participation because there is no power position in the arrangement. A rectangular table or a lectern and classroom arrangement may inhibit interaction.

7. *Prepare in advance for the meeting.* Have a short form of the agenda available for distribution at the meeting. Be certain that you have all of the supplies the group will need, such as chalk, flip-chart, markers, note pads, and pencils. If you plan to use audio-visual equipment, check in advance to be sure it is in working order.

## *Conducting an Effective Meeting*

Group leaders have more responsibilities than other members. Leaders must understand the problem-solving process the group will use so that deliberations can proceed in an orderly, constructive way. Leaders also should be well informed on the issues involved so that they can answer questions and keep the group moving toward its objective. The following check list should be helpful in guiding your behavior as a group leader.

- Prepare and present background information concisely and objectively.
- Encourage differences of opinions. Get conflict out in the open so that it can be dealt with directly.
- Urge all members to participate. If group members are reticent, you may have to ask them directly to contribute.
- Keep the discussion centered on the issue.
- Summarize what others have said to keep the group focused on the problem.
- At the close of a meeting, summarize what the group has accomplished.

As group leader, you may need to present the group's recommendations to the organization that appointed the group. *In this task, you function mainly as an informative speaker.* You should present the recommendations offered by the group, along with the major reasons for these recommendations. You should also mention any opposing reasons or reservations that may have surfaced during group deliberations. Your job in making this report is not to advocate, but to educate. Later, you may join in the discussion that follows your report with persuasive remarks that express your convictions on the subject.

## GUIDELINES FOR FORMAL MEETINGS

The larger the group, the more it may need formal procedures to conduct a successful meeting. Also, if a meeting involves a controversial subject, it is often wise to have a set of rules for conducting group business. Such guidelines help keep meetings from becoming chaotic and assure fair treatment of all participants. Many groups operate by **parliamentary procedure.**[10]

Parliamentary procedure establishes an order of business for a meeting and defines the way the group initiates discussions and reaches decisions. Under parliamentary procedure, a formal meeting proceeds as follows:

1. The chair calls the meeting to order.
2. The secretary reads the minutes of the previous meeting, which are corrected, if necessary, and approved.
3. Reports from group officers and committees are presented.
4. Unfinished business from the previous meeting is considered.
5. New business is introduced.
6. Announcements are made.
7. The meeting is formally adjourned.

All business in formal meetings goes forward by means of **motions,** which are proposals set before the group. Consider the following scenario. The chair of a group asks: "Is there new business?" A member responds: "I *move* that we allot $100 to build a Homecoming float." This member has offered a **main motion,** which proposes to commit the group to some action. Before the motion can be discussed, it must be seconded. If no one volunteers a second, the chair may ask, "Is there a second?" Another member will typically respond, "I second the motion." The purpose of a **second** is to assure that more than one person wishes to see the motion considered. Once a main motion is made and seconded, it is open for discussion. It must be passed by majority vote, defeated, or otherwise resolved before the group can move on to other business. With the exception of a few technical motions (such as "I move we take a fifteen-minute recess" or "Point of personal privilege—can we do anything about the heat in this room?"), the main motion remains at the center of group attention until resolved.

Let us assume that as the group discusses the main motion in our example, some members believe the amount of money proposed is insufficient. At this point, another member may say: "I move to amend the motion to provide $150 for the float." The **motion to amend** gives the group a chance to modify a main motion. It also must be seconded and, after discussion, must be resolved by majority vote before discussion goes forward. If the motion to amend passes, then the amended main motion must be considered further.

How does a group come to a decision on a motion? There usually is a time when discussion has pretty well played itself out. At this point the chair might say, "Do I hear a call for the question?" A **motion to call the question** ends the discussion, and requires a two-thirds vote for approval. Once the group votes to end discussion, it must then vote to accept or reject the motion.

At times, discussion of a motion may reveal that the group is deeply confused or sharply divided about an issue. At this point a member may move **to table the motion** or "to lay [the motion] on the table," as it is technically called. This can be a backdoor way to dispose of a troublesome or defective motion without the pain of further divisive or confused discussion. At other times, discussion may reveal that the group lacks vital information needed to come to an intelligent decision. At that point, we might hear from yet another member: "In light of our uncertainty on the cost issue, I move that we postpone further consideration of this motion until next week's meeting." The **motion to postpone consideration,** if approved, gives the chair a chance to appoint a committee to gather the information needed.

These are just some of the important motions and procedures that can help assure that formal group communication remains fair and constructive. For more information on formal group communication procedures, consult the authoritative **Robert's Rules of Order.**

**NOTES**

1. M. Kriesberg, "Executive Evaluative Administrative Conferences," *Advanced Management* 15 (1950): 15–17; S. L. Tubbs, *A Systems Approach to Small Group Communication* (Reading, Mass.: Addison–Wesley, 1978), p. 5.
2. Irving L. Janis, *Groupthink: Psychological Studies of Policy Decisions and Fiascoes,* 2nd ed. (Boston: Houghton Mifflin, 1982), p. 9.
3. Gerald M. Goldhaber, *Organizational Communication* (Dubuque, Iowa: William C. Brown, 1983), p. 263.
4. Harold Guetzow and John Gyr, "An Analysis of Conflict in Decision-Making Groups," *Human Behavior* 7 (1954): 367–82; Norman R. F. Maier and Richard A. Maier, "An Experimental Test of the Effects of 'Developmental' vs. 'Free' Discussion on the Quality of Group Decisions," *Journal of Applied Psychology* 41 (1957): 320–23.
5. For an overview of other methods, see Patricia Hayes Andrews and John E. Baird, Jr., *Communication for Business and the Professions* (Dubuque, Iowa: William C. Brown, 1989), pp. 256–64.
6. Donelson R. Forsyth, *Group Dynamics,* 2nd ed. (Pacific Grove, Calif.: Brooks/ Cole, 1990), pp. 286–87.
7. The problem-solving process described here is adapted from William C. Morris and Marshall Sashkin. "Phases of Integrated Problem Solving (PIPS)," *The 1978 Annual Handbook for Group Facilitators,* ed. J. William Pfeiffer and John E. Jones (La Jolla, Calif.: University Associates, Inc., 1978), pp. 109–16.
8. Adapted from David G. Smith, "D-I-D: A Three-Dimensional Model for Understanding Group Communication," *The 1977 Annual Handbook for Group Facilitators,* ed. John E. Jones and J. William Pfeiffer (La Jolla, Calif.: University Associates, Inc., 1977), p. 106.
9. Robert F. Bales, *Interaction Process Analysis: A Method for the Study of Small Groups* (Cambridge, Mass.: Addison-Wesley, 1950); *Personality and Interpersonal Behavior* (New York: Holt, Rinehart & Winston, 1970).
10. This discussion is based on Henry M. Robert, *Robert's Rules of Order* (New York: The Berkley Publishing Group, 1983).

APPENDIX

# B

# Speeches for Analysis

## SELF-INTRODUCTORY

*Rodney Nishikawa,* "Free at Last"
*Scott Champlin,* "My Twenty-First Birthday Party"

## INFORMATIVE

*Cecile Larson*, "The 'Monument' At Wounded Knee"
*Jane Doe,* "Rape by Any Other Name"
*Stephen Lee,* "The Trouble with Numbers"

## PERSUASIVE

*Bonnie Marshall*, "Living Wills: Insuring Your Right to Choose"
*Elizabeth Glaser,* "AIDS: A Personal Story"
*Mary Fisher,* "AIDS: A Personal Narrative"

## CEREMONIAL

*Bill Clinton,* "Inaugural Address"
*Elie Wiesel,* "Nobel Peace Prize Acceptance Speech"
*Bill Cosby,* "University of South Carolina Commencement Address"
*Ronnie Davis*, "The Trials of Malcolm X"

# Free at Last

## *Rodney Nishikawa*

Rod Nishikawa presented this sensitive and moving self-introductory
speech in his public speaking class at the University of California–Davis.
Although most of his classmates were aware of prejudice, Rod's personal
narrative — about his first encounter with prejudice as a child — introduced many of them to the Japanese-American culture and helped them
relate to the problem more closely. Rod's willingness to speak from the
heart helped transform his class into a creative, caring community.

Three years ago I presented the valedictory speech at my high school
graduation. As I concluded, I borrowed a line from Dr. Martin Luther
King's "I Have a Dream" oration: "Free at last, free at last, thank God
almighty we're free at last!" The words had only a joyful, humorous place in
that speech, but for me personally they were a lie. I was not yet free, and
would not be free until I had conquered an ancient enemy, both outside me
and within me — that enemy was racial prejudice.

The event in my life that had the greatest effect on me happened over
twelve years ago when I was eight years old. I was a shy, naive little boy. I
knew I was Japanese, but I didn't consider myself different from my friends,
nor did I realize anyone else noticed or even cared. But at least one person
did. The "bully" in our class made it a point to remind me by calling me a
"Jap." He told me I didn't belong in America, and that I should go back to
Japan.

It was hard for me to understand what he meant, because like my parents I was born here in this country. This was my home. I didn't know what
to do when I was taunted. All I can remember is going home after school
and crying as though my heart were broken. I told my mom that I wished I
wasn't Japanese, but that if I did have to be Japanese, why did I have to be
born in this country?

Of course my mother knew exactly how I felt. She was about the age I
was then when the Japanese attacked Pearl Harbor. She told me how she
too had experienced prejudice at school, but that the prejudice she encountered was over a hundred times worse. When my father came home from
work, my mom and I told him what had happened. Although my father was
understanding, he said that I would never know the meaning of true prejudice because I did not grow up on the West Coast during World War II.

My encounter with the school bully was the beginning of my personal
education about prejudice. What I have learned is that prejudice is not a
disease that infects only the least educated among us. Rather, it is a bad part

of human nature that lies buried deep within all of us. Some people, however, seem to enjoy their prejudice. These people like to feel good by putting others down. But I have also learned how to deal with such problems when they arise. It was the advice from my mother that helped me the most.

My mother explained to me the meaning of the Japanese word *gaman*. *Gaman* means to "bear within" or "bear the burden." It is similar to the American phrase "turn the other cheek," but it means more to "endure" than to "ignore." She told me that when I go back to school, I should practice *gaman* — that even if I am hurt, I should not react with anger or fear, that I should bear the burden within. She said that if I showed anger or fear it would only make things worse, but if I practiced *gaman* things would get better for me. She was right. When I went back to school, I remembered what she had said. I used *gaman*. I bore the burden within. It wasn't easy for an eight-year-old, but I did not show any anger. I did not show any fear to the bully, and eventually he stopped picking on me.

Prejudice has been a bitter teacher in my life, but *gaman* has been an even greater blessing. By learning how to practice it, I feel I have acquired a great deal of inner strength. Whereas Gary (another student in the class) said he is a "competitor," I believe I am a "survivor." I look around my environment, recognize my situation, and cope with it. Because *gaman* has been part of my daily life since I was eight years old, I rarely experience feelings of anger or fear — those negative emotions that can keep a person from really being "free."

Being freed from such negative feelings has also helped me to better understand and accept myself. When I first encountered prejudice, I was ashamed of who I was. I didn't like being different, being a Japanese-American. But as I've grown to maturity, I have realized that I'm really proud to be Japanese-American: Japanese by blood — with the rich culture and heritage of my ancestors behind me — and American by birth — which makes me equal to anyone in this room because we were all born in this country and we all share the same rights and obligations.

Practicing *gaman* has helped me conquer prejudice. Although my Japanese ancestors might not have spoken as boldly as I have today, I am basically an American, which makes me a little outspoken. Therefore, I can talk to you about racial prejudice and of what it has meant to my life. And because I can talk about it, and share it with you, I am finally, truly, "free at last."

## My Twenty-First Birthday Party

### *Scott Champlin*

Scott Champlin's self-introductory speech is noteworthy for its irony and for its exceptionally graphic use of language. Irony occurs when speakers reflect upon events that don't normally go together, such as celebrating one's birthday and participating in a military action. Scott's words, especially as he describes his parachute jump into the hostile night and his wound that "spun me around like a twisted yo-yo at the end of a string," help us to share his experience. The one ingredient missing from his speech is his interpretation of how this vivid experience affected his outlook and thinking. This ingredient might well have been supplied, however, in later speeches.

O n December 20th, 1989, I celebrated my twenty-first birthday. This event is typically a noteworthy occasion for most young adults in that they have reached that mark to which nearly all younger persons aspire — they are now legal!

Whereas most people choose to celebrate this occasion by testing the bounds of their newly acquired legal right to consume alcohol, I was indoctrinated into the ranks of legality in the belly of a C-130 aircraft two hours and four minutes away from a small, troubled country in South America with a dash one bravo parachute strapped to my back and a rucksack full of ammunition. The only beverage I consumed was a bitter bottle of reality.

Two hours into being twenty-one years old, I found myself shuffling to the back door of an airplane, about to jump into a country troubled by political tyranny and social injustice. The wind came rushing in at one hundred and twenty knots with an overwhelming noise as the door was opened. Yet, through it all I'd swear you could hear my heart pounding with the fury of wild horses. To the door I shuffled. My brain was awhirl with thoughts as my feet carried me through the thick loudness to the ever approaching door into the unknown. As I fell from the airplane, I was enveloped by an equally all-consuming silence scattered with an occasional CRACK, CRACK, or BOOM! I took some comfort in seeing my parachute fully inflated over my head. The easy part was over. The darkness of two o'clock in the morning was multiply penetrated by streaks of red marking the paths of tracer rounds as they cut their way through the night. Suddenly, I felt a surge of heat knock me in the right leg with a force that spun me around like a twisted yo-yo at the end of a string. Only when I landed did I realize what had happened. I had received my first birthday present — a 7.62-by-38-mm round from an AK47 assault rifle aimed by an unknown Panamanian Defense Force soldier. I was less than grateful. Fortunately, the wound was not debilitating so I could continue to celebrate my twenty-first birthday.

But where would I go, what would I do to celebrate this day in my life I had so looked forward to since high school? The opportunities were limited. The first place I wanted to go was out of the tall grass where the bullets whizzed by with whisping noises as they cut through the grass. As the bellies of the planes flying overhead continued to drop guests to my surprise party, and I continued to deliver a few presents of my own, the unwanted guests began to leave. My guess was they were unhappy that there was no cake.

The United States government chose to celebrate my twenty-first birthday under the guise of Operation "Just Cause." I can think of an endless number of better ways to celebrate one's coming of age, yet none quite so unique. How many people can say they started an international incident on the day they turned twenty-one?

## The "Monument" at Wounded Knee

### *Cecile Larson*

Cecile Larson's classroom speech serves two informative functions. First, it shapes the perceptions of the audience because of the way it describes the "monument" and the perspective it takes on the situation — most of her classmates had had little or no contact with Native Americans, and this might have been their first exposure to this type of information. Second, the speech serves the agenda-setting function in that it creates an awareness of a problem and thus increases its importance in the minds of the audience. The speech follows a spatial design. Cecile's vivid use of imagery and the skillful contrasts she draws between this "monument" and our "official" monuments create mental pictures that should stay with her listeners long after the words of her speech have been forgotten.

We Americans are big on monuments. We build monuments in memory of our heroes. Washington, Jefferson, and Lincoln live on in our nation's capital. We erect monuments to honor our martyrs. The Minute Man still stands guard at Concord. The flag is ever raised over Iwo Jima. Sometimes we even construct monuments to commemorate victims. In Ashburn Park downtown there is a monument to those who died in the yellow fever epidemics. However, there are some things in our history that we don't memorialize. Perhaps we would just as soon forget what happened. Last summer I visited such a place — the massacre site at Wounded Knee.

In case you have forgotten what happened at Wounded Knee, let me refresh your memory. On December 29, 1890, shortly after Sitting Bull had been murdered by the authorities, about 400 half-frozen, starving, and frightened Indians who had fled the nearby reservation were attacked by the Seventh Cavalry. When the fighting ended, between 200 and 300 Sioux had died — two-thirds of them women and children. Their remains are buried in a common grave at the site of the massacre.

Wounded Knee is located in the Pine Ridge Reservation in southwestern South Dakota—about a three-hour drive from where Presidents Washington, Jefferson, Theodore Roosevelt, and Lincoln are enshrined in the granite face of Mount Rushmore. The reservation is directly south of the Badlands National Park, a magnificently desolate area of wind-eroded buttes and multicolored spires.

We entered the reservation driving south from the Badlands Visitor's Center. The landscape of the Pine Ridge Reservation retains much of the desolation of the Badlands but lacks its magnificence. Flat, sun-baked fields and an occasional eroded gully stretch as far as the eye can see. There are no signs or highway markers to lead the curious tourist to Wounded Knee. Even the *Rand-McNally Atlas* doesn't help you find your way. We got lost three times and had to stop and ask directions.

When we finally arrived at Wounded Knee, there was no official historic marker to tell us what had happened there. Instead there was a large, handmade wooden sign—crudely lettered in white on black. The sign first directed our attention to our left—to the gully where the massacre took place. The mass grave site was to our right—across the road and up a small hill.

Two red-brick columns topped with a wrought-iron arch and a small metal cross form the entrance to the grave site. The column to the right is in bad shape: cinder blocks from the base are missing; the brickwork near the top has deteriorated and tumbled to the ground; graffiti on the columns proclaim an attitude we found repeatedly expressed about the Bureau of Indian Affairs—"The BIA sucks!"

Crumbling concrete steps lead you to the mass grave. The top of the grave is covered with gravel, punctuated by unruly patches of chickweed and crabgrass. These same weeds also grow along the base of the broken chain-link fence that surrounds the grave, the "monument," and a small cemetery.

The "monument" itself rests on a concrete slab to the right of the grave. It's a typical, large, old-fashioned granite cemetery marker, a pillar about six feet high topped with an urn—the kind of gravestone you might see in any cemetery with graves from the turn of the century. The inscription tells us that it was erected by the families of those who were killed at Wounded Knee. Weeds grow through the cracks in the concrete at its base.

There are no granite headstones in the adjacent cemetery, only simple white wooden crosses that tell a story of people who died young. There is no neatly manicured grass. There are no flowers. Only the unrelenting and unforgiving weeds.

Yes, Americans are big on monuments. We build them to memorialize our heroes, to honor our martyrs, and sometimes, even to commemorate victims. But only when it makes us feel good.

# Rape by Any Other Name

## *Jane Doe*

The student who presented this courageous informative speech in a public speaking class at Memphis State University gave us permission to reprint the text using the pseudonym "Jane Doe." Although the topic is quite sensitive and personal, it deals with an important problem that many college students must face. "Jane" handled the subject in good taste with a  matter-of-fact, unemotional presentation. Her introduction was especially effective. She used a telephone as a visual aid and presented the first part of the introduction with her hair pulled back and wearing dark glasses. To signal the change from male to female speaker in her introduction, "Jane" hung up the phone, removed the combs holding back her long hair, and took off the glasses. The use of dialogue and slang in the introduction added to its impact.

Yo, Kevin. Man, what's up? Did you go to that party Saturday night? You did? Man, did you see that girl in the blue dress? Yea, man, she was cool, the girl was wild! I had been lookin' at her all night, man, when a slow song came on and I asked her to dance. I knew she liked me by the way she kept smiling and looking at me. She told me her name was 'Jane' and so I said, 'Hey, Babe, why don't we go back to my room for a couple of drinks or something?' She said, 'Yeah,' man and I *knew* I was gonna make a move! Man, when we got back to my room, we sat on the bed and started kissin', then, man, when I started to lay her down on the bed, she started sayin' 'No.' I said, 'No? Hey babe if this isn't what you wanted then why'd you come up to the room?' Man, she started cryin' and stuff after. . . . You know girls don't want to seem too easy. But man, you could tell by the way she was lookin' in that dress *she wasn't no virgin!* . . . Hold on a minute, man." (Pause while the speaker clicks the phone over to call waiting.) "Hello? . . . Yes, this is he . . . Who? . . . Oh! . . . Jane . . . Hey, Baby. Yeah . . . You did *what? Pressing charges?* But . . . but . . . but . . . Hello . . . hello . . . hello . . . ."

"I met him at a party. He was really good-looking and had the nicest smile. I wanted to meet him, but I wasn't sure how. Then he came over and introduced himself to me. We danced and talked for a long time and found out that we had a lot in common. When he asked me to go to his dorm room for a drink, I didn't think anything of it, so I went. When we got there, the only place to sit was on his bed, so I did. He sat down next to me and after we'd talked a while, he kissed me. It wasn't bad, so I didn't stop him. But then, he pushed me down on the bed. I tried to get up and I told him to stop, but he wouldn't. He was so much bigger and stronger . . . I got scared and I started to cry. I froze and he raped me. When it was over, he kept asking me what was wrong . . . like what he did was okay . . . like what he did wasn't wrong! He drove me home and said he wanted to see me again. I'm afraid to see him again. I never thought anything like this would happen to me."

*Date rape.* What you've just heard was adapted from a brochure produced by the American College Health Association entitled *Acquaintance Rape.* Date rape — acquaintance rape — social rape — by any other name, it is still rape. We need to understand what it is, what causes it, and what its effects usually are. We need to know what we can personally do to keep date rape from happening, and what we should do if and when it does happen.

First, what is date rape and what causes it? Date rape is a forced or unwanted sexual relationship involving two people who know each other — who are friends or acquaintances. Most of the time the female victim is on a "date" with the rapist. She has voluntarily gone with him as opposed to having been forcefully abducted. And, although she knows the man involved and may consider him a friend, she does not want and she does not agree to a sexual relationship.

How can a social relationship, or a date, end up in a rape? What are some of the causes of date rape? Date rape typically occurs because of sex role stereotypes and poor communication between two people of opposite sexes. Many people firmly believe that men are competitive and aggressive and women are yielding and passive. When these stereotypes are treated as "just the way things are," then men may presume that men *should be* aggressive and forceful in relationships and that women *should be* passive and submitting. They turn a misinformed description into a prescription for behavior. There's also a potential for date rape when two people don't have a clear understanding of each other's sexual intentions and expectations. Date rape can happen because of mixed messages and learned violence. Mixed messages occur when a man, thinking a woman is playing hard to get, believes she really means "yes" when she says "no." Mixed messages may be communicated verbally such as through suggestive or flirtatious conversation — the verbal game-playing that goes on at parties. Mixed messages can also be communicated nonverbally through body language or in many cases by the way a woman dresses. On television and in the movies violence is often shown as a way to solve problems, so some men feel it's okay to use "a little force" to get what they want from a woman.

We've looked at what date rape is and some of the reasons why it happens, so now let's explore some of the effects of date rape. The female victim of a date rape may experience a loss of trust — particularly of men — and find it difficult to feel comfortable in close relationships. I can speak from my own experience in saying that date rape does have a devastating effect on future relationships. It's hard to be open and warm and friendly because you're always afraid it will happen again. The victim may feel guilty because she thinks maybe she did something to cause it or because she thinks she should have been able to prevent it. These negative feelings can cause some victims of date rape to experience depression or sexual adjustment problems that call for professional counseling. The man may also be considered a victim — in a way, like the guy in my opening example who didn't seem to realize that "no" means "no" — period. He may not be able to understand or accept that what he did was wrong. In that sense, he is a victim of his distorted beliefs. And if the female presses charges, he too may suffer from the consequences.

Date rape is real, and it is a problem, but it's a problem we can do a lot to keep from happening if both men and women learn how date rape can be avoided. One way to help prevent date rape is to always clearly express what *you* want before getting involved in a relationship with a person of the opposite sex. Know your limits. Beware of alcohol and drugs. It's hard to cope with a date rape situation. It's much harder to be in control if you're under the influence of these substances. Be aware of how much your date drinks, too. Avoid secluded places. *Don't* go to a beach, park, deserted bridge, or "make-out spot" with someone you've just met. Suggest meeting in public places like the mall or the movies when getting to know someone. Have your own transportation. Don't rely on your date for it (especially if you don't know him very well). Drive your own car, double date, or take the bus.

It's also important for each of us to know our individual rights and those of anyone we may be socially involved with. A woman may dress any way she pleases. If she is scantily clad and flirts, that doesn't necessarily mean, "Let's do it!" Even if she lets things advance to the point of having sex, she can change her mind at any time. It should not be assumed that if (1) "I paid for dinner!" or (2) we met at a beer party, or (3) we've had sex before, then it's okay to force someone into having sex.

Any instance of sexual assault, including date rape, should be reported to the authorities. Date rape is sometimes not seen as serious as "real rape" — or sexual assault by a stranger — BUT IT IS! Sometimes a woman thinks that she won't be believed if she reports the crime. She may be afraid that people will accuse her of "asking for it." But it is a crime, and it has to be reported. Next, the victim should go to a hospital immediately. *She should not shower, change clothes, douche, or even comb her hair!* Finally, the victim should get some type of emotional support, be it a friend, minister (whom I confided in about my situation), or if neither of these, there are rape crisis hotlines with compassionate counselors you can call.

Date rape, acquaintance rape, social rape, silent rape, or cocktail rape. By any name, date rape is and always will be considered a crime. So remember to be aware of what causes date rape so you will be alert to the danger signs. Know its effects before you let a dangerous situation go too far, and be aware that everyone plays a part in the control of date rape.

# The Trouble with Numbers

### *Stephen Lee*

Stephen Lee first presented this informative speech of explanation to his public speaking class at the University of Texas–Austin. Later, Stephen's speech won the Southern division of the 1991 Houghton Mifflin speaking contest. The speech is noteworthy for its use of testimony and its illustrative examples. It first gains and holds attention by the novelty of its introduction, as Stephen describes a mythical "average American." The speech is somewhat loosely structured around a categorical design, as Stephen reflects upon the "misuse, abuse, and general overuse" of statistics in various dimensions of modern life. Stephen's presentation skills — his timing, wry sense of humor, eye contact, vocal variety, and gesture — helped bring his speech to life. All in all, he offers a sprightly commentary that critiques our society's over-reliance on one of the basic forms of supporting materials, statistical knowledge.

Name, Bill Smith. Address, 103 Main Street, Smalltown, USA. Height, 5'11", weight, 185 pounds. Who is this person? Why, he's the average American. Bill makes a comfortable $32,000 each year. His car gets 18.9 miles to the gallon. He reads 4.2 novels every year, each with 482.73 pages. He receives 9.7 gifts every Christmas and he brushes his teeth 1.9 times every day. The average American.

Today it seems we hear a lot of this person. Someone who is supposedly like all of us and yet not like any of us. After all, how many men do you know with 2.7 children? No, Bill is by no means real. His composition is not one of flesh and blood. Instead Bill is the product of cold and heartless data. Born of a national almanac, Bill is nothing more than a statistic.

But the characteristics of Bill Smith and the way we interpret them are highly reflective of our society's misuse, abuse, and general overuse of statistics. As Darrell Huff tells us in his essay, *How to Lie With Statistics*, "Americans use statistics like drunks use lamp posts, for support instead of illumination." He was referring to the unfailing dependence that we Americans put on statistics. He continues: "We prefer to record and measure ourselves with numbers and what we can't measure we assume not to exist at all." But what are these mystic symbols and figures? And more importantly, how do they affect us? Humorist Artemus Ward once said, "It ain't so much what we know that gets us in trouble. It's the things we know that ain't so."

Now such was the case in the government. Our government is faulted for many problems. Statistical misuse is perhaps one of the greatest. This was clearly demonstrated in March of 1983 when the computation of the unemployment rate was changed to encompass military personnel. Now this had a significant impact, as the number changed from 10.6% to 10.1%. Some people said this was a political ploy of President Reagan, trying to make himself look good in the public spectrum, while others claimed this was a highly justified move since, after all, military personnel were employed. But I think there is a more important question that needs to be answered. Look at what happened to the number. It changed. Look at what happened to the way the number was computed. It changed, too. But what happened to the very real problem of civilian unemployment, which we all assumed this number to represent? It had not changed at all. It all goes back to what Lester T. Thurow said in his basic theory of economics. "A difference is only a difference if it truly makes a difference." Many times a difference in a number does not represent a difference in the real world. This was the case in the late 1970s when housing was taken out of the consumer price index. Now as contradictory as it might sound, while inflation continued to sky-rocket the inflation rate actually stagnated.

In our society we even misuse something as simple as a baseball statistic, denoting one player is good, batting .350, while another one bad, batting .150. But what do these figures tell us about his moral character, his interaction with other players, his leadership abilities — any of which any coach will tell you is necessary for the well-rounded player? While numbers may be convincing, so much of what they imply, as Ward said, simply "ain't so." Perhaps we can all relate to standardized tests, where the quality of one's education is measured by the quantity of correct circles on a piece of paper. You may not be aware of how misleading statistics are on the university level, but look closer when a university advertises that 95% of its needy students receive financial aid. It sounds good, but the truth behind this claim is the fact that the university is the one who determines who is needy, and thereby allocates aid accordingly.

Perhaps the greatest inadequacy surrounding statistics lies not in what is wrong with these numbers, but instead with the way we use them. Numbers are only numbers. Many times we forget this. We forget that there are very real humans and very real human conditions behind these statistics. And yes, we are all affected by them. The only solution to our statistical dilemma is to better understand what a statistic is and what a statistic is not. We need to more adequately comprehend what a statistic can do, but what a number cannot do.

So when you go home today, read your paper. Eat your meal, watch TV. You don't have to go looking for statistics. They're all around us. But this time be aware of them. Train yourself not to passively sit by as seemingly innocent numbers are flashed before your eyes. Learn to question what hides behind those numbers. I think it's interesting, and indeed fascinating, that statistics have come to dominate our decision making in America today. But don't get me wrong. I am not saying that statistics are bad, but that statistics can be misleading. And without careful management they can do more harm than good. Carl Tucker summed it up best in his book,

*The Data Game.* He wrote: "Statistics and lists are obviously useful tools. They, in their own way, can tell us what happened, but never why that mattered." And in the end that is the only question worth answering. So as you leave, remember: three-fourths of the people always comprise 75% of the population.

## Living Wills: Insuring Your Right to Choose
### *Bonnie Marshall*

Bonnie Marshall was a student at Heidelberg College in Ohio when she made the following persuasive presentation. Her speech is noteworthy for its use of opening narrative to heighten interest in the problem Bonnie was presenting. The speech is also strong in its use of personal and expert forms of testimony. Clearly, Bonnie had responsible knowledge of her subject. In her conclusion she makes excellent use of anaphora to underscore her message of personal responsibility. She presented the speech with great conviction, and its overall impact led to its selection as a finalist in the Midwest division of the 1991 Houghton Mifflin Public Speaking contest.

Harry Smith was a cranky, obstinate, old farmer. He loved bowling, Glenn Miller music, and Monday night football. He was also dying from cancer of the esophagus, which had metastasized to his lungs. He didn't like doctors and he liked hospitals and modern medicine even less. Harry used to say that he remembered when three square meals, mom's mustard plaster, and an occasional house call from Doc Jones was all anyone ever needed to stay healthy. Harry didn't want to live in pain, and he hated being dependent on anyone else; yet like so many others, Harry never expressed his wishes to his family. When Harry's cancer became so debilitating that he could no longer speak for himself, his family stepped in to make decisions about his medical care. Since Harry never told them how he felt, his children, out of a sense of guilt over the things they had done and the love they hadn't expressed, refused to let Harry die. He was subjected to ventilators, artificial feedings, and all the wizardry that modern medicine can offer. Harry did die eventually, but only after months of agony with no hope of recovery.

Harry's doctor, my husband, agonized too, over the decisions regarding Harry's care. He knew that the children were acting out of grief and guilt, not for Harry's benefit. Yet because Harry had not documented his wishes, his doctor had no choice but to subject Harry to the senseless torture that he didn't want.

We all know of a similar case that gained national attention. On December 26, 1990, Nancy Cruzan died. The tragic young woman who became the focal point for the right-to-die movement was finally allowed to die after eight long years and a legal battle that reached the hallowed halls of the Supreme Court. Nancy's battle is now over, yet the issue has not been resolved and the need for action is more urgent than ever. Since the Supreme Court ruling on June 25, 1990, public interest in this issue has skyrocketed. From July 1990 to November 1990, the last month statistics were available, the Society for the Right To Die answered 908,000 requests for information. By comparison, in November of 1989, the first month that the Society kept monthly statistics, they answered only 21,000 requests.

Today I would like to explore this problem and propose some solutions that we all can implement.

The *Cruzan v. Missouri* decision was significant because it was the first time that the Supreme Court had rendered an opinion on the right-to-die issue. However, the message from the Court is anything but clear and complete. As Justice Sandra Day O'Connor wrote in her concurring opinion, "Today we decide only that one state's practice does not violate the Constitution. . . . The more challenging task of crafting appropriate procedures for safeguarding incompetents' liberty interests is entrusted to the 'laboratory' of the states." So while the Court has for the first time recognized a "constitutionally protected liberty interest in refusing unwanted medical treatment," it has also given the power over this issue back to the states. According to the July 9, 1990 issue of *US News and World Report*, nine states, including Ohio, have no legislation recognizing the legality of living wills. Of the states that do have living will legislation, about one-half do not allow for the withdrawal of nutrition and hydration, even if the will says the patient does not want such treatment, according to Lisa Belken in the June 25th issue of the *New York Times*. Also according to the *Times*, only 33 states have health care proxy laws. Perhaps as a result of all this indecision and inconsistency, desperate patients with terminal illnesses will continue to seek out the "Dr. Deaths" of the medical community, those who, like Dr. Kevorkian of Michigan, are willing to surpass simply allowing the terminally ill to die, to actively bringing about death.

The right-to-die issue may seem far removed from you today, yet the American Medical Association estimates that 80–90% of us will die a "managed death." Even today, according to an editorial by Anthony Lewis in the June 29, 1990 *New York Times*, "The problem is far more acute and far-reaching than most of us realize. Almost two million people die in the United States every year, and more than half of those deaths occur when some life-sustaining treatment is ended." The decision to provide, refuse, or withdraw medical treatment should be made individually, personally, with the counsel of family, friends, doctors, and clergy, but certainly not by the state.

More and more however, these personal decisions are being taken away from patients and their families and instead are being argued and decided in courts of law. Perhaps it began with Karen Ann Quinlan. It certainly continued with Nancy Cruzan, and these decisions could be taken away from you, if we do not act now to insure that our right to refuse medical treatment is protected. And our right to refuse medical treatment includes the right to refuse artificial nutrition and hydration, just as it includes the right to refuse antibiotics, chemotherapy, surgery, or artificial respiration. According to John Collins Harvey, M.D., Ph.D from the Kennedy Institute of Ethics at Georgetown University, "The administration of food and fluid artificially is a medical technological treatment . . . Utilizing such medical treatment requires the same kind of medical technological expertise of physicians, nurses, and dietitians as is required in utilizing a respirator for treatment of respiratory failure or employing a renal dialysis machine for the treatment of kidney failure. This medical treatment, however, is ineffective, for it cannot cause dead brain cells to regenerate; it will merely sustain biological life and prolong the patient's dying. Such treatment is considered by many physicians and medical ethicists to be extraordinary." Additionally, the Center for Health Care Ethics of St. Louis University, a Jesuit institution, prepared a brief for the Cruzan case which states that "within the Christian foundation, the withholding and withdrawing of medical treatment, including artificial nutrition and hydration, is acceptable."

So what can we do to protect ourselves and assure that our wishes are carried out? My plan is fourfold. First, we in Ohio must urge our legislators to pass living will legislation. Representative Marc Guthrie from Newark, Ohio has drafted a living will bill, House Bill 70. We must urge our legislators to pass this bill, since it is more comprehensive than the Senate version and will better protect our rights on this crucial issue.

Secondly, we must draw up our own living wills stating our philosophy on terminal care. I propose the use of the Medical Directive, a document created by Drs. Linda and Ezekiel Emanuel. This document details twelve specific treatments that could be offered. You can choose different treatment options based on four possible scenarios. You can indicate either that you desire the treatment, do not want it, are undecided, or want to try the treatment, but discontinue it if there is no improvement. This directive, which also includes space for a personal statement, eliminates much of the ambiguity of generic living wills and provides clearer guidelines to your physician and family.

Third, designate a person to make health care decisions for you should you become incompetent. This person should be familiar with your personal philosophy and feelings about terminal care and be likely to make the same decisions that you yourself would make. You should name this person in a Durable Power of Attorney for Health Care, a legal document that is now recognized in the State of Ohio.

Fourth, have a heart-to-heart talk with your doctor and be sure that he or she understands and supports your wishes on terminal care. Have a copy of your living will and Durable Power of Attorney for Health Care placed in your medical file. Finally, for more information on living wills, you can contact: The Society for the Right To Die, 250 West 57th St., New York, NY 10107, or send $1.00 to the Harvard Medical School Health Letter, 164 Longwood Ave., Fourth Floor, Boston, MA 02115 for a copy of the Emanuels' Medical Directive form.

I am interested in this issue because, through my husband, I have seen patients suffer the effects of not having an advance directive. You need to ask yourself how you feel about terminal care, but regardless of your personal response, we all must choose to protect our rights on this issue. WE must choose to pressure our legislators to adopt living will legislation. WE must choose to draw up our own living wills and health care proxies. And most importantly, WE must choose to discuss this most personal and sensitive issue with our families and loved ones, so that in the absence of a legal document, or even with one, they may confidently make the decisions concerning our life and death that we ourselves would make. Not all patients end up like Nancy Cruzan or Harry Smith. Many people are allowed to quietly slip away from the pain and suffering of life. But that can only happen after the careful, painful deliberation of a grieving family, who can at least take comfort in the fact that they are carrying out their loved one's wishes.

## AIDS: A Personal Story

### *Elizabeth Glaser*

Elizabeth Glaser presented her tragic story before the Democratic National Convention in New York on July 14, 1992. Like Mary Fisher, whose speech follows in this text, she was not the stereotypical AIDS victim. Married to a prominent television director and actor, she had founded the Pediatric AIDS Foundation, which has raised $13 million for research in memory of her daughter, Ariel.

Unlike Mary Fisher's, hers is a speech of indictment, aimed at "leaders who say they care but do nothing." It is a fiercely partisan speech, as her attacks on Presidents Reagan and Bush indicate. Hers is also a persuasive speech that attempts to arouse a sense of urgency in listeners to support programs of AIDS research. Having lost one child already, she stands to lose another and her own life unless her listeners become involved.

Obviously, these two speeches — both quite moving and judged at the time to be successful — were given before different political audiences, which encouraged in turn different strategies, approaches, even purposes. Studied together, they can tell us much about how audiences and situations can shape speeches, and about the work of specific techniques. Read them carefully, and share your impressions with classmates.

I'm Elizabeth Glaser. Eleven years ago, while giving birth to my first child, I hemorrhaged and was transfused with seven pints of blood. Four years later I found out that I had been infected with the AIDS virus and had unknowingly passed it to my daughter, Ariel, through my breast milk and my son, Jake, in utero.

Twenty years ago, I wanted to be at the Democratic Convention because it was a way to participate in my country. Today I am here because it is a matter of life and death. Exactly four years ago my daughter died of AIDS. She did not survive the Reagan administration. I am here because my son and I may not survive four more years of leaders who say they care but do nothing.

I am in a race with the clock. This is not about being a Republican or an Independent or a Democrat. It's about the future for each and every one of us. I started out just a mom fighting for the life of her child. But along the way, I learned how unfair America can be today, not just for people who have HIV but for many, many people — poor people, gay people, people of color, children.

A strange spokesperson for such a group — a well-to-do white woman. But I have learned my lesson the hard way and I know that America has lost her path and is at risk of losing her soul. America, wake up. We are all in a struggle between life and death.

I understand the sense of frustration and despair in our country because I know first hand about shouting for help and getting no answer. I went to Washington to tell Presidents Reagan and Bush that much, much more had to be done for AIDS research and care and that children could not be forgotten.

The first time when nothing happened, I thought they just didn't hear me. The second time when nothing happened, I thought maybe I didn't shout loud enough. But now I realize they don't hear because they don't want to listen. When you cry for help and no one listens, you start to lose your hope. I began to lose faith in America. I felt my country was letting me down and it was.

This is not the America I was raised to be proud of. I was raised to believe that others' problems were my problems as well. But when I tell most people about HIV, in hopes that they will help and care, I see the look in their eyes — "It's not my problem," they are thinking.

Well, it's everyone's problem, and we need a leader who will tell us that.

We need a visionary to guide us — to say it wasn't all right for Ryan White to be banned from school because he had AIDS, to say it wasn't all right for a man or a woman to be denied a job because they are infected with this virus. We need a leader who is truly committed to educating us.

I believe in America, but not with a leadership of selfishness and greed, where the wealthy get health care and insurance and the poor don't.

Do you know how much my AIDS care costs? Over $40,000 a year. Someone without insurance can't afford this. Even the drugs that I hope will keep me alive are out of reach for others. Is their life any less valuable? Of course not.

This is not the America I was raised to be proud of, where rich people get care and drugs that poor people can't. We need health care for all. We need a leader who will say this and do something about it.

I believe in America, but not a leadership that talks about problems but is incapable of solving them. Two HIV commission reports with recommendations about what to do to solve this crisis are sitting on shelves, gathering dust. We need a leader who will not only listen to these recommendations but implement them.

I believe in America, but not with a leadership that doesn't hold government accountable. I go to Washington, to the National Institutes of Health, and say, "Show me what you're doing on HIV." They hate it when I come, because I try to tell them how to do it better. But that's why I love being a taxpayer—because it's my money and they must feel accountable.

I believe in an America where our leaders talk straight. When anyone tells President Bush that the battle against AIDS is seriously underfunded, he juggles the numbers to mislead the public into thinking we're spending twice as much as we really are.

While they play games with numbers, people are dying.

I believe in America, but an America where there is a light in every home. "A thousand points of light" just wasn't enough. My house has been dark for too long.

Once every generation, history brings us to an important crossroads. Sometimes in life there is that moment when it's possible to make a change for the better. This is one of those moments. For me, this is not politics. This is a crisis of caring. In this hall is the future—women, men of all colors saying, Take America back.

We are just real people wanting a more hopeful life. But words and ideas are not enough. Good thoughts won't save my family. What's the point of caring if we don't do something about it?

A President and a Congress that can work together so we can get out of this gridlock and move ahead, because I don't win my war if the President cares and the Congress doesn't or if the Congress cares and the President doesn't support the ideas.

The people in this hall this week, the Democratic Party, all of us can begin to deliver that partnership and in November we can all bring it home.

My daughter lived seven years and in her last year, when she couldn't walk or talk, her wisdom shone through. She taught me to love when all I wanted to do was hate. She taught me to help others when all I wanted to do was help myself. She taught me to be brave when all I felt was fear. My daughter and I loved each other with simplicity. America, we can do the same.

This was the country that offered hope. This was the place where dreams could come true, not just economic dreams but dreams of freedom, justice and equality.

We all need to hope that our dreams can come true. I challenge you to make it happen, because all our lives, not just mine, depend on it. Thank you.

# AIDS: A Personal Narrative

## *Mary Fisher*

Mary Fisher gave the following persuasive speech at the Republican National Convention in Houston, Texas, on August 19, 1992. The speech was remarkable for the situation in which it was presented and for the speaker. Up to this point in the convention, the religious right and the ultra-conservative wing of the party had dominated convention rhetoric with attacks on alternative lifestyles and praise for traditional family values. The GOP platform specifically opposed distribution of condoms and syringes to help prevent AIDS. This "preliminary tuning effect" was hardly ideal for a speaker who wished to arouse awareness and sympathy for AIDS sufferers.

Mary Fisher, however, did not fit the stereotypical image of an AIDS victim: she was not "the lonely gay man" or the infected drug user. Instead, she was introduced carefully in the rather uncomfortable convention atmosphere as a former aide to President Gerald Ford and as the daughter of Max Fisher, the honorary chairman of the Bush-Quayle National Finance Committee.

Unlike Elizabeth Glaser, Mary Fisher does not criticize previous national political leadership nor does she plead for programs of research. She asks her listeners instead to open their hearts to AIDS sufferers. *Are you human?* is her critical, challenging moment. Therefore, her speech can be studied for its use of proof by pathos before an initially wary audience, and for its effort to establish an identification linkage among herself, the audience, and other victims of AIDS.

Less than three months ago, at Platform Hearings in Salt Lake City, I asked the Republican party to lift the shroud of silence which has been draped over the issue of HIV and AIDS. I have come tonight to bring our silence to an end.

I bear a message of challenge, not self-congratulation. I want your attention, not your applause. I would never have asked to be HIV-positive. But I believe that in all things there is a purpose, and I stand before you, and before the nation, gladly.

The reality of AIDS is brutally clear. Two hundred thousand Americans are dead or dying; a million more are infected. Worldwide, forty million, sixty million, or a hundred million infections will be counted in the coming few years. But despite science and research, White House meetings and congressional hearings; despite good intentions and bold initiatives, campaign slogans and hopeful promises — it is, despite it all, the epidemic which is winning tonight.

In the context of an election year, I ask you, here, in this great hall, or listening in the quiet of your home, to recognize that AIDS virus is not a political creature. It does not care whether you are Democrat or Republican. It does not ask whether you are black or a white, male or female, gay or straight, young or old.

Tonight, I represent an AIDS community whose members have been reluctantly drafted from every segment of American society. Though I am white, and a mother, I am one with a black infant struggling with tubes in a Philadelphia hospital. Though I am female, and contracted this disease in marriage, and enjoy the warm support of my family, I am one with the lonely gay man sheltering a flickering candle from the cold wind of his family's rejection.

This is not a distant threat; it is a present danger. The rate of infection is increasing fastest among women and children. Largely unknown a decade ago, AIDS is the third leading killer of young adult Americans today. But it won't be third for long, because, unlike other diseases, this one travels. Adolescents don't give each other cancer or heart disease because they believe they are in love. But HIV is different.

And we have helped it along. We have killed each other—with our ignorance, our prejudice, and our silence. We may take refuge in our stereotypes, but we cannot hide there long. Because HIV asks only one thing of those it attacks: Are you human? And this is the right question: Are you human?

Because people with HIV have not entered some alien state of being. They are human. They have not earned cruelty and they do not deserve meanness. They don't benefit from being isolated or treated as outcasts. Each of them is exactly what God made: a person. Not evil, deserving of our judgment; not victims, longing for our pity. People. Ready for support and worthy of compassion.

My call to you, my party, is to take a public stand no less compassionate than that of the President and Mrs. Bush. They have embraced me and my family in memorable ways. In the place of judgment, they have shown affection. In difficult moments, they have raised our spirits. In the darkest hours, I have seen them reaching not only to me, but also to my parents, armed with that stunning grief and special grace that comes only to parents who have themselves leaned too long over the bedside of a dying child.

With the President's leadership, much good has been done. Much of the good has gone unheralded. As the President has insisted, "Much remains to be done." But we do the President's cause no good if we praise the American family but ignore a virus that destroys it. We must be consistent if we are to be believed. We cannot love justice and ignore prejudice, love our children and fear to teach them. Whatever our role, as parent or policy maker, we must act as eloquently as we speak, else we have no integrity.

My call to the nation is a plea for awareness. If you believe you are safe, you are in danger. Because I was not hemophiliac, I was not at risk. Because I was not gay, I was not at risk. Because I did not inject drugs, I was not at risk. My father has devoted much of his lifetime to guarding against another holocaust. He is part of the generation who heard Pastor Niemoeller come out of the Nazi death camps to say, "They came after the Jews and I was not a Jew, so I did not protest. They came after the Trade Unionists, and I was not a Trade Unionist, so I did not protest. Then they came after the Roman Catholics, and I was not a Roman Catholic, so I did not protest. Then they came after me, and there was no one left to protest."

The lesson history teaches is this: If you believe you are safe, you are at risk. If you do not see this killer stalking your children, look again. There is no family or community, no race or religion, no place left in America that is safe. Until we genuinely embrace this message, we are a nation at risk.

Tonight, HIV marches resolutely toward AIDS in more than a million American homes, littering its pathway with the bodies of the young. Young men. Young women. Young parents. And young children. One of the families is mine. If it is true that HIV inevitably turns to AIDS, then my children will inevitably turn to orphans.

My family have been a rock of support. My 84-year-old father, who has pursued the healing of the nations, will not accept the premise that he cannot heal his daughter. My mother refuses to be broken. She still calls at midnight to tell wonderful jokes that make me laugh. Sisters and friends, and my brother Phillip (whose birthday is today), all have helped carry me over the hardest places. I am blessed, richly and deeply blessed, to have such a family.

But not all of you have been so blessed. You are HIV-positive but dare not say it. You have lost loved ones, but you dared not whisper the word AIDS. You weep silently. You grieve alone.

I have a message for you. It is not you who should feel shame, it is we. We who tolerate ignorance and practice prejudice, we who have taught you to fear. We must lift our shroud of silence, making it safe for you to reach out for compassion. It is our task to seek safety for our children, not in quiet denial but in effective action. Some day our children will be grown.

My son Max, now four, will take the measure of his mother. My son Zachary, now two, will sort through his memories. I may not be here to hear their judgments, but I know already what I hope they are.

I want my children to know that their mother was not a victim. She was a messenger. I do not want them to think, as I once did, that courage is the absence of fear. I want them to know that courage is the strength to act wisely when most we are afraid. I want them to have the courage to step forward when called by their nation, or their party, and give leadership, no matter what the personal cost. I ask no more of you than I ask of myself, or of my children.

To the millions of you who are grieving, who are frightened, who have suffered the ravages of AIDS firsthand: have courage and you will find support. To the millions who are strong, I issue the plea: Set aside prejudice and politics to make room for compassion and sound policy.

To my children, I make this pledge: I will not give in, Zachary, because I draw my courage from you. Your silly giggle gives me hope. Your gentle prayers give me strength. And you, my child, give me the reason to say to America, "You are at risk." And I will not rest, Max, until I have done all I can to make your world safe. I will seek a place where intimacy is not the prelude to suffering.

I will not hurry to leave you, my children. But when I go, I pray that you will not suffer shame on my account. To all within the sound of my voice, I appeal: Learn with me the lessons of history and of grace, so my children will not be afraid to say the word AIDS when I am gone. Then their children, and yours may not need to whisper it at all.

God bless the children, God bless us all. Good night.

## Inaugural Address

### *Bill Clinton*

The Presidential Inaugural Address is one of the great ceremonial speech forms of American public life. Typically, the inaugural performs a number of vital functions, including

- celebrating the national experience, while reassuring the nation and the world community that a competent leader who respects the traditions of American government has taken up the reins of government;

- after a divisive political campaign, providing a unification ritual that reminds listeners of their shared national identity as a people, emphasizing common values;

- acknowledging the problems that people have, but offering hope that these problems can be solved by united action;

- sketching the direction and priorities of the next four years, while persuading listeners that the presidential agenda should also be *their* agenda;
- in the case of great inaugurals, such as Lincoln's Second Inaugural, offering a grandeur of vision or an eloquence of statement that lifts the spirit and redefines national purpose in unforgettable ways.

As you read the speech that follows, ask yourself how well the Clinton inaugural, presented on January 20, 1993, in Washington, D.C., performed these functions. To learn more about the inaugural address as a ceremonial form, see Karlyn Kohrs Campbell and Kathleen Hall Jamieson, *Deeds Done In Words: Presidential Rhetoric and the Genres of Governance* (Chicago: University of Chicago Press, 1990), pp. 14-36.

M y fellow citizens, today we celebrate the mystery of American renewal. This ceremony is held in the depth of winter, but by the words we speak and the faces we show the world, we force the spring. A spring reborn in the world's oldest democracy that brings forth the vision and courage to reinvent America.

When our founders boldly declared America's independence to the world and our purposes to the Almighty, they knew that America, to endure, would have to change. Not change for change sake but change to preserve America's ideals — life, liberty, the pursuit of happiness. Though we march to the music of our time, our mission is timeless. Each generation of Americans must define what it means to be an American.

On behalf of our nation, I salute my predecessor, President Bush, for his half-century of service to America.

And I thank the millions of men and women whose steadfastness and sacrifice triumphed over depression, fascism, and communism. Today, a generation raised in the shadows of the cold war assumes new responsibilities in a world warmed by the sunshine of freedom but threatened still by ancient hatreds and new plagues.

Raised in unrivaled prosperity, we inherit an economy that is still the world's strongest, but is weakened by business failures, stagnant wages, increasing inequality, and deep divisions among our own people.

When George Washington first took the oath I have just sworn to uphold, news traveled slowly across the land by horseback and across the ocean by boat. Now the sights and sounds of this ceremony are broadcast instantaneously to billions around the world. Communications and commerce are global, investment is mobile, technology is almost magical, and ambition for a better life is now universal. We earn our livelihood in America today in peaceful competition with people all across the earth. Profound and powerful forces are shaking and remaking our world. And the urgent question of our time is whether we can make change our friend and not our enemy.

This new world has already enriched the lives of millions of Americans who are able to compete and win in it. But when most people are working harder for less, when others cannot work at all, when the cost of health care devastates families and threatens to bankrupt our enterprises great and small, when the fear of crime robs law-abiding citizens of their freedom, and when millions of poor children cannot even imagine the lives we are calling them to lead, we have not made change our friend. We know we have to face hard truths and take strong steps, but we have not done so. Instead, we have drifted, and that drifting has eroded our resources, fractured our economy and shaken our confidence.

Though our challenges are fearsome, so are our strengths. Americans have ever been a restless, questing, hopeful people, and we must bring to our task today the vision and will of those who came before us. From our Revolution to the Civil War, to the Great Depression, to the civil rights movement, our people have always mustered the determination to construct from these crises the pillars of our history.

Thomas Jefferson believed that to preserve the very foundations of our nation we would need dramatic change from time to time. Well my fellow Americans, this is our time. Let us embrace it.

Our democracy must be not only the envy of the world but the engine of our own renewal. There is nothing wrong with America that cannot be cured by what is right with America. And so today we pledge an end to the era of deadlock and drift, and a new season of American renewal has begun.

To renew America we must be bold. We must do what no generation has had to do before. We must invest more in our own people — in their jobs and in their future — and at the same time cut our massive debt. And we must do so in a world in which we must compete for every opportunity. It will not be easy. It will require sacrifice. But it can be done and done fairly, not choosing sacrifice for its own sake, but for our own sake. We must provide for our nation the way a family provides for its children.

Our founders saw themselves in that light of posterity. We can do no less. Anyone who has ever watched a child's eyes wander into sleep knows what posterity is. Posterity the world to come — the world for whom we hold our ideals, from whom we have borrowed our planet, and to whom we bear sacred responsibility. We must do what America does best: offer more opportunity to all and demand more responsibility from all.

It is time to break the bad habit of expecting something for nothing from our government or from each other. Let us all take more responsibility, not only for ourselves and our families but for our communities and our country.

To renew America we must revitalize our democracy. This beautiful capital, like every capital since the dawn of civilization, is often a place of intrigue and calculation. Powerful people maneuver for position and worry endlessly about who is in and who is out, who is up and who is down, forgetting those people whose toil and sweat sends us here and pays our way.

Americans deserve better, and in this city today there are people who want to do better. And so I say to all of you here, let us resolve to reform our politics so that power and privilege no longer shout down the voice of the people. Let us put aside personal advantage so that we can feel the pain and see the promise of America. Let us resolve to make our government a place for what Franklin Roosevelt called "bold, persistent experimentation," a government for our tomorrows, not our yesterdays. Let us give this capital back to the people to whom it belongs.

To renew America, we must meet challenges abroad as well as at home. There is no longer a clear division between what is foreign and what is domestic. The world economy, the world environment, the world AIDS crisis, the world arms race — they affect us all.

Today, as an old order passes, the new world is more free but less stable. Communism's collapse has called forth old animosities and new dangers. Clearly, America must continue to lead the world we did so much to make.

While America rebuilds at home, we will not shrink from the challenges nor fail to seize the opportunities of this new world. Together with our friends and allies, we will work to shape change lest it engulf us. When our vital interests are challenged or the will and conscience of the international community is defied, we will act — with peaceful diplomacy whenever possible, with force when necessary.

The brave Americans serving our nation today in the Persian Gulf and Somalia, and wherever else they stand, are testament to our resolve.

But our greatest strength is the power of our ideas, which are still new in many lands. Across the world we see them embraced and we rejoice. Our hopes, our hearts, our hands are with those on every continent who are building democracy and freedom. Their cause is America's cause.

The American people have summoned the change we celebrate today. You have raised your voices in an unmistakable chorus, you have cast your votes in historic numbers, and you have changed the face of Congress, the presidency and the political process itself. Yes, you, my fellow Americans, have forced the spring.

Now we must do the work the season demands. To that work I now turn, with all the authority of my office. I ask the Congress to join with me. But no president, no Congress, no government can undertake this mission alone. My fellow Americans, you, too, must play your part in our renewal.

I challenge a new generation of young Americans to a sense of service — to act on your idealism by helping troubled children, keeping company with those in need, reconnecting our torn communities. There is so much to be done — enough, indeed, for millions of others who are still young in spirit to give of themselves in service, too.

In serving, we recognize a simple but powerful truth: We need each other and we must care for one another. Today we do more than celebrate

America; we rededicate ourselves to the very idea of America: An idea born in revolution and renewed through two centuries of challenge; an idea tempered by the knowledge that but for fate we, the fortunate and the unfortunate, might have been each other; an idea ennobled by the faith that our nation can summon from its myriad diversity the deepest measure of unity; an idea infused with the conviction that America's long, heroic journey must go forever upward.

And so, my fellow Americans, as we stand at the edge of the 21st century, let us being anew with energy and hope, with faith and discipline. And let us work until our work is done. The Scripture says, "And let us not be weary in well-doing, for in due season we shall reap if we faint not."

From this joyful mountaintop of celebration we hear a call to service in the valley. We have heard the trumpets, we have changed the guard. And now, each in our own way and with God's help, we must answer the call.

Thank you, and God bless you all.

## Nobel Peace Prize Acceptance Speech

### *Elie Wiesel*

Elie Wiesel delivered the following speech in Oslo, Norway, on December 10, 1986, as he accepted the Nobel Peace Prize. The award recognized his lifelong work for human rights, especially his role as "spiritual archivist of the Holocaust." Wiesel's poetic, intensely personal style as a writer carries over into this ceremonial speech of acceptance. He uses narrative very effectively as he flashes back to what he calls the "kingdom of night" and then flashes forward again into the present. The speech's purpose is to spell out and share the values and concerns of a life committed to the rights of oppressed peoples, in which, as he puts it so memorably, "every moment is a moment of grace, every hour an offering."

It is with a profound sense of humility that I accept the honor you have chosen to bestow upon me. I know: your choice transcends me. This both frightens and pleases me.

It frightens me because I wonder: do I have the right to represent the multitudes who have perished? Do I have the right to accept this great honor on their behalf? I do not. That would be presumptuous. No one may speak for the dead, no one may interpret their mutilated dreams and visions.

It pleases me because I may say that this honor belongs to all the survivors and their children, and through us, to the Jewish people with whose destiny I have always been identified.

I remember: it happened yesterday or eternities ago. A young Jewish boy discovering the kingdom of night. I remember his bewilderment, I remember his anguish. It all happened so fast. The ghetto. The deportation. The sealed cattle car. The fiery altar upon which the history of our people and the future of mankind were meant to be sacrificed.

I remember: he asked his father: "Can this be true? This is the 20th century, not the Middle Ages. Who would allow such crimes to be committed? How could the world remain silent?"

And now the boy is turning to me: "Tell me," he asks. "What have you done with your life?"

And I tell him that I have tried. That I have tried to keep memory alive, that I have tried to fight those who would forget. Because if we forget, we are guilty, we are accomplices.

And then I explained to him how naive we were, that the world did know and remain silent. And that is why I swore never to be silent whenever and wherever human beings endure suffering and humiliation. We must always take sides. Neutrality helps the oppressor, never the victim. Silence encourages the tormentor, never the tormented.

Sometimes we must interfere. When human lives are endangered, when human dignity is in jeopardy, national borders and sensitivities become irrelevant. Wherever men or women are persecuted because of their race, religion or political views, that place must — at that moment — become the center of our universe.

Of course, since I am a Jew profoundly rooted in my people's memory and tradition, my first response is to Jewish fears, Jewish needs, Jewish crises. For I belong to a traumatized generation, one that experienced the abandonment and solitude of our people. It would be unnatural for me not to make Jewish priorities my own: Israel, Soviet Jewry, Jews in Arab lands.

But there are others as important to me. Apartheid is, in my view, as abhorrent as anti-Semitism. To me, Andrei Sakharov's isolation is as much a disgrace as Iosif Begun's imprisonment. As is the denial of Solidarity and its leader Lech Walesa's right to dissent. And Nelson Mandela's interminable imprisonment.

There is so much injustice and suffering crying out for our attention: victims of hunger, or racism and political persecution, writers and poets, prisoners in so many lands governed by the left and by the right. Human rights are being violated on every continent. More people are oppressed than free.

And then, too, there are the Palestinians to whose plight I am sensitive but whose methods I deplore. Violence and terrorism are not the answer. Something must be done about their suffering, and soon. I trust Israel, for I have faith in the Jewish people. Let Israel be given a chance, let hatred and danger be removed from her horizons, and there will be peace in and around the Holy Land.

Yes, I have faith. Faith in God and even in His creation. Without it no action would be possible. And action is the only remedy to indifference: the most insidious danger of all. Isn't this the meaning of Alfred Nobel's legacy? Wasn't his fear of war a shield against war?

There is much to be done, there is much that can be done. One person — a Raoul Wallenberg, an Albert Schweitzer, one person of integrity, can make a difference, a difference of life and death. As long as one dissident is in prison, our freedom will not be true. As long as one child is hungry, our lives will be filled with anguish and shame.

What all these victims need above all is to know that they are not alone: that we are not forgetting them, that when their voices are stifled we shall lend them ours, that while their freedom depends on ours, the quality of our freedom depends on theirs.

This is what I say to the young Jewish boy wondering what I have done with his years. It is in his name that I speak to you and that I express to you my deepest gratitude. No one is as capable of gratitude as one who has emerged from the kingdom of night.

We know that every moment is a moment of grace, every hour an offering; not to share them would mean to betray them. Our lives no longer belong to us alone; they belong to all those who need us desperately.

Thank you Chairman Aarvik. Thank you members of the Nobel Committee. Thank you people of Norway, for declaring on this singular occasion that our survival has meaning for mankind.

## University of South Carolina Commencement Address

### Bill Cosby

Bill Cosby, one of the beloved entertainers of our time, delivered the speech that follows as a commencement address at the University of South Carolina on May 17, 1986. The speech sparkles with Cosby humor, humor that makes fun of the typical graduation address that invites graduates to "go forth . . . to change the world." Instead, Cosby's good-natured laughter brings a gentle realism to the graduation occasion. The "real world," he tells graduates, loves "fresh blood." Graduates now need to seek "maturity, that ability to read other human beings, that maturity to make a decision based on what is needed as opposed to what you want. . . ." He invites them to "find out where 'forth' is," and to seek an occupation in which they will be doing something they enjoy.

For all of the grads, obviously, this is supposedly your moment. However, for the first time in your lives, you carry other people with you. Specifically, Mom and Dad paved the way, whether all of it, some of it, half of it. It was a road that needed to be paved. The job you've done, studying; their job — taking care of tuition, fees, incidentals, "ask-a-dentals." This day that you'll receive your paper is a great day.

All across the United States of America, people are graduating. And they are hearing so many guest speakers tell them that they are going forth. As a parent I am concerned as to whether or not you know where "forth" is. Let me put it to you this way: We have paved a road — the one to the house was already paved. "Forth" is not back home.

Yes, we love you, and we are proud of you, and we are not tired of you, but you can make us tired. Nothing is worse than a daughter or son with a college degree still at home. "Forth" could be next door to us, with you paying the rent.

All of these years of college you've spent second-guessing, third-guessing great politicians, great doctors, great lawyers, great anybody — the way you would have done it. Now your chance is supposed to be here, but it isn't. And I'm speaking specifically to those who've graduated for the first time. I'm speaking to all of you who have your diploma and now are being told you're going forth, that you have an opportunity to change the world. My question is with what?

What noises are you going to make to get someone's attention? Those of us who graduated long before you have comfortable places and uncomfortable places, and if you think that your little diploma is going to take away what we've worked so hard to get, you're out of your mind. You can come out here if you want to, waving your little diploma — we didn't ask for it, your parents told you to get one.

So I'm saying to you, those people who are giving speeches across this nation — "Yes, you can make change and you can do this" — you can't do anything yet. You don't know how to do it. You don't know how to play the game out there. There are some old ones waiting for you.

Every person with a college diploma is not necessarily an overachiever. Don't you believe it! I've met some great underachievers — graduated from college — went on to graduate school. Some great underachievers — lawyers, some great underachievers — doctors, some great underachievers — engineers. You look at them and wonder how the hell they got a degree.

These are the people you're going to have to usurp. These are the people you're going to have to move out of the way so that you can do better, if you can do better. When you get your diploma today and you throw your hat in the air — some of you may be sitting out there with your cap and gown and nothing on underneath, passing a bottle of champagne around, and you are ready because you have a four-year degree. You have nothing. You have nothing.

You've made your parents very, very happy. Make them happier. Find out where "forth" is. However, the "real world" is waiting for you, and many thousands and thousands of people have been out here a long time and know how to play the game. We're waiting for you. We love fresh blood. We love nice clean-cut looking people. We'll run you around for about four years doing nothing. You say, "Well, I think I'm…." "No, not yet, just keep following me. I'm going to show you something else." Then you begin to wonder, you begin to doubt yourselves. I just want you to know the truth.

It's a happy, happy time today. Turn to your family; that's where love is. Those of you with younger sisters and brothers, you show them what you've done. As a parent I know that four years of college brings nothing more than a learned person in terms of books, tests, notes; but that maturity, that ability to read other human beings, that maturity to make a decision based on what is needed as opposed to what you want — there's no degree for that and there's no time specification.

Yes, the world needs leaders. But if any of you sitting there think that upon your walking out of this building with that paper and your parents smiling and you get into the car and you're going to have a party at so-and-so's house, and shaking of the hands — that does not give you a credit card into the big-spending world. It's a happy time for you. It's a time to get it together, collect your family, collect the love, and then collect yourselves because now comes the maturity of self, the decisions to be made. And it's a wonderful world out here. You look at these old faces back here — leaders — but look at what it's done to them.

As a parent, I get a great, great feeling about this because as a parent I realize how difficult it is to say "college" to a child. You can say it. And more and more as a parent, the old saying — I don't know how old it is but when you become a parent and the longer you remain a parent, the more old sayings keep coming — you don't know who said it, you just know it's old — "[You can] lead a horse to water, but you can't make him drink." That's one of my favorites so far.

Ladies and gentlemen, young ladies and gentlemen, this is not your world yet. You have to make it.

I had my own television show three times and failed. Yet, they remember this one, and they act like this is the only one I ever had. I had one show that lasted seven weeks. I was number 67 out of 63 shows for seven weeks when they unmercifully pulled the plug. I asked them to pull the plug at the end of the second week, but they wanted to punish me.

And so now through timing, hard work is not hard work when you're successful. Power is not felt when you're busy doing what you enjoy doing.

Do you hear me? Do you all hear me, these people here? Do you hear me? I just want to give you this message, because we don't have time to deal with words like that.

You're doing what you enjoy doing. We all know somewhere in these number of years you worked you did something where you just couldn't wait to get up. As a matter of fact, you didn't even go to sleep, you just couldn't wait. Whatever the project was, you didn't care what you put into it; you didn't care about the extra step you took because you weren't tired. You enjoyed it.

It isn't hard work, especially when you're enjoying it. You don't have time to think about power when you enjoy what you're doing. And so, if there is a message — which I think I've already given — [there is] the fun of knowing that "forth" is not back at your parents' home, the fun of knowing that now your work is cut out for you to mature and get on with whatever it is you think you want to do.

There are many people out there who graduated twenty, thirty-five, two years ago. You can take their place. But every year graduates someone who can take your place if you're not enjoying what you're doing.

I want to congratulate all of the parents who understand exactly what I'm saying. And on this particular day let me say to any parent, "If you want to come up here with your child and get that diploma, let it be today."

## The Trials of Malcolm X

### *Ronnie Davis*

Ronnie Davis presented the following ceremonial speech of tribute to Malcolm X in his class at Memphis State University. Such speeches typically emphasize two major techniques—identification, which helps the audience relate closely to the subject and speaker, and magnification, which helps listeners to appreciate the accomplishments of the subject. Ronnie's impressive array of quotations help magnify the importance of Malcolm X as a voice for the anger and bitterness within the African-American experience. Ronnie also traces the important phases of Malcolm's personal journey through degeneration, crime, rebirth as a Black Muslim, and final acceptance of the brotherhood and sisterhood of all people. To build audience identification, Ronnie might have drawn more clearly the meanings of these various phases of Malcolm's life as they contributed to his moral growth and expansion.

The purpose is to explain in detail the trials and tribulations of one man. The goal is to educate and to inform the audience of his life and times through various stages, from my point of view. You just can't sit through a movie for three-and-a-half hours and form a true understanding of a truly controversial subject. But to understand the man is to understand his struggle. Columnist Walter Winchell called him "a petty punk." *Time* magazine said that he was "an unashamed demagogue." And a *New York Times* editorial referred to him as being a "twisted man." As a matter of fact, he called himself "the angriest Negro in America." This man was none other than Malcolm X. To some he was misunderstood and considered a sinister, racist preacher who taught violence and spread malicious untruths. The media misconstrued and twisted his words. But to others, such as myself, he was a black hero who fought oppression at a time when being black was considered a crime.

Malcolm, in my perspective, was tired. He was tired of putting so much energy into the struggle and receiving so little in return. I can't stress this fact enough. To understand the man is to understand the struggle. He expressed his true feelings through his highly motivational, or should I say, colorful speeches, as referred to by our own Osborn text. For example, "We're not Americans. We're Africans who happen to be in America. We were kidnapped and brought here against our will from Africa. We didn't land on Plymouth Rock. Plymouth Rock landed on us." Other prominent figures expressed similar opinions about Malcolm. Black civil rights activists such as Ossie Davis, who delivered the eulogy at Malcolm's funeral, said that Malcolm was a prince, our own shining black prince who didn't hesitate to die because he loved us so. But as I stated before, to understand the man is to understand the struggle.

He was born Malcolm Little, the son of Louise and the Reverend Earl Little, at the University Hospital in Omaha, Nebraska on May 19, 1925. He was harassed, he and his family, throughout his life. His trouble began early when Malcolm's family was harassed by the Ku Klux Klan and his father was allegedly murdered by the same group. After the death of Malcolm's father his family was separated. This separation by the state welfare agency affected Malcolm's mother psychologically, ultimately resulting in her being committed and Malcolm's other brothers and sisters becoming wards of the state. Malcolm later said that "I truly believe that if ever a state social agency destroyed a family, it destroyed ours."

From the years of 1941 to 1952 Malcolm used the street name Detroit Red. These represented Malcolm's criminal years. During this time he met a friend, Shorty, after he moved to Boston to live with a half sister, Ella. Shorty taught him street lingo and how to survive in street knowledge. When Malcolm moved to Harlem in New York, he set his sights on bigger territory. He met a character named West Indian Archy, who at the time was a crime lord. This partner in crime was responsible for converting Malcolm into a drug dealer, a pusher, and a pimp.

From 1946 to 1952 Malcolm was incarcerated. Fellow inmates gave him the name of Satan because he cursed God. In Charlestown State Prison Malcolm met an inmate named Bimby. Bimby helped Malcolm to believe in himself and to obtain self-respect. He was then converted to the Nation of Islam, and introduced to the leader of that nation, who was the honorable Elijah Muhammad. This was Malcolm's turning point. Elijah Muhammad influenced the majority of Malcolm's work and later contributed to Malcolm's downfall.

During the years 1952 to 1963, Malcolm's radical years, Malcolm used the name Malcolm X. And these are the years for which he is most recognized. Malcolm's purpose during this time was to create black awareness. I guess you could consider him a black nationalist Muslim minister who exposed the racist barbarism of American life. His goal was to be a messenger for the honorable Elijah Muhammad, whom he represented in speeches at Harvard and before the United Nations.

Later Malcolm reached another turning point when he was separated from the Nation of Islam. During this time in 1964, he made a trip to Mecca, like all devout Muslims, during the hajj. He was reconverted there and began using a new name, El Haj Malik El Shabazz. His religion and his ideals were completely expanded when he returned to America. He had learned to embrace the brotherhood of all people. His final projects in the latter part of his life were to create his own Muslim Mosque Incorporated and to promote the Organization of Afro-American Unity. He was martyred on February 21, 1965, at the New York Audubon Ballroom, where he was felled by the bullets of four assassins.

In conclusion, I would like to state that Malcolm was a noble man who went through a series of changes. It takes more than just wearing a T-shirt or seeing the movie. You have to understand the man in order to understand his struggle.

# Glossary

**after-dinner speech** A brief, often humorous, ceremonial speech, presented after a meal, that offers a message without asking for radical changes in attitude or action. (15)

**alliteration** The repetition of initial consonant sounds in closely connected words. (10)

**amplification** The art of developing ideas by strategic repetition in a speech. (10)

**analogical argument** Creating a strategic perspective on a subject by relating it to something about which the audience has strong positive or negative feelings. (14)

**analogous color** Colors adjacent on the color wheel; used in a visual aid to suggest both differences and close relationships among the components represented. (9)

**analogy** A connection established between two otherwise dissimilar ideas or things. (12)

**analogy design** A pattern for a persuasive speech whose body consists of an extended comparison supporting the speaker's proposal. (13)

**anaphora** The use of the same initial wording in a sequence of phrases or sentences. (10)

**antithesis** A language technique that combines opposing elements in the same sentence or adjoining sentences. (10)

**archetypal metaphor** A metaphor that draws upon human experience that is common, intense, and enduring, and that arouses group feeling. (10)

**argument** A combination of evidence and proofs designed to produce a strong case for one side of an issue. (14)

**argument *ad hominem*** An attempt to discredit a position by attacking the people who favor it. (14)

**articulation** The manner in which individual speech sounds are produced. (11)

**assimilation** The tendency of listeners to interpret the positions of a speaker with whom they agree as closer to their own views than they actually are. (3)

**attitudes** Pre-existing complexes of feelings, beliefs, and inclinations that we have toward people, places, events, or ideas. (4)

**audience dynamics** The motivations, attitudes, beliefs, and values that influence the behavior of listeners. (4)

**bar graph** A kind of graph that shows comparisons and contrasts between two or more items or groups. (9)

**begging the question** Assuming that an argument has been proved without actually presenting the evidence. (14)

**beliefs** Things accepted as true about a subject. (4)

**bias** Prejudice or lack of objectivity resulting from self-interest in an issue. (1)

**body** The middle part of a speech, used to develop the main ideas. (2)

**body language** Communication achieved using facial expressions, eye contact, movements, and gestures. (11)

**boomerang effect** An audience's hostile reaction to a speech advocating too much or too radical change. (13)

**brainstorming** A group technique that encourages all members to contribute freely and creatively to the range of options available for consideration. (Appendix A)

**brief example** A specific instance illustrating a more general idea. (6)

**call the question** A motion that proposes to end the discussion on a motion and to bring it to a vote. (Appendix A)

**categorical design** The use of natural or traditional divisions within a subject as a way of structuring an informative speech. (12)

**categorical imprecision** Vague or careless wording of an argument's major premise. (14)

**causation design**  A pattern for an informative speech that shows how one condition generates, or is generated by, another. (12)

**ceremonial speech**  A group of speech types that emphasizes the importance of shared values. Includes the speech of tribute, the speech of acceptance, the speech of introduction, and the after-dinner speech. (1, 15)

**co-active approach**  A way of approaching reluctant audiences in which the speaker attempts to establish good will, emphasizes shared values, and sets modest goals for persuasion. (13)

**cognitive restructuring**  The process of replacing negative thoughts with positive, constructive ones. (2)

**commitment**  The dedication of the speaker to the subject of the speech and the well-being of the audience. (1)

**communication apprehension**  Concern or nervousness experienced before or during speaking in public. (2)

**communication environment**  The overall conditions in which communication occurs. (1)

**comparison and contrast design**  A pattern for an informative speech that relates an unfamiliar subject to something the audience already knows or understands. (12)

**competence**  The speaker's appearance of being informed, intelligent, and well prepared. (2)

**complementary color**  Colors opposite one another on the color wheel; used in a visual aid to suggest tension and opposition among various elements. (9)

**concluding remarks**  The speaker's final reflections on the meaning of the speech. (2)

**conclusion**  The last part of a speech, which should include a summary statement and concluding remarks (2); the proposition that follows the major and minor premises of a syllogism and directs the audience toward the speaker's point of view. (14)

**confusion of probability and certainty**  A fallacy in an argument in which something likely is passed off as something definite. (14)

**connotative meaning**  The emotional or attitudinal reactions evoked by certain words. (3)

**consciousness-raising function**  The result of a presentation that has made an audience more sensitive to an issue and more receptive to future persuasion. (13)

**constructive listening**  The role of the listener in the creation of meaning. Involves discovering the speaker's intention, tracing out the implications and consequences of the message, and applying the message to one's life. (3)

**contamination of the conclusion**  A kind of inductive error involving the use of irrelevant or emotionally loaded words. (14)

**contrast effect**  A tendency by listeners to distort the positions of a speaker with whom they disagree and to interpret those positions as even more distant from their own opinions than they actually are. (3)

**coordination**  The requirement that statements equal in importance be placed on the same level in an outline. (8)

**critical listening**  A learned skill that involves hearing, comprehending, analyzing, remembering, and responding to a message. (3)

**critical thinking**  An integrated way of assessing information, ideas, and proposals that calls not for accepting them at face value, but for exploring the grounds for these views, checking them against previous experience, and discussing them with knowledgeable others. (3)

**critique**  An evaluation of a speech. (3)

**cultural gridlock**  Occurs when the cultural differences in a group are so profound that the varying agendas, priorities, customs, and procedures create tensions that block constructive discussion. (Appendix A)

**culturetype**  A term expressing the values and goals of a group's culture. (10)

**deductive argument**  A kind of proof that begins with a generally accepted truth, connects an issue with that truth, and draws a conclusion based on the connection. (14)

**deliberation**  Allowing all sides to express their opinions before a decision is made. (13)

**demographic audience analysis**  A systematic study of such factors as the audience members' age, gender, educational level, group memberships, race, and social class. (4)

**denotative meaning**  The literal, dictionary definition of a word. (3)

**descriptive statistics**  Numbers demonstrating the size and distribution of an object or occurrence. (6)

**dialect**   A speech pattern associated with an area of the country or with a cultural or ethnic background. (11)

**dialogue**   Conversation that is reproduced exactly, rather than paraphrased. (6)

**either-or thinking**   A fallacy that occurs when the speaker informs listeners that they have only two options, only one of which is desirable. (14)

**empathetic listening**   Listening with a feeling of closeness to, or identity with, the speaker or others whom the speaker's words might affect. (3)

**enunciation**   The manner in which individual words are articulated and pronounced in context. (11)

**ethical consequences**   The positive or negative results of a speech for its listeners and for the causes and people it discusses. (1)

**ethos**   Those characteristics that make a speaker appear honest, credible, and appealing (1); a kind of proof created by a speaker's own favorable impression and by association with credible testimony. (14; Appendix A)

**eulogy**   A speech of tribute presented upon a person's death. (15)

**evidence**   Supporting materials used in persuasive speeches, including facts and figures, examples, narratives, and testimony. (14)

**example**   A verbal illustration for an oral message. (6)

**expert testimony**   Information derived from authorities within a field. (6)

**extemporaneous presentation**   A form of presentation in which a speech, although carefully prepared and practiced, is not written out or memorized. (1, 11)

**extended example**   A detailed illustration that allows a speaker to build impressions. (6)

**fact**   Verifiable unit of information. (6)

**factual example**   An illustration based on something that actually happened or that really exists. (6)

**fallacy**   An error in persuasion. (14)

**faulty analogy**   A comparison drawn between things that are dissimilar in some important way. (14)

**feedback**   The audience's immediate response to a speaker. (1)

**figurative analogy**   A comparison made between things that belong to different fields. (12)

**filtering**   Listening to only part of a message, the part the listener wants to hear. (3)

**flow chart**   A visual method of representing power and responsibility relationships. (9)

**formal outline**   The final outline in a process leading from the first rough ideas for a speech to the finished product. (8)

**formal power**   A perceived strength arising from a speaker's position or status. (2)

**gender stereotyping**   Generalizations based on oversimplified or outmoded assumptions about gender and gender roles. (4)

**general purpose**   A speech's overall function. (5)

**good form**   A primary principle of structure, based on simplicity, symmetry, and orderliness. (7)

**great expectation fallacy**   The mistaken idea that major change can be accomplished by a single persuasive effort. (13)

**groupthink**   Occurs when a single, uncritical frame of mind dominates group thinking and prevents the full, objective analysis of specific problems. (Appendix A)

**habitual pitch**   The level at which people speak most frequently. (11)

**hasty generalization**   An error of inductive reasoning in which a claim is based on insufficient or nonrepresentative information. (14)

**historical design**   A structure for an informative speech that uses a chronological narrative of the subject's background. (12)

**hyperbole**   A technique of language that employs exaggeration to make points and arouse feeling. (10)

**hypothetical example**   A representation of reality, usually a synthesis of actual people, situations, or events. (6)

**idea**   A complex of thoughts and feelings concerning a subject. (1)

**identification**   The close involvement of subject, speaker, and listener. (1, 15)

**ideograph**   A word conveying a group's basic political faith or system of beliefs. (10)

**image**   A mental picture created by the use of vivid examples. (10)

**impromptu speaking**   A talk delivered with minimal or no preparation. (11)

**incomparable percentages**  Comparisons offered as evidence even though the bases of comparison are unequal. (14)

**inductive argument**  The use of specific instances to build general conclusions. (14)

**inferential statistics**  Numbers employed to make predictions, show trends, and demonstrate relationships. (6)

**informal power**  A favorable impression created by a speaker's competence, integrity, decisiveness, and confidence. (2)

**information card**  A record of facts and ideas obtained from an article or book used in research. (5)

**informative speech**  Speech aimed at extending understanding. (1)

**integrity**  The quality of being ethical, honest, and dependable. (2)

**interference**  Any physical noise or psychological distraction that impedes the hearing of a speech. (1)

**internal summary**  Reminding listeners of major points already presented in a speech before new ideas are introduced. (7)

**introduction**  The first part of a speech, intended to gain the audience's attention and prepare it for the rest of the presentation. (2)

**inversion**  Changing the normal word order to make statements memorable and emphatic. (10)

**key-word outline**  An abbreviated version of a formal outline, used in presenting a speech. (2, 8)

**lay testimony**  Information that is derived from the firsthand experience of ordinary citizens. (6)

**likableness**  The quality of radiating goodness and good will and inspiring audience affection in return. (2)

**line graph**  A visual representation of changes across time; especially useful for indicating trends of growth or decline. (9)

**listening log**  A record of listening lapses kept by students to improve their attention spans. (3)

**literal analogy**  A comparison made between subjects within the same field. (12)

**logos**  A form of proof that makes rational appeals based on facts and figures and expert testimony. (14)

**magnification**  A speaker's selecting and emphasizing certain qualities about a subject in order to stress the values that they represent. (15)

**main motion**  A proposal that would commit a group to some specific action or declaration. (Appendix A)

**major premise**  A general truth that is part of a syllogism. (14)

**malapropism**  A language error that occurs when a word is confused with another word that sounds like it. (10)

**manuscript presentation**  A speech read from a manuscript. (11)

**marking**  Adding a gender reference when none is needed — e.g., "a woman doctor." (4)

**maxim**  A brief and particularly apt saying. (10)

**medium**  The channel that transmits the speaker's message, usually the air through which the sound travels. (1)

**memorized text presentation**  A speech that is committed to memory and delivered word for word. (11)

**message**  The fabric of words, illustrations, voice, and body language that conveys the idea of the speech. (1)

**metaphor**  A figure of speech in which anticipated words are replaced by new, surprising language in order to create a new perspective. (10)

**metonymy**  A language technique that evokes an idea by employing a term that is associated with it. (10)

**minor premise**  The claim made in a syllogism that an important idea is related to a generally accepted truth (or major premise). (14)

**mirror question**  A question that includes part of a previous response to encourage further discussion. (5)

**monochromatic color**  Variations in one color; used in visual aids to suggest changes in a subject. (9)

**motion**  Formal proposal for group consideration. (Appendix A)

**motion to amend**  A parliamentary move that offers the opportunity to modify a motion presently under discussion. (Appendix A)

**motivated sequence design**  A persuasive speech design that proceeds by arousing attention, demonstrating a need, satisfying the need, visualizing results, and calling for action. (13)

**motivation**  Internal forces that impel action and direct human behavior toward specific goals. (4)

**multisided presentation**  A speech in which the speaker's position is compared favorably to other positions. (13)

**myth of the mean**  The deceptive use of statistical averages in speeches. (14)

**mythos**  A form of proof that connects a subject to the culture and tradition of a group through the use of narratives. (14)

**narrative**  A story used to illustrate some important truth about a speaker's topic. (6)

**non sequitur fallacy**  A deductive error occurring when conclusions are drawn improperly from the premises that preceded them. (14)

**onomatopoeia**  The use of words that sound like the objects they signify. (10)

**open leadership style**  A leadership approach that encourages all sides to air their views and that resist premature closure on an issue. (10)

**optimum pitch**  The level at which people can produce their strongest voice with minimal effort and that allows variation up and down the musical scale. (11)

**orderliness**  A consistent pattern used to develop a speech. (7)

**parallel construction**  Wording an outline's main points in the same way in order to emphasize their importance and to help the audience remember them. (8)

**paraphrase**  A summary of something said or written. (6)

**parliamentary procedure**  A set of formal rules that establishes an order of business for meetings and encourages the orderly, fair, and full consideration of proposals during group deliberation. (Appendix A)

**participative communication**  The shared responsibility of the speaker and the listener for creating meaning. (3)

**pathos**  Proof relying on appeals to personal motives and emotions. (14)

**personification**  A figure of speech in which nonhuman or abstract subjects are given human qualities. (10)

**perspective by incongruity**  A language technique used to shock audiences into new ways of understanding; usually relies on extreme metaphors. (10)

**persuasive speech**  Speech intended to influence the attitudes or actions of listeners. (1)

**pictograph**  On a chart, a visual image symbolizing the information it represents. (9)

**pie graph**  A circle graph that shows the size of a subject's parts in relation to each other and to the whole. (9)

**pitch**  The position of a human voice on the musical scale. (11)

**plagiarism**  Presenting the ideas and words of others without crediting them as sources. (1)

***post hoc ergo propter hoc* fallacy**  A deductive error in which one event is assumed to be the cause of another simply because the first preceded the second. (14)

**postpone consideration**  A motion that defers discussion until some specified time when necessary information will be available. (Appendix A)

**precision**  Using information that is closely and carefully related to the specific purpose; particularly important when a topic varies widely from place to place. (5)

**preliminary tuning effect**  The effect of previous speeches or other situational factors in predisposing an audience to respond positively or negatively to a speech. (4)

**preparation outline**  A tentative plan showing the pattern of a speech's major parts, their relative importance, and the way they fit together. (8)

**presentation**  Utterance of a speech to an audience, integrating the skills of nonverbal communication, especially body language, with the speech content. (11)

**prestige testimony**  Information coming from a person who is highly regarded but not necessarily an expert on a topic. (6)

**preview**  The part of the introduction that identifies the main points in the body of the speech and presents an overview of the speech to follow. May follow the thematic statement or be part of the thematic statement itself. (5, 7)

**primary audience**  That person or persons who are capable of making the speaker's words effective. (4)

**principle of closure**  The need for a satisfactory end or conclusion to a speech. (7)

**principle of proximity**  The idea that things occurring together in time or space should be presented in the order in which they normally happen. (7)

**principle of similarity**  The principle that like things should be grouped together. (7)

**probe**  A question that asks an expert to elaborate on a response. (5)

**problem-solution design**  A persuasive speech pattern in which listeners are first persuaded that they have a problem and then are shown how to solve it. (13)

**pronunciation**  The use of correct sounds and of proper stress or accent on syllables in saying words. (11)

**proof**  An interpretation of evidence that provides reasons for listeners to change their attitudes or behaviors. (14)

**proxemics**  The study of how human beings use space during communication. (11)

**purpose**  The goal that a speech attempts to accomplish. (5)

**rate**  The speed at which words are uttered. (11)

**receiver**  The audience that processes the message. (1)

**recency**  Ensuring that the information in a speech is the latest that can be provided. (5)

**red herring**  The use of irrelevant material to divert attention. (14)

**refutative design**  A persuasive speech design in which the speaker tries to raise doubts about, damage, or destroy an opposing position. (13)

**reinforcer**  A comment or action that encourages further communication from someone being interviewed. (5)

**reliability**  The trustworthiness of information critical to the credibility of a speech. (5)

**research overview**  A listing of the main sources of information used in a speech and of the major ideas from each source. (7)

**response**  The audience's reaction, both immediate and delayed, to a speech. (1)

**responsible knowledge**  An understanding of the major features, issues, experts, latest developments, and local applications relevant to a topic. (5)

**rhetorical question**  A question that has a self-evident answer, or that provokes curiosity that the speech then proceeds to satisfy. (7)

**rhetorical style**  The unique way a speaker chooses and arranges words in a presentation. (10)

**Robert's Rules of Order**  The authoritative, traditional "bible" of parliamentary procedure. (Appendix A)

**second**  A motion must receive a "second" before group discussion can proceed. Assures that more than one member wishes to have the motion considered. (Appendix A)

**self-awareness inventory**  A series of questions that a speaker can ask to develop an approach to a speech of introduction. (2)

**sequence chart**  Visual illustrations of the different stages of a process. (9)

**sequential design**  A pattern for an informative speech that presents the steps involved in the process being demonstrated. (12)

**setting the agenda**  Employing information to create a sense of what is important. (12)

**sexist language**  The use of masculine nouns and pronouns when the intended reference is to both sexes, or the use of derogatory emotional trigger words when referring to women. (4)

**shock-and-startle technique**  A method of gaining attention and arousing the audience's curiosity about a topic. (7)

**simile**  A language tool that clarifies something abstract by comparing it with something concrete; usually introduced by *as* or *like*. (10)

**simplicity**  A desirable quality of speech structure. Suggests that a speech have a limited number of main points and that they be short and direct. (7)

**sleeper effect**  A delayed reaction to persuasion. (13)

**slippery slope fallacy**  The assumption that once something happens, an inevitable trend is established that will lead to disastrous results. (14)

**social leadership behavior**  Occurs when leaders focus upon building and maintaining positive, productive relationships among group members. (Appendix A)

**source**  The person who begins the communication process with intent to express an idea. (1)

**source card**  A record kept of the author, title, place and date of publication, and page references for each research source. (5)

**spatial design**   A pattern for an informative speech that orders the main points as they occur in physical space. (12)

**specific purpose**   The speaker's particular goal or the response that the speaker wishes to evoke. (5)

**speech of acceptance**   A ceremonial speech expressing gratitude for an honor and acknowledging those who made the accomplishment possible. (15)

**speech addressing attitudes**   Persuasive speech that attempts to form, reform, or reinforce audience attitudes. (13)

**speech of contention**   Persuasive speech that confronts the opposition by systematically refuting its claims. (13)

**speech of demonstration**   An informative speech aimed at showing the audience how to do something or how something works. (12)

**speech of description**   An informative speech that creates word pictures to help the audience understand a subject. (12)

**speech of explanation**   A speech that is intended to inform the audience about abstract and complex subjects, such as concepts or programs. (12)

**speech of inspiration**   A ceremonial speech directed at awakening or reawakening an audience to a goal, purpose, or set of values. (15)

**speech of introduction**   A ceremonial speech in which a featured speaker is introduced to the audience. (15)

**speech of tribute**   A ceremonial speech that recognizes the achievements of individuals or groups or commemorates special events. (15)

**speech urging action**   Persuasive speech that urges the audience to take action, either as individuals or as a group. (13)

**statistics**   Facts numerically expressed. (6)

**stock issues design**   A persuasive speech pattern that attempts to answer the major general questions a reasonable person would ask before agreeing to a change in policies or procedures. (13)

**straw man fallacy**   Understating, distorting, or otherwise misrepresenting the position of opponents for the sake of refutation. (14)

**stream chart**   A way of depicting how several forces can converge over the course of time. (9)

**subordination**   The requirement that material in an outline descend in importance from main points to subpoints to sub-subpoints to sub-sub-subpoints. (8)

**subpoints**   The major divisions within a speech's main points. (8)

**substance**   A quality possessed by a speech when it has an important message, a careful plan of development, and adequate facts, examples, and testimony. (1)

**sub-subpoints**   Divisions of subpoints within a speech. (8)

**sub-sub-subpoints**   Division of sub-subpoints within a speech. (8)

**summary statement**   The speaker's reinterpretation of the speech's main idea at the end of a presentation. (2)

**supporting materials**   The facts and figures, testimony, examples, and narratives that constitute the building blocks of successful speeches. (6)

**syllogism**   The basic structure of deductive reasoning, consisting of a major premise, a minor premise, and a conclusion. (14)

**symmetry**   Achieving a balance among the major parts of a presentation. (7)

**synecdoche**   A language technique in which part of a subject is used to represent the whole of it. (10)

**synergistic listening**   The process by which listeners respond fully and creatively to the speaker's words in order to find the richest possible meaning within them. (3)

**table the motion**   Suspends indefinitely the discussion of a motion. (Appendix A)

**task leadership behavior**   A leadership emphasis that directs the attention and activity of a group towards a specified goal. (Appendix A)

**testimony**   The employment of the observations, opinions, or conclusions of other people or institutions to enhance the credibility of a presentation. (6)

**textual graphics**   Visual presentation of key words in a speech using a chalkboard, posterboard, flip chart, transparency, slide, or handout. (9)

**thematic statement**   The speech's central idea. (2, 5)

**thoroughness**   Providing complete and accurate information about a topic. (5)

**toast**   A short speech of tribute, usually offered at celebration dinners or meetings. (15)

**transitions**   Connecting elements used in speeches. (7)

**tree chart**   A chart that demonstrates how a few things can grow into many over the course of time. (9)

**trigger word**   A term or word inspiring positive or negative emotions in listeners. (3)

**values**   Standards of desirable or ideal behavior. (4)

**verbatim**   Using the exact words of a source. (6)

**verifier**   A statement by an interviewer confirming the meaning of what has just been said by the person being interviewed. (5)

**visual aids**   Supplemental materials used to enhance the effectiveness and clarity of a presentation. (9)

**visualization**   The process of systematically picturing oneself succeeding as a speaker and practicing a speech with that image in mind. (2)

# Text Credits

**Page 26:** "Credo for Free and Responsible Communication in a Democratic Society." Reprinted by permission of the Speech Communication Association.

**Pages 53–54:** "Visualization: Is It More Than Extra-Attention?" by Joe Ayres and Theodore S. Hopf. Copyright by the Speech Communication Association. January 1989. Reproduced by permission of the publisher.

**Page 121:** "I Keep Six Honest Serving Men . . .," from *Just So Stories* by Rudyard Kipling. Copyright © 1921. Used by permission.

**Pages 165-166:** "Columbus Plus 500 Years: Whither the American Indian," by David Archambault, from *Vital Speeches of the Day* (1 June 1992). Reprinted with permission.

**Page 152:** "Health Care in the '80s: Changes, Consequences, and Choices," by William L. Kissick, M.D., from *Vital Speeches of the Day* 52 (15 Jan. 1986).

**Page 191:** "Patience, Persistence, and Perspiration," by Bob Lannom, from the *Parsons News Leader* (20 Sept. 1989). Reprinted by permission of the *Parsons News Leader*.

**Page 262:** "The Whiskey Speech," by N.S. Sweat, Jr., from William Raspberry, "Any Candidate Will Drink to That," *Austin American Statesman* 11 (May 1984). Reprinted with permission of N.S. Sweat, Jr.

**Page 265:** Reprinted from Claire Perkins, "The Many Symbolic Faces of Fred Smith: Charismatic Leadership in the Bureaucracy," *The Journal of the Tennessee Speech Communication Association* 11 (1985). Used by permission.

**Page 285:** "Malapropisms Live," collected by William J. Crocker, from *Spectra,* May 1986. Used by permission.

**Page 309:** "mehitabel and her kittens," by Don Marquis, from *the lives and times of archy and mehitabel.* Copyright 1927 by Doubleday and Company, Inc. Reprinted by permission of the publisher.

**Pages 437–438:** Speech prepared by Jesse Owens. Reprinted by permission of United Features Syndicate, Inc.

**Page 440:** Thanks for this story go to Professor Joseph Riggs, Slippery Rock University. Used by permission.

**Pages 444–445:** Speech by Dick Jackman. Copyright © 1985 by *Harper's Magazine.* All rights reserved. Reprinted from the March 1985 issue by special permission.

**Pages A3–A7:** Adapted by permission from pages 109–116 of *The 1978 Annual Handbook for Group Facilitators,* by J. William Pfeiffer and John E. Jones. Copyright © 1976 by West Publishing Company. All rights reserved.

**Pages B16–B19:** Presentation on AIDS at the 1992 Democratic National Convention by Elizabeth Glaser reprinted by permission of the Democratic National Committee and Elizabeth Glaser.

**Pages B19–B22:** Remarks on AIDS at the 1992 Republican National Convention by Mary Fisher reprinted by permission of the Republican National Committee.

**Pages B26–B28:** "Nobel Peace Prize Acceptance Speech," by Elie Wiesel. Copyright © The Nobel Foundation 1986. Used by permission.

**Pages B28–B31:** "University of South Carolina Commencement Address," May 1986, by Bill Cosby. Used by permission.

## Photo Credits

*Chapter 1:* **Page 2 (Opener),** Bob Daemmrich/The Image Works; **7,** David Young-Wolff/PhotoEdit; **20,** Harvey Finkle/Impact Visuals.

*Chapter 2:* **Page 28 (Opener),** Philip T. Dattilo; **33,** Bob Daemmrich/Stock, Boston, Inc.; **37,** Richard Swanson.

*Chapter 3:* **Page 58 (Opener),** Bob Daemmrich/The Image Works; **62,** Loren Santow/Impact Visuals; **68,** Kent Knudson/Stock, Boston, Inc.; **76,** Stacy Rosenstock/Impact Visuals.

*Chapter 4:* **Page 86 (Opener),** Rick Reinhard/Impact Visuals 1993; **90,** Paula Lerner; **107,** Rick Gerharter/Impact Visuals.

*Chapter 5:* **Page 116 (Opener),** Rob Crandall/Stock, Boston, Inc.; **130,** UPI/Bettman; **133,** Seth Resnick/Stock, Boston, Inc.; **140,** Peter Menzel/Stock, Boston, Inc.

*Chapter 6:* **Page 146 (Opener),** Barbara Alper/Stock, Boston, Inc.; **150,** Peter Andrews/Publiphoto/Picture Group; **164,** AP/Wide World Photos.

*Chapter 7:* **Page 172 (Opener),** Constantine Manos/Magnum Photos, Inc.; **189,** Asahi Shimbun; **196,** Jim Levitt/Impact Visuals.

*Chapter 8:* **Page 202 (Opener),** Matthew McVay/Stock, Boston, Inc.; **217,** Jennifer Waddell.

*Chapter 9:* **Page 230 (Opener),** Barbara Filet/TSW/Click-Chicago, LTD.; **243,** AP/Wide World Photos; **253,** David Shopper/Stock, Boston, Inc.

*Chapter 10:* **Page 258 (Opener),** Jeffrey D. Scott/Impact Visuals; **265,** Donna Binder/Impact Visuals; **278,** Wide World Photos, Inc.

*Chapter 11:* **Page 292 (Opener),** Philip Dattilo; **296,** Donna Binder/Impact Visuals; **301,** AP/Wide World Photos; **311,** Reuters/Bettman.

*Chapter 12:* **Page 324 (Opener),** Margot Granitsas/The Image Works; **330,** Loren Santow/Tony Stone Worldwide, LTD.; **341,** Ted Speigel/Stock, Boston, Inc.

*Chapter 13:* **Page 356 (Opener),** Wide World Photos, Inc.; **361,** Rick Reinhard/Impact Visuals; **372,** Tom McKitterick/Impact Visuals.

*Chapter 14:* **Page 392 (Opener),** Tim Lucas/f/Stop Pictures, Inc.; **396,** Dan Habib/Impact Visuals; **403,** The Thomas Gilcrease Institute of American History and Art.

*Chapter 15:* **Page 424 (Opener),** Jim Harrison; **433,** Mark Ludak/Impact Visuals; **439,** Jim Harrison.

# Index

*ABI/Inform Ondisc, 134*
*The Abortion Battle* (TV documentary), 407
Abstractions
explanation of, 336
personification of, 272–273
visualization of, 267–270
Abstract language, 19, 282
Abstracts, information from, 131–132
Acceptance
of persuasion, 361–363
speech of, 432–434
Accuracy
and biased sources, 21
delineation of fact, opinion, and inference, 21
and incomplete information, 21–23
and speaker's bias, 21
verification of, 140–142
Action
clarification of options for, 329
commitment to, 359–360, 360, 363, 369–371, 379
demonstration of need for, 369–370
encouragement through language, 266, 276–277
movement from attitude to, 369–371
plan of, 370–371
speeches urging, 372–373, 375 (fig.)
Active voice, 284
Activity, sustaining attention with, 332
Ad hominem argument, 415
Adversaries, and group identity, 265, 274
Advertising
credibility of, 73, 74
critical analysis of, 62
exploitation of human motivation, 101–105
ideas for topics from, 118–119
persuasive messages in, 401–402
and principle of retention, 333
unethical use of quotations, 157–158
use of language in, 271–272
Aesop's fables, 163
After-dinner speech, 438–441, 444–445
Age, as factor in audience response, 95
Agenda setting, by informative

speeches, 328–329
Agreement, with persuasion, 362–363, 363
"AIDS: A Personal Narrative" (Fisher), B19–B22
"AIDS: A Personal Story" (Glaser), B16–B19
Alcoholics Anonymous, 191
Aley, Anna, 389–391
Alger, Horatio, 273, 403
Alliteration
encouragement of action by, 277
language color and, 282
sustaining attention with, 331
Almanacs, information from, 133
American Cancer Society, 21, 402
American Council on Education, 5
American dream, mythos of, 404–405
American Heart Association, 32
American Medical Association, 73
*American Statistics Index,* 133
Amplification, 280–281
Analogous color scheme, for visual aids, 252
Analogy, use in informative speech, 340
Analogy arguments, 410–411
defective, 418–419
Analogy design
method of argumentation, 410
for persuasive speech, 382–384
Anaphora
encouragement of action by, 277
evocation of culturetypes by, 278
magnification, use in, 429
sustaining attention with, 331
Anecdotes
in conclusion, 197
in introduction, 189
*see also* Narratives
Angelou, Maya, 265 (fig.)
Antithesis
encouragement of action by, 277
language color and, 24
Anxiety, *see* Communication apprehension
Apathy, conquest with language, 264
Application, as goal of demonstration speech, 335
Archambault, David, 165
Archetypal metaphors
creation of group identity with, 275–276

encouragement of action by, 276
evocation of memory by, 279
and language color, 282
*Areopagitica* (Milton), 24
Argument(s), 362
ad hominem, 415
by analogy, 410–411, 418–419
deductive, 406–408, 416–417
defective, 416–418
definition of, 394, 406
definition of terms in, 411–412
inductive, 408–409, 417–418
refutation of, 373
Aristotle, 10, 23, 95, 230, 399, 426, 428
Articulation, 308
*Art Index,* 134
Ashe, Arthur, 161
Assassination attempt on President Reagan, 401
Assimilation, 67
Associative meaning, 64–65
Astaire, Fred, 440
Atlases, information from, 132
Attention
capturing with introduction, 187–192
disruption of, 63–66
feigning, 69–70, 71
improvement of, 66–67
in learning, 331–334
in persuasion, 362, 378–379
Attention span, 69, 71
Attitude(s)
control of, 69
creation of listening problems by, 67–69
in effective presentation, 295
as factor in audience response, 105–108
movement to action from, 369–371
speeches addressing, 371–372, 375 (fig.)
survey to elicit, 107–108, 108 (fig.)
Audience
adaptation of topic to, 116–117, 119, 120 (fig.)
capturing attention of, 187–192
consideration of, in outlining process, 210–211
creation of positive communication climate by, 50
critical skills of, 60–63, 72–82
determination of purpose by, 123, 124–125

Audience *(Cont.)*
establishing credibility with, 192–193
impression of speaker on, 31–35
involvement of, 16, 80 (fig.), 163, 166, 189–190
members as visual aids, 234
movement from attitude to action, 369–371
operation of persuasive process on, 361–364
overcoming reluctance of, 365–367
proximity of speaker to, 313
receptivity of, 10–11, 13–14, 32, 63–72
*see also* Audience dynamics; Communication environment; Demographic audience analysis
respect for, 284
response of, 9, 13
size of, speaker's adjustment to, 93
speaker's respect for, 7–8
target, 88–89
uncommitted, 368–369
*see also* Listener
Audience dynamics, 101–108
Audiotapes, as visual aid, 248–249
Audubon Society, 100
Authoritative sources, 414 (fig.)
collection of citations of, 132–133, 135
confirmation of information from, 153
credibility of, 73
demographic factors in selection of, 99
documentation of, 140
enhancement of speaker's prestige by, 32
*see also* Expert testimony
Average, illusion of, 413
Awareness, of persuasion, 362

Bacon, Francis, 261, 292, 294
Bad habits
control of, 71
creation of listening problems by, 69
Balance
in design of visual aids, 251–252
*see also* Symmetry
Baltz, Sandra, 56–57
Bar graph, as visual aid, 237, 238 (fig. 9.3)
*Bartlett's Familiar Quotations*, 133
Begging the question, 416
Behavior, change in response to persuasion, 363
Beliefs
change in response to persuasion,

363, 367, 371–372
common, celebration by persuasive speaker, 369
as factor in audience response, 105–108
Benefits
of constructive listening, 63
of critical listening, 61–63
of public speaking, 4–9
Bias
control of, 69
creation of listening problems by, 67
of information sources, 21
in informative speaking, 328
in interpretation of facts, 150–151
of speaker, 21
Bible, as source of mythos, 403
Bibliography
in formal outline, 223 (fig.), 223–224
for persuasive speech, 391
working, 135
Biden, Joseph R., Jr., 23
Biographical references, information from, 132
*Biography Index*, 134
Black, Hugo, 138
Body language
and effective presentation, 21
effective use of, 310–314
enhancement of speaker's power with, 34–35
exclusion from listening process, 69–70
and likableness of speaker, 33
listening to, 71
sustaining attention with, 332
Body of speech, 18
arrangement of main points in, 178–182
categorical pattern for, 180
closure principle in, 180–181
coherent relationship to other parts, 177
design of, 177–185
determination of main points for, 178, 179 (fig.)
formal outline of, 214 (fig.), 215–219, 220–222 (fig.)
for introductory speech, 40, 42–43
outline of, 45, 47
preparation outline of, 205–206, 207–210, 208 (fig.), 212–213 (fig.)
presentation within time limits, 176–177
preview in introduction, 193–194
proximity principle in, 179
separation from other parts, 215
sequential pattern for, 179

similarity principle in, 180
spatial pattern for, 179
supporting materials for, 182–185
use of narratives in, 165
*Book of Facts*, 133
Books, citation in bibliography, 223–224
Boomerang effect, 367
Brady, James, 401
Brainstorming, in problem-solving process, A4–A5
Brandeis, Louis D., 358
Breath control, 306
Brennan, William, 7
Brief examples, 160
Buckley, William E., 71, 151
Burke, Kenneth, 260
Bush, George, 105, 275, 331, 404
*Business Periodicals Index*, 132

Calling the question, in parliamentary procedure, A12
Card catalogs
computerized, 134
information from, 135
Cassirer, Ernst, 28, 424
Categorical imprecision, 416
Category
building arguments arranged by, 409
graphic demonstration of, 237
informative speech arranged by, 337
main points arranged by, 180
speech arranged by, 18, 40, 41
Causation design
for ceremonial speech, 429
for informative speech, 345
Cause-effect design, 40–41, 180–181, 186, 240
CD-ROM, 134
Center for Public Resources, 4
Ceremonial speech
of acceptance, 432–434
after-dinner, 438–441, 444–445
creation of identification by, 427–428, 438
design of, 429
humor in, 438–441
importance of, 426
of inspiration, 436–438
of introduction, 434–436
language of, 267, 277–278, 429, 433–434
magnification in, 428–429, 431, 433–434, 435
narrative for, 427, 430, 434, 437–438, 440
purpose of, 16, 17 (fig.)
recognition of heroes in, 427

Ceremonial speech (Cont.)
  renewal of group commitment in, 427–428
  samples of, 431, 437–438, 444–445
  techniques of, 427–429
  of tribute, 429–432
  types of, 429–441
Certainty, confusion with probability, 416
Chalkboard, as visual aid, 243–244
Chamber of Commerce, 100
Champlin, Scott, B4–B6
"Changing Relationships between Men and Women" (Sachs), 155
Charts
  making, 253
  presentation on flip chart, 245
  as visual aid, 239–241, 240 (fig.), 241 (fig.)
Chinese democracy movement, 273, 275–276, 284
Churchill, Sir Winston, 272
Claims
  support of, 149–151, 182–185, 398–406
  validity of, 73
Clarity, of language, 279–281
Clinton, Bill, 263, B22–B26
Closed-circuit television, 316
Closure principle
  in arrangement of main points, 180–181
  in ending speech, 195
Clothes
  and effective presentation, 313–314
  and likableness of speaker, 33–34
  for television presentation, 316
  as visual aid, 233
Co-active approach to persuasion, 365–366
Cognitive restructuring, 49
Coherence, as principle of structure, 177
Color
  of language, 281–282, 317, 416
  in television presentation, 317
  use in visual aids, 251–253
Combined design, for informative speech, 346
Comfort, need for, as factor in audience response, 102
Commitment
  to action, 359–360, 360, 363, 369–371, 379
  enhancement of speaker's power by, 35
  evaluation of, 80 (fig.)
  group, renewal of, 427–428
  removing barriers to, 368–369

self-characterization of speaker through, 38
  of speaker, 14–15
  to topic, 116
  visual aids as reflection of, 233
Communication, 9–14
  etymological relationship to community, 6
  idea in, 9, 11
  indispensability to democratic politics, 6–7
  listener's attitude toward, 68–69
  medium in, 9, 12–13
  message in, 9, 11–12
  receiver in, 9, 13
  response in, 9, 13
  source in, 9, 10–11
  successful, 294
Communication apprehension
  control of, 48–50
  visual aids as remedy for, 233
Communication climate, positive, 50
Communication environment, 9–10, 13–14
  adjusting to, 89–94
  of classroom, 30
  context of recent events, 92
  context of recent speeches, 90–92
  immediate adjustments to, 88, 90
  long-range adjustments to, 88
  place, 89–90
  purpose of occasion, 92–93
  size of audience, 93
  time of day, 89
Communication technology, video presentations, 316
Community
  celebration in public speech, 426, 431, 438
  etymological relationship to communication, 6
Comparison and contrast design, 237
  for ceremonial speech, 429
  for informative speech, 340–342
  use of inductive arguments in, 409
Competence, creating impression of, 31–32
Complementary color scheme, for visual aids, 252
Comprehension, of persuasion, 362
Computer, generation of visual aids with, 247, 248, 249 (fig.), 250, 251, 253, 254 (fig.)
Computerized search services, information from, 133–135
Computer search, 134
Conciseness, of language, 283–284
Concluding remarks, 44
Conclusion, 408
Conclusion of argument, 407–408
  defective, 418

Conclusion of speech, 18, 127, 195–198
  anecdotes in, 197
  coherent relationship to other parts, 177
  design of, 195–198
  formal outline of, 215 (fig.), 223 (fig.)
  functions of, 195
  for informative speech, 332
  for introductory speech, 40, 43–44
  memorization of, 297
  metaphor in, 197–198
  outline of, 45, 47
  for persuasive speech, 363
  preparation outline of, 206, 209 (fig.), 213 (fig.)
  presentation within time limits, 176–177
  questions in, 196–197
  quotations in, 197
  separation from other parts, 215
  use of examples in, 159
  use of language in, 277
  use of narratives in, 165–166
  writing out for presentation, 225
Concrete language, 19, 168, 282
  conversion of abstractions to, 268–269
Confucius, 260
Confusion of probability and certainty, 416
Congressional Record, 133
Connotative meaning, 64, 270–271
Consciousness-raising function, 367
Consequences
  concern for, 284
  of public speech, 21, 23
Consolidation, of persuasion, 363
Constructive listening
  benefits of, 63
  definition of, 61
  development of skills for, 75–79
  empathetic listening, 76–77
  synergistic listening, 77–79
Consumer Reports, 178, 179 (fig.)
Contamination of the conclusion, 418
Contention, speeches of, 373–374, 375 (fig.)
  defective design in, 419
  design of, 380–382
  use of inductive arguments in, 409
Context, adjustment of speaker to, 90–92
Contrast
  drawing proof from, 399
  sustaining attention through, 332
  see also Comparison and contrast design
Contrast effect, 67

Control, need for, as factor in audience response, 104
Conversation, similarity of effective presentation to, 46, 295, 299
Conversational presentation, for television, 316–317
Coordination, principle of structure, 215–217, 216–217
Correctness, of language, 282–283
Correlations, 152
Cosby, Bill, B28–B31
Cosmetics, for television presentation, 316
Counterarguments, development while listening, 69
Credibility
  and body language, 310
  enhancement with visual aids, 233
  establishment in introduction, 192–193
  and exaggeration, 74
  of examples, 162
  facts as support for, 149, 153
  fit of message with prior knowledge, 75
  of interview material, 135
  and misuse of language, 283
  of persuasive speaker, 366, 369
  of sources, 73, 140
  and speaker's adjustment to vocal characteristics, 300, 307–308, 309
  see also Ethos
Critical listening
  benefits of, 61–63
  definition of, 60–61
  guidelines for, 73–75
  importance of, 73
  learning to speak as aid to, 6
Critical thinking
  definition of, 72
  guidelines for, 73–75
  importance of, 73
Critique, guidelines for, 79–82
Crocker, William J., 283
Cultural benefits, of public speaking, 8–9
Cultural diversity, 8–9
Cultural gridlock, 462
Cultural sensitivity, and language, 284–285
Culturetypes
  creation of group identity with, 274
  evocation of memory by, 278
Cuomo, Mario, 164 (ill.)
Curiosity, as factor in audience response, 104
*Current Biography*, 132

Davis, Ronnie, B31–B33
Daydreaming, 64, 66, 103

Dean, Dizzy, 168
Debate theory, 377
Deductive arguments, 406–408
  cautions in using, 408
  defective, 416–417
Definitions, importance to arguments, 411–412
Delayed response, in communication process, 9
Deliberation, 358
Democratic politics
  indispensability of communication skills to, 6–7
  persuasion as requirement for, 358
  see also Chinese democracy movement
Demographic audience analysis, 94–101
  educational level, 97–98
  group affiliations, 98–100
  occupational groups, 98–99
  political affiliation, 99
  religious affiliation, 99–100
  social-group membership, 100
  sociocultural background, 100–101
Demonstration
  design of, 335, 342–343
  of persuasion, 363
  speech of, 335–336
Denotative meaning, 64, 270
Description, speech of, 334–335
  design of, 335
Descriptive statistics, 151
Design of speech
  analogy, 382–384, 410
  for body, 177–185
  categorical, 18, 40, 41, 180, 237, 337, 339–340, 409
  causation, 345, 429
  cause-effect, 40–41, 180–181, 186, 240
  for ceremonial speech, 429
  combined, 346
  comparison and contrast, 237, 340–342, 409, 429
  for conclusion, 195–198
  defective, 418
  effective, 17–19
  evaluation of, 80 (fig.)
  good form in, 174–177
  historical, 343–344, 429
  importance of outline to, 204
  for informative speech, 337–346
  for introduction, 40–44, 187–195
  motivated sequence, 105, 378–380
  for persuasive speech, 374–384, 375 (fig.)
  problem-solution, 180, 181, 186, 374–376, 409, 418

refutative, 380–382, 409
sequential, 18, 42, 179, 335, 342–343
spatial, 41, 179, 236, 337–339
stock issues, 376–378
Design of visual aids, 250–251
Devil terms, 274
Dewey, John, 426, 463
Dialect, 309–310
Dialogue, use in narratives, 166, 437
Dictionaries, consultation on pronunciation, 308
*Dictionary of American Biography*, 132
Directories, information from, 133
Dirkson, Everett McKinley, 152
Distance
  between speaker and audience, 313
  transcendence through language, 263
Distractions
  avoidance in effective presentation, 295
  in communication environment, 89
  control of, 66–67, 69
  creation of listening problems by, 65–66
  in video studio, 318
  visual aids as, 234–235, 236, 242, 253
Documentation, 140
Donne, John, 277

Education, importance of critical listening in, 63
Educational level, as factor in audience response, 97–98
Ehrlichman, John, 268
Either-or thinking, 418
Elevation, of speaker over audience, 313
Emerson, Ralph Waldo, 392
Emotion
  language, arousal through, 262–264, 270–273
  persuasive speech, arousal by, 360–361
  substitution for reasoning, 74
  see also Mythos; Pathos
Empathetic listening, 76–77
Emphasis
  in design of visual aids, 250
  see also Magnification
Employment
  importance of speaking skills for, 4–5
  see also Occupational groups; Work

*Employment Prospects for College Graduates*, 5
*Encyclopaedia Britannica*, 130
*Encyclopedia of associations*, 133
*Encyclopedia of education*, 130
*Encyclopedia of Religion and Ethics*, 130
*Encyclopedia of World Art*, 131
Encyclopedias, information from, 130–131
Enjoyment, need for, as factor in audience response, 105
"Entertainment syndrome," 71
Enunciation, 308
Equality, principle of, in presentation of main points, 177
Erasmus, 333
Ervin, Sam, 166
Ethical definitions, 412
Ethical listener, 24
Ethics
    evaluation of, 80 (fig.)
    hypothetical examples and, 162
    of persuasive speaking, 360, 362
    in public speaking, 20–24, 21
    in use of culturetypes, 274
    in use of testimony, 157–158
Ethos, 11, 32
    borrowing from experts, 155
    of guest speaker, 434–435
    proof by, 399, 399 (fig.), 401–402, 407, 409, 415
    *see also* Credibility
Evaluating speeches, criteria for, 14–21, 79–82
    audience involvement, 16, 80 (fig.)
    commitment, 14–15, 80 (fig.)
    ethics, 21, 80 (fig.)
    language use, 19, 80 (fig.)
    presentation, 20–21, 80 (fig.)
    purpose, 16, 80 (fig.)
    structure, 17–19, 80 (fig.)
    substance, 17, 80 (fig.)
    topic selection, 15–16, 80 (fig.)
Evaluation
    of examples, 162
    of facts and figures, 152–154
    of narratives, 166–167
    of practice sessions, 315–316
    of testimony, 157–158
    of vocal characteristics, 302
Evidence
    defective, 412–415
    definition of, 394
    effective use of, 394–399
    as foundation of persuasion, 362
    inappropriate, 415
    in proof by ethos, 401–402
    in proof by logos, 399–400

in proof by mythos, 402–405
in proof by pathos, 400–401
refutation of, 373, 380–382
use in persuasive speech, 365–366, 380, 381
Examples
    amplification with, 281
    arousal of emotion by, 271–272
    building arguments from, 409
    combination of statistical material with, 153
    communication of vast subjects through, 269–270
    contribution to speech's substance, 17
    demographic factors in selection of, 98, 100
    drawing proof from, 400–401, 405
    enhancement of speaker's authority by, 32
    evaluation of, 162
    in formal outline, 219
    in impromptu speaking, 296
    in introductory speech, 39, 42
    misuse of, 415
    in persuasive speech, 362, 370
    as supporting material, 159–160, 182, 183–184, 184
    sustaining interest with, 332
    types of, 160–162
    use in ceremonial speech, 432
    use in informative speech, 332, 343
    use in persuasive speech, 396–397
    use of, 163
Expert testimony
    building arguments from, 409
    collection in interview, 135–139
    definition of, 155
    drawing proof from, 402, 405
    evaluation of, 157–158
    in format outline, 219
    in persuasive speech, 369, 398–399
    as supporting material, 155–156, 182, 183, 185
    *see also* Authoritative sources
Explanation, speech of, 336–337
    design of, 336–337, 343, 345
Exposure, in persuasion, 362
Extemporaneous presentation, 20, 46, 295, 300
Extended examples, 160–161
Eye contact
    and audience size, 93
    and control of communication apprehension, 49–50
    effective use of, 310–312
    in manuscript presentation, 299
    use of chalkboard, 244

Facial expression, effective use of, 310–312
Fact(s)
    building arguments from, 409
    confusion with opinion, 21, 412
    contribution to speech's substance, 17
    critical analysis of, 73–74
    drawing proof from, 398–399, 405
    evaluation of, 152–154
    in formal outline, 219
    in introductory speech, 42
    listening exclusively for, 70–71
    misuse of, 412, 415
    as supporting material, 150–151, 182–183, 183
    use in persuasive speech, 395–396
    use of, 154
*Facts on File*, 131
Factual examples, 161
    use in persuasive speech, 396–397
Fallacies, 412–419
    non sequitur, 417
    post hoc ergo propter hoc, 417
    slippery slope, 412–413, 414 (fig.)
    statistical, 413
    straw man, 419
*The Fall of Public Man* (Sennett), 6
Faulty analogy, 418–419
Federal Express Company, 262–263
Federal Register, 133
Feedback
    and attitude of listener, 61
    in communication process, 9, 13
    false, 71
    influence of audience size, 93
    in practice sessions, 316
    prompting of speaker by, 61
    reinforcement of confidence by, 35
    in television, 317
    on use of voice, 306
Feinstein, Dianne, 159, 160, 433 (ill.)
Ferraro, Geraldine, 156
Figurative analogy
    use in informative speech, 340
    use in persuasive speech, 382–384
Figures, *see* Statistics
Films, as visual aid, 248–249
Filtering, 67
First Amendment, U. S. Constitution, 7, 358
Fisher, Mary, B19–B22
Flip charts
    design of, 250, 251
    drawing graphics on, 253
    as visual aid, 245, 246 (fig.)
Flow charts, as visual aid, 239, 240 (fig.)
Food and Drug Administration, 402

Form, *see* Design of speech; Good form
Formal outline, 211–224
  bibliography in, 223–224
  coordination in, 215–217, 216–217
  format for, 214–215 (fig.), 220–223 (fig.)
  practice with, 315
  separation of speech parts in, 215
  specification of theme and purpose in, 215
  subordination in, 215, 216–217
  support of main points, 219
  title for, 211
  wording of main points, 218–219
Foss, Joe, 417
"Free at Last" (Nishikawa), B3–B4
Friendship, need for, as factor in audience response, 103
Frontier, mythos of, 402, 403 (ill.)

Gender, as factor in audience response, 95–97
Gender stereotyping, 97
Generalization, hasty, 417–418
*General Periodicals Ondisc*, 134
General purpose of speech, 122–123, 126
Gestalt psychology, 174, 178
Gestures
  adjustment to audience size, 93
  and art of narratives, 167
  and effective presentation, 21
  effective use of, 312–313
  enhancement of speaker's power with, 35
  and likableness of speaker, 33
Glaser, Elizabeth, B16–B19
Goals, self-characterization of speaker through, 38
God terms, 274
Good form
  orderliness, 177
  as principle of structure, 174
  simplicity, 174–176
  symmetry, 176–177
Good Samaritan, parable of, 163
Gorbachev, Mikhail, 268
Gore, Albert, Jr., 279–280
Government documents, information from, 133
Grammar, faulty, 283
Graphics, as visual aid, 235–241
Graphs
  making, 253
  use of color in, 251
  use with informative speech, 351 (ill.)
  as visual aid, 236–238, 238 (figs.), 239 (fig.)

Gray, L. Patrick, 268
Great expectations fallacy, 367, 380
Greek architecture, 176
Greek rhetoric, 399
Grooming, and effective presentation, 313–314
Group affiliation
  as factor in audience response, 98–100
  renewal of commitment to, 427–428
Group identity
  celebration of, 426
  creation with language, 265–266, 273–276
  and cultural memory, 277–279
  mobilization on behalf of action, 361, 372
Group problem solving, A3–A13
  brainstorming in, A4–A5
  conducting effective meeting for, A11
  formal meetings for, A11–A13
  leadership in, A9–A11
  meeting plan for, A10–A11
  parliamentary procedure for, A12–A13
  participation in, A7–A8
  social leadership behavior in, A9–A10
  task leadership behavior in, A9
  *see also* Problem-solving process
Groupthink, A3
Gun control legislation, 417

Habits, *see* Bad habits
Habitual pitch, 302–303, 304
Handouts, 255
  computer-generated, 248, 250, 253
  design of, 250–251
  making, 253
  use with informative speech, 336, 355 (ill.)
  as visual aid, 246–247
Harvard Psychological Clinic, 102
Hasty generalization, 417–418
Hearing
  confusion with listening, 68
  definition of, 60
Hegel, Friedrich, 2
Hemingway, Ernest, 58
Henry, Patrick, 284
Heroes
  celebration by persuasive speaker, 369
  and group identity, 265, 273, 274
  recognition in ceremonial speech, 427
  and tradition, 267
Hillman, Ralph, 306

Historical design
  for ceremonial speech, 429
  for informative speech, 343–344
Hitler, Adolf, 62, 272, 428, 429, 437
Hobby, self-characterization of speaker through, 37–38
Homer, 6
Howell, Mary, 155
Huff, Stephen, 350–355
*Humanities Index*, 134
Humor
  adjustment of communication environment through, 91
  in ceremonial speech, 438–441
  use in introduction, 189
Hyperbole
  arousal of emotions through, 272
  encouragement of actions by, 276
  and language color, 282
Hypothetical examples, 161–162

Ideal model, for support of main points, 184
Ideas
  in communication process, 9, 11
  emphasis over style, 46
  sharing of, 327
Identification, 16, 33–34
  and body language, 313
  creation by ceremonial speech, 427–428, 438
  credibility as foundation for, 193
  intensification through lay testimony, 157
  in persuasive speech, 365
  and vocal characteristics, 307–308
Ideographs, 274
Illusion of the average, 413, 414 (fig.)
Images
  arousal of emotion by, 272
  descriptive, 335
  encouragement of action by, 276
  evocation of culturetypes by, 278
  and language color, 282
  in persuasive speech, 363, 369, 379
  use in ceremonial speech, 430
Immediate adjustments, to communication environment, 88, 90
Impromptu speaking, 295–297
Improved conversation, ideal of, 46
"Inaugural Address" (Clinton), B22–B26
Independence, need for, as factor in audience response, 104
Index cards
  recording of information on, 139–140

Index cards *(Cont.)*
  use in presentation, 224, 225
Indexes
  computerized, 133–134
  information from, 131–132
*Index to Journals in Communication Studies,* 132
Indiana University, 332
Inductive arguments, 408–409
  defective, 417–418
Inferences
  critical analysis of, 73–74
  justification of, 21
Inferential statistics, 151, 152
Informal power, 34
  creating impression of, 34
Information
  biased sources, 21
  collection of, 127–139
  distortion by listener, 67
  documentation of, 140
  evaluation of, 152–154
  as impetus to commitment, 368
  purpose of speech as, 122–123, 124, 127
  reporting of, 21
  retention of, 333–334
  sharing of, 326, 327
  specification of sources, 21–23
  as supporting material, 149–152
  testing of, 140–142
  use of, 154
  *see also* Evidence
Information card, 139–140, 140, 141 (fig. 15.5)
*The Information Please Almanac,* 133
Information retrieval service, 135
Informative speech
  agenda-setting role, 328–329
  clarification of options by, 329
  contrasted with persuasive speech, 359–361
  of demonstration, 335–336
  of description, 334–335
  design of, 337–346
  engagement of learning process by, 330–334
  of explanation, 336–337
  function of supporting material in, 149
  functions of, 327–329
  motivational appeals in, 101–102
  purpose of, 16, 17 (fig.)
  sample, 350–355
  shaping of perceptions by, 328
  sharing information and ideas in, 327
  topic selection, 116, 120–121
  types of, 334–337
  use of visual aids with, 232, 253

*Infotrac,* 134 & fig.
Inspiration, speech of, 436–438
Integration, in persuasion, 363, 426, 436
Integrity, creating impression of, 32–33
Intensity, sustaining attention through, 331
Interest(s)
  capturing with introduction, 187–192
  fit of topic to audience's, 119, 120 (fig.)
  fit of topic with speaker's, 116–117, 118 (fig.)
Internal summary, 186
*International Encyclopedia of the Social Sciences,* 131
Interviews
  advantages and limitations of, 135
  citation in bibliography, 224
  conducting, 137–139
  contacting interviewee, 135–136
  crystallization of main points from, 178, 179 (fig.)
  design of, 137
  preparations for, 135
Introduction of speech, 18
  adjustment to fit communication environment, 91
  anecdotes in, 189
  and audience involvement, 189–190
  capturing audience attention with, 187–192
  for ceremonial speech, 438, 440
  coherent relationship to other parts, 177
  design of, 187–195
  establishing speaker credibility, 192–193
  formal outline of, 214–215 (fig.), 220 (fig.)
  guidelines for technique selection, 194–195
  inclusion of thematic statement in, 127
  for informative speech, 331
  for introductory speech, 40, 41–42
  memorization of, 297
  outline of, 44–45, 47
  preparation outline of, 206, 208 (fig.), 212 (fig.)
  presentation within time limits, 176–177
  preview of main points in, 193
  quotations in, 188
  rhetorical questions in, 187–188
  separation from other parts, 215

  shocking audience in, 191–192
  subject related to personal experience, 191
  suspense in, 191
  use of examples in, 159
  use of language in, 277
  use of narratives in, 163
  use of testimony in, 156
  writing out for presentation, 225
Introductory speech
  body of, 40, 42–43
  ceremonial, 434–436
  concluding remarks in, 44
  conclusion of, 40, 43–44
  demographic information from, 94, 101
  development of, 39–44
  example of, 56–57
  examples in, 39, 42
  facts and figures in, 42
  as icebreaker, 31
  introduction to, 40, 41–42
  narratives in, 42
  natural sound in, 46
  outline of, 44–45, 46–47
  presentation of, 45–50
  self-inventory for, 36–39
  summary statement in, 43
  testimony in, 43
Introductory techniques for speech, 194–195
Inversion, encouragement of action by, 277
Involvement, of audience, 16, 80 (fig.), 163, 166, 189–190
Isocrates, 352

Jackman, Dick, 439, 444–445
Jackson, Jesse, 196–197, 264
Jargon, 280
Jefferson, Thomas, 190, 284, 369
Jesus, use of parables, 163
Jewell, Delorah Lee, 306
Jordan, Barbara, 439

Kaixi, Wuer, 275
Kennedy, John F., 189, 277, 303, 304–305, 369, 403
Key-word outline, 224–225, 225 (fig.)
  for introductory speech, 44, 46–47
  practice with, 315
King, Martin Luther, Jr., 156, 272, 276, 369, 412, 432–433, 433
Kipling, Rudyard, 119
Knowledge, prior, judging credibility of message against, 75
  *see also* Responsible knowledge

*Ladies' Home Journal,* 156
Lancaster, Melodie, 197

Language
  for abstract subjects, 267–270
  arousal of emotion by, 262–264,
    270–273
  and art of narratives, 168
  clarity of, 279–281
  color in, 281–282
  color of, 416
  for complex subjects, 269
  conciseness of, 283–284
  concreteness in, 282
  conquest of apathy with, 264
  conquest of opposing views, 270
  correctness of, 282–283
  demographic factors in selection
    of, 98–99
  descriptive, 334–335
  encouragement of action with,
    266, 276–277
  evaluation of, 80 (fig.)
  evocation of memory through,
    267, 277–279
  group identity created with,
    265–266, 273–276
  and likableness of speaker, 33
  limitations of, 232
  oral vs. written, 260–261, 298
  personal reactions to, 63–66
  power of, 23, 260–268
  sexist, 64, 97
  simplicity of, 176
  skillful use of, 19, 279–285
  stimulation of learning with, 331
  in television presentation, 317
  as tool of deception, 74, 280
  tools of, 267–279
  transcendence of distance
    through, 263
  transcendence of time through,
    262–264
  use in magnification, 429
  for vast subjects, 269–270
  visualization through, 261–262,
    267–270, 279
  wording of main points, 218–219
Larson, Cecile, B6–B7
Lay testimony
  definition of, 155
  drawing proof from, 402
  evaluation of, 158
  misuse of, 415
  as supporting material, 157, 183
  use in persuasive speech, 398
Leadership
  critical analysis of, 62
  display of, 426
  exercise by persuasive speaker,
    360
  in small groups, A9–A11
  speaker's role of, 11, 31
Learning

attention in, 331–334
engagement by informative speaking, 330–334
motivation of, 330–331
retention in, 333–334
Lee, Stephen, B11–B13
Library research, 129–135
  citation in bibliography, 223–224
  crystallization of main points
    from, 178, 179 (fig.)
  as source of speaker credibility,
    193
  use of reference room, 130–133
Library research materials
  abstracts, 131–132
  almanacs, 133
  atlases, 132
  biographical references, 132
  card catalogs, 135
  computerized search services,
    133–135
  directories, 133
  encyclopedias, 130–131
  government documents, 133
  indexes, 131–132
  periodicals, 132
  quotation collections, 132–133
  vertical file, 133, 135
  yearbooks, 133
Likableness, of speaker, 33–34
Lincoln, Abraham, 369
Line graph
  use of color in, 251
  as visual aid, 237–238, 239 (fig.),
    243 (ill.)
Listener
  attitude of, 60
  ethical responsibilities of, 24
  as receiver, 13
  see also Audience
Listening
  confusion with hearing, 68
  critical, 60–63, 72–75
  definition of, 60–61
  empathetic, 76–77
  synergistic, 77–79
  time devoted to, 61, 63
Listening log, 66, 71
Listening problems
  attitudes, 67–69
  bad habits, 69–72
  checklist, 64 (fig.)
  personal reactions, 63–67
Literal analogy
  use in informative speech, 340
  use in persuasive speech, 382
the lives and times of archy and
  mehitabel (Marquis), 307
"Living Wills: Insuring Your Right to
  Choose" (Marshall), B13–B16
Locke, John, 324

Logos, proof by, 398–399, 399 (fig.),
  409
Long, Luz, 437–438
Longinus, 272
Long-range adjustments, to commu-
  nication environment, 88
Loudness, of voice, 305–307
Loyola Marymount University, 92

Magazines
  ideas for topics from, 118
  indexes to, 132, 133–134
  information from, 132
  supporting material from, 151
Magnification, 428–429, 431,
  433–434, 435
Main motion, in parliamentary procedure, A12
Main points, 127
  arrangement of, 178–182
  determination of, 178, 179 (fig.)
  emphasizing in impromptu speak-
    ing, 296
  in formal outline, 214 (fig.), 215,
    216–219, 220–222 (fig.)
  in key-word outline, 224
  number of, 175–176
  organization with outline, 204
  phrasing of, 176, 218–219
  in preparation outline, 205–206,
    207–210, 208 (fig.), 212–213
    (fig.)
  presentation within time limits,
    176–177
  preview in introduction, 193
  substantiation with supporting
    materials, 182–185
  summary of, 186, 195
Major premise, 406, 408
  defects in, 416, 417
Malapropisms, 283
Malcolm X, 281
Manuscript presentation, 298–300
Maps
  design of, 250
  use of color in, 251, 252
  use with informative speech, 352
    (ill.)
  as visual aid, 236, 237 (fig.)
Marshall, Bonnie, 163, 164, B13–B16
Maxims, 284
McGee, Michael Calvin, 274
McGervey, John, 152
McGuire, William J., 361, 364, 367
Mean, myth of, 413, 414 (fig.)
Meaning
  associative, 64–65
  connotative, 64, 270–271
  creation of, participative commu-
    nication, 63
  denotative, 64, 270

Meaning *(Cont.)*
  and vocal characteristics, 301, 303, 304, 307
Media presentations, 318
Medium, in communication process, 9, 12–13
Meeting plan, for group problem solving, A10–A11
"Melting pot" theory of American identity, 8
Memorized text presentation, 297–298
Memorizing, of toasts, 432
Memory, evocation through language, 267, 277–279
Message
  in communication process, 9, 11–12
  critical analysis of, 60–63, 72–80
  reception of, 63–72
  substantiveness of, 17
Metaphor
  arousal of emotion by, 271, 272
  building arguments from, 410
  in conclusion, 197–198
  creation of group identity with, 275–276
  encouragement of action by, 277
  evocation of culturetypes by, 278
  evocation of memory by, 279
  inspirational, 438
  and language color, 282
  sustaining attention with, 332
  use in magnification, 429, 434
  visualization of abstractions through, 268–269
Metonymy, 269
  arousal of emotion by, 271
  encouragement of action by, 276
  and language color, 282
Mill, John Stuart, 358
Milton, John, 24
Minor premise, 406, 408
  defects in, 417
Mirror questions, use in interviews, 138
Mixed metaphor, 268
Models, as visual aids, 234, 235
Monochromatic color scheme, for visual aids, 252
Monroe, Alan, 378
*Monthly Catalog of United States Government Publications*, 133
"The 'Monument' at Wounded Knee" (Larson), B6–B7
Motions, in parliamentary procedure, A12–A13
Motion to amend, in parliamentary procedure, A12
Motivated sequence design, 105

for persuasive speech, 378–380
Motivation
  as factor in audience response, 101–105
  of learning, 330
Movement, effective use of, 312–313
Moyers, Bill, 280
Multiculturalism, theory of American identity, 8–9
Multisided presentation, 365, 366, 369
Murray, Henry A., 102
Murray, Patty, 196 (ill.)
Murrow, Edward R., 334
Myth of the mean, 413, 414 (fig.)
Mythos, proof by, 399, 399 (fig.), 402–405, 407, 418
"My Three Cultures" (Baltz), 56–57
"My Twenty First Birthday Party" (Champlin), B4–B6

Narratives
  building arguments from, 409
  creation of group identity with, 273–274
  demographic factors in selecting, 100
  drawing proof from, 400–401, 402–404, 405
  effective use of, 279
  emotive language in, 262–263
  evaluation of, 166–167
  function of, 149
  in introductory speech, 42
  misuse of, 415
  in persuasive speech, 363, 366–367, 369, 397
  as supporting material, 163–166, 183–184
  use in ceremonial speech, 40, 427, 430, 434, 437–438
  use of, 167–168
  *see also* Anecdotes
Nathanson, Dr. Bernard, 406–407
National Football Foundation, address to, 439, 444–445
*National Geographic Atlas of the World*, 132
National Institutes of Health, 155
*The National Newspaper Index*, 134
National Organization for Women, 100
*National Review*, 151
National Rifle Association, 417
Nation Press Club, 417
*NBC Handbook of Pronunciation*, 308
Nervousness, *see* Communication apprehension
"The New Madrid Earthquake Area"

(Huff), 350–355
*The New Republic*, 151
Newspapers
  consultation on pronunciation, 309
  expert testimony from, 155
  ideas for topics from, 118–119
  indexes to, 131, 134
  information from, 131
  morgue of, 133, 135
*Newsweek*, 118, 131
New York Stock Exchange, 96
*New York Times*, 309, 436
*New York Times Index*, 131
Nishikawa, Rodney, B3–B4
Nixon, Richard M., 268, 413
"Nobel Peace Prize Acceptance Speech" (Wiesel), B26–B28
Non sequitur fallacy, 417
Novelty, sustaining attention with, 332
Nurturance, need for, as factor in audience response, 105

Objects, as visual aid, 234–235
Occupational groups, correlation of audience response with, 97–98
  *see also* Employment; Work
O'Connor, Sandra Day, 96
Oglala Sioux, the, 6
O'Neill, Thomas P., Jr., 430
Onomatopoeia, 270
Openness, of persuasive speaker, 366–367
Opinion
  confusion with fact, 21, 412
  critical analysis of, 73–74
  minority, in democratic society, 358–359
  transformation of facts into, 150–151
Optimum pitch, 303, 304
Options
  choosing among, 359, 418
  clarification by informative speaking, 329
Orderliness, as principle of structure, 177
Outline
  extemporaneous speaking from, 20
  formal, 211–224
  importance to structure, 204
  for introductory speech, 44–45, 46–47
  key word, 224–225
  preparation, 205–211
  use of, in speaking, 48
Overhead projections, *see* Projections
Owens, Jesse, 428–429, 429, 430, 431, 436–437, 437–438

*The Oxford Dictionary of Quotations*, 133
*Oxford English Dictionary*, 134

Parallel phrasing
  sustaining attention with, 331
  use with main points, 219
Paraphrase
  in introduction, 188
  of testimony, 156
  use in narratives, 166
Parliamentary procedure, for formal meetings, A12–A13
Participative communication, 63
Pathos, proof by, 399, 399 (fig.), 400–401, 407, 409
Pauses, use of, 304–305
Pavlov, Ivan Petrovich, 114
Percentages, incomparable, 414 (fig.), 415
Perceptions, shaping by informative speech, 328
*Periodical Abstracts*, 134
Periodical indexes, *see* Indexes
Periodicals, *see* Magazines; Newspapers
Perot, Ross, 243 (ill.), 265, 273
Personal appearance, and effective presentation, 313–314
Personal benefits, of public speaking, 5–6
Personal experience
  acquisition of knowledge from, 128–129
  audience identification with speaker's, 34
  crystallization of main points from, 178, 179 (fig.)
  enhancement of speaker's authority by, 32
  organization of, 174
  relation of topic to, 189–190, 191
  self-inventory of, 36–39
  as source of speaker credibility, 193
Personal reactions
  control of, 66
  creation of listening problems by, 63–66
Personification
  arousal of emotion through, 272–273, 407
  encouragement of action by, 276
  evocation of culturetypes with, 278
  and language color, 282
Perspective by incongruity, 270
Persuasion
  acceptance of, 361–363
  age as factor in susceptibility to, 95
  agreement with, 363

attention in, 362, 378–379
awareness of, 362
comprehension of, 362
consolidation of, 363
demonstration of, 363
evidence supporting, 362
exposure in, 362
importance of, 358–359
integration of, 363, 426, 436
and language, 260
as purpose of speech, 122–123, 124–125
retention of, 363
utilization of, 363
Persuasive speech
  appeals to values in, 106, 365, 368–369
  boomerang effect in, 367
  building arguments in, 406–412
  challenges of, 364–371
  co-active approach to, 365–366
  conclusion of, 196–197
  consciousness-raising function, 367
  contrasted with informative speech, 359–361
  defective arguments, 416–418
  defective design, 418
  defective evidence, 412–415
  defective proofs, 415–416
  design of, 374–384, 375 (fig.)
  engagement of reluctant audience, 365–367
  function of supporting material in, 149
  great expectations fallacy, 367, 380
  language of, 265–266, 277
  motivational appeals in, 101–102, 105
  movement from attitude to action, 369–371
  multisided presentation in, 365, 366, 369
  power of speaker in, 34
  predisposition toward, as role of informative speaking, 328–329
  proving points in, 398–406, 399 (fig.)
  purpose of, 16, 17 (fig.)
  removing barriers to commitment, 368–369
  sample, 389–391
  sleeper effect, 367
  strengthening of speaker credibility, 369
  topic selection, 116, 121
  types of, 371–374, 375 (fig.)
  use of evidence in, 394–399
  use of shock technique, 191–192
  use of visual aids with, 232, 253

vital information in, 368
Peterson, Roger Tory, 270
Photographs, as visual aid, 241–242
Pictographs, 241
Pie graph
  use of color with, 252
  as visual aid, 237, 238 (fig. 9.2)
Pitch, 302–304
  and improper breathing, 306
  sustaining attention with, 332
  variety in, 307
Place, adjustment of speaker to, 89–90
Plagiarism, 21–23
Planned Parenthood, 407
Plato, 86, 172
Political affiliation, as factor in audience response, 99
Poster board
  design of, 250–251, 251
  drawing graphics on, 253
  use of color on, 252
  for visual aids, 236, 242, 245–246
Post hoc ergo propter hoc fallacy, 417
Postponing consideration, in parliamentary procedure, A13
Power, creating impression of, 34
Practice
  importance to effective presentation, 314–316
  of manuscript presentation, 298, 299
  of speech presentation, 20–21, 47–48, 49
  in use of body language, 312, 313
  use of outlines in, 224
  in use of voice, 303, 305, 306–307, 307
  for video presentation, 317–318
  with visual aids, 246, 248, 254
Precision of information, 141–142
Preliminary tuning effect, 90–91, 435
Preparation outline, 205–211
  for introductory speech, 44–45, 46–47, 48
  use in practice, 224
Presentation
  effective, 20–21, 294–295
  evaluation of, 80 (fig.)
  extemporaneous, 20, 46, 295, 300
  impromptu, 295–297
  of introductory speech, 45–50
  media, 318
  memorized, 297–298, 432
  methods of, 295–300
  multisided, 365, 366, 369
  practice for, 314–316
  reading from manuscript, 298–300
  tools for, 232–256
  use of outline in, 224–225
  use of voice in, 300–310

Presentation *(Cont.)*
video, 316–318
Presidential primaries, 1992 elections, 394
Prestige testimony
definition of, 155
evaluation of, 158
misuse of, 415
as supporting material, 156–157
use in persuasive speech, 398
Preview of topic, 193–194
Probability, confusion with certainty, 416
Probes, use in interviews, 138
Problem-solution design, 180, 181, 186
defective, 418
for persuasive speeches, 374–376
use of inductive arguments with, 409
Problem-solving process, A4–A7
defining problem, A4
evaluating solution options, A5–A6
generating solution options, A4–A5
planning for action, A6
planning for evaluation, A6–A7
*see also* Group problem solving
Progression, principle of, in presentation of main points, 176–177
Projections
computer-generated, 247, 248, 249 (fig.), 250, 253
design of, 250–251
making, 253
as visual aid, 247–248
Pronouns, inclusive, creation of group identity with, 273
Pronunciation, 308–309
Proofs, 362
building arguments from, 406–412
combination of methods, 405
defective, 415–416
definition of, 394
by ethos, 399, 399 (fig.), 401–402, 407, 409, 415
by logos, 398–399, 399 (fig.), 409
by mythos, 399, 399 (fig.), 402–405, 407, 418
by pathos, 399, 399 (fig.), 400–401, 407, 409
visual aids as, 232
*ProQuest*, 134, 135
Proxemics, 313
Proximity, principle of, in arrangement of main points, 179
*Public Affairs Information Service* (PAIS), 132
Purpose of occasion, adjustment of speaker to, 92–93

Purpose of speech
clarification of, 16
determination of, 122–127
evaluation of, 80 (fig.)
general, 122–123, 126
specific, 123–125, 125, 126
specification in thematic statement, 125–127

Questions
in conclusion, 196–197
interview, 137, 138
rhetorical, in introduction, 187–188
*The Quotable Woman*, 133
Quotation collections, 132–133, 188
Quotations
collections of, 132–133, 188
in conclusion, 197
documentation of, 139
in introduction, 188
rehearsing delivery of, 315
of testimony, 156, 157, 158
writing out for presentation, 225

Radio
as medium, 12
use of descriptive language on, 334–335
Rand Corporation, 133
"Rape by Any Other Name" (Jane Doe), B8–B10
Rate of speaking, 304–305
sustaining attention with, 332
variety in, 307
*Reader's Guide to Periodical Literature*, 132
Reading, presentation of speech by, 298–300
Reagan, Ronald, 157, 163, 266–267, 278 (fig.), 401
Reasoning
disregard of, 74
plausibility of, 74
*see also* Arguments
Receiver, listener as, 9, 13
Recentness of information, 141, 153, 158
Reception, of persuasion
*see also* Audience, receptivity of
Recognition, need for, as factor in audience response, 103
Red herring, 413, 414 (fig.)
Refutative design
for persuasive speech, 380–382
use of inductive arguments in, 409
Reinforcer, use in interviews, 138
Relevance
and retention, 333

sustaining interest through, 332–333
Reliability of information, 141
Religious affiliation, as factor in audience response, 99–100
Repetition
and clarity, 280–281
and retention, 333
sustaining attention through, 331, 333
Replacement
arousal of emotion by, 271
visualization of abstractions through, 268
Research, *see* Library research
Research overview, 178, 179 (fig.)
Response
in communication process, 9, 13
demographic factors affecting, 94, 95–101
environmental factors affecting, 89–94
influence of internal dynamics, 101–108
Responsible knowledge, 21–23, 42, 117
acquisition from library research, 129–135
acquisition from personal experience, 128–129
acquisition through interviews, 135–139
in informative speaking, 329
Retention
in learning, 333–334
of persuasion, 363
Revere, Paul, 278
Rhetorical questions, in introduction, 187–188
Rhetorical style, 279
*Rhetoric* (Aristotle), 399, 428
Richards, Ann, 438–439
*Robert's Rules of Order*, A13
Rogers, Ginger, 440
Roosevelt, Franklin D., 283, 301, 369
Roosevelt, James, 283
Roper poll, 103
Rowan, Katherine, 336–337
Rukeyser, Muriel, 146

Sachs, Bernice Cohen, 155
Safety, need for, as factor in audience response, 102–103
Sandburg, Carl, 283
Save the Children, 271–272
Second, in parliamentary procedure, A12
*Selected Rand Abstracts*, 133
Self-awareness inventory, 36–39
Seneca, 202
Sennett, Richard, 6

Sequence
arrangement of informative
speech in, 335, 342–343
arrangement of main points in,
179
arrangement of speech in, 18,
41–42
*see also* Motivated sequence design
Sequence charts, as visual aid,
240–241, 241 (fig.)
Sexist language, 64, 97
Sheridan, Richard, 283
Shock-and-startle technique,
191–192
Sierra Club, 100
*The Silent Scream* (film), 406–408
Similarity principle, in arrangement
of main points, 180
Simile
arousal of emotion by, 271
building arguments from, 410
use in magnification, 429
visualization of abstractions
through, 268–269
Simplicity, as principle of structure,
174–176
Sketches, as visual aid, 236
Sleeper effect, 367
Slides
computer-generated, 248, 250, 253
design of, 250–251
making, 253
as visual aid, 247–248
Slippery slope fallacy, 412–413, 414
(fig.)
Small groups, *see* Group problem
solving
Smith, Fred, 263
Smith, Margaret Chase, 159
Social benefits, of public speaking,
6–8
Social-group affiliation, as factor in
audience response, 100
Social leadership behavior, in
groups, A9
*Social Sciences Index*, 132, 134
Sociocultural background, as factor
in audience response, 100–101
Socrates, 411
Solomon, Martha, 402
Source, speaker as, 9, 10–11
Source card, 140, 141 (fig. 15.6)
Sources of information, acknowl-
edgement of, 21–23
Spatial design, 41, 179, 236
Speaker
listener's attitude toward, 67
as visual aid, 233
Speaker's Notes
analysis of speech setting, 94

application of persuasive process,
364
avoidance of plagiarism, 23
capturing audience attention, 192
challenge of uncommitted audience, 368
constructive listening, 78
creating a good public speech, 15
design of informative speech, 346
design of persuasive speech, 383
determination and arrangement of
main points, 181
development of arguments, 411
development of formal outline,
218
effective listening, 70
engagement of reluctant audience,
367
evaluation of examples, 162
evaluation of facts and figures,
154
evaluation of specific purpose,
124
evaluation of testimony, 158
focus of introductory speech, 39
guidelines for critical thinking, 75
interviewing for information, 139
introducing main speakers, 436
learning process, 333
long-range audience analysis, 106
making acceptance speech, 434
methods of presentation, 299
moving audience to action, 370
preparation of introductory
speech, 43
preparation of visual aids, 252
racism in language, 285
rehearsal of presentation, 315
sexism in language, 285
10 ways to control communication
apprehension, 50
topic selection, 122
use of evidence, 398
use of language, 271, 275, 280
use of narratives, 167
Speaking outline, *see* Key-word outline
Specific purpose of speech, 123–125,
125, 126
identification in formal outline,
215
simplicity of statement in, 176
statement in preparation outline,
205
Speech Communication Association,
98
Sperry Corporation, 63
Spontaneity, in television presentation, 318
*Statistical Abstract of the United
States*, 133

Statistics
contribution to speech's substance, 17
defective, 413
drawing proof from, 398–399
evaluation of, 152–154
in introductory speech, 42
as supporting material, 151–152,
182–183, 184
use in persuasive speech, 365,
381, 395–396
use of, 154
visual presentation of, 236–238
writing out for presentation, 225
Steinbeck, John, 271
Stepp, Laura, 397
Stevenson, Adlai, 413
Stock issues design, for persuasive
speech, 376–378
Stockton, California, shooting incident, 92
Stories, *see* Anecdotes; Narratives
Straw man fallacy, 419
Stream charts, as visual aid, 239–241
Structure
evaluation of, 80 (fig.)
*see also* Design of speech; Good
form
Subjects, *see* Topic
Subordination, as principle of structure, 215, 216–217
Subpoints
in formal outline, 214 (fig.), 215,
216, 219, 220–222 (fig.)
grouping under main points, 175
organization with outline, 204
in preparation outline, 206,
207–210, 208 (fig.), 212–213
(fig.)
Substance
body of speech as vehicle for, 177
evaluation of, 80 (fig.)
as prerequisite for good speech, 17
Sub-subsubpoints, in formal outline,
214 (fig.), 216, 220–222 (fig.)
Success, need for, as factor in audience response, 104–105
Summary
concluding speech with, 18, 195
in impromptu speaking, 296
internal, 186
in interviewing, 139
Summary statement, 43
Supporting materials
collection of, 127–139
defective, 412–415
documentation of, 140
drawing proofs from, 398–406,
399 (fig.)
evaluation of, 152–154, 157–158,
162, 166–167

Supporting materials (Cont.)
in formal outline, 214 (fig.), 216, 219
function of, 149
in impromptu speaking, 296
for introductory speech, 42–43
organization with outline, 204
in persuasive speech, 362, 363, 394–399
stimulation of learning with, 331, 332
substantiation of main points with, 182–185
types of, 149–168
validity of, 73
see also (for greater specificity) Examples; Fact(s); Narratives; Testimony
Supreme Court, U. S., record of opinions of, 133
Survey, of audience attitudes, 107–108, 108 (fig.)
Suspense, in introduction, 191
Syllogism, 406, 408
Symbols, accomplishments and events as, 430, 431
Symmetry
as principle of structure, 176–177, 196
see also Balance
Synecdoche, 269
arousal of emotion by, 271
encouragement of action by, 276
evocation of culturetypes by, 278
and language color, 282
Synergistic listening, 77–79
Synonyms, misuse of, 283

Tabling the motion, in parliamentary procedure, A12–A13
Taft, Mrs. Robert A., 236
Tape recorders, use in interviewing, 137
Target audience, 88–89
Task leadership behavior, in groups, A9
Teleprompter, in television presentation, 318
Television
adapting for, 316–317
generation of bad listening habits by, 69
ideas for topics from, 118
making presentation, 318
as medium, 12
use of concise language for, 284
Teresa, Mother, 429
Testimony
building arguments from, 409
contribution to speech's substance, 17

defective, 415
drawing proof from, 401–402, 405
evaluation of, 157–158
expert, 155–156, 157–158, 182, 183, 185, 219, 369, 398–399, 402, 405, 409
in format outline, 219
in introductory speech, 43
lay, 155, 157, 183, 398, 402, 415
in persuasive speech, 369, 395, 397–399
prestige, 155, 156–157, 398, 415
as supporting material, 155–158, 182–183, 183, 184, 185
types of, 155
use of, 158
Textual graphics
computer-generated, 248, 249 (fig.)
as visual aid, 241
Thematic statement, 41
identification in formal outline, 215
in preparation outline, 205
presentation in introduction, 193
revision in preparation outline, 206–207
simplicity of, 176
specification of purpose in, 125–127
Thompson, Mark, 161
Thorndike, Edward, 258
Thoroughness of information, 141
Time, transcendence through language, 262–263
Time limitations
conformity of speaker to, 123–124
structuring speech with regard to, 176–177
and use of concise language, 283, 284
Time magazine, 118, 131, 159, 404
Time of day, adjustment of speaker to, 89
Timing, in television presentation, 317
Title, for format outline, 211
Toasts, 431–432
Topic
analysis of, 119–121
appropriateness of, 15–16
cluttering with extraneous information, 152–153
complex, language appropriate for, 269
confidence of speaker in, 49
demographic factors affecting, 94, 95, 97, 98, 100
determination by audience, 88–89, 116–117
determination of rate of speaking by, 304

elaboration with supporting material, 149, 153, 155, 160
enthusiasm for, as prerequisite for effective presentation, 295
evaluation of, 80 (fig.)
final selection of, 121–122
fit with audience's interests, 119, 120 (fig.)
fit with speaker's interests, 117, 118 (fig.)
gathering information for, 127–142
ideas from popular media, 118–119
identification in formal outline, 215
of informative speech, 327, 329
listener's attitude toward, 67–68
listener's avoidance of complexity in, 70, 71
manageability of, 117
meaningfulness of, 116
natural division of, 180
preview of, 193–194
and psychodynamics of listener, 102, 103, 104, 105, 107
relation to personal experience, 189–190, 191
responsible knowledge of, 21–23
shaping by speaker's purpose, 122–127
statement in preparation outline, 205
vast, language appropriate for, 269–270
Topic inventory chart, 119, 120 (fig.)
Tradition
celebration of, 426
drawing proof from, 402–405
invocation through language, 267
need for, as factor in audience response, 104
Training materials, videotaped, 316
Transitions, 18–19, 127
in formal outline, 214 (fig.)
organization with outline, 204
into testimony, 158
use of, 185–187, 194, 195
use with combined design, 346
use with examples, 163
Transparencies
computer-generated, 247, 248, 249 (fig.), 250, 253
design of, 250–251
making, 253
as visual aid, 247–248
Tree chart, as visual aid, 239
Trends, 152
graphic representation of, 238
Treptow, Martin, 157
"The Trials of Malcolm X" (Davis), B31–B33

Tribute, speech of, 429–432
Trigger words, 64–65, 97
"The Trouble with Numbers" (Lee),
    B11–B13
Truman, Bess, 160
Truth
    discovery by audience, 163
    facts as, 149
Truth, Sojourner, 284
Twain, Mark, 305
Tylenol product-tampering inci-
    dents, 401–402

U. S. News & World Report, 279
Ueberroth, Peter, 92
Understanding
    as goal of demonstration speech,
    335
    as goal of explanatory speech, 336
Undex (United Nations Document
    Index), 133
United States Reports, 133
University of California-Davis, 92
"University of South Carolina Com-
    mencement Address" (Cosby),
    B28–B31
USA Today (newspaper), 100, 104,
    157
Utilization, of persuasion, 363

Values
    appeal to, in persuasive speech,
    365, 368–369
    celebration of, 426, 430, 431, 433,
    436
    drawing proof from, 402–405
    emphasis with magnification tech-
    nique, 428–429, 431
    as factor in audience response,
    99–100, 105–108
    self-characterization of speaker
    through, 39
Variety
    need for, as factor in audience re-
    sponse, 103
    in vocal characteristics, 307

Verbatim quotations, of testimony,
    156
Verifier, use in interviews, 138
Vertical file, information from, 133,
    135
Video presentations, 316–318
Videotapes, as visual aid, 248–249
Visibility, in design of visual aids,
    250
Visual aids, 232–256
    adjustment to audience size, 93
    advantages of, 232–233
    audiotapes as, 248–249
    bar graph as, 237, 238 (fig. 9.3)
    chalkboard as, 243–244
    charts as, 239–241, 240 (fig.), 241
    (fig.)
    computer-generated materials,
    247, 248, 249 (fig.)
    films as, 248–249
    flip chart as, 245, 246 (fig.)
    flow charts as, 239, 240 (fig.)
    graphics as, 235–241
    graphs as, 236–238, 238 (figs.),
    239 (fig.)
    guidelines for using, 253–255
    handouts as, 246–247
    line graph as, 237–238, 239 (fig.),
    243 (ill.)
    making, 253
    maps as, 236, 237 (fig.)
    models as, 234, 235
    objects as, 234–235
    people as, 233–234
    photographs as, 241–242
    pie graph as, 237, 238 (fig. 9.2)
    poster board for, 236, 242,
    245–246
    principles of color, 251–253
    principles of design, 250–251
    projections as, 247–248
    sequence chart as, 240–241, 241
    (fig.)
    sketches as, 236
    stream chart as, 239–241
    support of main points with, 183

sustaining attention with, 331, 332
    textual graphics as, 241
    tree chart as, 239
    use with informative speech, 336,
    351 (ill.), 352 (ill.), 355 (ill.)
    videotapes as, 248–249
Visualization, through language,
    261–262, 267–270, 279
Voice
    and art of narratives, 167
    in effective presentation, 21, 48
    effective use of, 300–310
    loudness of, 305–307
    pitch of, 302–304
    rate of speaking, 304–305
    speech patterns, 307–310
    sustaining attention with, 331, 332
    variety in, 307

Wall Street Journal, 155
Walters, Barbara, 308
Washington, George, 402
Washington Post, 397
Weaver, Richard, 149, 274
"We Don't Have to Live in Slums"
    (Aley), 389–391
Weight Watchers, 191
White, Velva, 161
Who's Who, 132
Wiesel, Elie, 90 (ill.), 433, 434,
    B26–B28
Wilhelm, Georg, 2
Wisconsin Office of Academic Af-
    fairs, 4
Work
    importance of critical listening in,
    63
    self-characterization of speaker
    through, 38
    see also Employment; Occupa-
    tional groups
The World Almanac, 133
World Book Encyclopedia, 130

Yearbooks, information from,
    133